Fourth Edition

LANGUAGE ARTS
Process, Product, and Assessment

Pamela J. Farris

Distinguished Teaching Professor
Northern Illinois University

WAVELAND

PRESS, INC.

Long Grove, Illinois

For information about this book, contact:
    Waveland Press, Inc.
    4180 IL Route 83, Suite 101
    Long Grove, IL 60047-9580
    (847) 634-0081
    info@waveland.com
    www.waveland.com

Photo Credits
Cover & p. 493: ©Bob Daemmrich/The Image Works; pp. xx, 38, 45, 473, 537, 549: courtesy of Northern Illinois University; pp. 14, 77, 125, 498: courtesy of Pamela J. Farris; p. 55: courtesy of NCTE; pp. 61, 554: courtesy of *Rochelle News-Leader*; p. 240 courtesy of *Rochelle News-Leader* (Jeff Robertson); pp. 68, 93, 188, 250, 264, 296, 324, 350, 395, 408, 419, 482: Skjold Photographs; pp. 116, 133, 199, 430: ©Ellen Senisi/The Image Works; p. 224: ©Dick Hemmingway; p. 301: ©Syracuse Newspapers/David Lassman/The Image Works

To

Dick and Kurtis

who provide encouragement, support,

patience, and love

Contents

7   Listening: A Receptive Skill

8   Writing: A Multidimensional Process   297

13   Extending the Language Arts Curriculum   549

Preface

Teaching is a daunting task. One must possess a deep passion for learning and genuine caring for students. With a less than adequate paycheck, one stretches to pay for the bare necessities of living and squeezes out a goodly measure to provide an ample classroom library and teaching materials that the school district doesn't furnish. Burning the midnight oil to create exciting lesson plans while striving to have students meet and exceed state and national standards, the exemplary teacher regularly encounters challenges. Serving as the facilitator and guide for learning, the exemplary teacher's classroom has children enthusiastically engaging in relevant language arts activities in which they are truly interested. Self-motivation drives students to pursue new knowledge. As Kathy Jongsma (2002, p. 62), so eloquently writes, "This school year, let's remember that our goal is to help students become joyfully literate and experience the pleasures and rewards that most of us associate with learning."

Approach

Language Arts: Process, Product, and Assessment, 4th edition, provides an overview of the six language arts: reading, writing, listening, speaking, viewing, and visually representing. Best described as a "meat and potatoes" textbook, the language arts are presented with a liberal selection of irresistible desserts—ideas that will entice students to read, write, listen, speak, view, and visually represent the world around them. From the first edition of this textbook to the current one, the purpose has been to present language arts theory and methodology in a palatable fashion with real classroom anecdotes from real teachers and at a modest cost. Hence, don't expect a CD showing "model" classroom instruction in which disruptive students have been removed or a Web site of activities to help you prepare for tests or write lesson plans. This textbook has been thoughtfully outlined to cover accepted theories and practices in language arts and present them in a straightforward, easy to grasp approach. Ideas for lesson plans, how to use technology, and where to find information on the Internet for yourself and your students are all included. Interdisciplinary instruction (the presenting of concepts and learning goals from more than one curricular content area) is strongly encouraged, as activities throughout the text demonstrate. Good teachers possess a wide variety of teaching strategies; hence, this book offers different strategies for teaching the language arts to meet the diverse student populations of our schools.

Organization

Assessment is said to drive the curriculum. Certainly it is at the forefront of the standards movement. Because assessment and evaluation play a major role in language arts instruction, it is presented and discussed early in the text. How students process the language arts via thinking is also critical. It, too, is presented early in the text so that the reader can develop a foundation for how students learn the language arts. Subsequent chapters present the various language arts in depth.

Standards

Standards are a vital aspect of teaching. Without standards set at local, state, and national levels, educators would have no specific goals to strive to meet with their students. Just as the Olympic runner or Tour de France biker needs the stopwatch to gauge success, so too do we need measures to mark the progress of our students. Thus, we use objectives and measure the outcomes of student achievement through rubrics, anecdotal records, tests, and other assessment means. Increasingly research points out that good teachers make a difference in student learning. Many states are moving to additional teacher accountability by tracking the teachers each student has during their school years and measuring each student's achievement on an annual basis. Ineffective teachers are being duly noted and required to improve their methodologies, while superior teachers are encouraged to share their instructional practices with peers.

The fourth edition includes a listing of the Standards for Reading Professionals—Revised 2003—as developed by the Professional Standards and Ethics Committee of the International Reading Association (2003) for each chapter. These standards for preparation programs for reading professionals target the knowledge and skills of teacher preparation candidates. Unlike the standards for good or exemplary teachers who have gained a vast amount of knowledge and skills from their own classroom experiences, engaging in professional development through attending conferences, workshops, and taking graduate coursework at universities, teacher education candidates need to possess a basic set of standards to enter the teaching force. Experienced teachers are seasoned professionals who should be expected to perform at higher levels of competence. The five standards for preservice teachers address the following:

1. Foundational Knowledge
2. Instructional Strategies and Curriculum Materials
3. Assessment, Diagnosis, and Evaluation
4. Creating a Literate Environment, and
5. Professional Development

This edition of *Language Arts: Process, Product, and Assessment* was developed with these standards in mind. Each chapter opener identifies the standards that it addresses.

Features

Readers will find the fourth edition a comprehensive language arts textbook. Upon turning the page to a new chapter, readers are invited into a classroom of a practicing teacher to learn the joys, triumphs, trials, and frustrations of teaching elementary and middle school students in the twenty-first century. At the end of the chapter there are questions and a reflective task designed to immerse the reader into how language arts should be taught.

Chapter objectives help readers focus on the concepts discussed. The six language arts are presented in a clear, concise manner that readers can readily comprehend. Anecdotes of actual teaching applications, instructional activities, and ways to use technology are interspersed throughout the textbook.

The fourth edition offers several features that preservice and in-service teachers have requested, containing teaching hints and mini lessons including:

- A plethora of developmentally appropriate instructional activities for reading, writing, listening, speaking, viewing, and visually representing
- In the Classroom boxes containing teaching hints and mini lessons
- The More You Know boxes with information designed to provide new and enriching information for teaching
- Chapter objectives to help the reader focus on topics
- Inclusion in each chapter of the Standards that it addresses
- Numerous assessment techniques including checklists, rubrics, and portfolios
- Brain research findings and the Multiple Intelligences as they relate to language arts instruction in elementary and middle school
- Theories, instruction, and teaching activities aimed at English Language Learners (ELLs)

- Instructional techniques and activities to meet the needs of special needs learners
- Current children's literature including a vast number of fiction and informational titles along with a listing of multicultural books
- An appendix listing notable award-winning titles
- Developmentally appropriate interdisciplinary activities and units of study
- Use of technology and Web sites to assist teaching language arts and other content areas
- Numerous examples of children's work to help readers understand what to expect from different ages and ability levels

Furthermore, the instructor's manual and test bank have been greatly expanded with numerous new class activities, resources, suggested readings, and discussion questions. A PowerPoint presentation for each chapter has been designed to enrich the teaching and learning experience.

These are just a few of the new features that enrich the textbook and make it a valuable instructional tool as well as a comprehensive language arts resource.

Acknowledgements

In writing this book, I observed and taught in a wide variety of elementary and middle school classrooms including those in urban, suburban, and rural school districts. I also contemplated the skills of several outstanding, exemplary teachers as they went about their work teaching hundreds upon hundreds of energized children. In particular, one third grader was so impressed with a writing lesson I had just taught, she asked if I do karaoke.

Many teachers shared a wealth of ideas, concerns, problems, and suggestions as we met in after school sessions to discuss problems they've encountered and successes they've had in teaching language arts. An untold number of stories, reports, books, and poetry composed by children were also shared. To those teachers and their students, I owe a great debt of thanks. In turn, I continue to learn from my undergraduate and graduate students as well as my colleagues. There are always new ways of thinking and learning to discover.

Dr. Mary Napoli of Pennsylvania State University-Harrisburg deserves a huge thank you for her thoroughness in critiquing the book. Conversations and bantering with my colleagues throughout the years aided in the creation of this book as did topics of discussion with leaders in the field at conferences.

My deep appreciation goes to Waveland Press: Jeni Ogilvie, editor, and Deborah Underwood Vasco, Katy Murphy, and Jan Weissman for all their assistance and guidance. Neil Rowe and Carol Rowe gave me encouragement and freedom, which added greatly to the development of this edition as well. Much appreciation goes to Richard Fluck and Kurtis Fluck for preparing the IM/TI and accompanying PowerPoint presentations for the chapters.

My hope is that readers of this book will come away with new insights and ideas that they will carry back to their classrooms to light up the eyes of their students—then all the time and effort put forth in writing it will have been worthwhile.

I teach because it is what I enjoy. Teaching is what I do best. And, most of all, teaching is what I love. Being in a classroom teaching is an electrifying experience as one witnesses students turn a glimmer of knowledge into a roaring flame. This happens day after day, year after year. What more exciting profession is there?

Pamela J. Farris
Distinguished Teaching Professor
Northern Illinois University

Reference

Jongsma, K. (2002). Instructional materials: Good beginnings! *The Reading Teacher, 56* (1), 62–65.

Teaching the Language Arts

> As adults we must keep in mind the wonder of childhood—the magic, the mystery, and the miraculous.
>
> —Lee Bennett Hopkins
> *Let Them Be Themselves*

PEERING INTO THE CLASSROOM
THE BEGINNING TEACHER

A bundle of energy best describes Stacie Rubens, a first-year teacher. And that's good because the first graders are extremely full of pep and vigor. It's up to Stacie to harness all of their energy and continue to motivate them to become avid readers and writers. Like all classrooms, Stacie's has a diverse population of students with different backgrounds and needs. Good teachers use relevant materials to teach language arts so students will not only acquire new skills and strategies but also be motivated to learn new literacy strategies.

Today Stacie is sharing *If You Give a Pig a Pancake* by Laura Numeroff (1998). She has all the *If You* books by Numeroff, but she selected this particular one to use in a lesson because it will help build her students' reading and writing skills. Today she is focusing on four letter combinations: -*ig*, -*uck*, -*ou*, and -*ake*. These are referred to in phonics as word chunks that are commonly found in English words. Stacie gathers her charges around her canvas camp chair that she refers to as "The Author's Chair." Students can share their stories or books written by others when they sit in this chair. To keep the students from crunching up and sitting on top of one another, Stacie has placed 26 carpet squares of four different colors—red, blue, green, and yellow—in rows on the floor. Each color represents a reading group that the child is assigned to for two-week rotations. The children quickly find their spots and plop their bottoms on the carpet squares.

"Today, girls and boys, we're going to read about a pig who comes to visit a little girl. What do you think will happen?" Stacie displays the cover of the book to the class.

Several eager students raise their hands.

"Elizabeth, what do you think will happen?" asks Stacie.

"The pig will make a mess."

"That's a good answer." Stacie places her hands on her hips, tilts her head slightly, and queries, "Why would a pig make a mess?"

More hands fly up.

"Carlos."

"Pig are dirty," Carlos says softly.

"Yes, Carlos, pigs can be very dirty. What else could cause a pig to make a mess?" asks Stacie, probing further. She looks over the students and calls on a student in the back of the group.

"James."

"It might knock something over."

"That would make a mess. What could be knocked over in a house?" Stacie asks. She points in rapid-fire fashion to five students. Their responses are animated.

"A lamp."

"A glass of milk."

"A chair."

"A TV set."

"A table."

"Wow, girls and boys, there are lots of things that a pig in the house or an apartment could knock over. Let's look at the title of our book. It is *If You Give a Pig a Pancake*. What do you think the pig will do in this book? Maria?"

"He'll eat it." Maria grins.

"How many of you think the pig will eat the pancake?"

Twenty-six hands reach for the ceiling. Stacie smiles and says, "Let's see what the pig does." And she reads the book to her alert listeners. After reading the book, Stacie asks what the pig wanted. Each student is given an opportunity to respond. Once children have been called on, they must keep their hands down. This gives the entire class a chance to participate. Quickly, Stacie writes on chart paper what the pig wanted.

"Whew!" she finally says. "That pig wanted a lot of things, didn't she? Let's read this list together." The class joins in with her as she points to and reads out loud the items listed: pancake, syrup, bubble bath, rubber duck, tap shoes, music, stamps, and tree house. Stacie hands out pictures of the items the pig requested that she drew on sticky notes before school. She calls on students to put the sticky note pictures next to the word(s) on the chart. Then the class rereads the list together.

Next Stacie says, "There are lots of great words for our Word Wall in this book. Let's see. Who was the main character?"

"The pig!" said the students enthusiastically.

Stacie writes "pig" on a rectangular piece of tagboard and underlines "ig." "Let's spell 'pig,' boys and girls."

In unison, the children spell out "P–I–G."

"Can you think of other words that end in -*ig*?"

Big, rig, jig, and twig are volunteered.

"Great job!" Stacie smiles. "Now let's do the same with another word." She continues with other words that she had previously selected for the lesson—*pancake, duck,* and *house*—underlining the respective frequently found English letter combinations of -*ake, -uck,* and -*ouse.*

The students spell each word out loud in unison and then offer other words with the same spelling combination (make, shake, take; stuck, tuck, truck; mouse, blouse). Stacie refers to these as "word chunks." The tagboard word strips are placed above the white board.

"Boys and girls, it's time for lunch. Everybody line up! Do you think we'll have pancakes for lunch?"

The class chuckles, and most of the students shake their heads. "When do we eat pancakes?" Stacie asks as she waits for the other first grade to pass by her classroom.

"Jamarcus?"

"Mrs. Rubens, I eat pancakes for breakfast!" he announces.

"Yes, pancakes taste great at breakfast, don't they? Gabriela, lead us to the cafeteria!"

The next day, Stacie again has her students sit around "The Author's Chair." The class rereads together the list of items the pig wanted. Stacie then rereads the book. At the end, she asks the students to revisit their Word Wall of tagboard words at the front and side of the classroom.

Stacie eyes the hands in the air. "Kelly, what's a word from our book?"

"Pancake!"

"Yes, pancake is a good word for us to start with today," Stacie explains. "Pancake is a special word called a compound word. That means it is made up of two smaller words, *pan* and *cake*. It is made up of two words, pan like we cook in and cake like we eat. Pan-cake."

"Let's put it up on our compound word list. Let's spell it together." Stacie points to the letters in the word pancake. "P–A–N–C–A–K–E. And what's the word boys and girls?" She writes the letters on the compound word chart for everyone to see.

"And what does this spell, girls and boys?"

"Pancake!"

"Pancake, that's right. Now let's write the two words that make up pancake on our Word Wall. What are the two words, David?"

"Pan and cake," answers David, an attention deficit disorder (ADD) student, who squirms and rocks back and forth on his knees. Stacie, understanding that David is fidgety, provides him with an opportunity to feel success from joining in the class discussion.

"Good job, David."

David grins and drops back quietly to his original seated position.

Stacie says, "You spell the words with me as I write them. Look up at pancake. How do we spell *pan?*"

"P–A–N," the class says in unison. "What chunk does pan have, Yvette?"

"The letters *an.*"

"Yes, those two letters *an.*" Stacie underlines the *an* in pan on the Word Wall. "What are some other word that have that *-an* combination? Terry?"

"Can."

Stacie points to Max who answers "Fan."

"Can and fan. And we could certainly use a fan today because it is hot in the classroom." Stacie smiles as the students wave their hands in front of their faces to fan themselves.

"Look, boys and girls, you have made fans out of your hands." She turns back to the Word Wall. "What about cake? Look up at pancake. Let's spell *cake.*"

A chorus sings out, "C–A–K–E."

"That's right, boys and girls. Does the word cake have a word chunk that we see a lot when we read? Rafe?"

"*Ake.*"

"Um, *ake.* Like what word, Angelica?" asks Stacie.

"Like take or make."

"Oh, yes, take and make. And what is the chunk we want to underline, Carlos?"

"*Ake.*"

"That's right, *ake.* Now boys and girls, my paper passers will be giving you each a piece of paper. Let's pretend that the pig visits us at our homes. Write a sentence telling what you would give the pig. Then draw a picture to show what you gave the pig. Look at our Word Wall for help with spelling. The list of things on our chart may help you come up with an idea of what you might give the pig." Stacie's first graders scurry back to their desks and get out their pencils and crayons as two students hand out blank sheets of white paper.

A few days later Stacie will share *If You Give a Mouse a Cookie* (Numeroff, 1985) and, on yet another day, *If You Take a Mouse to School* (Numeroff, 2002) in the same fashion—reading it one day and having her students identify the items the animals requested and the next day searching out words with word chunks that are missing from their Word Wall. Stacie will have the students point out words for their Word Wall such as *broom.* Then she'll reinforce the concepts with other words with the same spelling patterns such as *room* and *boom.* In the meantime, students will reread the books in their small reading groups. Stacie has purchased six paperback copies of each title for her classroom library as well as text sets of other titles appropriate for first graders. She uses these books to supplement the basal reader series her school district has adopted.

Stacie teaches the language arts as integrated subjects, which provides effective and efficient instruction. Her students better understand how to spell words, for instance, since they combine decoding and spelling. They relate listening and reading comprehension to their own writing and development of ideas. Depicting and noting visual clues aids their learning. By blending the language arts together, Stacie is preparing her students to incorporate skills from the various language arts as they need to use them.

Peering into the Classroom
Team Teaching

September is a marvelous time for Susan Johnson and Will Hilgert who team teach their fifth- and sixth-grade classes. Autumn is perfect for them to integrate language arts, science, and math in a pond study unit. Their fifth and sixth graders work together in small groups to study microorganisms, called protists, which eat food such as algae, bacteria, and other life forms. Students select from different kinds of protists—protozoans, amoebas, algae, and fungi—which type they want to study. After a couple of days of going to the library and writing notes about their protists, the group members then discuss what they've found. Each group then summarizes what they've researched, recording their findings on a chart. The next day, the class ventures out to a preserve where they gather specimens in a bag and pond water in buckets. Back at school, each group of students carefully examines the finds, making slides that are carefully scrutinized under microscopes. Pond water is placed in aquariums. The large, squirming bullfrog that Mohammad caught is placed in a large aquarium along with rocks and water. A screen top is devised by the other students in the group to serve as a lid, preventing the frog from taking an unexpected hop out of the container amid their research work. Naturally, both classes dub the bullfrog as the official mascot, and they devise a contest to name it.

It's Susan's first year teaching fifth and sixth graders, and she's pleased to be working with Will, a seasoned veteran. Even so, Will points out that, although they may know how they want to teach the unit they've planned, they will need to make some adjustments as the days go by to accommodate the different learning styles and preferences of students. Already Susan can detect different learning strategies being used by the students—Keisha prefers to write down in list form what she's learned, while Jamar uses short phrases and Anne writes out complete sentences and is very descriptive, just as she is when she talks about something. Tasha refuses to touch the bullfrog; Angie thinks it's "cool" to put live flies in the aquarium and watch the frog's tongue flash out and capture them. Paulo wants to do the math assignment first, converting the liquids from quarts to liters.

Most of the boys spend their time observing and talking about the protists while the girls take careful notes of what they have viewed. Susan makes a mental note that no two students are completely alike. When the frog deftly escapes and hops about the classroom to shrieks and giggles, she grins and adds to her mental note: they are all kids.

Chapter Objectives

The reader will:

✓ be able to list and define the language arts.

✓ be able to describe how the language arts are interrelated.

✓ understand the history of language arts instruction.

✓ understand balanced literacy instruction.

✓ understand the need to adjust language arts instruction so that every child can develop his or her language skills to full potential.

✓ understand different assessment methods.

Standards for Professionals

The following Standards will be addressed in this chapter:

Standard 1: Foundational Knowledge and Dispositions

1.1 Demonstrate knowledge of psychological, sociological, and linguistic foundations of reading and writing processes and instruction.

1.2 Demonstrate knowledge of reading research and histories of reading.

1.3 Demonstrate knowledge of language development and reading acquisition and variations related to cultural and linguistic diversity.

Standard 2: Instructional Strategies and Curriculum Materials

2.1 Use instructional grouping options (individual, small-group, whole-class, and computer based) as appropriate for accomplishing given purpose.

2.2 Use a wide range of instructional practices, approaches, and methods, including technology-based practices, for learners at differing stages of development and from differing cultural and linguistic backgrounds.

Standard 3: Assessment, Diagnosis, and Evaluation

3.1 Use a wide range of assessment tools and practices that range from individual and group standardized tests to individual and group informal classroom assessment strategies, including technology-based assessment tools.

3.2 Place students along a developmental continuum and identify students' proficiencies and difficulties.

3.3 Use assessment information to plan, evaluate, and revise effective instruction that meets the needs of all students, including those at different developmental stages and those from differing cultural and linguistic backgrounds.

3.4 Effectively communicate results of assessments to specific individuals (students, parents, caregivers, colleagues, administrators, policy makers, policy officials, community, etc.).

Standard 5: Professional Development

5.3 Work with colleagues to observe, evaluate, and provide feedback on each other's practice.

Introduction

This book presents the language arts—listening, speaking, reading, writing, thinking, viewing, and visually representing—from a balanced literacy approach. Viewing and visually representing are mentioned throughout the book with listening, speaking, reading, and writing each having their own chapters. Unless a teacher understands each specific language art, he will have difficulty teaching it to students. Likewise, the teacher must be knowledgeable of both phonics and children's literature as well as writing and listening. The book presents several activities at a variety of developmental levels from kindergarten through eighth grade that integrate many or all of the language arts. Integrating instruction is imperative to being an efficient and competent teacher.

According to Dixie Lee Spiegel (1992, p. 39), a leader in literacy research, "We are . . . *literacy* educators, not just reading teachers and occasionally writing teachers. Writing is increasingly viewed from the perspective of a process of communication, not as a set of mechanics to be mastered and then applied. Even very young children are being perceived as both writers and readers. . . ." Writing starts before children read and needs to be taught in kindergarten along with the other five language arts.

The language arts are best taught as integrated language modes; however, teachers need to understand fully each of the language arts. The integrated language arts curriculum is described by Vacca, Vacca, and Gove (2000, p. 55):

> An integrated language arts approach to instruction extends the concept of language experience throughout the grades by immersing students in reading, writing, talking, listening, and viewing activities. . . . Just as teachers believe that systems of language should not be separated and taught as isolated skills, so too do they believe that reading, writing, speaking, listening, and viewing should be taught in concert, not in separate lessons . . . the language arts support one another and are connected through the use of informative and imaginative literature.

In addition to being proficient in teaching writing, listening, speaking, viewing, and visually representing, the competent classroom teacher of language arts must also meet the Standards for Reading Professionals. Drawing from research findings in reading and reading instruction as well as professional expertise, the professional standards and ethics committee of the International Reading Association adopted a set of five primary standards, which were revised in 2003 (IRA, 2003, p. 1):

1. Foundational Knowledge and Dispositions
2. Instructional Strategies and Curriculum Materials
3. Assessment, Diagnosis, and Evaluation
4. Creating a Literate Environment
5. Professional Development

By meeting each of these standards, the reader meets the criteria for being a classroom teacher candidate. The inside cover of this textbook contains the complete set of standards. The beginning of each chapter contains the specific elements of the standards addressed in that chapter, so that readers can link the chapter information with these important standards.

The Development of the Language Arts

The language arts consist of listening, speaking, reading, writing, viewing, and visually representing (NCTE/IRA, 1996). The language arts are interwoven so as a child develops skills in one of the language arts, the others are also enhanced. Thus, the development of listening, speaking, reading, writing, thinking, viewing, and visually representing is concurrent and interrelated. Such development, however, is not sequential or linear in nature.

By the time a child reaches the age of two, many different classification systems have been developed, modified, and eliminated as the youngster seeks to bring order to his world. This order, or structure, greatly influences the child's perceptions of and reactions to the environment. For instance, the child learns that cats and dogs may be kept in the house whereas cows and horses must live in barns. The child also learns that he can, to some extent, structure the environment. For example, Kurtis, at age 20 months, discovered that he could not only select but also control which books his mother and father would read to him. He only had to first sort out the books that he wanted read and then stack them in the order he wanted them to be read. He would hand his mother or father a book to read and, upon its completion, clap his hands. Then he would pick up the next book in the stack and say, "Read it." Like adults who program their CD players to listen to songs in their own chosen order, Kurtis developed a similar preferred order to his listening pleasure, "programming" his parents rather than a CD player.

The thinking process is not only aided by the classification of information, but it is also facilitated by children's natural tendency to be curious. By capitalizing on this innate ability to experiment playfully—be it through manipulation of toy cars or Play-Doh, exploring a neighbor's backyard, pretending to be a superhero, or testing simple hypotheses by floating sailboats down a stream—thinking can be enhanced. When adults and other children interact with a child, such whimsical acts by the child can be further developed into observing, comparing, classifying, organizing, hypothesizing, applying, and summarizing (Strickland, 1977).

Children gain understanding of the printed word through their personal interactions with others. For example, three- and four-year-olds can identify places where their family frequently shops: Sears, Target, and those fast-food restaurants they love, Burger King and McDonald's. They know these words and others, because Mom or Dad tells them that is where they are going to shop or eat. Children obtain additional knowledge through their observations of adults and other children, as well as through their own oral and written experiences with language. Reading and writing are socially constructed, higher-order thinking skills. "Children develop these functions as they participate in authentic literacy practices and receive guidance in their 'zone of proximal development' from more knowledgeable members of the community—adults, older students, or more capable peers" (Kong & Fitch, 2002–2003, p. 354). Vygotsky (1978) first pointed out the "zone of proximal development" as being what the child can do on her own, as determined by her ability to problem solve, and what the same child can do under the guidance of an adult or more capable peer. Children, like adults, try to make sense of the world around them. They do so by moving from global generalities to specifics, using knowledge they have previously acquired.

Children increase their ability to listen, speak, read, write, view, and visually represent by becoming involved with language that is somewhat more mature than what they currently use (Johnson & Louis, 1987). This means teachers should use new vocabulary in class discussions, sharing the meanings of the new words and concepts. Read alouds, the sharing of a book by a teacher orally with a class and talking about it, also need to stretch students' vocabulary. Thus, reading aloud every day to students at every grade level is important as it helps students' comprehension and expands their knowledge base. Both fiction and informational texts should be shared at all grade levels. "The read aloud time will cause children to want to read. Once children have heard a good book read aloud, they can hardly wait to savor it again. Reading aloud thus generates further interest in books. Good oral reading should develop a taste for fine literature" (Huck, Hepler, Hickman, & Kiefer, 2004, p. 26).

In grades K–2, teachers devote much of the time, as Stacie does, to working with phonics to teach decoding and spelling. However, like Stacie, they need to stress comprehension, vocabulary, and writing. Research points out that "schools that focus entirely on teaching decoding skills in the early grades neglect the essential vocabulary knowledge that students need to be competent readers" (Juel, Biancarosa, Coker, & Deffes, 2003, p. 13). Students in grades K–8 need to practice their reading and writing skills as well as to hone new ones.

In addition to the above, the learning environment should provide ample opportunities for meaningful use of the language arts (Morrow, 2004). This means students should see language, hear language, and be given opportunities to experiment with language. Children need to use language in different settings and in different ways to develop their literacy skills to the fullest to become excellent communicators.

Historical Overview of the Teaching of the Language Arts

Historically, the teaching of the language arts in the United States began with an emphasis on oral language. In the 1700s, children learned the letters of the alphabet from hornbooks, which were shaped like Ping-Pong paddles and made of wood or cardboard. Today few hornbooks are left because children used them to hit paper wads or pebbles back and forth to each other. When stories were shared, they were read or told orally as family and friends gathered together in the evening. In those days, children learned to read primarily from the Bible or *The New England Primer,* a book filled with didacticism based on the religious ideas of that period.

Next to *The New England Primer,* Noah Webster's *The Elementary Spelling Book* was the most important textbook of the colonial period. More commonly referred to as the "Blue Back Speller," this book was handed down within families from sibling to sibling and generation to generation. Initially, children were instructed in single letter recognition. This was later combined with letter-sound correspondence, such as *ab* and *ac.* Word parts, such as *bab* and *bat,* were introduced next, and whole words, such as *babble* and *battle,* were presented as the last step before sentences. Thus, learning was from part to whole.

During this period, listening and speaking were not stressed. The primary listening skill was to "pay attention." Speaking was to occur only when the student was asked to recite or respond to the teacher's questioning. Students were "to be seen and not heard."

In the mid-1800s, William Holmes McGuffey created a graded reading series based on a controlled repetition of letters, sentence length, and vocabulary. Because copyright laws were less rigorous in those days, McGuffey borrowed pieces of literature from all over the English-speaking world to include in his readers. Noted authors such as William Shakespeare and Henry Ward Beecher had stories, parables, or poetry that fit McGuffey's didactic theme for the *McGuffey Eclectic Readers.* The texts more than hinted that if a child disobeyed his elders, fate would intervene and severe punishment would be dealt to the evildoer. Handwriting and, to a limited extent, spelling and writing were included in the lessons. Even though McGuffey earned a total of only $500 for his books, his work was the pioneering effort of what is known today as the basal reading series.

Although early writing instruction emphasized the correctness of the written product, no attempt was made to consider the writing process. Essays were common assignments for children in the upper-elementary grades. Every error was pointed out and marked as such.

Toward the end of the 1800s, reading instruction changed after a phonetics method was introduced. However, the emphasis on word analysis rather than comprehension resulted in teachers becoming dissatisfied and seeking another method for teaching reading. The phonetics approach was replaced by the "look-say" method, which required a child to learn words as "sight" words. In other words, children memorized the words so they could recall the words on sight.

During the early 1900s, reading continued to dominate language arts instruction. Technology was advancing and affecting society in general—indoor plumbing, electricity, the telephone, and the radio were advances that touched the masses. Reading, too, advanced as "scientific instruments" were used to evaluate the effectiveness of reading materials and methods. The introduction of standardized reading tests led to a multitude of research studies. Even today, standardized reading tests prevail in many school districts.

During this period, particularly around 1920, the emphasis on oral reading changed to that of silent reading. Later, during World War II, reading methodologies underwent careful analysis when it was discovered that many of the men drafted into the armed forces were illiterate. As a result, reading became a national concern at the end of World War II. The baby boom and the trend toward conservatism in the 1950s led to the very successful basal readers published by Scott Foresman, which centered on the middle-class lives of the mythical Dick and Jane and their pets, Spot and Puff. Children were usually divided into three reading groups, high, average, or low ability, in which they took turns listening to each other read short passages out loud as they followed the lifestyles of Dick and Jane and middle-class America.

The basal reader program included a reader and a teacher's manual. Later, a student workbook was added. Stories in the basal reader were written with a controlled vocabulary. Some publishers even attempted to present sentence patterns that paralleled children's oral language development. Around the middle of the 1950s, reading instruction again returned to a focus on phonics.

During the 1970s, the trend was toward humanism, with the key educational terms being *individualization* and *integration*. Children progressed at their own rates, not at a rate determined by their teacher. The language arts were taught as integrated subjects. For the first time, listening and speaking skills took the lead in early childhood grades as children were taught poetry and songs to share and enjoy. The language experience approach promoted by Roach Van Allen (1976), among others, emphasized individualization and integration of language arts instruction. "Personal language," or the language of the child, was the key to teaching language arts. The child would dictate a story to the teacher, who wrote it down word for word and read it back to the child. The child would read it again, thereby relating her own orally spoken words to the printed words on the paper.

In the 1980s, writing gained increased interest as researchers began to consider the relationship between reading and writing development. Rather than the end product, the process of writing was viewed as being of primary importance. Children were encouraged to read what they had written to classmates who listened and provided reactions. Once again, listening and speaking grew in importance. The process approach contends that a hierarchy of sub-skills does not exist in the development of the language arts.

A major publication appeared in 1984, entitled *Becoming a Nation of Readers: The Report of the Commission on Reading*, by Richard C. Anderson, Elfrieda H. Hiebert, Judith A. Scott, and Ian A. G. Wilkinson. The recommendations in the report included the need for parents to read to preschoolers and to support school-age children's interest in reading. In addition, teachers were encouraged to allow children more time for writing and independent reading. Phonics instruction, according to the report, was necessary for beginning reading.

In the 1980s, the whole language approach came into vogue as the child was encouraged to "take control" of his own learning through "empowerment." Children's literature and writing were moved to the forefront. Basal reader publishers took note of the holism-constructivism of whole language and began to change their materials from their previous behavioristic bent. According to Fuhler (1990, p. 312), new basal reading series at that time reflected "a concerted effort to include recognized children's authors, a variety of literacy genre, excerpts, and complete stories from award winning books to entice children to read." In addition, according to Fuhler, there was increased emphasis on the process of writing, asking thought-provoking questions, and using instructional techniques to teach effective reading strategies.

In the late 1980s, leaders in language arts still could not agree on how beginning reading should be taught—a phonics or a whole language approach. Because of the intensity of the controversy, the U.S. Department of Education funded a study by Marilyn Adams (1990) entitled *Beginning to Read: Thinking and Learning about Print* to examine the merits of both approaches. The summary concluded that beginning reading "programs for all children, good and poor readers alike, should strive to maintain an appropriate balance between phonics activities and the reading and appreciation of informative and engaging texts" (p. 125).

Practices varied between the traditional approach, which relied on textbooks and skills, and the nontraditional whole language approach, which emphasized learning processes and more choice and flexibility in instruction but provided less structure and direction for the classroom teacher. The whole language approach resulted in basal readers that emphasize process rather than product and acquisition of learning strategies rather than skills. Increasingly, children's literature is being used to teach reading and content area subjects such as science and social studies.

Many classroom teachers continued to rely on the basal reader as the predominant approach in the teaching of reading. Most teachers, however, adopted an integrated process approach to language arts instruction, incorporating reading, writing, listening, and speaking. Such a combination of approaches has a distinct advantage in that skills and strategies are learned in a relevant, real-life context (Duffy, 1992). This led to the addition of viewing and visually representing as the two most recent language arts.

In the mid-1990s, "balanced reading" was promoted as a combination or blend of phonics and reading comprehension instruction (Baumann, Hoffman, Moon, & Duffy-Hester, 1998; Farris, Fuhler, & Walther, 2004). The term "balanced reading" conjures up an equal dose of phonics literature-based reading instruction. Research findings pointed to 10 interrelated ideas for transforming the teaching and learning of reading (Sweet, 1995, pp. 1–5):

1. When reading, children construct their own meaning.

2. Effective reading instruction can develop engaged readers who are knowledgeable, strategic, motivated, and socially interactive.

3. Phonemic awareness, a precursor to competency in identifying words, is one of the best predictors of later success in reading.

4. Modeling is an important form of classroom support for literacy learning.

5. Storybook reading, done in the context of sharing experiences, ideas, and opinions, is a highly demanding mental activity for children.

6. Responding to literature helps students construct their own meaning, which may not always be the same for all readers.

7. Children who engage in daily discussions about what they read are more likely to become critical readers and learners.

8. Expert readers have strategies that they use to construct meaning before, during, and after reading.

9. Children's reading and writing abilities develop together.

10. The most valuable form of reading assessment reflects current understanding about the reading process and simulates authentic reading tasks.

The phrase "balanced reading" actually goes back several decades to the *Balanced Reading Programmes* of New Zealand in which the components of reading instruction include environmental design, assessment, modeling, guidance, interactivity, independence, practice, oral language acquisition, writing and reading processes, community building, and motivation. This concept of balanced reading is sometimes referred to as "Reading TO, WITH, and BY." In New Zealand, a cadre of instructional approaches is utilized: reading aloud, language experience (in which the child dictates a story to the teacher or an aide who writes it down, word for word), shared reading, guided reading, interactive writing, independent writing, and independent reading (Reutzel, 1998, 1999).

In 2002, the No Child Left Behind Act (NCLBA) was passed. Developed by members of President George W. Bush's administration and supported by Congress, No Child Left Behind was a $26.5 billion federal education law that was intended to make schools more accountable for reading and math instruction: by 2008, every third-grade student in America is supposed to be reading at the third grade level. For the first time in history, assessment instruments were designed to recognize results reported by minority groups. The tests were developed by each state to be administered to students in grades 3–12. Public schools that failed to test would not receive any federal funding (e.g., Title I, aid for free and reduced lunches). Unfortunately, the only language art mentioned in No Child Left Behind was reading, and phonics instruction was strongly encouraged. Listening, speaking, writing, viewing, and visually representing were not included. As a result, in some schools teachers felt pressured to focus on reading so that their students would perform well on the tests, thereby slighting the other language arts.

The Language Arts

Speaking

By the time children enter kindergarten, they have two expansive vocabularies: one for listening and one for speaking. Their listening vocabulary greatly exceeds their speaking vocabulary; however, they are easily able to carry on an adultlike conversation. These vocabularies have been shaped to a large extent by the children's experiential backgrounds. Early and frequent exposure to books; opportunities to visit stimulating places of interest such as

Children need to have the opportunity to share their oral skills. These students are doing storytelling before an audience in their school.

zoos, museums, and libraries; involvement in discussions with family members; and conversations about the television programs they watch are all important in the development of vocabulary and speaking skills.

In the classroom, speaking needs to be encouraged rather than discouraged. Research suggests that children will not benefit from being told about language and how it should be used; rather, they must be active users of language to master it (Fisher & Terry, 1990). Language play is a part of childhood, and children need to have many opportunities to experiment with it. For instance, Kurt, a five-year-old, described his reversible down vest as his "switcher vest" because he could wear it to school as a red vest, "switch" it, and wear it home as a blue vest.

All children need to interact with the teacher and their peers, but this is especially critical for children who are bilingual, language delayed, learning disabled, or mentally challenged. Educators agree that such children need a "language-rich environment." Activities that capitalize on these children's oral language skills are beneficial.

Writing

Writing, like reading, is acquired early by children, even before reading. Two-year-olds make pencil or crayon marks on paper, marks that are meaningful to them even though they are meaningless scribbles to adults. Like speaking, children grasp that making marks on an object is a way to share one's thoughts.

Writing is the most difficult language art to acquire because years of development are needed before this skill is mastered. In fact, some professional writers assert that it takes between 20 and 30 *years* to learn to write because of the complexity of writing. Whereas the reading process requires an individual to take symbols from the printed page and extract meaning from them, the writing process is more complicated. It incorporates a large number of skills: not only must a child initiate an idea, but the idea must be developed and expanded upon, modified or deleted, and organized so that it makes sense to the reader; moreover, correct grammar and spelling must be included and the handwriting must be legible. These are high expectations for children to meet! Indeed, when Frank Smith (1988) began observing children to better understand how they go about the process of writing, he said, "The first time I explored in detail how children learn to write, I was tempted to conclude that it was, like the flight of bumblebees, a theoretical impossibility" (p. 17).

Because of writing's many aspects, researchers have discovered that the writing process entails not only inventing and choosing ideas but also writing the first draft, editing and revising the draft, and finally, sharing the finished product with others.

Children enjoy writing, and they really want to write down their ideas and thoughts. However, when preschoolers and kindergartners begin to write, they lack spelling proficiency. This does not deter them in their eagerness to communicate with the world. If they don't know how to spell a word, they simply invent their own spelling. For instance, Paul, a kindergartner, wrote "I WT TWO A FD HS" for "I went to a friend's house." Other examples of this type of spelling include "ET" for "eat" and "LF" for "laugh." From the outset, children use invented or temporary spelling as a way to convey meaning, the most important part of the writing product. Through their invented spellings, they share imaginative stories and personal experiences.

A classroom teacher must be an advocate of writing and a master of the craft. Donald Graves (1983), a leader in the teaching of writing as a process, refers to the teacher as a craftsperson, "a master follower, observer, listener, waiting to catch the shape of the information" (p. 6). In essence, the teacher assists children in discovering their strengths and in learning from their failures. Teachers gently push and form children into writers, each with a unique style. The end results are children who are in control of their own writing—confident, self-assured writers who write for the love of writing.

Listening

Listening is the first language art that children acquire. The ability to hear and recognize sounds is actually a prenatal development. Amazingly, within two weeks after birth, a baby can distinguish its mother's voice from the voices of other adults. It even recognizes music that the mother listened to frequently during pregnancy.

Listening is often considered the neglected language art because it receives less instructional attention in the classroom than do the other language arts. Yet children are required to spend most of the school day listening. They must listen to the teacher to understand newly introduced concepts or directions for an assignment, to classmates during group and class discussions, to the librarian at story time, to announcements broadcast over the school's intercom, and so on. More time is spent listening than in any other language art, including reading.

Listening enables young children to develop a wide vocabulary, establish sentence patterns, and follow directions—all essential for developing speaking, reading, and writing skills. One aspect of listening, auditory discrimination or the ability to distinguish the difference between sounds, aids spelling and reading proficiency.

Both external and internal factors affect children's listening. For example, a sixth-grade class in Indiana had a teacher who had been born and reared in Connecticut. It took the students nearly six weeks before they could fully understand his dialect as well as keep up with his fast New England style of speech. In the meantime, the scores on their weekly spelling tests suffered. Schools located near airports or construction areas may have lots of background noise that drowns out speakers from time to time—another external hindrance.

In terms of internal factors, attitude, experiential background, vocabulary, ability to relate new knowledge to previously learned knowledge, and intelligence all play a role in listening. Moreover, emotional or physical problems may hinder listening.

Lessons in listening need to involve children as active listeners; for instance, discussing a book they've read or video they've seen gives children a purpose for listening. Such instruction requires the teacher to eliminate external hindrances to the listening process. The teacher must speak with clarity, adjust delivery speed to that which is comfortable for the majority of the class, carefully examine any dialect differences, present material in an orderly manner, and reduce classroom noise.

Reading

Ask a four-year-old what she wants to learn to do in school and the answer will most likely be, "learn how to read." Children consider reading a grownup, "big stuff" activity. Reading is a major step in learning, for it opens up a vast new world to youngsters and gives them independence as learners.

Reading and writing are interrelated and develop concurrently, secondary to listening and speaking, which are the two primary language skills. The development of the two secondary language skills in young children is called *emergent literacy*, meaning that there is in fact a continual emergence or recognition of the printed word. Homes that provide ample opportunities for young children to look at picture books and to hear the books read out loud by their parents or grandparents, to watch Mom and Dad read the local newspaper for items of interest or add an item to the weekly grocery list, and to explore literacy on their own by playing store and school are homes that foster literacy.

Research by Cochran-Smith (1984) and Taylor (1983) has shown that when such literacy surrounds the child, learning usually occurs. Adults should reinforce children by "praising what they have written and read" (Danielson, 1992, p. 279). Indeed, many children from home environments that foster literacy become readers and writers before entering kindergarten.

Having many firsthand and vicarious experiences greatly aids children in learning to read. Because reading is actually the processing of *meaning* from the printed page, children who have had a wide experiential background are better able to relate to and are more likely to be familiar with many reading topics. Smith (1978, 1992) claims that the child's world knowledge actually enriches a passage of text because less is required to identify a word or meaning from the text itself. Take for example, Timmy, a four-year-old. The word *Crest* on a tube of toothpaste was pointed out and Timmy was asked to read the word out loud. He looked at the word but didn't respond. Then Timmy was asked what kind of toothpaste it was, and he beamed and said, "Crest." Young children can "read" by recognizing commonly used household items, but they often fail to understand that such identification is reading. As children become competent, the reading process becomes progressively more automatic.

Reading can be so personal that it is almost as though the author wrote the words solely for the reader. It is not unusual for a child to laugh out loud at the antics of Judy Moody or try to help Nate the Great solve a mystery or ride a roller coaster of emotions while reading Karen Cushman's (1995) *The Midwife's Apprentice*. Whether the message is broad or narrow, happy or sad, informational or sublime, the reader can relate to the message intellectually and emotionally.

To become a good reader, children must become experienced with text. That is, they must be able to use word meaning and word order clues as well

When reading with a child, a parent should ask the child to predict what will happen next. Questions about characters and their actions may be included, as well as having the child note details in the illustrations.

as sound/symbol relationships to sample, infer, predict, and confirm/discon-firm their predictions. The goal of elementary and middle school teachers is to produce lifelong readers. "Proficient readers are experienced readers. They have read a wide variety of literature for a wide variety of purposes which has allowed them to become very familiar with a wide range of vocabulary, syntac-tic [word order] structures, content, background experiences, and authors' styles" (Martens, 1997, p. 608).

Advocates of teaching reading skills focus on teaching the three primary skills in isolated lessons: phonics (also referred to as phonetics), vocabulary, and comprehension. Other educators believe it is best to teach from a con-structionist point of view in that as they read, readers process language and relate it to their own prior experiences, knowledge, and culture. A third the-ory, balanced literacy instruction, promotes the need to combine reading and writing instruction. Balanced literacy instruction has six basic assumptions:

1. Reading, writing, speaking, and listening are considered merely differ-ent mediums through which the concept of language may be mani-fested in communication.

2. Learning to read and write is and ought to be a natural process like learning to speak.

3. Meaning is at the heart of learning to read and write.

4. Reading and writing instructions focus squarely on meaning by progress-ing from the whole to the parts and returning to the whole of language.

5. Learning to read and write are developmental processes.

6. Children learn to read in a supportive and rich literacy environment from the demonstrations of caring and informed people—not from pub-lished texts and instructional materials (Reutzel & Cooter, 1996, p. 57).

In order to teach the language arts effectively, teachers must strive to achieve balance in all areas of literacy instruction and make critical instruc-tional decisions. This requires that teachers be knowledgeable in several areas including assessment, comprehension instruction, children's literature, phon-ics instruction, and vocabulary instruction (Blair-Larsen & Williams, 1999).

As literacy instruction has evolved so too has direct instruction, or explicit teaching. In the 1980s when whole language was at its height of popularity, it was found that children from lower socioeconomic backgrounds struggled. Direct instruction of phonics and other skills aided such students in learning to read.

> Too often in classrooms, many students are left guessing how they should behave and what they should do to become successful readers and writers. Sometimes this is because teachers themselves are not clear about what students should do to learn; sometimes it is because teachers have not seen any advantage in explaining the purposes, processes, and outcomes to the learners; and sometimes it is because teachers have not realized their talk and their modeling has confused rather than enlightened their learners. . . . As teachers accept their responsibility in reducing students' confusion

about literacy learning, they are being challenged to look more closely at the processes of learning, and to be more precise in their teaching. (Hancock, 1999, p. vii)

A research summary by Moats (1999, pp. 7–8) of effective reading instruction points out the need for the following instructional practices:

- Direct teaching of decoding, comprehension, and literature appreciation
- Phoneme awareness instruction
- Systematic and explicit instruction in the code system of written English
- Daily exposure to a variety of texts, as well as incentives for children to read independently and with others
- Vocabulary instruction that encourages children to explore relationships among words and the relationships among word structure, origin, and meaning
- Comprehension strategies that include prediction of outcomes, summarizing, clarification, questioning, and visualization
- Frequent writing of prose to enable deeper understanding of what is read

According to Moats (1999, p. 6), to understand printed language well enough to teach it explicitly requires disciplined study of its systems and forms, both "spoken and written. The result of such research findings has been changes in teacher education preparation programs and professional developing for in-service teachers in the field."

Viewing

Over 200 years ago, John Amos Comenius, an advocate of educational cooperation and author of one of the first illustrated books for children, pointed out the need to include drawings and diagrams in textbooks for better understanding by children. Indeed, teachers have long encouraged beginning readers to use picture clues as they read. Inasmuch as our world today consists of a wide variety of visual media by which messages, ideas, and stories can be conveyed visually—such as print ads, TV shows, Web pages, movies—viewing is a major part of our lives. Thus, students need to learn how to comprehend such visual images and integrate such knowledge with knowledge gained from the other language arts.

In viewing picture books, the teacher can point out certain visual images. John Stewig (1992, p. 12) suggests that teachers follow three steps in sharing picture books so that children's visual literacy skills are developed:

1. Have the children bring their own background to bear on what they see. Have the students tell what they notice and how it compares with what they have experienced.
2. Have the children pay attention to individual units within the larger unit. For example, the use of color in an illustration, the borders of pictures in Jan Brett books, or the designs in the material of Ms. Frizzle's dress in the last illustration of a Joanna Cole's *Magic School Bus* book, or how the end papers of a picture relate to the text.

3. Last, have the children make aesthetic judgments about the relative merits of one picture book over another, giving reasons for their opinions.

Visual literacy is on the rise. Increasingly children's books are being made into movies and television programs. Consider *Babe*, *The Cat in the Hat*, *Harriet the Spy*, *Shiloh*, *Stuart Little*, and *Harry Potter and the Sorcerer's Stone*, all movies based on popular children's books. Now there are television shows as well: *Arthur*, *Franklin*, *Little Bear*, and *The Magic School Bus*. These are available for purchase or rental on tapes or DVDs at video stores. According to Joan L. Glazer (2000, p. 72):

> It is helpful to have children explain orally what they are seeing or have seen, how they have interpreted visual action and symbols. Media can be played and replayed so that children can check on their observations. Teachers have also found that with media, as with books, it is important to set, or have the children set, purposes for viewing and listening.

Visually Representing

Likewise, visually representing is crucial in that students share information in a visual way. For instance, students may use hula-hoops as Venn diagrams to show commonalities and differences between two versions of a folktale such as *The Three Little Pigs* or *Little Red Riding Hood*. A group of students may make a video production of an ad for a book. Hypertext may be used by a class in creating a brochure about projects for a science fair.

Visually representing is a natural for young children. They love to draw pictures of things they love: family, friends, pets, favorite parts of books. Certainly they enjoy illustrating their own stories.

Visually representing is an effective way to teach concepts. For instance, Maria Walther, a first-grade teacher, reads biographies about George Washington and Abraham Lincoln to her students during the week prior to President's Day. Then she places pictorial facial profiles of the two presidents on a bulletin board, carefully overlapping the two. Her students volunteer unique qualities about each man as well as qualities they shared. The shared qualities are inserted where Washington and Lincoln's heads overlap; unique qualities are placed on the faces of the respective presidents. The result is shown in figure 1.1.

Being able to represent a concept visually greatly improves children's understanding of that concept. Visually representing can be done in a myriad of ways including but not limited to art projects, flowcharts, and graphic organizers.

Examples of Using Language Arts

1. Here is an example of how Stacie Rubens used the language arts in first grade as part of her balanced literacy instruction.
   - **Listening.** The students listen as the teacher reads *If You Give a Pig a Pancake* (Numeroff, 1998).
   - **Speaking.** The students take turns talking about the book. They recall the different items that the pig requested.

- **Reading.** The teacher rereads *If You Give a Pig a Pancake* the next day. The students then suggest words to be added to the classroom Word Wall. For example, "pig" has the word chunk "ig" as found in words like "big" and "dig." Other words include "toy" with the "oy" chunk and "sticky" with "ick" as a chunk. All of the word chunks are underlined on the Word Wall.

- **Writing.** The students use invented spelling to write a sentence about what they would each give the pig if she came to visit them at their homes.

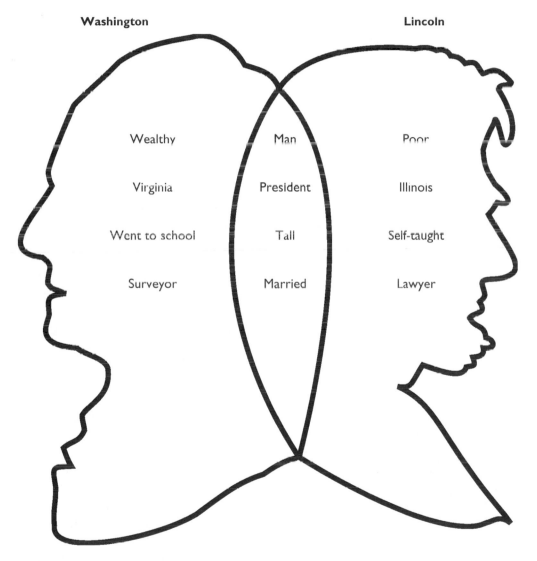

Figure 1.1   Venn diagram of George Washington and Abraham Lincoln

- **Viewing.** The students as a class make a graphic organizer of the items the pig requested. They list items under the categories food, clothing, toys, and other things.

- **Visually Representing.** The students draw pictures of what they would give the pig on the same pages as the sentences they wrote for writing. The pictures and sentences are displayed on the wall outside the classroom for other students and visitors to admire.

2. Here is an example using the language arts in a second-grade unit on Native Americans.

- **Listening.** The students listen as the teacher reads the Algonquin Indian version of *Cinderella* entitled *The Rough-Faced Girl* by Rafe Martin (1992). The students listen to each other in class discussion about how the book is similar and different from the French version of *Cinderella* with which they are familiar. (Note: The teacher a few days later shares several different versions of *Cinderella*—Korean, Egyptian, Irish, etc.—and has the students compare and contrast these versions as well in another literacy lesson.) After listening to *The Rough-Faced Girl*, the students then listen to Native American music from a CD.

- **Speaking.** The students take turns talking about the book and the songs. The teacher has given each student a colored feather to hold. When a student wants to say something, he holds up the feather. After the teacher calls on the student, the child then puts the feather in a headdress the class is making. Once a child has given up a feather, the child cannot reenter the discussion. This enables all of the students to engage in the discussion without a few children dominating it.

- Before they begin reading, the students select tribes to read about. Each group then makes a KWL chart about the tribe's culture with the help of the teacher. The chart lists K, what they already know about the tribe, and W, what they would like to learn about the tribe's culture.

- **Reading.** The students read books about Native American tribes from throughout North America. The students work in small groups of three or four.

- **Writing.** The students take notes on specific aspects of each tribe's lifestyle. Later in their small groups, they complete their KWL charts with L, what they have learned about their respective tribe's culture.

- **Viewing.** The students make Venn diagrams of how the tribes are alike and how they differ.

- **Visually Representing.** Each student makes a model of a typical home for a member of the tribe they have studied. The models are displayed in the school library for other students to admire.

3. The following is an example using the language arts in a fifth-grade study of *Harry Potter and the Sorcerer's Stone* (Rowling, 1997).

- **Listening.** Students listen as the teacher reads aloud the first chapter of *Harry Potter and the Sorcerer's Stone*. The students listen as classmates discuss their predictions as to what will come next in the story.

- **Speaking.** Students share their thoughts as to what they anticipate will happen next in the story. Such discussion occurs after the 1st, 4th, 7th, 10th, 13th, and 16th chapters of the book.

- **Reading.** Students read *Harry Potter and the Sorcerer's Stone* with a partner. The students are given specific chapters to read by a specific date so the class can discuss the book together.

- **Writing.** Students write dialogue journals. Two students "dialogue" in a notebook as they read the book. Their dialogue includes their reaction to the plot, to characters, and to the author's style.

- **Viewing.** In small groups, students select scenes to re-create as a drama. Each group writes a play based on the scene selected. They rehearse the play before they present it to the rest of the class.

- **Visually Representing.** The students stay in their viewing groups and use magazine pictures to make a collage about Harry Potter's adventures.

4. An example of using the language arts in an eighth-grade unit on *Holes* (Sachar, 1998) is given here.

- **Listening.** The class listens as the teacher uses "popcorn" oral reading to have students take turns reading the first two chapters of *Holes*. Students later listen as their peers share their views on the book.

- **Speaking.** Since Louis Sachar writes short, concise chapters, the teacher has the class read the book in chunks of seven chapters. At those points, students give their opinions on the book *Holes*. They discuss the humor and sadness depicted by the author in his telling of Stanley's plight at a juvenile detention center.

- **Reading.** Students read the remaining chapters of *Holes* individually. Sections of the book are shared as rereadings during class discussions. Students also read articles about the arrest of youths who are then sent to juvenile detention centers.

- **Writing.** Students keep simulated journals about what it would be like to be a Stanley or (for the girls) a Stella in a juvenile detention center. They are encouraged to comment on being homesick, missing family and friends, as well as anticipating what life will be like in their respective futures.

- **Viewing.** Students form their own groups to reenact selected scenes from the book.

- **Visually Representing.** Students make a "hole" out of a paper bag. Inside the hole, they write their favorite phrases, sentences, or paragraphs from *Holes*. These are then displayed on a bulletin board for the entire class and other classes of middle schoolers to see.

Characteristics of Competent Language Users

Teachers not only need to be familiar with each of the language arts but also need to become aware of the characteristics of competent language users. The Steering Committee of the Elementary Section of the National Council of Teachers of English (NCTE, 1996) identified seven characteristics of competent language users. These characteristics relate not only to the classroom but also to the way a child engages in language use throughout the day. These seven characteristics are:

1. **Personal Expression.** Students use language to express themselves as they make connections between their own personal experiences and those of their community and society. Such personal expression is demonstrated whenever they select books to read, topics they want to discuss, or ideas about which they want to write. In short, the students are creating their own personal voices.

2. **Aesthetic Appreciation.** Students use language aesthetically in talking with others, reading literature, writing, and enriching their lives.

3. **Collaborative Exploration.** Students use language as a learning tool as they work with peers to investigate concepts and ideas.

4. **Strategic Language Use.** Students use strategies they adopt or create as they share meaning through language.

5. **Creative Communication.** Students use text forms and genres (different types of literature and writing) creatively as they share ideas through language.

6. **Reflective Interpretation.** Students use language to organize and evaluate learning experiences, question personal and social values, and think creatively and critically.

7. **Thoughtful Application.** Students use language to solve problems, persuade others, and take action on ideas.

Interdisciplinary Instruction

Increasingly, schools are moving toward interdisciplinary instruction in which all content areas are taught in one thematic unit. This makes for learning experiences that are often more "personal, authentic, and inquiry-driven" (Whitin & Whitin, 1996, p. 84) and more relevant than those that rely solely upon science or social studies textbooks.

There are many successful elementary and middle school programs throughout the country that use an interdisciplinary approach to language arts instruction. For instance, Pope Elementary School in Pope, North Carolina, was recognized for its exemplary language arts program. Emily Kyser Ramey (1995, p. 418), principal of Pope Elementary, described her school as follows:

Language arts instruction is built on the research-based position that children learn to read by reading and being read to and that children learn to write by writing and reading the writing of others. Daily instruction integrates reading, writing, listening, and speaking activities with content area subjects. . . .

Daily time is provided for students to read silently from self-selected materials, to write in journals, and to read aloud to classmates. Learning logs, for subject areas such as science, math, and social studies, allow students to comprehend and summarize new information for themselves and provide additional text for individual and class reading.

Ramey (1995, p. 419) is careful to point out that teachers alone cannot make an outstanding language arts program, that there must be a

combined effort of parents, teachers, and administrators committed to a quality language arts program for all students. . . . Pope School strives to provide an integrated language arts program that promotes critical thinking, builds literacy, and helps to develop a lifetime love of reading.

Lafayette Township School in rural New Jersey, also recognized for its outstanding language arts program, views reading, writing, listening, and speaking as integral to the content areas—math, science, and social studies. Students at Lafayette Township have a portion of the school day set aside for silent reading and are read to regularly by their teachers. Writing is often combined with reading (Mahler, 1995).

Student Assessment

Teaching the language arts requires that the classroom teacher rely on a variety of assessment measures, including anecdotal records, checklists to indicate progress in a skill area, informal reading inventories, rubrics that specify what each assignment should contain, quizzes, and achievement and diagnostic tests.

Most teachers use a rubric at one time or another to let students know what is expected for an assignment. Rubrics are frequently used for writing assignments, projects, and dramatic reenactments. (See figures 1.2 and 1.3.)

In particular, writing lends itself to the use of rubrics. Once the focal point of the learning has been established and objectives have been created, the teacher can develop a rubric for the task. Many teachers have the students help formulate the rubric, which gets the class to buy into the task. Internet Web sites also provide rubrics that teachers can use. These Web sites include *www.rubistar.4teachers.org* or *www.teach-nology.com* and require the teacher to type in the lesson's objectives; the Web site will then create the rubric.

Anecdotal records are helpful measures. These may be notes recorded throughout the school day in a daily log, perhaps using a notebook, a clipboard, or a handheld electronic device. Interests, behaviors, academic work, and so on can all be included in anecdotal records. At the end of each day, the teacher may organize the notes by individual students and convert the notes to a computer disk. A quick and efficient means of organization is to use 4" × 6" index cards taped inside a photo album in a layered fashion. (See box 1.1 on p. 28.) After a student's card is full, it may be placed in a portfolio.

Although standardized achievement tests continue to be used in most school districts, portfolios have also become popular ongoing assessment measures. Standardized achievement tests are given once a year to evaluate how a group performs. Standardized achievement tests are summative measures—like a onetime photo that may or may not turn out to the individual's satisfaction. On the other hand, portfolios offer a series of "photos," or pictures of the child's achievement, over a period of time—a type of formative assessment during the year that becomes summative at semester or year-end and throughout a child's school career. Portfolios can contain an interest inventory (see box 1.2 on p. 29), writing samples from first draft through the final product, lists of

	Visual (9)	Delivery (14)	Elements of Report (10)

3	Original
	Clear message
	Attractive
	Easily understood
	Eye-catching
		Captures attention of audience
		Speaks clearly, loudly, and distinctively
		Uses good posture
		Presents serious demeanor
			Includes elements of report:
			    Setting
			    Characters
			    Problem
			    Events (3)
			    Conclusion details left open
			Follows logical and sequential order

2	Clear message
	Attractive
	Easily understood
		Speaks clearly, loudly, and distinctively
		Uses good posture
		Presents serious demeanor
			Contains 3+ of the elements
			Includes elements of report:
			    Setting
			    Characters
			    Problem
			    Events (3)
			    Conclusion details left open
			Follows logical and sequential order

1	Lacks clear message
	Unattractive
		Poor quality of speech
		Poor quality of overall presentation
			Contains 2+ of the elements
			Includes elements of report:
			    Setting
			    Characters
			    Problem
			    Events (3)
			    Conclusion details left open
			Follows logical and sequential order

0	No attempt	No attempt	No attempt

Written by Jones, B., Little, A., Marshall, N., Slack, P., & Parsons, S. (1998). Tifton, GA: Len Lastinger Elementary School, Tift County Schools. Used by permission.

Figure 1.2 Rubric: evaluating oral presentations: story (re)telling

books read independently and as part of classroom assignments, and videos and audio tapes of the student presenting a dramatic piece or reading poetry or a favorite passage from a children's book. Each item in the portfolio is dated.

Some schools require that each item in a portfolio have an attached index card describing why it is in the portfolio. The student and/or the teacher must then defend the piece. For instance a student may decide to put in a narrative

	Topics (7)	Ideas (7)	Sentence Structure (7)	Mechanics (4)
4	All 10 topics developed	Fresh ideas Focused Many details	Clearly written Complete Variety of length Descriptive	Few or no errors: Capitalization (beginning of sentences and proper nouns) Ending punctuation Commas Paragraphs indented Spelling
3	Eight topics developed	Fresh ideas Focused Several details	Most sentences clearly written Complete sentences Some variety of length Simple sentences	Some errors: Capitalization (beginning of sentences and proper nouns) Ending punctuation Commas Paragraphs indented Spelling
2	Six topics	Fresh ideas Some details Moves away from focus Ending punctuation	Some sentences unclear Some run-on sentences Fragments Little variety	Many errors ($+\frac{1}{2}$ sentences): Capitalization Ending punctuation Commas Paragraphs indented Spelling
1	Four topics	Incomplete ideas Few details Unfocused	Sentences not clear Frequent fragments No variety	Serious errors (all or most sentences): Capitalization Commas Paragraphs indented Spelling
0	No attempt	No attempt	No attempt	No attempt

Topics: Who are you? What do you look like? Where do you live? What is your family like? What (if any) type of pet do you have? What do you think about school? Who are your friends and why? Who is your favorite teacher and why? What bothers you? What do you wish?

Written by AbduLhadi, S., & Powell, A. (1998). Tifton, GA: Northside Elementary School, Tift County Schools. Used by permission.

Figure 1.3   Rubric: evaluating writing: narrative autobiography

writing selection because she had a well-developed character, or a science fair project about the human body including an illustration of the human digestive system that she drew.

1.1   In the Classroom: Teaching Hint

Anecdotal Record Keeping

The classroom teacher must stay abreast of students' reactions to activities and materials, their development of learning strategies, and their basic interests and dislikes. The development of self-discipline, an important life skill, should also be noted. In addition, it is important to maintain a record of students' physical well-being. Such information is useful to the teacher in that certain patterns tend to evolve; such patterns influence each child's development in the language arts as well as other curricular areas. These patterns may be shared with the parents during a parent-teacher conference. For instance, if a note indicates that Rod fell asleep in class three times in two weeks, the teacher should make a phone call to Rod's parents. Perhaps Rod stays up too late at night or has a medical problem.

A simple record-keeping device is a photo album designed to hold 4" × 6" photos in plastic flip sheets. When the album is opened, one set of flip sheets lies on each side. The teacher writes the child's name on the bottom left-hand side of a 4" × 6" index card and tapes it to a flip sheet. The students' names are placed in alphabetical order so that when the teacher wants to write a note about a particular child, the other cards are quickly flipped up and that student's card is ready for the teacher's note taking. When a card is filled, the tape is removed and the card is placed inside the plastic photo cover for future reference. Later, the cards may be placed in a student's portfolio. An index of student cards and sample cards are shown below.

Lisa A.	Hector L.		9/5 Brought her new public library card
Adam A.	Jimmy N.		9/6 Wrote a poem for social studies
Mark B.	Ty P.		9/14 Had trouble deciding which group to join
Jose B.	Carole P.		
Roberta B.	Leon P.		
Melinda C.	Eric R.		
Gary C.	Roberto S.		
Glenda D.	Susan S.		
Ivan F.	Harry T.		
Melissa H.	Jason T.		
Terry H.	Julie T.		
Jenny K.	Linda W.		
Linda L.			Lisa A.

Student Cards

9/5   Very happy about being back in school

9/6   Forgot homework

9/7   Brought homework from yesterday; worked well with Hector on writing project

9/8   Brought in a box turtle he found on way home from school

9/14   Requested to work with Hector and Eric on science project; Joked

9/16   Late to school

9/21   The science coop project turned out great; Mark complimented Hector and Eric on their work

Mark B.

9/6   Worked well with Ivan on writing up science experiment

9/8   Has trouble with writing topic sentences

9/13   Lost his library book

9/14   Found "   "   " in his locker
         Wrote a nice letter to Jason who was out ill.

Hector L.

1.2   In the Classroom: Teaching Hint

Portfolio Interest Inventory

Name:

I like to do:

1. _____
2. _____
3. _____

My favorite books are:

1. _____
2. _____
3. _____

Titles of books I'd like to read:

1. _____
2. _____
3. _____

I want to write about:

1. _____
2. _____
3. _____

I'd like to see videos about:

1. _____
2. _____
3. _____

Grade:

I like books about:

1. _____
2. _____
3. _____

My favorite authors are:

1. _____
2. _____

I've written about:

1. _____
2. _____
3. _____

I'd like to know more about:

1. _____
2. _____
3. _____

It is best to use a wide variety of assessment measures that are integral to the instruction process, not merely added on (see figure 1.4).

Assessment Methods	Objective Scoring	Subjective Scoring

Paper & Pencil	Tests
	    Multiple Choice
	    True/False
	    Matching
	    Fill-in-the Blank
		Essays, Reports

Performance (Process & Product)	Checklist or rubric of specific attributes present or absent in behaviors or products	Rating scale reflecting *degrees* of quality in behaviors or products
Personal Communication (Teacher & Student)	Closed-ended questions	Open-ended questions Portfolios Conferences

Figure 1.4   Various assessment methods

Individualized Educational Plans (IEPs)

Individualized Educational Plans (IEPs) are reports by a multidisciplinary team that typically includes a school psychologist, a special education resource teacher, a social worker, and the classroom teacher regarding a special education or inclusion student. Other members of the team may include the principal, speech/language therapist, adaptive physical education teacher (for motor skill development), school counselor, and school nurse. The child's parents or guardians must approve the final plan before it is put into action. The plan includes results of various assessment measures and an instructional plan to meet the needs of the student. Prior to its implementation, the multidisciplinary team meets with the child's parents or guardians to go over the instructional strategies the team has developed for the child. The parent or guardian's permission in writing needs to be obtained before the IEP can be implemented.

When working with a student whom the teacher suspects has special needs and requires assessment by a school psychologist, the teacher should keep careful documentation of the student's behavior patterns and academic work, which can be photocopied and kept in a file. The teacher should focus on education factors, which include academic/cognitive factors (speech and language should be separate categories), health/physical factors, and personal/social factors. The teacher must be careful to document the behavior in an objective manner. Keeping to the facts and not including opinions is critical. The information will assist the school psychologist in determining which tests to administer. Box 1.3 contains a checklist for the four areas of primary concern. Although the checklist is important, dated examples of the student's work and carefully maintained anecdotal records are essential.

1.3   In the Classroom: Teaching Hint

Checklist for Referring Students to School Psychologist

Student: _____   Birthdate: _____

Date: _____   Teacher: _____

Grade: _____   School: _____

I. Academic/Cognitive Factors

_____ 1. Academic difficulties

_____ Math

_____ Reading

_____ Writing

_____ Listening

_____ 2. Poor handwriting

_____ Manuscript   _____ Letter reversals (Indicate: _____)

_____ Cursive   _____ Poor letter formation (Indicate: _____)

_____ 3. Difficulty devoting attention to a task

_____ 4. Difficulty following directions

_____ 5. Difficulty moving from one activity to another

____ 6. Easily discouraged/frustrated
_____ Subject area

____ 7. Work completion
____ Fails to finish assignments
____ Fails to complete homework
____ Work is hurried
____ Works very slowly but finishes

____ 8. Poor retention of concepts

Comments:

II. Speech/Language Factors

____ 1. Articulation problems
Specify sounds

____ 2. Unable to blend sounds together
____ dr ____ bl ____ str ____ tr ____ other (Specify:)
____ Beginning sounds of words
____ Middle sounds
____ Final sounds

____ 3 Stuttering
____ 4. Poor grammar/usage
____ 5. Limited speaking vocabulary
____ 6. Limited listening vocabulary
____ 7. Incomplete sentences
____ Uses phrases rather than sentences most of the time
____ 8. Difficulty relating own ideas to topic presented to group or class
____ 9. Inappropriate responses to questions
____ 10. Difficulty following directions
____ Simple directions
____ Directions of two steps
____ Directions with three or more steps

Comments:

III. Health/Physical Factors

____ 1. Frequent absences
____ Frequent tardiness

____ 2. Health problems
____ Complains of (specify)

____ 3. Very restless, fidgety, active
____ 4. Looks pale, listless, lacks energy
____ 5. Poor motor coordination
____ 6. Growth lag
____ 7. Possible deficit:
____ Hearing
____ Visual

Comments:

continued

IV. Personal/Social Factors

____ 1. Withdrawn, timid, shy

____ 2. Poor interactions with peers

    ____ Can't engage in a conversation with a peer at recess or lunch

    ____ Disturbs others

    ____ Fights

____ 3. Lacks self control

    ____ Temper outbursts

    ____ Use of inappropriate language

    ____ Use of inappropriate names for peers, teachers

____ 4. Lacks control of emotions

    ____ Cries frequently

    ____ Frequently unhappy

    ____ Moody

____ 5. Low self-concept

____ 6. Exaggerates

    ____ Lies

    ____ Fantasizes

____ 7. Lacks empathy for others

    ____ Lacks concern for others

    ____ Tries to bully others

____ 8. Challenges authority/defiant

____ 9. Impulsive

____ 10. Behavior is often unpredictable

Comments:

Summary

The language arts consist of listening, speaking, reading, writing, viewing, and visually representing. Thinking is considered the seventh language art that undergirds them all. The development of the language arts is concurrent and interrelated. As teachers, we must understand each of the language arts individually so that we can better teach them in integrated fashion.

Today's emphasis is upon instruction in which beginning readers and writers learn phonics in tandem with reading for comprehension. Such a balanced approach aids writing development as well. Later, the upper-elementary and middle school students develop and fine-tune their language arts skills as they work with relevant, real-world materials.

Assessment plays an important role in language arts instruction because we as teachers use various measures to determine student strengths and weaknesses and then develop our instruction based on these findings in order to apply appropriate methodology. As teachers, we must also be attuned to the needs of all students, including those with special needs and those with diverse backgrounds.

Questions

1. How have the language arts changed?
2. What types of habits possessed by a speaker interfere with the audience's ability to listen?
3. How does the home environment help or hinder the development of emergent literacy?
4. What is balanced literacy (reading and writing) instruction?

Reflective Teaching

Flip back to the beginning of the chapter to the teaching vignette entitled "Peering into the Classroom." After rereading the vignette, consider the following questions: What characteristics (either implied or directly exhibited) does the teacher possess that you would like to develop? What strengths and weaknesses are revealed for the students described in this section? How would you meet the needs of students such as these?

Activities

1. Listen to young children as they play in a park or at a day care center. In what unique or unusual ways do they use words?
2. List several factors, both internal and external, that affect your own listening.
3. Ask an experienced teacher about what changes in reading/writing instruction have occurred over the last 15 to 20 years.

Further Reading

Adams, M. J. (1990). *Beginning to read: Thinking and learning about print*. Urbana, IL: Center for the Study of Reading.

Ainsworth, L. (1998). *Student generated rubrics: An assessment model to help all students succeed*. Palo Alto, CA: Dale Seymour Publications.

Akhaven, N. (2004). *How to align literacy instruction, assessment, and standards and achieve results you never dreamed possible*. Portsmouth, NH: Heinemann.

Bausch, L. S. (2003). Just words: Living and learning the literacies of our students' lives. *Language Arts, 80* (1), 223–229.

Gambrell, L. B., Morrow, L. M., Neuman, S. B., & Pressley, M. (Eds.). (1999). *Best practices in literacy instruction*. New York: Guilford.

Kong, A., & Fitch, E. (2002–2003). Using Book Club to engage culturally and linguistically diverse learners in reading, writing, and talking about books. *The Reading Teacher, 56* (4), 352–362.

Moats, L. C. (1999). *Teaching reading is rocket science: What expert teachers of reading should know and be able to do*. Washington, DC: American Federation of Teachers.

Routman, R. (2000). *Conversations: Strategies for Teaching, Learning, and Evaluating*. Portsmouth, NH: Heinemann.

Villaume, S. K., & Brabham, E. G. (2003). Phonics instruction: Beyond the debate. *The Reading Teacher, 56* (5), 478–482.

Vukelich, C., & Christie, J. (2004). *Building a foundation for preschool literacy: Effective instruction for children's reading and writing development*. Newark, DE: International Reading Association.

References

Adams, D., & Hamm, M. (2001). *Literacy in a multimedia age*. Norwood, MA: Christopher Gordon.

Allen, R. V. (1976). *Language experiences in communication*. Boston: Houghton Mifflin.

Anderson, R. C., Hiebert, E. H., Scott, J. A., & Wilkinson, I. A. G. (1984). *Becoming a nation of readers: The report of the Commission on Reading*. Washington, DC: National Institute of Education.

Baumann, J. F., Hoffman, J. V., Moon, J., & Duffy-Hester, A. M. (1998). Where are teachers' voices in the phonics/whole language debate? Results from a survey of U.S. elementary teachers. *The Reading Teacher, 51* (9), 636–650.

Blair-Larsen, S. M., & Williams, K. A. (1999). *The balanced reading program: Helping all students achieve success*. Newark, DE: International Reading Association.

Cochran-Smith, M. (1984). *The making of a reader*. Norwood, NJ: Ablex.

Cushman, K. (1995). *The midwife's apprentice*. New York: Clarion.

Danielson, K. E. (1992). Learning about early writing from response to literature. *Language Arts, 69*, (4), 274–280.

Duffy, G. (1992). Let's free teachers to be inspired. *Phi Delta Kappan, 73* (6), 442–447.

Farris, P. J., Fuhler, C., & Walther, M. (2004). *Teaching reading: A balanced approach for today's classrooms*. Boston: McGraw-Hill.

Fisher, C., & Terry, A. (1990). *Children's language and the language arts* (3rd ed.). Boston: Allyn and Bacon.

Fuhler, C. J. (1990). Let's move toward literature-based reading instruction. *The Reading Teacher, 43* (4), 312–315.

Glazer, J. L. (2000). *Literature for young children* (4th ed.). Upper Saddle River, NJ: Merrill/Prentice-Hall.

Graves, D. (1983). *Writing: Teachers and children at work*. Portsmouth, NH: Heinemann.

Hancock, J. (Ed.). (1999). *The explicit teaching of reading*. Newark, DE: International Reading Association.

Huck, C. S., Hepler, S., Hickman, J., & Kiefer, B. Z. (2004). *Children's literature in the elementary school* (8th ed). Boston: McGraw-Hill.

Kong, A., & Fitch, E. (2002-2003). Using Book Club to engage culturally and linguistically diverse learners in reading, writing, and talking about books. *The Reading Teacher, 56* (4), 352–362.

Johnson, T. D., & Louis, D. R. (1987). *Literacy through literature*. Portsmouth, NH: Heinemann.

Juel, C., Biancarosa, G., Coker, D., & Deffes, R. (2003). Walking with Rosie: A cautionary tale of early reading instruction. *Educational Leadership, 60* (7) 12–18.

Mahler, W. R. (1995). Practice what you preach. *The Reading Teacher, 48* (5), 414–415.

Martens, P. (1997). What miscue analysis reveals about word recognition and repeated reading: A view through the "Miscue Window." *Language Arts, 74* (8), 600–609.

Moats, L. C. (1999). *Teaching reading is rocket science: What expert teachers of reading should know and be able to do*. Washington, DC: American Federation of Teachers.

Morrow, L. M. (2004). Motivation: The forgotten factor. *Reading Today, 21* (5), 6.

NCTE Elementary Section Steering Committee. (1996). Exploring language arts standards within a cycle of learning. *Language Arts, 73* (1), 10–13.

NCTE/IRA. (1996). *Standards for the English language arts*. Urbana, IL: National Council of Teachers of English and International Reading Association.

Ramey, E. K. (1995). An integrated approach to language arts instruction. *The Reading Teacher, 48* (5), 418–419.

Reutzel, D. R. (1998–1999). On balanced reading. *The Reading Teacher, 52* (4), 322–323.

Reutzel, D. R., & Cooter, R. B. (1996). *Teaching children to read: From basals to books* (2nd ed.). Columbus, OH: Merrill.

Smith, F. (1978). *Comprehension and learning*. New York: Holt, Rinehart, & Winston.

Smith, F. (1988). *Joining the literacy club: Further essays in education*. Portsmouth, NH: Heinemann.

Smith, F. (1992). Learning to read: The never ending debate. *Phi Delta Kappan, 73* (6), 442–447.

Spiegel, D. L. (1992). Blending whole language and systematic instruction. *The Reading Teacher, 46* (1), 38–44

Stewig, J. (1992). Reading pictures, reading texts: Some similarities. *The New Advocate, 5* (1), 11–22.

Strickland, D. (1977). Promoting language and concept development. In B. Cullinan & C. Carmichel (Eds.), *Language and young children*. Urbana, IL: National Council of Teachers of English.

Sweet, A. P. (1995). *State of the art: Transforming ideas for teaching and learning to read*. Washington, DC: U.S. Department of Education.

Taylor, D. (1983). *Family literacy*. Norwood, NJ: Ablex.

Templeton, S. (1991). *Teaching the integrated language arts*. Boston: Houghton Mifflin.

Vacca, J. L., Vacca, R. T., & Gove, M. K. (2000). *Reading and learning to read* (4th ed.). New York: Addison, Wesley, Longman.

Vygotsky, L. (1978). *Mind in society: Development of higher psychological processes*. Cambridge, MA: Harvard University Press.

Whitin, D. J., & Whitin, P. E. (1996). Inquiry at the window: The year of the birds. *Language Arts, 73* (2), 82–87.

Children's Literature

Cohn, J. (1987). *I had a friend named Peter* (G. Owen, Illus.). New York: Morrow.

Martin, R. (1992). *The rough faced girl* (D. Shannon, Illus.). New York: Putnam.

Numeroff, L. (1985) *If you give a mouse a cookie* (F. Bond, Illus.). New York: Harper & Row.

Numeroff, L. (1991). *If you give a moose a muffin* (F. Bond, Illus.). New York: HarperCollins.

Numeroff, L. (1998). *If you give a pig a pancake* (F. Bond, Illus.). New York: HarperCollins.

Numeroff, L. (2002). *If you take a mouse to school* (F. Bond, Illus.). New York: HarperCollins.

Rowling, J. K. (1997). *Harry Potter and the sorcerer's stone*. New York: Scholastic.

Sachar, L. (1998). *Holes*. New York: Farrar, Straus, and Giroux.

Thaler, M. (1993). *The principal from the Black Lagoon*. New York: Scholastic.

Web Sites

www.4teachers.org

An invaluable site for both new and experienced teachers! It has tutorials, review tips on how to protect children from going to undesirable Web sites, lesson plans, rubric development, and more.

www.microsoft.com/education/Default.aspx

This site provides many classroom resources, such as lesson plans, templates, clip art, as well as professional learning resources.

www.nwrel.org

This site has assessments and lesson plans particularly focusing on writing.

www.teachnet.com

Language arts lesson plans and other teaching information is provided at this site.

www.lessonplansearch.com

A wide variety of lesson plans are listed at this site.

www.reading.org

This is the official web site of the International Reading Association and features lesson plans as well as information about the organization itself. IRA/NCTE position papers on important literacy topics are available here.

www.ncte.org

This is the official Web site of the National Council of Teachers of English and features lesson plans and information about the organization.

Other Web sites: Each state has its own department of education, which provides valuable information about standards for language arts, lesson plans, and assessment.

Children and Teachers in the Classroom

> Live a balanced life—learn some and think some and draw and paint and sing and dance and play and work every day some.
>
> —Robert Fulghum
> *All I Really Needed to Know I Learned in Kindergarten*

PEERING INTO THE CLASSROOM
A FOURTH-GRADE CLASS

The school doors open at 8:15 AM for yet another day of learning. Kim McNamara's fourth graders scurry into the classroom. Two girls offer their services to Miss McNamara to unpack the paperback book order that has just arrived. Other students quickly hang up their jackets and book bags and then head to one of the activity tables Miss McNamara has set up in the back of the classroom—a writing center on parodies, a table filled with humor and joke books, a computer with math games, and a science center with the materials necessary to make a homemade camera. Two students who were previously assigned the responsibility of feeding the classroom pets are carefully measuring the appropriate amounts of food for the two gerbils and an aquarium of guppies. Next, the two students will give the box turtle the houseflies they caught before school.

A few students go to a box labeled "Concerns" to scribble a brief note about problems they are struggling to overcome—for example, the death of a family cat or a lost necklace. Having changed their "concerns" from mental worries to tangible notes, they deposit their "concerns" for the day into the box; they will pick up the notes when school is over when they can try to resolve their problems without interfering with their learning.

It is only the fifth week of the school year, but all the children appear to be confident and at ease as they pursue the many different opportunities available to them. Electricity permeates the air as the children excitedly immerse themselves in the day's activities that Miss McNamara has carefully planned.

The classroom itself is enticing. Two bulletin boards offer variety and color, displaying timely themes that coincide with a learning goal of the class or of the school. The bulletin boards, which are changed biweekly, typically are working bulletin boards that the students can manipulate. One of the bulletin boards has parodies written by the students and Miss McNamara. The other is an action bulletin board with questions about photography, the current science topic.

Looking around the classroom, one observes library books, prominently displayed on chalk rails and tables, and colorful posters. There are writing and listening charts that succinctly give instruction. Three simple rules describing acceptable classroom behavior are listed above the chalkboard. Mobiles hanging overhead depict the students' favorite characters in recently read books. Clearly, students' attitudes and interests have been considered in the creation of the classroom environment.

A bell rings, signaling the official beginning of the school day. What was a silent classroom when Kim McNamara arrived at 7:30 AM has now become one marked by low murmuring voices, an occasional giggle followed by laughter, the rattling of papers and books as the students take their seats—the sounds of children readying themselves for a day of learning.

Only a year ago, Kim McNamara had been studying methods of teaching elementary students—learning techniques of instruction in language arts, reading, mathematics, science, and social studies, among other subjects. As she was learning theories about teaching, she was able to observe and participate with elementary students as part of her preservice teacher education program. But now Kim is *the teacher*. She must put theory into practice, making decisions that could affect her students for the rest of their lives. How well she is prepared, how much time she has devoted to planning the lessons, and how enthusiastic she is about each lesson are reflected in the learning of her students.

It didn't take Kim long to discover that as a teacher she is also a "student," learning something new about children and teaching every day. She has students with different cultural and ethnic backgrounds and a wide range of abilities and interests. According to Kim, "Teaching has proved to be a major challenge, the greatest I've ever encountered. But I've found that I love every minute of it!"

Kim has made a special attempt to communicate with each of her fourth graders. Prior to the beginning of school, she wrote a letter to each of her students introducing herself. She described her hobbies of playing golf and swimming as well as her interest in reading mysteries. Kim also asked what the students enjoyed doing after school. She asked each one to think of something he or she wanted to learn more about, promising to try to include it some time during the school year. Kim has continued the open communication pattern by regularly writing achievement notes to parents and students. Each student has a mailbox, encouraging rather than discouraging "note passing." "My goal is to be supportive of literacy (reading and writing). If a student writes a note and the recipient reads it, literacy has been reinforced and promoted," Kim states. "Communication has taken place between an author (the note writer) and the reader (the note's recipient)."

Kim closely monitors the pulse of her class as she meets the academic needs of her students in ways they find stimulating. Kim McNamara is aware that students have many needs and concerns that will change throughout the school year.

Chapter Objectives

The reader will:

✓ understand the importance of developing a good rapport with students.

✓ appreciate the need to acquire a variety of instructional approaches to interest students in language arts.

✓ understand that effective teaching requires close monitoring of individual and class performance.

✓ be able to apply a variety of classroom management approaches in teaching language arts.

Standards for Professionals

The following Standards will be addressed in this chapter:

Standard 1: Foundational Knowledge and Dispositions

1.1 Demonstrate knowledge of psychological, sociological, and linguistic foundations of reading and writing processes and instruction.

1.3 Demonstrate knowledge of language development and reading acquisition and variations related to cultural and linguistic diversity.

Standard 2: Instructional Strategies and Curriculum Materials

2.1 Use instructional grouping options (individual, small-group, whole-class, and computer based) as appropriate for accomplishing given purpose.

2.2 Use a wide range of instructional practices, approaches, and methods, including technology-based practices, for learners at differing stages of development and from differing cultural and linguistic backgrounds.

Standard 4: Creating a Literate Environment

4.1 Use students' interests, reading abilities, and backgrounds as foundations for the reading and writing program.

Standard 5: Professional Development

5.1 Display positive dispositions related to reading and the teaching of reading.

5.2 Continue to pursue the development of professional knowledge and dispositions.

5.3 Work with colleagues to observe, evaluate, and provide feedback on each other's practice.

5.4 Participate in, initiate, implement, and evaluate professional development programs.

Introduction

Teachers face ever-mounting challenges in trying to instruct their charges. Likewise, students encounter more choices and social problems today than ever before. Insightful teachers are aware of the home and community environments of their students. They must teach all students, including those whose cultural backgrounds, language, and cognitive or physical abilities present challenges to learning. This chapter discusses the needs of children as well as ways teachers can improve classroom management and organization for instruction.

Children and Their Teachers

It is just after lunch on the first full day of the new school year. Joe Blackburn's sixth graders are nearly spent. They are tired and sweaty from running at recess. According to Joe, his students are "out of school shape"—that is, they haven't had to sit quietly at desks and work for 30 minutes or more at a single setting in a hot classroom in September. While they eagerly engaged in the variety of learning activities Joe set up for the morning, they ran out of steam for learning. Joe's feeling out of "teaching shape" as well. Reaching for a book, Joe tells his class to sit back, relax, and listen. Gratefully, they follow the directions of their newly assigned teacher. Joe opens the book and reads aloud, "Chapter One. The Boy Who Lived." By the time Joe reaches page 17, the last page of the chapter, all 27 of his new students are rested and refreshed. And all are hooked on *Harry Potter and the Sorcerer's Stone* (Rowling, 1997), anxiously awaiting what will happen next.

Joe smiles. They'll find out but not until after lunch tomorrow. In the meantime, they've recovered the energy and enthusiasm for learning for the science experiment Joe's planned for them to do.

Patricia Wasley (1999) believes "teachers have an enormous responsibility to send children soaring off to self-confident and enthusiastic learning" (p. 9). In her research, Wasley found a strong relationship between students' interests and investment in their work at school and their teacher's repertoire of techniques for engaging them (Wasley, Hampel, & Clark, 1997). Wasley illustrates her point with this story of her eight-year-old great niece,

Hannah, and Sammy, Hannah's younger brother, when asked about their first day of school.

> Hannah twirled and whirled. "It was wonderful!" she said in a singsong voice, pirouetting around the deck. "I had such a good time! My teacher is the best, and we did lots of things, and some were very hard and I love her!"

> "What makes you love her? What made the day so wonderful?" My husband and I, both educators, were a little astounded by her enthusiasm for her first day of school.

> "First we read chapter books," she sang. "I *love* chapter books, and she reads so that you can *see* what is going on in your head, like the bubbles in cartoons. Then we planted lots of things to see how they grow. And then we did some math. It was review mostly, to make sure that we hadn't forgotten *everything* we learned last year. And there was lots of other stuff. She is just the best teacher, and she told me that I am very smart." Hannah was soaring in her excitement about her teachers, about her learning, about the prospect of another 179 days of school stretching before her like treats.

> Sammy, her six-year-old brother, sat at the picnic table looking down, swinging his legs.

> "So, Sammy, how was your first day?"

> "It was OK," he said in a whisper, not looking up, legs going faster. "What did you do?" we asked.

> "Well, first she told us what we couldn't do. We can't talk without raising our hands. We can't get up and walk around without raising our hands. We have to be nice to everybody. We have to do our work or we can't go out to play. . . ." His voice trailed off. Wisps of his summer freedom floated away. (p. 8)

Children possess a natural curiosity and desire to learn that is coupled with their wanting to be accepted by others. To kindergartners and primary grade children, their teacher is nothing short of a god. Young children are amazed to see their teacher, dressed in jeans and a sweatshirt, shopping at Wal-Mart or eating at Taco Bell. For them, it is difficult to conceive that their teacher is but a mere mortal.

The enthusiasm and energy that children have when they enter school must be nurtured by understanding teachers who set realistic but challenging goals. Teaching is not an easy profession, but it is a rewarding one in that teachers help others better their lives. Such satisfaction accompanies very few other career choices. To quote a saying found on a coffee mug in a teachers' lounge, "Those who can, teach. Those who can't, go into some lesser profession."

The inner need one human being has to help another is the essence of teaching. Some refer to this as an idealistic call to teaching, a conviction deeply rooted in one's soul to work to make life better for the generations that follow. Qualified, caring, and dedicated teachers are needed more than ever before in our nation's schools. Living in a complex, technological society, today's children encounter more problems and demands than any previous generation ever did. Yet children are resilient; given all their problems, as a group, they are survivors.

Schools are challenged to provide education and training that will prepare today's students to live full and productive lives in an ever-changing world. Students must become accustomed to life within a technological world requiring critical-thinking and problem-solving skills. According to Frank Smith (1988, p. 55), author and theorist within the field of literacy, "Children learn when they have opportunities and reason to use language and critical thinking personally. . . . Children learn from what is demonstrated to them, from what they see others doing." Being able to analyze, organize, and synthesize information will be essential in applying their knowledge to newly encountered situations. Many will be employed only to discover later that their labor skills or careers have become obsolete, necessitating the return to school for more education. Lifelong learning will become a necessity.

How do children and teachers adapt to the challenges? What makes an effective teacher of language arts? These questions are examined next.

Children and Their World

Children learn best when they are interested in the topic and are allowed to include their own previously gained knowledge as part of the learning setting (Guthrie, Wigfield, & Perencevich, 2003). Children also prefer to learn about what is relevant to themselves. They differ in their abilities and interests. For instance, in the United States and Canada, a six-year-old child is usually considered to be a first grader; however, society cannot dictate readiness. Many children attend preschool before entering kindergarten and have had opportunities to engage in social and oftentimes academic activities. For such children, the structure and demands of kindergarten and first grade are usually taken in stride. For children who lack the maturity needed to cope in school, this is not the case. "When children enter school before they are developmentally ready to cope with it, their chances for failure increase dramatically" (Uphoff & Gilmore, 1986, p. 11).

Children who are younger than their classmates, often the children with summer birthdays, are at a disadvantage in the classroom. Research indicates that older children in a grade are much more likely to score in the above-average range on achievement tests, whereas younger children in a grade are far more likely to fail at least one grade (Uphoff, 1985). Retaining, or failing, a child increases the risk by 40 to 50 percent that the student will drop out of school later (Riley, 1986). Research indicates that neither grade retention, even at lower grade levels, nor social promotion improves educational success. Intervention programs with sound instructional strategies are best to improve reading and writing skills (Jimerson & Kaufman, 2003).

Children's differences make the classroom interesting and teaching challenging. Consider Charles, a six-year-old who was driven to school by his mother on the first day of the school year. Charles held his mother's hand

Children possess a natural curiosity and desire to learn. Using technology capitalizes on that curiosity.

tightly while she talked to his teacher, Marilyn Wright. When Mrs. Wright asked Charles a question, Charles's mother would answer. When his mother began looking around the room for a place to sit, it was clear to Mrs. Wright that the mother intended to stay for the entire day. Upon informing Charles's mother that parents needed to complete paperwork in the principal's office, Mrs. Wright took Charles by the hand and led him to his desk. He sat quietly until time for the morning milk break. Charles held up the line because he couldn't decide whether he wanted chocolate or white milk. When asked, he volunteered that he *really* liked chocolate milk, but his mom didn't let him have it because if it spilled on his clothes it made a mess. As Charles reached for a carton of chocolate milk, Mrs. Wright winked at him and said, "Chocolate is my favorite, too." Charles shyly grinned and handed her the carton of chocolate milk before picking up another one for himself.

Over the next few weeks, it was apparent that Charles had had few opportunities to make choices. Little things, like getting mustard on his shirt or tearing a hole in the ever-so-thin first-grade writing paper, would upset him.

The same year Charles was in Mrs. Wright's first-grade classroom, Emily, whose family had just moved to the community, was too. The children had gone home at the close of the first day of school, and Mrs. Wright had kicked off her shoes to ease the pressure on her feet when Emily appeared in the classroom doorway. Wearing a dress that was inside out and socks that did not match, Emily burst into the classroom with a barrage of questions. She said, "Hi! My name is Emily. What's yours? Are you my teacher? Will you teach me how to read? I don't know how, so somebody has to teach me." When she finally stopped to catch her breath, Mrs. Wright managed to recover enough from this abrupt appearance of an apparent whirlwind to respond, "Well, Emily, I don't know if I'll be your teacher or Mrs. Johnson will be. But I do know that you'll learn to read. And you'll find that reading is a fun thing to do."

Mrs. Wright considered Charles her "toe tester," willing to stick his toe in the water but always being somewhat reluctant to do so, whereas Emily was her "plunger," willing to dive headfirst into anything. Shy, reserved Charles delighted in finding a library book on his desk that Mrs. Wright thought he might like. Boisterous Emily discovered that writing was a great outlet for expressing one's feelings. Throughout the year Emily enjoyed doing a "you write to me, I'll write to you" dialogue journal with Mrs. Wright. Both children met with success because they had a teacher who was responsive to their needs and interests despite their being so different.

Effective Teaching

"The act of teaching is always a dynamic interaction of individuals (teachers and teachers, teachers and learners, and learners and learners)" (Orlich et al., 1990, p. 3). As such, teaching is an exciting profession; every day in the classroom is unique. School is a place where children learn from the teacher, children learn from each other, the teacher learns from the children, and the teacher learns from other teachers. Learning is contagious!

But we know that beginning teachers have learning needs that "cannot be grasped in advance or outside the contexts of teaching" (Feiman-Nemser, 2003, p. 26). Nitty-gritty things like developing smooth transitions and maintaining momentum are honed in the classroom. Ball and Cohen (1999) point out that the need to learn how to think on one's feet, size up situations and decide what to do, study effects of the instruction one implements, and use what one has learned as part of planning for future instruction are teaching skills every teachers needs to possess.

Guiding Principles

Effective teachers are many things. One of the qualities that makes for a good teacher is the underlying determination to be a success within the classroom despite any obstacles that may arise. That is a daunting challenge indeed!

Ken Bain of the Searle Center for Teaching Excellence (2004) found that there are several general principles that guide outstanding classroom teachers:

- **Create a natural critical learning environment.** Students enjoy tackling questions and tasks that they find to be of interest to themselves.

Students learn to reason by examining evidence and the quality of their own thinking. In so doing, they make improvements on their own thinking. Students need to learn how to ask probing and insightful questions so teachers need to model such questions.

- **Get students' attention and keep it.** From the opening of the lesson through to its end, the teacher must make it appealing so students feel compelled to be engaged in the learning process. This means lessons must be interesting.

- **Start with where the students are, not where the textbook says they should be.** Start with the simple and move to the complex. Be certain students have a solid footing before you ask them to climb mountains. But once that footing is secured, start looking for a mountain and push them to get to the top.

- **Seek commitments.** Let students know that you expect them to listen, read, write, respond. Assignments are to be completed and handed in on time. And you grade them and hand them back in short fashion so they aren't waiting for days or even weeks. If they were absent, tell them that you missed seeing them. Don't miss a day of school to go shopping or on vacation. You're the model—don't let your students down.

- **Help students learn outside of class.** Write a weekly newsletter along with your students so parents and guardians will know what they are doing in school and what topics are coming up in the curriculum.

- **Create diverse learning experiences.** The school day, as mentioned earlier, should be structured and organized. However, learning experiences can vary. Re-creating a scene from a piece of historical fiction, writing letters to an author from your own state after reading the author's book, calling an astronaut on a speaker phone while studying a space unit all serve to motivate students to learn.

Other researchers have pointed out other aspects of being a successful teacher. For instance, teachers must be experienced readers, writers, and thinkers. "An experienced teacher can, at a strategic moment and with one question or observation, move a class discussion into an entirely different dimension. There is no way to become more experienced at doing this except by doing it" (Rosenthal, 1995, p. 118).

Effective teachers have perseverance. Rather than avoiding lessons that can be risky in lieu of the safety of convergent questions or work sheets, effective teachers tend to attempt to stretch their students—and their own teaching abilities as well. This requires a sense of optimism that they convey to the students and to fellow teachers. Mistakes are not highlighted in the classroom; everyone makes mistakes. Often mistakes lead to future successes. Thus, learning from one's mistakes becomes important.

Rosenthal and Jacobsen's classic (1968) study points out the need for teachers to have high expectations of their students. When teachers assume, sometimes even prior to meeting with their students, that they have a good class of "capable learners," the children tend to perform accordance with such corresponding teachers' expectations. Rosenthal and Jacobsen referred to this as the "self-fulfilling prophecy." Teachers in rural and urban schools particularly have to set the bar higher for their students according to Larry Cuban (2004), noted educational theorist and researcher. Cuban (2004, p. 65) writes, "[in] schools where low expectations reign, teachers have a special obligation to push students academically."

In addition to possessing the above qualities, effective teachers are aware of learning theories and their application. Two views of learning are prevalent today. The first, a direct approach to learning, tends to be quite organized and highly structured. The other view is the constructivist view, which states that learning is "continuous, spontaneous, and effortless; . . . learning occurs in all kinds of situations" (Smith, 1992, p. 432). Thus, constructivism deems learning to be holistic in nature. In addition, constructivism considers learning to be social rather than solitary, or as Smith writes, "we learn from the company we keep." Inspired, successful teachers tend to "analyze their particular situation and create instruction to meet the needs of that situation" (Duffy, 1992, p. 442). Thus, the best of both views of learning are adopted when needed and appropriate.

However, teachers must be careful not to get caught up in instructional methods and forget about the children. Bill Talbot, a teacher in Alberta, Canada, writes that "we also need to realize that the magic in teaching lies less in the strategies and methodology than it does in the rapport we have with our students" (1990, p. 56). Indeed research points out that students taught by caring, knowledgeable teachers perform higher than students taught by teachers who lack rapport or fail to try to understand their students and who lack the instructional skills their students need. It doesn't matter if a good teacher is teaching in a wealthy suburb or a poor inner-city school; that teacher's students will perform better than the students who have a teacher of average or less ability.

When the school day is geared toward providing students with maximum learning opportunities, teachers find that they themselves are more satisfied with their own teaching. This means that the teacher must create a classroom that has a warm environment that fosters learning, follow a curriculum that teaches important content and skills, and have high standards and expectations of students in the class (Lewis, 1986).

Daily Structure and Flexibility

During elementary school, children receive instruction in many subject areas: language arts (listening, speaking, reading, writing, and the visual arts), mathematics, science, and social studies. These content areas are usually given the most time and are typically taught daily. Although art, health, music, and physical education are not taught as often, they are still important parts of the elementary curriculum. (See box 2.1 for examples of daily schedules.)

Typically in early childhood education, particularly during kindergarten through grade 3, the major portion of the school day—often the entire morning—is devoted to language arts instruction. This includes the teaching of

2.1   In the Classroom: Teaching Hint

Organizing the School Day

Organizing the school day is one of a teacher's most important tasks. The classroom itself needs to be neat and orderly, and also enticing to students. Books and activities must be accessible and easily stored. Below are examples of two daily schedules.

First-Grade Classroom's Daily Schedule

8:10   Children arrive and put away coats. Papers are collected. Lunch count and attendance are taken. Pledge to the flag. Morning Message.

8:20   Read aloud—The teacher reads a book to the class, stopping to ask questions from time to time. The class may discuss the book after each chapter and at the end. (Most read alouds in first grade are picture books.)

8:30   Mini lesson—Short language arts lesson (listening, speaking, reading, writing and visual arts).

8:45   Big books—Teacher reads on Monday and Tuesday with children reading along orally the second time through. On Wednesday, the class reads the book together. On Thursday, students take turns reading the book in pairs. On Friday, students take turns reading the book.

9:00   Activity centers and four blocks—In groups of five, the students rotate through the five activity centers (reading and writing, math, science, social studies, and computer center). Groups rotate between activity centers every 20 minutes. Teacher works with one group at the table doing a four blocks language arts activity (guided reading, writing, working with words, and self-selected reading).

9:40   Restroom break.

9:50   Recess.

10:05   Activity centers and four blocks continued.

11:20   Preparation for lunch.

11:25   Lunch and recess.

12:15   Restroom break.

12:25   Book sharing by students and teacher (art on Monday; library on Wednesday).

12:45   Math.

1:15   Social studies (physical education on Tuesday and Thursday).

1:45   Restroom break.

1:55   Science (computer lab on Wednesday).

2:30   Sustained silent reading (Monday, Wednesday, and Friday). Journal writing (Tuesday and Thursday).

2:45   Review of what was learned during the day.

2:55   Preparation for dismissal.

3:00   Dismissal.

Fifth-Grade Classroom's Daily Schedule

8:15   Children arrive and put away coats. Papers are collected. Lunch count and attendance are taken. Teacher talks briefly with students who were absent the day before to catch them up. Pledge to the flag. Class meeting.

8:30   Mini lesson—Short language arts lesson (listening, speaking, reading, and writing).

8:45   Reading and writing (individual and group activities).

10:00   Restroom break.

10:10   Reading and writing continued (physical education on Monday; library on Thursday).

10:45   Sustained silent reading (art on Wednesday).

11:05   Social studies (music on Tuesday).

11:45   Preparation for lunch. Restroom break.

continued

11:55   Lunch and recess.
12:45   Restroom break.
12:55   Math.
 1:40   Read aloud—The teacher reads a book, such as a picture book or a portion of a novel, to the class and stops to ask questions or to discuss points along the way.
 1:55   Restroom break.
 2:05   Science (computer lab on Monday and Wednesday).
 2:45   Review of what was learned during the day.
 2:55   Journal writing.
 3:00   Preparation for dismissal.
 3:05   Dismissal.

Whenever possible, these teachers use an interdisciplinary approach. For instance, while studying the Revolutionary War, Civil War, and World War II, the fifth-grade teacher may devote most of the school day to social studies. The morning might involve reading, writing, listening, and speaking activities using historical novels, literature response journals, poetry, and songs of the era. The usual social studies period may be devoted to research time using the social studies textbook and library materials. Science might take into consideration the scientific developments of the period being studied (e.g., battlefield nurses, submarines, carbine rifles, and problems of poor sanitation during the Civil War). Math might involve calculation of supplies and troops, and economic considerations (e.g., the cost of funding the Revolutionary War and the use of script instead of money).

speaking, listening, reading, and writing. Language arts receives smaller time allotments in grades 4–8, but it still receives more attention than any other subject area. No Child Left Behind (see chapter 1) requires that elementary students have a minimum of 90 minutes per week of uninterrupted reading time.

Trying to fit all of the subjects into one school day is by no means easy. As Sue Sunberg, a student teacher, remarked, "It took me 3 weeks to figure out how to schedule everything. And then there are always unexpected interruptions—school pictures, a special convocation, a child who must leave for a dental appointment. If anything, a teacher must be flexible!" Sue adapted to the hectic world of the classroom by creating a "filler pack" as part of what she called her "teaching survival kit." She scoured professional journals and the Internet for learning activities that fit the curriculum and that took only a few minutes to do and used them to "fill" short time lapses between lessons or before lunch and recess.

Presenting new material and skills may occasionally require extra time. Sometimes students become so involved in a lesson, additional time is needed. Ron Lindberg found it difficult to predict how long a lesson would take, especially when he first began teaching.

> Sometimes I would plan for a 30-minute lesson only to find that the kids could complete it in 10 minutes. Over the years, I've adopted the whole language approach. This has enabled me to teach by bringing things that interest my sixth graders into the classroom. Rather than having several short lessons, I have large blocks of time for each subject area. Language arts is usually a two-hour segment in which we read, write, act out, share, react, discuss, reflect, and appreciate. We start out with a short review of

material, discuss and explain new skills, work on the task at hand, and close the period with sharing and more review.

It's not unusual for us to spend a few days on a social studies unit that includes reading, writing, and discussing so we cover both social studies and language arts. For example, we were discussing immigration in social studies and talked about the waves of immigrants that came from Europe in the 1800s and 1900s. Because there had been recent changes in the United States immigration laws, we talked about the economic and social impacts that immigration has on the United States today. Because my sixth graders love the work of Gary Paulsen, the class read *The Crossing* (1987). The book is about a Mexican orphan who illegally crosses the border into the United States, where he meets an alcoholic Vietnam veteran. The result was a discussion of illegal immigration, the economic and social problems of Latin American countries, and the role of the United States as a keeper of world peace. Language arts and social studies fit together perfectly in this instance.

Mr. Lindberg had high expectations of his students because *The Crossing* is a book that challenged their abilities. A few students found the book difficult to read, but their love of Paulsen's depictive writing style in his adventure books and the high interest maintained by their classmates gave them the motivation to continue reading the book. Mr. Lindberg believed that, given the opportunity, the students would succeed in reading the book and gaining from the vicarious experiences they encountered. The students' interactions with their classmates made the classroom an exciting environment. Students asked and responded to questions and sought out additional information about the cultural and geographic aspects of Latin America. They brought in newspaper clippings for a bulletin board display, shared television news reports, and debated the reporters' speculations. Learning took on an active role for every student in the class as well as for Mr. Lindberg.

In order for his students to better understand immigration and its effects on the economic environment as well as on society, Mr. Lindberg asked both convergent and divergent questions. He asked convergent questions, or those with a right answer, at the beginning of class discussions to help put the students at ease and set the stage for probing more deeply into the topic. When Mr. Lindberg began the initial discussion about immigration, he asked several convergent questions. What is immigration? Did any of the students want to share a story about a relative who immigrated to the United States? Did anyone know about contributions immigrants had made to this country? And so on. The students joined in the discussion. One student had a great-great-grandfather who made harnesses for horses; another had a relative who opened a hot-dog stand in Chicago at the turn of the century. Someone recalled that her great-grandmother took in other people's laundry to earn money to buy food for her family. The students enjoyed sharing stories about their families. Later they talked of discoveries that were made and buildings that were built by immigrants.

After asking several convergent questions, Mr. Lindberg began to interject divergent, open-ended questions into the discussion. These types of questions can have many right answers: there is no *one* correct answer. He pointed out that the United States has a large population and has problems taking care of its own citizens, including providing adequate health care for the entire population and fulfilling the needs of the homeless. Limited resources and hazards to the environment because of increased waste were mentioned as other examples of the effects of a growing population.

The class decided that thousands of people each year try to immigrate to the United States because of the freedom and opportunities it offers. Should the United States shut its gates to new immigrants? Or does the United States have an obligation to take care of those people who come to America because they want to live as we do? Students pointed out that their own community was becoming crowded. Jobs were still plentiful but many were low paying. Several students had noticed workers or shoppers in the area who didn't speak English. Was a new type of "slavery" being created, with the slaves being immigrants and migrant workers? The students took over the discussion completely as they began to address questions to the entire class. How do the workers who don't speak English understand their jobs and know what to do? Isn't it dangerous for them? Perhaps it is dangerous for others, too, if they make a mistake with chemicals, for example. Where do they live? How do they shop when product labels are in English? Today many immigrants provide services, such as being nannies, taxi drivers, or landscapers. Their work is hard to do. Many jobs are being exported from the United States to other countries such as India and Ireland. Is that fair? And what about athletes who immigrate to America? Several have scholarships to play basketball, run track, or participate in some other sport. If they are "really" good, they go pro and play in the NBA or NFL, taking a spot on a team that would otherwise go to a U.S. athlete who would make millions of dollars. Is that right?

As the students continued their initial discussion, they soon realized that immigration is a complex issue. The students decided to divide into groups and gather more information on the topic before their next discussion. Mr. Lindberg helped them select different aspects of immigration, which were then assigned to the groups. Each group was to report back to the class. Mr. Lindberg also sought out materials to use as references and monitored each group's progress.

By giving his students the opportunity to have frequent open-ended discussions about various topics, Mr. Lindberg encouraged them to develop their creative- and critical-thinking skills. By searching for information and analyzing it together in groups, the students discovered the importance of gathering data before reaching a conclusion.

Effective teachers like those described in this chapter instruct at levels that students can understand. They communicate by using clear, concise language to facilitate the learning process. By moving about and interacting with their students, teachers see to it that the classroom becomes an exciting learning environment. By asking and responding to questions as well as seeking additional information that the students provide, teachers can ensure that learning involves active participation by everyone in the classroom. Not only do effective teachers expect students to achieve, but such teachers develop activities and units of study that provide plenty of opportunities for students to succeed.

2.2   The More You Know

Locating Appropriate Resources

Teachers need to have access to teaching aids and materials beyond those available through their schools or school district curriculum libraries. There is a wealth of information for teachers on the Internet. The following are some Internet sites that target the needs of K–8 teachers. You need to be aware that Internet sites are constantly changing, so these sites may have changed since this was printed. You can also search the Internet under the topic of language arts instruction.

Internet Resources

www.amazon.com—Amazon.Com
Great site for book reviews of both professional and children's books.

www.ciera.org—Center for the Improvement of Early Reading Achievement
Cutting-edge research on emergent reading and writing is shared via this site at the University of Michigan.

www.srv.net/~gale/childrens.html—Children's Literature
Contains links to Web sites containing information for using books in the classroom and matching books with readers.

www.education-world.com—Education World
Search engine for locating over 100,000 Internet sites related to teaching and education.

www.reading.org—International Reading Association
Site of the largest professional organization for teachers of reading.

www.sll.ocps.net/lang_arts_03/language_arts.htm—Multilingual Student Education Services
This site contains a simplified guide for teachers of English to speakers of other languages.

www.loc.gov—Library of Congress
This is the general server for the largest library in the world. Government documents, rare books, and special exhibits can be accessed via this site.

http://tiger.coe.Missouri.edu/Resource.html
Links to Education Resources Lesson plans, thematic units, etc., can be found here.

www.wcom.com/marcopolo/—Marcopolo
The Marcopolo Web site contains standards-based K–12 Internet content in the language arts and other content areas.

http://www.ncbe.gwu.edu—National Clearinghouse on Bilingual Education
The latest research and trends in bilingual education are posted on this site.

www.ncte.org—National Council of Teachers of English
Web site of the National Council of Teachers of English, a K–college organization.

www.ncrel.org—North Central Regional Educational Laboratory
One of the 10 federally funded regional educational laboratories in the United States. This site has information about current research findings. In addition, sample language arts lessons using technology are available.

http://Poetryalive.com—Poetry Alive!
Site offers information about oral presentations of poetry in the schools.

Internet Sites for Student Use

www.ipl.org—Internet Public Library
Site offers "Youth" and "Teen" sections with reading, writing, math, science, social studies, and general homework help.

www.studyweb.com—Lightspan Network
This site has a huge index of information for schools.

continued

Besides having access to the Internet, teachers need to have their own professional library. A list of professional books in the areas of language arts and working with diverse student populations appears below:

Suggested Books for a Professional Library

Atwell, Nancie. (1998). *In the middle: New understandings about writing, reading, and learning* (2nd ed.). Portsmouth, NH: Heinemann. (Gr. 6–8)

Cunningham, Pat. (2000). *Phonics they use* (4th ed.). New York: Addison-Wesley. (Gr. K–5)

Farris, Pamela, Fuhler, Carol, & Walther, Maria. (2004). *Teaching reading: A balanced approach for today's classrooms.* Boston: McGraw-Hill. (Gr. K–8)

Harvey, S., & Goudvis, A. (2000). *Strategies that work.* Portland, ME: Stenhouse. (Gr. 3–6)

Jenkins, Carol Brennan. (1999). *The allure of authors: Author studies in the classroom.* Portsmouth, NH: Heinemann. (Gr. K–8)

Ovando, C. J., Collier, V. P., & Combs, M. C. (2003). *Bilingual & ESL classrooms: Teaching in multicultural contexts.* Boston: McGraw-Hill. (K–8)

Rief, Sandra F. (1993). *How to reach and teach ADD/ADHD children.* West Nyack, NY: Center for Applied Research in Education. (Gr. K–8)

Robb, Laura. (2003). *Teaching reading in social studies, science, and math: Practical ways to weave comprehension strategies into your teaching.* New York: Scholastic. (Gr. 2–8)

Rosencrans, Gladys. (1998). *Spelling book: Teaching children how to spell, not what to spell.* Newark, DE: International Reading Association. (Gr. 3–6)

Routman, R. 2000. *Conversations: Strategies for teaching, learning and evaluating.* Portsmouth, NH: Heinemann. (Gr. K–4)

Tompkins, Gail E. (2004). *Teaching Writing* (4th ed.). Columbus, OH: Merrill/Prentice-Hall. (Gr. K–8)

Wagstaff, J. (1999). *Reading and writing with word walls.* New York: Scholastic. (Gr. K–3)

Creating an Enticing Classroom Environment

Brain research suggests that an organized, structured classroom aids in student learning. Creating a classroom that entices the students to learn starts with a close examination of the room. Is there a bulletin board for displays that can change each month? File and storage cabinets? Tables for students to work on? What are the room's dimensions? Newer schools tend to have smaller rooms than those built in the 1900s. Putting four or six desks together to create rectangles saves space but students tend to chatter more. Fifth-grade teacher Paul Zackman places his students' desks in groups of four to six to form a table. At one end is a stack of large plastic vegetable containers, all identical in color. The top container holds the group's basal readers, the second container has math textbooks, the third has social studies textbooks, and the bottom container holds science textbooks. When Paul moves from one subject to another, a student from each group simply hands out the appropriate textbook. This leaves ample room in their desks for notebooks, supplies, and free reading books. To identify each group of students, Paul merely refers to the color of the bins (red, green, blue, yellow, or purple). By organizing desks in a table format, less time is wasted when small group activities are done. This is due to the fact that students have the opportunity to socialize more than if they were in rows. As Paul says, "Adults get to talk while they work, why not let kids?"

An organized classroom provides structure for children to learn efficiently.

Shelves or bins are needed for the classroom library; keep in mind that there should be seven books for each child and the books should be from a variety of genres—historical fiction, informational books, biographies, poetry, mysteries, fantasy, etc. Books can be stored in racks for older students or displayed on chalkboard ledges and in baskets for younger students in such a way that the picture book covers are visible.

Michelle Myers uses plastic milk crates to hold her hundreds of paperback books for her second graders. The books and crates are color coded (orange stickers for biographies, blue stickers for poetry, red stickers for informational books, etc.), so students can quickly put the books back into the proper crate. Each day, Michelle opens with the Morning Message that she, along with a student of the day, writes on the chalkboard and has the other students read along. Michelle writes down any unusual events that will take place during the day, such as a walking field trip to see a concert at the high school next door or a reading buddies day. Every day, Michelle fits in 15 minutes of free reading time for her students, which she refers to as "CPR"—"Cool People Read." Educators generally call this Self Selected Reading (SSR). In some parts of the country SSR is called DEAR—Drop Everything And Read—or RABBIT—Read A Book Because It's Terrific. During this free reading time, Michelle also reads a book, such as *The Tale of Despereaux* (DiCamillo, 2003), or another book or article so her students will see her as a reading model.

There also should be a space to display books written by the students themselves. Danny Brassell (1999), who teaches second-grade English language learners (ELLs), had his students create a "nuestra biblioteca"—their own library—by writing their own books about their families, pets, friends, and neighbors. Written in Spanish, the books were proudly shared by their authors. The classmates were eager to read the works written by peers.

If the teacher is to work with groups and individuals, literacy centers need to be created and maintained on a regular basis. While the teacher works with one group, the other groups rotate through the literacy centers. Each center has a focus: *writing center* (1) letter writing with pictures to use for postcards, chart of the proper format to write a friendly letter, envelopes, colorful kid friendly stationery; (2) examples of sentence patterns (for younger children, patterned books such as those by Bill Martin, Jr., and Eric Carle); (3) ideas for writing their own plays, short stories, etc.; *informational center* to accompany thematic units in science or social studies; *listening center* with books and accompanying cassette tapes; *poetry center* (1) a binder of poetry shared in choral reading in the class or favorites of the class, (2) for grades 2–8 poetry books; *fine arts center* with water paints, chalk, art books, etc.; *read the room center* for K–2 where the students move around the room reading the word wall, charts, titles of big books, student names on bins, etc.

Students can work independently or with a partner in the literacy centers without teacher assistance. The directions are clearly displayed, as are any rubrics for work to be accomplished. Finished work is placed in the appropriate bins near the teacher's desk. Throughout the year, literacy centers change slightly while others are replaced completely to enliven learning. Jennifer Nickolas adds a center on jokes, riddles, and limericks for her third graders during March. "Things begin to drag a bit. With the state tests looming, I like to see the kids kick back and have a tad bit of a giggle now and then. They all create a limerick that goes up on the bulletin board."

Literacy centers require that the teacher set the rules and create established routines. There should be no running to the teacher when she is busy with another student or group. Each morning the literacy centers are introduced with the rotation explained. By grouping students by colors and having their names on clothespins, the children can move themselves through the literacy centers each week by simply moving the clothespin on a clothesline. If it takes 20 minutes to complete a center, the students can do two centers a day or about 8–10 a week.

Diversity in the Classroom

All individuals are diverse—each person is unique in his or her own way. But in the United States, the term *diversity* frequently refers to people who are members of nondominant groups, such as those who are culturally, socioeconomically, racially, linguistically, physically, and cognitively different from those in dominant groups. Dominant group members, who tend to be white, middle- or upper-class, historically have enjoyed more political, social, economic, and educational advantages in U.S. society. In some cases, these advantages include the opportunity to attend schools whose curricula reflect their experiences, language, and learning styles. Unfortunately, often members of many nondominant groups either attend inferior schools or are expected to join and adapt to the learning environments designed for white, middle- or upper-class students. The result of inattention to the educational needs of diverse groups can be devastating. Consider that the rate of reading and writing failure among African American, Hispanic, limited-English speakers, and poor children ranges from 60 to 70 percent (Moats, 1999).

In order to meet the needs of a diverse student population it is important for teachers to recognize the types of diversity that are present. Academic and cognitive diversity, cultural diversity, and linguistic diversity exist in every classroom in every school.

Academic and cognitive diversity refer to learning pace or style. For instance, a particular child may require more time to understand a concept than her classmates. Another child may have strong listening comprehension, but weak reading comprehension, so listening to books on tape is helpful. The teacher may need to record science and social studies chapters from the textbooks in order for the child to learn efficiently and effectively. Still another child may have been reading fluently before he entered kindergarten. Gifted students need to be challenged but not frustrated. With the prevalence of academic and cognitive diversity, teachers must plan their methods of instruction accordingly. All students need to be motivated and kept interested in the subject matter.

Cultural diversity refers to the student's family, background experiences, and socioeconomic group (all of which are cultural elements) and how these factors differ from those of the dominant school population. This is complicated inasmuch as there is no one set "cultural background"—a Hispanic child may have been born in Mexico and moved to Texas, or born into a Hispanic family in a rural midwestern city, or even born into a Puerto Rican family in New York City. By definition, these children are of Hispanic descent but their culture, family, and primary language of Spanish will differ greatly. Likewise there is no one African American culture, no one Chinese culture, no one Irish culture, no one Russian culture. A middle-class child who moves into a lower-class neighborhood has a different cultural background than her peers. Her dress, home, toys, parental views on education may be unlike that of her peers. In some ways, we all come from different cultures. As teachers we must realize that each child is unique and needs to be accepted and appreciated. According to Kaser and Short (1998, p. 191):

> When children feel their cultural identities have no place in the classroom, they often reject the curriculum. . . . Children need to be constantly encouraged to share oral, written, and visual stories from their lives so that they can explore their own connections. Through this sharing of stories, they develop a sense of community that allows them to enter into dialogue with each other.

Linguistic diversity includes not only ELLs but English-speaking students with varying dialects, including African American students who speak Black English, also known as Ebonics, and students who possess dialects representative of the geographic location in which they currently live or previously lived. Consider that ELL students who speak Spanish as their first language may say "eshoe" for "shoe" and "eship" for "ship" because in Spanish, any consonant cluster beginning with "s" that starts a word has an "e" in front of it. Likewise, consider a child who calls a concoction made of milk, chocolate syrup, and ice cream all mixed together a "cabinet"; a student from New York refers to the same drink as a "soda," whereas the midwestern and western students would call the drink a "milk shake." Furthermore, the pronunciation of words differs as well by geographic area. In southern Ohio, Indiana, Illinois, and much of Kentucky and Missouri, the word "wash" is pronounced "warsh." Even in a large city like Boston or Chicago, the same word may be pronounced differently in different parts of the city.

Black English, or Ebonics, has been controversial in the schools. It is highly regular, predictable, and rule governed. But it is not accepted as standard English by the business world and mainstream society. The use of incorrect verb forms such as "they was" rather than "they were" and the use of double negatives such as "I don't got no" are examples of why Ebonics is not considered acceptable English. Speakers of Black English fail to pronounce the final consonant "l" so that "pool" becomes "poo." It is the teacher's job to accept the child's language and dialectical differences. The hardest instructional aspect is for the teacher to convey to the child that the language spoken at home is not inferior or subordinate to standard English, while helping the child move toward standard English in speaking and writing for more formal language settings.

Vacca, Vacca, and Gove (2000) suggest for linguistic diversity that the teacher consider dialectical differences in terms of reading strategies. Important elements include: the student's background knowledge (connecting what the student already knows to what she doesn't know), the student's language experiences (with beginning readers, write down exactly what the child says so the child will be able to make the connection between speech and writing a concrete experience), using culturally relevant materials (e.g., books in which the student's own ethnic background is portrayed), and an awareness and understanding of dialectical miscues (i.e., reading "doesn't" as "don't" has no effect on the author's intended meaning). With ELLs, they suggest focusing on authentic, relevant communication; maintaining dialogue journals between the teacher and student as well as between student and student; and creating activities that involve specific content areas (art, math, music, science, and social studies).

Diversity in the classroom requires a vast array of instructional beliefs and practices. For academic and cognitively diverse students, teachers must plan appropriate instruction to meet individual needs. For cultural diversity, the teacher needs to acquaint himself with the customs and traditions of both the community of the school and of the students in his classroom. In addition to finding and incorporating appropriate instructional materials in terms of multicultural literature and, if necessary, ELL materials, this might also include attending social events such as a local festival or a wedding of a relative of a student. The teacher needs to talk with people who work in the stores or recreation centers. Getting out and visiting the students and their parents or guardians in their homes is something every teacher should do at least twice during the school year. During the visit the teacher should convey his goals and expectations for the students as well as a genuine interest in their well-being and a desire to communicate with family members. The teacher must make every effort to convey an image of a supportive adult in the student's life and not come across as a nosy person who wants to know how the family lives or if they are illegal aliens.

Multicultural Considerations

In teaching elementary and middle school students, the teacher should be sensitive to diversity. In addition, the teacher must help the other students in the class develop a familiarity with and respect for different cultures. As Walker-Dalhouse (1992, p. 416) writes:

> The multicultural and multiethnic composition of our society today necessitates instruction that addresses the literacy needs of all of its people. Instruction must promote cultural awareness and a valuing of parallel cultures. Parallel culture is used here to denote equality in value and respect for the contributions of cultures co-existing within an area.

According to Sleeter and Grant (1988), there are five primary approaches to teaching children from and about different cultures and people with and about special needs.

The first approach is that of "teaching the exceptional and culturally different." Teachers focus on culturally different or exceptional children and attempt to apply teaching strategies that remediate deficiencies. Cultural background, language, learning style, and/or learning ability are believed to hinder these students in fitting into the mainstream of American society.

The second approach is one of "human relations." Teachers attempt to develop self-confidence in all students. The idea of a melting pot is promoted as students are encouraged to acquire tolerance toward other cultures and toward groups with special needs. Like the first approach, this one promotes assimilation into the mainstream of American society.

The third approach is that of "single-group studies." One group is selected and studied by the class. For example, African Americans might be studied during Black History Month (February). Supporters of this approach hope to reduce social stratification and thereby raise the status of the group being studied.

The fourth approach is one of "multicultural education" and has five goals (Gollnick, 1980, p. 142): to promote

1. the strength and value of cultural diversity;
2. human rights and respect for those who are different from oneself;
3. alternative life choices for people;
4. social justice and equal opportunity for all people;
5. equity in the distribution of power among groups.

This approach supports structural equality and cultural pluralism. Rather than being a "melting pot," American society is more reflective of a "tossed salad" in that each ingredient is individual and distinct, and each contributes a certain flavor and texture that enriches the end product.

The fifth approach is that of "education that is multicultural and social reconstructionist." Undoubtedly, this approach deals most directly with oppression and social structural inequality in the areas of disability, gender, race, and social class (Sleeter & Grant, 1988). With this approach, teachers attempt to make the entire curriculum multicultural. Discussions and units can revolve around current social issues and life experiences of the students themselves. For instance, why are so few buses accessible to people with disabilities? Why does the price of gasoline in predominately African American neighborhoods tend to be higher than in predominately white areas?

One of these approaches may be adopted as part of a school's elementary curriculum, and the language arts teacher may be asked to implement the approach, thus requiring a familiarity with different cultures and those with special needs.

Meeting the Learning Needs of Every Student

Children vary greatly in their learning needs. Thus every class has students with differing interests, abilities, and weaknesses. Some students are born with or have acquired a physical or mental disability that makes learning more challenging for them. There has been much debate among educators about inclusion of severe learning disabled or physically challenged students in the regular classroom. Many schools have chosen to include students who have disabilities or heightened challenges in the same classroom with those who do not. To help each student develop to the fullest, the classroom teacher must plan in advance how to approach the student's strengths and weaknesses.

Depending upon the particular disability, physically challenged students may or may not have greater difficulty with language arts than other children. For instance, Melissa, who was severely injured in an auto accident and suffered head and leg injuries, had trouble with language in all forms—speaking, listening, reading, and writing. She was evaluated as being mildly mentally retarded. Dave was injured in an accident and lost his right arm. His language skills were fine, but he had to learn to write with his left hand. Children with cerebral palsy usually have difficulty speaking, writing, and walking, but their thinking is not impaired.

Students who are academically challenged because of retardation tend to learn more slowly and need frequent opportunities to practice skills. Repetition and structure are very important. Such children need to learn the basic skills of listening, speaking, reading, and writing in order to communicate effectively with others. Concrete, hands-on activities should be stressed. Activities that they can relate to are important so that interest in learning is maintained. Pairing these students to work on projects with other students in the class benefits all of the students.

Students with one or more specific learning disabilities may have trouble with listening, speaking, reading, writing, and/or math. They may have trouble conversing with others, reading fluently, organizing their writing, and

In presenting his report for Women's History Month, this fifth grader is describing how he conducted his research study and compiled his results.

spelling. Their handwriting tends to be slow and often illegible to anyone but themselves. A computer, if available, can help speed up a learning disabled child's writing. Like low ability students, it is important to structure the learning experiences for learning disabled students.

Structure is also important for students with behavioral disorders, who often display inappropriate behavior both inside and outside the classroom. They may be overly assertive, aggressive, or disruptive—frequently or perhaps only occasionally. Often they are unhappy or depressed children. It is important to find learning activities that these children can do successfully. Praise and support from the teacher are essential. Developing such students' communication skills is crucial, particularly if the children recognize the need to communicate in a positive manner, both orally and in writing.

Students with attention deficit hyperactivity disorder (ADHD) also need structure as they have difficulty attending to activities and staying on task. The seating arrangement in the classroom should take into consideration the fact that they are very easily distracted. An activity center located near the door may result in the child wandering down the hallway, or if the child's seat is close to a window she may be easily distracted by activity outside, such as a squirrel in a tree. Like behavior disordered children, ADHD students tend to be disruptive and have mood swings. Some ADHD students are given medication to help them cope with the demands of a classroom structure, such as sitting quietly and working attentively.

Gifted students are academically talented but may not be equally proficient in all areas. A child may be brilliant in math and science but average in writing, especially if he isn't as motivated in that area. Spelling may be a problem if the gifted student is interested in getting ideas down on paper but not necessarily in having them spelled correctly. Some gifted students are underachievers because they lack motivation. Others may be outspoken and lack tolerance of other students, which can lead to difficulty in group work. The classroom teacher needs to find activities that challenge the gifted student and enrich his or her learning.

English Language Learners

Kari, a student teacher working in a second-grade classroom, was upset. "I was teaching a lesson that I had spent hours putting together and then Miguel laid his head down on his desk. He just stared at me. I think he's lazy or maybe he doesn't get enough sleep at home." Kari's diagnosis could be correct. Or she could be completely wrong. If an ELL student lays his head on his desk, it may be indicative that he is just overwhelmed trying to keep up with a language that is not yet his own.

The process of acquiring a second language can be described as an unfamiliar territory for the learner until she can use both his primary and secondary language effectively to communicate. For monolingual English teachers, instructing ELL students can be extremely challenging. Currently in the United States the fastest-growing population of children is Spanish speaking. Hence, elementary and secondary teachers need to be aware of how to meet the language needs of such students. According to Fránquiz and Reyes (1998), classroom teachers need to find ways of incorporating and utilizing the cultural and linguistic resources of their students. In addition, students themselves can be resources for their own learning.

Below is a list of language paradigms regarding second language acquisition (Fránquiz and Reyes, 1998, p. 218):

- Acquisition of linguistic varieties expands an individual's literate repertoire and increases cognitive flexibility.

- Linguistic and cultural differences are seen as "funds of knowledge" for building literacy in the classroom.

- Literate ways of thinking develop by actively engaging in the practices of a community of learners where interpersonal processes transform into intrapersonal ones.

- Language code "mixing" (i.e., use of two languages such as Spanish and English in a fully grammatical way within a single sentence or conversation) is seen as a meaningful verbal strategy and as an indicator of bilingual development.

- Speakers who codeswitch are sensitive to a relationship between language status and context.
- Codeswitching in an educational context (i.e., such as a classroom instructional setting) is an inclusionary, meaningful, and available strategy.
- Bilingualism/biliteracy is a living, desirable, functioning mode of communication in academic work and social contexts.

Teachers who follow the above paradigm will focus on the inclusion of children's own culture and language to create rich literacy communities in the classroom where learning takes place. By gaining confidence, ELLs will be more likely to attempt to use their second language while learning. Thus the teacher should focus on no more than one or two specific language skills that ELLs must have in order to develop proficiency. Teachers should also keep in mind that ELL students may have parents who are not literate in their primary language. Therefore, learning to read and write may not be reinforced at home.

There are many ways teachers can minimize the frustration that ELLs might experience and make them feel more comfortable in the classroom environment. Labeling classroom items in both the primary and secondary languages is important. Even events—lunch, recess, P.E., music, art—can be labeled. ELL students need lots of opportunities to work with partners and in small groups to converse in natural sharing of interests. Like all children, ELL students will learn from those students whose primary language is English. The more interaction they have, the better. ELL students also need time to listen and process language. When they are quiet, it is often that they are trying to understand or to create appropriate wording.

Books written in the student's primary language should be accessible in the classroom. Even better are parallel language books, for instance, books with the English version written on one side and the Spanish or Chinese version written on the other. Teachers can ask older students or community members who are proficient in both languages (even a student in an advanced high school Spanish class) to audiotape picture and chapter books in both languages and do the same for content area books such as math, science, and social studies. These audiotapes can be made accessible at a listening center where the ELL students freely visit. Typically school districts employ bilingual aides whenever possible, but when a family in tiny rural Steward, Illinois, adopted six children from Russia, between the ages of 6 months and 13 years, such an aide could not be found. A call to a university 35 miles away resulted in a core of Russian majors, all undergraduates eager to share their second language along with their first—English.

ELL students should be encouraged to bring in artifacts of their culture: clothing, food, music, dances, and toys. They can explain how these items relate to their culture and traditions. But the cultural focus should be more than food, families, and festivals; it should be relevant to everyday life, the culture's history, and its traditions.

Non-English-speaking students have varying needs. Spanish more closely resembles English than do the languages spoken by Native American or Asian American students. Hispanic students have to learn fewer vowel sounds and nine additional consonant sounds in acquiring English—far fewer than do Native American or Asian language speakers. However, there are still major language differences between English and Spanish, such as pronouns in English that don't exist in Spanish. In addition to language, non-English-speaking students encounter many cultural differences as previously discussed. Teachers need to be supportive of these students, and their families as well. Working in pairs or small groups is beneficial for such students as is providing a structured environment.

Summary

Children possess a variety of interests and have gathered a great deal of knowledge that needs to be tapped in the learning setting. By interacting with other students and their classroom teacher, students acquire new knowledge, incorporating it into their own knowledge bank. By probing to seek the answers to relevant questions about the world in which they live, children adopt new learning strategies and begin to rely on their creative- and critical-thinking skills.

Effective teachers respect their students. By learning within an atmosphere of warmth and trust, children possess a sense of security and of belonging. They can't wait to get to school, to be a part of class activities, to share ideas, and to learn new things. A well-organized classroom is student centered, with the teacher serving as a facilitator of the learning process.

Meeting the learning needs of all students becomes increasingly difficult each year and will probably continue to do so as more and more students with special needs enter the school system. Consider the fact that "crack babies," who suffer from learning problems caused by their mothers' drug addiction, are in school now, as are children who have learning problems because their mothers consumed an excess of alcohol while they were pregnant. The number of children raised by single mothers continues to increase; thus, many children lack a father figure and a male role model. Working parents may not have the time to talk with their children each day, let alone read to them and help them develop their writing skills. Consider, also, the child who comes from a model home environment but who lacks self-confidence. Our list of examples of children with diverse and special needs can go on and on; meeting the needs of *all students* will be a continual challenge for every teacher.

Questions

1. What types of experience have you had that you could share with students to enrich their lives?

2. How will you encourage students to work together and respect each other?

3. How will you deal with the diverse backgrounds and needs of your students?

4. What will a typical day be like in your classroom?

Reflective Teaching

Flip back to the beginning of the chapter to the teaching vignette entitled "Peering into the Classroom." After rereading the vignette, consider the following questions: What characteristics (either implied or directly exhibited) does the teacher possess that you would like to develop? What strengths and weaknesses are revealed for the students described in this section? How would you meet the needs of students such as these?

Activities

1. Observe a primary and an intermediate classroom. Note how the children are alike and how they differ culturally, emotionally, physically, and intellectually.

2. Develop a set of classroom rules that are brief, clear, and positive.

3. Create a way to introduce yourself to your students before the opening day of school.

4. Describe and illustrate how your classroom will look on the first day of school.

5. Search the Internet for language arts activities for the grade level you are doing your field experiences.

6. Plan a field trip to a nearby historical landmark. Try to integrate activities that include the language arts (listening, speaking, reading, and writing) with other curricular areas (math, music, science, and social studies).

7. Locate two articles concerning methodologies and strategies for teaching multicultural education. React to the articles in terms of your own beliefs about teaching.

8. Read an article about children with special needs and share it with your classmates.

Further Reading

Berger, R. (2003). *An ethic of excellence*. Portsmouth, NH: Heinemann.

Cuban, L. (2004). Meeting challenges in urban schools. *Educational Leadership, 61*, (7), 64–67, 69.

Farnan, N. (1996). Connecting adolescents and reading: Goals at the middle level. *Journal of Adolescent and Adult Literacy, 39* (6), 436–445.

Fay, K., & Whaley, S. (2004). *Becoming one community: Reading and writing with English language learners*. Portland, ME: Stenhouse.

Feiman-Nemser, S. (2003). What new teachers need to learn. *Educational Leadership, 60* (8), 25–29.

Morrow, L. M. (2002). *The literacy center: Contexts for reading and writing* (2nd ed.). Portland, ME: Stenhouse.

Winsor, P. J. T., & Hanson, J. (1999). Coming to know as teachers. *The Reading Teacher, 52* (8), 810–819.

References

Bain, K. (2004, April 9). What makes great teachers great? *Chronicle of Higher Education,* B7–B8.

Ball, D., & Cohen, D. (1999). Developing practice, developing practitioners: Toward a practice-based theory of education. In G. Sykes & L. Darling-Hammond (Eds.), *Teaching as the learning profession: Handbook of policy and practice* (pp. 3–32). San Francisco: Jossey Bass.

Brassell, D. (1999). Creating a culturally sensitive classroom. *The Reading Teacher, 52* (6), 651.

Cuban, L. (2004). Meeting challenges in urban schools. *Educational Leadership, 61* (7), 64–67, 69.

Duffy, G. (1992). Let's free teachers to be inspired. *Phi Delta Kappan, 73* (6), 442–447.

Feiman-Nemser, S. (2003). What new teachers need to learn. *Educational Leadership, 60* (8), 25–29.

Fránquiz, M. E., & Luz Reyes, M. D. (1998). Creating inclusive learning communities through English language arts: From chanclas to canicas. *Language Arts, 75* (3), 211–220.

Gollnick, D. M. (1980). Multicultural education. *Viewpoints in Teaching and Learning, 56,* 1–17.

Guthrie, J. T., Wigfield, A., & Perencevich, K. (2003). *Motivating reading comprehension.* New York: Erlbaum.

Jimerson, S. R., & Kaufman, A. M. (2003). Reading, writing, and retention: A primer on grade retention research. *The Reading Teacher, 56* (7), 622–635.

Kaser, S., & Short, K. (1998). Exploring culture through children's connections. *Language Arts, 75* (3) 185–191.

Lewis, A. C. (1986). The search continues for effective schools. *Phi Delta Kappan, 68* (4), 187–188.

Moats, L. C. (1999). *Teaching is a rocket science: What expert teachers of reading should know and be able to do.* Washington, DC: American Federation of Teachers.

Orlich, D. C., Kauchak, D. P., Harder, R. J., Pendergrass, R. A., Callahan, R. C., Keogh, A. J., & Gibson, H. (1990). *Teaching strategies: A guide to better instruction* (3rd ed.). Lexington, MA: Heath.

Riley, R. W. (1986). Can we reduce the risk of failure? *Phi Delta Kappan, 68* (4), 214–219.

Rosenthal, I. (1995). Educating through literature: Flying lessons from Maniac Magee. *Language Arts, 72* (2), 113–119.

Rosenthal, R., & Jacobsen, L. (1968). *Pygmalion in the classroom.* New York: Holt, Rinehart & Winston.

Sleeter, C. E., & Grant, C. (1988). *Making choices for multicultural education: Five approaches to race, class, and gender.* Columbus, OH: Merrill.

Smith, F. (1988). *Joining the literacy club: Further essays into education.* Portsmouth, NH: Heinemann.

Smith, F. (1992). Learning to read: The never-ending debate. *Phi Delta Kappan, 73* (6), 432–441.

Talbot, B. (1990). Writing for learning in school: Is it possible? *Language Arts, 67* (1), 47–56.

Uphoff, J. K. (1985). Pupil chronological age as a factor in school failure. Paper presented at the annual conference of the Association for Supervision and Curriculum Development, Chicago.

Uphoff, J. K., and Gilmore, J. (1986). Pupil age at school entrance-how many are ready for success? *Young Children, 41* (2), 11–16.

Vacca, J., Vacca., R., & Gove, M. K. (2000). *Reading and learning to read* (4th ed.). New York: Longman.

Walker-Dalhouse, D. (1992). Using African-American literature to increase ethnic understanding. *Reading Teacher, 45* (6), 416–423.

Wasley, P. (1999). Teaching worth celebrating. *Educational Leadership, 56* (8), 8–13.

Wasley, P., Hampel, R., & Clark, R. (1997). *Kids and school reform.* San Francisco: Jossey-Bass.

Children's Literature

DiCamillo, K. (2003). *The tale of Despereaux.* Cambridge, MA: Candlewick.

Paulsen, G. (1987). *The crossing.* New York: Orchard.

Rowling, J. K. (1997). *Harry Potter and the sorcerer's stone.* New York: Scholastic.

3

Strategies for Processing Language

> The child sees everything that has been experienced and learned as a doorway. So does the adult. But what to the child is an entrance is to the adult only a passage.
>
> —Friedrich Nietzsche
> *On the Future of Our Educational Institutions*

PEERING INTO THE CLASSROOM
A FIFTH-GRADE CLASS PROJECT

Walking into Paul Carter's fifth-grade classroom, one immediately becomes invigorated. His students have been working in groups of three, with each group having selected a state to study in depth. The success of each group's project requires that all three group members work together cooperatively. In addition, Paul wants to integrate his already crowded curriculum, so each group must respond to at least 7 of 10 questions that the class developed together and put on the white board. The questions range from historical and geographic information to climate to industry and economic status to famous people. Paul also requires that each presentation include something about the humanities, the social sciences, and the sciences. Each group must present its findings to the entire class and make a time capsule for next year's class to open.

Each group was allowed to select any state that had not already been chosen by another group. When two groups wanted the same state, California, they were given 10 minutes to formulate their reasons for wanting to examine that state. Each group presented its reasons to the rest of the class, who served as the jury. After much discussion, the class decided that California was sufficiently large for two reports, one on the northern area and one for the area south of Sacramento. Although Paul was a bit skeptical about how this would work out, he held his concerns in check. After all, this was a democratic process.

Shelly, Edwin, and Max had selected Indiana. Carefully, they prepared their time capsule: a Match Box Indianapolis-style race car, a poster of Jermaine O'Neal, a newspaper clipping of an Amish buggy with a "slow-moving vehicle" sign on the rear, a bottle of prescription drug capsules (empty) from Eli Lilly, a drawing of the political campaign slogan of William Henry Harrison ("Tippecanoe and Tyler Too"), a copy of a poem by James Whitcomb Riley, a cassette recording of Cole Porter's *Anything Goes*, and pictures of the boys' and girls' state high school basketball champs. Using a computer with a hypercard, Shelly, Edwin, and Max presented their overview of the state, which they had put together as text with short video clips on a CD. With actual video clips of a tornado touching down in a rural area, the group explained how tornadoes are formed and pointed out the devastating effects of tornadoes, which are common in Indiana in March and April. A film clip of a recent Indianapolis 500 race enabled the group to emphasize the economic benefits of a sporting event. With other film clips, a poster board of pictures of products manufactured or grown in the state, and their written report, the group members shared the information they believed would be the most beneficial to the class.

The other groups also had intriguing reports. The groups that selected Kansas and Montana were both stumped as to what existed in the way of the humanities in their states. The Kansas group went to the local art museum and discovered that the Cowboy Museum of Art is in Wichita, Kansas. The Montana group learned that Mel Gibson, Ted Turner, and other famous people have ranches in the state. Clearly, the integrated, cooperative learning activity Paul had hoped would be successful proved to be an excellent learning activity for the entire class.

Chapter Objectives

The reader will:

✓ be able to define and apply the ten Multiple Intelligences to language arts instruction.

✓ understand a variety of learning strategies for literacy and integrated instruction.

✓ understand the role of advance and graphic organizers in assisting students to understand newly presented concepts.

✓ be able to incorporate appropriate instructional strategies to use with culturally diverse and special needs students.

Standards for Professionals

The following standards will be addressed in this chapter:

Standard 1: Foundational Knowledge and Dispositions

1.1 Demonstrate knowledge of psychological, sociological, and linguistic foundations of reading and writing processes and instruction.

1.2 Demonstrate knowledge of reading research and histories of reading.

Standard 2: Instructional Strategies and Curriculum Materials

2.1 Use instructional grouping options (individual, small-group, whole-class, and computer based) as appropriate for accomplishing given purpose.

2.2 Use a wide range of instructional practices, approaches, and methods, including technology-based practices, for learners at differing stages of development and from differing cultural and linguistic backgrounds.

2.3 Use a wide range of curriculum materials in effective reading instruction for learners at different stages of reading and writing development and from differing cultural and linguistic backgrounds.

Standard 3: Assessment, Diagnosis, and Evaluation

3.2 Place students along a developmental continuum and identify students' proficiencies and difficulties.

3.3 Use assessment information to plan, evaluate, and revise effective instruction that meets the needs of all students, including those at different developmental stages and those from differing cultural and linguistic backgrounds.

3.4 Effectively communicate results of assessments to specific individuals (students, parents, caregivers, colleagues, administrators, policy makers, policy officials, community, etc.).

Standard 4: Creating a Literate Environment

4.1 Use students' interests, reading abilities, and backgrounds as foundations for the reading and writing program.

4.3 Model reading and writing enthusiastically as valued lifelong activities.

4.4 Motivate learners to be lifelong readers.

Introduction

Thinking and language are closely related and their development is largely concurrent. Children who can deal effectively with tasks requiring the use of thinking strategies are usually those who are proficient in listening, speaking, reading, and writing. For example, Tompkins (2004, p. 2) found that developmental trends in writing can be observed as children "learn to express more complex thoughts." Certainly teachers need to understand how students think and, in turn, how to develop instruction that will both meet standards and motivate students to learn the new concepts, skills, and strategies—a most difficult task indeed. Teachers play a critical role in student achievement. The No

Child Left Behind Act (NCLB) mandates that by the end of the 2005–6 school year every child will be taught by a "highly qualified" teacher. No one knows a child's learning strengths and weaknesses better than the classroom teacher. "Consensus is growing among school reformers that teachers are the most important school-related determinant of student achievement" (Berry, Hoke, & Hirsch, 2004, p. 685). In order to be a nurturing, caring teacher who can design and implement instruction, one must understand how children think and what motivates them to learn.

This chapter briefly discusses children's thinking processes: how information is gathered, interpreted, encoded, and related. By understanding the thinking processes, teachers can teach the language arts more efficiently and help students become effective communicators and independent thinkers as they solve problems and make critical judgments.

There are three basic theories of learning (see figure 3.1): The innative theory of learning suggests that the child at birth possesses the ability to acquire and develop language—like a new computer with a language program that adjusts to any human language. The constructivist learning theory suggests that children are born with the capacity to acquire language but need to interact in their environment with others to acquire and develop language. The behaviorist theory of learning suggests that through reinforcement, language is acquired by youngsters. Teachers need to be aware of these theories as they observe and work with diverse populations of students.

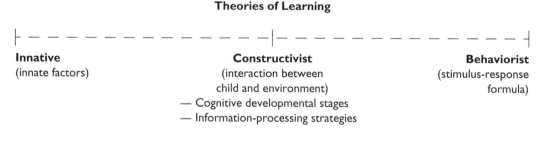

Figure 3.1   Theories of learning

Thinking and Language

Children progress through two phases of behavior as they develop thinking and language skills: egocentric and socialized. The vignette in box 3.1 demonstrates both egocentric and socialized behavior.

Egocentric and Socialized Behavior

During the egocentric phase, a young child plays with sounds and words for the sheer joy of it. Beth, a two-year-old, heard the word "no" from her

3.1   The More You Know

Our Own Stories on Baseball Cards and Literacy Acquisition
Pamela J. Farris

The spring before entering kindergarten, my son signed up to play T-ball, his first formal experience with a team sport. Kurtis was the youngest player on the team, and he dutifully attended practices, eagerly taking his turn at bat and not so eagerly attempting to catch the soft rubber ball. When the team's yellow and black "Pirate" shirts were handed out, with their accompanying yellow baseball caps with a black *P* insignia, Kurtis couldn't wait to get home, try them on, and see himself in the mirror.

Late afternoons that summer were spent at the diamond amidst other families of T-ball players. Conditions were idyllic. No one kept score. Every player got a turn at bat every inning. An out usually meant tears as the player rushed to a parent for a hug and consolation. No one struck out because strikeouts weren't part of the rules. No overly aggressive play was allowed and good plays received cheers from both teams' fans. Games concluded with the opposing players giving each other high fives along with a sincere "Good game." T-ball offered Kurtis the best of what sports have to offer.

After each game, the Pirates would gather around for a snack. During this period, the players socialized, talking about things that were important to them—the worm that the left fielder had found while standing in the outfield, a scraped knee or elbow, or weekly reports of scores on a variety of video games. Then one day, a player shared his baseball cards with the team.

Kurtis was taken in by the baseball cards, those colorful miniature information data banks that have been around for over a century. As the various noteworthy players and their teams were handed around to be duly admired, Kurtis became hooked. He had to have his own baseball cards.

A New Hobby Takes Form

On a trip to the local discount retailer with his dad, Kurtis selected his first packet of baseball cards. It didn't matter that he couldn't read any of the information or recognize any of the team logos; he was immeasurably content just to possess them. He would fan them out over the carpet before carefully examining each card.

As a mother, I felt this was a phase boys went through. As a professor of language arts and children's literature, I wasn't overly pleased that he was devoting hours to his baseball cards when he had literally hundreds of picture books in the house that had more substantial quality and content to peruse. I believe he should be pouring over Eric Carle's, Mem Fox's, and Steven Kellogg's work rather than Steve Avery's, Barry Larkin's, and Ryne Sandberg's statistics.

Kurtis began to identify the teams by their logos. The Cubs, his father's favorite team, and the Reds, my favorite team, were learned first, along with the Pirates of course. The next team he learned, perhaps because of seeing them so frequently on television, was the Braves, which became his favorite team. At first he referred to the New York Yankees as the New York Lincolns. After a couple of futile attempts to correct him, both his father and I gave up. If Kurtis wanted to refer to the Yankees as the Lincolns, that was fine. We knew what he meant.

As the season progressed, Kurtis's card collection grew from a few cards wrapped with a rubber band to a pile of cards in a small shoebox to finally filling a paper grocery sack. As the number of cards increased so did Kurtis's obsession with them. He wanted to know the names of all the teams and all the players. He invented games with them, playing his own modified version of T-ball in which everyone got to bat and no one kept score.

By late summer, Kurtis was collecting football and basketball cards as well. Every day he stacked and restacked his cards. He continued to seek out information. "What does this say?" "How do you spell Cowboys?"—or Reds or Bulls.

continued

Kurtis's Literacy Strategies Expand

Kurtis added writing to his daily review of his cards. By now he had created several new games. Each day would find him carefully copying the names of the teams and creating scoreboards for imaginary games. Kurtis would design a football field complete with the logo of the home team on the 50–yard line and the names of the teams printed in block letters in their respective end zones. He made lists of baseball and basketball teams and their opponents along with their scores, which he invented.

Before long Kurtis decided that the cards could be put in a variety of categories besides teams. He moved his collection to the basement family room, where he had plenty of space to sort out his new categories. Animals, birds, cowboys, and space were some of the new groupings Kurtis developed. For example, among his animal teams were the Chicago Bulls, Detroit Lions, Chicago Bears, Florida Marlins, Miami Dolphins, and Minnesota Timberwolves. There were always leftover teams that Kurtis couldn't find a category to designate. Kurtis referred to the Indiana Pacers as the "P-balls"—their logo being a *P* with a basketball in the center of the loop. The P-balls cards were always set aside along with the Green Bay Packers and Milwaukee Brewers—teams that Kurtis couldn't regroup into his categorical system.

There were also teams with unfamiliar names. He would ask either his dad or me, "What's a Padre?" or "What's a Dodger?" or "What's a Knick?" and we would diligently provide an explanation.

The more Kurtis categorized the teams, the more groupings he made. He moved to grouping by initial sounds—M for Mariners, Marlins, and Mets; R for Reds, Rockies, and Rangers. Then he began to question initial sounds and initial letters. "Why do the Giants and Jets start with different letters?" and "How come Expos doesn't start with X?"

The teams helped Kurtis to discover different parts of the United States and Canada as he located the different home cities of the teams on a map. He learned that some teams were named after cities—Boston Red Sox, Cleveland Indians, Philadelphia Phillies, San Francisco Giants—while others were named after states—California Angels, Colorado Rockies, Minnesota Twins, Texas Rangers.

With football cards, Kurtis discovered something new about the data offered—the linemen were "huge guys." He would sort out all the linemen and play a card game that he invented, a kind of variation of Old Maid and Euchre. Each player was dealt a stack of cards. Then one player would place a card on the table. The other player had to put a card down with a player who weighed more than the first player's card. If the players were the same weight, the taller (that is, bigger) player won. Prior to this, Kurtis could recognize numbers up to 100 and didn't really understand feet and inches in terms of height. Now he could accurately identify any three-digit number and had a better grasp of height as measured in feet.

As Kurtis's familiarity with the teams increased, he would walk past a game on television and note which teams were playing and tell us which players' cards he had from the two teams. He could draw all of the team logos and noted the different fonts used in their lettering. For instance, the Spurs, Kurtis pointed out to me, have a real spur in their name.

Literacy Lessons

Kurtis's love of sports cards taught me some valuable lessons. Although we had read him quality children's literature every day since birth, he needed other literary genres. Informational print on the sports cards was very important to him. The cards represented real people that he could occasionally see on television. The weights and heights represented real pounds and real inches of real human beings. The team logos were also important. Kurtis noticed them on the baseball caps, shirts, and jackets that he saw people wearing in the grocery store, the park, and the shopping mall.

Enthusiasm for and interest in the textual material overcame Kurtis's initial lack of experience and ability with the topic. He repeatedly and doggedly pursued literacy, determined to understand the cards that meant so much to him. Kurtis helped me realize that the reader's enthusiasm and interest are really far more important than the material itself.

Maybe the biggest lesson I learned was that sports cards and a child's imagination can be combined to foster literacy development. Categorization, recognizing words, learning to spell, and the identification of numbers are all important in literacy acquisition. Spring has arrived and Kurtis is eager for the T-ball season to begin. As for me, I'm heading to the store to purchase some more baseball cards for Kurtis.

Farris, Pamela J. (1995, April). On baseball cards and literary acquisition. *The Reading Teacher*. Reprinted with permission of the author and the International Reading Association.

parents many times, as do all children who reach the "terrible twos." After having yet another encounter with her parents and being told "no," Beth walked up to Herman, the family's basset hound who was lying peacefully in his bed, pointed a chubby finger at his nose, and said, "No! No! No!" Herman, the dog, may have been confused, but Beth probably felt a small tinge of satisfaction in being able to correct the dog's behavior, even if it did not need correcting. Such is egocentric behavior! Socialized behavior is important inasmuch as children learn from each other.

A child will engage in other egocentric behavior, such as talking out loud in a monologue. For instance, Kurtis, at 30 months of age, loved to sing in a bathtub filled with toys. He would invent songs by combining various sounds, ending each by throwing back his head and yelling out, "Yee ooo!" At that point, Kurtis would bow to his audience of toys and say, "Thank you, duck. Thank you, frog"—as if his yellow rubber duck and green plastic frog had given him a standing ovation.

Children may share their thoughts as they describe aloud each action they perform in doing a task or an activity. Five-year-old Cynthia was drawing along with her mother and nine-year-old sister. When her sister announced that she was drawing a house, Cynthia responded by telling everyone, "I'm going to draw a picture of a house." Her sister then mentioned that she was going to draw a pumpkin. Cynthia immediately proclaimed, "I'm going to draw a pumpkin by my house."

Social Context for Learning

Socialized behavior involves children's desire to share and acquire information. For instance, a child may volunteer to give a friend the directions for making a potato chip sandwich or tell the friend where to buy the most gummy bears for a dollar. Children will also respond to questions asked by others and ask questions themselves, expecting a response in return. Through such independent and assertive actions, they gain new insights and develop new concepts.

Lev S. Vygotsky (1962, 1978), a noted Russian psychologist, studied children's thinking and their acquisition of language. He believed that children are active participants in their own learning. In their early development they begin to move from being incapable of using language to being competent language users. As they make this transition, language stimulates their cognitive development, or thinking. "Gradually they begin to regulate their own problem-solving activities through the mediation of egocentric speech. In other words, children carry on external dialogues with themselves. Eventually external dialogue gives way to inner speech" (Vacca, Vacca, and Gove, 2000, p. 24).

The importance of social interaction is stressed in many ways. Vygotsky (1962) theorized that the gestures a baby makes in the crib are a form of language symbols that the child later turns into writing. Such gestures as waving Vygotsky referred to as writing in the air. Today, based on much of Vygotsky's work, sign language is taught to infants as young as six months old. For example, moving your hand to your mouth represents eating, an easily recognizable and transferable sign for six-month-old babies.

Vygotsky (1962) believed that meaning is created through interaction with other language users in the environment whereby meaning arises and is established in the mind of the child. Thus when children are in social situations such as playing dress up, pretending to prepare a meal, or digging in a sandbox with others, they use language as a tool to explore their world. In turn, when language is used in this way, children develop cognitively. According to Vygotsky (1978), children must be active participants if they are to develop as learners. They need to interact with the surrounding environment as well as be challenged and assisted by their teachers.

Vygotsky's findings pointed out that teachers should intercede between what students are able to do on their own independently and what they are capable of doing with assistance, encouragement, and prompting. When a teacher works with a child to accomplish a task he cannot yet complete independently this is referred to as the *zone of proximal development*. This has been described by Frank Smith (1988, pp. 196–197) as "everyone can do things with assistance that they cannot do alone, and what they can do with collaboration on one occasion, they will be able to do independently on another." Vygotsky (1978) suggested that once a zone of proximal development has been identified, a teacher, parent, or even a peer can help a child perform a task she would not be able to do alone. Consider, for instance, a parent teaching his child how to ride a bike or a young friend teaching another how to tie shoelaces. In both instances, verbalization of the task is important for the learner to internalize language in order to successfully complete the task, which, in these examples, entails motor skill development.

School and nonschool learning were differentiated by Vygotsky (1978). Spontaneous concepts are learned outside of school and are mostly concrete in nature. Scientific concepts are more abstract in nature and are learned principally in the school environment. However, scientific concepts are best learned when they are built on spontaneous concepts.

Vygotsky's belief that language use and social interaction play a significant role in developing a child's language ability and cognitive growth is important in teaching the language arts. "When children are immersed in reading and writing early in the schooling experience while receiving support from peers and adults, their learning clearly reflects this belief. Further, Vygotsky's theory obviously supports a child-centered and activity-oriented . . . curriculum, enabling children to negotiate the meaning of language while using language in a supportive learning environment" (Reutzel & Cooter, 1996, p. 35). Every student must have numerous opportunities to interact with others in order to develop proficiency in all six areas of the language arts as well as to develop cognitive skills.

Information Processing

The underlying assumption of information-processing theory is that the human memory is an "active, complex organizer, and processor of information" (Gredler, 1992, p. 160). The thinking process involves gathering, selecting, perceiving, organizing, encoding, storing, retrieving, and relating information. Thus, multiple operations, interpretations, and inferences are made before the brain constructs an entire picture of the exciting and complex reality.

Children, like adults, rely upon organized networks of information structures called *schemata* (singular, schema) to relate past experiences and previously gained knowledge to new situations. Schemata also provide the structure or format into which new information must fit in order to be understood and fill gaps or voids in information.

This baby will develop schemata based on the experiences it has growing up.

Concepts exist within a hierarchical framework of information that enables one to identify interrelationships among concepts. This framework functions as a type of "on-line" conceptual family tree. For instance, a child's concept of "home" may be part of a larger framework of "houses," which in turn is part of a still larger structure of "buildings." The schemata that children possess influence how they will interpret new information and experiences and, in turn, will ultimately have an impact on the learning process. For instance, a child who has read most of the *Little House* books by Laura Ingalls Wilder will have a much different interpretation of pioneer life than will a classmate who primarily reads mysteries. Likewise, a sixth grader who has grown up in Pennsylvania will have a much different interpretation of the Civil War than a sixth grader reared in South Carolina.

Three major developments have resulted from information-processing research. First, teachers must place greater emphasis on how children process information as they learn. Because each child brings a personal knowledge base to the learning situation, a teacher must take such a knowledge base into consideration. For example, both the child who has read several *Little House* books and the child who is not as familiar with life on the prairie may find Patricia MacLachlan's (1985) *Sarah, Plain and Tall* to be interesting and enjoyable reading. Both children will gain from the book but probably in different ways.

Second, teachers need to instruct children directly in developing problem-solving skills. Children should be taught ways in which they can organize knowledge and how they can correct mistakes in understanding. "Like writing, reading is an act of composition. When we write, we compose thoughts on paper. When we read, we compose meaning in our minds. Thoughtful, active readers use the text to stimulate their own thinking and to engage with the mind of the writer" according to Stephanie Harvey and Anne Goudvis (2000, p. 8). They suggest the use of FQR (facts, questions, response). Each student is given three different colors of sticky notes to write on as they read. When they encounter a fact, they write it down on a yellow sticky note. Questions that come to mind are written on blue sticky notes. A response, such as "Wow! 80% of the earth is covered by water. That's a lot of water!", is written on a pink sticky note. Students then place their sticky notes on the white board in one of the three categories—Facts, Questions, and Response. The group or class then discusses each of the categories. Thus, groups may select different subtopics within a broad topic, discuss them in their small groups, and then share the information with the entire class.

Third is the need to use semantic networks in both curriculum organization and the analysis of content. Through integrated instruction, the common concepts taught in more than one subject area are presented. For instance, knowledge of the cause of a thunderstorm, a scientific concept, was needed before the problem of being afraid of thunderstorms could be resolved.

Information processing requires that the teacher be aware of students' goals, experiences, and motivation and also demonstrate and teach problem-solving strategies. Because concepts acquired for language arts are likely to be similar to those for other content areas, the teacher should attempt to integrate the curriculum to develop and extend students' abilities to apply information-processing strategies. Such instruction is important in that recent cognitive research findings suggest that children are capable of higher-level thinking at a relatively young age.

> One of the most significant ideas emerging from recent research on thinking is that the mental processes we have customarily associated with thinking are not restricted to some advanced or "higher order" stage of mental development. Instead, "thinking skills" are intimately involved in successful learning of even elementary levels of reading, mathematics, and other subjects. Cognitive research on children's learning of basic skills such as reading and arithmetic reveals that cultivating key aspects of these thinking processes can and should be an intrinsic part of good instruction from the beginning of school. Thinking, it appears, must pervade the entire school curriculum, for all students, from the earliest grades. (Resnick & Klopfer, 1989, pp. 1–2)

In accordance with the foregoing statement, teachers must recognize that learning should be thinking and meaning centered. In other words, children are not recorders of information and knowledge but builders of knowledge structures.

The Nature of Intelligence: Multiple Intelligences

Howard Gardner (1993) states in his theory on Multiple Intelligences (MI) that there is not just one form of intelligence based on verbal and reasoning abilities, but that there are many different intelligences, each having a unique neurological pattern and course of development. With this expanding view, he redefined the concept of intelligence. According to Gardner, intelligence should be defined as follows:

> An intelligence entails the ability to solve problems or fashion products that are of consequence in a particular cultural setting. The problem-solving skill allows one to approach a situation in which a goal is to be obtained and to locate the appropriate route to that goal. The creation of a cultural product is crucial to capturing and transmitting knowledge or expressing one's views or feelings. The problems to be solved range from creating an end to a story to anticipating a mating move in chess to repairing a quilt. Products range from scientific theories to musical composition to successful political campaigns. (Gardner, 1993, pp. 7–8)

Gardner (1993) originally identified seven intelligences:

1. **Linguistic intelligence** involves sensitivity to the meaning of words; their order and syntax; the sounds, rhythms, and inflections of language; and the uses of language.

2. **Musical intelligence** consists of sensitivities to rhythm, pitch, and timbre. It also has an emotional component. Gardner relates musicians' descriptions of their abilities that emphasize an individual's

natural feel for music and not the reasoning or linguistic components of musical ability.

3. **Logical-mathematical intelligence** involves interaction with objects and is often called "scientific thinking." It includes deductive thinking and reasoning, discernment of logical or numerical patterns, and recognition of abstract patterns.

4. **Spatial intelligence** involves the capacity to perceive the physical world accurately, to perform transformations and modifications on these perceptions, and to produce or recreate forms.

5. **Body and kinesthetic intelligence** involves the ability to use the body in highly specific and skilled ways, both for expressive and goal-directed purposes.

6. **Intrapersonal intelligence** involves the ability to access one's own feelings and to label, discriminate, and symbolize one's range of emotions in order to understand behavior.

7. **Interpersonal intelligence** involves the ability to notice and make distinctions about other people's moods, temperaments, motivations, and intentions.

Gardner (1999) later added other intelligence categories.

8. **Naturalist intelligence** involves the ability to recognize and classify plants, minerals, and animals, including rocks and grass and all variety of flora and fauna. The ability to recognize cultural artifacts like company logos and cars may depend upon this intelligence.

9. **Existentialist intelligence** involves the capacity to ponder deep questions about the meaning of life and human existence. (Note: This intelligence is not often addressed in grades K–8.)

10. **Spiritualistic intelligence** involves the ability to make distinctions between appropriate and inappropriate behavior such as between what is right and wrong.

Gardner (2003) is still researching to determine if other intelligences exist, for example sexual intelligence.

According to Gardner (1993), much of the school day favors children who are skilled at reading and writing. It does not address the spatial intelligence skills of a student who could, for instance, operate a film projector after watching the teacher set it up once—the same student who may not be considered intelligent because his reading and writing skills are poor. Gardner believes that there are too many children whose educational needs are not being met because educators have too narrow a view with regard to who is intelligent. He thinks they need to broaden their definition of intelligence to include all of the intelligences and then include each of these when they plan their learning experiences for their students.

Also, Gardner states that "genuine understanding—going beyond repetitive learning and short answers" (1993, p. 27) should be the fundamental goal of education. To promote this understanding he proposes that education systems should increase learning activities that involve individual and group projects, apprenticeships, and hands-on experiences. Gardner states:

> Efforts to cover too much material doom the achievement of understanding. We are most likely to enhance understanding if we probe deeply in a small number of topics. And once the decision is made to "uncover" rather than "cover," it is possible to take advantage of our multiple intelligences. Put concretely, we can approach topics in a number of ways; we can make use of analogies and comparisons drawn from a range of domains; and we can express the key notions or concepts in a number of different symbolic forms. (Gardner, 2003, p. 9)

Also, he believes that schools should help children discover subject areas that interest them instead of just focusing on the learning of basic skills. In doing this he believes that children's senses of adventure, flexibility, creativity, and natural enthusiasm for learning will be enhanced instead of suppressed. This then would facilitate the attainment of a genuine understanding of whatever children would be learning and, therefore, would facilitate the transfer of this understanding to situations in everyday life.

In an interview (Checkley, 1997), Howard Gardner shared his opinion on how teachers can implement his theory of Multiple Intelligences. According to Gardner,

> linking the Multiple Intelligences with a curriculum that focuses on understanding is an extremely powerful intellectual undertaking. When I talk about understanding, I mean that students can take ideas they learn in school, or anywhere for that matter, and apply those appropriately in new situations. (p. 11)

There are many Multiple Intelligence curricular formats. Below are five formats outlined by Campbell (1997) that are based largely on students' interests, strengths, and talents. These include Multiple Intelligence-focused lesson designs, interdisciplinary curricula, student projects, assessments, and apprenticeships.

1. **Lesson designs**, or plans, can focus on all or some of the Multiple Intelligences. To initiate lesson planning, teachers should reflect upon the concepts they want to teach. At that point the intelligence(s) that seem most appropriate for communicating the content need to be identified. Teachers then develop a variety of activities utilizing the selected intelligences to teach the concept. This permits student choice. For example, in teaching about amphibians, a teacher may have the students work in small groups to create a poem, song, or rap about what they've learned and then present it to the class as a means of assessment.

2. **Interdisciplinary curricula** is a fairly common way for elementary and middle school teachers to incorporate the Multiple Intelligences. Learning centers or stations may be set up to teach a concept. Teachers on the Tulalip Indian Reservation in Marysville, Washington, have students rotate through such learning stations each morning. To learn about

photosynthesis, for example, "students might act out the process at one station, read about it at another station, and at others, sing about photosynthesis, chart its processes, discuss plant and human life cycles, and finally, reflect on events that have transformed their lives, just as chloroplasts transform the life cycle of plants" (Campbell, 1997, p. 14).

3. **Student projects** allow for self-directed activities. This places responsibility on the students for initiating and managing complex projects over a period of time. This is best done with elementary and middle school students by setting goals with accompanying dates by which the goals need to be accomplished. Here is an example of project guidelines for fourth to sixth graders:

   a. State your purpose or goal (e.g., I want to learn how dogs and cats are alike and how they differ).

   b. List at least four sources of information you will use (e.g., library books, the Internet, veterinarians, and cat and dog breeders).

   c. List at least five main concepts or ideas you'd like to research (e.g., How are cats and dogs alike in their skeletal build? How do they differ? How are they alike in terms of getting diseases? How do they differ? How are they alike in behavior? How do they differ?).

   d. Describe the steps you will use to research the information (e.g., go to the library, locate books on cats and dogs, read the books, and take notes on what you read; look up cat and dog food companies on the Internet; make an appointment to talk to a local veterinarian, create questions to ask, and take notes as well as record the interview; do the same thing with a local cat breeder and a local dog breeder).

   e. Draw an example of your display/presentation. Make sure that it is done in a creative way that will attract attention as well as share the highlights of your research. (Note: All students are required to use a folding project display board.)

   f. Do your research and keep notes in a spiral notebook.

   g. Write and edit the final draft of your paper.

   h. Develop your display/presentation.

   i. Write a one-page reflection piece describing what you learned about doing such a research project. This is how you evaluate your project.

4. **Assessments** can be done in a variety of ways. Students need to demonstrate what they have learned in ways other than paper and pencil tests. Videotaped presentations, flowcharts, role plays, song lyrics, quiz games, and other activities can be used to evaluate the knowledge, concepts, and skills gained.

5. **Apprenticeships** during elementary and middle school years aren't designed to mold students into a career path. Rather, they are intended to develop well-rounded individuals. Gardner (1993) suggests that each student should participate in three different apprenticeships: one in an

academic area such as science or social studies (e.g., learning how simple kitchen ingredients can be used in chemistry, making a rocket and flying it, or studying geography to determine how land forms and soil types influenced the location of cities), one in an art form or craft (e.g., studying different forms of media in Caldecott books or learning to make dream catchers), and one in a physical discipline such as dance or sports (e.g., learning to swing dance or how to play tennis). Some schools, such as Tilton Elementary, in Rochelle, Illinois, offer eight to ten such apprenticeships during the spring semester for three-week periods. These are taught by classroom teachers in grades four to six along with parents and community volunteers who possess certain expertise in one of the areas.

The above are but five suggestions of ways to integrate the Multiple Intelligences into the elementary and middle school curriculum. There are literally hundreds of other models that teachers have created.

Box 3.2 (on p. 84) contains two examples of using the multiple intelligences with a single book.

Stimulating Motivation in the Classroom

Children who are intrinsically motivated, that is to say those students who become engaged in an activity based on their interest in the activity itself, gain cognitive and emotional satisfaction that in turn leads them to invest a larger amount of time in doing the activity. However, extrinsic motivation, the participation in an activity based on external rewards, such as free pizzas, or external demands by others, results in children being engaged in the activity predominately as a means to the end of the task itself (Verhoeven & Snow, 2001). Research points out that curiosity, involvement, and the desire to be challenged are motivational constructs for comprehending narrative texts (Huei-yu Wang & Guthrie, 2004). "If we teach children to read and write but they have no desire to do so, we will not have achieved much. . . . Motivation to read and write and literacy ability go hand in hand. They must be nurtured simultaneously" asserts Lesley Mandel Morrow (2004, p. 6), respected researcher and former president of the International Reading Association. Morrow gives some specific suggestions for sparking student motivation to read and write.

1. *Create literacy-rich environments in your classroom.* There needs to be an abundance of reading and writing materials that are readily accessible to students. Lots of fiction and informational books of varying reading levels need to be in the classroom library along with many types of paper and writing tools. The classroom itself should be inviting with meaningful print on the walls in the form of posters and charts.

2. *Provide time for choice and collaboration.* Students need a place and ample time to make choices about in which literacy tasks they will participate. In short, students must be given opportunities to take on some of the

3.2   In the Classroom: Mini Lesson

Using the Multiple Intelligences with a Single Book

Second- and Third-Grade Levels

Demi. (1997). *One grain of rice: A mathematical folktale.* New York: Scholastic.

In ancient India, a raja orders the people to give him most of their rice. When a famine comes, the raja refuses to give up his rice to save the starving people. Rani, a girl in the village, devises a clever plan. Upon doing a good deed for the raja, he, in return, rewards her with the gift of her choosing. Quick-witted Rani asks for a grain of rice to be doubled each day for a month. The raja thinks Rani is foolish but she insists. So for 30 days, Rani receives a doubling of rice until it grows to more than one *billion* grains of rice, more than enough to save her village from starvation.

Here are accompanying multiple intelligence activities:

Linguistic. Write a letter to the raja to persuade him to give rice to the people.

Musical. Listen to music from India and make rice drums to accompany it.

Logical-Mathematical. Have the children solve math problems based on the story. For instance, how many grains of rice would Rani have on day 3? day 5? day 7?

Spatial. Divide students into groups of three. Give each group a plastic medicine cup, a thimble, and a milk carton (cleaned and dried out after lunch), along with a bag of rice. Have the students make a chart with each of them estimating how many grains of rice it takes to fill up each of the three containers.

Body/Kinesthetic. Have students act out how they would move the rice (i.e., carry it in their hands, in a cup, in a jar, in a bucket, in a big basket, with a cart, with elephants, etc.).

Intrapersonal. Have students write about how they would feel if they were in Rani's position.

Interpersonal. Have students predict how the raja will react when he discovers Rani's clever plan is a trick. Do they think the raja's behavior will change as a result of Rani's wise plan? (The class could debate this.)

Naturalistic. Compare and contrast different varieties of rice and where they come from.

Spiritualistic. Was Rani right in tricking the raja? Why or why not?

Fourth- to Eighth-Grade Levels

Jacqueline Glasgow (1999) suggests that the Multiple Intelligences can often be utilized in buddy journals with upper-elementary or middle school students. She had students do the following seven Multiple Intelligence activities and share them with their assigned partners via their buddy journals as they read the same novel.

Verbal/Linguistic. Write a biopoem about a main character in the book. The biopoem was to include what the character felt, loved, needed, feared, and gave as well as where the character lived. The students also wrote a found poem using words, phrases, and passages from the book.

Musical. The students selected a 30–second sound track or rap that related to their book.

Visual/Spatial. The students made a coat of arms and a story portrait, a one-page graphic where the students represent their understandings. For example, placing words that represent the character's feelings on an outline of a face.

Logical/Mathematical. The students mapped a story structure and created a character continuum.

Interpersonal. Students worked with their buddies to create a report sack containing items that related to the main character.

Intrapersonal. Students wrote a one-page reflective, evaluative paper that addressed the following questions: What were the benefits of the project? How did your cooperation with your buddy influence you, your reading, your writing, and your completion of the multiple intelligence projects?

Such Multiple Intelligence projects can enrich the curriculum and stretch students by requiring them to use higher-level thinking skills.

responsibility and control of their learning. If they want to read or write alone or work in collaboration with others, they can decide. According to Morrow (2004, p. 6), "studies have found that children accomplish more together than they could alone. Social interaction during collaborative work encourages interesting discussions and problem-solving."

3. *Read to your students.* A teacher who regularly reads to students with enthusiasm and expression from quality literature serves as a great example. All grade levels need to be read to. Reading aloud increases vocabulary and reading interest. After reading a selection, talk about it with the class. Have students predict what they think will occur next. For informational books, have them discuss what they want to discover and learn from the book.

4. *Relevant reading and writing is motivating.* Themes can be motivating for readers, especially when they are based around interesting ideas and topics that are relevant to the students' own lives.

5. *Have high expectations for student success.* Research findings point out that when students are challenged they will try hard to succeed and are quite apt to do so. Material that is too easy or too difficult tends to frustrate children, causing them to not give their best effort.

These suggestions will help to keep students as engaged learners. Viewing pictures and videos also engages and motivates children (and adults).

Viewing

One of the language arts is viewing. Over three hundred years ago, Comenius determined that illustrations assist students in understanding text. A few years ago researchers found that students retain 25 percent of the information given orally but 50 percent when a visual such as an overhead transparency or video is added. Now it is estimated that by combining a visual with the auditory, the retention rate of our students is as much as 80 percent. No wonder video games include audio effects!

Many classrooms today have projectors in which the teacher or a student may project a picture or illustration from a picture book on a screen so that everyone can readily view it, not just those students fortunate enough to be sitting in the front row. Viewing black and white photos of the plains Indians or the dust bowl or the soup lines of the Depression era creates a much different impact than just reading about such topics.

Picture Walks

A *picture walk* is an effective way to introduce a book to beginning readers. The teacher initially shares the cover of a picture book with the students and asks questions about it to activate prior knowledge. She then asks the students to generate predictions about what they think the book is about. The questions can be simple (who, what, where, when, why, and how). The teacher continues to do this as the students progress through the picture book as part of the guided reading technique (Clay, 1991; Fountas & Pinnell, 1996).

Use of picture walks should be greater with struggling readers in grades K–2. Older students who encounter difficulty reading also have been found to benefit from picture walks. Picture walks help with reading fluency as well as with comprehension of the story.

Reenactment

Although it is important for teachers to incorporate illustrations, other visual activities in lessons are also valuable learning assets. Having students act out vital scenes in the plot of a story or book helps them visualize the situation. For instance, this may involve an entire class of first graders as they re-create the sounds of farm animals in *Barnyard Banter* (Fleming, 1994). Or a large group of upper-elementary students may role-play as they reenact the scene in the house with the coffin where the German soldiers descend upon the group of Danes who were smuggling Jews to Sweden in *Number the Stars* (Lowry, 1989). A middle school group might write and deliver a reader's theater based on *Heartbeat* (Creech, 2004).

Having students act out specific scenes of books helps them develop their self-confidence as they perform in front of classmates. It can also nurture empathy for others if the teacher selects appropriate books. For example, Patricia Polacco's (1998) autobiographical account of being dyslexic and unable to read until a special teacher helps her is portrayed in her book *Thank You, Mr. Falker*. Another book that creates insight into the feelings of others is *The Tale of Despereaux* (DiCamillo, 2003), a Newbery Award winner. When young Despereaux travels through the castle, he learns about the feelings of others. In *Loser,* a book by popular author Jerry Spinelli (2002), a boy who fails at everything is mocked and given the nickname of "Loser" only years later to become the town hero. A book that causes both introspection and discussion is *The Jacket* (Clements, 2002). A quick read (only 89 pages) for fifth through seventh graders, it is the story of a middle schooler named Daniel who spots a black student wearing his brother's jacket. Daniel confronts the student and the principal intercedes. Daniel then learns his mother had given the jacket to the boy's grandmother, Daniel's family's cleaning lady. Daniel then thinks about his quick-to-judge decision and whom he chooses as friends.

Videos and DVDs

Viewing obviously includes the use of videos and DVD media. In studying about the Holocaust, Illinois eighth graders view the Steven Spielberg film *Schindler's List* and discuss it as a part of the state social studies curriculum. Viewing the movie *Shiloh*, based on Phyllis Reynolds Naylor's (1991) Newbery Award winning book of the same name, can help children better understand the devotion between Marty and the young beagle dog and Marty's failure to be completely honest with his parents. After viewing such films, it is critical for students to discuss their content either in small groups or with the entire class involved. This deepens student understanding of the concepts presented.

Concept Muraling

Ever aware of the visual world in which we live, children gravitate to images they recognize. *Concept muraling* is a direct instructional approach that visually represents the material to be taught. Using simplistic illustrations, the teacher presents an aural overview of the content area text to be studied in a form of visual representation. When used as a scaffolding technique, concept muraling can provide students with the basic concepts needed to comprehend content area text. For diverse and learning disabled learners, it can be a foundation from which other learning can springboard. Concept muraling relies upon presenting a simple pictorial overview of the concepts to be presented in a text. Because pictures present a pattern recognized holistically by the brain, students can grasp the meaning more readily than when solely reading or listening to text. Thus English language learners (ELLs), struggling readers, and students with disabilities interpret the meaning and assimilate it (Farris, Fuhler, & Walther, 2004).

To initiate concept muraling, the teacher scans the content area material for significant concepts to be presented, while keeping in mind benchmarks created by the local school district as well as standards set by the state. After reading the chapter of a content area textbook (i.e., science or social studies), a list of 6–8 major points may surface. Next the teacher creates a simple visual that can be used on an overhead for each concept. These visuals are organized in a logical progression. For instance, a concept mural of Abraham Lincoln might begin with a picture of a book to represent his limited formal schooling and his own desire to learn, with the next picture being a split rail fence to represent his farming background. The third illustration could be a desk to depict his law background. Other depictions might include an illustration of Stephen Douglas and Lincoln debating, a picture of a slave, an illustration of soldiers during the Civil War, a portrait of Lincoln as president, and a simple sign saying "Ford's Theatre." The teacher would choreograph these, starting with the upper left-hand corner of a transparency, going from left to right and down the page in a flowing manner that finishes up at the bottom right-hand corner of the overhead transparency. The teacher points to each illustration and presents up to three major points about each before moving on to the next picture. Any unfamiliar terms are written directly on the transparency and shared with the class so they encounter the text visually and aurally. All pictures are simple in nature as students tend to be distracted when too many details are present. The actual presentation time may be as little as 3 minutes to as long as 30 minutes, depending on the complexity of the concepts. (See box 3.3 on pp. 88–89 for an example of a concept mural in science and the accompanying concepts that the teacher presented orally.)

When the teacher completes the progression of the illustrations, the overhead transparency is then removed from the projector (or PowerPoint turned off; chart turned over). The teacher then points to the location of the first picture on the lighted overhead (or back of chart) and asks a student what the illustration was. Then the class contributes information about that picture. This process is continued with the second picture, then the third, and soon all

3.3   In the Classroom: Mini Lesson

Concept Muraling: Sea Turtles

The steps in concept muraling are first for the teacher to review the objectives of the lesson or unit, skim through the text the students are to read, and develop a summary of concepts to be presented. Next the teacher either locates pictures or clip art or makes simple drawings that relate to the concepts and makes a transparency, PowerPoint, or chart of the illustrations. Finally, the teacher writes a brief script that presents no more than three concepts per picture, with the total number of pictures being about four for kindergarten to eight for middle schoolers. In the script, new vocabulary terms are noted. The teacher orally presents the information about each picture by pointing to it on the overhead, PowerPoint, or chart and writing any new terms next to the appropriate picture after they have been introduced. The students then pronounce the word along with the teacher as he points to it.

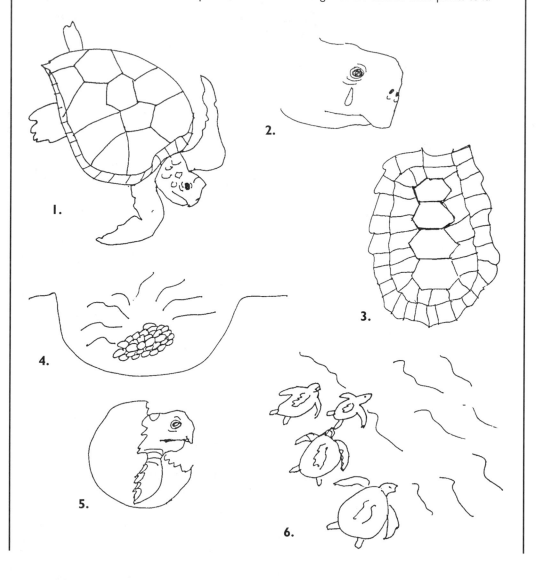

1.

2.

3.

4.

5.

6.

Sea Turtles Concept Mural (Grades 2–3)

(Note: The pictures are staggered beginning with the upper left-hand corner to the lower right-hand corner like a stream of thought meandering from the top to the bottom of the page. The teacher points to each picture before introducing the accompanying concepts.)

Script:

Picture One: Adult Sea Turtle

1. Sea turtles are reptiles that live in warm ocean waters.
2. They have strong flippers that make it a powerful and swift swimmer.
   a. Some can swim as fast as 20 mph
   b. They can swim 4 times faster than a human being
3. There are 8 kinds of sea turtles (teacher holds up hands and wiggles all 10 fingers and then folds thumbs into palm and has the students do likewise).
   a. The largest sea turtle is the *leatherback* (teacher writes on overhead/chart) and weighs 1,000 pounds
   b. *Ridley* sea turtles are the smallest (teacher writes on overhead/chart)
      i.   2 feet long
      ii. weigh 100 pounds
   c. *Loggerhead* sea turtles are found off the Atlantic coast
      i.   3–5 feet long
      ii. weight 400 pounds

Picture Two: Head of Sea Turtle

1. A sea turtle has keen senses.
   a. Hearing organs are behind the eye
   b. It can smell through its nostrils
   c. It can see far distances underwater
2. A sea turtle cries tears to rid its eyes of sea salt from the ocean's water
3. Unlike other kinds of turtles, a sea turtle can't pull its head and feet inside its shell for protection.
4. The sea turtle tears sea plants with its jaws and swallows the chunks whole.

Picture Three: Shell

1. Shell is hard and bony for protection
   a. Top of shell is *carapace* (teacher writes on overhead/chart and students pronounce)
      i.   Large scales called *scutes* (pronounced scoots) cover the carapace. These look like puzzle pieces. (teacher writes word on overhead/chart and students pronounce)
   b. The bottom of the shell is called the *plastron* (teacher writes on overhead/chart and students pronounce)
   c. The carapace and the plastron are connected by bridges.

Picture Four: Nest of Sea Turtle Eggs on Beach

1. Female sea turtles migrate every 2 years in late spring or summer
2. Return to the same stretch of beach where they were born.
   a. Only time they ever leave the ocean
   b. Dig a shallow pit in the sandy beach
   c. Lay about 100 eggs and cover them up with sand. This is a *clutch* (teacher writes word on overhead/chart and students pronounce).

Picture Five: The Sea Turtle Eggs Hatch

1. Two months after they were laid.
2. Baby sea turtles use an *egg tooth* (teacher writes on overhead/chart) like baby chicks and baby ducks to crack the shell and get out.

Picture Six: Baby Sea Turtles

1. During dark of night, baby sea turtles crawl with their flippers to the sea
2. Use the moon's reflection to find the seawater because the sky is brighter over water than land

Accompanying book: Gail Gibbons. (1995). *Sea turtles*. New York: Holiday House.

the pictures have been discussed. The overhead light is turned on again so the students may once again view the illustrations and any accompanying vocabulary words (Farris & Downey, in press).

At this point the students are teamed up to work on their concept muraling logs. Each student creates her own concept mural in a notebook in which the pictures are drawn and the vocabulary words written down. Next, the students read the accompanying chapter assignment in their textbooks. Typical class discussion of headings, textbook illustrations, sections of text, and so forth, occurs. Students may engage in other projects such as reading accompanying novels, researching reports, completing Web quests, and so on. At the end of the unit, the teacher once again pulls out the concept mural transparency and has the class contribute their previously gained knowledge along with additional information they have acquired through their reading and other assignments.

Concept muraling may be used with children as young as kindergarten. In such cases the teacher may elect to use only four simple illustrations from an informational book about animals, such as dogs, whales, or bunnies. After completing the concept muraling with the students, the book would then be read to the students later that same day. The next day the students would go back over the concept mural. Later in the week, the book would be reread by the teacher with immediate review of the concept mural.

Middle school students with learning disabilities or English language learners may find that having concept murals on smaller portions of a chapter rather than the entire chapter itself is more effective and less overwhelming. After being exposed to this process, learning disabled students and English language learners may use concept muraling as a method for sharing informational oral reports with the class, as concept muraling provides structure and organization.

Visually Representing

Students create meaning by developing visual texts to share information learned during an activity, such as writing in a literature response journal, participating in a literature circle, studying a thematic unit, or during some other learning activity. These visual texts may be illustrations, flowcharts, posters, story quilts, slide shows combining illustrations with readings of various passages, videos, or even hypertext productions using computer applications.

Visually representing opens the door to a multitude of creative ways to demonstrate one's learning. For example, a group of students may decide to read the same book and present it visually by making a mural of the major scenes of the plot. Another group may decide to make a comic strip and include dialogue from their book. A third group may elect to make a Y chart, dividing a poster into a Y with the main character, plot, and setting in the three parts of the Y. Each student in the group then writes something in each of the three sections of the Y chart. A fourth group may elect to do character representations. They draw a picture of the character's head, with the character's name written on his or her neck, and cut it out. On one half of the manila paper, the students write the character's thoughts inside a bubble or actual dialogue from the story in quotation marks. The character's face is drawn on the remaining half of the manila paper. The head is then thumb-tacked to a bulletin board. Other students can see the partial face of the character and read his thoughts or words.

Visual representation of concepts learned can be a motivating and challenging way for students to demonstrate their knowledge and understanding. It is also an effective alternative assessment measure to paper and pencil tests.

Teaching Models for Language Arts Instruction

The teacher must create a "learning tone" by using methodologies in which students are aware of which learning behaviors are accepted and which are not. The learning tone influences whether students will be active or passive learners. Learning requires children to rely on information processing as they build structures for making sense of the surrounding world (Harvey & Goudvis, 2000). As stated by Jensen and Roser (1990, p. 10), "readers and writers are thinkers: they analyze and synthesize; they compare and contrast; they assimilate and accommodate; they weigh and refine ideas." A good way to introduce students to this type of thinking process is to have them write a biographical poem. The biographical poem described in box 3.4 (on p. 92) is a good example of helping to get students to think about themselves and who they are.

Children must use what they themselves know about learning and apply that knowledge. As Wells (1990, p. 15) notes, "simply telling students to read more critically or to make their point more effectively in writing will be of no help unless they have developed an understanding of the mental activities involved." To put it more concisely, children must think about thinking.

This knowing about knowing and knowing how to know is called *metacognition*. Teaching children to use metacognition requires that teaching be indirect (Derry & Murphy, 1986). Children become responsible and accountable for their own learning as they monitor their own understanding and comprehension. They must know about knowing: how to know, when to know, and the reasons for knowing. Through opportunities to learn and apply various learning strategies, children can adopt the best study approach for a particular problem. Thus, learning becomes tactical as children are aware of and try to control their efforts to use particular learning strategies and skills (Jones, Palincsar, Ogle, & Carr, 1987; Verhoeven & Snow, 2001).

By capitalizing on children's past experiences and having them relate what they have already learned through observation, experience, and language, teachers will find that learning is facilitated. Through the sharing of such existing knowledge, especially at the beginning of a lesson, children further develop the framework of knowledge as they associate the new learning experience with older and more familiar ones.

Teachers, however, must be cautious in that cultural differences exist among learners, and these differences affect literate thinking. For instance, in Western culture we analyze a text based on the purpose it attempts to serve.

For example, one type of text attempts to persuade the reader to take action, as in to buy a particular product after reading an advertisement about that product. Another type of text conveys factual information, as in reference and do-it-yourself books. A third type of text depends on the emotional engagement between the reader and the author and the previous experience of the reader, as in novels, poetry, and so forth (Wells, 1990). It is possible that students from non-Western cultures have not been taught to think about or write texts that fit these types. Therefore those students' literate thinking processes may not be developed in the same way as their Western counterparts.

Some of the teaching models that aid students in their development of learning strategies include graphic organizers, nondirective teaching (constructivism), think alouds, and cooperative learning. A discussion of these models follows.

3.4   In the Classroom: Mini Lesson

Biographical Poem

In an attempt to become acquainted with students, the teacher may have them write an autobiographical poem at the beginning of the school year. For the teacher, this is also an opportunity for sharing some information about herself so that, in turn, the students get better acquainted with their teacher. Later in the year the students might write a biographical poem about historical figures or a main character in a novel (Hancock, 2000). The format for a biographical poem (Danielson, 1989, pp. 65–68) follows.

Title: First and last name
Line 1: First name
Line 2: Four traits that describe you
Line 3: Brother/sister of . . . (May substitute Son/daughter of)
Line 4: Lover of . . . (Gives names of three people or ideas)
Line 5: Who feels . . . (Gives three feelings)
Line 6: Who fears . . . (Give three items)
Line 7: Who would like to see . . . (Give three items)
Line 8: Resident of . . . (Give city and state)
Line 9: Last name only

Michael Pedersen
Michael
Smart, athletic, funny, musical
Brother of Pat and Phil
Lover of baseball, singing, and my dog
Who feels excited when the Mets win, happy when I go to Florida, and sad when it rains
Who fears high places, power blackouts, and black widow spiders
Who would like to see the movie *Batman,* a New York Knicks game, and Disneyland
Resident of Rochester, New York
PEDERSEN

—Michael Pedersen, Grade 4

Danielson, K. (1989). Helping history come alive with literature. *Social Studies 80,* 65–68.
Hancock, M. R. (2000). *A celebration of literature and response.* Upper Saddle River, NJ: Prentice-Hall.

The success of any lesson depends on student engagement and motivation. This teacher interacts with the students to continually and gently nudge them along in their learning.

Graphic Organizers

Graphic organizers are used by teachers to assist students in concept acquisition. They are ideas presented to students prior to, during, and after a lesson. The ideas serve to assist in the organization of the students' thinking as they acquire new concepts. Organizers may be opening comments or questions made by the teacher in initiating a lesson. Such comments or questions are targeted at focusing students' attention on the primary topic of discussion. Graphic organizers are written charts or semantic maps that may be partially developed at the beginning of a lesson or unit of study. Then, as the students learn more about the topic being studied, additional information is added. At the end of the learning activity, a graphic organizer may be created by each of the students to demonstrate what they have learned.

Ausubel (1963) developed the theory of organizers on the assumption that students can be assisted with concept development; providing information to students in this way will result in greater understanding and retention on their behalf. In Ausubel's opinion, if a child begins with the right "set" and is presented with material that is understandable, then meaningful learning can occur. It has been shown that students who have been exposed to graphic organizer techniques over a long period of time tend to be more adept at organizing ideas and information as a means to anchor content (Joyce, Showers, & Rolheiser-Bennett, 1987).

The way the subject matter is to be organized should parallel the way in which students organize knowledge in their own minds. Meaning, therefore, necessitates a connection of the new information with the existing knowledge of the child. The child must take an active role in the learning process because graphic organizers "explain, integrate, and interrelate" the new material of a lesson or assignment with previously learned material (Joyce & Weil, 1986).

Graphic organizers may be simple story maps in which the student illustrates the major events of the story or book from start to finish. For students in grades K–2, this might be a three-scene illustration—beginning, middle, and end—of a picture book. For older students, this might be four to eight significant scenes from a middle-grade reader or novel.

One extremely popular graphic organizer is the K-W-L. Developed by Donna Ogle (1986, 1989), the K-W-L chart stands for "What we **K**now," "What we **W**ant to know," and "What we **L**earned" about a specific topic. These charts are used by teachers and students at the beginning of a thematic unit of study. The teacher initiates class discussion about a topic by asking what the students already know about it. The teacher then writes the information on a K-W-L chart, which is displayed in the classroom throughout the unit of study. Next the teacher asks the students what they would like to know about the topic. As the unit progresses, the teacher and students fill in the last category—"What We Learned." The chart in Figure 3.2 was developed by a third-grade class for the topic "weather."

Some teachers add a fourth letter, "H," for "how," to the K-W-L chart, "How we can use what we've learned." The third graders who created the above K-W-L chart decided to keep a weather chart as well as predict changes in the weather by recording barometric measures three times each school day along

K	W	L
Different parts of the country have different climates.	What affects climate?	Nearness to the equator; El Niño.
Weather forecasters use different instruments for predicting the weather.	What is a barometer?	An instrument that measures air pressure.
There are different kinds of clouds.	What are the different kinds of clouds?	*Stratus*—flat. *Cumulus*—bumpy, look like cotton balls. *Cirrostratus*—very high stratus clouds. *Cumulonimbus*—cumulus clouds that rain or snow. *Nimbostratus*—raining stratus clouds.
	What causes the wind to blow?	Wind is moving air from a high air pressure region to a low-pressure region.

Figure 3.2   K-W-L organizer for a unit on weather

with noting the types of clouds in the sky. For kindergarten through third grade, K-W-L works best as K-W-W with the last letter representing "I wonder" with questions formulated about the topic (i.e., I wonder where rain comes from?).

Janet Richards and Nancy Anderson (2003) created another variation on K-W-L, which they use with kindergarten and first grade students as they read storybooks. What do I **S**ee? What do I **T**hink? What do I **W**onder? (S-T-W) is a visual literacy approach that prompts emergent readers to carefully examine storybook illustrations and devote greater attention to the subtle aspects of storybook illustrations, such as the look on a character's face, as with Maria's furtive glance as she tries on her mother's ring in *Too Many Tamales* (Soto, 1993) or the pert faces in *The Talking Eggs* (San Souci, 1989).

It is critical that the teacher model the behavior each time a new picture book is introduced. Beginning with the cover of the storybook, the teacher asks the students to consider a compelling aspect of the illustration. For the picture book *Peach and Blue* (Kilborne, 1993), the teacher might say, "I *see* a peach with a face (seeing). I *think* this must be a fantasy story because in real life peaches don't have faces (thinking). I *wonder* if the peach will talk in this story (wonder)?" One child observed an illustration later on in the book depicting Peach and Blue together on two lily pads as the sunlight is fading. He said, "I *see* Peach and Blue together, but they're not smiling. I *think* the colors the artist used are kind of sad. I *wonder* if something is going to happen to Peach and Blue" (Richards and Anderson, 2003, p. 442). This technique is useful for students with varying reading abilities and for English language learners. It can be used with older students for reading science and social studies content in textbooks or informational books. However, some children become overly preoccupied with the details and miss the whole gist of the picture.

Typically, a teacher will introduce a lesson, presenting all new concepts before the assigned reading. By using previously learned concepts and terminology as a means to introduce unfamiliar ideas, the teacher makes the acquisition of the new material easier for the students. The initiation of a study dealing with Middle Eastern people will require that the concepts of culture and religion be understood. A beginning lesson on reptiles will require that the idea of a reptile be comprehended.

Graphic organizers can be used during and after a lesson to help students develop concepts. Figures 3.3 through 3.6 on pp. 96–98 are examples of graphic organizers. An explanation accompanies each example. It is crucial for the teacher to model each graphic organizer so that the children will be able to use the visually representing technique on their own.

Nondirective Teaching (Constructivism)

Creating a classroom where students are self-directed requires that students be both self-motivated and confident learners. The goal of constructivist teaching is to facilitate student learning through the establishment of a stimulating classroom environment in which examining, probing, and questioning take place. Inquiry is the focus. Newly gained knowledge may influence the learner to reevaluate previous perceptions. This approach is used in many

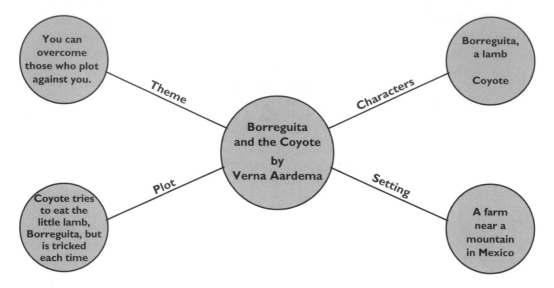

Aardema, Verna. (1991). *Borreguita and the coyote* (Petra Matthews, Illus.). New York: Knopf.

Figure 3.3   The spoke wheel. The spoke wheel is used to summarize what is known about one thing or character. The spokes serve as primary headings or categories.

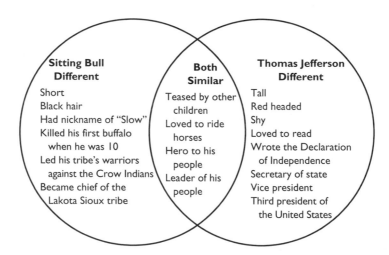

Bruchac, Joseph. (1994). *A boy called Slow: The true story of Sitting Bull* (Rocco Baviera, Illus.). New York: Philomel.
Giblin, James Cross. (1994) *Thomas Jefferson* (Michael Dooling, Illus.). New York: Scholastic.

Figure 3.4   Venn diagram. Two intersecting circles are used to include information about how two things or characters differ and how they are alike, as with the above information for Sitting Bull and Thomas Jefferson. For first graders two overlapping hula-hoops make an effective model. Words written on tagboard cards may then be placed in the three areas showing how the two items being compared are similar and different.

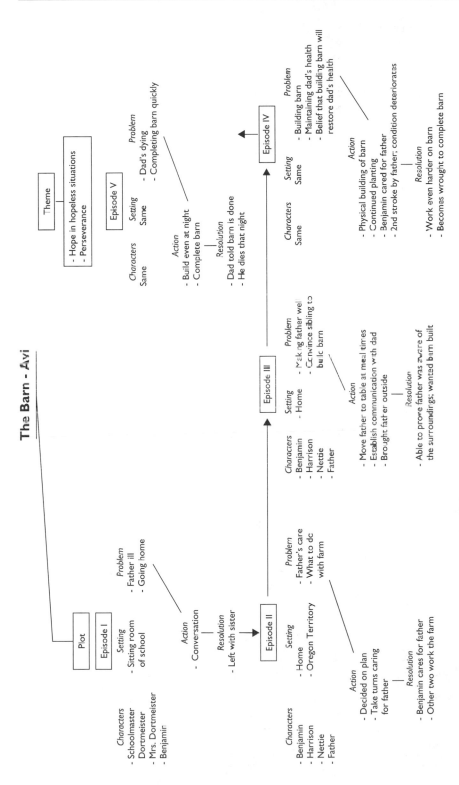

The Barn - Avi

Theme
- Hope in hopeless situations
- Perseverance

Plot

Episode I

Characters
- Schoolmaster Dortmeister
- Mrs. Dortmeister
- Benjamin

Setting
- Sitting room of school

Problem
- Father ill
- Going home

Action
- Conversation

Resolution
- Left with sister

Episode II

Characters
- Benjamin
- Harrison
- Nettie
- Father

Setting
- Home
- Oregon Territory

Problem
- Father's care
- What to do with farm

Action
- Decided on plan
- Take turns caring for father

Resolution
- Benjamin cares for father
- Other two work the farm

Episode III

Characters
- Benjamin
- Harrison
- Nettie
- Father

Setting
- Home

Problem
- Making father well
- Convince sibling to build barn

Action
- Move father to table at meal times
- Establish communication with dad
- Brought father outside

Resolution
- Able to prove father was aware of the surroundings; wanted barn built

Episode IV

Characters
Same

Setting
Same

Problem
- Building barn
- Maintaining dad's health
- Belief that building barn will restore dad's health

Action
- Physical building of barn
- Continued planting
- Benjamin cared for father
- 2nd stroke by father; condition deteriorates

Resolution
- Work even harder on barn
- Becomes wrought to complete barn

Episode V

Characters
Same

Setting
Same

Problem
- Dad's dying
- Completing barn quickly

Action
- Build even at night
- Complete barn

Resolution
- Dad told barn is done
- He dies that night

Avi. (1994). *The barn.* New York: Orchard Books/Richard Jackson.

Figure 3.5 Plot organizer. A plot organizer includes the episode and the characters, setting, and problem along with the action and resolution. A picture book may have only one episode whereas a novel may have several episodes.

classrooms because it forces the student to attempt to make sense of the surrounding world.

Constructivism requires that the teacher's role be one of facilitator. The teacher accepts all responses, feelings, and beliefs without judgment. As a warm, responsive individual, the teacher must be supportive and sincerely interested in the intellectual growth and welfare of all the students in the classroom. There is a "permissiveness" in the classroom: permission to learn without coercion or pressure from the teacher. Encouragement is offered freely by both the teacher and the student's peers.

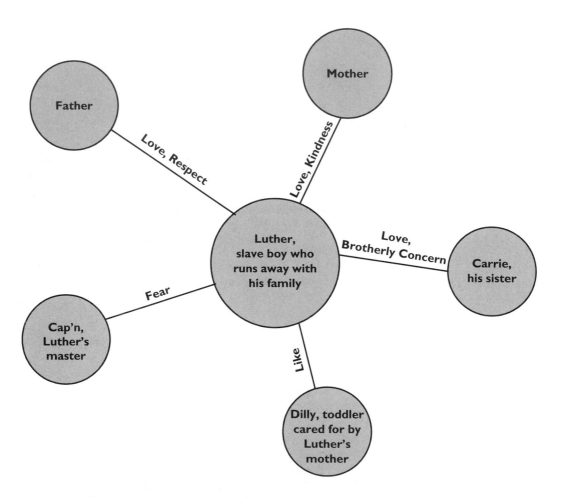

Turner, Glennette Tilley. (1994). *Running for our lives* (Samuel Byrd, Illus.). New York: Holiday House.

Figure 3.6   A character web. A character web can take different formats. It may be a circle, representing the main character, and have several surrounding circles, each representing another character. The student writes in the names of the characters with an arrow from the main character and the way that character feels or acts toward each of the other characters.

Student-centered group discussions play a major role in nondirective teaching. Conferences and interviews are commonplace; divergent thinking and self-evaluation are emphasized inasmuch as learning is highly personalized.

3.5   The More You Know

The Meaning of Time

One good example of constructivist teaching took place in a first-grade classroom in a small New Mexico town. The teacher asked her students to hurry and finish their work so they would be on time for lunch. This prompted one of her students to ask, "Who controls time?" The teacher responded with another question: "Who do you think controls time?" The students began looking at each other. No one knew. One boy raised his hand and said, "The mayor controls time." Other students disagreed, each volunteering the name of a person or persons whom they thought directed people's comings and goings.

Seizing the opportunity to use an inquiry approach, the teacher suggested that the students write letters to various individuals to find out who controls time. That afternoon, the students wrote to every important person in town: owners of businesses, politicians, religious leaders, municipal employees, and the like. Every one of the letters received a response, which the teacher read to the class before placing it on a "Who Controls Time?" bulletin board. A three-page, single-spaced letter from a judge explained the importance of time and promptness. Other individuals not only wrote letters but either arranged to visit the classroom or to provide a walking field trip through their places of work for the entire class. Paramedics demonstrated how they used medical equipment as quickly and efficiently as possible to save lives. A rancher discussed how cattle grow over a period of several months, and a postal employee explained how time is needed to get mail from different parts of the United States.

The first graders undoubtedly learned more about time from this nondirective teaching episode than they would have from any form of direct instruction. They also gained respect for community members—just as the community leaders gained an understanding of six-year-olds and how they think.

Think Alouds

The teacher can orally demonstrate his thinking process by talking about how he gains knowledge while reading; he gives students verbal clues that provide insights as to how he thinks. The verbal cues may refer to a vocabulary word, a twist in a plot, a particular concept, the feelings of the main character in a story, etc. The teacher reads a passage aloud to the class or group of students and then asks a question such as:

- What does the word _____ mean?
- Where did this story take place?
- I wonder who is _____?
- Why did the protagonist do that?
- How is this problem going to be resolved?

- What caused this event to happen?
- I wish I knew more about _____. He seems to be a key character.

The teacher then pauses a second to ponder the question and then talks out his thinking process as he orally responds to his own question. For instance, the teacher may say, "It reads, 'Jennifer had a mystique about her that enabled her to appear to know more than she really did.' What does 'mystique' mean? I think that perhaps the word 'mystique' means to have a special skill that others may not have." The teacher then may ask a second question that pertains to understanding the passage before moving on to the next section of the text.

Think alouds demonstrate to students how to find and interpret important information in a narrative or informational text. It helps if the students can see the text as the teacher reads it. Either have copies available for the students or make an overhead so that the students may follow along. Throughout the think aloud, students participate by giving a "thumbs up" sign if they agree with the teacher's thought processes or a "thumbs down" if they disagree. Throughout the think aloud it is important that the teacher demonstrate a sense of desire to discover the unknown, expressing pleasure whenever a question is successfully answered.

The teacher should also point out the various informational portions of the text and how to use them. During a think aloud, the teacher may demonstrate how to use one of the following:

- table of contents
- introduction to a chapter or book
- bold print, colored or italicized words
- titles and headings
- captions and labels
- charts, graphs, tables, and time lines
- maps
- fact boxes and sidebars
- diagrams
- size comparisons, magnifications, and cut aways
- bullets
- index
- glossary and pronunciation guide

Think alouds are a means where the teacher can point out important words that clue the reader. Words such as **because, since, although, beyond, rather, unlike, consequently, similar to, different than, however, as a result of,** and **compared with** should cause the reader to raise antennae and be alert because significant information is dead ahead.

After seeing the teacher demonstrate think alouds, students themselves can do likewise by using sticky notes to write their questions, thoughts, and reactions and place them on the text itself. Whenever an answer is discovered, the students jot it down on that question sticky note. Throughout the year, the teacher continues to demonstrate how to comprehend by using a think aloud.

Cooperative Learning

Teachers have three types of instructional goal structures from which to choose: competitive, individualistic, and cooperative (Johnson & Johnson, 1987). A competitive goal structure exists when students perceive that they can meet their own goals only if other students fail to meet their goals—for instance, listing the names of students by rank order according to their achievements on a spelling test. An individualistic goal structure exists when the students are able to achieve their learning goals independently of the goal achievements of other students—for example, learning how to correctly form a cursive capital *F*. Both competitive and individualistic goals structures are a major part of classroom instruction because students need to learn to compete for fun and to work autonomously (Johnson & Johnson, 1978).

Students can help one another in the learning process by working together in heterogeneous groups in which the success of each member depends on the success of each of the other group members. Such group interaction is more popularly referred to by educators as cooperative learning (Watson & Rangel, 1989). According to Slavin (1988), the collaboration of children attempting to accomplish a common task or goal is expected to produce a better finished product than would be produced if the students worked individually. Serving as a social model, cooperative learning requires that small groups be formed by the teacher for the purpose of unified investigation of a topic or development of a specific end product. Group investigation requires students to take an active part in planning what they will study and how. Groups are formed on the basis of interest in a topic. Each group member contributes to the investigation by seeking out needed information. The group gets together to synthesize and summarize the work and presents its findings to the entire class. Group investigation includes the following six stages (Sharan & Sharan, 1989–1990, pp. 17–21):

Stage 1: The topic to be investigated is identified, and students are organized into research groups.

Stage 2: The investigation is planned in the groups.

Stage 3: The investigation is carried out by group members.

Stage 4: Each group synthesizes and summarizes information and prepares a final report.

Stage 5: Each group presents its final report to the class.

Stage 6: Each group's investigation, including the process used and its products, are evaluated.

Students may be encouraged to form their own groups without direct teacher influence after they have experienced cooperative learning and understand the associated requirements; however, most cooperative learning groups are formed across ability levels (Meloth, 1991). For cooperative learning to be effective, (1) the children must work toward a group goal and (2) the achievement of the goal must depend on the individual learning of *all* group members (Slavin, 1988). Thus the group goal must be both challenging and attainable.

Because cooperative learning is the sharing of knowledge among peers and ultimately helping the other members of the group master academic material, divergent thinking is fostered and valued. Through the verbalization of both new ideas and previously acquired information, decision making and the ability to compromise are promoted along with the sharpening of speech and investigative skills. Conducive to activating and stimulating children's prior knowledge (Flood, 1986), cooperative learning enables children to share their thoughts and ideas in a type of group brainstorming. Cooperative learning also contributes to concept attainment (Johnson & Johnson, 1985) because students can introduce new concepts and ideas, explaining and interpreting them for their group colleagues.

If students of different ethnic backgrounds are grouped together, cultural awareness along with the knowledge base is expanded (Slavin, 1983). However, because of the students' diverse backgrounds, the accomplishment of the final goal will probably require additional time. A commonality of beliefs and experiences serves as a type of "shorthand form of communication" whereby each of the group's participants can assume certain responses or agreements without the need for discussion or negotiation (Ouchi, 1981). Nevertheless, participation within a successful group, despite the varying extent of each child's actual performance and contributions, allows for an increased self-perception of ability, satisfaction, and pride, as well as increased peer esteem (Ames, 1981).

Research findings suggest that cooperative learning improves academic performance for all students, enhances ethnic interactions, and increases proficiency in English for second-language students (Watson & Rangel, 1989). Three elementary teachers in Minnesota who have used cooperative learning with their students for a combined 23 years have found that cooperative learning can benefit all students, low ability, mainstreamed, or gifted (Augustine, Gruber, & Hanson, 1989–1990).

Cooperative learning is often based on common interests. For example, a group of students may wish to read the same book, discussing it within the cooperative group on a daily basis until they have completed the book. Mrs. Wells's class of inner-city students had one small group of sixth-grade boys who decided to read *Sounder* (Armstrong, 1969). Although the boys were close friends and inseparable on the playground, their reading skills varied widely. Still, they made up their minds that they were going to read *Sounder* together. Mrs. Wells got multiple copies of the book for the group, but before she gave the boys the books, she had them create some guidelines for studying and discussing it. Together, the boys decided to write down any questions they had as they read the book and to talk about them the next day when they met as a group. Any new words or parts of the book they especially liked, they also jotted down in their notebooks. The group members decided to pace themselves by reading and sharing a chapter a day.

3.6 In the Classroom: Mini Lesson

Sequencing Events

After reading Mary Ann Hoberman's (1978) classic, *A House Is a House for Me*, have the students get into groups of four. Give each group the following materials:

2 green paper plates
a can of chocolate frosting
a package of graham crackers
a plastic knife
8 pieces of red licorice
a variety of colors of small gumdrops
thin, 2-inch pretzels
sentence strips

Have the children make a house for their group. When the houses are complete, have each group write the directions for building their house on sentence strips. Younger children may dictate their directions to the teacher or a parent volunteer.

This is also a good activity to do with reading buddies from another grade level. The older student can assist the younger student in building the house. Then the younger student can give the instructions in the correct sequence to the older child. The following is an example dictated by a group of first graders:

First we made the floor. Next we used icing to add the walls. Then we put on the ceiling and the roof. Then we made doors and windows and a sidewalk. Last, we made trees and a chimney.

Hoberman, M. A. (1978). *A house is a house for me* (B. Frasier, Illus.). New York: Viking.

The boys became engrossed in *Sounder* and by far surpassed their daily reading goal. Even though none of the boys had ever been to a farm or even outside the large northern city in which they lived, their interest in southern rural living intensified as they progressed through the book. One of the boys saw an analogy between *Sounder* and *Uncle Tom's Cabin* (Stowe, 1852), which he had seen on television as a late, late movie. Tim, the poorest reader in the group, was the first to notice that Armstrong did not refer to any of the characters by name except for the dog, Sounder, and individuals outside the described family.

When the group began daily discussions, Mrs. Wells would occasionally join the students. She made a few suggestions, but primarily she listened to their interactions. Later in the class sessions, she would find herself working with other children but still listening to the *Sounder* group's conversation because of the boys' high level of enthusiasm and excitement.

In their discussions and sometimes arguments, the boys' vocabularies grew. They were now using words such as *prejudice, empathy,* and *apathy;* by reading and rereading passages, they were able to make comparisons and interpretations. In using their newly acquired skills, they selected one passage as the most powerful in the book and shared it with the entire class. The passage described the boy, now grown, remembering his father and faithful coon dog, Sounder, as they were in the prime of life, a time prior to the tragedies that befell the family and resulted in the deaths of his father and dog. The boy knows that he will forever remember the deep voice of Sounder echoing through the night.

When the boys finished *Sounder*, they were emotionally spent. The lower-ability readers had kept up with the other members of the group in their readings throughout most of the book. Realizing how draining the book had been for the boys and trying again to utilize the advantages of cooperative group interaction, Mrs. Wells suggested that they read another book together. She provided copies of *Be a Perfect Person in Just Three Days!* by Stephen Manes (1984), a humorous book lacking the complex literary merit of *Sounder*. Mane's book enabled the boys to laugh together, and because they were such good friends, they readily shared personal stories of embarrassing situations when they appeared to be "cool" and to have everything under control. The boys later read two other books together as a group.

Drama, storytelling, and writing each lend themselves to cooperative learning. For example, a writing activity may require students in a group to formulate questions for investigation of a particular subject; group members must then conduct research and contribute information for the purpose of uncovering the answers. Each student may write a portion of the final report to be read to the class. The lesson plan on organizing information (see box 3.7) reveals a method for making cooperative writing an enjoyable experience as students work together to solve a mystery.

Questioning Strategies

Questions need to be posed effectively by the teacher in a timely, supportive manner. We know that by asking simple low-level recall questions initially, students can then respond correctly to more difficult, higher-level questions than if the higher-level questions were asked first. Think of the brain like a car in Minnesota in January. After it is started and warmed up, it can go 65 mph. But if you start it and try to drive it immediately, the engine will probably chug or even die on the road. Or consider this. Did you ever take a test when the first test item was extremely difficult? Then the next test item was even harder? By the third item which you knew something about, you were second guessing yourself. Student performance has to do with confidence level. Thus, there is something to that old adage, "success begets success."

"Curiosity spawns questions. Questions are the master key to understanding. Questions clarify confusion. Questions stimulate research results. Questions propel us forward and take us deeper . . ." (Harvey & Goudvis, 2000, p. 81). Good questions help keep students focused on the topic, keep them engaged, and help them monitor their understanding (Farris, Fuhler, & Walther, 2004). By modeling good questions, teachers assist students in probing for more information. Why did that character dislike the new student? How did the setting influence the plot? And so on. In turn, students must be given frequent opportunities to develop and ask their own questions.

3.7   In the Classroom: Mini Lesson

Organizing Ideas for Writing

Objective: To stress the importance of organizing information in writing

Subjects: Language arts (writing, listening, speaking, and reading)
Social studies

Prepare different clues for the same crime and make six copies of each clue. Mix the clues and place three different clues in an envelope, so that each student will have one envelope containing three clues.

On a piece of colored cardboard, write the following questions:

When did the theft take place?

Where did the theft occur?

How was the money taken without anyone noticing?

What was the robber's motive?

Who stole the money?

Display the questions for all the students to see. Tell the students they are to play detective and solve the crime by answering all five questions. Then randomly divide the class into groups of five students each. Give each student an envelope containing three clues. The groups will have 10 minutes to solve the mystery, trying to answer as many of the questions as possible.

Each group member must read the clues in his or her envelope to the other four members of the group. After all the clues have been read, group members may begin their discussion

At the end of 10 minutes, ask for answers to the five questions. Unless the clues clearly point out the answers, probably two or fewer responses will be correct and the crime will go unsolved. At this point, ask the students why they did not (or did) solve the robbery. What strategy would have helped the group solve the case? Move from solving the mystery to modeling the importance of organizing facts. (Note: Organize the clues. Point out that when a person reads, it helps if the information is organized. This is true for letters, recipes, newspaper accounts of a crime, and so forth.) The next day, move to expository writing using this organizational approach to writing a descriptive piece.

As another demonstration of organizing information, on an overhead transparency prepared in advance, show the students 20 different factual statements about the life of George Washington, from his childhood to his farewell address as president. Then have each group organize the facts into categories, labeling each category. The groups should organize the statements and, afterward, share their categories with the class by explaining how and why they selected their categories. As a final step, have each group tie together the statements in one of the categories and write a paragraph for that category.

For K–2 learners and for struggling readers, research reveals that the most effective and efficient procedures for teaching students to generate their own questions are those that are both concrete as well as easy to use (Stahl, 2004). Young children should be taught to use signal words.

Who?

What?

Where?

When?

Why?

How?

These signal words are effective for being a good listener, speaker, reader, writer, and viewer.

Generic question stems also aid students in acquiring knowledge and greater comprehension. Below are some generic question stems:

How are ___ and ___ alike?
What is the main idea of _____?
How is _____ related to ____?
Why is it important that _____?

Both the list of signal words and generic question stems should be placed on charts in large enough print to be visible to students as they engage in language arts activities. Periodically, the teacher should review the signal words and generic questions with the class, modeling her own use of these two strategies. At the beginning of the school year, the signal questions work at all grade levels; however, after two to three weeks, upper-elementary and middle schoolers need to press on to develop more complex questions that require higher level thinking skills. Signal questions, however, are a good gauge for students to use in evaluating their own writing and speaking.

3.8   In the Classroom: Teaching Hint

Wonder Books

Students in grades 1–8 can create their own "Wonder Books" by using an inexpensive spiral notebook to write down what they wonder. They then can write down research questions and read to find the answer to their questions. In grades 1–3, students can divide the page into two columns, one for Questions and the other for Facts. As a prereading activity as well as during their reading, they can generate questions and write them down in their Wonder Books. When they discover the answers to their questions, they jot them down next to the question (Harvey & Goudvis, 2000). Wonder Books are especially effective when used with informational books. Students can work as partners reading the same book together, or two different books on the same topic.

Wonder Books can be combined with concept muraling for a content area of study such as in science or social studies. It is best to give the students an inexpensive spiral notebook (often costing $.25 or less at a back-to-school sale by discounters) for each topic being studied so that the pages don't become ratty and tiny bits of paper end up on the floor.

Topics may include the human body with sections on the brain, the circulatory system, bones, and so forth, or the Industrial Revolution with sections on inventions, economics, and important figures and leaders.

Before and during each unit of study, students write down their "I wonder" questions and then leave a space to write the response or answer as they gain new knowledge.

Developing Higher-Level Thinking Skills

Children process information and utilize it through different levels of thinking. Bloom's (1956) taxonomy of education provides such a hierarchy of thinking processes (see box 3.9).

3.9   In the Classroom: Teaching Hint

Bloom's Taxonomy of Education and Children's Literature

Bloom's categories begin with the most basic and move up the hierarchy, ending with the most complex. Included with each is a brief description of how the teacher can develop and reinforce each of these cognitive skills using a selected piece of children's literature.

1. **Knowledge** *Recalling information that has been presented*
   Example: Giving the sequence of events in *My Great Aunt Arizona* (Houston, 1992)

2. **Comprehension** *Understanding, translating, interpreting, or extrapolating information.*
   Example: Making generalizations about Lilly's feelings toward her teacher in *Lilly's Purple Plastic Purse* (Henkes, 1996)

3. **Application** *Abstracting and applying the information by using principles to problem solve.*
   Example: Inferring traits of characters in *Poppleton: Book One* (Rylant, 1997)

4. **Analysis** *Breaking down complex information or ideas into simple parts to discover how the parts relate to each other or are organized.*
   Example: Predicting the outcome of *Pink and Say* (Polacco, 1994) with one-third of the book still to be read

5. **Synthesis** *Breaking information down and putting it together in a new way*
   Example: Interpreting the personal conflict of slave owners and the slaves at Christmas in *Christmas in the Big House, Christmas in the Quarters* (McKissick & McKissick, 1994)

6. **Evaluation** *Making judgments, usually against a standard*
   Example: How do people react to homeless people like the boy in *Fly Away Home* (Bunting, 1991)? Why?

Bunting, E. (1991). *Fly away home* (R. Himler, Illus.). New York: Clarion.
Henkes, K. (1996). *Lilly's purple plastic purse.* New York: Greenwillow.
Houston, G. (1992). *My great aunt Arizona* (S. Lambe, Illus.). New York: HarperCollins.
McKissick, P., & McKissick, F. (1994). *Christmas in the big house, Christmas in the quarters* (J. Thompson, Illus.). New York: Scholastic.
Polacco, P. (1994). *Pink and Say.* New York: Philomel.
Rylant, C. (1997). *Poppleton: Book one* (M. Teague, Illus.). New York: BlueSky/Scholastic.

It is important to realize that the six levels of Bloom's taxonomy can be used to formulate questions for most children's literature, from wordless picture books to adolescent novels. In many instances, it is possible, for example, to use a picture book to question children at both lower levels of thinking (knowledge, comprehension, and application) and higher levels (analysis, synthesis, and evaluation). For example, consider the following use of Jon Scieszka's (1989) classic, *The True Story of the Three Little Pigs*:

Knowledge:	What did the wolf want to borrow?
Comprehension:	Why did the wolf eat the first little pig?
Application:	Why did the wolf become angry with the third little pig?
Analysis:	Why wouldn't the newspaper reporters believe the wolf's story?
Synthesis:	Why do you think the wolf frequently got into trouble?

Evaluation: Do you think the wolf was clever or dumb? Tell why you think so, giving examples from the book to back up your opinion.

Formulating good questions is an art and a science. It requires preparation prior to teaching the lesson itself. Creating and asking the lower-level questions is a rather simple task; an elaborate list can be developed quite quickly. In the case of *Peter Rabbit* (Potter, 1982), for instance, one might ask: What color was Peter's coat? What did Mrs. Rabbit tell her children before she left to go shopping? Where did Peter go? What did Peter eat in the garden? What did Mr. McGregor hold in his hand as he chased Peter? Where did Peter hide? Who encouraged Peter to get up and run? What did Peter leave in Mr. McGregor's garden? And so on.

Asking such lower-level questions may appear to be almost a waste of time; however, such questions do have value in discussions. By initially answering basic questions, children tend to be more apt to answer higher-level questions. This is because in providing correct responses to the easier questions, students actually become more confident overall. Starting out with higher-level, rigorous questions often intimidates students, especially those who are insecure or shy to respond.

Lower-level questions tend to be closed-ended in that either a right or wrong response exists. For example, the question "What did Peter leave in the garden?" was answered by Tim, who said, "his coat and shoes." This was the

3.10   In the Classroom: Mini Lesson

Problem Solving

Problem solving can be an effective group thinking activity for children of all grade levels. The books listed below are excellent choices for problem-solving activities. The teacher reads to the point in the text where the problem has been firmly established. The teacher then divides the class into groups of three students and instructs them to resolve the problem. The groups must first brainstorm for ideas and then select one idea that will best solve the problem. Each group then writes its solution down and shares it with the class.

Goble, P. (1988). *Iktomi and the boulder*. New York: Orchard/Watts. This book tells the story of Iktomi, a Plains Indian, who is vain and manipulative. Iktomi gets into trouble when a boulder begins chasing him and won't let him escape. Children in the intermediate grades will enjoy solving this problem.

Johnston, T. (1994). *Amber on the mountain* (R. Duncan, Illus.). New York: Dial. Amber becomes friends with Anna, who teaches her to read. When Anna returns to the city, Amber must find a way to communicate with her.

Lasky, K. (2000). *Vision of beauty: The story of Sarah Breedlove Walker* (N. Bennett, Illus.). Boston, MA: Candlewick. Older readers will enjoy this picture book biography. Sarah is the first child born to her parents after slavery is ended. By age seven, she is orphaned. Her problem is how to work her way up to be a success in business and to do something to help others at the same time.

Pfister, M. (1992). *The rainbow fish*. New York: North-South Books. The rainbow fish is the most beautiful fish in the ocean but must discover how to be happy.

response the teacher sought. However, Sarah interpreted the closed-ended question in a more open manner when she suggested, "He also left behind his courage"; this was quite a divergent and insightful response for a six-year-old. Although both Tim and Sarah gave correct responses to the same question, clearly their levels of thinking were markedly different.

Higher-level, open-ended questions require more thought in relating and interpreting information. Why do you think the author/illustrator included a robin in many of the pictures with Peter? Was Mrs. Rabbit cautious? Why or why not? Do you think Peter visited the garden again on another day? Why or why not? Such questions obviously have more than one correct response and are worthy of discussion time. The question "Was Mrs. Rabbit cautious?" can be answered by both yes and no. Jordan believed Mrs. Rabbit was very conservative in her lifestyle, asserting, "Yes, she's cautious, because she took an umbrella with her. She also took time to clearly warn her children of the dangers of Mr. McGregor's garden." However, Ginger believed otherwise and said, "No, she would have taken her children with her when she shopped if she was cautious." Which child is correct? Both have valid arguments. Does a right answer exist for this question?

Culturally Diverse and Special Needs Students

Teaching strategies for processing language that are geared toward culturally diverse and special needs students are an absolute must for all classroom teachers. ADD, ADHD, ELL, LD, mildly mentally retarded students, and struggling readers and writers generally need structure because often they have not developed the ability to structure internally on their own. This may be true of gifted students as well because they are intensely interested in focusing on one thing, often neglecting other assignments or content areas. Thus it is important to list the steps in an assignment and post them prominently in the room. When the child is doing individual or group work, write lists of steps on a sticky note and place it on the child's desk or table. Have the child cross out each item as it is completed. This will give a feeling of accomplishment to the student.

Previewing what is going to be taught in a lesson is helpful to such students but the preview should be kept to the point. For instance, "Today, we're going to learn how to interview senior citizens. First, we'll think of questions to ask them about their families. Then we'll ask them questions about changes they've seen in their lifetimes. These could be inventions, sports, or some other area." Concept muraling, explained earlier in this chapter, can be used to both preview and review a unit of study.

In addition to specific, straightforward directions, learning challenged and gifted children often need reminders. Lots of repetition and practice are helpful. Direct instruction in which a teacher presents the information orally and students listen has proved to be very beneficial. "At-risk students often begin school academically behind. But the highly structured setting of the direct instruction approach can help these children catch up" (Engelmann, 1999, p. 77). Because at-risk students enter school behind the others, they must achieve more than the average student each year in order to keep up. This is a difficult challenge for such students. Engelmann (1999) points out that such students in fourth grade often have not mastered skills they were expected to attain by the end of first grade. For instance, some of the words that poor or lower-ability readers in fourth grade often confuse are *a/the, what/that, when/then, of/for,* and *was/said.*

Recording reading material for the students to listen to at a listening center and/or permitting them to dictate reports and other writing assignments into a tape recorder, with either a classroom aide or volunteer transcribing the information and typing it for them, are other techniques. Caution should be given that some students can become dependent upon using such techniques and fail to attempt to use other literacy strategies.

One key the teacher must keep in mind on a daily basis is the emotional aspect of learning. Culturally diverse and special needs students need to be motivated just as other students do. By making learning enjoyable and pleasurable, they will be more excited than if they constantly encounter boredom or frustration.

Summary

Because of the close relationship between language and thinking, instructional procedures need to consider the thinking processes in the teaching of language arts. By gaining an understanding of how children think, teachers can help students become more effective and efficient in their learning. Children need to develop strategies for learning that enable them to utilize prior knowledge along with their problem-solving capabilities. Teachers assist by having lessons with social interaction. In addition, activities based on the different multiple intelligences help students with different learning styles and strengths.

Graphic organizers, constructivism, thing alouds, and cooperative learning are teaching models that can be used in language arts instruction to enhance student learning for all students depending on the skill being taught. All four models necessitate much planning by the teacher prior to the presentation of a lesson or the organization of a study group. Visual representation through concept muraling and graphic organizers greatly assist average, ELL, and struggling readers to grasp new concepts and understandings.

Teachers and students need to develop good questioning strategies in order to expand their own learning. The posing of both lower- and higher-level questions can greatly enhance the development of children's thinking skills. Bloom's (1956) taxonomy of education objectives offers a hierarchy of thinking processes that can be used across the curriculum.

Questions

1. How would you incorporate cooperative learning in your classroom?
2. What is an organizer? Give an example of an organizer.
3. What is a schema and how does it affect a child's learning?
4. As a teacher, how would you model problem solving?
5. Name the levels of Bloom's taxonomy and define each level.
6. What is the difference between emphasizing lower-level questions and emphasizing higher-level questions?
7. What strategies work well with special needs students?

Reflective Teaching

Flip back to the beginning of the chapter to the teaching vignette entitled "Peering into the Classroom." After rereading the vignette, consider the following questions: What characteristics (either implied or directly exhibited) does the teacher possess that you would like to develop? What strengths and weaknesses are revealed for the students described in this section? How would you meet the needs of students such as these?

Activities

1. Develop questions based on Bloom's taxonomy for a children's book.
2. Prepare three advance organizers for chapter 3.
3. Observe your own learning strategies for a week. Write down the ways in which you use your prior knowledge and problem-solving techniques to study for another class.
4. Pretend you are a famous person and model problem solving from that person's perspective—for example, Eisenhower and the D-day invasion of Europe; Rosa Parks and her decision of where to sit on the bus; Martin Luther King and the march in Selma, Alabama; and Sandra Day O'Conner and her decision to accept the appointment to become the first woman Supreme Court justice.

Further Reading

Farris, P. J. (2004). *Elementary and middle school social studies: An interdisciplinary and multicultural approach.* Boston: McGraw-Hill.

Glasgow, J. N. (1999). Recognizing students' Multiple Intelligences in cross-age buddy journals. *English Journal, 88* (6), 88–96.

Orange, C., and Horowitz, R. (1999). An academic standoff: Literacy task preferences of African American and Mexican American male adolescents versus teacher-expected preferences. *Journal of Adolescent and Adult Literacy, 43* (1), 28–39.

Richards, J. C., & Anderson, N. A. (2003). What do I *See?* What do I *Think?* What do I *Wonder?* (STW): A visual literacy strategy to help emergent readers focus on storybook illustrations. *The Reading Teacher, 56* (7), 442–443.

Thames, D. G., & York, K. C. (2003). Disciplinary border crossing: Adopting a broader, richer view of literacy. *The Reading Teacher, 56* (7). 602–610.

Wilhelm, J. D. (2001). *Improving comprehension with think-aloud strategies: Modeling what good readers do.* New York: Scholastic.

References

Ames, C. (1981). Competitive versus cooperative reward structure: The influence of individual and group performance factors on achievement attributions and affect. *American Educational Research Journal, 18* (3), 273–288.

Augustine, D. K., Gruber, K. D., & Hanson, L. R. (1989–1990). Cooperation works! *Educational Leadership, 47* (4), 4–7.

Ausubel, D. (1963). *The psychology of meaningful verbal learning.* New York: Grune & Stratton.

Berry, B., Hoke, M., & Hirsch, E. (2004). The search for highly qualified teachers. *Phi Delta Kappan, 85* (9), 684–689.

Bloom, B. (1956). *Taxonomy of education objectives.* New York: David McKay.

Campbell, L. (1997). How teachers interpret MI theory. *Educational Leadership, 55* (1), 14–19.

Checkley, K. (1997). The first seven . . . and the eighth: A conversation with Howard Gardner. *Educational Leadership, 55* (1), 8–13.

Clay, M. (1991). Introducing a new storybook to young readers. *The Reading Teacher, 45* (4), 264–273.

Derry, S. J., & Murphy, D. A. (1986). Designing systems that train learning ability: From theory to practice. *Review of Educational Research, 56* (1), 1–39.

Engelmann, S. (1999). The benefits of direct instruction: Affirmative action for at-risk learners. *Educational Leadership, 57* (1), 77, 79.

Farris, P. J., & Downey, P. (In press). Concept muraling: Dropping visual crumbs along the instructional trail. *The Reading Teacher.*

Farris, P. J., Fuhler, C., & Walther, M. (2004). *Teaching reading: A balanced approach for today's classrooms.* Boston: McGraw-Hill.

Flood, J. (1986). The text, the student, and the teacher: Learning from exposition in the middle schools. *The Reading Teacher, 40* (8), 414–418.

Fountas, I. C., & Pinnell, G. S. (1996). *Guided reading: Good teaching for all children.* Portsmouth, NH: Heinemann.

Gardner, H. (1993). *Frames of mind: The theories of multiple intelligences.* New York: Basic Books.

Gardner, H. (1999). *Intelligence reframed.* New York: Basic Books.

Gardner, H. (2003, Apr. 2). *Multiple intelligences after twenty years.* Paper presented at the American Educational Research Association, Chicago.

Gavan, E. M. (1994). Who's in control? Is there enough "empowerment" to go around? *Language Arts, 71,* 192–199.

Glasgow, J. N. (1999). Recognizing students' multiple intelligences in cross-age buddy journals. *English Journal, 88* (6), 88–96.

Gredler, M. E. (1992). *Learning and instruction: Theory into practice* (2nd ed.). New York: Macmillan.

Gursky, D. (1992). The unschooled mind. *The Education Digest, 58,* 27–29.

Harvey, S., & Goudvis, A. (2000). *Strategies that work*. Portland, ME: Stenhouse.

Huei-yu Wang, J., & Guthrie, J. (2004). Modeling the effects of intrinsic motivation, extrinsic motivation, amount of reading, and past reading achievement on text comprehension between U.S. and Chinese students. *Reading Research Quarterly, 39* (2), 162–187.

Jensen, J. M., & Roser, N. L. (1990). Are there really 3 R's? *Educational Leadership, 47* (7), 7–12.

Johnson, D. W., & Johnson, R. T. (1978). Cooperative, competitive, and individualistic learning. *Journal of Research and Development in Education, 12* (1), 3–15.

Johnson, D. W., & Johnson, R. T. (1987). *Learning together and alone: Cooperative, competitive, and individualistic learning*. Englewood Cliffs, NJ: Prentice Hall.

Johnson, R. T., & Johnson, D. W. (1985). Student-student interaction ignored but powerful. *Journal of Teacher Education, 36* (1), 22–26.

Jones, B. F., Palincsar, A. S., Ogle, D. S., & Carr, E. G. (1987). *Strategic teaching: Cognitive instruction in the content areas*. Elmhurst, IL: North Central Regional Educational Laboratory.

Joyce, B., Showers, B., & Rolheiser-Bennett, C. (1987). Staff development and student learning: A synthesis of research on models of teaching. *Educational Leadership, 45* (2), 12–23.

Joyce, B., & Weil, M. (Eds.). (1986). *Models of teaching*. Englewood Cliffs, NJ: Prentice Hall.

Meloth, M. S. (1991). Enhancing literacy through cooperative learning. In E. H. Hiebert (Ed.), *Literacy for a diverse society* (pp. 172–183). New York: Teachers College Press.

Morrow, L. M. (2004). Motivation: The forgotten factor. *Reading Today, 21* (5), 6.

Ogle, D. M. (1986). K-W-L: A teaching model that develops active reading of expository text. *The Reading Teacher, 39* (7), 564–570.

Ogle, D. M. (1989). The know, want to know, learn strategy. In K. D. Muth (Ed.), *Children's comprehension of text: Research into practice* (pp. 205–223). Newark, DE: International Reading Association.

Ouchi, W. (1981). *Theory Z: How American business can meet the Japanese challenge*. Reading, MA: Addison-Wesley.

Resnick, L. B., & Klopfer, L. E. (1989). Toward the thinking curriculum: An overview. In L. B. Resnick & L. E. Klopfer (Eds.), *Toward the thinking curriculum: Current cognitive research*. Arlington, VA: Association for Supervision and Curriculum Development.

Reutzel, D. R., & Cooter, R. B., Jr. (1996). *Teaching children to read: From basals to books* (2nd ed.). Columbus, OH: Merrill.

Richards, J. C., & Anderson, N. A. (2003). What do I *See*? What do I *Think*? What do I *Wonder*? (STW): A visual literacy strategy to help emergent readers focus on storybook illustrations. *The Reading Teacher, 56* (7), 442–443.

Sharan, Y., & Sharan, S. (1989–1990). Group investigation expands cooperative learning. *Educational Leadership, 47* (4), 17–21.

Slavin, R. E. (1983). *Cooperative learning*. New York: Longman.

Slavin, R. E. (1988). Cooperative revolution catches fire. *School Administrator, 45* (1), 9–13.

Smith, F. (1988). *Understanding reading* (4th ed). Hillsdale, NY: Erlbaum.

Stahl, K. (2004). Proof, practice, and promise: Comprehension strategy instruction in the primary grades. *The Reading Teacher, 57* (7), 598–609.

Tompkins, G. (2004). *Teaching writing: Balancing process and product*. (4th ed). Columbus, OH: Merrill.

Vacca, J. L., Vacca, R. T., & Gove, M. K. (2000). *Reading and learning to read* (4th ed). New York: Addison-Wesley.

Verhoeven, L., & Snow, C. (2001). *Literacy and motivation.* New York: Erlbaum.

Vygotsky, L. S. (1962). *Thought and language.* Cambridge, MA: MIT Press.

Vygotsky, L. S. (1978). *Mind in society.* Cambridge, MA: Harvard University Press.

Watson, D., & Rangel, L. (1989). Can cooperative learning be evaluated? *School Administrator, 46* (6), 8–11.

Wells, G. (1990). Creating conditions to encourage literate thinking. *Educational Leadership, 47* (6), 13–17.

Children's Literature

Armstrong, W. (1969). *Sounder.* New York: Harper & Row.

Avi. (1994). *The barn.* New York: Orchard/Richard Jackson.

Clements, A. (2002). *The jacket* (M. Henderson, Illus.). New York: Simon & Schuster.

Creech, S. (2004). *Heartbeat.* New York: Joanna Colter Books.

DiCamillo, K. (2003). *The tale of Despereaux.* Cambridge, MA: Candlewick.

Fleming, D. (1994). *Barnyard banter.* New York: Holt.

Kilborne, S. (1994). *Peach and Blue* (S. Johnson & L. Fancher). New York: Knopf.

Lowry, L. (1989). *Number the stars.* Boston: Houghton Mifflin.

MacLachlan, P. (1985). *Sarah, plain and tall.* New York: Harper & Row.

Manes, S. (1984). *Be a perfect person in just three days!* New York: Bantam.

Naylor, P. R. (1991). *Shiloh.* New York: Atheneum.

Polacco, P. (1994). *Pink and Say.* New York: Philomel.

Polacco, P. (1998). *Thank you, Mr. Falker.* New York: Philomel.

Potter, B. (1982). *The complete works of Peter Rabbit.* New York: Warne.

San Souci, R. (1989). *The talking eggs: A folktale from the American South* (J. Pinkney, Illus.). New York: Dial.

Scieszka, J. (1989). *The true story of the three little pigs* (L. Smith, Illus). New York: Viking.

Soto, G. (1993). *Too many tamales.* New York: Putnam.

Spinelli, J. (2002). *Loser.* New York: Joanna Colter Books.

Stowe, H. B. (1852). *Uncle Tom's cabin.* New York: Viking.

Children's Literature
Opening Windows to New Worlds

Read to Them

Read to them
　Before the time is gone and stillness
　fills the room again.
Read to them.

What if it were meant to be that you
　were the one, the only one, who could
　unlock the doors and share the magic
　with them?
What if others have been daunted by
　scheduling demands, district
　objectives, or one hundred other
　obstacles?

Read to them
Be confident Charlotte has been able to
　teach them about friendship, and
　Horton about self-worth;
Be sure the Skin Horse has been able to
　deliver his message.

Read to them
Let them meet Tigger, Homer Price,
　Aslan, and Corduroy;
Take them to Oz, Prydain, and
　Camazotz;
Show them a Truffula Tree.

Read to them
Laugh with them at Soup and Rob, and
　cry with them when the Queen of
　Terabithia is forever lost;
Allow the Meeker Family to turn
　loyalty, injustice, and war into
　something much more than a
　vocabulary lesson.

What if you are the one, the only one,
　with the chance to do it?
What if this is the critical year for even
　one child?

Read to them
Before the time, before the chance, is
　gone.

　　　　　　　　　　　—Steven L. Layne

PEERING INTO THE CLASSROOM
A DIVERSE CLASSROOM

Books! Books! Books! Maria Walther's first-grade classroom has over a thousand books that she has purchased or obtained from paperback book clubs in addition to the many published books her students have written during the school year. Maria jokes that it would be nice if the local children's bookstore could be considered a "dependent" on her and her husband's 1040 IRS form. Maria teaches in a neighborhood school in Aurora, Illinois. Typically she has a diverse group of six- and seven-year-olds in her first-grade class ranging from students with Down syndrome to ADD and ADHD to low-ability and average-ability up to gifted students. There are students from many different cultures as well—African American, Chinese, Hispanic, and those with family roots established generations ago in Western Europe.

Maria knows young children need to get their hands on books and pour over them. So she provides a generous quantity and variety for them to explore. In the beginning of the year there may be only one or two students who can actually "read" a simple picture book. But every child can appreciate and gain from viewing the illustrations. Like many teachers, Maria reads to her class daily—usually several times a day. The school day opens with a poem that students are given for their "Poetry Book," a binder that holds all the poetry collected throughout the year. In June, the Poetry Books are bound by a parent volunteer and sent home with the students to read and reread as they so desire. One favorite poem is Margaret Wise Brown's "I Like Bugs." According to Maria, "The kids absolutely LOVE this poem. And I do, too." Later in the day, Maria reads a picture or chapter book to her students. Maria primes the pump by introducing the book, perhaps relating the book to another one by the same author or to something the class has been taught. When she opens the book and begins to read aloud, one can hear a cotton ball drop—so intent are the students in listening to their teacher.

Maria is always on the lookout for new books for her classroom library. She points out that most of her books came from book club orders. "That's the least expensive way to accumulate new books. Hardbacks cost $15 and teachers don't make much money so we have to look for ways to stretch our dollars." Book clubs always offer the latest award-winning books plus those that are popular with children. Another advantage of book clubs is that they provide a variety of genres, or types, of books. Biographies, informational books, folktales, fantasy, historical novels, contemporary realistic fiction, and poetry are all available. And, as Maria points out, there are some categories that kids can't resist buying from the book clubs even though they are not quality literature—books on the latest movie or cartoon sensations. Books of jokes and riddles are useful in providing comic relief during the day.

Critical to Maria's students' success is knowing what kind of books each child needs and making it available at the appropriate time. The Down syndrome student needs books with simple language and pictures. These include board books such as *Where's Spot?* (Hill, 1980) and simple pattern books like

Brown Bear, Brown Bear, What Do You See? (Martin, 1964; 1983), *Panda Bear, Panda Bear, What Do You See?* (Martin, 2003), and *Chicka Chicka Boom Boom* (Martin & Archambault, 1989). The latter two books are also enjoyed by all of her other students at the beginning of the school year. For the average-ability students, *Good Dog, Carl* (Day, 1985) is an excellent starting point for the beginning of the school year. For her upper-ability students who can already read, Maria searches out chapter books such as the *Little Bear* series by Else H. Minarik and *Henry and Mudge* books by Cynthia Rylant.

With such a huge collection of books, it is easy for Maria to develop thematic units. For instance, she has five books on Christopher Columbus's first voyage to America (her personal favorite is *Follow the Dream: The Story of Christopher Columbus* (Sis, 1991). Maria has over 10 different titles for her penguin unit and four simply written books about Martin Luther King's life. During September, she teaches a unit on apples. Says Maria, "It helps that Johnny Appleseed was born on September 26." This is perfect timing for sharing *Johnny Appleseed* (Kellogg, 1988), who in the mid-1800s planted apple seeds in Pennsylvania, Ohio, Indiana, and Illinois. She reads aloud *Apples* (Robbins, 2002), an informational book. Maria also reads *The Life and Times of the Apple* (Micucci, 1992) as her students learn about grafting, the various parts of an apple blossom, varieties of apples, harvesting apples, and how the fruit is used. After a field trip to a local orchard, the students bring in different kinds of apples to make apple butter—a delicious ending to a very thorough unit of study.

For her thematic units, Maria likes to buy hardbacks because of their durability as well as a few paperbacks of the same titles for her students to read at school or take home to share with their families. According to Maria, "Children like to read, or have someone read to them, books that are shared in class by the teacher. This is great because it reinforces not only concepts that were taught but helps the students become fluent readers on their own." This is an important goal of all teachers, not just first-grade teachers such as Maria.

Chapter Objectives

The reader will:

✓ become familiar with the different genres of children's literature.

✓ become familiar with the different aspects of a book including characterization, plot, setting, theme, and author's style.

✓ be able to develop activities to accompany quality children's literature.

Standards for Professionals

The following Standards will be addressed in this chapter:

Standard 2: Instructional Strategies and Curriculum Materials

2.3 Use a wide range of curriculum materials in effective reading instruction for learners at different stages of reading and writing development and from differing cultural and linguistic backgrounds.

Standard 4: Creating a Literate Environment

4.1 Use students' interests, reading abilities, and backgrounds as foundations for the reading and writing program.

4.2 Use a large supply of books, technology-based information, and nonprint materials representing multiple levels, broad interests, and cultural and linguistic backgrounds.

4.4 Motivate learners to be lifelong readers.

Introduction

In the picture book, *The Bee Tree* (Polacco, 1993), Grandpa says to Mary Ellen, his granddaughter:

> There is such sweetness inside of that book too! . . . Such things . . . adventure, knowledge and wisdom. But these things do not come easily. You have to pursue them. Just like we ran after bees to find their tree, so you must also chase these things through the pages of a book. (unpaged)

Teachers must introduce students to a variety of quality literature and then offer ample opportunities for them to engage in free reading for enjoyment and enrichment. "Reading literature for pleasure offers several benefits. First, readers pay attention to those aesthetic qualities of texts that entertain or please the ears. We can also identify with familiar experiences captured in stories. This enhances meaning-making. In transacting personal meanings, we gain ownership of the text and create our own texts from the reading experience" (Yenika-Agbaw, 1997, p. 446).

"Literature educates the imagination, provides language models, and molds the intellect. The heritage of humankind lies in books; we endow students with the key to their legacy when we teach them to read," according to Beatrice Cullinan (1987, p. 6). Adams (1990) supports this view in writing that "the single most important activity for building the knowledge and skills eventually required for reading appears to be reading aloud to children" (p. 46). Children make the greatest strides in acquiring such knowledge and skills when the vocabulary and syntax are slightly above the child's own level of language development (Chomsky, 1972). Indeed, research indicates that a single oral reading of a book may result in new word meanings being acquired by young children (Elley, 1989). According to Cullinan and Galda (2003), "Children's books contain beautiful language and outstanding art, providing their young readers with wonderful examples of symbolic thought. The act of reading books develops children's facility with language as they pore over carefully crafted prose and poetry" (p. 6).

Consider, for instance, Jamal, age 22 months, who became quite familiar with *Brown Bear, Brown Bear, What Do You See?* by Bill Martin, Jr. (1964/1983). While watching television, Jamal and his mother observed a new commercial that contained several different colorful scenes; the last of these was a lingering shot of a goldfish in a fishbowl next to a stack of encyclopedias. Jamal's mother pointed to the television screen and said, "fish." Jamal looked at the screen, then up at his mother and said, "goldfish." As far as Jamal's mother knew, the only other goldfish with which he was familiar was the one in *Brown Bear, Brown Bear, What Do You See?* Yet Jamal was confident he could correctly categorize the fish as a goldfish.

The content of children's literature can expand a child's knowledge and understanding of the surrounding world. "Our children must be taught about the world and ethical values that are generally considered to be important in our culture, such as the sanctity of human life, justice, integrity, respect for the dignity of the individual, honesty, and the importance of family" (Honig 1988, p. 235).

Quality literature should be not only read aloud but also read by students themselves. Students should read it, respond to it, create their own meanings from what they have read, and share their findings and understandings with peers. "Any avid reader feels the urge to share a good book with somebody immediately after finishing it" (Steiner & Steiner, 1999, p. 19). Teachers need to provide lots of opportunities for student sharing. During grand conversations (Daniels, 1994), classmates form small groups and share their personal reactions to a book. Typically, upper-elementary and middle school students will describe how a book relates to real life, even their own lives. Another approach is literature circles that offer small group interaction in which each group member takes on a specific role in reacting to the book. Both grand conversations and literature circles are discussed later in this chapter.

Reading should be both educational and enjoyable. In other words, literature can be the central means of teaching reading, or it can be used in conjunction with a basal reading program. According to Huck (1996), "Teachers must know literature to help children find the right book for them. And . . . they need an understanding of children's responses to books and ways to help them link books to their own personal experience" (p. 30). This chapter discusses the various aspects of selecting and integrating literature into the elementary curriculum.

Important Literary Elements

In choosing literature for elementary students to read, the classroom teacher must be familiar with five important literary elements: (1) characterization; (2) plot; (3) setting, both time and place; (4) theme; (5) author's style; and (6) for picture books and some informational books, illustrations. Although a book typically contains all five of these, one element may be emphasized more than the others. Each literary element is described below.

Characterization

The development of characterization is crucial because children often identify with and have empathy for a character, and that character may not necessarily be a main character. It is important that characters be believable, having both good and bad qualities. Henry and Ramona in the books by Beverly Cleary and Harry, Hermoine, and Ron in J. K. Rowling's *Harry Potter* series display honesty, humor, and bravery as well as jealousy, unhappiness, and fear. Their behavior is predictable to a large extent in that it is quite normal for children their age to demonstrate such feelings.

Unlike characters who fail to mature and are considered "flat" characters, Beverly Cleary's and J. K. Rowling's characters grow and learn from their successes and failures in life as well as from other characters. Because of the humanness of such characters, children find it easy to relate to them, often reading several of the books in the series as a result of the kinship they develop. Other books that exemplify strong characterization are Kevin Henkes' (1996) classic *Lilly's Purple Plastic Purse*, Polly Horvath's (2001) *Everything on a Waffle*, Mildred Taylor's (1995) *The Well*, and Louis Sachar's (1998) *Holes*. In *Bridge to Terabithia* (Paterson, 1977), children can relate to Jess and Leslie's friendship and empathize with Jess when tragedy strikes Leslie. *Out of the Dust* (Hesse, 1997) shares the hardships of the Great Depression from a child's perspective.

A character may be developed by the author through that character's actions, thoughts, and conversations with other characters; through other characters' thoughts about that character; and/or through narration. By sharing and discussing books that develop characters through one or more of these methods, children can acquire insights into the personalities and beliefs of different characters. Such insights are beneficial for children in that they can use them to understand people in real life.

Plot

The plot is what a story is all about. A good plot contains, in some measure, action, conflict, intrigue, and resolution. For example, consider folktales and fairy tales, stories that were handed down orally for generations before they were written down. They contain action, intrigue, and conflict that is resolved at the end of the story. Such tales have been handed down from parent to child for generations, and many are as popular today as when they were first told hundreds of years ago. For children, the plot needs to begin to unfold early in a book. A good beginning is essential to maintaining children's interest. Typically, the conflict and accompanying intrigue are introduced after the reader has gained some information about the main character(s), and the resolution comes at the end of the book. Because children prefer order and predictability, most children's literature follows chronological order; that is, events are described in the order in which they occur.

In biographies, the plot typically begins with the character at a certain age and then describes events during a specific time in the character's life. Caldecott Award winning *Snowflake Bentley* (Martin, 1998) shares the determination of a boy who became known worldwide for his research on snowflakes. Pam Muñoz Ryan's (2002) *When Marian Sang* depicts the essence and dignity of Marian Anderson's life as a opera singer. Authors noted for their biographies include David Adler and Jean Fritz who write for both primary and upper-elementary children while Russell Freedman, Jim Murphy, and Diane Stanley target mid-elementary through middle school readers.

Cumulative tales such as *Henny Penny, The Gingerbread Boy,* and *The House That Jack Built* are examples of chronological order in picture books. *When I First Came to This Land* (Ziefert, 1998) are cumulative tales that describe the events in chronological order and also review the events as they take place. A most unusual twist is that of Nancy Andrews-Goebel's (2002) *The Pot that Juan Built,* which presents the life of Juan Quezada, the premier potter in Mexico, in cumulative tale fashion with accompanying explanatory text. Informational text does not need to be dull and boring as proven in Madeline Dunphy's (1994) *Here Is the Tropical Rainforest,* a beautifully illustrated science book on ecology told as a cumulative tale complete with lyrical words.

4.1   The More You Know

Stories about Pigs

In recent years, pigs have become increasingly popular; in fact, March 1 has been declared "National Pig Day." Perhaps the most favorite pig story of all time is that of the infamous humble pig, Wilbur, in the middle reader *Charlotte's Web* by E. B. White (1952). Below is a sampling of picture books about pigs.

Axelrod, A. (1997). *Pigs go to market* (S. McGinley-Nally, Illus.). New York: Simon & Schuster. (1–3). Math activities reign as the pigs dress up and head for the supermarket.

Lowell, S. (1992). *The three little javelinas* (J. Harris, Illus.). New York. Scholastic. (K–3). This is the Southwestern U.S. version of *The Three Little Pigs* in which the pigs are called javelinas (pronounced ha-ve-LEE-nas), the Spanish word for "wild pigs," and the culprit is a coyote, not a wolf.

Marshall, J. & Sendak, M. (1998). *Swine lake.* New York: HarperCollins. (K–3). An unkempt wolf attends the "Swine Lake" ballet at the New Hamsterdam Theater. He is unable to resist joining the pig ballerinas on stage.

McPhail, D. (1993). *Pigs aplenty, pigs galore!* New York: Dutton, (K–1). When the narrator of the book investigates sounds of feeding in the kitchen, he finds pigs throughout his house. This book includes lots of rhyming words and repetitive patterns for children to repeat.

Numeroff, L. (1998). *If you give a pig a pancake* (F. Bond, Illus.). New York: HarperCollins. (K–2) When a pig drops by and asks for a pancake, trouble follows.

Scieszka, J. (1989). *The true story of the 3 little pigs! by A. Wolf* (L. Smith, Illus.). New York: Viking. (1–3). This is the hilarious version of the three little pigs as told by the much maligned wolf. This is the book that launched Jon Scieszka (rhymes with Fresca) from successful classroom teacher to bestselling children's author.

Teague, M. (1994). *Pigsty.* New York: Scholastic. (1–3). Wendell Fultz's bedroom is so messy that it is a real pigsty. But Wendell doesn't mind until pigs start showing up in his room. Then Wendell devises a plan to clean up his room—with his new friends helping along the way.

Trivizas, E. (1993). *The three little wolves and the big bad pig* (H. Oxenbury, Illus.). New York: Maxwell Macmillan. (K–3). Once upon a time there were three cuddly wolves who were told by their mother to go out and build a house for themselves but to beware of a big bad pig. This is a delightful twist on an old tale.

Wiesner, D. (2002). *The three pigs.* New York: Clarion. (1–3). A delightful tale of the swine siblings.

These picture books are great to share with children in grades K–3. After reading the books aloud to the class, students can then compare and contrast the characters as well as the story lines in a class discussion.

Plot conflict may be of several different types: (1) person against person, (2) person against nature, (3) person against self, and (4) person against society. An example of person against person is Elisa Carbone's (1998) *Starting School with an Enemy*. Sarah moves to a new school and immediately makes an enemy. A book with the plot conflict of person against nature is *Ghost Canoe* by Will Hobbs (1997), which describes how a 14-year-old boy attempts to rescue survivors of a sailing ship that breaks up on the rocks of Cape Flattery, Washington, during a fierce storm. Conflict, or tension, between a character and nature is commonplace in intermediate-level books. Consider these timeless classics: *Hatchet* (Paulsen, 1987), *Island of the Blue Dolphins* (O'Dell, 1960), and *Julie of the Wolves* (George, 1972).

In *Choosing Up Sides* (Ritter, 1998), a boy faces an inner conflict about whether to play baseball and pitch left-handed, which his religion believes is evil, or to follow his father's religious beliefs. For the plot conflict of person versus society, students will enjoy reading *Wringer* by Jerry Spinelli (1997), a story of a boy who dreads turning 10 years old because he will be forced to "wring" the necks of pigeons at the town's annual Pigeon Shoot. *Loser*, also written by Spinelli (2002), raises emotions in his novel about Donald Zinoff, the butt of all jokes and a failure at everything until he rescues a missing boy.

Appropriate for young children, a thought-provoking example of conflict between character and society is Patricia Beatty's (1981) *Lupita Mañana* and Pam Muñoz Ryan's (2000) *Esperanza Rising*, a Pura Belpré winner, which describe the plight of impoverished illegal immigrants who enter the United States by crossing the Mexican border. In reading Kate DiCamillo's (2000) *Because of Winn-Dixie*, intermediate elementary students will examine society's influence on what is and what is not proper cultural behavior.

By reading books with different types of plot conflict, children are encouraged to examine their own strengths and weaknesses and, hopefully, to gain acceptance and understanding of themselves. Moreover, children often mature in their interactions with peers and adults as they acquire increased awareness of cultural and social influences.

Setting

Setting refers to both time and place. The development of characterization and plot can be dependent upon the geographic location and time period in which a story occurs. Multisensory experiences are evoked through careful descriptions that connect time and place with plot and characters. For instance, consider pioneer life in the United States. In *Aurora Means Dawn*, a picture book, Scott Russell Sanders (1989) tells of a family traveling through the Ohio River Valley in the 1800s to settle in Aurora. The setting of time and place are crucial as the author describes the family's hardships, hopes, and dreams. *Who Came Down That Road?* (Lyon, 1992) poses a young child's question to his mother, who responds with answer after answer. The boy's great-great-grandparents, as well as Union soldiers in the Civil War, pioneers, Shawnee and Chippewa Native Americans, buffalo, bear, elk, mastodons, and woolly mammoths all came down that road in Kentucky.

Dioramas can be made from file folders and construction paper to represent settings from various picture books or novels.

In Pam Conrad's (1987) *Prairie Songs,* a novel set in the late 1800s on the Nebraska prairie, the reader encounters the importance of the setting in the book's opening. Conrad describes the prairie as a giant plate and two children as two peas on that plate. The book goes on to describe how some pioneers loved the prairie and the hardships that accompanied life there, whereas others found that the prairie offered only loneliness and despair (see figure 4.1, p. 128).

Two picture books that also portray life on the prairie are *A Fourth of July on the Plains* (Van Leeuwen, 1998) and *Prairie Town* (Geisert & Geisert, 1998). Young Jesse is traveling on the Oregon Trail in 1852. He recalls the Fourth of July celebrations back home with flags waving, cannons shooting, speeches, and games. The wagon train decides to create its own Fourth of July picnic when it stops near Sweetwater River. Children can compare and contrast the Independence Day settings. *Prairie Town* is set in the early 1900s and shares a year's events in the small rural town. Students need to pay close attention to the changes that take place in town throughout the year.

In some instances, a setting may be deliberately vague in terms of location and/or time; the story might have occurred in any location, for example. In such a case, setting obviously contributes little to the plot. However, when the setting is specific, details must be accurate and realistic. This is especially true for biographies and historical fiction.

Theme

The theme of a book is the central idea of the story. In other words, it is the point or meaning the author wants to convey to the reader. For instance, E. B. White (1952) uses friendship as the theme for *Charlotte's Web*, while Jeanette Winter (1988) focuses on the desire for freedom and the Underground Railroad in *Follow the Drinking Gourd*. The importance and value placed on knowing how to read is depicted in Eve Bunting's (1989) *The Wednesday Surprise*, which tells about Anna, who spends every Wednesday evening reading books to her illiterate grandmother. At the end of the book, Anna and her grandmother throw a surprise birthday party for Anna's father; the biggest surprise occurs when Grandma reads to them. Three moving books about life and death that are appropriate for fifth through eighth graders are Gary Paulsen's (1987) *Hatchet*, a story of survival, Cynthia Rylant's (1993) *Missing May*, and Karen Hesse's (1997) *Out of the Dust*.

Camille Yarbrough's (1989) *The Shimmershine Queens* tells the story of a black inner-city fifth grader who gets the lead in a school play. Yarbrough uses the themes of confidence and motivation to illustrate how dreams can be achieved despite challenges and problems.

Style

Style refers to the author's word choice and sentence construction. Repetition, for example, is a style often used in writing picture books, such as Nancy White Carlstrom's (1986) *Jesse Bear, What Will You Wear?* Rhyme is also commonly found in picture books, such as *Quacky, Quack-Quack!* by Ian Whybrow (1991) and Nancy Shaw's (1986) delightful *Sheep in a Jeep*.

Authors of books for students in the intermediate grades sometimes emphasize images through word usage. This may involve the description of characters or setting. A humorous or suspenseful thread may continue throughout a story's plot. In realistic fiction, such as Gary Paulsen's (1987) very popular *Hatchet*, the author uses engaging language. Cullinan and Galda (1999, p. 226) suggest that the language for realistic fiction should have a "rhythmic, melodic quality appropriate to the theme, the setting, and the characters." Or as one children's literature editor put it, the language should sing! The style for a biography differs somewhat from that of realistic fiction in that facts are presented; however, the writing still must be engaging. Consider the language of *Abigail Adams: Witness to a Revolution* (Bober, 1995), of *The Wright Brothers: How They Invented the Airplane* (Freedman, 1991), or of *Mother Teresa: Helping the Poor* (Jacobs, 1991). Certainly the style of writing for nonfiction must present information and facts in a refreshing way, such as in Milton Meltzer's (1990) *Brother Can You Spare a Dime?*, a book about the Great Depression, or William Jay Jacobs's (1990) *Ellis Island: New Hope in a New Land*.

Children may become familiar with an author's style and want to read every book the author has written. This is often the case with authors Beverly Cleary, Kevin Henkes, Steven Kellogg, Lois Lowry, Phyllis Reynolds Naylor, Katherine Paterson, and Gary Paulsen, among others. Classroom teachers can promote an author's works by simply reading a chapter or captivating passage from a selection and providing additional copies of the book (known as text sets) as well as other works by the same author. In essence, this is an attempt by the teachers to broaden their own interests and familiarize themselves with various authors while trying to entice the children to discover new works of literature.

Illustrations

Illustrations in picture books, as well as in informational books, must add to and extend the story and/or concept being presented. Both art quality and visual appeal to children are important when considering illustrations. If the illustrations fail to keep the child interested in the story, they are not appropriate.

Illustrations vary greatly because of the wide variety of media available to artists. Still, each illustrator carves out his own characteristic style. For instance, Jan Brett (1990) includes delicate borders in her books, such as in *The Mitten: A Ukrainian Folktale*, whereas Tomie dePaola (1975, 1988) is noted for his folk art as portrayed in *Strega Nona* and *The Legend of the Indian Paintbrush*. Eric Carle uses collage, relying on vividly colored sheets of tissue paper that he tints in his own studio. Good examples of Carle's work are in *Brown Bear, Brown Bear, What Do You See?* by Bill Martin, Jr. (1964/1983) and Carle's (1969) own, *The Very Hungry Caterpillar*. Lois Ehlert, like Carle, relies upon vivid colors in her work. Her books include *Eating the Alphabet* (1989), *Color Zoo* (1989), and *Fish Eyes: A Book You Can Count On* (1990). Cartoons have recently become in vogue in children's books with the popularity of Betsy Lewin's illustrations in Doreen Cronin's (2000, 2002, 2003) *Click, Clack, Moo: Cows that Type* and its sequels, *Giggle, Giggle, Quack* and *Duck for President*.

The softness of watercolors is used by award-wining illustrator Jerry Pinkney in Robert San Souci's (1990) *The Talking Eggs* and Patricia McKissack's (1988) *Mirandy and Brother Wind*, both of which were Caldecott honor books. The artwork of Lane Smith accentuates the bizarre antics in author Jon Scieszka's (1989, 1992, 1995) books, *The True Story of the Three Little Pigs*, *The Stinky Cheese Man: And Other Fairly Stupid Tales*, and *Math Curse*. In *Squids Will Be Squids* (Scieszka & Smith, 1998), the authors play on Aesop's fables. Certainly the cultural influences on an author's life emerge in the illustrations. For instance, Ed Young (1989, 1992) was born in China, and his art clearly reflects his roots in his books *Lon Po Po* and *Seven Blind Mice*.

Like teachers, children need to discover and develop an understanding of literary elements. This can begin as early as kindergarten with a discussion about characterization in *Don't Fidget a Feather* (Silverman, 1994). Five-year-olds are quick to point out the bad qualities of the fox. They are equally adept at noting the positive characteristics of the two young friends, Duck and Goose.

The literary elements are summarized as follows:

Characterization: Characterization is what the author reveals about an individual character. Characters should be believable, having both good and bad qualities. The author develops characterization through narration, dialogue, and the actions and thoughts of the characters.

Plot: The plot is the action (not necessarily physical), or story, of the work. It usually consists of conflict, intrigue, and resolution.

Setting: The setting consists of both time and place.

Theme: The theme is the central idea or point the author wishes to convey.

Style: Style involves the author's word choice and sentence structure.

Illustrations: Illustrations support the story by extending and reflecting its meaning.

First graders may be introduced to a literary web. Rather than include all literary elements, it is better to focus on one element at a time; this allows students to grasp and understand one element before being introduced to another. For instance, with appropriate books, the teacher can explain theme as a simple literary element to young students. Mary Ann Hoberman's classic (1978) *A House Is a House for Me* delightfully describes and illustrates different types of houses found in nature. Her book is appropriate for a science lesson with a theme of shelter. After the teacher reads the book to the class, students can discuss the different names and types of homes that were mentioned. The students might also bring in houses made of different objects and create a shelter display in the classroom.

Literary webs for upper-primary and intermediate students should include all of the literary elements. Figure 4.1 presents the components of such a web.

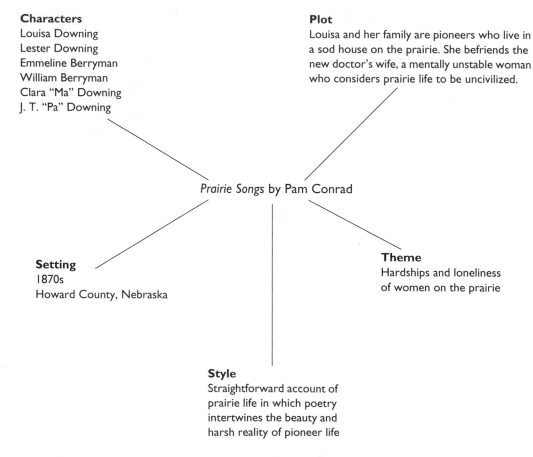

Characters
Louisa Downing
Lester Downing
Emmeline Berryman
William Berryman
Clara "Ma" Downing
J. T. "Pa" Downing

Plot
Louisa and her family are pioneers who live in a sod house on the prairie. She befriends the new doctor's wife, a mentally unstable woman who considers prairie life to be uncivilized.

Prairie Songs by Pam Conrad

Setting
1870s
Howard County, Nebraska

Theme
Hardships and loneliness of women on the prairie

Style
Straightforward account of prairie life in which poetry intertwines the beauty and harsh reality of pioneer life

Figure 4.1   Literary web

Picture Books

Picture books are books in which the pictures are as important as, if not more important than, the accompanying text (Sutherland & Hearne, 1984). In fact, picture books may be just that, books containing only pictures and no accompanying text. Such books are called wordless picture books. The story is told completely through the illustrations. This requires the reader to gather, interpret, and relate information from artwork or photographs. Because only illustrations are included in a wordless picture book, the characters, setting (usually place rather than time), and plot must all be conveyed through the illustrations. Such books often provide opportunities for children to develop their storytelling skills while at the same time expanding their oral language skills. *Rosie's Walk* (Hutchins, 1968) and *A Boy, a Dog, and a Frog* (Mayer, 1971) are considered as classics. Eric Carle's (1997) *From Head to Toe* as well as Judy Hindley's (2002) *Do Like a Duck Does* are simple books that ask readers to do movements. Carle's (2003) *Slowly, Slowly, Said the Sloth* has great visualization.

Picture books may also be fairy tales, a form of traditional literature. Contemporary realistic fiction is a popular form of picture books by such authors as Eve Bunting and Patricia Polacco. Fantasy picture books have been popularized in recent years by Chris Van Allsburg and David Wiesner. Historical topics may be the focus of picture books as well, as in George Ella Lyon's, Peter Sis's, and Ann Turner's works.

Picture books can be excellent sources of information for young children. In *Can You Find Me? A Book about Animal Camouflage* (1989), Jennifer Dewey, a naturalist as well as an author and an illustrator, describes the survival techniques of animals in their use of camouflage to avoid predators. Even seemingly ordinary events of nature can prove to be interesting information. For instance, Anne Rockwell's (2002) *Becoming Butterflies* or Jonathan London's (2001) *Crocodile: Disappearing Dragon* will hook students to discover more about these amazing creatures.

Although picture books are typically associated with preschoolers and students in the primary grades, many picture books are best suited for older students. For example, *Lincoln: A Photobiography* (Freedman, 1987) and *My Hiroshima* (Morimoto, 1990) are appropriate for students in intermediate grades and middle school.

Students of all grade levels can analyze and compare picture books. For example, when presented with several versions of a folktale such as *Little Red Riding Hood* or *The Three Billy Goats Gruff,* children can discuss the commonalities of the stories as well as how the authors and illustrators differ in their interpretations. Appropriate stories can also contribute to science and/or social studies discussions. For instance, William T. George's *Box Turtle at Long Pond* (1989) can be part of a discussion of ecology and the life cycle of animals.

An underlying theme, such as trickery and deception, may also emerge. In *Tops and Bottoms* by Janet Stevens (1995), a lazy bear is tricked by a clever hare who offers to give the bear half of all he grows on the bear's land—either the tops or bottoms of the crop. Such a theme of underlying trickery goes undetected by most kindergarten and first-grade students, and even some intermediate-grade students. Only through discussion and the sharing of similar stories do students discover the underlying theme. Other enjoyable picture books that provide good discussion topics are *Miss Spider's Tea Party* (Kirk, 1994), *Pete's a Pizza* (Steig, 1998), *The Dumb Bunnies* (Denim, 1994), *Cinder Edna* (Jackson, 1994), and for younger students, *Hilda Must Be Dancing* (Wilson, 2004).

Picture books offer examples of a wide variety of media. Children's aesthetic development can be enhanced through their exposure to illustrations done in acrylics, block prints, chalk, collage, ink, and watercolors. Whether it be the intricate details of the line drawing in David Macaulay's (2003) *Mosque* or the cut paper illustrations of David Wisniewski's (1991) *Rain Player*, children can discover new ways to examine their world by analyzing the illustrations in picture books.

Research findings suggest that children who were read to at home while they were still preschoolers have an advantage in terms of literary development over those peers who were not read to at home. This is particularly evident in children's early attempts to read and write (Taylor & Dorsey-Gaines, 1988; Teale & Sulzby, 1985). According to Roser, Hoffman, and Farest (1990, p. 554), "children from economically disadvantaged homes enter school with fewer exposures to the tools of literacy and [are] more 'at risk' relative to their literacy acquisition." Because of this, early childhood teachers must become familiar with picture books in order to share a wide variety of topics and create a rich literary environment in the classroom.

Suggested Books for Emergent and Beginning Readers

Wordless Picture Books
Aliki. (1995). *Tabby, a story in pictures*. New York: HarperCollins.
Day, A. (1998). *Follow Carl*. New York: Farrar.
Hoban, T. (1997). *Look book*. New York: Greenwillow.
Weisner, D. (1991). *Tuesday*. Boston: Clarion.

Concept Books
Burningham, J. (1994). *First steps: Letters, numbers, colors, opposites*. Cambridge, MA: Candlewick.
Carle, E. (1977). *The grouchy ladybug*. New York: Crowell.
Ehlert, L. (1990). *Fish eyes: A book you can count on*. San Diego: Harcourt.
Garne, S. T. (1993). *One white sail: A Caribbean counting book*. New York: Simon.
Hoban, T. (1998). *So many circles, so many squares*. New York: Greenwillow.
Jonas, A. (1995). *Splash*. New York: Greenwillow.
Tafuri, N. (1997). *What the sun sees/what the moon sees*. New York: Greenwillow.

Predictable Books
Asch, F. (1981). *Just like daddy*. Upper Saddle River, NJ: Prentice Hall.
Aylesworth, J. (1994). *My son John* (D. Frampton, Illus.). New York: Holt.
Brown, M. W. (1947). *Goodnight, moon* (D. Hurd, Illus.). New York: Harper & Row.

Carle, E. (1984). *The very busy spider*. New York: Philomel.
Fleming, D. (1994). *Barnyard banter*. New York: Holt.
Fox, M. (1987). *Hattie and the fox* (P. Mullins, Illus.). New York: Bradbury.
Lindberg, R. (1990). *The day the goose got loose* (S. Kellogg, Illus.). New York: Dial.
Martin, B. (1964/1983). *Brown bear, brown bear, what do you see?* (E. Carle, Illus.). New York: Holt.
Van Laan, N. (1998). *So say the little monkeys* (Y. Heo, Illus.). New York: Atheneum.
Ziefert, H. (1998). *I swapped my dog* (E. Bolam, Illus.). Boston: Houghton Mifflin.

Beginning to Read—Picture Books

Brown, M. (1980). *Arthur's Valentine*. New York: Little Brown.
Cherry, L. (2003). *How groundhog's garden grew*. New York: Blue Sky/Scholastic.
dePaola, T. (1975). *Strega Nona*. New York: Simon & Schuster.
Freeman, D. (1968). *Corduroy*. New York: Viking.
Hall, D. (1979). *Ox cart man*. (B. Cooney, Illus.). New York: Viking.
Henkes, K. (1993). *Owen*. New York: Greenwillow.
Kvasnosky, L. M. (2004). *Frank and Izzy set sail*. Boston: Candlewick.
Paul, A. W. (1998). *Hello toes! Hello feet!* (N. B. Westcutt, Illus.). New York: DK Ink.
Pilkey, D. (1993). *Dogzilla*. San Diego: Harcourt Brace.
Rathman, P. (1995). *Officer Buckle and Gloria*. New York: Putnam.
Rylant, C. (1985). *The relatives came* (S. Gammell, Illus.). New York: Bradbury.
Steig, W. (1998). *Pete's a pizza*. New York: HarperCollins.
Walker, S. (1998). *The 18 penny goose*. (E. Beier, Illus.). New York: HarperCollins.

Beginning to Read—Chapter Books

Avi. (1997). *Finding Providence: The story of Roger Williams* (J. Watling, Illus.). New York: HarperCollins.
Cameron, A. (1997). *More stories Huey tells* (L. Toft, Illus.). New York: Farrar.
Haas, J. (2001). *Runaway Radish* (M. Apple, Illus.). New York: Greenwillow.
Lobel, A. (1970). *Frog and toad are friends*. New York: Harper & Row.
Rylant, C. (1998). *Henry and Mudge in the family trees: The fifteenth book of their adventures* (S. Stevenson, Illus.). New York: Simon.

Genre

Genre here refers to the different categories that comprise children's literature. These include traditional literature, modern fantasy, contemporary realistic fiction, historical fiction, biography and autobiography, informational books, and poetry. Each genre is described below.

Traditional Literature

Traditional literature has its roots in oral stories that were handed down from generation to generation even before writing came into existence. Religion and heroes are common themes. Usually a heroic deed results in overcoming an adversary by cunning or trickery.

Traditional literature includes folktales, such as cumulative tales *(The House that Jack Built)*, humorous tales *(The Princess and the Pea)*, beast tales *(Beauty and the Beast)*, and wonder or magic tales *(Jack and the Beanstalk)*. Traditional literature also includes fables (Aesop's *The Lion and the Mouse*), myths (Jane Yolen's *Wings*, 1991), and legends (Tomie dePaola's *The Legend of the Indian Paintbrush*, 1988). *You Read to Me, I'll Read to You: Very Short Fairy Tales to Read Together* (Hoberman, 2003) is a delightful book for shared reading.

Traditional literature allows children to distinguish easily between goodness and evil through the deeds and actions of the characters: heroes are good through and through, whereas villains are rotten to the core. Because such literature is based on conflict and its resolution, children can be encouraged to create and develop their own solutions to the problems depicted in the stories.

Sharing traditional literature is an excellent way to enable children to appreciate the contributions of various cultures. For instance, Lawrence Yep's (1989) *The Rainbow People*, a collection of Chinese folktales, and John Bierhorst's (2002) *Is My Friend at Home? Pueblo Fireside Tales*, can enrich children's knowledge of life in another country and the beliefs of the people who live there.

Modern Fantasy

Modern fantasy involves the creation of a time and a place where the unbelievable becomes believable. The plot may be outrageous, yet within the context of the fantasy it becomes imaginable. Characters in modern fantasy may be real people who have imaginary experiences, animals who take on human characteristics, personified toys, or even supernatural beings.

The setting of modern fantasy may be in the past, but most often it is in the present or the future. Traveling through time and space is common, as in Chris Van Allsburg's (1985) picture book *The Polar Express* and David Wiesner's *Tuesday* (1991). *The Giver* (1993) by Lois Lowry is a science fiction novel that describes a futuristic Utopian society. *Ghost Canoe* (Hobbs, 1997) is a popular fantasy with middle schoolers. The *Harry Potter* series by J. K. Rowling has captured the imagination of millions of children in the U.S., Canada, and Great Britain. The series by Rowling includes *Harry Potter and the Sorcerer's Stone* (1998), *Harry Potter and the Chamber of Secrets* (1999), *Harry Potter and the Prisoner of Azkaban* (1999), *Harry Potter and the Goblet of Fire* (2002), and *Harry Potter and the Order of the Phoenix* (2003).

Contemporary Realistic Fiction

The characters, setting, and plot of contemporary realistic fiction are believable in that they could appear in real life. Although the story is invented by the author and is therefore fictitious, it appears to be true. Contemporary realistic fiction offers children insights into the personal and social values of our culture and permits them to become actively involved in the dilemmas and the triumphs of the characters. Growing up, family life, and friendship are all themes of contemporary realistic fiction. Animal, sports, and humorous stories also fall into this category.

J. K. Rowling's *Harry Potter* has brought resurgence to the reading of fantasy.

Popular authors of contemporary realistic fiction include Betsy Byars (*The Cybil War*, 1981, and *The Night Swimmers*, 1980), Beverly Cleary (*Ramona the Pest*, 1968), Sharon Creech (*Walk Two Moons*, 1994), Phyllis Reynolds Naylor (*Shiloh*, 1991), Richard Peck (*A Long Way from Chicago*, 1998), Jerry Spinelli (*Maniac Magee*, 1990), and Lawrence Yep (*Dragon's Gate*, 1994). A child may read a book by one of these or other authors only to follow it by another book by the same author. This may continue until the student has completed all of the author's works contained in the school library.

In some instances an author may write one or more sequels to a book. Beverly Cleary is a prime example with her many books about Ramona growing up. In *Ramona's World*, Cleary (1999) continues the adventures of Ramona as she enters fourth grade. Cleary also wrote a sequel to *Dear Mr. Henshaw* (1983), a story about how an author helps a boy, Leigh, overcome problems related to his parents' divorce. The sequel, *Strider* (1991), finds Leigh as an adolescent who adopts an abandoned dog that Leigh names "Strider." Gary Paulsen's survival series featuring Brian is quite popular with children.

Contemporary realistic fiction often deals with actual problems. For instance, Ann Cameron's (1988) *The Most Beautiful Place in the World*, the story of Juan, an abandoned Guatemalan boy, could actually take place today. The tragedy of the effects of Alzheimer's disease is portrayed in Vaunda Micheaux Nelson's (1988) *Always Grandma*. The turmoil in Hong Kong between ancient ties and modern trends is the subject of Riki Levinson's (1988) *Our Home Is the Sea*. Such books can be tied to current events and provide enrichment for class discussions.

Historical Fiction

In historical fiction, the characterization, setting, plot, and theme must be realistic. The characters must be developed through dialogue, which poses a problem if a real person is included as a major character. For this reason, many authors of historical fiction include famous historical characters as background characters, relying upon fictitious characters to carry the plot. The setting, both time and place, needs to be authentic in every detail. Such exactness often necessitates considerable research on the part of the author. Descriptions of everyday life must be realistic depictions of the daily routines that existed at that particular time. In *Back Home*, Gloria Pinkney (1992) accurately portrays a rural setting—North Carolina in the 1950s.

The plot of a piece of historical fiction may involve a real historical event or one that could have taken place given detailed information from the period. In *Drylongso*, for example, Virginia Hamilton (1992) portrays a boy who performs "water witching"—finds water with a dowsing rod (a forked stick) during a drought. Plots in this genre frequently center around personal conflicts.

Most works of historical fiction have simple, basic themes that are as relevant for today's children as they were for those who lived in the time period in which the work is set. In stressing the need to use children's literature in social studies, Billig (1977, p. 857) writes, "When a social studies unit arises spontaneously out of honest interest and curiosity, the depth of understanding that develops is immeasurably greater than that resulting from an often irrelevant teacher-imposed assignment." This is due, according to Billig, to the human element that exists in historical fiction but is absent from social studies textbooks.

An example of an informative, historically accurate book for kindergartners through second graders is Kate Waters's (1989) *Sarah Morton's Day: A Day in the Life of a Pilgrim Girl*. The story is based on actual people who lived in Plymouth, Massachusetts, in 1627. Sarah Morton's day begins with the crowing of the rooster and continues with making breakfast, feeding the chickens, and learning verses from the scripture. Sarah also has time for playing, singing, and sharing dreams and secrets with her best friend, Elizabeth. *Emma and the Silk Train* (Lawson, 1998) is a picture book based on the silk trains that raced down the tracks setting records to get the cloth to its destinations. Young Emma longed for a silk dress. When a silk train derails, Emma risks her life to pull a bolt of silk from the river.

Biography and Autobiography

A biography is a book written about the life of or a period of the life of a person. An autobiography is a book written by the person herself or himself. Biographies should depict their subjects accurately rather than present only the good points of their subjects. As with historical fiction, biographical writing requires much research by the author. A good example of a well-researched birth to death biography is *Follow the Dream: The Story of Christopher Columbus* (1991) written and illustrated by Peter Sis, who used fifteenth-century maps as a basis for mapping out Columbus's journey in this picture book. *Shake Rag* (Littlesugar, 1998; illustrated by F. Cooper) depicts the life of Elvis Presley in a very detailed account of his youth before he became a star. A noted biographer is Diane Stanley, who does picture-book biographies including *Leonardo da Vinci* (Stanley, 1996) and *Joan of Arc* (Stanley, 1998). Her works always include a bibliography and an author's note.

Biographies are excellent ways to present history, especially because so many good ones have been written for children. Biographies for children have featured artists, scientists, and sports heroes, among others. Wendy Towle's (1993) *The Real McCoy: The Life of an African-American Inventor* describes the problems encountered by Elijah McCoy, inventor of the automatic oil cup, which became standard equipment on locomotives. Because his invention was the best of its kind, engineers referred to it as "the real McCoy." *Young Mozart* (Isadora, 1998) portrays the famous musician's life and leading musicians of that period.

Whereas biographies are prevalent, autobiographies written for children are in short supply. Jean Fritz is one of the few children's contemporary literature authors who has shared her childhood experiences via her autobiography, *Homesick: My Own Story* (1982). *A Girl from Yamhill, a Memoir* (1988) is the title of Beverly Cleary's autobiography, and Roald Dahl (1984) called his book *Boy: Tales of Childhood.* Tomie dePaola's (1989) *The Art Lesson* describes the author's own experiences in school as he developed his early artistic skills. In this auto-biography, dePaola tells of the first-grade teacher who insisted that he use a box of eight crayons rather than his box of 64 because the teacher believed it was unfair for dePaola to have a box of 64 crayons when his classmates had boxes of eight. Richard Peck and Laura Ingalls Wilder are two other authors who have shared their childhood experiences through their works. Despite the fact that there are so few autobiographies for children, children delight in writing their own autobiographies. Clearly, this is an area that needs additional publications (see box 4.2, p. 136).

Informational Books

Factual material makes up informational books: the how to, where to, and why books. These books range from directions for making a birdhouse and caring for pets to how computers are made and what it is like to travel in space to the history of Troy and the heroic deeds of famous generals. In particular, boys become riveted to informational books from kindergarten on. Brozo (2002) writes that boys should be given nonfiction, informational books during free time as he has observed "they shift their postures from complacency and dis-engagement to involvement and curiosity" (p. 17). Ideally the sharing of informational books begins in kindergarten and first grade where both a story picture book and an informational book are shared each day as a read aloud.

Informational books need to be accurate and should not mislead students. The writing should pique students' curiosity and complement the photographs or illustration. *A Drop of Water* (Wick, 1997) takes readers into the scientific world of water with brief, captivating text describing the wonders of this liquid accompanied by breathtakingly incredible photography. Older readers will enjoy the eye-catching photographs and informative text of *Hidden Worlds: Looking Through a Scientist's Microscope* (Kramer, 2001). Clare Walker Leslie's (1991) *Nature All Year Long* provides detailed information about hibernation, migration, plants, and weather in an engaging text. This book is presented as a calendar of events that occur in nature. Breathtaking photographs of earth from space are combined with a narrative that describes our environment in *Seeing the Earth from Space* by Patricia Lauber (1990). A book that needs to be pointed out to students is Mark Kurlansky's (2001) *The Cod's Tale*,

---

4.2   In the Classroom: Mini Lesson

Biography Presentation (Grades 4–6)

Name _____
Date _____

Description: For this assignment, you will need to read a biography or an autobiography about a person of your choice. Be sure to check your person with Mrs. Towner. Your final presentation must give the class important and inteiresting information about the person. To present the information, you may read from a paper or you may memorize it and act it out for the class. You may wish to bring in some artifacts to share with the class. These may be a picture of the person and/or examples of the person's work (a picture painted or a song composed). For this final presentation, you must dress up as the person.

Requirements:
_____ I checked with Mrs. Towner about the person I want to report about.
_____ I read a biography or autobiography.
_____ I have written a few paragraphs about the person to read to the class.
_____ I have a costume to wear that is typical for my person to have worn.

Optional:
_____ I memorized my presentation and will act it out for the class.
_____ I have artifacts to share with the class.

Biography Presentation Rubric

Name: _____
Famous Person: _____

	Yes	No
I checked my book with Mrs. Towner.		
I wore a costume that would be typical for my person to have worn.		
My presentation consisted of some interesting facts about my person.		
Optional—I brought some artifacts pertaining to my person.		
Optional—I acted out my presentation.		
Comments		

which provides a thumbnail sketch of the impact of this one variety of fish on the history of the world.

During the past 20 years, informational books have taken a change for the better. Joanna Cole's marvelous Magic School Bus science series provides information in a cartoon format that is very intriguing to second through fourth graders. This series is also available in Spanish. Young readers enjoy the numerous books by Gail Gibbons who has written books about fire engines, lighthouses, photography, tropical rain forests, and several other topics. In *The Honey Makers* (Gibbons, 1997), each step of a bee's life is carefully depicted and examined. *Soaring with the Wind: The Bald Eagle* (Gibbons, 1998) portrays the grandeur of our national emblem including how it hunts its prey, finds a mate, forms its nest, and hatches out its young. Intermediate and middle school students will find that the works of prolific scientist and writer Seymour Simon give detailed, accurate scientific facts in a colorful picture-book format. For most of his books, Simon includes actual photographs of his subject. Simon has authored over 150 books, with over 90 named outstanding science books for children. Two of his popular subjects are the human body and space.

Informational books can portray the drama of history without misleading students. Gillian Osband's (1991) *Castles*, a pop-up book, provides students with accurate and fascinating descriptions of how castles were built. The three-dimensional book illustrated by Robert Andrew portrays actual life in castles during medieval times, including the reasons for moats and how catapults worked during battles. This book is of interest for children from early childhood through middle school. Sheila Cowing (1989) gives children an accurate historical overview of the American Southwest in *Searches in the American Desert*. The book begins with the Spanish explorers seeking the seven cities of gold during the 1500s and continues through the story of Brigham Young and the Mormons and on to current times.

A good example of a book that focuses on a narrow historical period is Rhoda Blumberg's (1989) *The Great American Gold Rush*, which depicts the migration of people to California between 1848 and 1852 as "gold fever" set in. Blumberg presents interesting details and asides about individuals who journeyed to California to become rich, all of which adds to children's historical perspective of the period. In addition Blumberg covers the treatment of minorities during the Gold Rush. Jim Murphy's (1993) *Across America on an Immigrant Train* depicts the true story of Robert Louis Stevenson's trip in 1879 to the West Coast. Students learn from Stevenson's journal entries about the harshness of rail travel during that period. Jennifer Armstrong's (1998) *Shipwreck at the Bottom of the World* uses impressive language to describe Shackleton's plight. The award-winning *Surviving Hitler: A Boy in the Death Camps* (Warren, 2002) is a superb choice for a World War II unit.

Some informational books can be interactive. For instance, a good book for sharing with five- and six-year-olds is *The M&M's Counting Book* (McGrath, 1994). In this book, children learn how to count to 12 and to add. Of course, children delight in subtraction—that's when they get to eat the M&M's! *Shape Up!* (Adler, 1998) introduces children to triangles and other polygons while fractions are featured in *Fraction Action* (Leedy, 1994).

In informational works, facts should be clearly distinguishable from theory, and the most recent findings and information should be included. Because of this and because of limited funding for book purchases, school libraries generally have difficulty obtaining informational books that reflect the cutting edge of science and technology (see box 4.3).

4.3   In the Classroom: Teaching Hint

Tracing the Journeys of Explorers

A good geography and cartography lesson for students in grades four through eight is to trace the journeys of explorers. For lan d travels, raised relief maps help students understand the difficulties encountered by the exploration party.

Students also benefit from considering the primitive m aps that were available to the explorers, many of which were highly speculative. For instance, Lewis and Clark had heard of the Missouri River, but upon their arrival at the fork of the Missouri and the Platte, they had no idea which fork was the larger Missouri River and which was the smaller Platte River. As a result, the expedition had to temporarily split up into two parties to determine which river to follow, thus costing valuable travel time.

Two good trade books to use for this activity are listed below.

Fritz, J. (1994). *Around the world in 100 years: From Henry the Navigator to Magellan* (A. B. Venti, Illus.). New York: Putnam. (4–8). Jean Fritz has written an interesting view of 10 explorers including Diaz, da Gama, and Balboa. She places them in the context of the time period in which they lived. The observations and fascinating facts included about each explorer will keep students reading and talking about this book. The illustrations, unfortunately, are a bit lacking.

Roop, P., & Roop, C. (Eds.). (1993). *Off the map: The journals of Lewis and Clark* (T. Tanner, Illus.). New York: Walker. (4–8). This book traces, through their own journal entries and excerpts, the journey of William Clark and Meriwether Lewis as they explored the territory of the Louisiana Purchase. At the beginning of the book, the editors include the letter from President Thomas Jefferson authorizing the expedition. An epilogue summarizes the return journey of the expedition and offers intriguing information regarding the fates of the members of the expedition.

Historical novels can also be used in teaching social studies, especially geography. Here is an example:

Van Leeuwen, J. (1995). *Bo.und for Oregon* (J. Watling, Illus.). New York: Dial. (3–6). Nine-year-old Mary Ellen Todd and her family leave their Arkansas home and set out for the Oregon Territory in 1852. The difficulties and excitement they encounter along their journey are recounted in this book. Students can trace the family's trip and note geographic differences along the way.

Poetry

Children take to poetry as they naturally love the rhythm and rhyme of language. Poetry can be humorous, reflective, insightful, and descriptive. Above all, it offers diversity of themes. The first encounter most young children have with poetry comes through the sharing of Mother Goose rhymes. Later, rhymes and chants of the playground extend the playful, teasing side of poetry to children.

Unlike the other genres described in this chapter, poetry requires that each and every word be accountable for its existence in the poem. This is because a word carries more meaning in the shorter passages of poetry than the same word does in prose.

Based on the use of connotative rather than denotative meanings, poetry is often abused by teachers, particularly at the junior and senior high school levels, who insist that their students dissect poetry to find the poet's intent and "true" meaning. Such analysis usually results in the destruction of the desire to read and share poetry. Poetry ceases to be enjoyable when the reader is expected to be accountable for the reasons why each word in the poem was selected for use by the poet.

Elementary children delight in the sharing of humorous poetry. They relish the poetry in *Something Big Has Been Here* (1990) and *The New Kid on the Block* (1984) both by Jack Prelutsky. His *Poems of A. Nonny Mouse* (1991) is an excellent collection for encouraging children to write their own poetry. Another popular poet is Shel Silverstein and his classic *Where the Sidewalk Ends* (1974). For primary grades, Bruce Lansky's (1995) *A Bad Case of the Giggles* is delightful. Middle- and upper-level students particularly delight in poetry about sports in Arnold Adoff's (1986) *Sports Pages*, a book of poetry boys and girls can enjoy.

Feelings and reflections about life are popular poetic themes; certainly Shel Silverstein's poetry continues their popularity. *The 20th Century Children's Poetry Treasury* (Prelutsky, 1999) is a poetry collection that shares the joys, problems, and turmoil of being a child. *In Our Backyard Garden* by Eileen Spinelli (2004) offers fresh, insightful poems about family members. *Laughing Tomatoes (Jitomates Risueños)* (Alarcón, 1997) presents poems about spring in both English and Spanish.

Poetry should be included in the various content areas. For instance, a wide variety of poetry is appropriate for inclusion in science lessons, including Paul Fleischman's (1988) Newbery Award winning *Joyful Noise: Poems for Two Voices*, which contains poems that verbally re-create the unique sounds of insects. A delightful poetry book about insects, sea creatures, birds, reptiles, amphibians, and mammals is Jack Prelutsky's (1997) *The Beauty of the Beast*. *Earth Verses and Water Rhymes* by J. Patrick Lewis (1991) contains poetry that celebrates nature. Its simple language, combined with bold, double-page prints, provides rich images of the natural world. Myra Cohn Livingston's (1984) *Sky Songs* tells of the tranquility of a peaceful summer day and the "grumble and growl" of a thunderstorm. Livingston's *Up in the Air* (1989), a collection of poems about flying, contains a poem that describes the snow-covered mountain ranges. Jack Prelutsky's (1988) *Tyrannosaurus Was a Beast* is popular with children who are captivated by prehistoric creatures and is appropriate for introducing this theme in science.

Social studies also lends itself to the sharing of poetry. Virginia Driving Hawk Sneve (1989) collected poetry from American Indian children for her book *Dancing Teepees: Poems of American Indian Youth*. The poetry in this collection covers a variety of topics and includes pieces from oral tradition and contemporary works.

4.4   The More You Know

Poetry Anthologies

Children love poetry if it is shared in an enjoyable way. Teachers need to include poetry throughout the school day so that children can learn the power of word choice.

The following is a list of poetry anthologies along with suggested grade levels:

Alarcón, F. X. (1997). *Laughing tomatoes/Jitomates risueños* (M. C. Gonzalez, Illus.). San Francisco: Children's Book Press. (3–5)

Booth, D. (1990). *Voices on the wind* (M. Lemieux, Illus.). New York: Morrow. (K–4)

Carle, E. (1989). *Animals, animals*. New York: Philomel. (K–3)

Carlson, L. M. (1994). *Cool salsa: Bilingual poems on growing up Latino in the United States*. New York: Holt. (6–8)

Cassedy, S. (1993). *Zoomrimes: Poems about things that go* (M. Chessare, Illus.). New York: Harper-Collins. (K–2)

Chandra, D. (1993). *Rich Lizard and other poems* (L. Bowman, Illus.). New York: Farrar, Strauss, & Giroux. (K–4)

Clinton, C. (1998). *I, too, sing America* (S. Alcorn, Illus.). Boston: Houghton Mifflin. (3–5)

Colen, K. (1995). *Peas and honey: Recipes for kids (with a pinch of poetry)* (M. Victor, Illus.). Honesdale, PA: Boyds Mills. (3–6)

de Regniers, B. S. (1988). *Sing a song of popcorn*. New York: Scholastic (1–5)

Fisher, A. (1986). *When it comes to bugs* (C. & B. Degan, Illus.). New York: Harper & Row. (1–4)

Fleischman, P. (1988). *Joyful noise: Poems for two voices* (E. Beddows, Illus.). New York: Harper & Row. (3–8)

Goldstein, B. (1989). *Bear in mind*. New York: Penguin. (K–3)

Gollub, M. (1998). *Cool melons turn to frogs—the life and poems of Issa* (K. G. Stone, Illus.). New York: Lee and Low. (4–7)

Greenfield, E. (1988). *Under the Sunday tree*. New York: Harper & Row. (K–3)

Hoberman, M.A. (1991). *Fathers, mothers, sisters, brothers*. Boston: Little, Brown. (K–6)

Hopkins, L. B. (1988). *Side by side poems to read together*. New York: Simon & Schuster. (1–4)

Hopkins, L. B. (1990). *Good books, good times!* New York: Harper & Row. (1–5)

Hopkins, L. B. (1994). *April bubbles chocolate* (B. Root, Illus.). New York: Simon & Schuster. (K–5)

Hopkins, L. B. (2002). *Hoofbeats, claws and rippled fins: Creature poems* (S. Alcorn, Illus.). New York: HarperCollins. (2–4)

Hughes, L. (1994). *The dream keeper and other poems* (B. Pinkney, Illus.). New York: Knopf. (3–8)

Lansky, B. (1997). *No more homework! No more tests!* (S. Carpenter, Illus.). New York: Meadow-brook. (3–6)

Lansky, B. (1998). *Happy birthday to me* (S. Carpenter, Illus.). New York: Meadowbrook. (3–6)

Lansky, B. (1998). *Miles of smiles* (S. Carpenter, Illus.). New York: Meadowbrook. (3–6)

Larrick, N. (1990). *To the moon and back*. New York: Dell. (K–5)

Levy, C. (1994). *A tree place* (R. Sabuda, Illus.). New York: McElderry. (4–8)

Lewis, J. (1994). *July is a mad mosquito* (M. W. Hall, Illus.). New York: Atheneum. (3–8)

Livingston, M. C. (1993). *Roll along: Poems on wheels*. New York: McElderry. (K–3)

Livingston, M. C. (1994). *Riddle-me rhymes* (R. Perry, Illus.). New York: McElderry. (K–2)

McNaughton, C. (1994). *Making friends with Frankenstein: A book of monstrous poems and pictures*. New York: Candlewick. (K–up)

Meltzer, M. (2003). *Hour of freedom: American history in poem* (M. Nadel, Illus.). Honesdale, PA: Wordsong. (5–8)

Mora, P. (1996). *Confetti* (E. O. Sanchez, Illus.). New York: Lee & Low. (2–5)

Prelutsky, J. (1983). *Random House book of poetry*. New York: Random House. (K–8)

Prelutsky, J. (1984). *The new kid on the block*. New York: Greenwillow. (2–6)

Prelutsky, J. (1994). *The dragons are singing tonight* (P. Sis, Illus.). New York: Greenwillow. (K–5)

Prelutsky, J. (Ed.). (1999). *The 20th century children's poetry treasury* (M. So, Illus.). New York: Knopf. (K–2)

Silverstein, S. (1974). *Where the sidewalk ends*. New York: Harper & Row. (1–7)

Silverstein, S. (1981). *A light in the attic*. New York: Harper & Row. (K–6)

Silverstein, S. (1996). *Falling up*. New York: HarperCollins. (K–6)

Stevenson, J. (1995). *Sweet corn*. New York: Greenwillow. (3–5)

Walton, R. (1995). *What to do when a bug climbs in your mouth and other poems to drive you buggy* (N. Carlson, Illus.). New York: Lothrop, Lee & Shepard. (K–6)

Wong, J. (2003). *Knock on wood: Poems about superstitions* (J. Paschis, Illus.). New York: McElderry. (3–8)

Yolen, J. (2002). *Wild wings: Poems for young people* (J. Stemple, Illus.). Honesdale, PA: Wordsong. (3–5)

According to Hancock (2004), teachers should "savor the flavor and message of poetry as you select and share the wealth of this genre with children of all ages" (p. 116).

A summary of the genres of children's literature is presented here:

Traditional literature:	Traditional literature includes folktales, wonder or magic tales, humorous tales, beast tales, fables, myths, and legends.
Modern fantasy:	Modern fantasy consists of stories that rely on the creation of time and place to make the unbelievable become believable.
Contemporary realistic fiction:	Contemporary realistic fiction consists of fictitious works in which the characters, setting, and plot are believable and could actually appear in real life.
Historical fiction:	Historical fiction consists of fictitious works in which the characters, setting, and plot are realistically presented in terms of the historical authenticity of the period being described.
Biography and autobiography:	A biography is a nonfiction account of someone other than the author. An autobiography is an author's account of some or all of his or her own life.
Informational works:	Informational works are nonfiction books. These may include how-to books or reference books.
Poetry:	Poetry books are typically collections of poetry by one or several poets. The poems may have the same or different themes.

Multicultural Literature

In the book *Growing Up Literate: Learning from Inner-City Families* (Taylor & Dorsey-Gaines, 1988), the authors point out that children from economically disadvantaged homes who were read to by their parents or some other significant adult developed literacy knowledge and skills. The adoption of a literature-based reading program in a Brownsville, Texas, school district in which more than 80 percent of the students were Hispanic resulted in significantly improved student reading scores (on a state test) in five of the six schools in the district (Roser et al., 1990). Clearly, the sharing of literature with children of various cultural backgrounds is essential. As Stotsky (1992, p. 56) writes, "teachers are responsible, in a highly multireligious and multiethnic society, for creating and cultivating common ground through the literature they teach in all its many forms."

Until recently, the overwhelming proportion of children's literature represented white middle-class America. With the number of minority authors increasing, the number and quality of multicultural children's books have greatly increased. With the advent of many new books in this important area, more have found their way into the classroom.

Through the sharing of multicultural literature with all children, different cultures and races can be better understood, and the development of stereotypical images can be avoided. Minority children need to have positive role models and to become more familiar with their own culture (Bishop, 1992). All children need to understand and tolerate differences in cultures and beliefs.

Quality multicultural children's literature should have the same essential ingredients as quality children's literature in general: well-developed characters, strong plots, recognizable settings, and positive themes. Other characteristics may include minority characters who have a good self-concept and plots that are realistic. If the work is a picture book, the illustrations should be representative of the culture.

In selecting children's literature, teachers need to consider the contributions of various racial and ethnic groups. African Americans, Asian Americans, Hispanics, Jewish Americans, and Native Americans have all contributed to children's literature in significant ways (Cullinan & Galda, 2003). "When children are left on their own, they generally choose literature that is familiar and that reflects their own interests and culture. Therefore, it is important for teachers to expose children to literature that reflects many cultures, themes, and views" (Bieger, 1996, p. 309). In poetry, for instance, Lulu Delacre's (1989) *Arroz Con Leche: Popular Songs and Rhymes from Latin America* offers elementary children insight into the cultures of neighboring countries. Julius Lester's (1989) *How Many Spots Does a Leopard Have?* is a collection of African and Jewish folktales that have universal themes to which children can relate: magic, bravery, loyalty, and vanity.

Norton (1990) suggests that upper-elementary and middle school teachers may want to adopt a five-phase model for studying multicultural literature: (1) traditional literature of varying genres; (2) traditional tales from one area;

(3) autobiographies, biographies, and historical nonfiction; (4) historical fiction; and (5) contemporary fiction and poetry. By starting with traditional literature and moving through the other four phases, the class can become quite familiar with one cultural group. At the conclusion of the fifth phase, another cultural group can be selected and the process repeated.

Criteria for Selecting Multicultural Literature

Selecting multicultural literature for children is not an easy task for teachers. For some ethnic groups, such as African Americans, there is a multitude of children's literature available from which to choose. However, for other cultures, such as Latvian, there are few titles available. The areas of Asian American and Latino children's literature can be confusing to teachers because these are conglomerates of many cultural groups. For instance, Asian American children's literature includes not only Chinese and Japanese children's books but also Cambodian, Indonesian, Korean, Laotian, Malaysian, Thai, and Vietnamese, among others. Likewise, Hispanic includes Cuban, Dominican, Mexican, Nicaraguan, and Puerto Rican, as well as the South American countries—all very different cultural groups.

Cullinan and Galda (2003, p. 357) suggest that teachers look for books representing culturally diverse groups that:

1. avoid stereotypes;
2. portray the cultural groups and their values in an authentic way;
3. use language that reflects standards set by local usage;
4. validate children's experience;
5. broaden our vision;
6. invite reflection.

Through discussing and sharing multicultural literature with each other, teachers can become more familiar with appropriate titles to share with students.

There should be enough books available to give students different perspectives on issues and historical events, such as the Native American view on the European settlement of North America, both on the eastern seaboard and in the Southwest. In addition, books should be available that correct distortions of information (Bishop, 1992), such as the fact that many Native Americans died, not at the hands of pioneers and soldiers, but from illnesses such as small pox, a disease brought to North America by Europeans.

A Listing of Multicultural Literature

Following is a list of suggested African American, Asian American, Hispanic, and Native American multicultural books.

African American

Bryan, A. (1991). *All night, all day: A child's first book of African-American spirituals*. New York: Macmillan/Atheneum. (3–8)

Burchard, P. (1995). *Charlotte Forten: A black teacher in the Civil War*. New York: Crown. (4–7)

Collier, J., & Collier, C. (1981). *Jump ship to freedom*. New York: Delacorte. (5–8)

Cox, C. (1993). *The forgotten heroes: The story of the Buffalo Soldiers*. New York: Scholastic. (5–8)

Golenbeck, P. (1990). *Teammates* (P. Bacon, Illus.). Orlando, FL: Gulliver. (3–8)

Grimes, N. (2002). *Talkin' about Bessie: The story of aviator Elizabeth Coleman* (E. B. Lewis, Illus.). New York: Orchard. (3–6).

Hamilton, V. (1985). *The people could fly: American black folktales* (L. Dillon & D. Dillon, Illus.). New York: Knopf. (3–8)

Hamilton, V. (1992). *Drylongso* (J. Pinkney, Illus.). San Diego: Harcourt Brace. (3–6)

Hansen, J. (1986). *Which way freedom?* New York: Walker. (5–8)

Harris, J. C. (1986). *Jump! The adventures of Brer Rabbit*. Orlando, FL: Harcourt Brace Jovanovich. (K–8)

Haskins, J. (1993). *Get on board: The story of the Underground Railroad*. New York: Scholastic. (5–8)

Hoffman, M. (1991). *Amazing Grace* (C. Birch, Illus.). New York: Dial. (K–3)

Hopkinson, D. (1993). *Sweet Clara and the freedom quilt* (J. Ransome, Illus.). New York: Knopf. (2–5)

Hoyt-Goldsmith, D. (1993). *Celebrating Kwanzaa* (L. Midgale, Illus.). New York: Holiday. (K–8)

Isadora, R. (1991). *At the crossroads*. New York: Greenwillow. (3–5)

Kimmel, E. A. (1994). *Anansi and the talking melon* (J. Stevens, Illus.). New York: Holiday. (K–3)

Knutson, B. (1990) *How the guinea fowl got her spots: A Swahili tale of friendship*. New York: Carolrhoda. (K–2)

Lasky, K. (2000). *Vision of beauty: The story of Sarah Breedlove Walker* (N. Bennett, Illus.). Boston, MA: Candlewick. (3–6)

Lawrence, J. (1993). *The great migration: An American story*. New York: HarperCollins. (3–6)

Mettger, Z. (1994). *Till victory is won: Black soldiers in the Civil War*. New York: Lodestar. (5–9)

Mollei, T. M. (1995). *Big boy*. (E. B. Lewis, Illus.). New York: Clarion. (K–3)

Myers, W. D. (1988). *Scorpions*. New York: Harper & Row. (5–8)

Myers, W. D. (1991). *Now is your time!: The African-American struggle for freedom*. New York: HarperCollins. (4–8)

Pinkney, A. D. (1993). *Seven candles for Kwanzaa* (B. Pinkney, Illus.). New York: Dial. (K–up)

Ringgold, F. (1991). *Tar beach*. New York: Crown. (1–3)

Ringgold, F. (1992). *Aunt Harriet's Underground Railroad in the sky*. New York: Crown. (1–4)

Shange, N. (2004). *Ellington was not a street* (K. Nelson, Illus.). New York: Simon & Schuster. (3–6)

Asian American

Cassedy, S. & Suetake, K. (Trans.). (1992). *Red dragonfly on my shoulder* (M. Bang, Illus.). New York: HarperCollins. (K–3)

Choi, N. S. (1991). *Year of impossible goodbyes.* Boston: Houghton Mifflin. (4–8)

Coerr, E. (1993). *Sadako* (E. Young, Illus.). New York: Putnam. (3–8)

Compton, P. A. (1991). *The terrible eek* (S. Hamanaka, Illus.). New York: Simon & Schuster. (1–3)

Conger, D. (1987). *Many lands, many stories: Asian folktales for children.* New York: Tuttle. (3–5)

Dunn, M., & Ardath, M. (1983). *The absolutely perfect horse.* New York: Harper & Row. (3–6)

Hamanaka, S. (1990). *The journey: Japanese Americans, racism, and renewal.* New York: Orchard. (4–7)

Haugaard, E. C. (1995). *The revenge of the forty-seven samurai.* Boston: Houghton Mifflin. (6–8)

Hong, L. T. (1991). How *the ox star fell from heaven.* New York: Albert Whitman. (4–6)

Jiang J. L. (1998). *The red scarf.* New York: Harper Trophy. (6–8)

Johnson, R. (1992). *Kenji and the magic geese* (J. Tseng & M. Tseng, Illus.). New York: Simon & Schuster. (K–2)

Lord, B. B. (1984). *In the year of the boar and Jackie Robinson.* New York: Harper & Row. (4–6)

Morris, W. (1992). *The future of Yen-Tzu* (F. Henstra, Illus.). New York: Atheneum. (1–4)

Nhuong, H. Q. (1982). *The land I lost: Adventures of a boy in Vietnam.* New York: Harper & Row. (4–8)

Park, L. S. (2001). *A single shard.* New York: Clarion. (6–8)

Partridge, E. (2003). *Kogi's mysterious journey* (A. Sogabe, Illus.). New York: Dutton.

Salisbury, G. (1994). *Under the blood-red sun.* New York: Delacorte. (6–8)

Say, A. (1990). *El chino.* Boston: Houghton Mifflin. (4–8)

Say, A. (1993). *Grandfather's journey.* Boston: Houghton Mifflin. (K–3)

Shea, P. D. (1995). *The whispering cloth* (A. Riggio & Y. Yang, Illus.). Honesdale, PA: Boyds Mills. (K–2)

Siberell, A. (1990). *A journey to paradise.* New York: Henry Holt. (4–6)

Surat, M. M. (1983). *Angel child, dragon child.* Racine, WI: Carnival/Raintree. (3–5)

Uchida, Y. (1993). *The bracelet* (J. Yardley, Illus.). New York: Philomel. (K–2)

Wallace, I. (1984). *Chin Chiang and the dragon's dance.* New York: Atheneum. (3–7)

Yacowitz, C. (1992). *The jade stone* (J. H. Chen, Illus.). New York: Holiday. (1–3)

Yee, P. (1990). *Tales from gold mountain: Stories of the Chinese in the new world* (N. Ng, Illus.). New York: Harper & Row. (4–8)

Yep, L., (1989). *The rainbow people* (D. Wiesner, Illus.). New York: HarperCollins. (4–8)

Yep, L. (1993). *Dragon's gate.* New York: HarperCollins. (5–8)

Hispanic

Aardema, V. (1991). *Borreguita and the coyote: Tale from Ayutia, Mexico.* New York: Knopf (K–3)

Ada, A. F. (1998). *Under the royal palms: A childhood in Cuba*. New York: Atheneum. (6–8)

Ada, A. F. (2002). *I love Saturdays y domingo* (E. Savadier, Illus.). New York: Atheneum. (1–3)

Ancona, G. (1994). *The piñata maker/El piñatero*. San Diego: Harcourt. (K–8)

Anzaldua, G. (1993). *Friends from the other side/Amigos del otro lado*. Chicago: Children's Book Press. (1–7)

Andrews-Goebel, N. (2002). *The pot that Juan built* (D. Diaz, Illus.). New York: Lee & Low. (K–4)

Bunting, E. (1990). *The wall*. (R. Himler, Illus.). New York: Clarion. (3–8)

Charles, F., & Arenson, R. (1996). *A Caribbean counting book*. Boston: Houghton Mifflin. (K–1)

Cisñeros, S. (1994). *Hairs/Pelitos*. New York: Apple Soup/Knopf. (K–3)

Clark, A. N. (1980). *Secret of the Andes*. New York: Viking. (4–8)

De Gerez, T. (1981). *My song is a piece of jade: Poems of ancient Mexico in English and Spanish*. Boston: Little, Brown. (3–8)

dePaola, T. (1980). *The lady of Guadalupe*. New York: Holiday. (3–6)

Dorros, A. (1991). *Abuela*. New York: Dutton. (4–8)

Gershator, P., & Gershator, D. (1998). *Greetings, sun*. New York: Richard Jackson Books. (K–2)

Gonzalez, L. M. (1996). *The bossy gallito (rooster): A traditional Cuban folktale*. New York: Scholastic. (Available in both English and Spanish.) (K–3)

Hausman, G., & Wolff, A. (1998). *Doctor bird: Three lookin' up tales from Jamaica*. New York: Philomel. (2–3)

Isadora, R. (1998). *Caribbean dream*. New York: Putnam. (1–3)

Krull, K. (2003). *Harvesting hope: The story of Cesar Chavez* (Y. Morales, Illus.). San Diego: Harcourt. (3–5)

Mohr, N. (1993). *All for the better: The story of El Barrio*. Dallas: Steck-Vaughn. (2–5)

Mora, P (1995). *The desert is my mother/El desierto es mi madre*. (D. Leshon, Illus.). Houston: Piñata. (2–4)

Mora, P. (1998). *Delicious hulabaloo/Pachanga deliciosa*. (F. Mora, Illus.). (Arte Público Pre-Los Angeles. (3–5)

Myers, W. D. (1996). *Toussaint L'Ouverture: The fight for Haiti's freedom*. New York: Simon & Schuster. (6–8)

O'Dell, S. (1981). *Carlota*. Boston: Houghton Mifflin. (5–8)

Palacios, A. (1993). *¡Viva Mexico!: The story of Benito Juarez and Cinco de Mayo*. Cleveland, OH: Modern Curriculum Press. (2–5)

Pitre, F. (1993). *Juan Bobo and the pig: A Puerto Rican folktale* (C. Hale, Illus.). New York: Lodestar. (1–4)

Rodriguez, G. M. (1994). *Green corn tamales/Tamales de elote* (G. Shepard, Illus.). Tucson, AZ: Hispanic. (K–3)

Roe, E. (1991). *Con mi hermano—with my brother*. New York: Bradbury. (5–8)

Ryan, P. M. (2000). *Esperanza rising*. New York: Scholastic. (5–7)

Shute, L. (1995). *Rabbit wishes*. New York: Lothrop, Lee, & Shepard. (1–4)

Soto, G. (1990). *Baseball in April and other stories*. San Diego: Harcourt. (3–6)

Soto, G. (1992). *Neighborhood odes* (D. Diaz, Illus.). San Diego: Harcourt. (2–4)

Soto, G. (1993). *Too many tamales* (E. Martinez, Illus.). New York: Putnam. (K–3)

Tamar, E. (1996). *American City Ballet.* New York: Harper Trophy. (5–8)

Villaseñor, V. (1994). *Walking stars: Stories of magic and power.* Houston: Piñata.

Winter, J. (1991). *Diego.* New York: Knopf. (5–8)

Native American

Baylor, B. (1975). *A god on every mountain top: Stories of southwest Indian mountains.* New York: Scribner's. (3–6)

Baylor, B. (1978). *The other way to listen.* New York: Scribner's. (K–8)

Bierhorst, J. (1979). *A cry from the earth: Music of the North American Indians.* New York: Four Winds. (K–8)

Bierhorst, J. (1983). *The sacred path: Spells, prayers, and power songs of the American Indians.* New York: Four Winds. (K–8)

Bierhorst, J. (1995). *The white deer.* New York: Morrow. (2–up)

Bierhorst, J. (1997). *The dancing fox* (M. K. Okheena, Illus.). New York: Morrow. (2–5)

Bierhorst, J. (1998). *The deetkatoo* (R. H. Coy, Illus.). New York: Morrow. (4–6)

Bruchac, J. (1993). *Fox song* (P. Morin, Illus.). New York: Philomel. (K)

Bruchac, J. (1995). *Gluskabe and the four wishes* (C. Nyburg, Illus.). New York: Cobblehill. (1–3)

Bruchac, J. (1998). *The arrow over the door* (J. Watling, Illus.). New York: Dial. (1–4)

Bruchac, J., & London, J. (1992.). *Thirteen moons on turtle's back* (T. Locker, Illus.). New York: Philomel. (1–4)

Carey, V. S. (1990). *Quail song: A Pueblo Indian tale* (I. Barnett, Illus.). New York: Putnam. (K–4)

Cherry, L. (1991). *A river ran wild.* Orlando: Harcourt Brace Jovanovich. (K–8)

Cohen, C. L. (1988). *The mud pony: A traditional Skidi Pawnee tale* (S. Begay, Illus.). New York: Scholastic. (3–7)

De Felice, C. (1990). *Weasel.* New York: Macmillan. (5–8)

Dorris, M. (1992). *Morning girl.* New York: Hyperion. (3–5)

Ekoomiak, N. (1990). *Arctic memories.* New York: Holt, Rinehart, & Winston. (4–6)

Freedman, R. (1988). *Buffalo hunt.* New York: Holiday. (3–8)

Freedman, R. (1992). *Indian winter* (K. Bodmer, Photo.). New York: Holiday. (5–up)

Fritz, J. (1983). *The double life of Pocahontas.* New York: Putnam. (3–7)

George, J. C. (1983). *The talking earth.* New York: Harper & Row. (4–8)

Goble, P. (1988). *Iktomi and the boulder: A Plains Indian story.* New York: Orchard. (K–4)

Goble, P. (1990). *Dream wolf.* New York: Bradbury. (1–3)

Goble, P. (2001). *Storm maker's tipi.* New York: Atheneum. (2–3)

Goble, P. (2003). *Mystic horse.* New York: HarperCollins. (1–3)

Gregory, K. (1990). *The legend of Jimmy Spoon.* Orlando, FL: Harcourt Brace Jovanovich. (4–8)

Hoyt-Goldsmith, D. (1991). *Pueblo storyteller* (L. Migdale, Photo.). New York: Holiday. (1–4)

Larrabee, L. (1993). *Grandmother Five Baskets* (L. Sawyer, Illus.). Tucson, AZ: Harbinger. (3–8)

Martin, R. (1992). *The rough faced girl* (D. Shannon, Illus.). New York: Scholastic. (K–4)

Moore, R. (1990). *Maggie among the Seneca.* New York: HarperCollins. (5–6)

O'Dell, S. (1988) *Black star, bright dawn.* Boston: Houghton Mifflin. (5–8)

Paulsen, G. (1988). *Dogsong.* New York: Bradbury. (5–8)

Phillips, N. (2000). *A braid of lives: Native American childhood.* New York: Clarion. (4–7)

Rodanos, K. (1992). *Dragonfly's tale.* New York: Clarion. (5–8)

Rodanos, K. (1994). *Dance of the sacred circle.* New York: Little, Brown. (3–5)

Seymour, T. V. N. (1993). *The gift of changing woman.* New York: Henry Holt. (3–5)

Sneve, V. (1989). *Dancing teepees: Poems of American Indian youth.* New York: Holiday. (4–8)

Sneve, V. (1994). *The Nez Perce: A first Americans book.* New York: Holiday. (2–6)

St. Romain, R. A. (2003). *Moon's cloud blanket* (J. C. Waites, Illus.). New Orleans: Pelican.

Strete, D. K. (1990). *Big thunder magic* (G. Brown, Illus.). New York: Greenwillow. (K–4)

Van Laan, N. (1993). *Buffalo dance: A Blackfoot legend* (B. Vidal, Illus.). Boston: Little, Brown. (1–8)

Wisniewski, D. (1991). *Rain player.* New York: Clarion. (K–3)

Yolen, J. (1992). *Encounter* (D. Shannon, Illus.). San Diego: Harcourt Brace. (3–8)

Other Multicultural Works

Aamundsen, N. R. (1990). *Two short and one long.* Boston: Houghton Mifflin. (4–8)

Ashabranner, B. (1991). *An ancient heritage. The Arab-American minority* (P. S. Conklin, Photo.). New York: HarperCollins. (5–8)

Clinton, C. (2002). *A stone in my hand.* Cambridge, MA: Candlewick. (5–8)

Heide, F. P., & Gilliland, J. H. (1990). *The day of Ahmed's secret* (T. Lewin, Illus.). New York: Lothrop, Lee, & Shepard. (K–3)

Koja, K. (2003). *Buddha boy.* New York: Farrar, Straus & Giroux. (7–8)

Langton, J. (1985). *The hedgehog boy: A Latvian folktale* (I. Plume, Illus.). New York: HarperCollins. (2–4)

Lankford, M. D. (1992). *Hopscotch around the world* (K. Milone, Illus.). New York: Morrow. (1–2)

Mayers, F. (1992). *A Russian ABC.* New York: Abrams. (K–4)

Philip, N. (1991). *Fairy tales of Eastern Europe* (L. Wilkes, Illus.). New York: Clarion. (K–8)

Reed, D. C. (1995). *The Kraken.* Honesdale, PA: Boyds Mills. (3–6)

Shea, P. D. (2003). *The carpet boy's gift: A true story of Pakistan.* New York: Tilbury House. (5–8)

Silverman, E. (2003). *When the chickens went on strike: A Rosh Hashanah tale* (M. Trueman, Illus.). New York: Dutton.

Thematic Units

Developing a unit around a particular theme is an excellent way to allow children to delve into a specific area and share their findings and reactions with classmates. Such an activity allows every student to make a significant contribution to the group regardless of the student's reading ability or thinking skills.

The possibilities for thematic units are seemingly endless. An early-childhood level teacher may decide to have a thematic unit on dinosaurs. The following books could be made available for students to read:

Aliki. (1988). *Dinosaur bones*. New York: Crowell. (1–2)

Arnold, C. (1989). *Dinosaur Mountain: Graveyard of the past* (R. Hewlitt, Photo.). New York: Clarion. (1–4)

Barton, B. (1989). *Dinosaurs, dinosaurs*. New York: Crowell. (K–2)

Barton, B. (1990). *Bones, bones, dinosaur bones*. New York: HarperCollins. (K–2)

Dixon, D. (1990). *The first dinosaurs* (J. Burton, Illus.). New York: Dell/Yearling. (1–3)

Dodson P. (1995). *An alphabet of dinosaurs* (W. D. Barlowe, Illus.). New York: Scholastic. (2–5)

Donnelly, L. (1989). *Dinosaur beach*. New York. Scholastic. (K–2)

Gibbons, G. (1987). *Dinosaurs*. New York: Holiday. (1–3)

Gibbons, G. (1988). *Dinosaurs, dragonflies, and diamonds: All about natural history museums*. New York: Four Winds. (1–4)

Lauber, P. (1989). *The news about dinosaurs*. New York: Bradbury. (1–4)

Lindsay, W. (1998). *American Museum of Natural History: On the trail of dinosaurs*. New York: DK Publishing. (2–5)

Murphy, J. (1987). *The last dinosaur* (J. A. Weatherby, Illus.). New York: Scholastic. (2–4)

Nolan, D. (1994). *Dinosaur dream*. New York: Aladdin. (2–3)

Norman, D. (1987). *When dinosaurs ruled the earth*. Portsmouth, NH: Heinemann. (5–6)

Otto, C. (1991). *Dinosaur chase* (T. Hurd, Illus.). New York: HarperCollins. (1–3)

Pallotta, J. (1991). *The dinosaur alphabet book* (R. Masiello, Illus). Watertown, MA: Charlesbridge. (K–2)

Pfister, M., & Moreno, J. (1995). *Destello el dinosaurio*. New York: North South Books. (2–5)

Strickland, P., & Strickland H. (1994). *Dinosaur roar!* New York: Dutton. (K–1)

Wilhelm, H. (1988). *Tyrone the Horrible*. (New York: Scholastic. (1–3)

Yolen, J. (1990). *Dinosaur dances* (B. Degen, Illus.). New York: Putnam. (1–3)

Microsoft's (1998) CD-Rom program *Dinosaurs* offers a nice complement in the form of an informational interactive computer program.

Thematic units are especially appropriate for social studies and can be based on famous adventurers, pioneer life, historical figures, historical events, and so on. Such a unit need only entail the literary element of characterization.

By choosing to read about a particular time period and setting, such as the colonial period in America, including the Revolutionary War, several possibilities exist: discussing the life of the common people (farmers, fishers, itinerant salespeople, shopkeepers, teachers, and the like), the cultural differences between the people who lived in the cities and those who lived on farms, the customs and beliefs of the period, and so on.

American Colonial Period Books

Following is a list of books appropriate for a thematic unit on the colonial period in America, including books about the southeastern and southwestern parts of what is now the United States.

Famous Colonists

Bober, N. S. (1995). *Abigail Adams: Witness to a revolution*. New York: Atheneum. (6–up)

Chandra, D., & Comora, M. (2003). *George Washington's teeth* (B. Cole, Illus.). New York: Farrar, Straus, & Giroux. (K–3)

Davidson, M. (1988). *The story of Benjamin Franklin*. New York: Dell. (3–6)

Fleming, C. (2003). *Ben Franklin's almanac*. New York: Atheneum. (2–4)

Fritz, J. (1974). *Why don't you get a horse, Sam Adams?* (T. S. Hyman, Illus.). New York: Coward-McCann. (2–5)

Fritz, J. (1975). *Where was Patrick Henry on the 29th of May?* (M. Thomes, Illus.). New York: Putnam. (2–5)

Fritz, J. (1976). *Will you sign here, John Hancock?* (T. S. Hyman, Illus.). New York: Coward-McCann. (2–5)

Fritz, J. (1978). *What's the big idea, Ben Franklin?* (M. Thomes, Illus.). New York: Coward-McCann. (2–5)

Gilolin, J. C. (1992). *George Washington* (M. Dooling, Illus.). New York: Scholastic. (3–5)

Marrin, A. (2001). *George Washington and the founding of a nation*. New York: Dutton. (4–6)

Monsell, H. A. (1989). *Thomas Jefferson*. New York: Aladdin. (3–6)

Schanzer, R. (2003). *How Ben Franklin stole the lightning*. New York: HarperCollins. (3–5)

Siegal, B. (1989). *George and Martha Washington at home in New York* (F. Aloise, Illus.). New York: Four Winds. (2–5)

Wallner, A. (1994). *Betsy Ross*. New York: Holiday. (2–5)

Wallner, J., & Wallner, A. (1990). *A picture book of Benjamin Franklin*. New York: Holiday. (1–5)

Wallner, J., & Wallner, A. (1990). *A picture book of George Washington*. New York: Holiday. (1–5)

White, F. M. (1987). *The story of Junipero Serra: Brave adventurer*. New York: Dell. (4–8)

Colonial Life

Anderson, J. (1984). *The first Thanksgiving* (G. Ancona, Photo.). New York: Clarion. (2–4)

Ayer, E. H. (1993). *The Anasazi.* New York: Walker. (5–8)

Blos, J. W. (1979). *A gathering of days: A New England girl's journal, 1830–32.* New York: Scribner's. (4–6)

Clapp, P. (1968). *Constance: A story of early Plymouth.* New York: Lothrop, Lee, & Shepard. (3–6)

Dalgliesh, A. (1991). *The courage of Sarah Noble* (L. Weisgard, Illus.). New York: Aladdin. (3–6)

Finkelstein, N. H. (1989). *The other 1492: Jewish settlement in the New World.* New York: Scribner's. (5–8)

George, J. C. (1993). *The first Thanksgiving* (T. Locker: Illus.). New York: Philomel. (1–6)

Maestro, B. (1998). *The new Americans: Colonial times 1620–1689* (G. Maestro, Illus.) New York: Lothrop, Lee & Shepard. (1–7)

Early Colonies

Bosco, P. I. (1992) *Roanoke: The story of the lost colony.* New York: Millbrook. (4–6)

Bowen, G. (1994). *Stranded at Plimoth Plantation.* New York: HarperCollins. (3–7)

Clifford, M. L. (1993). *When the great canoes came* (J. Haynes, Illus.). New York: Pelican. (5–8)

Dorris, M. (1994). *Guests.* New York: Hyperion. (5–8)

Goor, R., & Goor, N. (1994). *Williamsburg: Cradle of the Revolution* (R. Goor, Photo.). New York: Atheneum. (3–6)

Wade, L. (1991). *St. Augustine: America's oldest city.* New York: Rourke. (3–5)

Revolutionary War

Avi. (1980). *Encounter at Easton.* New York: Pantheon. (5–8)

Avi. (1984). *Fighting ground.* Philadelphia: Lippincott. (5–8)

Bliven, B., Jr. (1987). *The American Revolution.* New York: Random House. (5–8)

Collier, J. L., & Collier, C. (1974). *My brother Sam is dead.* New York: Macmillan. (6–8)

DePauw, L. G. (1994). *Founding mothers: Women of America in the Revolutionary era.* Boston: Houghton Mifflin. (4–8)

Edwards, S. (1985). *George Midgett's war.* New York: Scribner's. (5–8)

Forbes, E. (1943). *Johnny Tremain* (L. Ward, Illus.). Boston: Houghton Mifflin. (4–8)

Johnson, N. (1992). *The battle of Lexington and Concord.* New York: Four Winds. (4–8)

Kroll, S. (1994). *By the dawn's early light: The story of the Star Spangled Banner.* New York: Scholastic. (3–8)

Longfellow, H. W. (2003). *Paul Revere's ride: The landlord's tale* (C. Santore, Illus.). New York: HarperCollins. (4–8)

Peacock, L. (1998). *Crossing the Delaware* (W. Lyon, Illus.). New York: Atheneum. (3–6)

Reit, S. (1990). *Guns for General Washington.* San Diego: Harcourt Brace. (3–7)

Rinaldi, A. (1993). *The fifth of March: A story of the Boston massacre.* San Diego: Harcourt. (5–8)

St. George, J. (1997). *Betsy Ross: Patriot of Philadelphia* (S. Meret, Illus.). New York: Henry Holt. (3–6)

Thomson, S. L. (2003). *Stars and stripes: The story of the American flag* (B. Dacey & D. Bandelin, Illus.). New York: HarperCollins. (K–3)

Turner, A. (1992). *Katie's trunk* (R. Himler, Illus). New York: Macmillan. (2–5)

Louisiana Purchase and the Journey of Lewis and Clark

Adler, D. (2003). *A picture book of Lewis and Clark* (R. Himler, Illus.). New York: Holiday House. (1–4)

Ambrose, S. (2003). *This vast land: A young man's journal of the Lewis and Clark expedition.* New York: Simon & Schuster. (5–8)

Blumberg, R. (1998). *What's the deal? Jefferson, Napoleon, and the Louisiana Purchase.* Washington, D.C.: National Geographic. (6–8)

Bruchac, J. (2000). *Sacajawea: The story of bird woman and the Lewis and Clark expedition.* New York: Scholastic. (5–8)

Edwards, J. (2003). *The great expeditions of Lewis and Clark by Private Reubin Field, member of the Corps of Discovery* (S. W. Comport, Illus.). New York: Farrar, Straus, & Giroux. (2–5)

Kroll, S. (1996). *Lewis and Clark, explorers of the west.* New York: Holiday House. (3–5)

Milton, J. (2001). *Sacajawea; Her true story* (S. Hehenberger, Illus.). Boston: Houghton Mifflin. (1–3)

Smith, R. (2001). *The Captain's dog: My journey with the Lewis and Clark tribe.* Orlando, FL: Harcourt. (5–8)

Witchcraft

Aronson, M. (2003). *Witch-hunt: Mysteries of the Salem witch trials* (S. Anderson, Illus.). New York: Atheneum. (6–8)

Jackson, S. (1987). *The witchcraft of Salem Village.* New York: Random House. (4–8)

Lasky, K. (1994). *Beyond the burning time.* New York: Blue Sky. (7–up)

Rinaldi, A. (1992). *A break with charity: A story about the Salem witch trials.* New York: Gulliver. (5–8)

Speare, E. G. (1971). *The witch of Blackbird Pond.* New York: Dell. (4–8)

Integrating the Curriculum

Thematic units provide a means for having a completely integrated curriculum. Because thematic units can combine a variety of genre of children's literature, such as informational books, contemporary realistic fiction, picture books, and poetry, children discover that topics can be written about in a variety of ways. By integrating the curriculum, teaching becomes more efficient and more relevant for the student.

The following In the Classroom boxes describe thematic units. Box 4.5 focuses on science as first graders investigate turtles. This unit, designed by Kristin Jung, a first-grade teacher, includes listening, drama, art, math, and writing activities. Box 4.6 focuses on social studies as fourth graders use a constructivism/inquiry approach to learning about the Underground Railroad. This unit was created by Lisa Vogt, a fourth-grade teacher. Box 4.7 is an example of a thematic unit also focusing on social studies with the Middle Ages as the primary topic. This thematic unit is appropriate for upper-elementary/middle school students.

4.5   In the Classroom: Mini Lesson

Thematic Unit in Science (First Grade)

A good science topic can evolve around the different kinds of turtles. Kristin Jung, a first-grade teacher in Clarendon Hills, Illinois, designed the following thematic unit on turtles for her first-grade class. The unit includes informational books, picture books, and poetry. In addition, Kristin incorporates math activities. Students learn about the different types of turtles through the books shared in read alouds and from viewing videotapes. The students compare and contrast the various types of turtles (i.e., box, sea, and loggerhead). Students use turtle puppets in storytelling. For art projects, the students make turtles from paper plates and hatchlings from felt and rocks. The diagram below presents a circular web of this study.

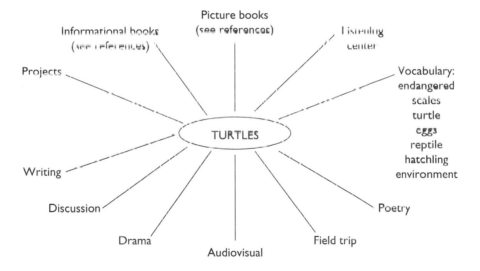

Listening Center
Students listen to fiction and nonfiction turtle stories, as well as watch videos/filmstrips on turtles.

continued

Poetry and Drama

Each child makes a finger puppet and recites a turtle poem, such as the following:

"The Little Turtle" by Vachel Lindsay

There was a little turtle.
He lived in a box.
He swam in a puddle.
He climbed on the rocks.
He snapped at a mosquito.
He snapped at a flea.
He snapped at a minnow.
And he snapped at me.
He caught the mosquito.
He caught the flea.
He caught the minnow.
But he didn't catch me.

Writing

- Each student writes a story about the life cycle of a sea turtle and illustrates the story.
- Each student writes her own "Franklin" story using the original stories as a framework. Student stories are "published" into finished books.
- The students write about the characteristics of reptiles (see example below) and draw accompanying pictures.
- The children write about turtles using a framed sentence structure.
- Each child writes an individual report and draws a realistic picture of the turtle he is researching.
- Every student writes about the trip to the aquarium.

Reptiles

A reptile has _____.
A reptile is _____.
A reptile _____.
A reptile breathes with _____.
A _____ is a _____.

Art Projects

- The children make turtles out of paper plates.
- Each student makes a hatchling out of felt and a rock.
- Each child makes a diorama of the turtle's habitat and places her hatchling inside the diorama.

Math

The children do a number of math worksheets related to turtles. These sheets correspond to what the students are currently learning in math.

Field Trip

The two first-grade classes go to the Shedd Aquarium in Chicago. The children attend a lab where they learn about sea turtles and why they are endangered. The children also get to see a stuffed hawksbill turtle and some products that are made from sea turtles. The students look at some freshwater turtles and are able to touch the carapace and plastron. After the lab, students tour the galleries and pay special attention to the turtles. The children get to see the diver feeding the various sea creatures in the big tank. This trip is one of the culminating activities for the turtle unit.

Turtle Tea

Finished projects are presented at a "Turtle Tea," to which the children's parents are invited. After the tea, parents are invited back to the classroom to see all of the projects their children have done during the turtle unit. Cookies and juice are served in the rooms, as well.

Audiovisual Aids

What is a reptile? (1977). A National Geographic Filmstrip, National Geographic Society, Washington, DC 20036.

Chickens aren't the only ones. A Reading Rainbow Video, Great Plains National (GPN), P.O. Box 80669, Lincoln, NE 68501.

Poetry

Lindsay, V. (1920). "The little turtle." New York: Macmillan.

Silverstein, S. (1981). "Turtle." *A light in the attic.* New York: HarperCollins.

Picture Books

Bampton, B. (Illus.). (1994). *Turtle egg pop-ups.* New York: Golden Books/Western.

Berger, M. (1992). *Look out for turtles!* (M. Lloyd, Illus.). New York: HarperCollins.

Bourgeois, P. (1986). *Franklin in the dark* (B. Clark, Illus.). New York: Scholastic.

Bourgeois, P. (1989). *Hurry up, Franklin* (B. Clark, Illus.). New York: Scholastic.

Bourgeois, P. (1991). *Franklin fibs* (B. Clark, Illus.). New York: Scholastic.

Bourgeois, P. (1992). *Franklin is lost* (B. Clark, Illus.). New York: Scholastic.

Bourgeois, P. (1993). *Franklin is bossy* (B. Clark, Illus.). New York: Scholastic.

Bourgeois, P. (1994). *Franklin is messy* (B. Clark, Illus.). New York: Scholastic.

Bruchac, J. & London, J. (1992). *Thirteen moons on turtle's back: A Native American year of moons* (T. Locker, Illus.). New York: Philomel.

Bryan, A. (1989). *Turtle knows your name.* New York: Atheneum.

Florian, D. (1989). *Turtle Day.* New York: Crowell.

George, W. (1989). *Box turtle at Long Pond* (L. B. George, Illus.). New York: Greenwillow.

Greenfield, E. (1992). *Sister Yessa's story* (C. Ewart, Illus.). New York: HarperCollins.

Leedy, L. (1993). *Tracks in the sand.* New York: Doubleday.

Stoddard, S. (1995). *Turtle time* (L. Munsinger, Illus.). Boston: Houghton Mifflin.

Tate, S. (1991). *Tammy Turtle: A tale of saving sea turtles* (J. Melvin, Illus.). Nags Head, NC: Nags Head Art.

Wood, D. (1992). *Old turtle* (C. K. Chee, Illus.). Duluth, MN: Pfeifer-Hamilton.

Informational Books

Ancona, G. (1987). *Turtle watch.* New York: Macmillan.

Arnold, C. (1994). *Sea turtles* (M. Peck, Illus.). New York: Scholastic.

Arnosky, J. (2000). *All about turtles.* New York: Scholastic.

The Cousteau Society. (1992). *Turtles.* New York. Simon & Schuster.

Fichter, G. S. (1993). *Turtles, toads, and frogs* (B. H. Ambler, Illus.). New York: Western.

Fowler, A. (1992). *Turtles take their time.* Chicago: Children's Press.

Gibbons, G. (1991). *Sea turtles.* New York: Morrow.

Jahn, J. (1987). *A step by step book about turtles.* Neptune City, NJ: T. F. H. Publications.

Kaufman, E., & Kaufman, E. (1989). *Sea animals.* Los Angeles: Price Stern Sloan.

Knox, C. (Illus.). (1983). *Animal world: The turtle.* Windermere, FL: Rourke Enterprises.

Lambert, D. (1983). *Reptiles.* New York: Gloucester.

Lepthien, E. (1996). *Sea turtles.* Chicago: Children's Press.

McCleery, P. R. (1988). *The turtle lady.* Austin, TX: Texas Geographic Interests.

Pallotta, J. (1989). *The yucky reptile alphabet book* (R. Masiello, Illus.). Watertown, MA: Charlesbridge.

Pope, J. (1985). *A closer look at reptiles.* New York: Gloucester.

Rudloe, J. & Rudloe, A. (1994). In a race for survival. *National Geographic, 185* (2), 95–121.

Stone, L. M. (1993). *Sea turtles.* Vero Beach, FL: Rourke Corp.

White, C. (1986). Freshwater turtles-designed for survival. *National Geographic, 169* (1), 40–58.

Source: Kristin Jung, first-grade teacher, Walker School, 120 S. Walker Ave., Clarendon Hills, IL 60514. Reprinted by permission.

4.6   In the Classroom: Mini Lesson (Fourth Grade)

Theme Cycle Units

Theme cycles are units in which the students and the classroom teacher select topics of study together. According to Altwerger and Flores (1994), theme cycles allow students to be at the center of learning as they ask critical questions, engage in meaningful problem posing and problem solving, and create and re-create knowledge. Students are actively involved as they share the collective knowledge of the class, select areas of interest, seek out resources, and plan learning experiences.

Below is a theme cycle developed by Lisa Vogt and her fourth-grade class as part of a unit of study on the Civil War. The students elected to become more familiar with the Underground Railroad because some of the original stations had been located in the area near their school. The figure that follows the background on the Underground Railroad presents a circular web of this study.

Altwerger, B., & Flores, B. (1994). Theme cycles: Creating communities of learners. *Primary Voices*, K–6, 2, 2–6.

Taking the Train to Freedom—Underground Railroad Study

As early as the sixteenth century, Western European nations constructed a uniform slavery system in the Western Hemisphere. This process was composed mainly of people of African origins. Through the notorious slave trade, Africans were dispersed and forced to labor on sugar, tobacco, and rice plantations throughout the Americas and Caribbean. In the 1600s and 1700s, slave labor played a vital role in the history of the British North American colonies. Beginning with Massachusetts and Virginia colonies in 1641 and 1660 respectively, slavery was legalized and regarded as essential to the colonial economy. As white colonists began to petition for freedom and human rights from the British government, this same sentiment was echoed by enslaved blacks. Those who voiced strong opposition to slavery campaigned for the destruction of the system. Although some blacks received liberation through legal suits, those who remained in bondage took considerable risks to gain freedom by escaping from their masters. This method, known as the "Underground Railroad," became a major impetus leading to the eradication of the "peculiar institution"—Slavery.

The Underground Railroad originated during the colonial era as slaves sought ways to escape the inhumane treatment of bondage. Neither "underground" nor a "railroad," this secretive system was not initially organized, but arose when escaped slaves sought refuge in unclaimed territories and newly settled colonies. With the assistance of agents such as the Quakers, free blacks and Native Americans, [slaves] were able to gain their freedom. The efforts of the "underground" promoted the enactment of local fugitive slave laws that were a response to the growing concerns of slaveholders who had lost numerous servants. But as the nation continued to struggle over the morality of slavery, the invention of the cotton gin in 1793 accorded the South justification to perpetuate slavery since it was viewed imperative to its economy.

The abolition movement of the early 1800s set its goal on exterminating slavery. To do so, abolitionists designed the "underground" into a well-organized system. Through the use of secret codes, "stations," "conductors," and "railways," runaway slaves usually traveled to their destinations by night either alone or in small groups. Guided by the North Star, their plans did not entail standard routes since it was necessary to prevent capture; thus waterways, back roads, swamps, forests, mountains, and fields were used to escape. While in flight, slaves hid in barns, caves, cellars, and even boxes or wagons and aboard ships. Food and shelter were provided at "stations" which were maintained by noted "conductors" such as William Still, Levi Coffin and Frederick Douglass. Moreover, Presbyterian, African Methodist Episcopal, African Methodist Episcopal Zion, and the United Methodist churches gave refuge to escapees. Once runaways achieved their freedom, a few like Harriet Tubman, known as a "Moses" to her people, returned to assist fellow slaves and loved ones to liberty. Singlehandedly, Tubman made 19 trips to the South and led more than 300 slaves out of bondage.

continued

By the 1850s, anti-slavery sentiment had reached its peak, and the "underground" program was challenged by slaveholders through a revised Fugitive Slave Act. This law, which called for the return of runaways, jeopardized the status of [ex-slaves], especially those who resided in northern states. Escape routes thus were no longer limited to northern midwestern regions and the federal territories of the United States. More than 100,000 American slaves sought freedom in these areas as well as in Canada, Mexico, and the Caribbean. The Underground Railroad remained active until the end of the Civil War as black [slaves] continued to use the system to flee the horrors of slavery.

From National Parks Service, *Taking the Train to Freedom.* Copyright © 1997. Reprinted by permission.

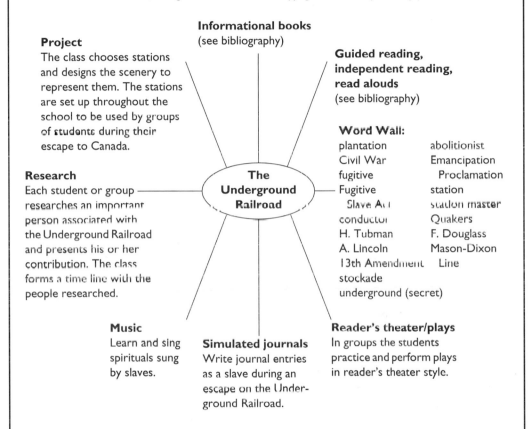

Informational books
(see bibliography)

Project
The class chooses stations and designs the scenery to represent them. The stations are set up throughout the school to be used by groups of students during their escape to Canada.

Guided reading, independent reading, read alouds
(see bibliography)

Research
Each student or group researches an important person associated with the Underground Railroad and presents his or her contribution. The class forms a time line with the people researched.

The Underground Railroad

Word Wall:

plantation	abolitionist
Civil War	Emancipation
fugitive	Proclamation
Fugitive	station
Slave Act	station master
conductor	Quakers
H. Tubman	F. Douglass
A. Lincoln	Mason-Dixon
13th Amendment	Line
stockade	
underground (secret)	

Music
Learn and sing spirituals sung by slaves.

Simulated journals
Write journal entries as a slave during an escape on the Underground Railroad.

Reader's theater/plays
In groups the students practice and perform plays in reader's theater style.

Underground Railroad Chronology

1607	Jamestown, Virginia, settled by English colonists.
1619	Twenty Africans are shipped to Jamestown, Virginia, on Dutch ships.
1641	Massachusetts colony legalizes slavery.
1642	Virginia colony enacts law to fine those who harbor or assist runaway slaves.
1660	Virginia colony legalizes slavery.
1741	North Carolina colony enacts law to prosecute any person caught assisting runaways.
1775	The Pennsylvania Abolition Society is established to protect fugitives and freed blacks unlawfully held in bondage.
1776	North American colonies declare independence from Great Britain.
1777–1804	Northern states abolish slavery through state constitutions.
1787	Northwest Ordinance prevents slavery to exist in the new federal territories. Free

continued

	African Society of Philadelphia, an abolitionist group, is organized by Richard Allen and Absolm Jones.
1793	Fugitive Slave Act becomes a federal law. Allows slaveowners, their agents or attorneys to seize fugitive slaves in free states and territories.
1794	Mother Bethel African Methodist Episcopal Church is established in Philadelphia, PA.
1800	Nat Turner and John Brown are born. Gabriel Prosser stages an unsuccessful slave insurrection in Henrico County, VA.
1804	Underground Railroad is "incorporated" after slaveowner, Gen. Thomas Boudes of Columbia, PA, refuses to surrender escaped slave to authorities.
1816	Seminole Wars begin in Florida as a result of many slaves taking refuge with Seminole Indians.
1818	As a response to the Fugitive Slave Act (1793), abolitionists use the "underground" to assist slaves to escape into Ohio and Canada.
1820	Missouri Compromise admits Missouri and Maine as slave and free states, respectively. The measure establishes the $36°30^1$ parallel of latitude as a dividing line between free and slave areas of the territories.
1821	Kentucky representatives present resolution to Congress protesting Canada's reception of fugitive slaves.
1822	Former slave Denmark Vesey performs a slave uprising in Charleston, SC.
1829	Black abolitionist, David Walker issues *David Walker's Appeal*. Afterwards, several slave revolts occurred throughout the South.
1830	Levi Coffin leaves North Carolina, settles in Indiana and continues abolitionist activities.
1831	William Lloyd Garrison prints first issues of his anti-slavery newspaper, *The Liberator*. Black entrepreneur and abolitionist Robert Forten becomes chief financial supporter of the publication. Nat Turner stages insurrection in Southampton County, VA.
1832	Louisiana presents resolution requesting Federal Government to arrange with Mexico to permit runaway slaves from Louisiana to be reclaimed when found on foreign soil.
1834	National Antislavery Society organizes Underground Railroad as a response to proslavery argument.
1838	Underground Railroad is "formally organized." Black abolitionist, Robert Purvis, becomes chairman of the General Vigilance Committee and "president" of the Underground Railroad.
1842	Supreme Court rules in *Prigg v. Pennsylvania* that state officials are not required to assist in the return of fugitive slaves.
1845	Frederick Douglass prints *Narrative of the Life of Frederick Douglass,* an account of his slave experience and escape to freedom.
1847	Douglass edits anti-slavery newspaper, the *North Star.*
1849	Harriet Tubman makes her escape from Maryland.
1850	Compromise of 1850 attempts to settle slavery issue. As part of the Compromise, a new Fugitive Slave Act is added to enforce the 1793 law and allows slaveholders to retrieve slaves in northern states and free territories.
1852	Harriet Beecher Stowe's *Uncle Tom's Cabin* is published as a response to the pro-slavery argument.
1857	Supreme Court declares in *Scott v. Sandford* that blacks are not U.S. citizens, and slaveholders have the right to take slaves in free areas of the country.
1859	John Brown's failed raid on federal arsenal and armory in Harper's Ferry, Virginia, which was aimed at starting a general slave insurrection.
1860	Republican candidate Abraham Lincoln is elected President of the United States.
1861	Civil War begins.

continued

1863	President Lincoln issues the Emancipation Proclamation which declares "all persons held as slaves within any st ate . . . be in rebellion against the United States shall be then . . . forever free."
1865	War ends.
	Thirteenth Amendment is amended to the U.S. Constitution abolishing slavery permanently.

From National Parks Service, *Underground Railroad Chronology*. Copyright © 1997. Reprinted by permission.

Underground Railroad Activities

Vocabulary Word Wall

The students and teacher generate this list together. Here are several possibilities:

plantation	Quakers
abolitionist	Harriet Tubman
Civil War	Frederick Douglass
Emancipation Proclamation	Abraham Lincoln
fugitive	Mason-Dixon Line
Fugitive Slave Act	Thirteenth Amendment
station, stationmtaster, conductor	stockade underground (meaning secret)

Reader's Theater

The following stories are written in play format with stage directions and can be performed as plays. The first play listed is directly related to the Underground Railroad. The second and third plays listed relate to Martin Luther King, Jr.'s birthday and the Civil Rights Movement, which we recently studied. The students choose their parts and practice before reading to the class.

Frederick Douglass: The Douglass "Station" of the Underground Road

Martin Luther King, Jr.: In the Footsteps of Dr. King

Rosa Parks: The Unexpected Heroine

Simulated Journals

The students write in their journals as "slaves" telling of their attempts to escape on the Underground Railroad. This is Amy's diary entry portraying herself in the role of a slave.

Under Ground Railroad

It is 1837. I an a slave but a very lucky one. I know how to read and wright. It is 3:00 in the morning and I haven't got caught yet. Last time I ran away I only lasted until 1:00. My slave is very mean. We only get 10 min. to eat lunch. Oh and by the way my name is Yotchy. My masters name is Mr. oops. I mean Master Kincan. When we are in bed we make fun of him and we say master canon. We also make fun of our own names too because our master named us. My realname used to be Amy. We hate our names. Sometimes when we have meetings all he talks about is how bad we work never how good I'm glad I'm free. Until morning mabey. Mabey I can lye myself. I only need a couple more dollars. Oh joy it is 5:00. Every one is going to get up now. Well mayby I could be lucky. like Yoma. She is free somewhere in Canida. Mabey I will go there. I'm going that way Oh no its morning. I better start to run. Well here I go. Oh great there is a slave cature. I beter hide. Trouble time. I hope he is not looking for me. I better take a run for it. One, two, three go! He hasn't seen me yet. Oh no he saw me. He's running tord me. I better find a place to go fast. ever wors he has a wgon I know I will stop & run the other way. Then it will take him longer to turn around. I hate myself for running away. go faster you legs. aaaaaah! stay away from me. I'm about to die! Oh so its Yotchy that run away this time. Ya I'm sorry. Yo well your . . . ouch! foot is coming off. THE END!

continued

Music

During music class, the music teacher discusses the history of spirituals with the students. After the students have had time to learn the songs, all the classes are put together to perform the songs on the day of the "Escape" (see Projects). Possible songs to learn are:

"Wade in the Water"

"Somebody's Knocking at Your Door"

"Who Built the Ark?"

"Swing Low, Sweet Chariot"

"Oh, Won't You Sit Down?"

Research

The students choose a person involved with the Underground Railroad and research his or her contributions and importance. This can be done individually, in pairs, or in small groups. The students present the information to the class as an "interview" with the famous person, as a news report about the person, or by dressing up as the person. The class then uses the information to form a time line sequencing the important people and their contributions.

Projects

The students plan and design the scenery for Underground Railroad stations. Eight stations are planned and set up throughout the school hallways. Using their knowledge of the types of places used as hideouts and stations on the Underground Railroad, the students design the scenery and signals (which indicate a safe or unsafe station). Scenery is hung throughout the school hallways and two "stationmasters" are assigned to each station. Two of the eight stations are deemed "unsafe." The unsafe stations rotate throughout the "escape." In groups of three or four, students are "released" from one end of the school and must safely travel the "Underground Railroad" to Canada (the gym) on the other end of the school. Along the way the students must stop at at least four stations. (If a group reaches Canada without four punches in their card they are considered to have starved.) If the station they choose to stop at is a safe station, their card is punched and the group continues. If they choose to stop at an unsafe station, their card is collected and they must return to the "captured slaves" room. Very few groups make it to Canada, and they must work together to look for signals and keep track of the stations passed!

Possible stations:	*Possible signals:*
Forest	Lanterns hung a certain way or in a certain place
Cemetery	Quilts displayed
House/cabin	
Riverboat	
Wagon	
Cave	
Barn	

Bibliography

Picture Books

Bial, R. (1995). *The Underground Railroad.* Boston: Houghton Mifflin—photo essay that is appropriate for all levels of readers.

Edwards, P. D. (1998). *Barefoot: Escape on the Underground Railroad* (H. Cole, Illus.). New York: HarperCollins—picture-book format.

Hopkinson, D. (1993). *Sweet Clara and the freedom quilt* (J. Ransome, Illus.). New York: Knopf—picture-book format.

Levine, E. (1988). *. . . . If you traveled on the Underground Railroad* (L. Johnson, Illus.). New York: Scholastic—question and answer, picture-book format, excellent read aloud.

Ringgold, F. (1992). *Aunt Harriet's Underground Railroad in the sky* (F. Ringgold, Illus.). New York: Crown—picture-book format.

continued

Stein, R. C. (1981). *The story of the Underground Railroad* (R. Canaday, Illus.). Chicago: Children's Press.

Nonfiction

Brill, M. T. (1993). *Allen Jay and the Underground Railroad* (J. L. Porter, Illus.). Minneapolis: Carolrhoda—easy reading level, good read aloud or guided reading for less able readers, novel format.

Cosner, S. (1991). *The Underground Railroad.* New York: Venture—advanced reading level, useful for teacher information.

Haskins, J. (1993). *Get on board: The story of the Underground Railroad.* New York: Scholastic—excellent nonfiction book for read aloud or guided reading.

Biographies

Carlson, J. (1989). *Harriet Tubman: Call to freedom.* New York: Fawcett Columbine—read aloud or guided reading.

Sterling, D. (1954). *Freedom Train. The story of Harriet Tubman.* New York: Scholastic—read aloud or guided reading.

Fiction

Armstrong, J. (1992). *Steal away.* New York: Orchard—novel.

Rappaport, D. (1991). *Escape from slavery: Five journeys to freedom* (C. Lilly, Illus.). New York: HarperCollins—contains five short stories mentioned in many of the nonfiction books listed above.

Turner, G. I. (1994). *Running for our lives* (S. Byrd, Illus.). New York: Dutton. Novel.

Folktales

Cohn, A. L. (1993). *From sea to shining sea: A treasury of American folklore and folk songs.* New York: Scholastic—has a section entitled "I've Been Working on the Railroad" that contains several folktales and songs.

Hamilton, V. (1985). *The people could fly: American Black Folktales* (L. and D. Dillon, Illus.). New York: Knopf—has a section entitled "Carrying the Running-Aways and Other Slave Tales of Freedom" that contains six short stories.

Reader's Theater Plays

Turner, G. Tilley. (1989). *Take a walk in their shoes* (E. C. Fax, Illus.). New York: Dutton.

Songs

Crook, E., Reimer, B., & Walker, D. S. (1985). *Music.* Englewood Cliffs, New Jersey: Silver Burdett.

Reimer, B., & Hoffman, M. E. (1985). *Music.* New Jersey: Silver Burdett.

Staton, B., Staton, M., Davidson, M., Kaplan, P., & Snyder, S. (1991). *Music and you.* New York: Macmillan.

Map of Slave States—1860

A free map of the slave states depicting the various Underground Railroad routes to Canada, Mexico, and the Caribbean can be obtained by writing to the following address:

Underground Railroad Study Project
National Park Service
Denver Service Center—Eastern Team
P.O. Box 25287
Denver, CO 80225

or by calling (800)524–6878 and asking for the project historian, Underground Railroad.

From Lisa Vogt. *Underground Railroad.* Reprinted by permission.

4.7 In the Classroom: Mini Lesson

Thematic Unit on the Middle Ages (Grades 6–8)

Until recent years, there have been relatively few trade books available about the Middle Ages for children to read. Certainly the "age of chivalry" greatly interests children. This unit was designed for students in grades six through eight.

The entire class reads Karen Cushman's (1995) *The Midwife's Apprentice* and engages in the integrated activities as outlined in the figure that follows. At the conclusion of these activities, each student selects and reads a second novel about the Middle Ages (such as *Catherine, Called Birdy*) and keeps a literature journal to record reactions and responses. Students are paired with someone who is reading the same book. They read and write in their response journals, then exchange journals to share their thoughts and reactions on the same material. They meet with their partners each day or every other day to discuss the book.

Books

Bellairs, J. (1989). *The trolley to yesterday.* New York: Dial. (4–8). This time-warp story takes Johnny and his friend, Fergie, back to 1453 and the Byzantine Empire. The two friends arrive in Constantinople just prior to the Turkish invasion.

Cushman, K. (1994). *Catherine, called Birdy.* New York: Clarion. (6–8). Birdy is 14 and she faithfully keeps a diary of her experiences in England in 1290. The diary spans a one-year period during which Birdy's father attempts to marry her off for money or land. This is a Newbery Honor Book.

Cushman, K. (1995). *The midwife's apprentice.* New York: Clarion. (4–8). The setting is the Middle Ages where a young orphan must fend for herself until she becomes apprenticed to a midwife. The book provides very accurate descriptions of details of the period.

Konigsburg, E. L. (1973). *Proud taste for Scarlet and Miniver.* New York: Atheneum. (4–8). Illustrated by the author, this historical-fiction novel focuses on Eleanor of Aquitaine. Proud Eleanor is waiting for her young husband, King Henry II, to join her in heaven. Henry had died before Eleanor, but had not yet been judged favorably by the angels. While she waits, Eleanor reflects upon the various events of her life. Children will find this book to be both interesting and amusing.

Osband, G., & Andrew, R. (1991). *Castles.* New York: Orchard. (K–8). This pop-up picture book is filled with information that will intrigue students. Early designs of castles, including how they expanded over the years, are depicted. In addition, castle life is discussed as well as the life of knights. Ten castles still in existence within a variety of European countries are portrayed and described.

Temple, F. (1994). *The Ramsay scallop.* New York: Orchard. (7–8). Thirteen-year-old Elenor is betrothed to Thomas—a marriage designed to join their parents' estates. When they are reluctant to wed, Father Gregory sends Elenor and Thomas on a pilgrimage to Ramsey, Spain, where they receive a scallop shell. This book is targeted at the mature reader.

Winthrop, E. (1985). *The castle in the attic.* New York: Holiday. (4–7). William receives an old, realistic model of a castle as a gift from the housekeeper. She warns him that it is very special. This fantasy will appeal to students interested in magic and the wizards of the Middle Ages.

continued

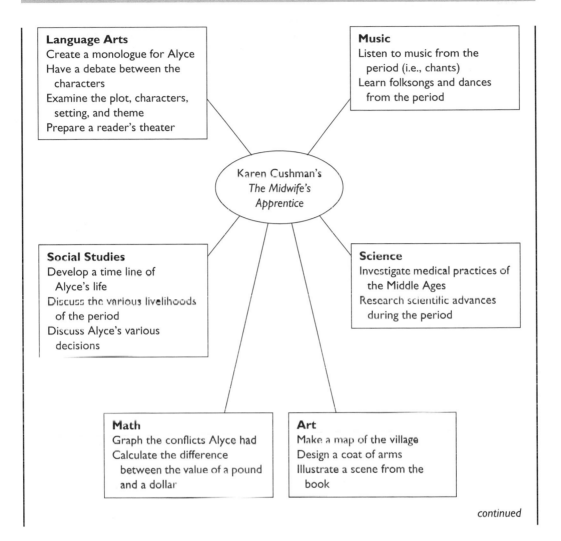

Language Arts
Create a monologue for Alyce
Have a debate between the
  characters
Examine the plot, characters,
  setting, and theme
Prepare a reader's theater

Music
Listen to music from the
  period (i.e., chants)
Learn folksongs and dances
  from the period

Karen Cushman's
*The Midwife's
Apprentice*

Social Studies
Develop a time line of
  Alyce's life
Discuss the various livelihoods
  of the period
Discuss Alyce's various
  decisions

Science
Investigate medical practices of
  the Middle Ages
Research scientific advances
  during the period

Math
Graph the conflicts Alyce had
Calculate the difference
  between the value of a pound
  and a dollar

Art
Make a map of the village
Design a coat of arms
Illustrate a scene from the
  book

continued

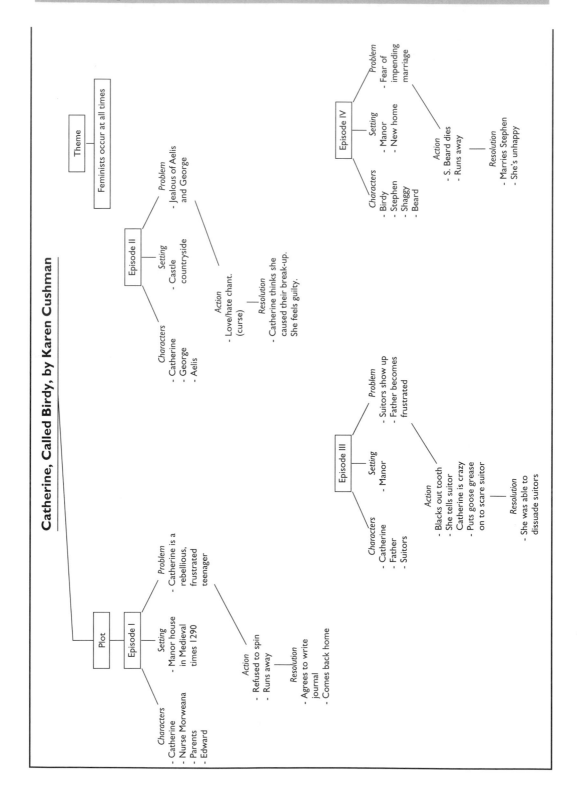

Catherine, Called Birdy, by Karen Cushman

Theme
Feminists occur at all times

Plot

Episode I

Setting
- Manor house in Medieval times 1290

Characters
- Catherine
- Nurse Morweana
- Parents
- Edward

Problem
- Catherine is a rebellious, frustrated teenager

Action
- Refused to spin
- Runs away

Resolution
- Agrees to write journal
- Comes back home

Episode II

Setting
- Castle countryside

Characters
- Catherine
- George
- Aelis

Problem
- Jealous of Aelis and George

Action
- Love/hate chant. (curse)

Resolution
- Catherine thinks she caused their break-up. She feels guilty.

Episode III

Setting
- Manor

Characters
- Catherine
- Father
- Suitors

Problem
- Suitors show up
- Father becomes frustrated

Action
- Blacks out tooth
- She tells suitor Catherine is crazy
- Puts goose grease on to scare suitor

Resolution
- She was able to dissuade suitors

Episode IV

Setting
- Manor
- New home

Characters
- Birdy
- Stephen
- Shaggy
- Beard

Problem
- Fear of impending marriage

Action
- S. Beard dies
- Runs away

Resolution
- Marries Stephen
- She's unhappy

Literature Circles

Literature circles have become popular with many teachers in that they foster both independent reading and writing as well as collaborative learning (Daniels, 1994; Kroll, & Paziotopoulos, 1991). Literature circles are a hands-on approach that promotes reading and discussion. Literature circles are groups of three to nine students who have read the same story, picture book, or novel and who have gathered to talk about their feelings, reactions, and responses, both written and oral, to what they have read. For young students in kindergarten through third grade, the teacher is usually present during the discussion to lend support but not to dominate the discussion. For older students, the teacher is nearby, usually roaming between groups, to provide support or resolve a problem if needed. However, the students lead the discussion because the goal of literature circles is to ensure that students converse with each other rather than talk only to the teacher. The long-term goal of literature circles is that children will become lifelong readers and will enjoy sharing their interest in reading with relatives, friends, and colleagues.

Discussions in literature circles enable students to consider different aspects of a book: characters, plot, setting, theme, and author's style. According to Kaser and Short (1998), "through this sharing of stories, they develop a sense of community that follows them to enter into dialogue with each other. Dialogue involves thinking out loud with others so that their ideas and connections are considered reflectively and critically" (p. 191). Such dialogue "provides children with multiple perspectives as they enter the story world of the book and share their interpretations with each other. They make connections to their lives and cultural identities and examine other possible worlds through the characters in books and the talk of their peers" (Kaser & Short, 1998, p. 191).

The following seven benefits of literature circles are outlined by Scott (1994):

1. Literature circles help students converse about literature.

2. Sharing personal responses to literature is essential for students to understand what they have read.

3. Literature circles use the social nature of the classroom to invite reading, extend thinking, and prolong involvement with text.

4. Because there is no ability-grouping with literature circles, they promote an acceptance of other students' ideas, strengths, and responses.

5. As students participate in literature circles, they can see their own growth as they learn to participate in literature circles.

6. Literature circles support the kind of skills students will need in the future in the workforce and as community leaders.

7. Literature circles help develop reading strategies and proficiency in responding to text in different ways.

A literature circle may last for a day on a picture book or basal reader story or two to three weeks on a novel. A literature circle can require between one to two hours of class time each day, depending on the reading level of the material, the reading ability of the students, the degree of experience students have had leading their own discussions without adult supervision, and how well organized the teacher is initially.

Literature Circles with Beginning Readers: Initiating Grand Conversations

The role of literature circles with beginning readers has been questioned. Some first- and second-grade teachers believe that six- and seven-year-olds lack the level of sophistication to discuss children's literature. Other teachers believe that the main focus of first-grade literature instruction should relate to decoding and use of patterned language in children's literature. Actually six- and seven-year-olds can engage in small group discussions, or literature circles, after having read the same book or several different books with a single theme such as friendship or sharing. The goal should be for students to listen carefully and think deeply along with their peers to create understandings that go beyond those of the individual students within the group (Short, 1995, 1997). Such discussion or dialogue is referred to as "grand conversations" and includes both inquiry and critique (Peterson & Eeds, 1990).

In introducing grand conversations, the teacher should model a book that the students are familiar with before the entire class. For instance, after reading a familiar picture book or story aloud to the class, the teacher may share a favorite part of the story and then ask students to share their favorite portions. The teacher may then elaborate on how the story relates to his own life. Michael Boll, a first-grade teacher, read a version of *The Three Bears* to his class. Then he shared with the class that his favorite part was when the chair was broken, because he was the youngest of four kids and every toy he got was used or broken. After a number of his students related the story to their own lives, Michael had the class illustrate their favorite portion of the folktale as a type of story response.

Hancock (2004) suggests being careful to select appropriate picture books that will sustain grand conversations with beginning readers. She suggests that such books meet the following four criteria:

1. a well-crafted story with a meaningful theme;
2. a book with sufficient depth to provide discussion;
3. the inclusions of memorable language;
4. diverse characters in real-world situations (p. 200).

By using picture books with children as characters, young students more readily see relationships between their own lives and those of characters in the books. Some good books to begin with are:

Henkes, K. (1992). *Chrysanthemum*. New York: Greenwillow. (K–2)
Hesse, K. (1999). *Come on, rain!* (J. J. Muth, Illus.). New York: Scholastic. (2–4)
Polacco, P. (1994). *My rotten redheaded older brother*. New York: Simon & Schuster. (2–4)

Singer, M. (1999). *Josie to the rescue* (S. D. Schindler, Illus.). New York: Scholastic. (2–4)

Although narratives are often the first genre to be shared via literature circles and grand conversations, some nonfiction books and biographies in the areas of science and social studies are applicable. Here are some to use with beginning readers.

Aliki. (1993). *Communication.* New York: Greenwillow. (K–2)
Bunting, E. (1999). *Butterfly house* (G. Shed, Illus.). New York: Scholastic. (1–3)
Gibbons, G. (1997). *The honey makers.* New York: Holiday House. (1–3)
Gibbons, G. (2002). *Tell me, tree.* New York: Little, Brown. (1–3)
Martin, J. B. (1998). *Snowflake Bentley* (M. Azarian, Illus.). Boston: Houghton Mifflin. (1–3)

The teacher should read one of these books aloud and have the class engage in a grand conversation in which he models the process. Then, depending upon the reading ability of the students, the teacher may opt to read other books aloud to the class or have the students read the books on their own, or do both before the next discussion occurs.

Beginning Bilingual Readers and Grand Conversations

Beginning bilingual readers are struggling to acquire a second language in addition to learning to read and write. Grand conversations can be used with beginning bilingual readers as an effective means of discussion. Martinez-Roldan and López Robertson (2000) suggest starting by dividing the class by primary languages. For instance, the teacher may read *Donde Viven los Mon struos* (Sendak [trans. Mlawer, 1999], 1963) to the Spanish-speaking students and the English version, *Where the Wild Things Are* (Sendak, 1963), to the native English speakers.

As the teacher reads the two books aloud, she tapes the stories for the students to use later at a listening center. Next, on a Word Wall, the teacher writes words that are offered by the students as being important to the story in both Spanish and English. The Word Wall might look like this:

English	*Spanish*
Max	Max
mother	mama
boat	bote
monsters	monstruos
quiet	quietos
ruckus	festejos

The students then share their feelings about monsters during a grand conversation. Later, they read along with their teacher's recording at the listening center. It is important to have a sufficient number of books in both English and Spanish so that the children have their own books with which to follow along. An accompanying art activity might be to have the students make monster masks and then, using drama, act out the story. This will enhance the children's language learning as well as make it a memorable, fun experience.

There are several books that can be used in this fashion. *Diez Deditos: Ten Little Fingers* (Orozco, 1997), contains play rhymes and action songs from Latin America that are presented in both Spanish and English. Here are other picture books for sharing with first through third graders that have parallel Spanish/English:

Anzaldua, G. (1993). *Friends from the other side/Amigos del otro lado*. San Francisco: Children's Book Press. (2–4)

Anzaldua, G. (1995). *Prietita and the ghost woman/Prietita y la llorona*. San Francisco: Children's Book Press. (2–4)

Mora, P. (1997). *Tomás and the library lady*. New York: Knopf. (English version) (3–6)

Mora, P. (1997). *Tomás y la señora de la biblioteca*. New York: Knopf. (Spanish version.) (3–6)

Listen to the Desert/Oye al Desierto (Mora, 1994) and the complete series of *The Magic School Bus*, available from Scholastic books in both English and Spanish, are excellent pieces of nonfiction literature to teach science to second-language learners.

Intermediate and Middle School Readers and Grand Conversations

Like beginning readers, intermediate and middle school students can benefit from the richness of talking about books. By this point, the teacher need only model from time to time as the students themselves take over the literary discussion. Hancock (2004) suggests that grand conversations are a reflection of the child's cognitive and social development. Considering these elements, she has found that grand conversations tend to proceed developmentally as follows:

- impressions and personal responses to the book (i.e., favorite parts, initial enjoyment of the book);
- connections to personal experiences and other book titles (i.e., text-to-life and text-to-text connections);
- specific conversational focus (i.e., critical dialogue, careful consideration of others' thoughts, focus on specific aspect of the book);
- expansion and textual support of personal responses and building off of participant comments; and,
- determination of focus for next meeting (i.e., a starting point for the next day's conversation) (p. 200).

Before letting students loose to discuss a book, the teacher needs to establish certain parameters to serve as guides. The next section will explain the roles of the students during the literature circle experience.

Organizing Literature Circles

Implementing literature circles can appear to be overwhelming at first. Thus it is important for the teacher to become organized and to plan out the activity before plunging into the activity with the students. The size of the group itself must be considered. With six or seven students in a group, more topics are covered, but the pace is usually fast and furious with the participants all vying to engage in the discussion. With three or four students, the pace slows down but the context is covered in greater depth. Thus, groups of four to five students tend to be the most popular.

The following are methods of establishing structure and providing guidance for students as they engage in literature circles.

Read Aloud

Each literature circle begins with a read aloud. What is selected to be read aloud by the teacher may differ with each book as well as with each grade level. For instance, the introduction or first chapter of a chapter book or novel may be most appropriate for third graders through eighth graders whereas a page or two of a picture book may be most appropriate for first or second graders. In some cases, a small portion of the text somewhere in the middle of the book may be the best choice. It largely depends on the book and the ability level of the students. The teacher may decide, for instance, to read the prologue or introduction from Lois Lowry's (1993) *The Giver*, Jerry Spinelli's (1990) *Maniac Magee*, or J. K. Rowling's (2003) *Harry Potter and the Order of the Phoenix* to a fifth- or sixth-grade class, or Jack Gantos's (2000) *Joey Pigza Loses Control* or Richard Peck's (1998) *A Long Way from Chicago* to a seventh- or eighth-grade class to entice them into the story.

A good picture book to start literature circles with kindergartners or first graders is Denise Fleming's (1993) *In the Small, Small Pond*, as children enjoy the delightful rhyming that describes the activities of the animals in a pond. Mem Fox's (1988) *Koala Lou* is also a good choice as children at this age may question their mother's love for them. Literature circle choices to use with first and second graders are Lynn Cherry's (1990) *The Great Kapok Tree* and Jim Arnosky's (2000) *A Manatee Morning*. Gail Gibbons (1994) *St. Patrick's Day* is a good nonfiction book for first through third graders, particularly because by March 17, St. Patrick's Day, most first graders can read this book on their own.

Picture books can be used for literature circles from kindergarten through middle school. In fact, some teachers prefer to begin with a picture book for introducing literature circles to upper-grade students. Jane Yolen's (1987) classic *Owl Moon* opens with an intriguing first page that makes for a good, albeit brief, read aloud that works well with third and fourth graders. Katherine Paterson's (1994) *Flip Flop Girl*, the story of a girl who moves to a new town, and Ruby Bridges's (1999) *Through My Eyes* are good choices.

The Fortune-Tellers, by Lloyd Alexander (1992), the story of a carpenter who accidentally becomes a fortune teller and marries a wealthy merchant's daughter in the process, is a great humorous story to use for a literature circle. Other types of picture books lend themselves to literature circles, as well. Allan Say's (1993) *Grandfather's Journey*, the biography of Say's Japanese grandfather's life in Japan and the United States, makes for an interesting discussion of life before and after World War II in both countries. Patricia Polacco's (1994) *Pink and Say* is the actual Civil War story of Polacco's great grandfather, Say, who had his life saved by an African American Union Army soldier, Pinkus, and Pinkus's mother, both of whom died in helping Say. *Pink and Say* can be used in literature circles with children from second through eighth grade. Newbery Award winners are often superb choices for fourth- through eighth-grade literature circles.

Response and Reaction

After reading a portion of the text aloud, the teacher divides the students into pairs and lets them spend two minutes discussing the material that was read, encouraging them to give open, honest responses and reactions.

Share (Teacher Evaluates)

Three or four students share the main focus of the discussions they had with their partners. This enables the teacher to determine to what extent the students are on target with the assignment because information is received from three to four different sets of students.

Form Groups

The teacher divides students into groups of four or five. Consideration needs to be given to students' interests, skills, and behavior. A list of the groups and of which students will be assigned to each group should be established *before* starting the read aloud, preferably the night before so changes can be made before school begins in the morning.

Assign Students Roles

The teacher gives each student a role to play in the group. This, too, should be prepared beforehand, as organizing students by group saves time involved in handing out assignment sheets.

Obviously, the size of the group will determine to some extent the roles assigned. For a group of three students in grade three and higher, the role assignments may double. For instance, one student may be both the discussion leader and the passage master, whereas another student may be the character captain and the summarizer, and the last student may be the connector and the illustrator. The book itself may dictate that certain roles be included and others not be included. Also the teacher may want to change the roles used for different stories or books in order to keep the activity fresh and interesting for students. The roles are as follows:

Discussion Leader: This student is responsible for keeping everyone on task, taking charge of the interchange as the group decides how they will get the tasks accomplished. Later this student monitors each group member's progress and serves as a troubleshooter if a group member needs help. The discussion leader writes a brief summary of what went on *in* the group.

Character Captain: This student jots down responses about the actions and thoughts of the characters in the story.

Scene Setter: This student tracks and describes the different scenes in the story, describing the importance of each.

Passage Master: This student notes and shares important passages *in* the story, explaining why they are significant.

Literary Critic: This student responds to literary questions about the book or book chapter. The student is given a worksheet with the following questions listed at the top:

- In what way is this book or book chapter important?
- What does it provide in terms of the following:

significant ideas or points?

character development?

plot development?

setting (time and/or place)?

theme?

writer's style?

- How does this chapter fit into the book?
- If this chapter were to be eliminated from the book, what essential elements would need to be put into other chapters?

Illustrator: This student creates an art project that reflects the content of the material read in the book, for example a major scene in the story or chapter. The art project may be a collage, a comic strip, a drawing, a computer graphic, a clay sculpture, or some other art medium.

Word Reporter: This student finds seven or eight unfamiliar words or words used in an unfamiliar context in each chapter. Each word is jotted down on a sheet of paper along with the page number on which it appeared. The word reporter also writes down the sentence in which it was used. When the group meets to discuss what they have read, the word reporter shares the words. The group then determines which three or four words need to be shared with the entire class.

Connector: This student makes connections between the book and real life.

Summarizer: This student briefly summarizes the key points of the story.

All Students in Group (Optional): All of the students keep a literature response journal to record the reactions and responses as they read. This may be a shared role.

Clarify Student Roles

The teacher selects a student from each group to read aloud the task description for his *or* her role until all the roles have been shared. After each task description has been read aloud, the teacher invites questions. Each role is clarified before moving on to the next one. Before sending the groups off to read the chapters and then to meet as a group, the teacher emphasizes that the discussion is to involve everyone.

Assign Reading

At this point, students read the assignment, for instance chapters 1 through 3, keeping their roles in mind. As they read, they take notes. If students finish reading the material before others in the group (and someone always finishes quite a bit ahead of the remainder of the group), they jot down possible discussion topics for the group or their own reactions to the material they read.

Groups Meet and Share

The groups meet for at least 15 minutes to talk about what they have read and their responses to the material. While the students are meeting in their groups, the teacher drifts from group to group, noting reactions as well as offering assistance when needed. (See figure 4.2.)

Reconvene the Class and Debrief

The teacher focuses the initial discussion on the content of the material the students have just read. Then, students are encouraged to share their personal reactions and responses to the book. Finally, students discuss the roles they played in their respective groups (Daniels, 1994).

Extension Activities

The teacher assigns extension activities for each group. The following are examples of creative projects:

- Semantic map of the relationships between characters
- Mural
- Clay sculpture
- Illustration
- Diorama
- Audiotape advertisement to promote the book
- Videotape of a readers' theater based on lines from the book
- Play based on a portion of the book
- Written report (particularly if the book is nonfiction)
- Biography of the author's life
- Panel debate
- Letters of correspondence between characters
- Diary of the main character or a supporting character
- Poem based on the events of the book

The timetable below shows how one teacher incorporates literature circles into his class. With older students such as fourth through eighth graders, each group may establish its own timetable to accomplish its goals.

Literature Circle Weekly Timetable

Monday

Read Aloud—Chapter 1	5–10 minutes
Response and Reaction	2 minutes
Share (Teacher Evaluates)	5 minutes
Form Groups	2 minutes
Assign Students Roles	2 minutes
Clarify Student Roles	3 minutes
Assign Reading—Chapters 2–5	1 minute
Reading Time	40 minutes

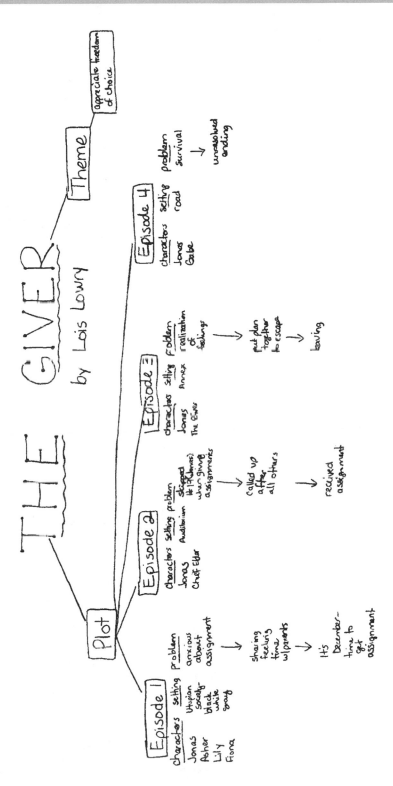

Figure 4.2   Semantic web of *The Giver*. This is part of the culminating project of a literature circle for a group of middle school students.

Tuesday

Groups Meet and Share   20 minutes
Reconvene the Class/Debrief   15 minutes

Wednesday

Assign Students Roles   2 minutes
Clarify Student Roles   3 minutes
Assign Reading—Chapter 6–10 (end of book)   1 minute
Reading Time   30–45 minutes

Thursday

Groups Meet and Share   20 minutes
Reconvene the Class/Debrief   15 minutes

Friday

Extension Activities   50 minutes

Suggestions for Initiating Literature Circles

Perhaps the easiest way to begin incorporating literature circles in the classroom is to use picture books or short stories. On the first day, the teacher reads aloud and then has the class discuss their reactions to the read aloud. Groups and roles are assigned and each role is carefully explained. The students then are given a short story or picture-book reading assignment. As they read, they perform the tasks corresponding to their assigned roles. Then the students meet in groups and share their reactions and responses to what they have read. They also share what they have done to complete the tasks assigned to their roles. The class reconvenes and shares with the teacher, who supervises the final debriefing. The next day, the students stay in the same groups but are given different roles to perform. This process continues until all students have had a chance to serve in each of the different roles.

Marianne Kroll and Ann Paziotopoulos (1991) use literature circles with kindergarten and first-grade students. They modify the literature circle by adding a "quiet voice monitor," a child who is given a red circle to place in the middle of his or her group when the discussion becomes too loud. Students start with wordless picture books and record their reactions by drawing pictures in a notebook. With kindergartners and first graders, the teacher remains with the group throughout the literature circle activity. Thus, only one group is engaged in the literature circle activity at a time. The other students are working at other activities, such as math, science, computers, and art.

When Kroll and Paziotopoulos perform a read aloud, they select from one of several bookmarks they have made. For example, they use bookmarks labeled "magic" for *Cinderella*. Later, when the students read in their groups, they put a magic bookmark at the places in the story where the fairy godmother uses magic.

At the kindergarten and first-grade level it is important to assign each group a different book so that children learn about four or five different books during the class sharing and debriefing stage. This helps keep the attention level high during class discussion time. Copies of all the books shared are available for the children to read or to take home for their parents to read to them. Some teachers find that recording the books and placing the books and audiotapes in the listening center after the class discussion is an effective way to motivate students to read.

In using literature circles at the middle school level, Jill Scott (1994), a middle school teacher, found that to begin with modest hopes is the best route. By starting with short stories and moving gradually to novels, students aren't overwhelmed by the tasks and are more willing to become involved in their group's discussion. At first, students tend to be somewhat reserved as they attempt to figure out exactly what is expected of them as part of the literature circle activity. After two or three times through literature circles, the students become more confident and take charge of their own learning.

Suggested Children's Literature for Literature Circles—Grades 3–8
Avi. (1991). *Nothing but the truth*. New York: Avon. (6–8)
Bauer, M. D. (1986). *On my honor*. Boston: Houghton Mifflin. (6–8)
Bauer, M. D. (1994). *A question of trust*. Boston: Houghton Mifflin. (3–5)
Crowe, C. (2002). *Mississippi trial, 1955*. New York: Phyllis Fogelman Books. (6–8)
Hahn, M. D. (1991). *Stepping on the cracks*. New York: Avon. (3–5)
Hesse, K. (1998). *Just juice*. New York: Scholastic. (3–5)
Holcomb, J. K. (1998). *The Chinquapin tree*. Tarrytown, NY: Cavenish. (5–7)
Lowry, L. (1993). *The giver*. Boston: Houghton Mifflin. (6–8).
MacLachlan, P. (1985). *Sarah, plain and tall*. New York: Harper & Row. (3–4)
Myers, W. D. (1996). *Slam!* New York: Scholastic. (6–8)
Park, L. S. (2001). *A single shard*. New York: Clarion. (6–8)
Taylor, M. (1990). *Mississippi bridge*. New York: Bantam. (3–4)
Warner, S. (1998). *Sort of forever*. New York: Knopf. (5–7)

Literature Response Journals

As more and more teachers attempt to incorporate literature into the elementary curriculum, children are increasingly being asked to respond to literature through writing and discussion. The literature response journal enables a child to write down his or her own feelings, thoughts, predictions, hunches, and reactions while reading a piece of literature. "Teaching students to respond strongly to text requires not only that they have opportunities to respond freely, but also that they be guided to a greater insight and appreciation of literary works and literature as a whole" (Wyshynski & Paulsen, 1995, p. 260). As Hancock (1992, p. 38) writes, "Although a traditional book report may reveal final interpretation of text, the literature response journal reflects the thought process on the mental journey to that final conclusion."

In the journal, a notebook kept solely for the purpose of responding to literature, the student jots down her notation and the page number of the book that provokes the notation. The teacher routinely reads each child's literature response journal, writing positive comments and thought-provoking, open-ended questions to the child. Only the child and the teacher share the journal. In short, "written response establishes the permanence of the reader's passing ideas, enabling him or her to revisit and build from them through continual growth in the understanding of and appreciation for literature" (Hancock, 2004, p. 211).

Rather than requiring students to provide a summary and critique of what they read—as was the case with a traditional book report—the literature response journal allows students the freedom to interact with the author and/or characters. As the children read, they gather information and make predictions that turn out to be either correct or incorrect. Then they formulate new predictions as they gain additional information in a meaning-making process. Langer (1990) refers to this as "envisionment building"; children's understanding changes and expands as they progress through a piece of literature and, after they have completed it, as they contemplate it and discuss it with others. Thus, envisionments are "a function of one's personal and cultural experiences, one's relationship to the current experience, what one knows, how one feels, and what one is after. . . . Each envisionment includes what the individual does and does not understand" (Langer, 1995, p. 9).

The following four guidelines for assisting children in envisionment building as they write in their literature response journals have been adapted from Langer (1990, p. 815):

1. **Initial understandings.** Begin with a question that encourages the children to respond to the story.

2. **Developing understandings.** Ask questions that help the students move beyond their initial understandings in ways that are meaningful to them. Such questions should strive to elicit deeper responses from the students, guiding them toward an exploration of motivation, cause and effect, implication, and so on.

3. **Reflecting on personal experiences.** Ask questions that help the students to relate what they are reading to their own knowledge and/or personal experiences—for example, to other books they have read or real-life experiences they have had.

4. **Elaborating and extending.** After the children have worked through their own understandings, encourage them to critique what they have read. Encourage them to analyze and evaluate it and also to compare it with other works that are similar in nature or perhaps by the same author. The students can also apply literary elements at this point.

Donna Werderich's pie chart (figure 4.3 on p. 177) summarizes ways to prompt students to do literature responses. Literature response journals are being used with preschoolers as young as age four. The children listen to the teacher or a parent read a story and then they draw their responses (Danielson, 1992). These children will continue to include their own illustrations in their literature response journals, along with their written responses, through middle childhood.

Response Facilitators

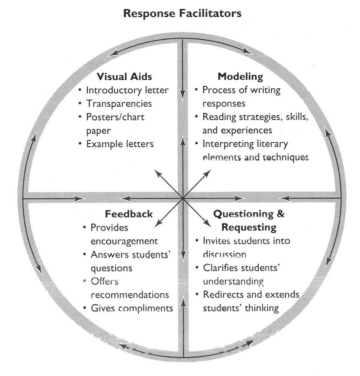

Donna E. Werderich. (2004). Unpublished doctoral dissertation. Northern Illinois University. Used by permission. (Figure graphic was designed by Leonard Walther.)

Figure 4.3 Response facilitators

After teachers introduce students to literature response journals, parents can become involved. Carol Fuhler (1994), a middle school teacher, and Katie Howe, an elementary teacher, invited parents of their students to keep their own literature response journals as they read the same novels as their children. Each evening the parents and their children shared their reactions with each other in the comfort of their own homes, building good connections between school and home.

Book Talks

"This book is the best ever!" "What an awesome book!" "I wish the book went on forever!" Statements such as these from students spur on peers to read—and relish—the same titles. But what about the books never taken off the shelf? Teachers have to roll up their sleeves and hone their marketing tools as they promote the reading of quality literature. Called by some the "blessing" of the books, teachers subtly endorse books by doing a variety of things. Sharing the first couple of chapters of a book as a read aloud and then declaring an inadequate amount of time to finish it before a holiday break but having a half a dozen copies available for those students who want to check it out while school is not in session is effective. So is the technique of reading the entire book to the class (one day for a picture book; several days for a novel or more difficult informational book) and then leaving a copy in the reading center for students to peruse. Putting ten titles from various genres each week into a picnic basket and then sharing them briefly on a Monday morning works wonderfully too. The following pointers will be helpful:

- Read the book before you try to promote it. Otherwise it will come off phony, like a vegetarian promoting the Atkins diet. If you don't have time to read every word, skim through it or go to the "Booktalks" Web site of previously prepared booktalks created by classroom teachers *www.nancykeane.com/booktalks*. Keep in mind that you set the tone for book talks.

- Be theatrical! Prepare an entrance that students will recall years later. Nancy Leifheit, a fifth grade teacher, wore earmuffs and rollerblades as she whizzed in with a basket of books and chocolate chip cookies. The topic of the books she shared? Why inventions of course! Go to garage sales and pick up items. A fish shower curtain, a few seashells, and a Hawaiian shirt completes an ocean theme. An adventure theme can be decking out in a hiker's vest, jeans, and hiking boots. An old choir robe accompanied by a wand and a cone-shaped hat made out of poster board transforms you into the "book wizard" (Farris, Fuhler, & Walther, 2004).

- Have the book in hand when you share it. Wave it around for all the students to see. Better yet, have an extra copy or two in the reading center.

- If there is an intriguing or interesting part at the beginning of the book, tag it with a sticky note and read it aloud. Don't read too much though—just enough to pique students' curiosity.

- Select one aspect to highlight—the main character, an exciting scene, an interesting discovery or fact (in case of an informational book), or a humorous incident.

- Brevity is the key to book talks. If you are sharing several books at one time, five or six sentences per book will suffice.

Summary

Children's literature should be a central part of the language arts curriculum. By sharing and discussing quality literature, children learn to *appreciate* and *enjoy* reading—two essential elements to becoming lifelong readers.

By understanding the literary elements of characterization, plot, setting, theme, and author's style, children discover the different components of literature and learn to appreciate more fully the value of reading books. Exposure to the various literary genres widens a child's knowledge base through vicarious experiences and often leads to new-found reading.

The use of thematic units in children's literature enables children to gain increased knowledge in specific topics and areas. Because children's literature offers several choices of how information is presented, children often are more eager and motivated to read books than textbooks in a content area.

Literature circles promote reading, discussion, and cooperation among students. Literature response journals help children in the meaning-making process as they relate their previous knowledge and experiences to what they are presently reading. In addition, they may use the information presented in a book to make predictions about what may take place later in the book. Finally, as they reflect on what they have read, the students may analyze and evaluate the work as they compare it with other works they have read.

Questions

1. Define the five literary elements of children's literature.
2. Why is it important for children to be exposed to a variety of genres?
3. How can children's literature add to the teaching of content-area material?
4. How does traditional literature differ from contemporary realistic fiction?
5. Select a grade level and describe how you would establish a literature circle "grand conversation."

Reflective Teaching

Flip back to the beginning of the chapter to the teaching vignette entitled "Peering into the Classroom." After rereading the vignette, consider the following questions: What characteristics (either implied or directly exhibited) does the teacher possess that you would like to develop? What strengths and weaknesses are revealed for the students described in this section? How would you meet the needs of students such as these?

Activities

1. Select a contemporary realistic fiction book that you read as a child. Reread it and think about your reaction to it today as compared with your reaction when you first read it.
2. Select a book that has won a Newbery Medal. Read it and consider the book's literary elements as you do so.
3. Prepare a thematic unit for a particular grade level.
4. Spend a morning or afternoon in the children's section of the public library. Observe how children select books, how they interact with their parents in discussing their selections, and what kinds of questions they ask the children's librarian.

Further Reading

Kaser, S. & Short, K. (1998). Exploring culture through children's connections. *Language Arts, 75* (3), 185–192.

Martinez-Roldan, C. M., & López-Robertson, J. M. (2000). Initiating literature circles in a first-grade bilingual classroom. *The Reading Teacher, 53* (4), 270–281.

Smith-D'Arezzo, W. (2003). Diversity in children's literature: Not just a black and white issue. *Children's Literature in Education, 34* (1), 75–94.

Tiedt, I. (2002). *Tiger lilies, toadstools, and thunderbolts: Engaging K–8 students with poetry.* Newark, DE: International Reading Association.

Young, T. (2004). *Happily ever after: Sharing folk literature with elementary and middle school students.* Newark, DE: International Reading Association.

References

Adams, M. J. (1990). *Beginning to read: Thinking and learning about print.* Urbana: University of Illinois, Center for the Study of Reading.

Bieger, E. M. (1996). Promoting multicultural education through a literature-based approach. *The Reading Teacher, 49* (4), 308–313.

Billig, E. (1977). Children's literature as a springboard to content areas. *The Reading, Teacher, 30* (6), 855–858.

Bishop, R. S. (1992). Multicultural literature for children: Making informed choices. In V. Harris (Ed.), *Teaching multicultural literature* (pp. 37–54). Norwood, MA: Christopher Gordon.

Brozo, W. (2002). *To be a boy, to be a reader: Engaging teen and preteen boys in active literacy.* Newark, DE: International Reading Association.

Chomsky, C. (1972). Stages in language development and reading exposure. *Harvard Educational Review, 42* (1), 1–33.

Cullinan, B. (1987). Inviting readers to literature. In B. Cullinan (Ed.), *Children's literature in the reading program.* Newark, DE: International Reading Association.

Cullinan, B., & Galda, L. (2003). *Literature and the child* (5th ed.). Orlando, FL: Harcourt Brace.

Daniels, H. (1994). *Literature circles: Voice and choice in the student-centered classroom.* York, ME: Stenhouse.

Danielson, K. E. (1992). Learning about early writing from response to literature. *Language Arts, 69* (4), 274–280.

Elley, W. B. (1989). Vocabulary acquisition from listening to stories. *Reading Research Quarterly, 24* (2), 174–187.

Farris, P. J., Fuhler, C. J., & Walther, M. (2004). *Teaching reading: A balanced approach for today's classrooms.* Boston: McGraw-Hill.

Fuhler, C. (1994). Response journals: Just one more time with feeling. *Journal of Reading, 37,* 400–408.

Hancock, M. R. (1992). Literature response journals: Insights, beyond the printed page. *Language Arts, 69* (1), 36–42.

Hancock, M. R. (2004). *A celebration of literature and response* (2nd ed.). Upper Saddle River, NJ: Prentice Hall.

Honig, B. (1988). The California reading initiative. *The New Advocate, 1* (4), 235–240.

Huck, C. (1996). Literature-based reading programs: A retrospective. *The New Advocate, 9* (1), 23–34.

Kaser, S., & Short, K. (1998). Exploring culture through children's connections. *Language Arts, 75* (3), 185–192.

Kroll, M., & Paziotopoulos, A. (1991). *Literature circles: Practical ideas and strategies for responding to literature.* Portsmouth, NH: Heinemann.

Langer, J. (1990). Understanding literature. *Language Arts, 67* (8), 812–816.

Langer, J. A. (1995). *Envisioning literature: Literary understanding and literature instruction.* New York: Teacher's College.

Martinez-Roldan, C. M., & López-Robertson, J. M. (2000). Initiating literature circles in a first-grade bilingual classroom. *The Reading Teacher, 53* (4), 270–281.

Microsoft. (1998). *Dinosaurs* (CD-Rom). Seattle, WA: Microsoft.

Norton, D. (1990). Teaching multicultural literature in the reading curriculum. *The Reading Teacher, 44* (1), 28–40.

Peterson, R., & Eeds, M. (1990). *Grand conversations: Literacy groups in action.* Richmond Hill, Ontario, Canada: Scholastic.

Roser, N. L., Hoffman, J. V., & Farest, C. (1990). Language, literature, and at-risk children. *The Reading Teacher, 43* (8), 554–559.

Scott, J. (1994). Literature circles in the middle school. *Middle School Journal, 26* (2), 37–41.

Short, K. (1995). Foreword. In B. Campbell Hill, N. J. Johnson, & K. L. Schlick Noe (Eds.), *Literature circles and response* (pp. ix–xii). Norwood, MA: Christopher-Gordon.

Short, K. (1997). *Literature as a way of knowing.* York, ME: Stenhouse.

Steiner, S., & Steiner, J. (1999). Navigating the road to literacy. *Book Links, 8* (4), 19–24.

Stotsky, S. (1992). Whose literature? America's! *Educational Leadership, 49* (4), 53–56.

Sutherland, Z., & Hearne, B. (1984). In search of the perfect picture book. In P. Barron & J. Burley (Eds.), *Jump over the moon.* New York: Holt, Rinehart, & Winston.

Taylor, D., & Dorsey-Gaines, C. (1988). *Growing Up literature: Learning from inner-city families.* Portsmouth, NH: Heinemann.

Teale, W., & Sulzby, E. (Eds.). (1985). *Emergent literacy: Writing and reading.* Norwood, NJ: Ablex.

Wyshynski, R., & Paulsen, D. (1995). Maybe I will do something: Lessons from coyote. *Language Arts, 72* (4), 258–264.

Yenika-Agbaw, V. (1997). Taking children's literature seriously: Reading for pleasure and social change. *Language Arts, 74* (6), 446–453.

Children's Literature

Aardema, V. (1975). *Why mosquitoes buzz in people's ears* (L. Dillon & D. Dillon, Illus.). New York: Dial.

Adler, D. A. (1998). *Shape up: Fun with triangles and other polygons* (N. Tobin, Illus.). New York: Holiday.

Adoff, A. (1986). *Sports pages* (R. Kuzma, Illus.). Philadelphia: Lippincott.

Alarcón, F. X. (1997). *Laughing tomatoes and other spring poems/Jitomates risueños y otros poemas de primavera* (M. C. Gonzalez, Illus.). San Francisco: Children's Book Press.

Alexander, L. (1992). *The fortune-tellers.* New York: Philomel.

Andrews-Goebel, N. (2002). *The pot that Juan built* (D. Diaz, Illus.). New York: Lee & Low.

Armstrong, J. (1998). *Shipwreck at the bottom of the world.* New York: Crown.

Arnosky, J. (2000). *A manatee morning.* New York: Simon & Schuster.

Beatty, P. (1981). *Lupita mañana.* New York: Morrow.

Bierhorst, J. (2002). *Is my friend at home? Pueblo fireside tales* (W. Lamb, Illus.). New York: Farrar, Straus, & Giroux.

Blumberg, R. (1989). *The great American gold rush.* New York: Bradbury.

Blume, J. (1970). *Are you there God, It's me Margaret.* New York: Bradbury.

Blume, J. (1972). *Tales of a fourth grade nothing* (R. Doty, Illus.). New York: Dutton.

Blume, J. (1973). *Deenie.* New York: Bradbury.

Bober, N. S. (1995). *Abigail Adams: Witness to a revolution.* New York: Atheneum.

Brett, J. (1990). *The mitten: A Ukrainian folktale.* New York: Putnam.

Bridges, R. (1999). *Through my eyes.* New York: Scholastic.

Bunting, E. (1989). *The Wednesday surprise* (D. Carrick, Illus.). New York: Clarion.

Byars, B. (1980). *The night swimmers* (T. Howell, Illus.). New York: Delacorte.

Byars, B. (1981). *The Cybil war* (G. Owens, Illus.). New York: Viking.

Cameron, A. (1988). *The most beautiful place in the world* (T. B. Allen, Illus.). New York: Knopf.

Carbone, E. (1998). *Starting school with an enemy.* New York: Knopf.

Carle, E. (1969). *The very hungry caterpillar.* New York: Philomel.

Carle, E. (1997). *From head to toe.* New York: HarperCollins.

Carle, E. (2003). *Slowly, slowly, said the sloth.* New York: HarperCollins.

Carlstrom, N. W. (1986). *Jesse Bear, what will you wear?* (B. Degan, Illus.). New York: Macmillan.

Cherry, L. (1990). *The great kapok tree.* San Diego: Gulliver/HBJ.

Cleary, B. (1968). *Ramona the pest* (L. Darling, Illus.). New York: Morrow.

Cleary, B. (1983). *Dear Mr. Henshaw* (P. O. Zelinsky, Illus.). New York: Morrow.

Cleary, B. (1988). *A girl from Yamhill, a memoir.* New York: Dell.

Cleary, B. (1991). *Strider* (P. O. Zelinsky, Illus.). New York: Morrow.

Cleary, B. (1999). *Ramona's world* (A. Tiegreen, Illus.). New York: Morrow.

Cleaver, V., & Cleaver, B. (1969). *Where the lilies bloom* (J. Spanfeller, Illus.). Philadelphia: Lippincott.

Cleaver, V., & Cleaver, B. (1971). *I would rather be a turnip.* Philadelphia: Lippincott.

Clinton, C. (1999). *I, too, sing America: Three centuries of African American poetry* (S. Alcorn, Illus.). New York: Scholastic.

Conrad, P. (1987). *Prairie songs* (D.S. Zudeck, Illus.). New York: Harper & Row.

Cowing, S. (1989). *Searches in the American desert.* New York: McElderry.

Creech, S. (1994). *Walk Two Moons.* New York: HarperCollins.

Creech, S. (1998). *Chasing redbird.* New York: HarperCollins.

Cronin, D. (2000). *Click, clack, moo: Cows that type* (B. Lewin, Illus.). New York: Simon & Schuster.

Cronin, D. (2002). *Giggle, giggle, quack* (B. Lewin, Illus.). New York: Simon & Schuster.

Cronin, D. (2003). *Duck for president* (B. Lewin, Illus.). New York: Simon & Schuster.

Dahl, R. (1984). *Boy: Tales of childhood.* New York: Puffin.

Day, A. (1985). *Good dog, Carl.* New York: Farrar, Straus, & Giroux.

Delacre, L. (1989). *Arroz con leche: Popular songs and rhymes from Latin America.* New York: Scholastic.

Denim, S. (1994). *The dumb bunnies* (D. Pilkey, Illus.). New York: Blue Sky.

dePaola, T. (1975). *Strega Nona.* New York: Simon & Schuster.

dePaola, T. (Reteller). (1988). *The legend of the Indian paintbrush.* New York: Putnam.

dePaola, T. (1989). *The art lesson.* New York: Putnam.

Dewey, J. (1989). *Can you find me? A book about animal camouflage.* New York: Scholastic.

DiCamillo, K. (2000). *Because of Winn-Dixie.* Cambridge, MA: Candlewick

Dunphy, M. (1994). *Here is the tropical rainforest* (M. Rothman, Illus.). New York: Hyperion.

Dygard, T. J. (1978). *Winning kicker.* New York: Morrow.

Ehlert, L. (1989). *Color zoo.* New York: HarperCollins.

Ehlert, L. (1989). *Eating the alphabet.* San Diego: Harcourt

Ehlert, L. (1990). *Fish eyes: A book you can count on.* New York: HarperCollins.

Epstein, S., & Epstein, B. (1989). *Bugs for dinner? The eating habits of neighborhood creatures.* New York: Macmillan.

Fleischman, P. (1988). *Joyful noise: Poems for two voices.* New York: Harper & Row.

Fleischman, P. (1996). *Dateline: Troy.* New York: HarperCollins.

Fleming, D. (1993). *In the small, small, pond.* New York: Henry Holt.

Fleming, D. (1994). *Barnyard banter.* New York: Henry Holt.

Fox, M. (1985). *Wilfrid Gordon McDonald Partridge* (J. Vivas, Illus.). San Diego: Harcourt.

Fox, M. (1988). *Koala Lou* (J. Devas, Illus.). San Diego: Harcourt Brace.

Freedman, R. (1987). *Lincoln: A photobiography.* New York: Clarion.

Freedman, R. (1991). *The Wright brothers: How they invented the airplane* (W. & O. Wright, Photo.). New York: Holiday.

Fritz, J. (1982). *Homesick: My own story.* New York: Putnam.

Gantos, J. (2000). *Joey Pigza loses control.* New York: Farrar, Strauss, & Giroux.

Geisert, B., & Geisert, A. (1998). *Prairie town.* Boston: Houghton Mifflin.

George, J. C. (1959). *My side of the mountain.* New York: Dutton.

George, J. C. (1972). *Julie of the wolves* (J. Schoenherr, Illus.). New York: HarperCollins.

George, J. C. (1979). *River Rats, Inc.* New York: Dutton.

George, J. C. (1989). *Shark beneath the reef.* New York: Harper & Row.

George, W. T. (1989). *Box turtle at Long Pond* (L. B. George, Illus.). New York: Greenwillow.

Gibbons, G. (1994). *St. Patrick's Day.* New York: Morrow.

Gibbons, G. (1997). *The honey makers.* New York: Morrow.

Gibbons, G. (1998). *Soaring with the wind. The bald eagle.* New York: Morrow.

Gollub, M. (1998). *Cool melons turn to frogs: The life and poems of Issa* (K. G. Stone, Illus.). New York: Lee & Low.

Green, N. (1974). *The hole in the dike* (E. Carle, Illus.). New York: Crowell.

Hamilton, V. (1992). *Drylongso* (J. Pinkney, Illus.). San Diego: Harcourt Brace

Henkes, K. (1993). *Owen.* New York: Greenwillow.

Henkes, K. (1996). *Lilly's purple plastic purse.* New York: Greenwillow.

Hesse, K. (1997). *Out of the dust.* New York: Holt.

Hill, E. (1980). *Where's Spot?* New York: Putnam.

Hindley, J. (2002). *Do like a duck does* (I. Bates, Illus.). Boston: Candlewick.

Hobbs, W. (1989). *Bearstone.* New York: Atheneum.

Hobbs, W. (1997). *Ghost canoe.* New York: Atheneum.

Hoberman, M. A. (1978). *A house is a house for me* (B. Fraser, Illus.). New York: Viking.

Hoberman, M. A. (2003). *You read to me, I'll read to you: Very short fairy tales to read together* (M. Emberley, Illus.). New York: Little, Brown.

Hoffman, M. (1991). *Amazing Grace* (C. Binch, Illus.). New York: Dial.

Holman, F. (1986). *Slake's limbo.* New York: Dell.

Horvath, P. (2001). *Everything on a waffle.* New York: Farrar, Straus & Giroux.

Hutchins, P. (1968). *Rosie's walk.* New York: Greenwillow.

Hughes, T. (1985). *The iron giant.* New York: Harper & Row.

Isadora, R. (1998). *Young Mozart.* New York: Viking.

Jackson, E. (1994). *Cinder Edna* (K. O'Malley, Illus.). New York: Lothrop, Lee, & Shepard.

Jacobs, W. J. (1990). *Ellis Island: New hope in a new land.* New York: Macmillan/Scribner's.

Jacobs, W. J. (1991). *Mother Teresa: Helping the poor.* New York: Millbrook.

Kellogg, S. (1986). *Best friends.* New York: Dial.

Kellogg, S. (1988). *Johnny Appleseed.* New York: Morrow.

Kendall, C. (1959). *The Gammage Cup* (E. Blegvad, Illus.). New York: Harcourt Brace Jovanovich.

Kennedy, X. J. (1985). *The forgetful wishing well: Poems for young children*. New York: Atheneum.

Kirk, D. (1994). *Miss Spider's tea party*. New York: Scholastic.

Kraus, R. (1971). *Leo the late bloomer*. New York: Windmill.

Kramer, S. (2001). *Hidden worlds: Looking through a scientist's microscope* (D. Kunkel, Photographer). Boston: Houghton Mifflin.

Kurlansky, M. (2001). *The cod's tale* (S. D. Schindler, Illus.). New York: Penguin Putnam.

Lansky, B. (Ed.). (1995). *A bad case of the giggles* (S. Carpenter, Illus.). New York: Meadowbrook.

Lauber, P. (1990). *Seeing the earth from Space*. New York: Orchard.

Lawson, J. (1998). *Emma and the silk train* (P. Mombourquette, Illus.). Buffalo, NY: Kids Can Press.

Leedy, L. (1994). *Fraction action*. New York: Holiday House.

Leslie, C. W. (1991). *Nature all year long*. New York: Greenwillow.

Lester, H. (1994). *Three cheers for Tacky*. Boston: Houghton Mifflin.

Lester, J. (1989). *How many spots does a leopard have? And other tales* (D. Shannon, Illus.). New York: Scholastic.

Levinson, R. (1988). *Our home is the sea* (D. Luzak, Illus.). New York: Dutton.

Lewis, C. S. (1950). *The lion, the witch, and the wardrobe* (P. Baynes, Illus.). New York: Macmillan.

Lewis, J. P. (1991). *Earth verses and water rhymes* (R. Sabuda, Illus.). New York: Atheneum.

Littlesugar, A. (1998). *Shake rag: From the life of Elvis Presley* (F. Cooper, Illus.). New York: Philomel.

Livingston, M. C. (1984). *Sky songs*. New York: Holiday.

Livingston, M. C. (1989). *Up in the air* (L. E. Fisher, Illus.). New York: Holiday.

Llewellyn, C. (1998). *The best book of bugs*. New York: Kingfisher.

London, J. (2001). *Crocodile: Disappearing dragon* (P. Morin, Illus.). Boston: Candlewick.

Lowry, L. (1989). *Number the stars*. Boston: Houghton Mifflin.

Lowry, L. (1993). *The giver*. Boston: Houghton Mifflin.

Lyon, G. E. (1992). *Who came down that road?* (P. Catalano, Illus.). New York: Orchard.

Macaulay, D. (2003). *Mosque*. Boston: Houghton Mifflin.

Martin, B., Jr. (1964; 1983). *Brown bear, brown bear, what do you see?* (E. Carle, Illus.). New York: Holt, Rinehart, & Winston.

Martin, B., Jr. (2003). *Panda bear, panda bear, what do you see?* (E. Carle, Illus.). New York: Henry Holt.

Martin, B., &. Archambault, J. (1989). *Chicka chicka boom boom* (L. Ehlert, Illus.). New York: Simon & Schuster.

Martin, J. B. (1998). *Snowflake Bentley* (M. Azarian, Illus.). Boston: Houghton Mifflin.

Mayer, M. (197 1). *A boy, a dog, and a frog*. New York: Dial.

McGrath, B. B. (1994). *The M&M's counting book*. Watertown, MA: Charlesbridge.

McKissack, P. (1988). *Mirandy and Brother Wind* (J. Pinkney, Illus.). New York: Knopf.

McKissack, P., & McKissack, F. (1994). *Christmas in the big house, Christmas in the quarters* (J. Thompson, Illus.). New York: Scholastic.

Meltzer, M. (1990). *Brother can you spare a dime?* New York: Facts on File.

Micucci, C. (1992). *The life and times of the apple*. New York: Scholastic.

Mora, P. (1994). *Listen to the Desert/Oye al desierto* (F. Mora, Illus.). Boston: Clarion.

Morimoto, J. (1990). *My Hiroshima*. New York: Viking.

Murphy, J. (1993). *Across America on an immigrant train*. New York: Clarion.

Murphy, J. (1995). *The great fire*. New York: Scholastic.

Naylor, P. R. (1991). *Shiloh*. New York: Dell.

Nelson, V. M. (1988). *Always Grandma* (K. Uhler, Illus.). New York: Putnam.

O'Dell, S. (1960). *Island of the blue dolphins.* Boston. Houghton Mifflin.

Orozco, J. L. (1997). *Diet deditos* (E. Kleven, Illus.). New York: Dutton.

Osband, G. (1991). *Castles* (R. Andrew, Illus.). New York: Orchard.

Paterson, K. (1977). *Bridge to Terabithia.* New York: Harper & Row.

Paterson, K. (1994). *Flip flop girl.* New York: Harper Collins

Paulsen, G. (1987). *Hatchet.* New York: Viking.

Peck, R. (1998). *A long way from Chicago.* New York Dial.

Pilkey, D. (1990). *'Twas the night before Thanksgiving.* New York: Orchard.

Pinkney, G. (1992). *Back home* (J. Pinkney, Illus.). New York: Dial.

Polacco, P. (1993). *The bee tree.* New York: Philomel.

Polacco, P. (1994). *Pink and Say.* New York: Philomel.

Prelutsky, J. (1984). *The new kid on the block* (J. Stevenson, Illus.). New York: Greenwillow.

Prelutsky, J. (1988). *Tyrannosaurus was a beast.* New York: Greenwillow.

Prelutsky, J. (1990). *Something big has been here* (J. Stevenson, Illus.). New York: Greenwillow.

Prelutsky, J. (1991). *Poems of A. Nonny Mouse* (H. Drescher, Illus.). New York: Dragonfly.

Prelutsky, J. (ed.) (1994). *The 20th century children's poetry treasury* (M. So, Illus.). New York: Knopf.

Prelutsky, J. (1997). *The beauty of the beast* (M. So, Illus.). New York: Knopf.

Ritter, J. (1998). *Choosing up sides.* Honesdale, PA: Boyd's Mill.

Robbins, K. (2002). *Apples.* New York: Atheneum.

Rockwell, A. (2002). *Becoming butterflies* (M. Halsey, Illus.). Aurora, IL: Walker.

Rowling, J. K. (1998). *Harry Potter and the sorcerer's stone.* New York: Scholastic.

Rowling, J. K. (1999). *Harry Potter and the chamber of secrets.* New York: Scholastic.

Rowling, J. K. (1999). *Harry Potter and the prisoner of Azkaban.* New York: Scholastic.

Rowling, J. K. (2002). *Harry Potter and the goblet of fire.* New York: Scholastic.

Rowling, J. K. (2003). *Harry Potter and the order of the phoenix.* New York: Scholastic.

Ryan, P. M. (2000). *Esperanza rising.* New York: Scholastic.

Ryan, P. M. (2002). *When Marian sang* (B. Selznick, Illus.). New York: Scholastic.

Rylant, C. (1993). *Missing May.* New York: Orchard.

Sachar, L. (1998). *Holes.* New York: Farrar, Straus, & Giroux.

Sanders, S. R. (1989). *Aurora means dawn.* New York: Bradbury.

San Souci, R. (1990). *The talking eggs: A folktale from the American south* (J. Pinkney, Illus.). New York: Dial.

Say, A. (1993). *Grandfather's journey.* Boston: Houghton Mifflin.

Scieszka, J. (1989). *The true story of the 3 little pigs* (L. Smith, Illus.). New York: Viking.

Scieszka, J. (1992). *The stinky cheese man: And other fairly stupid tales* (L. Smith, Illus.). New York: Viking.

Scieszka, J. (1995). *Math curse* (L. Smith, Illus.). New York: Viking.

Scieszka, J., & Smith, L. (1998). *Squids will be squids* (L. Smith. Illus.). New York: Viking.

Sendak, M. (1963). *Where the wild things are.* New York: Harper & Row.

Sendak, M. (T. Mlawer, trans.). (1963/1999). *Donde viven los monstruos.* New York: Scholastic.

Shaw, N. (1986). *Sheep in a jeep.* Boston: Houghton Mifflin.

Silverman, E. (1994). *Don't fidget a feather* (S. D. Schindler, Illus.). New York: Macmillan.

Silverstein, S. (1974). *Where the sidewalk ends.* New York: Harper & Row.

Sis, P. (1991). *Follow the dream: The story of Christopher Columbus.* New York: Knopf.

Sneve, V. D. H. (1989). *Dancing teepees: Poems of American Indian youth* (S. Gammell, Illus.). New York: Holiday.

Spinelli, E. (2004). *In our backyard garden* (M. Ramsey, Illus.). New York: Simon & Schuster.

Spinelli, J. (1990). *Maniac Magee*. New York: Little, Brown.

Spinelli, J. (1997). *Wringer*. New York: HarperCollins.

Spinelli, J. (2002). *Loser*. New York: Joanna Colter Books.

Stanley, D. (1996). *Leonardo da Vinci*. New York: Morrow.

Stanley, D. (1998). *Joan of Arc*. New York: Morrow.

Steig, W. (1998). *Pete's a pizza*. New York: HarperCollins.

Stevens, J. (1995). *Tops and bottoms*. San Diego: Harcourt Brace.

Taylor, M. (1995). *The well*. New York: Dial.

Taylor, T. (1969). *The cay*. New York: Doubleday.

Taylor, T. (1981). *The trouble with Tuck*. New York: Doubleday.

Tessendorf, K. C. (1989). *Along the road to Soweto: A racial history of South Africa*. New York: Atheneum.

Towle, W. (1993). *The real McCoy: The life of an African-American inventor* (W. Clay, Illus.). New York: Scholastic.

Van Allsburg, C. (1981). *Jumanji*. Boston: Houghton Mifflin.

Van Allsburg, C. (1985). *The polar express*. Boston: Houghton Mifflin.

Van Leeuwen, J. (1998). *A Fourth of July on the plains* (H. Sorensen, Illus.). New York: Dial.

Waber, B. (1972). *Ira sleeps over*. Boston: Houghton Mifflin.

Warren, A. (2002). *Surviving Hitler: A boy in the death camps*. New York: HarperCollins.

Waters, K. (1989). *Sarah Morton's day: A day in the life of a Pilgrim girl* (R. Kendall, Photo.). New York: Scholastic.

White, E. B. (1952). *Charlotte's web* (G. Williams, Illus.). New York: Harper & Row.

Whybrow, I. (1991). *Quacky, quack-quack!* (R. Ayto, Illus.). New York: Four Winds.

Wick, W. (1997). *A drop of water*. New York: Scholastic.

Wiesner, D. (1991). *Tuesday*. New York: Clarion.

Wilson, K. (2004). *Hilda must be dancing* (S. Watts, Illus.). New York: McElderry.

Winter, J. (1988). *Follow the drinking gourd*. New York: Knopf.

Wise, W. (1993). *Ten sly piranhas* (V. Chess, Illus.). New York: Dial.

Wisniewski, D. (1991). *Rain player*. New York: Clarion.

Wood, D., & Wood, A. (1984). *The little mouse, the red ripe strawberry, and the big hungry bear*. New York: Child's Play International.

Yarbrough, C. (1989). *The shimmershine queens*. New York: Putnam.

Yep, L. (1989). *The rainbow people* (D. Weisner, Illus.). New York: Harper & Row.

Yep, L. (1994). *Dragon's gate*. New York: Putnam.

Yolen, J. (1987). *Owl moon* (J. Schoenherr, Illus.). New York: Philomel.

Yolen, J. (1991). *Wings* (D. Nolan, Illus.). Orlando, FL: Harcourt Brace Jovanovich.

Young, E. (1989). *Lon Po Po*. New York: Philomel.

Young, E. (1992). *Seven blind mice*. New York: Philomel.

Ziefert, H. (1998). *When I first came to this land* (S. Taback, Illus.). New York: Putnam.

Web Sites

www.ala.org/alsc (American Library Association)

> This site includes the home pages for the Caldecott Medal (for the best illustrated U.S. picture book) and the Newbery Medal (for the most distinguished contribution to children's literature). In addition, the home pages for the Coretta Scott King Award (one given annually to an African American author and another to an African American illustrator for outstanding and inspirational contributions to children's and young adult's literature) and the biennial Pura Belpé Award (for the

Latino/Latina writer and illustrator whose work best affirms, celebrates, and portrays the Latino cultural experience for children and young adults) are located on this site.

www.nancykeane.com/booktalks (Booktalks)

This site contains book talks that have been developed by classroom teachers. A real time saver if you haven't got the time to read the books before you present them to your students.

Oral Language
Developing the Base of Expression

> Reading and writing float on a sea of talk.
>
> James Britton
> "Writing and the Story World"

PEERING INTO THE CLASSROOM
TEACHING DIVERSE LEARNERS

First-grade teacher Suzette Abbott understands how to involve in class activities students who are different or speak another language. She, too, was once the student who was the "outsider" when over two decades ago she arrived from South Africa. Although she spoke English, her culture was very different from that of her classmates. Suzette Abbott (Abbott & Grose, 1998) writes, "I have always tried as a teacher to draw into the class those children who are potentially 'outsiders,' to assure that they are not seen as less knowledgeable or capable because they are different or speak another language" (p. 175).

Typically Suzette has children from a wide variety of places—African nations, China, the Caribbean, and Central and South American countries as well as students born in the United States. From the beginning of the school year, Suzette tries to demonstrate an interest in her students by establishing a relationship with their parents. This is particularly important with the parents of English Language Learners (ELLs). Suzette meets them or calls and talks with them on the phone rather than send notes home with the children who may lose them or forget to pass them along. Suzette's primary goal is to show the parents her interest in the children's special qualities, to ease any concerns they may have, and to gather information that may help her in her teaching.

Two aides make Suzette's job somewhat easier. Born in China and educated at Wellesley College in Massachusetts, Mrs. Lu is in her 80s. The other volunteer, Mrs. Lopez, is a parent of one of Suzette's students and arranges her work schedule so she can spend some time each week in the classroom. These two ladies often serve as translators for Suzette and her ELL students as well as work with the students and their emergent writing.

This year there are three English Language Learners. Yen, who is quiet and serious in demeanor, has lived in the United States for two years. He works hard to speak, read, and write English and speaks Mandarin Chinese at home. Newly arrived from China, Ming has a mischievous smile and does not know any English. Both Chinese boys, Yen and Ming, attend Chinese School on Saturdays and both follow the achievements of Yao Ming, their hero on the basketball court. Another new student to the school is Maria, who moved to the United States during the summer from her native Venezuela. She is fluent in Spanish but speaks no English. There are other cultures and languages represented in the class as well. For instance, Anna's mother is Romanian, Andreas is Greek, Estella is Puerto Rican, and Kim's mother is Korean.

In order to make all of her students more comfortable in her classroom, Suzette quickly sets up a schedule and a routine. The room is filled with word cards labeled in English (black ink), Spanish (green ink), and Chinese (blue ink). The colors help her six-year-olds distinguish among languages. Because many Chinese schools now use an alphabetic phonetic approach to teach reading and writing, Suzette keeps in mind that phonics helps Yen and Ming not only in learning English but also in learning to write Chinese. For Ming and Maria, class discussions are trying times as they become frustrated in their attempts to make sense of the English language that their classmates and Suzette are using. Ming even goes so far as to lie down on the floor and tune out the entire conversation. Upon observing this and without any prompting by Suzette, Yen explains to Ming in Chinese what is taking place.

Reading aloud is a daily part of Suzette's teaching. Children are encouraged to look at the many picture books in the classroom. When Suzette finds a picture book written in a bilingual format of English and Spanish, she shares it with the class. Suzette reads in English and Mrs. Lopez in Spanish. Three such books are *Moon Rope* (Ehlert & Prince, 1992), a Peruvian legend, *Vejigante Masquerader* (Delacre, 1993), a story about a Puerto Rican boy who dresses up in costume for the Fiesta during Carnival, and *Margaret and Margarita* (Reiser, 1993), about a girl who speaks English and another who speaks Spanish. Other books with both English and Spanish in a bilingual format are *The Desert Is My Mother/El Desierto es mi Madre, Listen to the Desert/Oye al Desierto,* and *Uno, Dos, Tres: One, Two, Three* by Pat Mora (1994, 1994, 1996). *Jingwei Filling the Sea* (Jiannan, 1991), with Chinese and English texts side by side, was brought in for Suzette and Mrs. Lu to read together to the students.

"Good teaching emerges from the teacher's solid convictions, identification of a goal, and adherence to that goal through the flow of classroom life" (Abbott & Grose, 1998, p. 181). In Suzette's classroom, students understand the purpose of oral and written language. They also learn the way people across cultures use language to communicate meaning to others as well as to make sense of the world around them.

Chapter Objectives

The reader will:

✓ appreciate the contributions of other languages to English.

✓ be able to differentiate between phonology, morphology, syntax, and semantics.

✓ understand the major components of language acquisition.

✓ be able to apply a variety of instructional approaches to meet the needs of special needs students.

✓ be able to apply use-appropriate instructional techniques with second-language acquisition students.

Standards for Professionals

The following Standards will be addressed in this chapter:

Standard 1: Foundational Knowledge and Dispositions

1.1 Demonstrate knowledge of psychological, sociological, and linguistic foundations of reading and writing processes and instruction.

1.2 Demonstrate knowledge of reading research and histories of reading.

1.3 Demonstrate knowledge of language development and reading acquisition and variations related to cultural and linguistic diversity.

1.4 Demonstrate knowledge of the major components of reading (phonemic awareness, word identification and phonics, vocabulary and background knowledge, fluency, comprehension strategies, and motivation) and how they are integrated in fluent reading.

Standard 2: Instructional Strategies and Curriculum Materials

2.1 Use instructional grouping, options (individual, small-group, whole-class, and computer based) as appropriate for accomplishing given purpose.

2.2 Use a wide range of instructional practices, approaches, and methods, including technology-based practices, for learners at differing stages of development and from differing cultural and linguistic backgrounds.

2.3 Use a wide range of curriculum materials in effective reading instruction for learners at different stages of reading and writing development and from differing cultural and linguistic backgrounds.

Standard 3: Assessment, Diagnosis, and Evaluation

3.1 Use a wide range of assessment tools and practices that range from individual and group standardized tests to individual and group informal classroom assessment strategies, including technology-based assessment tools.

3.2 Place students along a developmental continuum and identify students' proficiencies and difficulties.

3.3 Use assessment information to plan, evaluate, and revise effective instruction that meets the needs of all students, including those at different developmental stages and those from differing cultural and linguistic backgrounds.

3.4 Effectively communicate results of assessments to specific individuals (students, parents, caregivers, colleagues, administrators, policy makers, policy officials, community, etc.).

Standard 4: Creating a Literate Environment

4.1 Use students' interests, reading abilities and backgrounds as foundations for the reading and writing program.

4.2 Use a large supply of books, technology-based information, and nonprint materials representing multiple levels, broad interests, and cultural and linguistic backgrounds.

4.3 Model reading and writing enthusiastically as valued lifelong activities.

4.4 Motivate learners to be lifelong readers.

Standard 5: Professional Development

5.1 Display positive dispositions related to reading and the teaching of reading.

5.2 Continue to pursue the development of professional knowledge and dispositions.

5.3 Work with colleagues to observe, evaluate, and provide feedback on each other's practice.

5.4 Participate in, initiate, implement, and evaluate professional development programs.

Introduction

On a chilly winter morning, Tyler, age three, is talking to his mother as he is getting dressed. "Yestermorning when I got up I had pancakes for breakfast. Today I want rooster corn flakes." His mother nods in the affirmative, translating Tyler's "yestermorning" into yesterday morning and "rooster corn flakes" into Kellogg's corn flakes. When she touches his bare leg with her cold hands, Tyler cries out, "Hey, you're colding me!" The acquisition of language enables children to demonstrate their feelings, needs, and desires verbally and to acquire the social skills of our culture.

Although English is the primary language used in schools in the United States, roughly one in four teachers use both English and Spanish during the school day. Throughout the world, English is spoken by about 800 million people, half of whom speak it as their native language. As the most widely spoken and written language, English is the first global language to exist (McCrum et al., 1986). By 2025, 51 million people or 18 percent of the population of the United States, will speak Spanish (Helman, 2004).

In this chapter, the history of the English language, including influences by other cultures and languages, as well as American dialects, is discussed. How children acquire language is also examined.

The Development of English

Like most languages, English has an oral base. English is considered a hybrid language in that it has continuously borrowed words from other languages as a result of trade, wars, and cultural revolutions. English can be broken down into three periods: Old English (600 to 1100), Middle English (1100 to 1500), and Modern English (1500 to today). Approximately one-fourth of all English words used today can be traced to Old English origins.

English is a member of the Indo-European language family, the common source of languages spoken by a third of the world's population (figure 5.1 on p. 194). The Indo-European language family can be broken down into several branches. The Italic branch of the Indo-European family tree, for example, includes French, Italian, Portuguese, and Spanish. The framework for the English language was primarily created by the Celtic and Germanic branches.

The Celts were one of the earliest peoples to migrate to the British Isles. "True British" are those people who are descendants of the Celts. These include the Irish, Scots, and Welsh. When Julius Caesar arrived in the British Isles in 55 BC, Celts met his boat. Other Roman legions followed Julius Caesar to the British Isles, but when the Roman Empire fell in AD 410, the legions left but only after they had made a major mark on the culture and landscape. Their engineering of major roadways linked cities for trade and communication purposes.

The next major invaders of the British Isles were the Angles, Saxons, and Jutes, those Germanic raiders who sailed from Denmark and Germany in AD 449. Like the American Indians in America, the Celts were driven westward by the invaders. The Angles, Saxons, and Jutes terrorized the inhabitants. "The English language arrived in Britain on the point of a sword" (McCrum et al., 1986, p. 60).

Time passed and the Angles and Saxons became an agrarian people. Therefore, the Anglo-Saxons developed terms such as *sheep, shepherd, earth, plough, ox, swine,* and *calf.* Other familiar words, including *laughter, mirth, coat, hat, glove, man, wife, child, here, there, you, the,* and *is,* are also of Anglo-Saxon origin. Indeed, it is almost impossible to write or speak a sentence without including Anglo-Saxon words.

Because the Anglo-Saxons were largely an illiterate people, theirs was an oral culture. Relying on speech and memory, they created poems, shared stories, and sang ballads, all of which helped to perpetuate "Englisc" in "Englaland."

In AD 597, St. Augustine brought Christianity to England, which was predominantly pagan at the time. The building of churches and monasteries led to the improvement of education in England, for the monks taught a wide range of subjects, including arithmetic, poetry, and Latin. From Latin, English has borrowed such words as *angel, cap, beet, cheese, mass, relic, school,* and *wine.* The Anglo-Saxons contributed the words God, heaven, and hell to Christianity.

Scandinavian peoples, the Vikings, were the next to invade England. These Vikings, or Danes as the Anglo-Saxons called them, raided the British Isles in AD 793, plundering the gold and silver of the monasteries. Such raids continued throughout the ninth century, until the Danes were defeated by King Alfred the Great's army in AD 878. Unlike the Celts, whose language had little

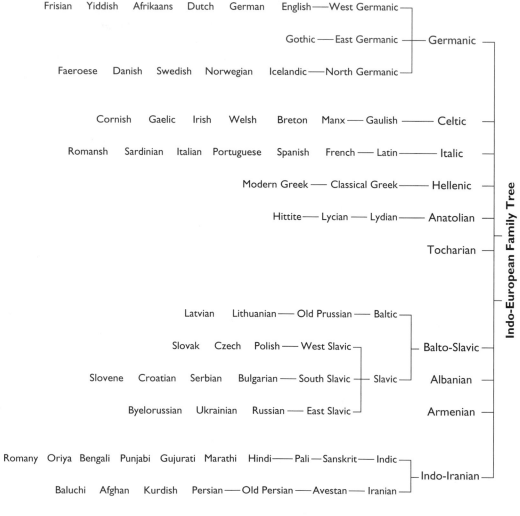

Figure 5.1   English is a member of the Indo-European language family.

influence on English, the Danes contributed nearly a thousand words to the English language. *Hit, birth, leg, knife, daughter, neighbor, slaughter, sky, still, skin, steak,* and *want* are some of the most frequently used Danish terms today. The *kn-* and silent *-gh* came from Danish.

King Alfred the Great was able to unite more of England than any previous ruler. He ordered the monasteries and schools that the Danes had destroyed to be rebuilt. Most important, King Alfred adopted English as the official language of the land, using it to create a sense of identity for the country. As a result, books were translated into English, and King Alfred ordered a history to be written to preserve the common heritage of the English people. Therefore, King Alfred is greatly, if not solely, responsible for saving and preserving the English language.

The next major invasion came in 1066, when the Normans, under the command of William the Conqueror, landed at Hastings. The English royal family and court were destroyed in an ensuing battle, leaving the control of England to the French. Thus, French became the official language of the land and eventually French words such as *attorney, lieutenant, justice, stamp, envelope, felony, colonel, nobility,* and *sovereign* came into the English language.

When the French finally left England in 1244, a majority of the English people still spoke Anglo-Saxon, not having given in to their Norman rulers and adopted French. For example, the people of the villages and farms continued to speak of *calf, ox,* and *swine,* whereas the Normans referred to the same animals as *veal, beef,* and *pork.* Nevertheless, French words still permeate the language of the kitchen: *pâté, sauté, mutton, braise, broil, cuisine, roast, soufflé,* and *croissant.*

After the French returned to France, the English were never again successfully invaded. However, the English language was still pervious to change. Trade, wars, and the discovery of new lands provided it with new words from which to borrow. Englishman William Caxton ventured to Germany to examine the Gutenberg printing press, a remarkable machine that had movable type. So impressed was Caxton that in 1475 he produced in Bruges (in what is now Belgium) the first book printed in English. Well aware of the importance of such a printing press, entrepreneur Caxton returned to England to set up his own press in Westminster, where he printed more than a hundred books in English.

The development and use of the movable-type printing press was important because it not only increased the opportunity for the common folk to read and write but also standardized spelling. Prior to the mass production of books, people who could read and write were gentry. Words were spelled at the writer's whim, sometimes being spelled four or five different ways in a single letter.

As the English empire grew, so did the language, as sailors, soldiers, and traders encountered the peoples of other nations. From the Dutch, a great sailing people, came *yankee, yacht, keel, deck, schooner, freight, cruiser, cookie, toy,* and *tub.* The Italians provided *design, opera, cello, violin, piano, volcano, torso, cartoon, cash, carnival,* and *broccoli.*

The German language, despite being from the same branch of the Indo-European language family as English, has lent English relatively few words. Among those are *delicatessen, hamburger, frankfurter,* and *dollar.*

From Spanish come several frequently used words, including *alligator, banana, canoe, cocoa, potato, ranch, rodeo*, and *tomato*. Also from Spanish come the weather terms *hurricane* and *tornado* and the names for those infamous pesky insects *cockroach* and *mosquito*.

English has borrowed from Arabic *algebra, candy, lemon, orange, sugar*, and *magazine*. *Bagel, ebony, cherub*, and *sapphire* are inherited Hebrew terms. From African languages come *gorilla, jazz, chimpanzee*, and *voodoo*.

Not many words have been borrowed from Asian languages, largely because of the centuries of limited Asian contact with the Western world. From Indian come *cot, khaki, bungalow, loot*, and the sport of kings, *polo*. Malayalam gave us *teak*, a type of wood. From Chinese come *tea* and *chow mein*. Japanese has lent *bonsai, kimono, jujitsu*, and *sushi*. However, most of the Japanese terms that English-speaking people use are trade names: Honda, Nissan, Sony, Yamaha, and the like.

Native Americans provided some state names, notably *Illinois* and *Florida*. Many United States city names also derive from Native American words. For example, *Chicago* comes from a Native American word meaning "place that smells like onions." *Manhattan* translates into the "place where all got drunk." Perhaps the Indians were even prescient in the naming of Peoria, Illinois, now a city that manufactures large earth-moving equipment. *Peoria* means the "place of great beasts." *Maize, caucus, skunk, raccoon*, and *wampum* are other donated American Indian terms.

Some words have entered English through inventions or the use of names of individuals. The word *jeans* was coined from the Italian term *Genoa fustian*, a combination of the name of a city and a type of twilled cloth used for work clothes. Levis take their name from Levi Strauss, a San Francisco merchant during the 1849 California Gold Rush. Strauss sold jeans made of a heavy-duty denim to prospectors who preferred durable, comfortable clothing.

The word *watt*, a unit for measuring electricity, comes from the inventor James Watt. Although Watt is often incorrectly referred to as the inventor of the steam engine, he did devise an efficient steam engine. Watt is also responsible for the word *horsepower*, a unit of measurement for determining the rate of the power of engines. The Fahrenheit and Celsius temperature scales are named after their founders. Gabriel Fahrenheit was a German physicist who supported his study by making meteorological instruments, and Anders Celsius, a Swede, was an astronomer.

The Indians of Virginia had a word meaning "one who advises or talks," *cawcaw-aasough*. John Smith, who was befriended by Pocahontas, the Indian princess, learned this term in the early 1600s and began to pronounce it as *caucus*. Approximately 150 years later, the word *caucus* became widely used to describe political meetings.

Some words entered the English language quite by accident. A London clerk misread the label on a consignment of cloth from Scotland, writing down *tweed* instead of *twill*. Perhaps the clerk was unable to read the handwriting on the label or was thinking of the River Tweed in Scotland, home of a large textile industry. And sometimes a product becomes identified with a brand name. The words *Coke, Kleenex, Scotch tape, Xerox,* and *Nike* are only a few examples. Technological advancements always bring new words; from wheel to cart to wagon to car to SUV to Hummer, our everyday language is influenced by new developments.

English is an ever-changing language in which new words are constantly being added and some old ones are occasionally dropped.

Aspects of Language

Language, according to Noam Chomsky (Putnam, 1994–1995, p. 331), is "an essential component of the human mind, a crucial element of the human essence." The study of language is called linguistics. A linguist is a person who studies language, being predominantly interested in language as it relates to human behavior.

Linguists study language through a variety of means, including phonology, morphology, syntax, and semantics. According to Hymes (1971), the individual who knows the phonology, morphology, syntax, and semantics of a language, as well as its rules for social language use, has acquired communicative competence.

Phonology

Phonology refers to the sounds of language. A phonological system includes all of the important or most commonly used sounds, the rules for combining sounds to make words, and stress and intonation patterns.

The sounds of a language are called phonemes and are represented by symbols called graphemes. A *phoneme* is the smallest unit of speech that makes a difference in sound to a listener or a speaker of a language. For example, if you say the words *bat, cat, hat,* and *sat* aloud, you will notice that their initial phonemes, or sounds, signal different meanings. If you substitute the phoneme /d/ for /t/, the words also change in meaning; that is, the words become *bad, cad, had,* and *sad.*

English has approximately 42 phonemes. Because of dialectical differences, this number may be slightly greater or smaller, depending on the geographic area of the United States in which one lives. For example, *park* is pronounced with a distinctive /r/ sound in most of the country, whereas in the Boston area the /r/ sound is much softer, almost inaudible.

Because phonemes are actually sounds, they are represented by symbols called *graphemes,* as mentioned earlier. The graphemes used in English are the 26 letters of the alphabet, which are sometimes used in various combinations to represent the phonemes contained in words. For example, the sound of /f/ is written as *f* in the words *fish, football,* and *fox.* In some words the /f/ phoneme is written *ff* as in *staff* and *puff.* In other words the /f/ phoneme is written as *gh* as in *laugh* and *tough.* The combination of *ph* represents the /f/ sound in *phenomenon, phone,* and even the word *phoneme* itself.

Morphology

The forms or structures of a language are referred to as *morphology*. A *morpheme* is the smallest unit of meaning in a language, meaning that cannot be broken down into any smaller parts. Words consist of one or more morphemes. The words *crop, galaxy,* and *neighbor* each consist of one morpheme, called a *free* morpheme because it can stand alone. Morphemes that cannot stand alone are called *bound* morphemes because they are always found attached to free morphemes. Bound morphemes are most easily identified when they are attached to the beginning or end of a word as in *happiness, freely,* and *impure.* As defined, then, the bound morphemes for these three words are *-iness, -ly,* and *im-,* respectively.

Syntax

Syntax, or the syntactic system, is the arrangement of words into meaningful phrases, clauses, and sentences; it is the grammatical rule system of a language. A knowledge of syntax allows a speaker or writer to take a basic sentence such as "The girl opens the present" and make *transformations* of it: "The girl opened the present." "Did the girl open the present?" "The girl did not open the present." "Wasn't the present opened by the girl?" This knowledge of syntax not only enables the speaker or writer to generate large numbers of new sentences but also to recognize those that are not grammatically acceptable, such as "The present opened the girl."

Semantics

The study of word meanings is known as semantics. Meaning is the most important thing about language. A person's semantic development occurs at a slower pace than does her development of phonology, morphology, and syntax. Indeed, learning new word meanings is a lifelong process.

The list below presents a summary of the aspects of language:

Bound Morpheme:	Morpheme that cannot stand alone, such as the affix, *-un*
Free Morpheme:	Morpheme that can stand alone, such as the word *drink*
Grapheme:	A symbol that represents the smallest unit of sound in a language (a phoneme); in English, a letter or combination of letters of the alphabet
Morpheme:	The smallest unit of meaning in a language
Morphology:	The forms or structures of a language
Phoneme:	The smallest unit of sound in a language—for example /p/ as in *pig,* in English, one of 42 units of sound
Phonology:	The sounds of a language
Semantics:	The meaning of words in a language
Syntax:	The arrangement of words in a language

Children's Language Acquisition and Development

The sound of human speech distinctively differs from other sounds. The human voice, even though it may not be that of a parent, is more effective in quieting a crying two-week-old baby than other sounds, such as bells, whistles, or rattles. Indeed, videotape analyses of day-old infants indicate that the infants' bodily movements change in direction and in rhythm in response to the sound of the human voice significantly more than to the sound of disconnected vowels or to tapping sounds (Condon & Sander, 1974). These early responses to speech lead to the acquisition of language in the young child.

The oldest recorded account of a study of language acquisition comes from Herodotus, a contemporary of Sophocles. Herodotus, who lived from about 484 to 425 BC, wrote of a shepherd ordered by an Egyptian king to raise two children by caring for their needs but not speaking to them. The king wanted to prove that the children would develop the language of the Egyptians all by themselves (Gleason, 1985). The king was obviously a believer in the innatist theory of language development.

In an interview, Noam Chomsky said that "a stimulating environment is required to enable natural curiosity, intelligence, and creativity to develop,

Exposure to picture books as preschoolers and toddlers assists language development as it builds semantics and syntax as well as phonological skills.

and to enable biological capacities to unfold" (Putnam, 1994–1995, p. 331). The development of speech in children is summarized in the chart below. This development is the same for children throughout the world regardless of the language. French and Thai children babble between the ages of three and six months just as children who grow up in English-speaking countries do. Children who are language delayed because of mental retardation nevertheless still acquire language in the same order as children of average or above-average intelligence.

At birth, a baby is capable of producing sounds, none of which are articulate or understandable. The infant is not yet equipped to produce speech. However, within a relatively short time, the baby refines vocalization until the first word is produced.

Newborns are usually exposed to large amounts of stimulation: auditory, visual, and tactile. They quickly learn to distinguish human voices from environmental noises. By two weeks of age, infants can recognize their mother's voice. Between one and two months of age, infants start producing "human" noises in the form of cooing as they make sounds that have a vowel-like *oo* quality. They use intonation. Soon they can understand some simple words and phrases.

Development of Speech

Crying	Birth
Cooing, crying	1–2 months
Babbling, cooing, crying	3–6 months
First words	8–14 months
First sentences (telegraphic speech)	18–24 months
Simple syntactic structures	3–4 years
Speech sounds correctly pronounced	4–8 years
Most semantic distinctions understood	9–11 years

Babbling

About midway through their first year, babies begin to babble. This sign of linguistic capacity is indicated when they repeat consonant-vowel combinations such as *na-na-na* or *ga-ga-ga*. Unlike cooing, babbling tends to occur when the babies are not attempting to communicate with others; in fact, some babies actually babble more when they are alone than when people are present in the room with them (Nakazima, 1975).

During babbling, babies do not produce all possible sounds; they produce only a small subset of sounds (Oller, 1980). Indeed, sounds produced early in the babbling period are seemingly abandoned as experimentation begins with new combinations of sounds. Research by Oller and Eilers (1982) has shown that late babbling contains sounds similar to those used in producing early words, such as *da-da-da* in English.

Semantic Development

Young children first acquire meaning in a content-bound way, as a part of their experiences in the world that are largely related to a daily routine.

Mother may say, "It's story time," but the youngster is already alerted by the picture book in Mother's hand. "It's time for you to take a bath" may not convey the message by itself; the time of day or evening and the presence of a towel, washcloth, and toys for the tub also give clues. Because the sharing of stories and baths are a regular part of the child's daily routine, the young child has mapped out language in terms of observations (McNamara, 1972).

Around the first birthday, babies produce their first words. Typically, *dada, mama, bye-bye,* or *papa* are characteristic first words for English speakers; they all have two syllables that begin with a consonant and end with a vowel.

Because youngsters' first words convey much meaning for them, most first words are nouns or names: *juice, dada, doggie,* and *horsie.* Verbs such as *go* and *bye-bye,* in this case meaning to go, quickly follow. Content-laden words dominate children's vocabulary at this age, and they possess few function words such as *an, through,* and *around.*

The use of one word to convey a meaningful message is called a *holophrase.* For instance, "cookie" means "I want a cookie."

First words may be overapplied. "Doggie" may refer to a four-legged animal with a tail. The neighbor's pet cat would also qualify. Tony, age 14 months, lived next to a large cattle-feeding operation. *Cow* was one of his first words. When Tony saw a large dog or horse, he immediately identified the animal as a "cow." Later, Tony refined his definition to refer only to female cattle as "cows."

Semantic development in children is interesting because speaking and listening abilities can vary with the same child. Maya, an 18-month-old, was playing when her uncle pointed to a clock and asked, "What's that?" Getting no response, he pointed to other objects in the room: the television set, the fireplace, and a table. Each time her uncle asked, "What's that?" Maya merely looked at him. He decided she didn't know the names of the objects. To test his theory, he tried a new line of questioning. He asked Maya: "Where's the table? Where's the clock? Where's the fireplace? Where's the television set?" Each time, Maya pointed to the correct object. Maya's listening vocabulary exceeded her speaking vocabulary. In the next few months, she began using the names of the same objects in her speaking vocabulary, as the objects became more important to convey messages.

Young children initially use language only as a tool for social interaction, according to Vygotsky (1962). Later, they use language both in talking aloud during play and in verbalizing their intentions or actions.

Holophrastic and Telegraphic Speech

After producing their first words, children rapidly develop their vocabulary, acquiring about 50 words in the next 6 months. At this time, children begin putting words together to express even more meaning than that found in a single word. In this way, children convey their thoughts, but they omit function words such as articles and prepositions. When a child says a one-word utterance, such as "juice" or "cookie," meaning "I want more juice" or "I want a cookie," it is referred to as a *holophrase.* When a child says "more juice" to express the desire for additional juice to drink, this two-word utterance is called *telegraphic speech* because they resemble telegrams that adults would send.

The limited number of words in telegraphic speech permits children to get their messages across to others very economically. For instance, Braden, age 20 months, says, "More milk" instead of, "I want another glass of milk." The resultant message is essentially the same as the more elaborate sentence.

The basics of language development are:

Babble:	The combination of a consonant sound and a vowel sound that is repeated: "da-da-da"
Holophrastic speech:	A one-word utterance first used by children between the ages of 12 and 18 months to convey meaning: "Juice" for "I want more juice"
Telegraphic speech:	Two-word utterances first used by children between 18 and 24 months of age to convey meaning: "Doggie allgone" for "The dog is gone"

Overgeneralization

Young children acquire the grammatical rules of English, but often they tend to *overgeneralize*. For example, a three-year-old may refer to "mouses" and "foots" rather than mice and feet. "Camed" may be substituted for came and, similarly, "falled" for fell. Such overgeneralization indicates evidence of the creativity and productivity of the child's morphology because these forms are neither spoken by an adult nor heard by the child.

In early childhood, children tend to invent new words as part of their creativity. Clark (1981, 1982) observed children between the ages of two and six years and found that they devised or invented new words to fill gaps in their vocabularies. Clark found that if children had forgotten or did not know a noun, the likelihood of word invention increased. "Pourer" was used for *cup* and "plant-man" for *gardener* in such instances. Verbs are often invented in a similar fashion, yet the verbs tend to evolve from nouns the children know. One four-year-old created such a verb from the noun *cracker* when she referred to putting soda crackers in her soup as "I'm cracking my soup" (Clark, 1981, p. 304).

Children often substitute words that they know for words that are unfamiliar to them. Three-year-old Sarah was taken by her grandmother to see *The Nutcracker*. After intently watching the ballet for a period of time, young Sarah inquired, "Is that the can opener?"

Children tend to regularize the new words they create, just as they overgeneralize words they already know. Thus, a child may refer to a person who rides a bicycle as a "bicycler," employing the frequently used *-er* adjective pattern rather than the rare, irregular *-ist* form to create the word *bicyclist* (Pease & Gleason, 1985).

Semantic development occurs at a slower rate than do phonological development and syntactic development. The grammar, or syntax, of a five-year-old approaches that of an adult. The child can actually carry on a sensible conversation with an adult. There are only a few grammatical patterns, such as the passive voice and relative clauses, yet to be acquired at this age (Chomsky, 1969).

By age four, a child understands all the sounds in a language; however, the child may be eight years old before he is able to produce the sounds correctly. For example, Jeff, age three and a half, was going shopping with his mother and her friend Penny. While they were waiting for his mother to get ready, Penny noticed that Jeff had a wallet and some money. She asked Jeff what he planned to buy. Jeff said, "A purse." "A purse?" Penny asked. To this question, Jeff insisted, "No, I want a purse." Because the boy seemed to enjoy playing with trucks and cars, Penny was quite confused, so she changed the conversation. At the shopping mall, Penny volunteered to help Jeff with his shopping. She asked Jeff to show her what he wanted to buy, thinking perhaps a carrying case for miniature cars was what he had in mind. Jeff led her to a large display of blue, red, and white things in the department store. Penny smiled and said, "You want a Smurf!" Jeff beamed, "Yes, I want a purse." Jeff obviously could distinguish the difference between the words *Smurf* and *purse* when someone else said them, but the words sounded identical to him when he produced them.

Even when children are older they may have difficulty articulating what they have heard older children and adults say. Consider Madison, who was upset when her mother picked her up from kindergarten. "Mommy, I had an awful day. It was just everotating! Zachary said he loved me!"

Children in kindergarten through third grade may not be able to articulate all of the consonants of English correctly. The list below indicates the developmental order for the correct pronunciation of English consonants. A second- or third-grade teacher should not be overly concerned, for example, if some students are unable to produce the /r/ sound, because it is typically the last sound to be acquired. A good book to share with first graders to encourage them to articulate the "r" sound correctly is the humorous *Hooway for Wodney Wat* by Helen Lester (1999).

Acquisition of Consonant Sounds

Age (years)	*Consonant*
3½	p, m, b, w, h
4½	d, t, n, g, ng (ring), k, ch, y
5½	f
6½	l, th (voiced—this), sh, zh (azure)
7½	s, z, th (unvoiced—thick), r

From Flood and Salus, 1984, p. 26.

The Functions of Language

Halliday (1975, p. 7) describes children's language development as a process by which they progressively "learn how to mean." Thus, through interactions with others, children learn how to convey meaning through speech.

According to Halliday (1975, pp. 19–21), seven functions of language are used by children. These are listed below.

1. **Instrumental:** Children use language to satisfy personal needs and to get things done.
2. **Regulatory:** Children use language to control the behavior of others.
3. **Personal:** Children use language to tell about themselves.
4. **Interactional:** Children use language to get along with others.
5. **Heuristic:** Children use language to find out about things, to learn things.
6. **Imaginative:** Children use language to pretend, to make believe.
7. **Informative:** Children use language to communicate information to others.

Children develop proficiency with language as their need to use it develops. Therefore, the interactions they have with other people, both adults and children, their own interests, and the meaning that language has for them all impact upon their language development.

Many children acquiring a first language progress similarly in the development of phonology, morphology, syntax, and semantics, as discussed earlier. However, some children have problems with language acquisition. These problems may be of a physical nature, such as sensory deficits in hearing or sight, or they may be related to cognitive problems. This results in delayed language acquisition. However, language activities for normal children at younger ages can be used with older language-delayed children. These include concept muraling and picture walks (see chapter 3).

Language in the Classroom

Knowing how each child uses language both in and out of school can help teachers develop an effective language program (see box 5.1). Kindergartners, for instance, view language as having a functional purpose. "They use language to ask, tell, report, discuss, negotiate, test, direct" (Searfoss, 1988, p. 4). Therefore, language should be used for genuine, relevant purposes in actual social contexts.

Children need to interact with each other and the teacher in acquiring background knowledge and information. By creating a learning situation in which children can closely observe and examine an object, for instance, the teacher allows them to compare it to things with which they are already familiar. Discussions should not be limited to concrete objects. Children's literature provides a variety of information. By reading to children, the teacher is providing them with an opportunity to envision a story's actions and characters in their minds.

Quality children's literature should be shared with children of all ages, from birth through elementary school. Children in kindergarten through third grade enjoy finger plays such as the "Let's Go on a Bear Hunt." They learn the parts of the body from actively participating in songs such as the "Hokey Pokey." Nursery rhymes and short poems encourage them to play with lan-

5.1   In the Classroom: Teaching Hint

Language Development of Emergent Literacy Child

Name: _____   Teacher: _____

Age: _____   Grade: _____   Date: _____

	Always	Sometimes	Never
Has no speech defects (i.e., stuttering, articulation disorders)			
Pronounces consonant sounds correctly			
Pronounces consonant blends correctly			
Pronounces consonant digraphs correctly			
Pronounces short vowels correctly			
Pronounces long vowels correctly			
Pronounces diphthongs correctly			
Can successfully use one-word sentences			
Can successfully use two-word sentences			
Can successfully use three or more word sentences			
Can identify words that rhyme			
Can identify familiar environmental sounds			
When engaged in a conversation with adults, can understand their language and respond			
When engaged in a conversation with another child, can understand the language and respond			
Can follow oral directions			
Has a good vocabulary			
Uses a variety of sentence patterns (syntactical/grammatical structures)			
Can be understood by adults			
Can be understood by other children			
Enjoys talking with adults			
Enjoys talking with other children			
Teacher comments:			

guage. Children at this level can expand their oral language skills with word-less books as they become adept at telling the story in their own words and elaborating on the illustrations they particularly enjoy. As mentioned earlier, the predictability of patterned books makes them popular with beginning readers because they "know" to a great extent what will happen on the next page.

When the teacher encourages children to retell a story that they have recently heard, they not only expand their oral language but also gain a sense of story structure. Once they have attained a sense of story structure, they can concentrate on the actions within the story, making interpretations and predictions. The retelling of a story requires that thought be blended with language, resulting in the enhancement of both (Hayes, 1989). Literature response journals are also beneficial as children use emergent writing and drawings initially and move on to writing to describe their reactions to a story (Danielson, 1992).

The retelling of stories is valuable in that the teacher can use it for both the instruction and the assessment of oral language complexity and comprehension (Morrow, 1988). A child's retelling may provide the teacher with a more accurate measure of the child's understanding of a story than answers to questions the teacher might ask the child. However, the teacher must be cautious when evaluating students who have had little practice in retelling stories. The teacher should tell such children beforehand that they will be asked to retell the story after it is read to them.

Language study can also take the form of word study as students discover how words came into the English language as a result of migration, trade, or wars. Students can research the names of states and their capitals or various inventions as part of a social studies lesson. Following this, the students might investigate the origins of their own last names. They can place pins in a map of the world to show where their names originated.

Dialects

A linguistic variation of the English language that is regional and differs distinctively from standard English is called a *dialect*. Three major dialects exist within the United States: Northern, Midland, and Southern. The Midland region is generally broken down into North Midland and South Midland, depending on whether major influence comes from the Northern or Southern dialect. Each major dialect area, in turn, is divided into regional areas. For example, eastern New England has speech patterns quite different from those of the remainder of the Northern region. The Southern dialect of East Texas differs from that of Alabama and South Carolina. This holds true for the other major dialects as well.

In addition to regional dialects, there are social dialects, those speech variations correlated with social class, age, occupation, religion, and recreational preferences. Each individual's speech is a composite of regional and social dialect characteristics (Myers, 1984).

There are 26 dialects in the United States; surprisingly enough, however, they are neither as numerous nor as distinctive as dialects in other countries. For example, Great Britain, a country about the size of the state of Oregon, has a greater number of dialects than does the entire United States. In addition, the dialects of Great Britain differ more than the American dialects do. The strongest U.S. dialects are found largely in those areas that were settled first, that is, the original 13 colonies. The advent of radio and television and increasing geographic mobility has resulted in less variation among American dialects. Broadcasting networks have become nonregional in trying to neutralize dialects. News anchor people are often the first to introduce words to the country, thereby eliminating the possibility of any dialectical differences.

Dialects differ in three possible ways: in phonology, in semantics, and in syntax. In the Midwest, the /r/ sound is pronounced clearly, as in *horse* or *earth*, and it may even intrude, as in "warsh" (wash). In eastern New England, on the other hand, the /r/ sound is often lost as in "pahk" (park) or "father" (farther). In the southern states of Georgia and South Carolina, "lahg" (log) rhymes with "fahg" (fog) but not with *hog* or *dog*, which sound more like "hawg" and "dawg." Dropping the ends of words is a common occurrence in the Southern dialect but can also be found in the South Midland dialect. "Goin'" for *going* and "runnin'" for *running* are commonplace.

Semantic differences affect dialects too. Is it a skillet, a frying pan, or a spider? Do you get water from a tap or a faucet? Do you drink water from a water fountain, a spigot, a drinking fountain, or a bubbler? Do you eat green beans, snap beans, or string beans?

Syntactic differences among dialects are less common. In the South Midland dialect some plurals are omitted: "2 year" rather than "2 years." In the North Midland dialect, *by* is sometimes used instead of *to*: "I'm going *by* the bank and the cleaner's." Double negatives are found in the speech of some south Midland and Southern natives but also in the speech of some working-class people in other dialect regions.

A teacher should not identify any one regional dialect as superior to the others. In teaching language, a teacher should respect a child's dialect but also convey to all students the need to develop standard English for the social and working worlds.

The acquisition of standard English can be accomplished without the loss of a dialect. Both are beneficial, depending on the setting in which language is used. To avoid teaching standard English is to shackle students by limiting their future employment possibilities. For example, the child who says, "I ain't got no pin" for "I don't have a pen" will not be welcomed as an accountant, secretary, or medical doctor, if such usage continues after the child becomes an adult. The role of the teacher is to help better the lives of students, which requires that the teacher be accountable for improving language skills when necessary.

Black English or Ebonics

Black English or Ebonics is a vernacular dialect spoken by many African Americans in the United States. This dialect is highly predictable and regular.

Phonological characteristics include the deletion of final /t/ and /l/ sounds, as in *past* becoming "pass" and *pole* becoming "po." The /r/ sound is frequently omitted, as when *Paris* becomes "pass." As in the Southern dialect, the final consonant is often dropped as in "goin'" for *going*. The glide is deleted with long vowels and diphthongs as in "rod" for *ride* and "spall" for *spoil*. The glide is added with short vowels such as "hiyat" for *hit*. Other pronunciation differences include "aks" for *ask* and "wif" for *with*.

Common syntactic differences of black English include nonstandard verb forms *was* for *were* and *is* for *are*. The variant *be* becomes a finite verb: "She *be* sick" or "He *be* mad at you." Many sentences are expressions of the future: "I'm *gonna* get you a present" or "He's goin' to do it."

Semantic differences include the words *cool* for *good* and *heavy* for *powerful*. Many African American families do not assign nicknames to their children. For example, Edward should not be called Ed but only Edward, the name given to him at birth.

In the late 1990s, there was a movement initiated in Oakland, California, to have Black English or Ebonics treated as a foreign language in the schools. If recognized as such, public schools would have been granted substantial funding to help African American students acquire mainstream or standard English. The movement failed. At the same time, California was cutting back on state funding of bilingual education programs in its schools.

Multicultural Considerations

The pluralistic nature of our society yields a large number of cultural and language variations. The classroom teacher needs to take such variations into consideration (see box 5.2). Some children from minority groups, just as some children from the majority white culture, have language deficits. However, not all minority children have a language deficit and should not be prejudged as language deficient. As Flores, Cousin, and Díaz (1991, p. 370) note: "One of the most pervasive and pernicious myths about 'at-risk' students is that they have a language deficit. This myth is reserved not for just bilingual and non-English-speaking students. It is also commonly held about African Americans and other minorities." The fact is that they possess a language and are acquiring English in addition. Thus it is critical not to hold such students back in content area instruction such as math, science, and social studies while they are developing their oral and written English literacy skills.

Language arts instruction for minority and ELL students that is most effective and efficient has been a major area of study by researchers. Research from Finland points out that "parents' overall high confidence in their children's academic competencies seem to foster their children's use of a task-focused rather than a task-avoidance achievement strategy" (Aunola, Nurmi, Niemi, Lerkkanen, & Rasku-Puttonen, 2002, p. 342). Culture does play a major role in parent-teacher interactions. In the Latino culture, it is considered the teacher's responsibility to teach the child and thus the child is less likely to get parental help with projects or homework than a child from an Asian or Polish family, for instance.

"In some classrooms, the way in which literacy is embedded in routines and social interactions is at odds with how language is used among students' social activities in the home" (Sheehy, 2002, p. 278). This may impact language development in one's home or first language as well as acquisition of another language. Cope and Kalentzis (1993), Delpit (1995), and Martin (1989) argue that a process or constructivist approach to language instruction for reading and writing is only suitable for students from middle-class, mainstream American families. They point out that direct instruction based on skill acquisition is superior for many minority and ELL children. Struggling readers and writers need greater guidance and structure that direct instruction offers with, for instance, emphasis on decoding and spelling skills.

Teachers must keep in mind that "when children feel their cultural identities have no place in the classroom, they often reject the curriculum, resist learning, and may eventually drop out of school" (Kaser & Short, 1998, p. 191). The teacher must be cautious and not misinterpret a child's spoken language for lack of comprehension. Thus it is important that teachers not consider teaching a remediation for students with linguistic differences in race/ethnicity but to view linguistic and cultural differences as funds of knowledge for building literacy in the classroom (Fránquiz & de la Luz Reyes, 1998). Requiring that English

---

5.2 The More You Know

Spoken Languages Present in One Urban School District

Below is a list of 64 first languages, other than English, spoken by students in Elgin School District Unit 46, a large suburban school district of 28,000 students located just outside of Chicago. Although Spanish and Laotian are spoken by large numbers of students, there are many languages, such as Gaelic and Sioux, for which there are five students or less represented.

Afrikaans (Taal)	Finnish	Kannada	Sindhi
Albanian	French	Khmer/Cambodian	Sioux
Amharic	Gaelic	Korean	Slovak
Arabic	German	Lao	Slovenian
Armenian	Greek	Latvian	Spanish
Assyrian	Gujarati	Lithuanian	Swedish
Bengali	Haitian Creole	Malayalam	Taiwanese
Bisayan	Hebrew	Marathi	Tamil
Bulgarian	Hindi	Norwegian	Telugu
Burmese	Hindustani	Pilipino (Tagalog)	Thai
Chinese-Cantonese	Hmong	Polish	Tibetan
Chinese-Mandarin	Hungarian	Portuguese	Turkish
Czech	Iroquoian	Punjabi	Ukrainian
Danish	Italian	Romanian	Urdu
Dutch	Jamaican	Russian	Vietnamese
Farsi (Iranian)	Japanese	Serbian/Croatian	Yugoslavian

be the only language used in the classroom can lead to self-doubt on the part of linguistically and culturally diverse learners (Donato, 1997). Even if the teacher does not know the student's first language, there are ways to include the child and his language as part of a lesson or learning activity. As increasing numbers of linguistically different students are in our classrooms, it is important that teachers use appropriate methods of instructional acts of inclusion.

A good example is presented by Fránquiz and de la Luz Reyes (1998). A first-grade teacher was presenting a lesson on the sense of sound to her students. The students were to reach inside "mystery bags" containing a variety of objects. Then the chosen student was to feel inside her bag, shake it, and give verbal clues to the other students to help them figure out the object. When Margarita, an ELL student, took her turn, she reached into the bag and shook it. A classmate yelled out, "It's money!" Margarita remained silent as she poured the pennies out of the bag. She remained silent as other students described the items in their "mystery bags." Finally one student had an object that no one could identify. Finally Margarita smiled but did not speak. When prompted by her teacher to say the word in Spanish, Margarita said softly "*Canicas.*" The teacher repeated the word for the class to hear, "*Canicas.* I have learned a new word in Spanish, *canicas.*" Then the teacher held up the objects from the bag—marbles.

When working with ELLs, teachers must be sensitive to the fact that such children are often uncertain and tentative in using their newly acquired words, phrases, or sentences. "The process of acquiring a second language can be described as an in-between state, an uncertain terrain one crosses as one becomes bilingual" (Fránquiz & de la Luz Reyes, 1998, p. 216).

Delpit (1995) advocates that teachers should balance skills and attention to mainstream English in teaching African American, Spanish, or other linguistically different students. Students also need lots of opportunities to use mainstream English in safe, relevant contexts so that they can feel comfortable communicating with peers as well as later on with strangers. The following sections describe differences between Spanish, Asian, and Native American influences on English.

Spanish-Influenced English

One in four U.S. teachers instruct in two languages, typically English and Spanish. Children who speak Spanish as their first language have difficulty adjusting to the nine English consonants that do not exist in Spanish: *v, j, z, sh, ng, zh* as in *measure, th* voiced as in *then, th* unvoiced as in *with,* and *r* as in *rabbit.* The pronunciation of the /s/ sound in consonant clusters becomes a separate syllable as in "es-hoe" for *shoe* and "es-hip" for *ship.* There is also a tendency to substitute long vowels for short vowels and for vowel digraphs such as *caught* to be pronounced as "coat." Spanish has four consonants that do not exist in English: *r (rancho), x (examen), ñ (mañana),* and the rolling *r (perro).* Sometimes these consonants are substituted when a Spanish-speaking child becomes confused in speaking English. English and Spanish languages also share some of the same consonant sounds as outlined in figure 5.2.

p	pat	t	tall	k	king	b	basket
	puerto		todo		kilo		bebida

d	dish	g	give	f	family	s	sing
	dar		gusto		falta		seda

y	yes	m	moon	n	nice	ch	church
	yo		madre		nota		mucho

l	lady	w	wing
	lado		Oaxaca

From Muriel Saville-Troike, and R. C. Troike, *A handbook of bilingual education*. Washington, DC: Teachers of English to Speakers of Other Languages: Copyright © 1971. Reprinted by permission.

Figure 5.2   Consonant phonemes shared in English and Spanish

Some consonant sounds are distinct to English and may cause problems in speaking and spelling for Spanish-speaking students who attempt to acquire them (Helman, 2004). Figure 5.3 points out these differences as well as English consonant blends that are not in Spanish.

Distinct English sound	May be pronounced	May be spelled as
/d/ as in den	*then*	dem (them)
/j/ as in joke	*choke*	gob (job)
/r/ as in rope	(rolled r) *rope, wope*	waipen (ripen)
/v/ as in van	*ban*	surbing (serving)
/z/ as in zipper	*sipper*	sivalais (civilize)
/sh/ as in shell	*chell*	ched (shed)
/th/ as in thick	*tick*	tenk (think)
/zh/ as in treasure	*treachure*	chesher (treasure)

English consonant blend	Sample English word	English consonant blend	Sample English word
st	star	tw	twice
sp	spirit	qu (kw)	quick
sk/sc	scar	scr	scrap
sm	small	spl	splash
sl	sleep	spr	spray
sn	snack	str	straight
sw	swim	squ (skw)	square

From Lori A. Helman. (2004, February). Building on the Sound System of Spanish: Insights from the alphabetic spellings of English-language learners, *The Reading Teacher, 57* (5), 452–460. Used by permission of Lori A. Helman and the International Reading Association.

Figure 5.3   English consonant sounds and consonant blends not in Spanish

Final consonant and consonant blend sounds are frequently substituted by first-language Spanish speakers and writers (Helman, 2004). These include the following:

Final sound	Spelling Error	Final sound	Spelling Error
-rd	har (hard)	-ng	sirvin (serving)
-st	tos (toast)	-ng	chopen (shopping)
-sk	as (ask)	-z	praes (prize)
-t	tha (that)	-mp	lanpa (lump)

Vowel sounds may have the same sound but be spelled differently in English than in Spanish. The schwa sound (found in words such as *develop* and *aloof*) is the most common English vowel sound, but it doesn't occur in Spanish. If a vowel sound doesn't exist in the child's home language, the child will most likely try to use the closest sounding native language vowel as a substitute. English has nearly twice as many vowel sounds as Spanish. Spanish does not have four short-vowel sounds from English (*man, pen, tip, up*), *r*-controlled vowels (e.g., *hard, her, shirt*), or the vowel sounds of *au, aw,* and *ou* (e.g. *caught, awful,* and *would*) (Goldstein, 2001).

Several syntactic differences between Spanish and English can be described. The native Spanish speaker's omission of verb endings when speaking English is very common, as in "He *go* to the store" and "She *play* a joke." Likewise, because subject pronouns do not occur in Spanish, native Spanish speakers sometimes eliminate them in English: "She is the new girl" becomes "Is the new girl." An article in Spanish indicates both the gender and number (singular or plural) of the noun that follows it. In Spanish, inanimate objects are either masculine or feminine. In English, such objects are neuter, having no gender whatsoever.

The possessive in Spanish necessitates the use of *de* (*of* in English) immediately preceding the possessor, such as "el libro de Juan," meaning "Juan's book." The /s/ sound at the end of a word denotes a plural, never a possessive as it sometimes does in English.

Spanish-speaking students frequently omit contractions or use them incorrectly in English. Particularly difficult for the Spanish-speaking child to acquire are those contractions that involve a change in the vowel sound of a word. For example, if the Spanish-speaking child knows the words *does* and *not*, then *doesn't* is more easily acquired than knowing *will* and *not* and producing *won't* as the contraction.

Negation in Spanish requires that a negative be used before the verb, resulting in a double-negative construction. Thus, double negatives are commonly used by Spanish-speaking children as they acquire English: "He no have nothing." Although such a construction is required in Spanish, it is not acceptable in English. Prepositions that are correctly used in the Spanish language are often—upon translation—incorrectly used according to standard English rules, such as when "*in* or *at* the table" is substituted for "*on* the table."

For example, the word *mosquito* is a true cognate because it is a word in both English and Spanish and has the same meaning in both languages. The word for *special* in Spanish differs slightly in its spelling *(especial)* from its English counterpart, but it has the same meaning and is considered a true cognate (see box 5.3). Semantic differences pertain to the many false cognates that exist within Spanish and English. Because the Spanish word *pan* (bread) and the English word *pan* (a cooking container) mean something very different, *pan* is a false cognate. Even though the Spanish word *fabrica* appears to be similar to the English word *fabric*, the two words are not true cognates because *fabrica* means factory in Spanish, and *fabric* in English refers to material.

One very costly example pertaining to a false cognate in the English and Spanish languages was an American firm's introduction of an economical car into Spanish-speaking countries several years ago. The company had sold several hundred thousand of the cars in the United States and expected the model to sell well in Mexico and the Central American countries. Potential foreign buyers would look the car over and take it for a test drive, but few actually purchased the car. This lack of sales was later related to the car's name, Nova, which in Spanish means "no go."

In addition to the phonological, syntactic, and semantic differences between Spanish and English, nonverbal differences exist. In order to show respect, young children of Spanish heritage are taught to avoid looking directly into the eyes of the teacher. However, around the time of puberty, boys are encouraged to be more independent of women, and therefore they may begin to challenge the authority of female teachers or classroom aides.

5.3   The More You Know

English and Spanish True Cognates

Many words that look alike are in both the English and Spanish languages. Because English and Spanish are related languages a number of words have identical (or almost identical) meanings. They are considered to be true cognates. Of course they do not always sound the same when spoken in Spanish, but the similarity will surprise you. Here are a few.

accident	el accidente	balcony	el balcón
active	activo	bank	el banco
agriculture	la agricultura	beefsteak	el biftec
algebra	el álgebra	bland	blando
ambulance	la ambulancia	bottle	la botella
America	la América	calendar	el calendario
animal	el animal	calm	la calma
appetite	el apetito	candle	la candela, la vela
application	la aplicación	capital	la capital
April	abril	cent	el centavo
arch	el arco	center	el centro
artist	el artista	check	el cheque
attention	la atención	chocolate	el chocolate
August	agosto	circle	el circulo
automobile	el automóvil	civil	civil

continued

class	la clase	habit	el hábito
column	la columna	hamburger	la hamburguesa
comical	cómico	hero	el héroe
company	la compañia	history	la historia
compartment	el compartimiento	honor	el honor
conversation	la conversación	hotel	el hotel
correct	correcto	hour	la hora
coupon	el cupón	humid	hùmedo
cream	la crema	humor	el humor
culture	la cultura	hungry	hambre
dance	la danza, el baile	idea	la idea
day	el día	illustration	la ilustración
decent	decente	important	importante
delicious	delicioso	industry	la industria
designation	la designación	information	la información
difficult	difícil	instant	el instante
direction	la dirección	intelligent	inteligente
distance	la distancia	interesting	interesante
doctor	el doctor	invitation	la invitación
document	el documento	island	la isla
effect	el efecto	jacket	la chaqueta
electric	eléctrico	jasmine	jazmín
enormous	enorme	jeep	el jeep
entrance	la entrada	June	junio
error	el error	justice	la justicia
family	la familia	lake	el lago
famous	famoso	lamp	la lámpara
favor	el favor	language	el lenguaje
figure	la figura	large	largo
film	el film	legal	legal
filter	el filtro	lemon	el limón
final	final	lemonade	la limonada
flower	la flor	lesson	la lección
forest	la floresta, el bo	license	la licencia
form	la forma	lime	la lima, el limón
fortune	la fortuna	limit	el límite
fountain	la fuente	line	la línea
fresh	fresco	liquid	el líquido
fruit	la frutafuture	liquor	el licor
future	el futuro	list	la lista
gallery	la galería	map	el mapa
garden	el jardín	March	marzo
gas	el gas	margarine	la margarina
—gas station	la gasolinera	medicine	la medicina
government	el gobierno	melody	la melodía
grain	el grano	menu	el menú
grand	gran	metal	el metal
grease	la grasa	meter	el metro
group	el grupo	minute	el minuto
guide	el guía	modern	moderno

continued

moment . . . . .el momento
—just a moment . . . . un momento
motor. . . . . el motor
museum . . . . el museo
music . . . . la música
name. . . . . el nombre
nation . . . . la nación
native . . . . .nativo
natural . . . . .natural
necessary . . . . .necesario
new. . . . . .nuevo
no, not . . . . no
normal . . . . .normal
north . . . . el norte
notice. . . . . la noticia
notion. . . . . la noción
novel. . . . . la novela
November . . . . .noviembre
number. el número
nylon. . . . . .el nilón
object . . . . el objeto
occasion . . . . la ocasión
occupied. . . . . ocupado
ocean . . . . .el océano
office. . . . . la oficina
olive . . . . la oliva, la aceituna
opera . . . . la ópera
opportunity . . . . .la oportunidad
ordinary . . . . ordinario
original . . . . .original
package. . . . . el paquete
page . . . . .la página
paint . . . . la pintura
pair . . . . el par
—pair of shoes. . . . . .un par de zapa
pajamas. .los pijamas
pants. . . . . los pantalones
paper . . . . el papel
pardon .el perdón
park . . . . el parque
part. . . . . la parte
passenger . . . . .el pasajero
passport . . . . el. pasaporte
peace . . . . .la paz
period. . . . . el período
person . . . . la persona
piano. . . . . el piano
plan. . . . . el plan
plant . . . . .la planta
plate . . . . el plato

point . . . . el punto
—viewpoint . . . . el punto de vis
police. . . . . la policía
port. . . . . .el puerto
possible. posible
practice. la práctica
precious . . . . precioso
precise. . . . . preciso
prepare . . . . preparar
present . . . . presente
price . . . . el precio
problem. . . . . el problema
product. . . . . .el producto
professor. . . . . el profesor
program . . . . el programa
prohibited . . . . prohibido
promise. . . . . la promesa
prompt . . . . pronto
pronunciation . . . . .la pronunciación
public. . . . . público
radio . . . . la radio
rapid . . . . rápido
rare . . . . raro
reason . . . . .la razón
receipt. el recibo
recipe . . . . la receta
region . . . . la región
regular. regular
religion . . . . la religión
repair. .la reparación
repeat . . . . repitir
—please repeat. . . . . repita por favor
reservation . . . . .reservación
residence. . . . . la residencia
respect . . . . el respeto
rest . . . . el resto
restaurant . . . . .el restaurante
rich . . . . rico
rose. . . . . la rosa
route . . . . la ruta
sack . . . . .el saco
salary. . . . . el salario
salmon. el salmón
salt. . . . . la sal
sandal . . . . la sandalia
sardine. la sardina
sauce . . . . .la salsa
season . . . . la escuela
second. .la segunda
secretary. . . . . la secretaria

continued

section	la sección	train	el tren
selection	la selección	tulip	el tulipán
September	septiembre	tunnel	el túnel
service	el servicio	typical	típico
soup	la sopa	union	la unión
South American	sudamericano	unit	la unidad
Spanish	español	university	la universidad
state	el estado	used	usado
—United States	los Estados Unidos	utensil	el utensilio
station	la estación	vacancy	la vacante
—train station	la estación del tren	vacation	la vacación
statue	la estatua	valid	válido
study	el estudio	valley	el value
sure	seguro	value	el valor
tavern	la taberna	vanilla	la vainilla
taxi	el taxi	various	varios
—taxi driver	el taxista	vast	vasto
tea	el té	vehicle	el vehículo
—teatime	la hora del té	verb	el verbo
telegram	el telegrama	version	la versión
telegraph	el telégrafo	vinegar	el vinagre
—telegraph office	la oficina telegráfica	violet	la violeta
telephone	el teléfono	violin	el violín
television	la televisión	visa	la visa
temperature	la temperatura	visit	visitar
tennis	el tenis	vitamin	la vitamina
terrace	la terraza	vocabulary	el vocabulario
time	el tiempo	voice	la voz
toast	el pan tostado	volume	el volumen
tomato	el tomate	yacht	el yate
total	total	yard	la yarda
tourist	el turista	zebra	la cebra
towel	la toalla	zero	cero
tower	la torre	zoo	jardin zoológic
traffic	el tráfico		

Asian-Influenced English

Asian children who attend school in the United States come from varying backgrounds. Since the end of the Vietnam War and the return of Hong Kong to China, there has been a large influx of Southeast Asian immigrants into the United States. Initially, most of the families came from the upper-social-class structure. Many of them, especially the fathers, had been educated in English-speaking schools. Later, families from the middle and lower classes immigrated to the United States. Although children of upper-class families may have been taught some English, most of the children from the middle- and lower-class Southeast Asian families had little or no familiarity with the

English language. Because of large investments by Japanese companies in American corporations and Japanese ownership of factories and businesses in the United States, children of Japanese corporate executives have moved to the United States with their families. These children have been attending public and private American schools and have had to learn English. Asian children who attempt to acquire English as a second language are at a disadvantage because few true cognates exist in Asian languages and English. The Thai word *fit*, unlike its English counterpart, means "is the wrong size." The word *seminar* is also a false cognate for the Laotian people. In English, a seminar is a meeting of a small group of people to discuss a topic or issue; however in Laotian, a seminar is a gathering of a small group of people who have been brainwashed by the Communists. *Bun* means rice noodle in Vietnamese, unlike the bread product it represents in English. Thus, when beginning to learn English as a second language, Asian students are faced with a difficult task.

Asian languages are tonal in quality. For example, by saying a single sound in Thai, the speaker can produce up to eight different words merely by changing intonation or pitch of voice. This tonal quality makes Asian languages difficult for English-speaking people to acquire. Nevertheless, a study by Chang and Watson (1988) reports that despite the major differences in phonemes in the Chinese and English languages, children were found to use the same cognitive activities (predicting, confirming, and integrating information) in reading Chinese materials as they use in reading English materials.

The syntax of Asian languages differs from that of English. Thai speakers talk of watching a "white and black TV" or ask for the "pepper and salt," as opposed to English speakers watching a "black and white TV" and asking for "salt and pepper." In giving directions, the Thai speaker says "eastnorth," not "northeast" as the English speaker does.

Nonverbal communication plays a major role in the teaching of Asian children. Most early childhood teachers in the United States have their students form a circle by "holding the hands of your neighbors"; however, in most Asian cultures boys are not allowed to hold the hands of girls. In some Asian cultures, children are taught not to cross their legs because this results in their toes pointing toward the teacher. Such a position is thought to be disrespectful because the feet are considered the most unholy part of the body. Parallel to this, some Asians believe that it is a discourtesy for the teacher to touch or pat a child's head because the head is considered the most holy part of the body.

Native American Languages

There are over 40 Native American languages that are prevalent in the United States. The Cherokee and Navaho languages, for example, were used for sending coded messages by the Army during World War II. Native American languages differ in syntax and semantics from tribe to tribe. The sounds, or phonology, of the languages also differ.

Native American children are taught to be quiet and not to speak unnecessarily. They hold great respect for adults and will not look the teacher in the eye out of this respect. Native American children are taught to work cooperatively and may automatically help a classmate with an activity even though the activity was designed to be done individually.

One mistake that some teachers make is to assume that the Native American tribes work together and in unison. There are still bitter differences between some tribes. For instance, a Navaho child may greatly resent being seated by a Hopi child, and vice versa. In addition, the folktales of one tribe may be offensive to another tribe.

Codeswitching

Codeswitching is the use of two languages simultaneously or interchangeably. Thus a speaker may alternate two linguistic codes (languages) in a fully grammatical way within a single sentence or conversation. For example, Felix and Ramon, middle school students and Spanish native language speakers, were talking about a football game between the Chicago Bears and the Tampa Bay Buccaneers. Both boys used English nouns (i.e., blitz, linebacker) with a few verbs (i.e., punt) commonly used in football although the rest of their sentences were in Spanish. Codeswitching is actually an indication of some degree of competence in two languages even if bilingualism is not yet attained (Durán, 1994).

Codeswitching, according to Crowell (1998), is the alternating use of two languages at the word, phrase, clause, or sentence level. As such, codeswitching is a "distinctive characteristic of bilingual communities. It occurs between friends and family members and is used to help tell stories, identify speakers as members of the same language community, and define social roles of the speakers" (p. 229). An example of codeswitching in children's book is Gary Soto's (1996) *The Old Man and His Door* (appropriate for grades one and two), the story of an old man who never listened carefully. When his wife asks him to bring a *puerco*, a pig, to a barbeque, the old man instead brings a *puerta*, a door. Another example is Soto's (1996) *Off and Running*, the story of a fifth-grade class election. This story is for older readers.

Evaluating Language Development

"Children's language processes are energized and sustained by meaningful (purposeful) use of language in varied situations. Sensible activities, and the people and things entailed in those activities, provide support for children's language learning" (Dyson, 1991, pp. 26–27).

Although extensive evaluation of children's language in varied situations is not possible in the classroom, teachers can use informal means to assess language development. For example, at the beginning of the school year, a kindergarten teacher takes each student aside for a short time while the other children are busy engaging in other planned activities. The teacher shows each child a picture of a young boy playing with a collie dog and a rubber ball and asks the child to tell the story behind the picture. Some children will identify the objects in the picture. Others will give short, descriptive phrases, and still others will greatly elaborate on the scene, with long, interesting stories evolving. The teacher then notes each child's progress and develops language activities according to needs. By taping and dating the responses, the teacher can later compare the student's progress.

Another opportunity for informal assessment involves the teacher's observing a child as she gives directions to another student and then noting whether the directions were clear and concise. The teacher may note whether the listening student was able to work through the directions provided by the first child. By using a natural, informal assessment exercise or activity that is closely related to the context in which it takes place, the teacher can judge students' progress by means of a previously established set of criteria. The criteria can be shared with students so that they can judge their own progress as well (Pinnell, 1991).

Teachers can note language problems during informal and formal conversations in the classroom. Articulation, lisping, and stuttering problems are often readily noticeable. Detecting dialectical differences and incorrect usage may require more time. Barr (1990) suggests that teachers frequently keep records about a young bilingual student's talk, noting significant gains in the child's acquisition of English.

Devising a checklist for usage errors can be effective but limited to those categories included. The most obvious errors should be eliminated first. For example, if the children constantly use "ain't" and double negatives such as "He don't do nothing," it is pointless to try to make them distinguish between "shall" and "may." Begin where the children are and go from there.

Conferences between the teacher and child are a very effective way to discover language abilities. This is particularly true if the teacher has empathy for the child and asks questions in a sensitive, supportive manner. As Barr (1990, p. 246) writes, "Sympathetic questioning and listening can enable children to share their sense of where they are doing well and where they are having problems."

Summary

The English language is the most widely spoken language in the world, and it is always changing. As it has done for centuries, English continues to borrow words from other languages. In addition, new words are created and become a part of the language and the culture.

The sounds and meanings of a language are studied in phonology and morphology. Children discover the rules governing the arrangement of words in a language, or its syntax, before they master word meanings, or semantics. Children who learn English as a second language encounter new sounds of consonants and vowels, new word meanings, and unfamiliar syntactical patterns, thereby making it a difficult task.

By incorporating language activities throughout the curriculum, teachers can guide their students' language development and expansion to increase their communicative competence.

Questions

1. How are semantics, syntax, and phonology related?
2. What is unique about your dialect?
3. How does culture influence language?
4. What languages have had the most influence on English? Why?
5. How has English changed in recent years?
6. How would you encourage children to expand their language use in your classroom?
7. How can teachers aid second-language students if they cannot speak the language?

Reflective Teaching

Flip back to the beginning of the chapter to the teaching vignette entitled "Peering into the Classroom." After rereading the vignette, consider the following questions: What characteristics (either implied or directly exhibited) does the teacher possess that you would like to develop? What strengths and weaknesses are revealed for the students described in this section? How would you meet the needs of students such as these?

Activities

1. Make a list of five slang terms, and their meanings, that were used by your parents or grandparents. Share the words with classmates.
2. Make a list of five terms that are unique to a particular occupation.
3. Develop an activity based on your language and cultural heritage to share with your students. (For example, you might use folktales that can be acted out.)
4. Develop methods for teaching English to non-English-speaking students.
5. Make your own list of poems and folktales from different cultures.
6. Plan a United Nations' Day in which your students can share their cultural heritages through dress, food, song, presentations about national heroes and famous people, and games.

Further Reading

Abbott, S., & Grose, C. (1998). "I know English so many, Mrs. Abbott": Reciprocal discoveries in a linguistically diverse classroom. *Language Arts, 75* (3), 175–184.

Fránquiz, M. E., & de la Luz Reyes, M. (1998). Creating inclusive learning communities through English language arts: From chanclas to canicas. *Language Arts, 75* (3), 211–220.

Helman, L. A. (2004). Building on the sound system of Spanish: Insights from the alphabetic spellings of English-language learners. *The Reading Teacher, 57* (5), 452–460.

Johnaron, P. (2004). *Choice words: How language affects children's learning.* Portland, ME: Stenhouse.

Labov, W. (2003). When ordinary children fail to read. *Reading Research Quarterly, 38* (2), 128–131.

Mates, B. F., & Strommen, B. F. (1996). Why Ernie can't read: Sesame Street and literacy. *The Reading Teacher, 49* (4), 300–307.

Smolkin, L. B., & Suina, J. H. (1996). Lost in language and language lost: Considering Native language in classrooms. *Language Arts, 73* (3), 166–172.

References

Abbott, S., & Grose, C. (1998). "I know English so many, Mrs. Abbott": Reciprocal Discoveries in a linguistically diverse classroom. *Language Arts, 75* (3), 175–184.

Aunola, K., Nurmi, J. E., Niemi, P., Lerkkanen, M. K., & Rasku-Puttonen, H. (2002). Developmental dynamics of achievement strategies, reading performance, and parental beliefs. *Reading Research Quarterly, 37* (3), 310–327.

Barr, M. (1990). The Primary Language Record: Reflection of issues in evaluation. *Language Arts, 67* (3), 244–253.

Britton, J. (1983). Writing and the story world. In B. Kroll & G. Wells (Eds.), *Explorations in the development of writing.* New York: Wiley.

Chang, Y. L., & Watson, D. J. (1988). Adaptation of prediction strategies and materials in a Chinese/English bilingual classroom. *The Reading Teacher, 42* (1), 36–44.

Chomsky, C. S. (1969). *The acquisition of syntax in children from 5 to 10.* Cambridge, MA: MIT Press.

Clark, E. V. (1981). Lexical innovations: How children learn to create new words. In W. Deutsch (Ed.), *The child's construction of language.* London: Academic Press.

Clark, E. V. (1982). The young word maker: A case of innovations in the child's lexicon. In E. Wanner & L. R. Gleitman (Eds.), *Language acquisition: The state of the art.* New York: Cambridge University Press.

Condon, W. S., & Sander, L. W. (1974). Neonate movement is synchronized with adult speech: Interactional participation and language acquisition. *Science, 183,* 99–101.

Cope, D., & Kalentzis, M. (1993). The power of literacy and the literacy of power. In D. Cope & M. Kalentzis (Eds.), *The power of literacy: A genre approach to teaching writing* (pp. 63–89). Pittsburgh, PA: University of Pittsburgh Press.

Crowell, C. G. (1998). Talking about books: Celebrating linguistic diversity. *Language Arts, 75* (3), 228–235.

Danielson, K. E. (1992). Learning about early writing from response to literature. *Language Arts, 69* (4), 274–280.

Delpit, L. (1995). *Other people's children.* New York: New Press.

Donato, R. (1997). *The other struggle for equal schools: Mexican Americans during the civil rights era.* Albany, NY: State University of New York Press.

Durán, L. (1994). Toward a better understanding of codeswitching and interlanguage in bilinguality: Implications for bilingual instruction. *Journal of Educational Issues of Language Minority Education, 14,* 19–88.

Dyson, A. H. (1991). Faces in the crowd: Developing profiles of language users. In J. A. Roderick (Ed.), *Context-responsive approaches to assessing children's language* (pp. 20–31). Urbana, IL: National Council of Teachers of English.

Flood, J., & Salus, P. H. (1984). *Language and the language arts.* Englewood Cliffs, NJ: Prentice Hall.

Flores, B., Cousin, P. T., & Díaz, E. (1991). Transforming deficit myths about learning, language, and culture. *Language Arts, 68* (5), 369–379.

Fránquiz, M. E., & de la Luz Reyes, M. (1998). Creating inclusive learning communities through English language arts: From chanclas to canicas. *Language Arts, 75* (3), 211–220.

Gleason, J. B. (1985). Studying language development. In J. B. Gleason (Ed.), *The development of language.* Columbus, OH: Merrill.

Goldstein, B. (2001). Transcription of Spanish and Spanish-influenced English. *Communication Disorders Quarterly, 23* (1), 54–60.

Halliday, M. A. K. (1975). *Learning how to mean: Exploration in the development of language.* London: Edward Arnold.

Hayes, D. (1989). Children as storytellers. *Reading Horizons, 29* (2), 139–146.

Helman, L. A. (2004). Building on the sound system of Spanish: Insights from the alphabetic spellings of English-language learners. *The Reading Teacher, 57* (5), 452–460.

Hymes, D. (1971). Competence and performance in linguistic theory. In R. Huxley & E. Ingram (Eds.), *Language acquisition: Models and methods.* London: Academic Press.

Kaser, S., & Short, K. (1998). Exploring culture through children's connections. *Language Arts, 75* (3), 185–192.

Martin, J. (1989). *Factual writing.* London: Oxford University Press.

McCrum, R., Cran, W., & MacNeil, R. (1986). *The story of English.* New York: Viking.

McNamara, J. (1972). Cognitive basis of language learning in infants. *Psychological Review, 79* (1), 1–13.

Morrow, L. M. (1988). Retelling stories as a diagnostic tool. In S. M. Glazer, L. W. Searfoss, & L. M. Gentile (Eds.), *Reexamining reading diagnosis: New trends and procedures.* Newark, DE: International Reading Association.

Myers, D. L. (1984). *Understanding language.* Upper Montclair, NJ: Boynton/Cook.

Nakazima, S. A. (1975). Phonemicization and symbolization in language development. In E. H. Lenneberg & E. Lenneberg (Eds.), *Foundations of language: Vol. 1. A multidisciplinary approach.* New York: Academic Press.

Oller, D. K. (1980). The emergence of the sounds of speech in infancy. In G. H. Yeni-Komshian, J. F. Kavanaugh, & C. A. Ferguson, (Eds.), *Child phonology: Vol. 1. Production.* New York: Academic Press.

Oller, D. K., & Eilers, R. E. (1982). Similarity of babbling in Spanish- and English-learning babies. *Journal of Child Language, 9* (3), 565–577.

Pease, D., & Gleason, J. B. (1985). Gaining meaning: Semantic development. In J. B. Gleason (Ed.), *The development of language.* Columbus, OH: Merrill.

Pinnell, G. S. (1991). Interactive assessment: Teachers and children as learners. In J. A. Roderick (Ed.), *Context-responsive approaches to assessing children's language* (pp. 79–96). Urbana, IL: National Council of Teachers of English.

Putnam, L. R. (1994–1995). An interview with Noam Chomsky. *The Reading Teacher, 48* (4), 328–333.

Saville-Troike, M. R., & Troike, R. C. (1971). *A handbook of bilingual education.* Washington, D.C.: Teachers of English to Speakers of Other Languages.

Searfoss, L. W. (1988). Winds of change in reading instruction. *Reading Instruction Journal, 31* (1), 2–6.

Sheehy, M. (2002). Illuminating constructivism: Structure, discourse, and subjectivity in a middle school classroom. *Reading Research Quarterly, 37* (3), 278–308.

Vygotsky, L. W. (1962). *Thought and language.* Cambridge, MA: MIT Press.

Children's Literature

Delacre, L. (1993). *Vejigante masquerader*. New York: Scholastic.

Ehlert, L., & Prince, A. (1992). *Moon rope*. New York: Scholastic.

Jiannan, F. (1991). *Jingwei filling the sea*. Beijing: Dolphin Books.

Lester, H. (1999). *Hooway for Wodney Wat* (L. Munsinger, Illus.). Boston: Houghton Mifflin.

Mora, P. (1994). *The desert is my mother/El desierto es mi madre* (D. Lechon, Illus.). Santa Fe: Piñata Books.

Mora, P. (1994). *Listen to the desert/Oye al desierto* (F. Mora, Illus.). New York: Clarion.

Mora, P. (1996). *Uno, dos, tres: One, two, three* (B. Lavalee, Illus.). New York: Clarion.

Reiser, L. (1993). *Margaret and Margarita, Margarita y Margaret*. New York: Scholastic.

Soto, G. (1996). *Off and running* (E. Velasquez, Illus.). San Diego: Harcourt Brace.

Soto, G. (1996). *The old man and his door* (J. Cepeda, Illus.). New York: Putnam.

Speaking
The Oral Expression of Thoughts

> Language learners must invent and try out the rules of language for themselves through social interaction as they move toward control of language for meaning.
>
> —Glenellen Pace
> "When Teachers Use Literature for Literary Instruction:
> Ways That Constrain, Ways That Free"

PEERING INTO THE CLASSROOM
RE-CREATING A FAVORITE STORY THROUGH DRAMA

Vicki is crouched on the classroom floor, pretending to be a very quiet young cricket. Some of her classmates are pretending to be other insects: Jeremy is a big cricket; Cory, a locust; Paul, a praying mantis; Jennifer, a worm; Susan, a spittle bug; Matthew, a cicada; Darrin, a bumblebee; Sherry, a dragonfly; Nate, a luna moth. The other students in the class are pretending to be mosquitoes. These five- and six-year-olds are reenacting a story their teacher just read to them, Eric Carle's (1990) *The Very Quiet Cricket*. The very quiet cricket encounters the different insects, each of which make a noise except for the beautiful luna moth. The very quiet cricket learns to appreciate silence as well as to "chirp" to another cricket. At the end of the informal drama, smiles of delight wreathe the children's faces. They have not only been involved in a drama but have discovered new knowledge about insects in a most enjoyable way.

Chapter Objectives

The reader will:

✓ become familiar with language settings.

✓ become familiar with various forms of creative dramatics.

✓ understand the various components of storytelling.

✓ develop strategies for teaching oral language skills.

Standards for Professionals

The following Standards will be addressed in this chapter:

Standard 1: Foundational Knowledge and Dispositions

1.1 Demonstrate knowledge of psychological, sociological, and linguistic foundations of reading and writing processes and instruction.

1.3 Demonstrate knowledge of language development and reading acquisition and variations related to cultural and linguistic diversity.

1.4 Demonstrate knowledge of the major components of reading (phonemic awareness, word identification and phonics, vocabulary and background knowledge, fluency, comprehension strategies, and motivation) and how they are integrated in fluent reading.

Standard 2: Instructional Strategies and Curriculum Materials

2.1 Use instructional grouping options (individual, small-group, whole-class, and computer based) as appropriate for accomplishing given purpose.

Standard 4: Creating a Literate Environment

4.1 Use students' interests, reading abilities, and backgrounds as foundations for the reading and writing program.

4.2 Use a large supply of books, technology-based information, and nonprint materials representing multiple levels, broad interests, and cultural and linguistic backgrounds.

4.3 Model reading and writing enthusiastically as valued lifelong activities.

4.4 Motivate learners to be lifelong readers.

Introduction

Oral language allows for the sharing of thoughts and ideas with others. Young children who are proficient in using oral language tend to become good readers and possess a tendency to become good writers as well (Loban, 1976; Tiedt et al., 1983). Providing children with opportunities and situations in which they are encouraged and even required to express themselves results in the expansion of their oral language. Such a fostering of conceptual development creates a language need; thus, *as* the complexity of children's thoughts and problem-solving abilities increases, so too does the need for language to clarify, categorize, conjecture, evaluate, interpret, synthesize, and summarize. These are all strategies for learning. Thus, thinking and language are interwoven and should be nurtured as such in teaching.

In this chapter, speaking, drama, and storytelling are examined. In addition, reader's theater and choral speaking are considered along with the elements of intonation—pitch, stress, and juncture.

The Importance of Oral Language

Children need to be free to discuss their knowledge, thoughts, and feelings with each other, for they have much to share. According to Berlin (1990, p. 159), "Language, we are now beginning to see, does not simply record our experience, it actually shapes it, structuring it in a way that determines what we see and do not see, what we know, who we are and who we are not." In a longitudinal empirical study of language and literacy development, it was found that reading and writing success is very much dependent on oral language skills. Therefore we need to place greater emphasis on vocabulary and on language-rich classroom environments, particularly in preschool and primary classrooms (Snow, Dickinson, & Tabors, 2002). Cindy Shultz Rosenbloom (1991, p. 54), a kindergarten teacher in Ohio, does just that as she writes: "Not only does language shape experience, but in my classroom language and literature guide the development of the curriculum."

Children enter kindergarten with knowledge gained from their own firsthand experiences and from vicarious experiences as they are read to by others. As speakers, kindergartners have engaged in both numerous and varied conversations with peers, siblings, parents, and other adults. The school curriculum, however, emphasizes the printed rather than the spoken word despite the fact that 90 percent of our language use is oral in nature (Stoodt, 1989). At this time, children are expected to be competent oral language users because they have been talking fluently for years prior to entering school. Although their speaking vocabularies are large and their formed grammatical structures are quite sophisticated, attention needs to be given to the development of the expressive, oral language skills from kindergarten through the elementary grades and beyond. Research indicates that children benefit from engagements in both informal and formal talk throughout the school day (Heath, 1983).

Speaking is important for the development of the other language arts: thinking, reading, writing, and listening. Thinking is actually enhanced by one's need to organize, conceptualize, clarify, and in some instances, simplify thoughts, feelings, and ideas as they are shared orally. Speaking facilitates reading, especially in the area of vocabulary acquisition, as children add new words to their speaking repertoires and simultaneously to their reading vocabularies. Storytelling, a form of language sharing in which children can participate and which they enjoy, provides young children with a basic grasp of the important elements of a story: plot, characters, setting (both time and place), and theme. These elements are not only present in the simple texts children complete as "beginning readers," but also in many of the materials they will encounter as "mature readers."

Oral language often supports writing, especially as young children are exposed to writing's initial stages. When undertaking a writing task, children often talk to themselves; such talk serves various functions. Some children engage in self-dialogue as they write, later using punctuation (exclamation points and underlining, for example) as graphic representations of intonation (Graves, 1983). Other children talk to themselves as they generate their writing ideas in a type of oral evaluation of the soundness of their own creative efforts. Thus, self-dialogue is used as a means of analysis of a written product (Dyson, 1981). Even as adults, people tend to read their written product aloud when the writing task is an important one.

Students at all grade levels need to engage in discussions about their individual pieces of writing. Having opportunities to talk with peers about a topic or idea prior to writing a first draft enables students to refine their thoughts about the writing piece. Thus, when discussion precedes the writing event, the quality of the written product improves. This is true because the writer has probably analyzed, elaborated, questioned, and to some extent justified thoughts and ideas prior to putting them down on paper.

After students have completed a writing assignment, the teacher should set aside time for a sharing of efforts. At this point, the discussions should focus primarily on the positive aspects of each of the finished pieces; this allows all the students to benefit from one another's successes. Students can give a supportive statement and then ask a constructive question about the writing piece. This necessitates frequent modeling by the teacher to demonstrate good questions.

Finally, speaking is important to the development of listening because good speakers actually tend to be good listeners; they are genuinely interested in what others say. In addition, good speakers not only have content worthy of sharing with others but are also effective in utilizing the special oral language skills of fluency, intonation, and style. They "invite" others to listen to them by projecting an enticing message. Clearly, these skills are demonstrated by network news anchor people who tend to articulate clearly, delivering news stories at a steady but brisk pace free of hesitations or pauses.

Because oral language skills contribute to thinking, reading, writing, and listening, teachers need to guide children's refinement of oral material presented. This can be done through teacher modeling and the oral sharing of quality literature. It is also beneficial for teachers to ask students meaningful questions that focus on content. Clearly, children need to engage in oral language activities in order to gather and share information as well as to react to new experiences. Students need ample opportunities to engage in meaningful dialogue as part of the learning process, something that they will be required to do on a daily basis as adult members of the nation's workforce.

Speaking and listening have been added to many states' standards requirements. According to James M. Brewbaker (1997, p. 81):

Without a great deal of warning or preparation, many English teachers find themselves in the position of being responsible for an expanded English curriculum that includes not only the traditional language arts of writing and reading but also the "new" language arts of speaking, listening, and media literacy. This pa. idigm shift that overtly includes and elevates the position of oral language arts in the English classroom is largely the result of the standards movement at both the national and state levels.

Effective teachers recognize that "the quality of teacher-student interactions and collaborative talk, especially during scaffolded teacher assistance periods, can hasten students' development" (Block & Pressley, 2002, p. 3).

Speaking includes both spontaneous informal speech, such as talking in work groups, responding in a class discussion, and participating in interviews, as well as giving a formal delivery of a presentation orally such as an oral report on a topic in science or social studies. Mary Beth Monahan (2003, p. 206) asserts that we should encourage our class to be "always on the lookout for language—exploring how and why we use language in certain situations and with particular people, investigating how language is used to confer or deny power, and considering the voices that we adopt as speakers and writers." Monahan has her students keep a notebook where they jot down examples of language use that they hear in everyday conversations (e.g., she used sarcasm to gain power in that discussion) or in their reading (e.g., the author used language to subordinate others and maintain social inequalities such as when an elderly African American must refer to a storekeeper as Mr. Wallace while he in turn is addressed by his first name).

Language Settings

Speaking is typically classified according to four types of settings: formal, informal, ceremonial, and intimate (Klein, 1977). In a formal setting, oral presentations, which include political speeches, homilies, and lectures, must be prepared in advance and presented in a serious tone.

An informal setting does not require such prior preparation of speeches or messages. Rather, the informal atmosphere is more casual and relaxed as individuals engage in conversation. Because conversations often shift from topic to topic, speakers must be alert to all the interactions within a conversation. The demands of keeping up with the discussion while preparing additional comments can make speaking in informal settings more rigorous than speaking in formal ones.

Ceremonial settings involve events of cultural importance, such as those of a legal or religious nature. Weddings, baptisms, graduations, and court trials are all examples of ceremonial settings.

In an intimate setting, people know each other very well. Speaking in this type of setting can involve two close friends, three classmates, or five teammates, all of whom are familiar with the language and behavior of the other speakers. Indeed, the way an individual pronounces a word or sighs conveys a certain meaning within an intimate setting; yet the same pronunciation or the same sigh would probably not be interpretable in any other setting. Because an intimate setting tends to be the most private of the four types, such an atmosphere is not commonplace in the elementary school classroom, although it is perhaps found within one-to-one conferences between teacher and student or in small class groups that have been established after the students have become familiar with one another.

When talking with family and friends, the conversation flows freely. In such a situation, it is perfectly acceptable to use one's dialect in lieu of standard English or, in the case of English as second language learners, to use one's first language. Teachers must convey that the different language settings influence how and what we use when we speak. Consider the following circumstances:

- *A child whose first language is Arabic is talking with her grandfather.* Most likely the child's grandfather only knows Arabic.

- *A middle schooler talking with friends after school uses slang and some mild profanity.* Like it or not, slang and profanity are part of the popular culture of today's society. As teachers we cringe when we hear it from students but such language plays a prominent role in current movies and television shows such as *South Park* and *The Simpsons*.

- *A student speaking in an Appalachian dialect with his grandmother.* Oftentimes we revert to our original dialects in a type of "remembering our upbringing," or put another way, in order to not offend our older relatives who are less educated than we have become. Thus by using the dialect of our roots, we are doing a kind of "dialectical codeswitching" in an attempt not to embarrass our family and friends. This may occur with African Americans, Chinese, Southerners, Bostonians, New Yorkers, Puerto Ricans, Texans, and others as they talk with old friends and family from their former neighborhood or town.

Because students are most accustomed to and comfortable with informal language settings, it is logical to begin oral language instruction with conversations and discussions.

There are three steps to encourage informal speaking participation by all students:

1. both teacher and students should expect every student to speak orally every day in every content area;

2. the teacher should establish classroom procedures and practices that make universal speaking a reality; and,

3. students should be given information and tools to prepare them to speak and engage in discussions (Goulden, 1998).

From the first day of class, the teacher needs to call on those students who volunteer as well as those who fail to raise their hands. This sets up the pattern that everyone will be called upon at any time by the teacher. The teacher needs to give the class ample wait time, that is, at least five seconds, after asking a question so that the students can formulate their responses in their minds.

In some instances, the teacher may establish students as good conversationalist role models for the class. Individuals outside the classroom setting, such as school personnel, area community leaders, or television personalities, may also serve as role models. Even characters from children's literature may be included as role models, as exemplified by Marc Brown's Arthur character, Charlotte in E. B. White's (1952) *Charlotte's Web*, or J. K. Rowling's Harry Potter and friends.

Conversational Skills

A good conversationalist must have oral language skills and an ability to think clearly and quickly. Interpersonal skills are also important inasmuch as conversation consists largely of personal reflections and therefore requires the sensitivity of all the participants. The participants in a conversation are collaborators; in addition to contributing thoughts, they must consider the ideas and feelings of others simultaneously. In effect, a good conversationalist is a well-rounded juggler who listens to and perceives another's input, composes an accompanying oral presentation, and adjusts to the emotional climate of the conversation itself.

The conversation process requires each participant to:

1. consider what has been said and anticipate what may be exchanged later in the conversation;
2. put thoughts and ideas together in a clear and concise manner, carefully selecting words and sentence structure before directly contributing to the conversation;
3. detect relationships between discussed items and relate these to previously gained knowledge;
4. make others in the conversation feel comfortable enough to ask questions or make comments;
5. contribute to but do not dominate the conversation;
6. highlight positiveness when helping to bring the conversation to a satisfactory conclusion.

Mrs. Pierce, a third-grade teacher, reviewed these six points with her students. One student, Garth, offered his summary of the conversation process by saying, "Don't talk, unless you have something to say." His comment was immediately countered by Nathan, who said, "Everybody has something important to say." After some discussion, the class decided that the two statements were good rules that everyone should follow. On a chart at the front of the classroom, Mrs. Pierce wrote both statements as a reminder of what is considered appropriate behavior when one is engaged in conversation.

Effective speaking necessitates having many varied opportunities to converse. Because such encounters must be both meaningful and purposeful, the teacher and students need to establish and meet progressive goals that can be attained through verbal interaction.

Knowing what the conversation process involves is not enough for students; rather, they must be interactive participants in meaningful conversation on a daily basis so that they can develop the oral language skills deemed necessary for a good conversationalist. To this end, a teacher must plan motivating activities whereby children will discuss their thoughts, feelings, and beliefs, and are allowed to do so in an environment of trust and acceptance. As Nathan stated, everyone has something to contribute; what he failed to say, however, was that criticism must be honest and nonthreatening. By having respect for each individual's contributions to a conversation, all students feel secure with the knowledge that their own opinions and statements will not be ridiculed in any way.

Intonation

Intonation includes the stress, pitch, and juncture of spoken language. By age two, children use intonation naturally, albeit unconsciously. When no one was paying attention to two-year-old Richie, who had gotten his foot caught in a bucket, he called out, "Help, please!" Intonation can bring words to life with an element of excitement or create an atmosphere of death. Children need to understand how intonation can convey meaning to the listener.

Stress, also referred to as accent, is the emphasis one gives to sounds, words, or phrases as one speaks. Consider the sentence "I love hamburgers." If the sentence is read aloud three times, with the emphasis on a different word each time, the meaning changes. When one emphasizes the word *I*, the focus falls on the individual person as the one who loves hamburgers. Emphasizing *love* gives the listener the impression that the individual is deeply infatuated with hamburgers as a food. Emphasizing *hamburgers* gives the impression that burgers are one of the great delicacies of the culinary world.

Pitch, or tone, is the melodic effect of language whereby the tone of voice rises and falls. When French is spoken, one's attention is easily drawn to the beautiful, melodic sounds of the French language. Although, to the unaccustomed ear, Vietnamese appears to be a jumbled conglomeration of high- and low-pitched sounds; this language, like other Asiatic languages, actually utilizes tone as a way to convey different meanings of words with the same sounds. In English, pitch is used to change an ordinary statement into an exclamation or a question. Using the same sentence from above, "I love hamburgers," a speaker can change pitch at the end of the sentence to make it either an exclamation or a question.

Juncture is a pause between sounds, words, or phrases. In essence, juncture serves as punctuation for oral language. Pauses, which are made at comma, semicolon, and period stops without change in the use of stress or pitch, may also serve to distinguish points for emphasis. Examples of the emphatic use of juncture include "I planned to watch the game, [pause] but the cable went out on my television set" or "John [pause] will provide us with an explanation of the events."

This "highlighting" effect can be achieved with "I love hamburgers." By pausing after the first word, the speaker clearly stresses who loves hamburgers, whereas a slight hesitation after the second word allows for full expression of the speaker's fondness for hamburgers.

Figure 6.1   Intonation and its qualities

Oral Interpretation of Poetry and Prose

Oral interpretation is the way in which poetry and prose are spoken or read aloud. The speaker or reader sets the rhythm, tempo, or cadence for the selection and by using the components of intonation—stress, pitch, and juncture—presents the poem or prose in a certain way. Oral interpretation is an enjoyable speaking activity in which every child can participate.

Because there is no single right or wrong way to interpret children's literature, oral interpretation encourages creativity and experimentation with language and its sounds. As McCauley and McCauley (1992) put it, "Children must feel free to take risks" (p. 530). Thus oral interpretation develops positive attitudes toward speaking and fosters cooperative learning.

Children who have learning disabilities or other reading problems often find a kind of refuge in oral interpretation in that it is generally a group activity. Analogous to the individual who sings off key yet feels secure in singing with the rest of the church congregation, the student who lacks fluency in oral reading can join a small group of classmates as they orally interpret children's literature and feel quite comfortable, if not competent.

The popularity of rap music has freed some children not only to participate in oral interpretation but also to compose their own rap and then present it to the class. For instance, the following rap was created by a group of nine- and ten-year-old boys:

> **Don't Pollute the Air**
> We need to protect the environment
> Keeping it clean just makes sense
> Then the air we breathe stays clean and clear
> No bad smog our lungs to fear
> So don't burn trash or drive polluting cars
> And at night we'll be able to see the stars
> Acid rain won't kill the trees
> And we'll live longer healthfully
> —Max, Travis, and Tork

Language Play, Fluency, and Children's Literature

Language play and reading fluency go hand in hand. Critical to beginning readers' success is the rapid transition from attending to words letter-by-letter (or chunks) to being able to readily recognize the entire word. Lots of language play enhances oral familiarity with words and aids word recognition when the language play is shared through charts or displayed in other ways. Writing patterned language from songs such as "I Love the Mountains" or "Twinkle, Twinkle Little Star," or poetry such as "I Like Bugs" by Margaret Wise Brown, or books like *Brown Bear, Brown Bear, What Do You See?* (Martin, 1968) or *Chicken Soup with Rice* (Sendak, 1969) on large charts or putting it in booklets that the children can keep in their desks to pull out and share with a partner from time to time aids fluency and word recognition.

Lots of children's books encourage language play. Consider the classic *Alexander and the Terrible, Horrible, No Good, Very Bad Day* (Viorst, 1972). What terrific synonyms for "rotten!" Many picture books offer playful language for children to share. Pamela Duncan Edwards is noted for her language play picture books such as *Some Smug Slug* (1996) and *Four Famished Foxes and Fosdyke* (1995), which feature alliteration. Her *Ed and Fred Flea* (1999) plays on homonyms such as "flea" and "flee." Another of Edwards' frolicsome word-play books is *Honk* (1998). Although these are enjoyable for primary-grade students, such books can also serve as models for intermediate students.

Choral Speaking and Reading

Choral speaking and reading are enjoyable activities for children. Choral reading itself "never fails to excite children's interest in reading regardless of their age, reading level, or level of language proficiency... [for] children whose first language is not English [they] are able to read choral reading selections with little difficulty" (McCauley & McCauley, 1992, p. 527). Generally, oral interpretation in the elementary grades begins with choral speaking and reading. Mother Goose rhymes provide appropriate material for kindergartners and first graders inasmuch as young children tend to be familiar with the various verses. A Mother Goose rhyme can be introduced as an oral interpretation activity in the following manner:

1. Introduce the class to the verse of the rhyme.
2. Have the class say the verse together.
3. Have the students repeat the verse while clapping their hands to the rhythm. If drums are available, the teacher can have two students tap out the rhythm on these instruments.
4. Divide the verse into alternating sections, with a student assuming the role of the leader and the remainder of the class taking the group role. The entire class should respond at the "all" prompt.
5. Have the children suggest various ways that voices could be changed and used within the rhyme. For example, whispering the words or having the group say the words softly and the leader speak loudly might be

mentioned. After each suggestion, the class could perform the verse by incorporating the changes.

As an alternative, students could be divided into two groups of equal size, with one group reciting the nursery rhyme itself and the other group softly repeating a refrain (for instance, "tick tock" for "Hickory, Dickory, Dock" or "meow, meow" for "The Three Little Kittens").

Some picture books lend themselves to choral reading. Bill Martin, Jr., and John Archambault's (1989) delightful book *Chicka Chicka Boom Boom* introduces children to the lowercase letters of the alphabet. The refrain is "Chicka chicka boom boom, will there be enough room?" Because all 26 letters of the alphabet have a role in this book, young students can recite the book together, with each member of the class taking a letter and the entire class joining in the refrain. Another example is *Pumpkin, Pumpkin* by Jeanne Titherington (1986), which is a descriptive, science-oriented story that is simplistic enough for five- and six-year-olds to perform as a choral reading activity. This tale centers upon the natural progression from pumpkin seed to blossom to pumpkin. *Yo! Yes?* by Chris Raschka (1993), a superb choral reading choice for six- and seven-year-olds, is a story about an African American boy and a white boy who meet on the street and become friends. Poetry can be shared together as Pam Muñoz Ryan's (2002) "Hello Ocean," which shares the aesthetic aspects of a beach. "Sandy grains in a salty drink/are best for fish and whales I think. I lick the drops/still on my face;/I love the way/the ocean tastes."

Choral reading of poetry takes on new meaning for middle- and upper-grade students because for many it is the first time they begin to acquire a true appreciation of poetry and the poets who write it. "Children usually dislike talking about poetry, often because they feel the need to construct a 'right' interpretation" (McClure, 1995, p. 117). Engaging in choral reading of well-loved poems allows children the enjoyable experience of focusing on the images, rhyme, and rhythm created by the poet. For instance, children relish Jack Prelutsky's poem "A Remarkable Adventure" in *Something Big Has Been Here* (1990). In the poem, a child describes a wild and absurd adventure that happened to coincide with precisely the time he should have been doing his homework. The child elaborately explains to his teacher why he doesn't have his homework. Other humorous contemporary poetry that lends itself to choral reading or speaking can be found in two of Prelutsky's other works (1982, 2000) *The Baby Uggs Are Hatching* and *It's Raining Pigs and Noodles*, Rebecca Kai Dotlich's (2003), *In the Spin of Things: Poetry of Motion*, and in Shel Silverstein's (1974, 1981) *Where the Sidewalk Ends* and *A Light in the Attic*.

Older children, who are somewhat sophisticated and enjoy a wide range of choral speaking experiences, will delight in the choral readings to be found within Paul Janeczko's (2001) collection, *Dirty Laundry Pile: Poems in Different Voices*. For poetry of a more frightening nature, Prelutsky's (1980) *The Headless Horseman Rides Tonight* contains 12 poems about giants, poltergeists, and zombies, all of which can be used for either choral reading or speaking.

Older children often relate to poetry such as the poem "Somebody Said That It Couldn't Be Done" (printed in Sloyer, 1983). Divide the class into two groups and have them present a choral reading of this anonymously written work as follows:

All:	Somebody Said It Couldn't Be Done
All:	Somebody Said It Couldn't Be Done
Group 1:	But he, with a grin replied
Group 2:	He'd never be one to say it couldn't be done— Leastways not 'til he tried.
Group 1:	So he buckled right in, with a trace of a grin;
Group 2:	By golly, he went right to it.
Group 1:	He tackled The Thing That Couldn't Be Done!
All:	And he couldn't do it!

Serious poetry should also be included in choral speaking as children begin to examine their own feelings and emotions. As Georgia Heard (1989, p. 14) notes, "Poems come from something deeply felt." Sometimes one child's experiences or questions will provide the opportunity for sharing poetry about real life.

Songs as Choral Language

Poetry is often the basis of song lyrics. Students in grades three through eight are capable of using the melodies of songs with which they are familiar to write new lyrics based on concepts currently being studied. For instance, the teacher can require that the song contain five facts. A group of fourth graders used the melody of the Everly Brothers' *Cathy's Clown* to come up with a "song summary" of what they had learned in a science unit on space. The following song is called "Asteroids":

Asteroids
(Sing to tune of Everly Brothers' "Cathy's Clown")

Here they come, Asteroids
Mini planets in the sky
Don't know how they got there
But there they are, Asteroids

There are several different types
Stony iron meteorites
Pock marked with craters
Very dark in color
Carbonaceous chondrites

Here they come, Asteroids
Mini planets in the sky
Don't know how they got there
But there they are, Asteroids

Made of hydrocarbon
Oldest material around
Iron nickel alloy
Melted planetary bodies
Big ones weigh several tons

Here they come, Asteroids
Mini planets in the sky
Don't know how, they got there
But there they are, Asteroids
Asteroids, Asteroids

Karaoke tapes are available for purchase in the music departments of large discount stores. Usually recently recorded songs by current pop and country artists are available, something that is highly motivational for middle school students. Other options include having the students write their verses to favorite theme songs from television (i.e., rather than "Here's the Story of a Man Named Brady" it becomes "Here's the Story of an Amphibian." "Meet the Flintstones" becomes "Meet the Pioneers"). Country-and-western songs, such as those sung by Alan Jackson, Kenny Chesney, George Strait, or Shania Twain, are easier for students to adapt, as many are repetitive in nature and slow in tempo.

Reader's Theater

Reader's theater, which is unique to choral reading and speaking techniques, allows for student portrayal of individual literary characters through oral interpretation. The written script may be based on either an entire book, such as a picture book, or an episode within a longer work, such as a novel. In essence, then, reader's theater becomes an informal reading of various dialogues woven together through narration.

Reader's theater is a formalized dramatic presentation of a piece of literature. According to Young and Ferguson (1995, p. 496), reader's theater is "a presentation of fiction, nonfiction, or poetry that is expressively and emotionally read aloud by several readers, and contributes to improved reading fluency, comprehension, and confidence." Students select a script or develop their own from a piece of literature. They then rehearse and stage the presentation.

Staging a reader's theater requires that some preparations take place. Scripts need to be placed in sturdy ring binders. Each reader's lines need to be marked with a highlighter. The readers must be taught to look down at the script with their eyes, not moving their heads. In the case of a long passage that goes from one page to the next, the latter portion can be photocopied and both pages placed side by side in the binder. This prevents the reader from having to turn the page in the midst of reading (Shepard, 1994).

The readers themselves should wear smocks: simple, large rectangular pieces of cloth with holes for the head and snaps or velcro fasteners on both sides, or T-shirts that are the same color. To give an even more professional appearance, T-shirts can have the school name and "Reader's Theater Group" printed on them. Having the readers dress alike gives them a neutral appearance so that the message of the literature comes across rather than an array of different dress styles and colors. Stools are more useful than chairs and should be of varying heights to reflect the heights of different characters (for instance, a tall stool for the donkey and a short chair for the dog). In addition, stools need to be sturdy so they can be used to stand on. Some stories call for the use of a stepladder. A colored sheet attached to the chalkboard can be used as a backdrop. Other props can be used, such as a basket, plastic ivy hanging down from the ceiling to represent a beanstalk, a pot for cooking vegetables—all depending on the particular story. Because reader's theater relies heavily on mime as well as what is read, props are kept to a minimum.

The readers may stand or sit. Because children doing a reader's theater for the first time may be a bit nervous, sitting tends to lessen the anxiety level. The readers should hold their binders rather than set them on music stands or lecterns. The binder can rest in the palm of the left hand of right-handed students and the right hand of left-handed students so that the free hand can be used for gesturing.

Students should work on focusing. The narrator will focus on, or look toward, the audience while the characters look at whomever they are talking with according to the story. Other means of focus are also appropriate. The character may look off into the distance, as if out a window, while sharing her own thoughts. In some instances characters may turn to talk directly to the audience.

The positions on the stage should be assigned based on the characters. Those who have similar viewpoints should be placed together. Readers with the most lines should be on the far left and far right of the cast. Rather than entering and exiting as in plays, simply stepping forward, standing, or, if seated on stools, leaning slightly forward before speaking can serve as an entrance (and reversing the action as an exit).

Reader's theater should begin with one student introducing the title and the author, and another student giving a brief introduction of the story itself. The introduction should be a hook and not give the plot or the ending, away. At the end of the reader's theater, the readers should become quiet so that a pause comes over the room. Then in unison, the readers close their scripts, stand, and bow to the audience.

Start with commercially prepared scripts or scripts developed from picture books. Then the students can move toward making their own scripts from favorite passages. After an appropriate story has been chosen, the material must be adapted and transposed into a script for the reader's theater. The characters' dialogue is taken directly from the story. The narrator, or story-teller, is given dialogue that consists of the story's descriptive passages. This narration provides the audience with the story's introduction, mood, theme, and conclusion. The student assigned this task must weave the tale from beginning to end with smooth transitions so that the audience can follow the story line. Sometimes characters are mentioned in descriptive passages but do not engage in the story's dialogue. In such instances, direct dialogue can be developed for the characters, who will then have formal speaking parts within the script.

The material used for reader's theater must capture children's attention. Lively and/or suspenseful plots with compelling and interesting characters allow students to readily interpret both personalities and story lines. Such materials become both enticing and exciting as a medium of experimentation within oral interpretation. Stories centered around long, drawn out narratives cause children to quickly lose their eagerness to participate. Typically, a book that lends itself to reader's theater has an abundance of dialogue interspersed with brief, descriptive paragraphs.

Generally, children can easily relate to themes deemed appropriate to reader's theater: stories of compassion, generosity, greed, and honesty. Such themes prevail with picture books, making them excellent sources of material. A few suggested picture books for young students include Arnold Lobel's (1970) *Frog and Toad Are Friends,* Steven Kellogg's (1991) *Jack and the Beanstalk,* and William Steig's (1977) *Caleb & Kate.* Students will also enjoy Charlotte Huck's (1989) *Princess Furball,* Ellen Jackson's (1994) *Cinder Edna,* Robert Munsch's (1980) *The Paper Bag Princess,* Tomie dePaola's (1982) *Strega Nona's Magic Lessons,* and Vera B. Williams's (1983) *A Chair for My Mother.* Older students can write scripts from such books as *With Every Drop of Blood* (Collier & Collier, 1994), *Sarah Bishop* (O'Dell, 1980), *Number the Stars* (Lowry, 1989), *A Single Shard* (Park, 2001), and *Crispin: The Cross of Lead* (Avi, 2002).

Storytelling

Storytelling has received renewed interest in recent years, both in the classroom and in society as a whole. Storytelling abilities can benefit the development of both conversational and dramatic communication skills. Also through storytelling, children develop new awareness of meaning (Nicholson, 1992). According to Karla Hawkins Wendelin (1991, p. 181):

> Engaging students in storytelling activities develops communication skills and encourages shared learning experiences. Telling stories enhances oral language and sharpens listening. Speaking ability is improved through attention to articulation, clarity, and volume. Poise and confidence in speaking before a group are acquired in the accepting environment of the classroom. Students experiment with various intonations and reflect a range of emotions in their voices. They are faced with the need to select just the right word to convey a thought. As they manipulate language, they also listen to, evaluate, and appreciate the expression of others.

The Storytelling Process

The storytelling process consists of six sequential stages. The first stage is the *selection of a story* that appeals to the storyteller and is appropriate for the intended audience in terms of theme and mood. The second stage is the *analysis of the story's characters and plot.* The third stage is the *experimentation with intonation and gestures* to depict the story. *Telling the story through scenes,* particularly with a set introduction and conclusion, is the fourth stage. The fifth stage is the *telling of the story in rehearsal before the actual presentation to a live audience,* and the final stage is presentation to a live audience.

Stage 1: Become familiar with the story and determine its appropriateness for the intended audience.
        a. Select a story that appeals to you. The story should be one that so captures your attention that you want to share it with someone else.

Two bilingual students in Mike Ellis' sixth-grade class at May School tell stories in English and Spanish to preschoolers in the Head Start program. They are assisted by two classmates.

b. Read the story at least twice, paying particular attention to the plot. The plot should be straightforward, easy to follow, and without complexities, all of which might distract listeners. The theme should be apparent rather than hidden, and the theme and the mood of the story should be appropriate for the audience's age level.

Stage 2: Analyze characters and plot.

a. Because characters should be believable and any character differences in personalities and traits should be easy to portray, consider closely the traits and personalities of the characters. How do the characters relate to one another? What purpose does each character serve in the story? How would each character look? What type of movement and voice is appropriate for the various characters? Experiment with the development of each individual character's voice and physical appearance until you are satisfied with his or her representation.

Stage 3: Use oral interpretations and gestures in the story's presentation.

a. Read the story aloud to discover interesting phrases that must be retained for the story's complete effect. Such phrases may help the listener create visual images. For example, in *The Teeny Tiny Woman*, a Brothers Grimm folktale, the phrase "teeny tiny" is used as an adjective for all the objects: teeny tiny house, teeny tiny hat, teeny tiny gate, teeny tiny bone, and so on. The repetition of "teeny tiny" makes the story "visually" dramatic for the listener.

    b. Incorporate gestures that add to rather than distract from the story. For example, the portrayal of a giant requires one to stand straight and tall, keep arms out from the sides, and appear as if looking down on individuals of smaller stature. Likewise, leaning over, clasping hands together, and swinging them back and forth creates the image of an elephant walking through the jungle.

Stage 4: Note the story's sequence of events and create an established introduction and conclusion.

    a. Take note of the primary scenes of the story. Don't attempt to memorize the story word-for-word; instead, rely on the highlighted scenes and settings to progress through the story.

    b. Develop a set introduction and conclusion. The events in the middle of the story can be changed, but the story's beginning and ending must follow the story line.

    c. Create an alluring introduction so that listeners will be compelled to follow the story throughout. Although introductions are usually brief, they establish both the setting (time and place) and the theme of a story. In the same way, folktales, which tend to begin with "Once upon a time in a forest there lived a . . . ," become quite enchanting to young children.

    d. The conclusion should bring closure to the story. Detail the outcomes for all characters in such a way that listeners are not left wondering whether the story is complete.

Stage 5: Rehearse the story without an audience.

    a. Using a mirror, cassette recorder, or video recorder, practice telling the story several times before presenting it to others. This mastery scheme requires time and several repetitions before you will actually feel at ease in presenting the work to an unfamiliar audience.

Stage 6: Present the story to a live audience.

    a. When sharing a story with an audience, eliminate distractions as much as possible. For example, if a storyteller stands before patterned curtains or a window facing a playground or street, the audience may have difficulty concentrating on the story. Similarly, one's dress or mannerisms can interfere with the presentation.

Fables, fairy tales, folktales, and fantasies appeal to children in the primary grades. Appropriate titles include Aesop's fables; the "Jack" tales of Great Britain and Appalachia (of which *Jack and the Beanstalk* is the most famous); *The Five Chinese Brothers*; *The Princess and the Pea* and *The Ugly Duckling*, both in *Hans Christian Andersen: His Classic Fairy Tales* (1974); and Laura Numeroff's (1991)

If You Give A Moose A Muffin. Children in the intermediate grades enjoy E. J. Bird's (1990) *The Blizzard of 1896,* as well as selections from the books of Beverly Cleary, Virginia Hamilton, and Edgar Allan Poe.

Based on oral language tradition, storytelling is an excellent way to combine speaking and listening and to present lessons in music, social studies, and even science at all grade levels. American folktales are the root of the "salad bowl" culture, and their timeless characters become vivid and alive through storytelling. Popular stories for social studies include stories about Johnny Appleseed, Molly Pitcher, John Henry, Mike Fink, Paul Bunyan, and Annie Oakley. Similarly, children can easily visualize the four voyages of Columbus when Jean Fritz's (1980) *Where Do You Think You're Going, Christopher Columbus?* is used as the basis for storytelling. Fritz's biographies of the founding fathers also make excellent sources for storytelling in the area of social studies instruction.

6.1   The More You Know

Storytelling Resources

Bauer, C. F., & Bredeson, L. (1993). *Caroline Feller Bauer's new handbook for storytellers: With stories, poems, magic, and more.* Chicago: American Library Association. This is a valuable resource as it offers a comprehensive overview of storytelling.

Bauer, C. F. (1997). *Leading kids to books through puppets (mighty easy motivators/Caroline Feller Bauer).* Chicago: American Library Association. Great book for primary-grade teachers! Everything from making puppets from popsicle sticks and cereal boxes or using stuffed animals to creating a simple stage from a cardboard box and an old sheet is covered. Lots of practical, easy-to-follow ideas.

Livo, N. J., & Rietz, S. A. (1991). *Storytelling folklore sourcebook.* Denver: Libraries Unlimited. This resource contains a compendium of story elements (characters, objects, activities, motifs, and memory devices) for teachers and storytellers. A good book for use with intermediate and middle school students.

One of the leading collectors of stories for children as well as a foremost storyteller herself is Margaret Read MacDonald. Her collections contain stories from throughout the world. Below is a list of some works by Margaret Read MacDonald:

Bookplay: 101 creative themes to share with young children (1995)
Celebrate the world: Twenty tellable folktales for multicultural festivals (1994)
Ghost stories from the pacific northwest (1995)
The girl who wore too much: A folktale from Thailand (1998)
Peace tales: World folktales to talk about (1992)
Pickin' peas (1998)
The round book: Rounds to sing or play (1998)
The skit book: 101 skits for kids (1990)
Slop! A Welsh folktale (1997)
The storyteller's startup book: Finding, learning, performing, and using folktales (includes *Twelve tellable tales*) (1993)
Twenty tellable tales (1991)
When the lights go out: Twenty scary tales to tell (1988)

Both legends and unfamiliar cultures can be explored through the sharing of such stories as Verna Aardema's (1981) *The Riddle of the Drum: A Tale from Tizapaán, Mexico;* Joseph Bruchac's (1995) *Gluskabe and the Four Wishes;* Joyce Cooper Arkhurst's (1964) *The Adventures of Spider: West African Folktales;* and Taro Yashima's (1955) *Crow Boy.* Because such tales range from simplistic to relatively complex, children with learning disabilities and those who are slow learners can just as readily find a story for storytelling as the more academically talented or gifted students. Providing children with the opportunity to experience a fascination with other cultures may help them understand and accept others' differences more easily.

6.2   In the Classroom: Mini Lesson

Tall Tales

America has produced several folk heroes and accompanying tall tales about them. Steven Kellogg's (1988) *Johnny Appleseed* shares the legacy of the real-life character and his work planting apple trees on the frontier. At the end of the book, Kellogg includes a mural of some of the tall tales about Johnny Appleseed. The teacher should read the book to intermediate-grade students. Afterward, the students should locate a tall talle about another American folk hero and tell it to the class.

To further expand the use of tale tales, divide the students into groups of four and have them create their own tall tale character. Give each group three feet of cfash register tape (you can purchase at the office supply store expensively), and have them take turns writing the adventures of their character. They then use art supplies to create a head, arms, and feet to attach to the tape to represent their character. The groups then share their respective tall tales and pin their stories and illustration on the bulletin board for all to enjoy.

Kellogg, S. (1988). *Johnny Appleseed.* New York: Morrow.

Puppets

Puppets are an effective device for children to use during storytelling to develop self confidence. By using a hand puppet, a child can tell a simple story to the class or a small group of children without feeling pressured. Children love to manipulate and play with puppets, which seem to be regarded as cousins to their beloved stuffed animals. Puppets can be made from a variety of sources: paper bags, construction paper glued to wooden sticks or rods, paper towel rolls, socks, buttons, movable eyes, cloth, felt, pipe cleaners, pencils, yarn, grass, sticks, and other materials. Puppets infuse the story's characters with life. Commercially prepared puppets can be purchased from zoos (for animal puppets), book companies (for character puppets such as Arthur and Clifford, the big red dog), and school supply stores.

Typical favorites are hand puppets made of discarded socks or gloves. Puppets can be made for favorite books. For instance, for *The Very Hungry Caterpillar* (Carle, 1971), a caterpillar can be made from a green kneesock and two white buttons for eyes. A butterfly cut out of a small piece of yellow felt can be folded and hidden in the toe of the sock until the end of the story. The fruit, leaf, and other food mentioned in the story can be cut out of 12-inch felt squares. Each piece of food should have a slit in it so that the caterpillar can "eat" through it as it goes over the child's hand. At the end of the story, the child removes the caterpillar and pulls out the butterfly to show to the audience. An empty refrigerator or washing machine shipping box can be transformed into a puppet theater. Children can invite other classes to their performances.

Felt, Flannel, and Magnetic Boards

Felt and magnetic boards on stands offer structure for storytelling. Characters and aspects of a setting (ex. houses made of straw, sticks, and bricks) can be created to add to the story. Velcro strips glued to the back of felt or heavy paper can be secured on the felt board. To make a felt or flannel board, get a large sheet of cardboard. Cut two sections in the desired size. If a large board is desired, consider using thin plywood and hinging two sections together. If cardboard is used, glue the two pieces together and let stand overnight. Cover with a piece of felt or flannel that is one color. Keep in mind white felt or flannel gets dirty easily while black is often too dark for the figures to be distinguished. Green or sky blue are neutral colors and make a good background. The figures, houses, trees, etc., should be stored in plastic boxes by story so they will be readily accessible for storytelling.

When telling a story using a felt or flannel board, set it on a stand or the chalk railing and gather the students in a semicircle around you. Position yourself where everyone can see the board. Prior to telling the story, have the figures in the order in which they appear in the story and the props for the initial setting (trees, boat, lake, etc.) already on the board. Keep the figures out of the students' sight until you are ready to place them on the board. Place them in a box or in a carpenter's apron tied around your waist. As you tell the story keep your head at eye level of the students and look into their eyes. A common problem with beginning storytellers is that they talk to the board and not to their audience. Saying the words in the direction of the board will hinder the audience's understanding of the story.

Most classroom *white boards* are also magnetic so adhering a small magnet to a prop will suffice in keeping it from moving during the storytelling. When making magnetic figures, be aware that the heavier the figure or prop, the more likely it will slide down the magnetic board during the retelling. Thus, paper props work best for magnetic board storytelling.

If the story is simple in actions (e.g., *The Three Bears*, *The Three Little Pigs*, *The Emperor's New Clothes*, or *Henry and Mudge*), felt and magnetic boards make great accompaniments as there are few characters and the settings are simple. Complex stories with lots of action don't lend themselves to felt and magnetic board telling, as often the audience gets confused as to what is exactly taking place in the story.

Felt, flannel, and *magnetic boards* are useful in having children retell stories. It helps with comprehension, sequencing, and vocabulary development as well as the development of oral language skills. Youngsters often want to make their own stories and figures, so having additional boards on a smaller scale can be useful.

Flip Charts

Flip charts can be used for storytelling. The teacher uses the pages of a flip chart to illustrate several scenes of a story. The first page is the title of the story, followed by the setting up of the problem, then followed by the first action, second action, third action, and so on until the story's resolution. The main ideas are thereby introduced with each of the subsequent pictures. The charts can be drawn by hand. For those teachers who lack artistic skills, photocopy the pictures and make them into transparencies. Then using the overhead projector, copy the pictures on to the chart paper using a pencil. Trace over the pencil marks later with different colors of markers. Flip charts can also use a variety of materials that can be glued on to the chart paper: straw for a thatched roof, rice for rain, nylon net for a fish net, cloth for clothing or curtains, bark for tree trunks, a quarter for the moon, spaghetti to make a house, dried beans or peas for seeds, etc.

Roll Stories

Roll stories begin with the illustration of the title. Each scene is then illustrated using the same dimensions. Students need to be reminded to leave a short blank space between scenes. Shoeboxes placed on their sides with two toilet tissue rolls secured with pencils make terrific roll story theaters. Students can cut sheets of chart paper and tape to the tissue rolls before they begin drawing. A template can be used to designate the size of each illustration.

Using Objects from the Stories

Some stories can be told by having the *objects* from the story itself. For instance, Janet Stevens' (1995) *Tops and Bottoms* describes how wily Rabbit slyly outwits Bear when he offers to plant crops for Bear. When Bear says he wants tops, Rabbit plants radishes, carrots, and potatoes. When Bear says he wants bottoms, Rabbit plants beans, tomatoes, and cabbages. When Bear wants both tops and bottoms, Rabbit wisely plants corn. Hiding these vegetables in a basket, the storyteller removes them as the story progresses. A similar object story is Marcia Brown's (1947) classic, *Stone Soup*. The end of which the class can make a pot of soup.

6.3   In the Classroom: Teaching Hint

Shadow Puppetry

Shadow puppetry is an enjoyable form of storytelling for children. By using an overhead transparency projector to create silhouettes on a screen, students can share a favorite story with an audience. To make the screen, purchase an inexpensive white window shade (the kind that rolls up). Secure the shade with weather stripping to a frame made out of 1- by 2-inch wood. Reinforce the corners of the frame with L braces screwed into the wood. Secure the screen to a table or a teacher's desk by using two C clamps.

To make the projection work, set the overhead transparency projector on a table about 12 feet in front of the screen and turn it on. Objects can be projected from both the top of the overhead

continued

projector and from immediately behind the screen. For instance, by placing a blue overhead transparency on the projector, the screen appears blue. A 3-inch cardboard cutout of a sea monster laid on top of the transparency gives the appearance of a giant sea monster in a blue ocean on the screen. If a student stands just behind the screen and pretends to be swimming, the shadow on the screen will look as though the sea monster is after the "swimmer."

Colored transparencies can create a very dramatic effect. A red transparency on the overhead projector with strips of blue and yellow transparencies overlaid on top gives the beauty of a sunrise. Similarly, keeping the blue transparency on the top and adding a green transparency on the lower portion of the projector will produce the appearance of a blue sky and green grass. One- to two-inch cutouts of covered wagons can give the impression of a wagon train moving across the prairie. Tiny toy or stuffed animals can also be placed on the transparency and larger stuffed animals can be held up by a puppeteer just behind the screen.

Other variations are suggested by David Wisniewski (1995), a puppeteer and author/illustrator of picture books. Wisniewski suggests placing a plastic vine on the bottom edge of the transparency screen and pushing it up and across the screen to give the appearance of the beanstalk growing in *Jack and the Beanstalk*. At the same time, a puppeteer can stand behind the large screen and pretend to be Jack climbing the beanstalk while the narrator reads the story.

Wisniewski (1995) also suggests using lace, moving it across the overhead transparency screen as another puppeteer stands behind the large screen and jogs in place. This gives the appearance of a person running. Wax paper on the lower part of the overhead transparency screen gives the appearance of ground. By tilting the wax paper at an angle, a hill appears—good for using with a story such as *Blueberries for Sal* (McCloskey, 1948). By moving the wax paper up and down quickly, it appears that an earthquake is taking place or that a giant is walking nearby. By moving the wax paper slowly up and down, the impression is that of water and waves. By tearing the wax paper into jagged edges and overlaying them, a mountain range appears. Crinkled wax paper looks like a spider's web. When a piece of plain wax paper covers the entire transparency screen, fog appears on the large screen. A wax paper background can give the illusion of a snowy appearance for a story such as *The Polar Express* (Van Allsburg, 1985).

Figures that represent the characters of a story can be created from cardboard cutouts covered with black paper (Wisniewski, 1995). Small figures may be placed directly on the projector, whereas large figures may be held by a puppeteer behind the screen. Arms and legs can be attached to the cutouts with brass tacks, then manipulated using umbrella ribs from discarded umbrellas. Cardboard cutouts can also be attached to a puppeteer's headband with Velcro. For instance, the profiles of a princess, a prince, and a frog may be attached to puppeteers' headbands for the story *The Frog Prince*.

Students can have fun devising their own props and making innovations on the various stories that they elect to present. Clear transparency rolls and transparency marking pens can be used to make background scenery for a story such as *Strega Nona Meets Her Match* (dePaola, 1993) or *Sukey and the Mermaid* (San Souci, 1992). Cutting out wax paper frogs and placing them on blue overheads, in combination with cardboard profiles of other characters, can create the story *Tuesday* (Wiesner, 1991). Older students delight in creating new adventures and mysteries for Harry Potter and the students of Hogwarts.

dePaola, T. (1993). *Strega Nona meets her match.* New York: Putnam.

McCloskey, R. (1948). *Blueberries for Sal.* New York. Viking.

San Souci, R. D. (1992). *Sukey and the mermaid* (B. Pinkney, Illus.). New York: Four Winds.

Van Allsburg, C. (1985). *The polar express.* Boston: Houghton Mifflin.

Wiesner, D. (1991). *Tuesday.* Boston: Clarion.

Wisniewski, D. (1995, March). *From shadow to silhouette.* Speech presented at the Northern Illinois University's Children's Literature Institute, DeKalb, IL.

Discussions as Small Group Activities

Children should learn to engage in group discussions at an early age. With kindergartners and primary-grade students, the best way to introduce discussions is for the teacher to serve as the discussion guide. Until children become familiar with the discussion process, and often this is not until the third or fourth grade, they need direction and organization from the classroom teacher.

When initially arranging small discussion groups of five to seven children, the teacher should consider the interests and personalities of the individual students. The very first time such discussion groups are created, shy students should not be placed with children who like to dominate conversations. Children with attitude problems, particularly those in the upper grades, need to be assigned to groups carefully; the teacher should avoid combining students who are overly disruptive. According to Wieneck and O'Flahavan (1994, p. 491) the classroom teacher needs to "consider the social, interpretive, and reading abilities of each student, and use this information to create heterogeneous groups." They go on to say that the teacher should lead the group discussion and then coach students to lead their own discussions. In doing so, it is a good idea to have the students begin with something in common, such as a selection of quality literature. Well-developed story elements maintain students' interest, are more easily understood, and help students to make predictions and inferences, thereby facilitating student discussion. Stories from basal readers tend to be short; thus, these are particularly helpful when initiating group discussions in the classroom.

After the groups have been formed, students must be introduced to various discussion methods (some are discussed below). Then, members of a group decide how their assignment or task will be completed; at this time, a group-appointed leader, often a more assertive student, issues individual responsibilities to each member. Although a time frame may be established for the lengthier projects of the upper grades, the first attempts at group discussion should be short, concrete, straightforward, and motivating for each student. Since discussion groups are direct, cooperative learning endeavors, tasks that are enticing will promote students' willingness to complete their portions of the assignment successfully.

Brainstorming

Brainstorming, a process used by discussion groups, occurs when all participants contribute ideas or possible resolutions to a real or proposed problem. No idea is rejected; rather, all suggestions are accepted and recorded in writing. Usually the time allowed for such interaction is limited, perhaps no more than five minutes. Here are some possible problems or situations that might be investigated:

- If you were locked inside a Six Flags theme park or Walt Disney World, how would you get out without assistance?

- If you won the lottery and wanted to establish a foundation for worthy children's causes, which causes would you want to include?
- How many uses can you suggest for the following items: empty soda cans, railroad ties, old school buses, drinking straws, foam hamburger containers, and old sneakers?
- In what ways can students be encouraged not to drop out of school?
- How might you be able to get positive publicity for your school?
- Why does the school need a science lab for conducting experiments?

After students have brainstormed and compiled a list of several possible solutions to an indicated problem or situation, they are ready to reach a consensus. Such problem-solving interaction involves the careful consideration and examination of all suggestions until only two or three possible solutions remain. The group must be able to justify each of these in terms of viability.

Assignments that rely on brainstorming with consensus-building outcomes are most effective when the students can directly relate to the problem or situation. Indeed, real-life dilemmas are appropriate problems for students to attempt to resolve.

Panel Discussions and Debates

After gaining experience in brainstorming and consensus building, students are ready for the more formal presentations of panel discussions and debates. In panel discussions, a group of three to five students is assigned a specific topic to be presented before a designated audience. The duty of each of the panel members is to develop an individual oral report about a particular aspect of the main topic through research and group discussion. One student assumes the responsibility of serving as the panel leader or moderator. This position requires that the student not only present the first or the last report but also coordinate the group's work and the order of the presentations and give the introductory and concluding statements.

For debates, each group member must be familiar with information about a relevant problem or issue in order to develop answers to questions posed by the rest of the class. A formal debate, which requires that each participant give an opening statement, allows the participants to ask each other questions. Therefore, the researching of facts and figures to be used in a response becomes especially important to the support of one's argument. Because of the level of sophistication involved, debates are not usually introduced until about the fifth grade. If they are introduced earlier, students depend on emotional pitches rather than sound, credible facts, and opinions.

Recording student discussions and/or debates in both audiotape and videotape forms enables the teacher to assess students' oral language usage during discussions. It can also provide a direct, effective way to evaluate student contributions in small established groups without having to monitor the group's activities personally.

Drama as Creative Play

Drama is a natural extension of creative play in which all youngsters engage at an early age. In essence, drama is an experiment in socialization on the child's part; the child pretends or engages in "make believe" play in the simulation of real-life experiences: managing a store, attending school, protecting the community as a police officer, celebrating special events with tea parties, and the like. Unusual adventures tend to be imagined as well: rescuing survivors from a capsized ship, designing and manning a space vehicle that is going to Mars, sailing to China in search of ancient treasure, and so on. Such dramatic play permits children to have opportunities to deal with reality and to practice appropriate, social behavior. By providing an escape from reality, on the other hand, drama also enables children to examine and explore new behaviors and situations. Dramatic play has been found to make important contributions to children's early reading and writing development (Christie, 1990). Children depend on memory, imagination, observation, and interactions with others as they create new ways of behaving and communicating (Wagner, 1988). They step outside themselves and assume new roles, which may be ones they have observed firsthand, such as the role of mother or storekeeper, or through some form of media, as represented by Barbie or cartoon characters, for example.

Proponents of dramatics have cited the many benefits of this creative form, including improved critical and intuitive thinking skills, concentration, and reading comprehension (Gray, 1987), as well as associated improvements in vocabulary development, speech, and self-concept. Moreover, the use of drama can also personalize knowledge and yield aesthetic pleasure (Siks, 1983). A study conducted by Smilansky (1968) found that sociodramatic play served as a means of extending the intellectual development of underprivileged children in the areas of vocabulary, speech quality, and sentence length.

In particular, drama enhances youngsters' speech because tone of voice and expression are essential components of an oral presentation. Typically, certain roles have specific, rhetorical requirements: the student who portrays Little Bear's mother in Minarik's *Little Bear* (1978) must use a soft voice to express tenderness and sensitivity, whereas the child depicting the Big, Bad Wolf in *The Three Little Pigs* must possess a loud, booming-with-confidence voice. Audibility and clarity must be highlighted. Children need to learn to project their voices and articulate their words so that the presentation can be understood by the audience.

Burgess (1984) believes that drama has a great contribution to make to the language arts. Because of drama's needs for abstract thinking and complete cooperative interactions, Burgess supports the notion that drama aids the general development of language.

Drama as a Process

Portraying a character enables a child to internalize language and "become" that character, if only for a few minutes. As McCaslin (1984) writes,

"The story one plays makes a lasting impression. Therefore, the opportunity to become well acquainted with good literature, through dramatizing it, is a major value." Through personification, drama becomes a means of deepening one's understanding of a portion of good literature.

The dramatic process requires a child to use both personal and literary experience to prepare for role playing. Like each of the characters, the plot must be thoroughly understood because it provides clarity and direction for a story or play. Haine (1985) states that through drama, the story is imagined. The student becomes engaged with it, may struggle with unfamiliar concepts

Teachers often have students use creative dramatics to reenact a picture book story. This girl is portraying the main character in *Too Many Tamales,* by Gary Soto.

or with her own reaction to it, and will ultimately shape it with her own particular interpretation. Thus, the key events, images, and themes of the story are processed as they are acted out in a drama.

Using drama as a process in the elementary grades requires the following six steps:

1. Select a good story that the students will enjoy and be motivated to dramatize. The story should be one the children can relate to in terms of their own knowledge and experiences.

2. Have the students identify the story's characters and discuss ways that those characters may have appeared, talked, felt, and reacted within the story's various events. If a character has any unique characteristics, they should be noted accordingly.

3. Have the students describe the main scenes or events that occur in the story. Then have the students choose the scene or scenes they want to perform within a drama

4. For each scene selected, have the students sequence the actions that occurred. Questions to be considered here are, "What are the essential actions of the scene?" and "What actions can be omitted without detracting from the scene's importance?"

5. Assign character roles to the students and review the predominant characteristics of the individuals whom they are portraying.

6. Have students dramatize the scene or scenes selected by presenting their own interpretations or versions of them. They can invent their own dialogue for informal dramatics or prepare lines to read as script for formal dramatics. In addition, they may use props for greater realism.

Language Expansion and Extension in Drama

The dramatic medium enables children to practice and extend their language in a meaningful context. According to Heathcote (1983), drama permits many different styles and language levels to be used and examined by children. The teacher must pay close attention to language as it is used by students during dramatic play. By considering overall content, style, tone, and vocabulary, the teacher can develop appropriate language models for the students. Such models aid children in processing oral language at both the informal and formal levels of speech. As the students manipulate language, they do so consciously and unconsciously. Thus, when they are speaking, they subconsciously monitor what they say and how they say it, a form of metalinguistic awareness (Morgan & Saxon, 1988).

Types of Drama

In the elementary classroom, drama is usually limited to three major types: pantomime, improvisation, and formal drama. These types are described in the rest of this chapter.

Pantomime

Pantomime relies solely on nonverbal behavior to communicate meaning. Through gestures and movements, an individual carries out a drama that symbolizes not only actions but thoughts and feelings as well. The use of such facial expressions and body movements has always been important on stage, where audiences must view and interpret the actions from afar. It is logical, then, for the gestures and actions used in pantomime to be more accentuated and detailed. For example, a person pantomiming the drinking of a cup of coffee may first go through the motions of slowly adding sugar and cream and then carefully stirring the mixture.

As children become aware that different expressions demonstrate different emotions, they learn how to make appropriate facial expressions to send a certain message to an audience. A range of emotions can be demonstrated facially, beginning with happiness, sadness, and fear and advancing to bewilderment, astonishment, apathy, empathy, and indifference. As children become more astute in observing nonverbal behavior, they are able to add body language and movements to particular facial expressions. For example, a shrug of the shoulders can represent uncertainty, and palms open upward with arms outspread becomes an appeal for help. Such motions add meaning to the associated facial representations.

Young children may be introduced to pantomime as an activity in which the entire class can participate. Consider having the students pretend that they are the following:

- A stick floating down a quiet brook
- Lambs friskily playing and jumping in the warm sunshine
- Leaves gently falling to the ground in autumn
- A kitten trying to find its way down a dark stairwell
- An adult making a snowman after a snowstorm

After the entire class has engaged in a few pantomime activities such as these, have the children individually work on different activities. There is one difficulty in working with kindergartners and first graders on pantomime: They often get excited and announce their role while performing. For example, six-year-old Karin burst forth in the middle of a pantomime of *The Three Billy Goats Gruff* with "I'm the troll who owns the bridge that the goats want to cross."

Here are some other pantomime situations that are appropriate for young children:

- Taking pictures with a video camcorder
- Shopping for groceries
- Cleaning out a closet
- Raking leaves into piles and jumping in the pile
- Flying a kite
- Scoring a touchdown but losing a shoe in the process
- Finding a winning lottery ticket

Children are very innovative and clever in creating facial expressions and actions for silent portrayals. Younger students can select events to depict from stories they have recently read, or they can attempt a pantomime of favorite characters from popular children's literature. Older students can be challenged in pantomiming individuals currently in the national and international news, including political leaders, television and movie stars, and sports figures.

Improvisation

After children feel confident in their pantomimic skills, improvisation should be introduced. Improvisational drama allows the students to now add dialogue to their dramatic skills repertoire. Although students' initial attempts at dialogue will be brief and stilted, later tries will flow more fluently, as the children become accustomed to using it. For this reason, improvisational situations should be devoid of complexity until the students are comfortable with using dialogue. Children often wish to improvise an excerpt from a story. The emphasis here should not be on memorization of the text but on the extemporaneous use of dialogue and imagination to share a scene from the story.

Favorite characters from books are excellent sources for student improvisation. Before having the students improvise the chosen characters, ask them to consider the characters' descriptions: What type of appearance did the character present? How did the character stand and walk? How old was the character? How did the character dress? How did the character speak? What voice qualities did the character possess? What was the character doing in the scene? What kind of person was the character? Did the character possess any unique characteristics?

Below are children's literature selections with characters for improvisation.

Primary Level

Allard, H. (1978). *Miss Nelson is missing* (J. Marshall, Illus.). New York: Scholastic.

Aylesworth, J. (1992). *Old black fly* (S. Gammell, Illus.). New York: Henry Holt.

Bang, M. (1999). *When Sophie gets angry, really, really, angry*. New York: Scholastic.

Hutchins, P. (1982). *Don't forget the bacon*. New York: Farrar, Straus & Giroux.

Kirk, D. (1994). *Miss Spider's tea party*. New York: Scholastic.

Rohman, E. (2002). *My friend Rabbit*. Brookfield, CT: Roaring Book Press.

Rosa-Casanova, S. (2001). *Mama Provi and the pot of rice* (R. Roth, Illus.). New York: Atheneum.

Trivizas, E. (1993). *The three little wolves and the big bad pig* (H. Oxenbury, Illus.). New York: Scholastic.

Wood, A. (1984). *The napping house* (D. Wood, Illus.). Orlando, FL: Harcourt Brace Jovanovich.

Intermediate Level

DiCamillo, K. (2003). *The tale of Desperaux*. Cambridge, MA: Candlewick.

Duffy, J. (1989). *The Christmas gang* (B. McClintock, Illus.). New York: Scribner.

Myers, W. D. (1987). *Fast Sam, cool Clyde and stuff*. New York: Puffin Viking.

Newman, R. (1984). *The case of the Baker Street irregular*. New York: Atheneum.

Pearson, K. (1990). *The sky is falling*. New York: Viking.

Rylant, C. (1992). *Missing May*. New York: Orchard.

Spinelli, J. (1990). *Maniac Magee*. Boston: Little, Brown.

Middle School Level

Avi. (2002). *Crispin: The Cross of Lead*. New York: Hyperion.

Curtis, C. P. (1999). *Bud, not Buddy*. New York: Delacorte.

Lowry, L. (2002). *Gathering blue*. Boston: Houghton Mifflin.

Peck, R. (2000). *A year down yonder*. New York: Penguin/Putnam.

Rupp, R. (2002). *The waterstone*. Cambridge, MA: Candlewick.

Sachar, L. (1998). *Holes*. New York: Delacorte.

Children who are self-conscious or for whom English is a second language may be reluctant to become involved in an improvisational activity. It is important that the teacher remain patient while still encouraging them to participate. Having an entire class share folktales, with students who do not speak English as a first language contributing a folktale from their own culture, can work well.

Improvisation authorizes students to develop their own oral language interpretations of a story. Therefore, a Greek myth or a Korean or Norwegian folktale may easily be transformed into the local vernacular. Without the structured language restrictions of having a required text from which to speak, children are free to use and ultimately expand their speaking skills in terms of fluency, content, and vocabulary.

Props may be used in improvisation along with accompanying sounds. Props may also be used to stimulate improvisations. Students can be divided into small groups of three or four members, with each group selecting an item from a "prop box." The goal for each group is to create an improvisation about the chosen item. Suggested props include a key chain, a cane, a wallet, a computer disk, a ring, a letter in a sealed envelope, a rabbit's foot, a necklace, a flashlight, and a small wooden box.

Props could also include articles of clothing, although remnants of material can serve the same purpose very effectively. The latter offer more versatility and are likely to be machine washable and therefore inexpensive to clean. For example, a large piece of drapery material can serve as a serape for a character in a Spanish folktale, a robe for a Roman senator, or a cape for a queen. Smaller pieces of cloth can be used as belts to tie the material in place. The inclusion of props in the improvisational process helps children become more aware of their creative potential and encourages them to be inventive in their thinking.

Formal Drama

Formal drama is more structured than improvisation as students either read written dialogue or recite dialogue that has been memorized for the dramatization. Some students enjoy the challenge of remembering lines; however, most children find it time-consuming and tedious, with additional pressure being placed on them. Rather than being natural in their deliveries, many children will appear to be stiff and uncomfortable. For these reasons, children should be permitted to read their characters' dialogue just as the narrator would read the narration.

A play for primary children to act out is the well-known *Frog Went A-Courting: A Musical Play in Six Acts* (Catalano, 1998). As children get older, they enjoy writing new scenes for favorite books such as those read as a literature circle activity. Students select the characters and setting before creating their plot. They then write the dialogue for the narrator and characters.

When using the formal dramatic process with children in the lower grades, San Jose (1988) suggests that the story drama be emphasized. The first step in story drama is to have an opening discussion about the story. In this discussion, the students share with one another what they already know about the story's setting, characters, and theme while always seeking additional information supplied by the teacher through maps and other illustrations. Next, the teacher or a designated student reads a portion of the story aloud; this is followed by questions, which are designed to check for understanding of the characters, setting (time and place), and plot. At this point, the students are asked these questions: Who could be telling the story, and how should the story evolve? Are there direct, natural parts of the story that could serve as narratives or dialogue? Are there any actions or movements that could be pantomimed by a few of the actors? In describing the foregoing steps, San Jose (1988) recommends that children be encouraged to contribute their own ideas to activities involving role playing, interpreting characteristics, and problem solving.

Books appropriate for drama are listed below.

Primary Level

Bursik, R. (1992). *Amelia's fantastic flight*. New York: Holt.

Cameron, A. (2002). *Gloria rising* (L. Toft, Illus.). New York: Farrar, Straus, & Giroux.

Dooley, N. (1991). *Everybody cooks rice* (P. J. Thornton, Illus.). Minneapolis, MN: Carolrhoda.

Kellogg, S. (1989). *Yankee Doodle*. New York: Four Winds.

Lester, J. (1998). *Black cowboy, wild horses: A true story* (J. Pinkney, Illus.). New York: Dial.

Rascol, S. (2004). *The impudent rooster* (H. Berry, Illus.). New York: Dutton.

Rylant, C. (1982). *When I was young in the mountains*. New York: Dutton.

Sanders, S. R. (1989). *Aurora means dawn* (J. Kastner, Illus.). New York: Bradbury.

Yolen, J. (1998). *Raising Yoder's barn* (B. Fuchs, Illus.). New York: Little, Brown.

Intermediate Level

Bierman, C. (1998). *Journey to Ellis Island: How my father came to this land* (L. McGraw, Illus.). New York: Hyperion.

Cushman, K. (1996). *Ballad of Lucy Whipple*. Boston: Clarion.

Gross, V. T. (1991). *The day it rained forever: A story of the Johnstown flood* (R. Himler, Illus.). New York: Viking.

Hickman, J. (1978). *ZoarBlue*. New York: Macmillan.

Hooks, W. H. (1983). *Circle of fire*. New York: Atheneum.

Lowry, L. (1989). *Number the stars*. New York: Dell.

Morrison, T. (2004). *Remember: The journey to school integration*. Boston: Houghton Mifflin.

Naylor, P. H. (1991). *Shiloh*. New York: Atheneum.

Soto, G. (1990). *Baseball in April and other stories*. Dan Diego: Harcourt.

Turner, A. (1987). *Nettie's trip south* (R. Himler, Illus.). New York: Macmillan.

Williams, C. L. (1998). *If I forget, you remember*. New York: Doubleday.

Middle School Level

Creech, S. (2004). *Heartbeat*. New York: HarperCollins.

Eckert, A. W. (1998). *Return to Hawk's Hill*. New York: Little, Brown.

Fine, A. (2002). *Upon cloud nine*. New York: Delacourt.

Leapman, M. (1998). *Witnesses to war: Eight true-life stories of Nazi persecution*. New York: Viking.

Paulsen, G. (1998). *Soldier's heart*. New York: Delacorte.

Rosenburg, M. (1994). *Hiding to survive: Stories of Jewish children rescued from the Holocaust*. New York: Clarion.

Spinelli, J. (2004). *Milkweed*. New York: HarperCollins.

Videotaping Performances

Videotaping children during both informal and formal drama exercises aids youngsters in improving their verbal and body movement skills. Although there is a natural tendency toward self-consciousness initially, by watching themselves on tape children become increasingly more aware of oral language habits that detract from the overall message they wish to convey. For example, Becky, a third grader, would unconsciously insert the phrase "you know" in a majority of her conversational pauses. A videotape of her portrayal of a character from a basal reader story made her recognize how distracting this phrase could be. Yet such success is most often affiliated with one's age. It is important to note that as children approach puberty, they become increasingly self-conscious; therefore, it is advantageous to familiarize students with this medium in the early elementary grades, when they are less reluctant to participate.

Because videotape cameras and VCRs are readily available in most school districts, teachers should regularly use them to enable students to perceive themselves as others see them. By becoming involved in the analysis of their own dramatic performances, students are better able to modify and adapt their role playing for better character portrayal.

Students may be asked to use the following questions during their self-evaluations:

1. Is my voice strong?
2. Do I pronounce the words carefully?
3. Do I have any distracting mannerisms, either in my oral language or my body language?
4. Do I speak clearly?
5. Do I speak at a pace that is easily understood, with few or no hesitations and pauses?
6. Do I make usage errors?

Media, Technology, and Creative Dramatics

Aftefr students have had experience with formal dramatics by participating in a role for which they have either read or memorized the lines, they should be encouraged to write their own plays. Third grade teachers in San Angelo, Texas, and Pittsburg, Kansas, teamed up to have their students study the Chisholm, Santa Fe, and Goodnight Trails as longhorn cattle were driven by cowboys over the cattle trails to ship from rail yards in Kansas. The unit included information on the life of cowboys and the Old West including cowboy songs, the breaking of horses, cowboy poetry, and telling tall tales around the campfire. Each class selected a tall tale to study such as *Sally Ann Thunder Ann Whirlwind Crockett* (Kellogg, 1999) or *Pecos Bill* (Kellogg, 1992). After reading the book, the students were divided into groups of three to create their own tall tale play. The students developed their characters and wrote the dialogue for one or two scenes. After rehearsing and honing the lines, the students next made puppets for characters and used cardboard boxes to create their stage. Puppets were made of paper and Popsicle sticks, pipe cleaners, straws, pencils, milk cartons, plastic toy animals and people, movable eyes, felt, buttons, and other materials. After a "dress rehearsal," each group presented their plays on the stages they had decorated with cloth and construction paper. Some had music or sound effects in the background.

The performances were taped with a digital video camera, downloaded to the computer, and burned onto CDs. Besides having copies in the computer center, each student was given a CD to take home as a permanent reminder of their playwright and performance efforts. In addition, one copy was put in the library for other grades to view. The classes then exchanged their plays via the

---

6.4 In the Classroom: Mini Lesson

Oral Language Activities

1. Have a "demonstration fair" in which every child demonstrates and explains to the class a skill or technique he or she possesses. Suggestions include making yogurt, building and riding a skateboard, or creating cartoons with video recorders.

2. Have students collect jokes and riddles to share with their classmates.

3. Have a day for book characters when each student dresses as his or her favorite character and responds to questions asked by classmates about the character.

4. Develop parallel panel discussion groups with upper-grade students who read books that have the same topic but opposite viewpoints.

5. Have students videotape their storytelling of a favorite part of a book.

6. Using a cassette recorder, have students "read" their own interpretation of a wordless picture book and share the tapes with students who share the same native language.

7. Have pairs of students design and describe a science experiment and present it to the class or videotape it.

Internet. The third-grade students also took their stages and puppets to the other classrooms and shared their creative dramatics expertise, which spurred a sixth grade class to take on a similar play-writing project. They used claymation characters that they patiently modified for frame-by-frame videotaping to make the characters appear to move across and around a small cardboard box stage.

A picture presentation is another example of teaming creativity with technology to produce a drama. An entire class can read a story, with each student illustrating one portion or event depicted. The drawings are then numbered, and each student writes the lines to be read for his "scene." Students who are more proficient writers can serve in an oversight capacity, such as "director," supervisor of the script writing, narrator, or mentor to assist struggling readers and writers. Using a video camera to project each scene on a TV screen as the student reads the lines written for a particular scene, the students present the story in cartoon form.

Other uses of media can be collages, dioramas, corner scenes that illustrate three major scenes from the story, facial stories in which the character is illustrated as a face with the opposite side being the person's thoughts and actions written out in phrases.

Special Needs and English Language Learners

Language experiences are critical for special needs students as often they have not had ample opportunities to engage in listening to quality literature read aloud by a good oral reader or participate in conversations that require higher-level thinking. Drama and reader's theater provide outlets for such children, which in turn provide a boost to their self-esteem. Choral speaking and reading enables special needs students to be part of a successful group experience.

Special needs learners who are language delayed possess a limited speaking vocabulary. Likewise, they tend to have smaller listening, reading, and writing vocabularies than their peers. Oral language activities are important in helping these learners learn and use new words.

For the ELLs, choral speaking and reading are essential if they are to learn the structure of English as well as the proper pronunciation of words. Small group reading is one way to help such students. A good source of poetry is Pat Mora's (1996) *Confetti*. One of the poems in this book is entitled "Can I, Can I Catch the Wind." This is a marvelous poem to use with ELL students because the phrase "Can I, can I catch the wind" is repeated throughout the poem. This gives students a solid repetitive base from which they can readily add the additional prepositional phrases (e.g., up in the air, above the clouds). In particular this is crucial for ELLs who have Spanish as their first language because they are unfamiliar with some English prepositions and prepositional phrases that aren't present in their own home language.

Choral speaking and reading that invites actions and movement are beneficial to ELLs. For limited-speaking ELLs, Jean Marzollo's (1990) *Pretend You're a Cat* is good book to introduce choral speaking along with actions. Although

ELLs, like special needs students, may take some time to get the rollicking verse down, they will enjoy the kinesthetic and linguistic linkage as they pretend they are cats, bees, squirrels, and other animals. The well-loved *Let's Go on a Bear Hunt* (Rosen, 1989) engages children in a kinesthetic and linguistic tandem as they hike, swim, climb trees, scramble up hills—all to find the bear. They then must scurry through the actions in reverse as they hustle to arrive safely back home.

For middle school ELLs, articulation can be a problem. In particular, final sounds are frequently not pronounced, and the word is in effect left hanging in midair. Choral reading of popular song lyrics can be helpful, for instance, the English versions of songs by the Puerto Rican singer, Ricky Martin, or Miami's Gloria Estefan for Spanish-speaking students. Frank Sinatra is a noted singer who clearly articulated every syllable in the words of a song's lyrics. Make available song lyrics and give students the opportunity to sing along while these singers croon in the background.

Summary

Speaking is a vital language art inasmuch as children who are adept in the use of oral language tend to become good thinkers, readers, writers, and listeners. Unfortunately, many teachers fail to provide children with the opportunities they need to develop such skills. Through conversations and discussion groups, children enhance their speaking skills.

The inclusion of oral language activities such as discussions, choral reading and speaking, reader's theater, storytelling, and dramatics enables children to discover and share new information, refine oral language, and develop confidence in their ability to communicate orally. Even students with language disorders and learning disabilities can successfully participate in various speaking activities.

Questions

1. How would you introduce intonation to second graders? Sixth graders?

2. How would you select a story for use as formal drama in your classroom?

3. What elements should be part of one's conversational habits?

4. What are the three aspects of intonation and why are they effective?

5. Describe the four language settings and how you would introduce third graders to each.

6. Which of your favorite picture books would be best suited to pantomime by first or second graders? Why?

7. If your fifth-grade students have had limited experiences with speaking, what speaking activity would you introduce them to first? How would you introduce it?

Reflective Teaching

Flip back to the beginning of the chapter to the teaching vignette entitled "Peering into the Classroom." After rereading the vignette, consider the following questions: What characteristics (either implied or directly exhibited) does the teacher possess that you would like to develop? What strengths and weaknesses are revealed for the students described in this section? How would you meet the needs of students such as these?

Activities

1. Observe children as they engage in a conversation on the playground and then in the classroom. Record usage errors and slang. How does their language differ in the two settings?

2. Find a story that would be appropriate for storytelling. Refer to the storytelling process described on pp. 239–241 to refine your storytelling techniques and then present the story to a group of children.

3. Collect poems for choral reading and speaking activities in which the entire class could participate.

4. Develop a list of children's books with social studies and/or science themes that would be appropriate for either improvisation or formal drama.

5. Develop a media presentation for your language arts methods class in which you relate a theory to practice.

6. Collect objects for a prop box.

7. Attend a storytelling festival. Note the different delivery techniques the storytellers use: gestures, stress, pitch, juncture, props, and so on.

8. Suppose that a fourth-grade student in your class has severe language problems in terms of usage. Develop a plan to assist the student on a one-to-one basis and in small group work.

Further Reading

Christie, J. F. (1990). Dramatic play: A context for meaningful engagement. *The Reading Teacher, 43* (8), 54.

Commeyras, M. (1994). Were Janell and Neesie in the same classroom? Children's questions as the first order of reality in storybook discussions. *Language Arts, 71* (7), 517–523.

Flynn, R. M., & Carr, G. A. (1994). Exploring classroom literature through drama: A specialist and a teacher collaborate. *Language Arts, 71* (1), 38–43.

Goldberg, M. (2001). *Arts and learning: An integrated approach to teaching and learning in multicultural and multilingual settings.* Portsmouth, NH: Heinemann.

McCauley, J. K., & McCauley, D. S. (1992). Using choral reading to promote language learning for ESL students. *The Reading Teacher, 45* (7), 526–533.

Monahan, M. B. (2003). "On the lookout for language": Children as language detectives. *Language Arts, 80* (3), 206–214.

Nelson, O. (1989). Storytelling: Language experience for meaning making. *The Reading Teacher, 42* (6), 386–391.

Wiencek, J., & O'Flahavan, J. F. (1994). From teacher-led to peer discussions about literature: Suggestions for making the shift. *Language Arts, 71* (7), 488–498.

References

Berlin, J. A. (1990). The teacher as researcher: Democracy, dialogue, and power. In D. A. Daiker & J. Morenberg (Eds.), *The writing teacher as researcher* (pp. 153–166). Portsmouth, NH: Boynton/Cook.

Block, C. C., & Pressley, M. (2002). *Comprehension instruction: Research-based best practices.* New York: Guilford.

Brewbaker, J. M. (1997). On Tuesday morning: The case for standards for the English language arts. *English Journal, 86* (1), 76–82.

Burgess, T. (1984). The question of English. In T. Burgess (Ed.), *Changing English: Essays for Harold Rosen.* London: Heinemann.

Christie, J. (1990). Dramatic play: A context for meaningful engagements. *The Reading Teacher, 43* (8), 542–545.

Dyson, A. H. (1981). Oral language: The rooting system for learning to write. *Language Arts, 58* (7), 776–784.

Goulden, N. R. (1998). Implementing speaking and listening standards. Information for English teachers. *English Journal, 87* (1), 90–96.

Graves, D. (1983). *Writing: Teachers and children at work.* Portsmouth, NH: Heinemann.

Gray, M. A. (1987). A frill that works: Creative dramatics in the basal reading program. *Reading Horizons, 28* (1); 5–11.

Haine, G. (1985). In the labyrinth of the image: An archetypal approach to drama in education. *Theory into Practice, 24* (3), 187–192.

Heard, G. (1989). *For the good of the earth and sun: Teaching poetry.* Portsmouth, NH: Heinemann.

Heath, S. B. (1983). Research currents: A lot of talk about nothing. *Language Arts, 60* (8), 999–1007.

Heathcote, D. (1983). Learning, knowing, and languaging in drama. *Language Arts, 60* (6), 695–701.

Klein, M. (1977). *Talk in the language arts classroom.* Urbana, IL: National Council of Teachers of English.

Loban, W. (1976). *Language development: Kindergarten through grade twelve* (Research Report No. 18). Urbana, IL: National Council of Teachers of English.

McCaslin, N. (1984). *Creative drama in the classroom.* New York: Longman.

McCauley, J. K., & McCauley, D. S. (1992). Using choral reading to promote language learning for ESL students. *The Reading Teacher, 45* (7), 526–533.

McClure, A. A. (1995). Fostering talk about poetry. In N. L. Roser & M. G. Martinez (Eds.), *Book talk and beyond.* Newark, DE: International Reading Association.

Monahan, M. B. (2003). "On the lookout for language": Children as language detectives. *Language Arts, 80* (3), 206–214.

Morgan, N., & Saxon, J. (1988). Enriching language through drama. *Language Arts, 65* (1), 34–40.

Nicholson, H. H. (1992). Stories are everywhere: Geographical understanding and children's fiction at Key Stages I & II. *Reading, 26* (1), 18–20.

Rosenbloom, C. S. (1991). From Ox-cart man to little house in the big woods: Response to literature shapes curriculum. *Language Arts, 68* (1), 52–61.

San Jose, C. (1988). Story drama in the content areas. *Language Arts, 65* (1), 26–33.

Shepard, A. (1994). From script to stage: Tips for reader's theatre. *The Reading Teacher, 48* (2), 184–186.

Siks, G. B. (1983). *Drama with children* (2nd ed.). New York: Harper & Row.

Sloyer, S. (1983). *Reader's theater: Story dramatization in the classroom.* Urbana, IL: National Council of Teachers of English.

Smilansky, S. (1968). *The effects of sociodramatic play on disadvantaged preschool children.* New York: Wiley.

Snow, C., Dickinson, T., & Tabors, S. (2000). *Preventing reading difficulties in young children.* Washington, DC: National Academy Press.

Stoodt, B. (1989). *Teaching language arts.* New York: Harper & Row.

Tiedt, I. M., Bruemmer, S., Lane, S., Stelwagon, P., Watanabe, K., & Williams, M. (1983). *Teaching writing in K–8 classrooms.* Englewood Cliffs, NJ: Prentice Hall.

Wagner, B. J. (1988). Research currents: Does classroom drama affect the arts of language? *Language Arts, 65* (1), 46–55.

Wendelin, K. H. (1991). Students as storytellers in the classroom. *Reading Horizons, 31* (3), 181–188.

Wiencek, J., and O'Flahavan, J. F. (1994). From teacher-led to peer discussions about literature: Suggestions for making the shift. *Language Arts, 71* (7), 488–498.

Young, T. A., & Ferguson, P. M. (1995). From Anansi to Zomo: Trickster tales in the classroom. *The Reading Teacher, 48* (6), 490–503.

Children's Literature

Aardema, V. (1981). *The riddle of the drum: A tale from Tizapán, Mexico* (T. Chen, Illus.). New York: Four Winds.

Andersen, H. C. (1974). *Hans Andersen: His classic fairy tales* (E. Haugaard, Trans.; M. Hague, Illus.). New York: Doubleday.

Arkhurst, J. C. (1964). *The adventures of Spider: West African folktales.* Boston: Little, Brown.

Avi. (2002). *Crispin: The cross of lead.* New York: Hyperion.

Bird, E. J. (1990). *The blizzard of 1896.* Minneapolis, MN: Carolrhoda.

Bruchac, J. (1995). *Gluskabe and the four wishes* (C. N. Shrader, Illus.). New York: Cobblehill.

Carle, E. (1971). *The very hungry caterpillar.* New York: Crowell.

Carle, E. (1990). *The very quiet cricket.* New York: Philomel.

Catalano, D. (1998). *Frog went a-courting: A musical play in six acts.* Honesdale, PA: Boyds Mills Press.

Collier, J. L., & Collier, C. (1994). *With every drop of blood.* New York: Delacorte.

Cushman, K. (1996). *The ballad of Lucy Whipple.* Boston: Clarion.

Dotlich, R. K. (2003). *In the spin of things: Poetry of motion* (K. Dugan, Illus.). Honesdale, PA: Wordsong/Boyds Mills Press.

dePaola, T. (1982). *Strega Nona's magic lessons.* San Diego, CA: Harcourt Brace Jovanovich.

Edwards, P. D. (1995). *Four famished foxes and Fosdyke* (H. Cole, Illus.). New York: Hyperion.

Edwards, P. D. (1996). *Some smug slug* (H. Cole, Illus.). New York: HarperCollins.

Edwards, P. D. (1998). *Honk* (H. Cole, Illus.). New York: Hyperion.

Edwards, P. D. (1999). *Ed and Fred Flea* (H. Cole, Illus.). New York: Hyperion.

Fritz, J. (1980). *Where do you think you're going, Christopher Columbus?* (M. Thomes, Illus.). New York: Putnam.

Huck, C. (1989). *Princess Furball* (A. Lobel, Illus.). New York: Greenwillow.

Jackson, E. (1994). *Cinder Edna* (K. O'Malley, Illus.). New York: Lothrop, Lee, & Shepard.

Janeczko, P. B. (Ed.) (2001). *Dirty laundry pile: Poems in different voices* (M. Sweet, Illus.). Boston: Houghton Mifflin.

Kellogg, S. (1991). *Jack and the beanstalk.* New York: Morrow.

Kellogg, S. (1992). *Pecos Bill.* New York: Harper Trophy.

Kellogg, S. (1999). *Sally Ann Thunder Ann Whirlwind Crockett.* New York: Harper Trophy.

Lobel, A. (1970). *Frog and toad are friends.* New York: Harper & Row.

Lowry, L. (1989). *Number the stars.* Boston: Houghton Mifflin.

Martin, B. (1968). *Brown bear, brown bear* (E. Carle, Illus.). New York: Holt.

Martin, B., Jr., & Archambault, J. (1989). *Chicka chicka boom boom* (L. Ehlert, Illus.). New York: Simon & Schuster.

Marzollo, P. (1990). *Pretend you're a cat* (J. Pinkney, Illus.). New York: Dial.

Minarik, E. H. (1978). *Little Bear.* New York: Harper & Row.

Mora, P. (1996). *Confetti: Poems for children* (E. O. Sanchez, Illus.). New York: Lee & Low.

Munsch, R. N. (1980). *The paper bag princess* (M. Martchenko, Illus.). Toronto, Canada: Annick.

Numeroff, L. (1991). *If you give a moose a muffin* (F. Bond, Illus.). New York: HarperCollins.

O'Dell, S. (1980). *Sarah Bishop.* Boston: Houghton Mifflin.

Park, L. S. (2001). *A single shard.* New York: Clarion.

Prelutsky, J. (1980). *The headless horseman rides tonight* (A. Lobel, Illus.). New York: Greenwillow.

Prelutsky, J. (1982). *The baby uggs are hatching* (J. Stevenson, Illus.). New York: Greenwillow.

Prelutsky, J. (1990). *Something big has been here* (J. Stevenson, Illus.). New York: Greenwillow.

Prelutsky, J. (2000). *It's raining pigs and noodles* (J. Stevenson, Illus.). New York: Greenwillow.

Raschka, C. (1993). *Yo! Yes?* New York: Orchard.

Rosen, M. (1989). *Let's go on a bear hunt* (H. Oxenbury, Illus.). New York: McElderry Books.

Ryan, P. M. (2001). *Hello ocean* (M. Vachula, Illus.). New York: Levine/Scholastic.

Silverstein, S. (1974). *Where the sidewalk ends.* New York: Harper & Row.

Silverstein, S. (1981). *A light in the attic.* New York: Harper & Row.

Steig, W. (1977). *Caleb & Kate.* New York: Farrar, Straus, & Giroux.

Titherington, J. (1986). *Pumpkin, pumpkin.* New York: Greenwillow.

Viorst, J. (1972). *Alexander and the terrible, horrible, no good, very bad day* (D. Cruz, Illus.) New York: Atheneum.

White, E. B. (1952). *Charlotte's web.* New York: Harper & Row.

Yashima, T. (1955). *Crow boy.* New York: Viking.

Listening
A Receptive Skill

> Listening is the language skill with which we all begin the learning process, and which we depend on throughout life.
>
> —Iris M. Tiedt and Sidney W. Tiedt
> *Contemporary English in the Elementary School*

PEERING INTO THE CLASSROOM
LISTENING TO STORIES OF OURSELVES

The fourth graders were silent, save for a single voice. Lupe was sitting on a stool reading the story that she had written to the class. Her classmates sat mesmerized as she described how her family came from Mexico to live with her uncle in the United States. Some children nodded understandingly when she told them about leaving her pet dog behind with her grandmother. Her classmates laughed when she read about the car breaking down in front of an auto parts store. Her story about her journey held her classmates' interest, and they listened intently. Sharing time is important as it helps to build a community of listeners in the classroom.

Chapter Objectives

The reader will:

✓ understand the four different levels of listening.

✓ understand the importance of being a good listening model for students.

✓ develop strategies for organizing for listening.

✓ develop instructional methods for each of the four levels of listening.

✓ be able to create directed listening and directed listening-thinking activities.

Standards for Professionals

The following Standards will be addressed in this chapter:

Standard 1: Foundational Knowledge and Dispositions

1.4 Demonstrate knowledge of the major components of reading (phonemic awareness, word identification and phonics, vocabulary and background knowledge, fluency, comprehension strategies, and motivation) and how they are integrated in fluent reading.

Standard 2: Instructional Strategies and Curriculum Materials

2.2 Use a wide range of instructional practices, approaches, and methods, including technology-based practices, for learners at differing stages of development and from differing cultural and linguistic backgrounds.

2.3 Use a wide range of curriculum materials in effective reading instruction for learners at different stages of reading and writing development and from differing cultural and linguistic backgrounds.

Standard 3: Assessment, Diagnosis, and Evaluation

3.1 Use a wide range of assessment tools and practices that range from individual and group standardized tests to individual and group informal classroom assessment strategies, including technology-based assessment tools.

3.3 Use assessment information to plan, evaluate, and revise effective instruction that meets the needs of all students, including those at different developmental stages and those from differing cultural and linguistic backgrounds.

Standard 4: Creating a Literate Environment

4.3 Model reading and writing enthusiastically as valued lifelong activities.

4.4 Motivate learners to be lifelong readers.

Introduction

Lupe shared her story with her classmates in a formal listening setting, but most listening settings are informal. According to Graves (1991), there are many "literate occasions," opportunities to listen and observe. Children must be taught how to listen and observe so that they can understand, appreciate, and evaluate the information presented to them.

Listening is one of the methods by which humans attempt to make sense of the surrounding world. By allowing us to hear and interpret environmental sounds, listening serves as an aural vehicle for comprehension development. Goss (1982a) defines listening as a process that organizes what is heard and establishes those verbal units to which meaning can be applied.

Listening is a language art that actually begins prior to birth and continues to be an important, interactive process throughout life. A fetus responds to various tones of music or to its mother's voice; within a few weeks after birth, the infant reacts to the sounds of both parents and siblings, as well as to sounds in the surrounding environment. The spoken language of others is converted into meaning as the months go by, and eventually the baby distinguishes among the names for self, other individuals, and objects.

Typically, listening receives much less emphasis in the classroom than do the other language arts. According to Carole Cox (1999, p. 151), "relatively little attention has been paid to teaching listening, even though active approaches to doing so have been demonstrated to improve students' listening ability." As Shane Templeton (1998, p. 136) writes, "There is little question that listening is the language art least attended to—not only in school but probably in our society as well." One possible explanation for the neglect of instruction in this area is that teachers generally have received little or no training in how to teach listening, and they lack the self-confidence to try (Funk & Funk, 1989) Another problem is that even experts in the field cannot agree upon a single definition of listening.

Determining whether a child has not only heard but actually "listened" to an oral message is difficult. The teacher's questioning of a child may result in incorrect responses either because of the child's failure to listen or the child's misunderstanding or misinterpretation of the question itself. Likewise, a child may give a correct response based upon previous knowledge without having listened to the presented message. As a result, the teacher may believe the child understood the question when, in fact, the child did not. Research studies conducted with first through third graders found that children will often indicate that they understand a message even though it is actually incomplete or ambiguous (Ironsmith & Whitehurst, 1978). Moreover, most children within each grade level will avoid seeking additional information by questioning the speaker when their understanding is poor or weak (Cosgrove & Patterson, 1977).

Children should be taught listening strategies explicitly, with ample opportunities to put them to use so that they eventually become automatic. This is best done when the instruction causes the children to think first about sound and then move on to the higher levels of listening awareness and ability (Templeton, 1998). While direct instruction is the best way to teach listening, it is critical that the teacher model listening by being a good listener. Perhaps the best known superb listener is Oprah Winfrey, who shows interest, empathy, and support as she listens. She listens and uses what she learns to ask pertinent questions of the speaker. Teachers need to follow her lead!

The listening process itself consists of three primary steps: (1) receiving the auditory input, (2) attending to the received auditory input, and (3) interpreting and interacting with the received auditory input. The first step involves the reception of the spoken message, for hearing the message alone does not necessarily guarantee understanding. When a listener receives a spoken message, other sounds must either be ignored or removed from the foreground. This technique, sometimes referred to as masking, allows the listener to mask or block out other sounds that are present in the surrounding environment.

The second step in the listening process, attending to the auditory input, requires the listener to concentrate on what is being presented by the speaker. Attending to this spoken message is both mentally and physically exerting, as demonstrated by the measurement of an individual's pulse rate during rest and during the attending step of the listening process. Attending while listening results in a faster pulse rate.

In the third step of the listening process, interpreting and interacting with the auditory input, the listener does not simply gather and file away information; rather, the listener takes in the spoken coded information and ultimately must classify, compare, and relate it to previous knowledge. According to Aronson (1974), this third listening step involves a rapid predict-then-confirm strategy. In the event that the listener is familiar with what the speaker is talking about, predictions can be made much more easily. Thus, at this point, on the basis of any internally developed findings, the listener may challenge the validity of, and even reject, the newly gained knowledge. Therefore, listening is described as an active, not a passive, process.

After the listener has accurately received an aural message, thinking and responding can proceed beyond the communicated event itself. According to Lundsteen (1979), the listener may respond by classifying parts of the message in terms of time, space, position, degree, and so on; ranking information according to relevance or importance; making comparisons and/or contrasts; predicting; sequencing; recognizing cause-effect relationships; using critical evaluation; appreciating the qualities of drama, tone, and rhythm; and engaging in problem solving.

This chapter describes the different purposes for listening and suggests appropriate teaching methods for successfully developing children's listening abilities and strategies.

Factors in Effective Listening

Teachers must recognize the importance of listening within the classroom. At the elementary level, especially in the lower grades, academic success is primarily related to the child's listening abilities. Generally speaking, however, students hear only 50 to 60 percent of the teacher's message to them (Blankenship, 1982; Strother, 1987). Research now indicates that when a visual is presented with an auditory message, the retention rate may improve to as much as 80 percent. Similarly, a study conducted by Weaver (1972) rated the success of requiring students to recall information that had just been presented orally by their classroom teachers. Weaver found that students in the lower grades tended to score higher overall on the recall task than did their older, more experienced counterparts. For example, first graders were able to recall the presented instructions at a rate of 90 percent and second graders at a rate of 80 percent; however, seventh and eighth graders scored 43.7 percent, and high school students scored only 28 percent. The study's results can be explained in terms of several factors. Younger children devote more attention to their teachers than do junior and senior high school students, and for kindergartners through second graders, listening is the primary means of obtaining information because they have limited reading skills. Older students are more apt to believe that they can predict what their teachers will say, and therefore they tune out what is actually being said. In addition, emotional concerns and problems as well as outside interests and activities often distract older students and reduce listening efficiency.

Children typically enter school possessing the basic, lower-level listening skills of recall and recognition. Nevertheless, a lack of concentration because of either external or internal distractions can cause a student to respond incorrectly to a lower-level question. Although it is common for teachers to ask only lower-level questions, teachers should try to help students attain higher-level listening skills by asking them higher-level questions as well.

Box 7.1 on p. 270 presents a checklist that teachers can use to evaluate both the lower- and higher-level listening skills of elementary students. This checklist can be used at all grade levels throughout the school year to monitor each student's proficiency development in listening. Teachers can also use it as a self-check as they talk with their students.

Teachers can incorporate several other techniques in assisting students to become better listeners. Since children must attend to the speaker in order to listen effectively, a teacher can promote this behavior by creating an atmosphere that permits students to concentrate on the listening task. Interruptions should always be kept to a minimum, and any outside noise must be reduced. Teaching in a classroom adjacent to a busy street or intersection requires more changes in one's instructional practices than does teaching in an appropriate, acoustically designed and engineered facility. Direct teacher intervention for helping students become effective listeners includes the following:

- Speak with clarity.
- Speak directly to the students and avoid speaking when writing on the chalkboard.
- Watch the students' faces to ascertain whether or not they understand what you are saying.
- Begin with an overview of the material, present it in a straightforward and logical sequence, and close with a summary.
- Give clear, concise instructions and avoid ambiguity.
- Encourage students to ask questions.

7.1   In the Classroom: Teaching Hint

A Checklist of Listening Skills

Student Name _____

Length of Message

Listening Skills	Sentence	Paragraph	Short Story
Recall knowledge			
Recognize knowledge			
Follow oral directions			
Comprehend/understand			
Apply knowledge			
Summarize			
Recognize cause and effect			
Problem solve/predict			
Evaluate/judge			

Listener Distractions	Present	Not Present
Background noise		
Quiet classroom		
Low volume by speaker		
Outside problems		
Length of presentation		

Comments:

- Stress important material through repetition.
- Use visual aids such as charts, models, notes on the chalkboard, and overhead transparencies.

Funk and Funk (1989) give four suggestions for developing listening skills in the elementary classroom. First, the teacher should provide a purpose for listening. Second, a classroom atmosphere that is conducive to listening should be created. Third, the teacher should provide follow-up experiences soon after the listening activity. Fourth, the teacher should include instructional techniques that promote listening. These simple guidelines can be used to teach listening throughout the school day. According to Funk and Funk, some of the best opportunities for teaching listening occur during art, music, physical education, science, and social studies, but they certainly apply language arts activities as well.

The Teacher as Listener

Children quickly become aware of the individual listening abilities and tolerance of their teachers and respond accordingly. The teacher who eagerly awaits student contributions finds children willing to disclose their thoughts in lively, often animated discussions, which in themselves encourage creative and divergent thinking. Such a teacher uses a particular series of open-ended questions; in this way, the teacher helps students develop necessary links between the questions, which in turn foster their skills in connecting ideas and in inferring, comparing, contrasting, and evaluating ideas. The opposing instructional style finds the teacher seeking only the correct response to a closed-ended question; therefore, the teacher is less apt to be a good listener. Through the teacher's nonverbal language, including tone of voice and facial expressions, students receive the message that "the answer" is the only acceptable response.

Teachers should conduct periodic self-checks of their own listening. For example, if teachers notice that they talk to students more often than they listen to them, teachers can take steps to modify this behavior. As mentioned at the beginning of this chapter, teachers should conduct such self-checks because they should be "model" listeners (Leverentz & Garman, 1987), conveying empathy and sincere interest to a speaking child. Paley (1986) believes that the key to becoming a model listener is curiosity. She states, "when we are curious about a child's words and our responses to those words, the child feels respected" (p. 127).

Levels of Listening

There are four levels of listening: (1) marginal or background, (2) appreciative, (3) attentive, and (4) critical or analytical. Each level, which students use on a daily basis, is discussed in the following sections.

Marginal Listening

The least demanding yet most frequent type of listening is described as *marginal* or *background listening*. Marginal listening occurs, for example, when one is able to distinguish between someone's voice and the noise from a busy street. Teachers continuously use marginal or background listening to ensure

---

7.2   In the Classroom: Mini Lesson

Background Listening

Kindergarten and first-grade students are not always aware of background noise. To acquaint them with this phenomenon, read them Charlotte Zolotow's (1980) book *If You Listen*. Afterward, have the class recall the sounds the little girl in the story heard when she listened carefully, as her mother told her to do. Next have the class listen for sounds in the classroom, and then go outside and have them listen to and identify sounds heard on the playground. What noises can the students identify without seeing what is causing the noises? Examples include a dog barking in the distance and the siren of a police car or fire engine.

Zolotow, C. (1980). *If you listen* (M. Simont, Illus.). New York: Harper & Row.

that all is going well in another part of the classroom, where too much quiet or noise could signal disruptions in learning. Yet in today's electronic world, some students find that they can study more successfully with available background noise, particularly if that noise is rock music. For such students, a quiet classroom can actually inhibit the learning process.

Appreciative Listening

Appreciative listening occurs when an individual listens to a reader, speaker, singer, or music for enjoyment. As such, it is aesthetic in nature. Appreciative listening includes listening to actors in a dramatic play, a friend telling a funny story, a person describing the San Francisco earthquake and fire, a popular rock group's album, or a trite but appealing radio commercial. Whereas music classes provide students with an environment in which to learn how to appreciate various rhythms, lyrics, styles, and types of music, the development of a comparable appreciation of speaking is rarely found in the elementary classroom. However, children must witness the use of stress, pitch, and juncture by effective speakers in order to become better listeners. Likewise, they should be made aware of the tone, mood, speaker's style, and audience's influence on the listening setting. Listening to tapes of authors reading their own writings presents students with a different perspective from which to consider various works.

To serve as effective models for speaking, teachers must develop their oral reading and storytelling expertise. In addition, they should also model good listening habits for the various levels of listening. In reality, many teachers demonstrate appreciative listening quite poorly, in part because of a lack of training in this area.

Teachers tend to overlook the need for the development of appreciative, aesthetic listening skills, whether one is listening to the oral reading of a sentence or paragraph from a novel or to the choral reading of a short poem by students. Although most teachers stress the oral production of language, they often fail to recognize the intricacies necessary for appreciative listening within the same work. Teachers should begin to instruct kindergartners and first graders in techniques of imagery formation. For instance, teachers can assist these students in both visualizing a story's descriptive passages and orally sharing their "images" with the class. Other appreciative listening skills that teachers can help develop in younger children include identifying the rhythm of poetry as it is read, evaluating the effects of various speeds of delivery on a poem's meaning, and developing an ability to describe the tone and mood of selected pieces of writing. (These same activities could also be applied to folk songs.)

There are many benefits to appreciative listening. This level of listening allows for the sharing of quality literature with children, thereby introducing them to new concepts and experiences. When a variety of books are used, children are exposed to different literary genres that can widen their reading interests. When unfamiliar terms or unusual sentence patterns are read aloud, children are encouraged to broaden their language experiences.

7.3   In the Classroom: Mini Lesson

Story Time and Story Journals

Appreciative listening can be coordinated with journal writing. Because the oral sharing of books with students is an event that occurs almost daily in elementary classrooms, having students react directly to a story makes for an effective appreciative-listening activity. After selecting a book with an intriguing, fast-paced plot that is almost guaranteed to captivate and maintain a child's interest, read it to the class in a dramatic fashion. Upon completion of the story, have the students write down and illustrate their reactions to it (Farris, 1989). Although some young children may only wish to draw and others may only want to write their responses, they should be encouraged to attempt both.

An example of a story journal written after a first-grade class listened to the teacher read Mercer Mayer's (1969) *There's a Nightmare in My Closet* appears below. The child's journal is written in invented spelling.

My pet most r.
My liaf is nias I hav a
pet you will not bu leav it what
it is. it is a mosts his
naem is spiek he likes
grhij I no it is schaenj
but it is not. he is mi
pel the end.

Here is the translated version:
My Pet Monster
My life is nice. I have a
pet you will not believe it what
it is. It is a monster. His
name is Spike. He likes
garbage. I know it is shocking
but it is not. He is my
pal. The end.

Older students tend to write more sophisticated story journal entries. Typically, these children will relate to one of the primary characters in a book by writing creative letters or descriptions from a particular character's point of view. A good book to share with third through sixth graders is *Bunnicula Strikes Again!* by James Howe (1999).

Farris, P. J. (1989). Storytime and story journals: Linking literature with writing. *New Advocate, 2* (1), 179–185.
Howe, J. (1999). *Bunnicula strikes again!* (A. Daniel, Illus.). New York: Atheneum.
Mayer, M. (1969). *There's a nightmare in my closet.* New York: Dial.

Books that are appropriate for appreciative-listening story journals are listed here.

Primary Level

Ballads and Folksongs
Ackerman, K. (1988). *Song and dance man* (S. Gammell, Illus.). New York: Knopf.
Allison, C. (1987). *I'll tell you a story, I'll sing you a song.* New York: Delacorte.
Kennedy, X. J., & Kennedy, D. (compilers). (1999). *Knock at a star.* (K. Weinhaus, Illus.) New York: Little, Brown.

Growing Up
Cole, J. (1987). *Norma Jean, jumping bean.* New York: Random House.
Hoberman, M. A. (1986). *A house is a house for me.* New York: Scholastic.
Jeram, A. (1995). *Contrary Mary.* Cambridge, MA: Candlewick.
Lester, H. (1994). *Three cheers for Tacky* (L. Munsinger, Illus.). Boston: Houghton Mifflin.
Lindbergh, R. (2004). *Our nest.* (J. McElmurray, Illus.). Cambridge, MA: Candlewick.
Scheller, M. (1992). *My grandfather's hat* (K. Narahashi, Illus.). New York: McElderry.
Schulman, J., & Boughton, S. (Eds.). (1998). *The 20th century children's book treasury: Picture books and stories to read aloud.* New York: Knopf.
Waddell, M. (1992). *Can't you sleep, Little Bear?* (B. Firth, Illus.). Cambridge, MA: Candlewick.

continued

Science
dePaola, T. (1975). *The cloud book.* New York: Holiday.
Hadithi, M. (1987). *Crafty chameleon* (A. Kennaway, Illus.). Boston: Little, Brown.
Tregebov, R. (1993). *The big storm.* New York: Hyperion.
Yolen, J. (1987). *Owl moon* (J. Schoenherr, Illus.). New York: Philomel.

Social Studies
Fritz, J. (1978). *What's the big idea, Ben Franklin?* (M. Tomes, Illus.). New York: Coward-McCann.
Smithsonian. (1999). *When the rain sings: Poems by young Native Americans.* New York: Simon & Schuster.
Stevens, C. (1982). *Anna, Grandpa, and the big storm* (M. Tomes, Illus.). Boston: Houghton Mifflin.
Ringgold, F. (1999). *If a bus could talk: The story of Rosa Parks.* New York: Simon & Schuster.
Winter, J. (1988). *Follow the drinking gourd.* New York: Knopf.

Math
Atherlay, S. (1995). *Math in the bath* (M. Halsey, Illus.). New York: Simon & Schuster.
Bolam, E. (1997). *Mother Goose math.* New York: Viking.
Jonas, A. (1995). *Splash!* New York: Greenwillow.
Pinczes, E. J. (1995). *A remainder of one* (B. MacKain, Illus.). Boston: Houghton Mifflin.

Upper-Elementary and Middle School Levels

Growing Up
Avi. (1994). *The barn.* New York: Avon.
Choi, S. N. (1991). *The year of impossible goodbyes.* Boston: Houghton Mifflin.
Fleishman, P. (1994). *Mind's eye.* New York: Holt.
Paterson, K. (1994). *Flip-flop girl.* New York: Lodestar.
Paulsen, G. (1999). *Alida's song.* New York: Delacorte.

Science
Floca, B. (2000). *Dinosaurs at the ends of the earth.* New York: Dorling-Kindersley.
Simon, S. (1998). *Muscles.* New York: Scholastic.
Lasky, K. (2003). *The man who made time travel* (K. Hawkes, Illus.). New York: M. Kroupa Books.
Williams, T. T., & Major, T. (1984). *The secret language of snow* (J. Dewey, Illus.). New York: Sierra Club/Pantheon.

Social Studies
Bunting, E. (1994). *Smoky night* (D. Diaz, Illus.). San Diego: Harcourt Brace.
Goble, P. (1987). *Death of the iron horse.* New York: Bradbury.
Greenwood, B. (1994). *A pioneer sampler* (H. Collins, Illus.). New York: Ticknor & Fields.
Hendershot, J. (1987). *In coal country* (T. B. Allen, Illus.). New York: Knopf.
Lakin, P. (1994). *Don't forget* (T. Rand, Illus.). New York: Tambourine.
Rodanas, K. (1992). *Dragonfly's tale.* New York: Clarion.

Math
Schwartz, D. M. (1998). *G is for googol: A math alphabet book* (M. Moss, Illus.). New York: Scholastic.
Scieszka, J. (1995). *Math curse* (L. Smith, Illus.). New York: Viking.

Attentive Listening

The next level of listening, *attentive listening,* is efferent in nature as the listener is seeking information that in many instances must be remembered. Attentive listening requires concentration and interaction on the part of the listener to ensure comprehension of the spoken message. At this level, the listener must categorize, examine, relate, question, and organize information in order to understand it and also to be able to apply it in the future. Attentive listening might involve obtaining oral directions to an unfamiliar location, watching the six o'clock news on television, getting a phone number from directory assistance, or attending a lecture on water safety. Yet because a suitable strategy is required to receive a particular type of message, the listener must know a message's purpose prior to hearing it.

Once students understand the purpose for listening, they must develop a system by which to understand a spoken message thoroughly. Although it is usually impossible to recall the exact words of a message, the listener can comprehend a message by remembering its primary points. Children can be taught the attentive-listening strategies described next.

The listener can relate a speaker's message to personal, previously gained knowledge. In doing this, the listener must categorize and organize information. Prior to listening, students need to recall what they already know about the particular topic. Using familiar corresponding material as a base, students should try to correlate a speaker's points with this information. In view of the fact that one can listen at a faster rate than one can speak, time becomes available to the listener for making such correlations while at the same time attending to the message as it is delivered.

Sequencing a story's events is a common listening activity in the lower grades. In this activity, students are encouraged to visualize the major actions or scenes in their proper order. To assist students, a teacher might give each student a blank sheet of paper and direct the students to fold the sheet in half twice to make a small "book." After the students unfold the books and place them on their desks, the teacher asks the class to listen closely to and remember the four main events in a short story, which the teacher then reads aloud. After reading the story, the teacher instructs the students to illustrate the four scenes, one in each section of their books.

Speakers can and do provide valuable assistance for attentive listening. If a speaker prepares a listener via a cursory outline of what is going to be said, the listener then has a framework for gathering information as it is delivered. This

---

7.4   In the Classroom: Mini Lesson

Attentive Listening

After sharing a read aloud, give each student a 3" × 5" colored index card with a question about the book on one side and an answer for another question on the other side. Start with one student reading the question he was given. The child with the card that has the answer then responds. That child then reads the question on the card she is holding, and so on.

In order to prepare the cards, write a question on the first index card and the answer on the next card. Set the first card aside. Then write each remaining question on a card and the answer for each on the next index card in the stack. When you reach the last card, put the answer to the last question on the first card that you set aside earlier.

This listening activity can also be used to review science concepts or a social studies chapter.

is exemplified by the speaker who announces that a lecture will contain three main highlights before identifying them. In this way, the framework or learning pegs are positioned for the listener.

InQuest, a comprehension procedure developed by Mary Shoop (1986) for use in both listening and reading, encourages students in third grade and above to mentally question an oral message while listening to it. InQuest involves the use of spontaneous drama as a means of stimulating attentive listening. Because Shoop's approach motivates students to actively monitor what they already know and do not know during listening, this form of metacognition fosters a "sensitivity to comprehension." In the InQuest procedure, the teacher reads a story, stopping at critical points. When he reaches one of these points, the teacher announces that a spontaneous news conference is to take place and designates one or two of the students as the story's main characters and the remainder of the students as investigative reporters. Seeking to interpret the story's events, the investigative reporters question the main characters and then evaluate their answers. In sifting through the interview information, the investigative reporters attempt to anticipate and predict upcoming events in the story.

Students in the intermediate grades should also learn how to take notes. Attentive listening requires that students get the facts correct and understand them. As such it is appropriate to teach note-taking skills as part of attentive listening. A mini lesson in which the teacher models note-taking skills is important. After showing a short video, 5 to 10 minutes in length, on a topic currently being covered in one of the curricular areas, the teacher should use an overhead projector to identify the topic (usually the gist of the topic is established in the title of the video). Next, the teacher should point out the main ideas that were presented. Typically educational videos give a brief overview listing the main ideas to be presented at the beginning of the film. The teacher should then list the main ideas under the primary topic. Under each main idea would be placed supporting ideas. Below is an example of the format of such note taking:

Topic: _____

Main Idea: _____

    Supporting Idea: _____

    Supporting Idea: _____

    Supporting Idea: _____

Main Idea: _____

    Supporting Idea: _____

    Supporting Idea: _____

    Supporting Idea: _____

Main Idea: _____

    Supporting Idea: _____

    Supporting Idea: _____

    Supporting Idea: _____

It must be pointed out to students that not every main idea will have three or even two supporting ideas. This is why the traditional outlining format with its structure outlined below often fails to work, frustrating students in the process.

    I. Topic
      A. Main Idea
        1. Supporting Idea
        2. Supporting Idea
          a. Minor Supporting Idea
          b. Minor Supporting Idea

After modeling note taking for viewing a video, with the principal topic and supporting ideas, the teacher should read a short nonfiction piece from a children's magazine such as *Cobblestone* (United States history, grades 4–6), *Calliope* (world history, grades 6–8), or *KidsDiscover* (science, grades 4–6). This time the students apply the just-modeled note-taking techniques individually at their

---

7.5 In the Classroom: Mini Lesson

Summarizing Information

Both science and social studies require students to become familiar with scientists, explorers, and their respective discoveries. One attentive-listening activity that reinforces such learning involves the use of questioning to probe for information. Because this technique utilizes the five "W" questions—who, what, when, where, and why—the activity can be successfully used with students in grades 2–8.

Write the questions on an 8" × 10" piece of tagboard or thick cardboard and also on the chalkboard in the following order: When? Where? Who? What? Why? (Because elementary students have difficulty establishing a reference point for the settings of events—both times and places—they will answer the when and where questions first; this establishes a framework for the analysis of the remaining information.) Next, announce to the students that you are going to read a short paragraph and that they are to remember the information necessary to answer the five posted questions.

After dividing the class into pairs, give one pair of students the cardboard that contains the "W" questions and send them down the hallway, beyond the range of hearing the passage as it is read. Read the paragraph to the remaining students. Then have the two students in the hallway return to the room and ask the written questions of their peers. Using the information offered by their classmates, the two students are to converse and ultimately summarize the paragraph for the class. Continue with new paragraphs of information and new partners until all students have summarized a paragraph read to the remainder of the class.

The paragraph to be read may be taken directly from the students' science or social studies textbook or from any other source. The length and complexity of a paragraph should be appropriate to the students' grade level, however.

own desks. Then as a group, the main ideas and supporting ideas can be shared, with the teacher again writing the information on an overhead transparency for all to see and discuss. This reinforces the note-taking procedure.

Students should be alert to a speaker's clues given at the beginning of a presentation. Most speakers indicate the primary areas to be covered. For instance, if students expect a message to contain three main categories, they could write an appropriate category title at the top of each of three sheets of paper or at the top of each of three columns on a single sheet. Then, while listening to the speaker's delivery, they can take brief notes in the form of phrases or single words within each category (see figure 7.1 on p. 279).

7.6   In the Classroom: Mini Lesson

Hunt Like an Eagle

This listening activity is based on a Native American game used to teach children hunting skills. As children played this game, the elders of the tribe watched and, based on each child's performance in the game, selected those who were ready to go on a real hunt for wild game.

The role of hunter of a tribe was an honored one in that a child had to demonstrate worthiness. The elders sent out only those who were prepared to hunt because the hunter who lacked the necessary skills could become the hunted and be hurt or even killed.

Children had to learn to listen and to use their other senses—smell and touch. They had to think and react quickly. They had to learn to move quietly and to sit silently. The children also had to learn to observe and to develop strategies based upon what they learned in order to get their "prey."

Before this activity is begun, the class has to practice sitting silently. A hunter will have to sit for a long time before the prey comes along. In addition, the hunter needs to be constantly ready to complete the task. If the hunter is distracted by another noise, scratches his or her nose, or stretches, the prey may be alerted and dart off into the woods. The hunter then will be left with no food for dinner.

To do this activity, have the children sit on the floor cross-legged in a large circle. One child is selected to be the eagle and is blindfolded. The eagle must be honest and tell if he or she can see out the blindfold. If the eagle lies, the others playing the game will know. The elders will not choose that child to be a hunter because the child will have proven that he or she cannot be trusted.

The eagle is seated in the center of the circle with the prey (a small stuffed animal for early childhood-level students or a keychain of keys for middle-level students). The teacher serves as the tribal elder and points to a child to be the hunter. The object is for the hunter to take the eagle's prey without being detected. The eagle catches the hunter by pointing directly at the hunter before the prey is taken away. If the hunter is caught by the eagle, the hunter goes back to the circle and a new hunter is chosen. If the hunter is successful in taking the prey and returning to the circle, that child becomes the eagle.

Critical Listening

Critical or *analytical listening* requires a listener to evaluate and judge information; the listener must therefore become a reflective processor of a message. Like attentive listening, critical or analytical listening is efferent in

Name: Terry Smith

North Carolina Notes—Jeremy's oral report

Famous Citizens	*History (Facts)*	*Products*
—Sir Walter Raleigh	12th state	tar
—Virginia Dare—1st white	1st colony—Roanoke	tobacco
child born in U.S.	Cherokee Indians	furniture
	Southern state	
	1st airplane flight of Wright	
	brothers at Kitty Hawk	

Figure 7.1   Terry's notes are a summary of his classmate Jeremy's oral report on North Carolina.

nature; however, the listener must evaluate the information and make judgments or decisions. Unlike literal comprehension, which is commonly emphasized in attentive listening, reflective processing requires the development of extensive inferences, cause and effect comparisons, and evaluations and judgments of both the message and the speaker. Such involvement is much more complex than that found within the other listening levels and is more dependent on the child's higher thinking skills (Goss, 1982b).

At first glance, it might appear that adults practice critical listening more often than children do because adults make important decisions on the basis of individual analyses of oral input. Voting for a presidential candidate, buying a new car, or selecting which new movie to see depends largely on personal critical reaction to and interpretation of oral messages. However, children also use critical listening on a frequent basis. For example, when a child offers a compromise in a dispute between friends or decides to buy a toy after listening to a television advertisement, she is demonstrating a result of critical listening.

Because of the numerous situations and experiences that demand critical listening skills, children must develop an ability to analyze auditory messages at an early age. Young children have been found to be easily misled and influenced by others, particularly by older individuals and commercially prepared media advertisements that prompt them to purchase (or to have their parents purchase for them) various goods or services. Research findings indicate, however, that when those problems inherent in aural messages are made more prominent and noticeable, children are better able to identify them (Pratt & Bates, 1982; Stein & Trabasso, 1982). In one study, Baker (1983) discovered that if children were told prior to their listening that the materials contained problems and, in turn, were given specific examples of those problems, then children improved in their identification of such problems overall. Thus, it is important that children be able to recognize propaganda techniques. Because there are several propaganda techniques, it is recommended that they be introduced to children a few at a time, with clear, specific examples accompanying each. Box 7.7 on pp. 280–81 describes and provides examples of the propaganda techniques that children in the intermediate grades can be taught to recognize.

7.7   The More You Know

Propaganda Techniques

Appeal to the Elite

The speaker, usually an advertiser, uses flattery to persuade the listener to do something: "Since you are obviously intelligent and money is probably no problem for you, why not take a look at this deluxe children's swing set [or European sports car or gourmet cookware or imported choco-late]." The idea behind this technique is to make listeners believe they are perceived as bright and wealthy and therefore deserve whatever the speaker is selling.

Bandwagon

The speaker appeals to people's, especially children's, desire to "belong," to be part of the in-group. The aim of the speaker who says "everybody's wearing black sneakers this year" is to con-vince the listener to wear black sneakers, too.

Card Stacking

The speaker purposely presents only one side of an issue in an attempt to persuade listeners to share his or her specific viewpoint or opinion. Unless listeners obtain additional information on the issue, they cannot respond to the message objectively.

Glittering Generality

The speaker makes broad and dazzling—but unsubstantiated—claims about a product's quality or an individual's character: "Vote for John Doe because he's simply the brightest and best student you could have for class president!" The critical listener will want to know in what specific ways John Doe is the "brightest" and the "best."

Name-calling

Youngsters find name-calling an easy technique to identify because it frequents both the play-ground and the neighborhood. As a propaganda technique, name-calling occurs when, for example, one candidate uses a derogatory name to label another candidate: "My opponent is nothing more than a bleeding-heart liberal."

Plain Folks

The plain folks technique is used most frequently by politicians in order to gain voter confi-dence. The speaker emphasizes that he or she is similar to the so-called common man: hardwork-ing, apple-pie-eating, taxpaying, and quite ordinary. Former U.S. Senator Sam Ervin used this technique when he described himself as "an ol' country boy." Although he was a country boy, he also possessed a Harvard law degree obtained with honors. Likewise, former Chicago Mayor Jane Byrne would wear a fur coat in the city's annual Saint Patrick's Day parades except during election years, when she wore a less expensive cloth coat.

Rewards

The inclusion of "free" prizes in boxes of cereal or offers for laundry detergent rebates can entice individuals to purchase such products. Similarly, low-interest-rate loans for cars or free mer-chandise for opening a long-term savings account can serve as rewards for buying large-ticket items. Yet a consumer must be wary of such gimmicks and decide whether he or she really needs or wants what must be purchased to obtain the token gift and whether that gift actually inflates the purchase price of the product.

Testimonial

Having a well-known personality serve as a product spokesperson can help convince listeners that the particular item is the one to buy. If a famous athlete, film star, or musician endorses a product, people are more likely to purchase it. Such advertisements may try to convince the lis-tener to buy everything from articles of clothing to health insurance. Typically, the celebrity will relate to particular listeners through age similarity (for example, a retired television star advertising life insurance for the elderly) or some shared interest (for example, a professional baseball player promoting a baseball glove to sports-minded students). The listener must determine whether or not the famous individual has the qualifications to assess the product adequately before deciding to purchase it.

Transference

Children and adults often confuse transference with the testimonial inasmuch as both techniques depend on famous individuals to promote products. The implication of the transfer technique is that listeners identify directly with the celebrities and their attributes. For example, a listener might believe that using the same antiperspirant that a football star is "pitching" will transform the listener into a big, strong, handsome athlete; likewise, a listener may decide to use the toothpaste touted by a movie superstar, believing that his smile will be as attractive as the movie star's and will attract the opposite sex. The fallacy, however, is that the product will produce the desired result.

Critical and analytical listening requires higher-level thinking skills because students are being asked to make judgments. Below are inquiry strategies that students need to adopt for critical, analytical listening along with suggested books to read at the intermediate and middle school levels:

- **Categorize.** Statements (fact or opinion), characters (antagonist or protagonist), events, time periods, and so on.
  Charley Skedaddle (Beatty, 1987, grades 4–5); *Who comes with cannons?* (Beatty, 1992, grades 6–8)

- **Cause and Effect.** Give reasons why something occurred; if-then scenarios; words such as "because," "therefore," and "as a result" serve as clues for the listener.
  How do apples grow? (Maestro, 1992, grades 3–5); *A nation torn: The story of how the Civil War began* (Ray, 1990, grades 4–8);

- **Describe.** List characteristics, features, and examples.
  Spiders (Gibbons, 1992, grades 2–4); *Eyes and ears* (Simon, 2003, grades 4–8)

- **Explain What Happened.**
  It's a hummingbird's life (Kelly, 2002, grades 2–4); *Come to the ocean's edge: A nature cycle book* (Pringle, 2003, grades 5–8)

- **Generalize to Real Life.**
  Shades of gray (Reeder, 1989, grades 4–6); *Bread and roses: The struggle of American labor, 1865–1915* (Meltzer, 1990, grades 6–8)

- **Compare/Contrast.**
  Surprising sharks (Davies, 2003, grades 2–4); *Hana's suitcase: A true story* (Levine, 2003, grades 6–8)

- **Make predictions.** Support with evidence from what you've heard.
  When Marian sang: The true recital of Marian Anderson, the voice of a century (Ryan, 2002, grades 2–4); *Secrets of the deep revealed* (Dipper, 2003, grades 5–8)

- **Problem and Solution.**

  If you traveled west in a covered wagon (Levine, 1986, grades 2–4); *Jungle rescue: Saving the new world tropical rain forest* (Miller & Berry, 1991, grades 6–8)

Graphic organizers, such as those presented in chapter 3, are useful for applying inquiry strategies, because students can visually represent concepts gained through their critical listening.

The four levels of listening are summarized as follows:

Marginal:	Being aware of noise or voices in the background
Appreciative:	Listening for pleasure and enjoyment
Attentive:	Listening to understand and interpret a speaker's message
Critical:	Listening to analyze, judge, and evaluate a speaker's message

Guidelines for Developing Listening Strategies

According to Funk and Funk (1989, pp. 660–662), teachers can help students develop good listening strategies by following four steps:

1. Provide a purpose for listening: Let students know what they are to listen *for*—not just what they are to listen to.

2. Create an atmosphere for listening by eliminating distractions, providing interesting lead-up activities, and being flexible in arranging student seating for all listening activities.

3. Provide follow-up experiences to listening activities.

4. Use teaching strategies that promote positive listening habits in which students must listen not only to the teacher but to each other.

Brent and Anderson (1993, p. 124) believe that "the keys to meaningful listening instruction are to identify the needed skill or strategy, teach it effectively, provide supervised practice, review strategies periodically, and assist children in selecting the most appropriate strategies in a variety of situations." Brent and Anderson go on to suggest the following classroom opportunities that teachers can provide so students can practice effective listening:

Author's Chair. Have a student read aloud from her own work or a selected piece from children's literature in front of the class. The other students listen carefully and then ask the student questions about what was read.

Reading Aloud to the Class. The teacher selects a variety of different materials to read to the class throughout the school year. For instance, in reading a novel to the class, the teacher may ask the students to predict what they think will happen based solely on the title of the book. Later, as they listen, students can make new predictions and validate their old ones. Students can also recall details and main events or summarize the story. In pairs, the students can take turns retelling the story.

Writing Workshop. During a writing workshop, children engage in several tasks that necessitate the use of listening skills. These include asking questions to clarify details, critiquing another student's story, and listening to other students' suggestions for improvement of a piece of writing.

Cooperative/Collaborative Groups. These group activities will not succeed if the members do not use good listening skills. As they begin such an activity, students need to be reminded to use encouraging and supportive comments after each group member shares information.

Reader's Theater. In reader's theater, a story or short passage from a book is converted into a script for reading aloud. Portions may be read in unison and other parts may be read individually. This requires attentive listening by all of the students.

Retelling. Students who read different books about the same topic, such as the westward movement, Native Americans, or World War II, may retell the story in small groups, thereby sharing the information they gleaned.

Brent and Anderson (1993) stress the importance of integrating listening throughout the school day and encourage the application of listening strategies in meaningful, integrated situations, rather than in isolation.

Instructional Approaches

The process of listening is somewhat similar to that of reading in terms of the importance of literal and inferential comprehension. Critical thinking plays a major role in both critical listening and critical reading. A study by Pearson and Fielding (1982) suggests that the instruction of children in certain reading comprehension skills will aid listening comprehension in the areas of inference and prediction formation.

Reading to young students is a common occurrence in most schools. Some teachers find it useful as a relief activity when students become distracted or "fidgety" and need a change of pace. Typically, upper-grade elementary teachers are hesitant to pursue this means with older and more sophisticated students. Yet a research study by Mendoza (1985) indicated that 74 percent of all surveyed students in the intermediate grades admitted that they enjoyed being read to by their teachers. A study of high school students by Bruckerhoff (1977) found that such reading activities that these students encountered in elementary school fostered positive attitudes toward reading. On this same line, Boodt (1984) found that enhanced listening skills positively enhanced the reading performance of intermediate-grade remedial students.

Frick (1986) believes that motivational levels are heightened when one reads to upper-elementary students. She emphasizes that the teacher's personal interest and enthusiasm for reading are shared through reading aloud and these positive feelings are conveyed to student listeners. Within such an atmosphere, children want to respond to the orally presented material and, ultimately, to read it for themselves.

There have been numerous studies of children who have listened to an oral reading of a text while simultaneously reading the text themselves. Indeed, this is the way a large portion of the population learns to read: following along as a young child while being read to by a parent or sibling. Such a process aids emergent literacy. In fact, if when driving in a car, a parent reads the name of a discount store aloud or repeats the message on a billboard to a child, soon the young passenger will be able to connect the aural input with the visual clues. Voila! The child is reading.

An informal study by Chomsky (1976) centering around third-grade students with reading difficulties led her to conclude that if children read along concurrently as a work is being read aloud by an adult, major improvements occur in the children's reading skills. Students in Chomsky's study were actually able to memorize picture books through repeated listening-while-reading sessions. Janiak (1983) suggests that students with reading problems engage in class choral readings, with the teacher serving as leader. Unfortunately, most current studies describe reading-while-listening activities that involve the use of recorded readings, thereby fixing the reading rate and ignoring the children's needs to read at faster or slower rates. As might be expected, such studies have been inconclusive in terms of the value of simultaneous reading and listening (McMahon, 1983).

Especially needed are read alouds with informational books and oral sharing activities such as concept muraling (see chapter 3) in order for struggling readers to acquire content area knowledge. Comprehending informational books can be difficult. Whereas narrative text usually follows a familiar story structure, expository text is written in different patterns (Benson, 2003; Livingston, Kurkjian, Young, & Pringle, 2004). By sharing the different patterns through read alouds and discussing or modeling the appropriate strategies for comprehension and vocabulary development, teachers give students the opportunity to develop informational thinking strategies.

According to Moss (1995, p. 123), "Exposure to nonfiction read alouds has the ever-widening effect of a pebble thrown into a pond." She offers five reasons for using nonfiction books as read alouds.

1. Nonfiction read alouds allow children to experience the magic of the real world.

2. Nonfiction read alouds sensitize children to the patterns of exposition.

3. Nonfiction read alouds provide excellent tie-ins to various curricular areas.

4. Nonfiction read alouds can promote personal growth and move children to social response.

5. Most importantly, reading nonfiction aloud whets children's appetites for information, thus leading to silent, independent reading of this genre (pp. 122–123).

Moss suggests that in selecting a quality nonfiction book for a read aloud (see box 7.8), teachers need to "consider the five A's":

1. the authority of the author;

2. the accuracy of the text content;

3. the appropriateness of the book for children;

4. the literary artistry; and

5. the appearance of the book (p. 123).

7.8   The More You Know

Quality Nonfiction Books for Read Alouds

Burleigh, R. (1991). *Flight: The journey of Charles Lindbergh* (M. Wimmer, Illus.). New York: Philomel. (1–8) Charles Lindbergh's preparation for and actual solo flight across the Atlantic Ocean are described as are his feelings of fright and loneliness.

Burleigh, R. (2002). *Into the air: The story of the Wright brothers' first flight* (M. Wimmer, Illus.). San Diego: Silver Whistle/Harcourt. (2–5) The story of Orville and Wilbur Wright's development of the airplane.

Cone, M. (1992). *Come back, salmon: How a group of dedicated kids adopted Pigeon Creek and brought it back to life*. New York: Sierra Club. (2–5) This book has an ecological theme that will encourage students to help preserve our natural resources.

Cummings, P. (1992). *Talking with artists*. New York: Bradbury. (3–8) This book presents children with insights into what it is like to be an artist as provided by several different artists themselves.

Fleischman, P. (1993). *Bull Run*. New York: HarperCollins. (4–8) From a firsthand viewpoint, the battle of Bull Run is described. Good details and descriptions are provided.

Freedman, R. (1987). *Lincoln: A photobiography*. New York: Clarion. (3–8) This book won the Newbery Award. Freedman has the knack of blending historical facts with poignant photos. A teacher could use almost any of his books for nonfiction read alouds.

Hamilton, V. (1993). *Many thousand gone: African Americans from slavery to freedom*. New York: Knopf. (3–8) Virginia Hamilton describes the lives of numerous African Americans, some famous, some forgotten.

Kurlansky, M. (2002). *Cod, the fish that changed the world*. New York: Simon and Schuster. (3–5). A delightful romp through the ages with the history of this important fish.

Lightfoot, D. J. (1992). *Trail fever: The life of a Texas cowboy* (J. Bobbish, Illus.). (3–6) This book vividly describes the daily life of a cowboy during the height of the great cattle drives in the 1880s.

Montgomery, S. (2004). *The tarantula scientist*. Boston: Houghton Mifflin. (3–6) This is an alluring book about the field of arachnology.

Murphy, J. (1995). *The great fire*. New York: Scholastic. (4–8) The 1871 Chicago fire is described based on accounts from the O'Leary family, in whose barn the fire started, and James Hildreth, a former politician who saved Chicago by blowing up parts of the city, thus preventing the fire from spreading from one set of buildings to another. Also depicted is Julia Lemo, a widow who saved her five children and her elderly parents.

Walker, S. (1994). *Volcanoes!* St. Paul, MN: Carolrhoda. (2–6) This book is just one in a series of science books that accurately describe natural phenomena.

Wechsler, D. (2003). *Bizarre bugs*. Honesdale, PA: Boyds Mills Press. (2–5) Like its companion, *Bizarre birds*, this book is filled with facts. Great key vocabulary to share with children to expand their word knowledge.

Organizing for Listening

When children engage in conversation with a partner or in a small group, a brief mini lesson on the aspects of conversational listening is beneficial. According to Dorothy Grant Hennings (2000, p. 165), in order to increase *metacommunicative awareness*—children's explicit awareness of the "rules" of discourse—students need reminders from the teacher. Hennings suggests that the teacher say such things as "remember to be respectful of others' ideas by listening closely and not interrupting. Give your buddy a fair share of the speaking time; don't be a timehog. Try to respond in terms of what your buddy has been saying." The same rules apply to *grand conversations* during which students discuss ideas, topics, or issues about which they are currently reading.

Grand conversations can revolve around children's literature, both fiction and nonfiction, as well as issues in the content areas such as science and social studies. For example, ecology may be discussed by second graders during a grand conversation. If it is a classwide discussion, the teacher may initially set some rules such as raising one's hand before speaking and everyone has to have an opportunity to speak before anyone can make a second statement. Difficult topics can be the subjects of grand conversations in small groups in the upper grades: comparisons of the emperors of Rome, ethical issues in medicine, and the appropriateness of current legislation before Congress or rulings before the U.S. Supreme Court. Certainly the newspaper and television can provide a catalyst as students discuss local, state, national, and international current events. A summarizer should be appointed to present the major points—pro, con, and neutral—brought out during the group's grand conversation. The summarizer should change daily to give all students the opportunity to listen attentively and critically. Note taking should also be encouraged.

During group work, some students often dominate the conversation, and there is always the student who lingers on a topic too long. One way to prevent this with third through eighth graders is to assign duties to two members of the group. One student serves as the "woofer." This student's role is to say "woof woof" when a student is dominating the conversation. The second student serves as the "tweeter." This student "tweets" whenever a student lingers too long on a topic or takes the group off task.

Special Needs Students and Listening

Special needs students may require additional reminders of the proper "rules" of conversation. Some low-achieving and ADD students are easily distracted so they need to be told to keep an eye on the current speaker. According to Francine Falk-Ross (1997, p. 210), inclusion children may have severe problems adhering to the general routines of classroom discourse. Such children may need help from a speech and hearing specialist or a resource room teacher who assists them with their responses by "guiding their language participation within and on the periphery of the classroom."

Students with auditory learning disorders, that is, problems processing oral language, need to focus on each speaker. Here, too, students need to look directly at the face of the speaker. Children with hearing disorders should be placed in a location in the group where they can see all speakers as well as not be distracted by other sounds such as hallway traffic.

Low achievers need explicit listening instruction in order to develop listening comprehension.

> Techniques like the five-finger retelling might provide a concrete means for fostering the inclusion of story structure elements with young children. In the five-finger retelling each finger is used as a prompt to tell about a particular story element (characters, setting, problem, plot, resolution). This can be taught with a poster as a reminder. (Stahl, 2004, p. 600)

Visual imagery helps poor comprehenders store and retrieve information. Students should be encouraged to "paint a picture in their minds" of the major points. The teacher then engages the students in extensive discussion about the images they created.

Gifted students often tend to dominate the conversation. After all they are recognized by their peers as being knowledgeable. Thus, classmates tend to let the gifted students take a topic and run with it. The teacher needs to intercede when this occurs. In turn, gifted students are often extremely good listeners and can serve as models for their peers.

English Language Learners (ELLs) and Listening

We tend to talk at a rapid pace that makes it very difficult for English language learners to comprehend what we are saying. They have to not only "catch" the sounds of English, but also translate those sounds into meaningful language. ELLs need to engage frequently in conversations with fluent English speakers if they are to develop their second language skills. It is critical that the teacher give a mini lesson on how to determine if someone is failing to understand what is being said. Does the person wrinkle the forehead? Go off on a tangent apart from the topic of the conversation? Look confused? The mini lesson should also include how the listening comprehension problem can be resolved—repeat slowly what you just said, say it another way, or ask the person what he doesn't understand. This works for ELLs as well as all students.

Directed Listening Strategies

In addition to the approaches of reading to students and the reading-while-listening activities, two other strategies concerned with listening instruction have been developed in recent years: the directed listening activity (DLA) and the directed listening-thinking activity (DL-TA). Both the DLA and DL-TA are structured techniques used in the presentation of listening materials. The DLA is appropriate for use with individuals, small groups, or an entire class, while the DL-TA is best suited for use with groups of six to eight students.

Directed Listening Activity

The *directed listening activity* follows the traditional format of basal reader lessons; however, rather than reading, a student listens to the text as it is read. The student is required to (1) prelisten, (2) listen, and (3) follow up (Cunningham, Cunningham, & Arthur, 1981). Before the actual listening event, the student is provided with or, in some instances, must determine the purpose, establish goals, and select an appropriate listening skill. A DLA permits the teacher and students to focus on the development of specific skills, such as determining the main idea, summarizing, understanding new vocabulary through denotation or connotation, categorizing, sequencing, identifying cause and effect, evaluating, and so on. A DLA is useful in assisting lower-achieving students and those with learning disabilities as well as children for whom English is a second language. Below are suggested steps for a directed listening activity.

1. Select a text that has a clear plot and a logical, straightforward sequence.
2. Share the purpose for listening with the students.
3. Give suggestions that will aid comprehension of the material. For example, have students relate the material to previous knowledge, noting major details and the like.
4. Present the material without distractions.
5. Have students follow up their listening by sharing their understanding of the material with the class. (This also provides closure to the activity.)

Teachers generally fail to delineate clearly the reasons for listening before they give students a listening assignment. Without such a base, students are unable to choose a strategic plan in accordance with the listening task. Lacking the opportunity to develop a variety of listening strategies, children will develop only one: recall of all the aural input. Obviously, such a tactic is not only ineffective and inefficient but also frustrating to students. Teacher direction prior to any listening activity greatly alleviates undue tension and fosters sharpened listening skills.

Once goals have been established, a listener is better able to progress through the second phase of the DLA: organizing and classifying information and forming inferences about the content of a message. Finally, in the follow-up stage, the listener reacts to the aural message. Such retrospection fosters critical thinking: the ability to critique, evaluate, and judge the message.

One example of a DLA is an activity in which a teacher tells the students that they will listen to three fables and subsequently match each fable with its corresponding moral. As instructed, the students are to listen to each fable and attempt to grasp its main idea. The actual association of each fable with its correct moral constitutes the follow-up. Box 7.9 on pp. 289–290 contains a DLA in which students cooperatively participate.

7.9 In the Classroom: Mini Lesson

Cooperative/Collaborative Attentive Listening

This DLA is appropriate for students in grades 2–8. Divide the students into groups of six and give each group member one-sixth of a paper circle that is eight inches in diameter. Next, inform the students that they are to listen carefully to a folktale as it is read aloud because each group of students must determine the six main events of the folktale. Once a group has identified the six events, have each group member illustrate one of the events on his or her sixth of the circle. (Note: The number of students per group along with the corresponding number of events may be changed, depending on class size or number of significant events in a particular folktale.)

When a group has completed its illustrations, each member describes his or her illustration of one event. Then the events are put in sequence and the story is retold. Each group's final product becomes a completed circle of six pie-shaped illustrations that tell the story in clockwise order, starting at the 12 o'clock position. When glued to bright-colored construction paper, the completed circles make an effective bulletin board display.

This activity can be extended into the writing arena by having each student write the first draft of a story and then illustrate each event in the story. By drawing the various scenes and placing them in a desired sequence, students can modify and refine a story before they begin the final writing.

Following are some suggested folktales for cooperative attentive listening:

Aylesworth, J. (2001). *The tale of tricky fox* (B. McClintock, Illus.). New York: Scholastic.

Brothers Grimm. (1978). *The fisherman and his wife* (E. Shub. Trans.; M. Laimgruber, Illus.), New York: Greenwillow.

Farris, P. J. (1996). *Young Mouse and Elephant: An East African Folktale* (V. Gorbachev, Illus.). Boston: Houghton Mifflin.

Kellogg, S. (1991). *Jack and the beanstalk.* New York: Morrow.

Kellogg, S. (1995). *Sally Ann Thunder Ann Whirlwind Crockett.* New York: Morrow.

Kimmel, E. A. (1996). *The magic dreidels: A Hanukkah story* (K. Krenina, Illus.). New York: Holiday House.

Rascol, S. (2004). *The impudent rooster* (H. Berry, Illus.). New York: Dutton.

Scieszka, J., & Smith, L. (1998). *Squids will be squids: Fresh morals, beastly tales.* New York: Viking.

The figure on the following page depicts the story of *Young Mouse and Elephant: An East African Folktale* as drawn by a group of six third graders. The story begins as Young Mouse brags that he is the strongest animal. His grandfather then tells him that Elephant is the strongest animal. Young Mouse goes off to seek out Elephant and the adventure and fun begin.

continued

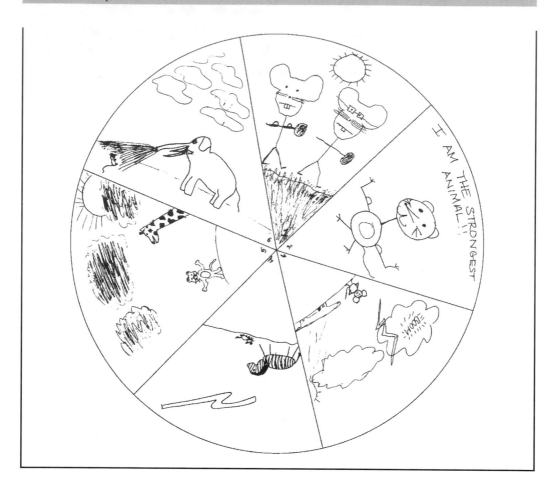

Directed Listening-Thinking Activity

As mentioned earlier, a good listener is able to anticipate portions of an upcoming message. The same is true for the good reader who can predict what is to come next in the text. The *directed listening-thinking activity* (DL-TA) depends on children's abilities to be active, critical listeners, participants who relate to prior knowledge and experiences (Stauffer, 1975).

During a DL-TA, the teacher reads a portion of a story and then stops at a critical point in the action. At this time, the students make predictions concerning upcoming events on the basis of information obtained through listening as well as that acquired through personal knowledge and experience. Most stories contain clues that provide listeners or readers with insights as to potential outcomes. When children gain experience in recognizing and interpreting these clues, they become aware of subtleties they might otherwise miss or ignore when participating in a DLA. After the students have shared all of their predictions with each other, the teacher continues to read the text until he reaches another important point in the story's plot. Any students who now feel their earlier predictions were incorrect must formulate new hypotheses based on the additional information they have just been given. The variety of experiential backgrounds present in any given classroom may result in varying predictions. Then the students must defend and justify their anticipatory statements. The sharing of clues or insights gained through listening to the story can aid students in this activity. The steps involved in a DL-TA are listed below. Box 7.10 contains a content area DL-TA lesson.

1. Divide the class into groups of 6 to 10 students to ensure good discussion interaction. In groups of this size, all or nearly all of the students will be able to share their predictions about the story they will hear.

2. Select a story with a clear plot and clearly delineated scenes.

3. Plan to make between 2 and 5 stops or pauses as you read the story, each immediately before you reach a critical point in the action of the story.

4. At each stop, have students summarize what has already taken place and then predict what is to occur next.

5. Accept all predictions without judgment; that is, do not classify the predictions as either right or wrong. Instead, encourage the children to defend and explain their predictions using their previously gained knowledge and experiential backgrounds.

6. Read the next portion of the story and review the predictions made earlier. Have the students confirm or deny their previously made predictions before they anticipate forthcoming events.

7. Encourage all children to join in the discussion; however, do not let the discussion become removed from the story or otherwise prolonged to the point where it diminishes the activity's stimulating nature.

7.10   In the Classroom: Mini Lesson

Listening in the Content Areas

Children need to be able to recognize links between history and science. To help them do this, the teacher may read Alice Fleming's (1988) *The King of Prussia and a Peanut Butter Sandwich* to students in second or third grade. The book tells the story of the Mennonites who were forced to leave Prussia and eventually settled in Kansas, where they introduced winter wheat from which bread is made. Using the DL-TA approach, the teacher encourages the students to make predictions about the title of the book, namely, how the King of Prussia is connected to a peanut butter sandwich.

After the DL-TA has concluded, the teacher places students in small groups, instructing each group to develop a story about a similar link between history and science. The teacher may provide hints as to possible topics and also give some direction as to where students can find appropriate information.

Another title (appropriate for fifth through eighth grades) that links history and science is *The Man Who Made Time Travel* by K. Lasky (2003). It is the story of the prize given to the person who could accurately measure longitude and make travel safer for seafaring ships.

Fleming, A. (1988). *The King of Prussia and a peanut butter sandwich* (R. Himler, Illus.). New York: Scribner.
Lasky, K. (2003). *The man who made time travel* (K. Hawkes, Illus.). New York: Melanie Kroupa Books.

Summary

Listening is an interactive process in which the listener attempts to relate previously gained knowledge to the aural message received from the speaker. In doing this, the listener classifies, organizes, sequences, evaluates, challenges, and accepts or rejects the speaker's message.

The purposes for listening differ from situation to situation. The four levels of listening are marginal, appreciative, attentive, and critical. Marginal listening occurs when one is aware of the presence or absence of background noise, such as music piped into an elevator. Appreciative listening is the act of enjoying aural input, whether it be music, a lecture, or a poetry reading. Attentive listening occurs when the goal is to comprehend and understand the aural message. In critical listening, the listener attempts to comprehend the message and also to evaluate it.

The directed listening activity (DLA) and the directed listening-thinking activity (DL-TA) are methods teachers can use to help children develop their listening abilities. The DLA can be used with a single student or an entire class. The DL-TA is best suited for small groups of students.

The DLA involves prelistening, listening, and follow-up. A purpose for listening is established before the activity begins. Students recall their previous knowledge about the topic and, in some cases, share that knowledge with other members of the group prior to the listening task. After the students have listened, closure is brought to the activity with a follow-up measure, such as a discussion or task based on the listening activity.

The DL-TA is designed to stimulate the use of higher-level thinking skills and to encourage divergent thinking. The teacher reads a story, stopping at pivotal points throughout. The students review what has occurred up to each point and make predictions based on clues from the story and their own experiential background as to what will occur next in the story.

For younger children, listening may be the most important language art in the learning process. As they grow older, listening seemingly diminishes in importance in the classroom. However, teachers at all grade levels must ensure that all students develop lower- and higher-level listening skills to their fullest.

Questions

1. Consider the three primary steps of the listening process in terms of the following children: (a) a fourth grader with a slight hearing loss, (b) a first grader who is learning English as a second language, and (c) a sixth grader who has recently learned that his parents are planning to divorce. How are those situations alike and how do they differ?

2. What elements are important in the teaching of critical listening?

3. How can outside factors interfere with a child's listening potential?

4. What should a teacher do to reduce distractions in the classroom and thereby improve students' listening ability?

5. Compare and contrast the four levels of listening and the role each plays in the primary grades and in the intermediate grades.

Reflective Teaching

Flip back to the beginning of the chapter to the teaching vignette entitled "Peering into the Classroom." After rereading the vignette, consider the following questions: What characteristics (either implied or directly exhibited) does the teacher possess that you would like to develop? What strengths and weaknesses are revealed for the students described in this section? How would you meet the needs of students such as these?

Activities

1. Observe a first-grade class and a sixth-grade class. Note the listening differences between the students in the two grades.

2. Appreciative listening receives little attention in most classrooms. Design a lesson that incorporates appreciative listening into the teaching of a subject other than language arts.

3. Record several political campaign commercials and have intermediate-grade elementary and middle school students identify the propaganda technique(s) used in each.

4. For one entire day, note your own personal strengths and weaknesses as a listener.

5. Develop a directed-listening activity and a directed thinking-listening activity for the grade level of your choice.

6. Find five different listening activities in various professional journals (*Instructor*, *The Reading Teacher*, etc.). Identify which activities are most appropriate for the directed listening activity and for the directed thinking-listening activity.

Further Reading

Armstrong, W. (1997–1998). Learning to listen. *American Educator, 21*, 24–25, 47.

Brent, R., & Anderson, P. (1993). Developing children's classroom listening strategies. *The Reading Teacher, 47* (2), 122–126.

Gallas, K. (1992). When the children take the chair: A study of sharing time in a primary classroom. *Language Arts, 69* (3), 172–182.

Johnson, N. J., Giorgis, C., Bonomo, A., Colbert, C., Conner, A., Kauffman, G., & King, J. (2000). Language of expression. *The Reading Teacher, 53* (7), 600–608.

Mandlebaum, L. H., & Wilson, R. (1989). Teaching listening skills in the special education classroom. *Academic Therapy, 24* (4), 449–459.

Moss, B. (1995). Using children's nonfiction tradebooks as read alouds. *Language Arts, 72* (2), 122–126.

References

Aronson, D. (1974). Stimulus factors and listening strategies in auditory memory: A theoretical analysis. *Cognitive Psychology, 6* (1), 108–132.

Baker, L. (1983). *Children's effective use of multiple standards for evaluating their comprehension.* Unpublished manuscript, University of Maryland, College Park.

Benson, V. (2003). Informing literacy: A new paradigm for assessing nonfiction. *The New England Reading Association, 39* (1), 13–20.

Blankenship, T. (1982). Is anyone listening? *Science Teacher, 49* (9), 40–41.

Boodt, G. (1984). Critical listeners become critical readers in reading class. *The Reading Teacher, 37* (4), 390–394.

Brent, R., & Anderson, P. (1993). Developing children's classroom listening strategies. *The Reading Teacher, 47* (2), 122–126.

Bruckerhoff, C. (1977). What do students say about reading instruction? *Clearing House, 51* (3), 104–107.

Chomsky, C. (1976). After decoding, what? *Language Arts, 53* (3), 288–296, 314.

Cosgrove, J. M., & Patterson, C. J. (1977). Plans and development of listener skills. *Developmental Psychology, 13* (5), 557–564.

Cox, C. (1999). *Teaching language arts: A student- and response-centered classroom* (3rd ed.). Boston: Allyn & Bacon.

Cunningham, J. W., Cunningham, P. M., & Arthur, S. V. (1981). *Middle and secondary school reading.* New York: Longman.

Falk-Ross, F. (1997). Developing metacommunicative awareness in children with language difficulties: Challenging the typical pull-out system. *Language Arts, 74* (7), 206–216.

Frick, H. A. (1986). The value of sharing stories orally with middle school students. *Journal of Reading, 29* (4), 300–303.

Funk, H. D., & Funk, G. D. (1989). Guidelines for developing listening skills. *The Reading Teacher, 42* (9), 660–663.

Goss, B. (1982a). Listening as information processing. *Communication Quarterly, 30* (4), 304–307.

Goss, B. (1982b). *Processing communication.* Belmont, CA: Wadsworth.

Graves, D. (1991). *Discover your own literacy.* Portsmouth, NH: Heinemann.

Hennings, D. G. (2000). *Communication in action: Teaching literature-based language arts* (7th ed.). Boston: Houghton Mifflin.

Ironsmith, M., & Whitehurst, G. J. (1978). The development of listener abilities in communication: How children deal with ambiguity. *Child Development, 49* (2), 348–352.

Janiak, R. (1983). Listening/reading: An effective learning combination. *Academic Therapy, 19* (2), 205–211.

Leverentz, F., & Garman, D. (1987) What was that you said? *Instructor, 96* (8), 66–70.

Livingston, N., Kurkjian, C., Young, T., & Pringle, L. (2004). Nonfiction as literature: An untapped goldmine. *The Reading Teacher 57* (6), 584–591.

Lundsteen, S. W. (1979). *Listening: Its impact at all levels on reading and the other language arts.* Urbana, IL: National Council of Teachers of English.

McMahon, M. (1983). Development of reading-while-listening skills in the primary grades. *Reading Research Quarterly, 19* (1), 38–52.

Mendoza, A. (1985). Reading to children: Their preferences. *The Reading Teacher, 38* (6), 522–527.

Moss, B. (1995). Using children's nonfiction tradebooks as read alouds. *Language Arts, 72* (2), 122–126.

Paley, V. G. (1986). On listening to what children say. *Harvard Educational Review, 56* (2), 122–131.

Pearson, P. D., & Fielding, L. (1982). Research update: Listening comprehension. *Language Arts, 59* (6), 617–629.

Pratt, M. W., & Bates, K. R. (1982). Young editors: Preschool children's evaluation and production of ambiguous messages. *Developmental Psychology, 18* (1), 30–42.

Shoop, M. (1986). InQuest: A listening and reading comprehension strategy. *The Reading Teacher, 39* (7), 670–674.

Stahl, K. A. D. (2004). Proof, practice, and promise: Comprehension strategy instruction in the primary grades. *The Reading Teachers, 57* (7), 598–609.

Stauffer, R. (1975). *Directing the reading-thinking process.* New York: Harper & Row.

Stein, N. L., & Trabasso, T. (1982). What's in a story? Critical issues in comprehension and instruction. In R. Glaser (Ed.), *Advances in instructional psychology* (Vol. 2). Hillsdale, NJ: Erlbaum.

Strother, D. B. (1987). Practical applications of research on listening. *Phi Delta Kappan, 68* (8), 625–628.

Templeton, S. (1998). *Teaching the integrated language arts* (3rd ed.). Boston: Houghton Mifflin.

Weaver, C. H. (1972). *Human listening: Process and behavior.* Indianapolis, IN: Bobbs-Merrill.

Children's Literature

Beatty, P. (1987). *Charley Skedaddle.* New York: Morrow.

Beatty, P. (1992). *Who comes with cannons?* New York: Morrow.

Davies, N. (2003) *Surprising sharks* (J. Croft, Illus.). Cambridge, MA: Candlewick.

Dipper, F. (2003). *Secrets of the deep revealed: Fantastic see-through pages.* New York: DK.

Gibbons, G. (1992). *Spiders.* New York: Holiday.

Kelly, I. (2002). *It's a hummingbird's life.* New York: Holiday House.

Levine, E. (1986). *If you traveled west in a covered wagon.* New York: Scholastic.

Levine, K. (2003). *Hana's suitcase: A true story* (G. Morton, Illus.). Toronto: Second Story Press.

Maestro, B. (1992). *How do apples grow?* New York: HarperCollins.

Meltzer, M. (1990). *Bread and roses: The struggle of American labor, 1865–1915.* New York: Facts on File.

Miller, C. G., & Berry, L. A. (1991). *Jungle rescue: Saving the new world tropical rain forest.* New York: Atheneum.

Pringle, L. (2003). *Come to the ocean's edge: A nature cycle book* (M. Chesworth, Illus.). Honesdale, PA: Boyds Mills Press.

Ray, D. (1990). *A nation torn: The story of how the Civil War began.* New York: Dutton.

Reeder, C. (1989). *Shades of gray.* New York: Harper Trophy.

Ryan, P. (2002). *When Marian sang.* New York: Simon & Schuster.

Simon, S. (2003). *Eyes and ears.* New York: Scholastic.

Wechsler, D. (2003). *Bizarre bugs.* Honesdale, PA: Boyds Mills Press.

Writing
A Multidimensional Process

> The teaching of writing demands the control of two crafts, teaching and writing.
>
> —Donald Graves
> *Writing: Teachers & Children at Work*

PEERING INTO THE CLASSROOM
WRITER'S WORKSHOP

Twenty-eight heads are bent over desks. Pencils make scratching noises as they fly across the paper. Taking a brief break from her own writing to make certain everyone is on task, Mrs. Lee Donnelson watches her fourth-grade charges engage in writing about a memorable family experience. Writer's workshop is moving full speed ahead. When Lee took the status of the class just prior to releasing her students to write, she discovered that the topic had spurred a wide variety of thoughts by her students. Kyle, for example, decided to write about his family's acquisition of a new Labrador puppy, while Zeke was drafting a piece about his family's trip to their native Mexico. Maria decided to write about her grandmother coming from Venice, Italy, to live with her family. For Alvaro the choice was simple: a fire had destroyed his family's trailer, but a fireman rescued Alvaro's pet cat. Other students had interesting ideas as well: a vacation trip to the Grand Canyon, a visit with a great aunt just before she passed away, going to a football game, a family going caroling during a snowfall, and so forth. After the drafts are written and polished, students will share their writing with the class. This is an opportunity for both students and Lee to get to know each other better. Because Lee is sensitive to her students' writing, they feel free to share sensitive thoughts knowing they won't be ridiculed or teased by peers.

Lee herself chose a topic close to her heart—being taught by her father how to drive the family car—a stick shift no less—and running into her younger brothers' carefully constructed igloo. Like many teachers, Lee often writes on the same topic as her students. She shares her work with her class and asks for suggestions for improvement. From time to time, Lee starts a piece of writing from scratch on an overhead and shares aloud her thoughts as she writes. Lee refers to this as "'mind opening-mine walking.' It's like I let the students see inside my head, how the wheels go around. It's like going through a mine field for a teacher as you share your inner thoughts and there are times when the wheels inside your head don't go around. You're stumped for an idea. Or you can't even think of how to spell the simplest of words. Ugh!!!!"

Chapter Objectives

The reader will:

✓ understand the aspects of the writing process: prewriting, writing, rewriting, and publishing.

✓ learn how to use the elements of writer's workshop.

✓ appreciate the need to teach students about audience and voice.

✓ understand the different types of writing—narrative, expository, and poetic.

✓ grasp the developmental differences in writing.

Standards for Professionals

The following Standards will be addressed in this chapter:

Standard 1: Foundational Knowledge and Dispositions

1.1 Demonstrate knowledge of psychological, sociological, and linguistic foundations of reading and writing processes and instruction.

1.2 Demonstrate knowledge of reading research and histories of reading.

1.3 Demonstrate knowledge of language development and reading acquisition and variations related to cultural and linguistic diversity.

Standard 2: Instructional Strategies and Curriculum Materials

2.1 Use instructional grouping options (individual, small-group, whole-class, and computer based) as appropriate for accomplishing given purpose.

2.2 Use a wide range of instructional practices, approaches, and methods, including technology-based practices, for learners at differing stages of development and from differing cultural and linguistic backgrounds.

2.3 Use a wide range of curriculum materials in effective reading instruction for learners at different stages of reading and writing development and from differing cultural and linguistic backgrounds.

Standard 3: Assessment, Diagnosis, and Evaluation

3.3 Use assessment information to plan, evaluate, and revise effective instruction that meets the needs of all students, including those at different developmental stages and those from differing cultural and linguistic backgrounds.

Standard 4: Creating a Literate Environment

4.1 Use students' interests, reading abilities, and backgrounds as foundations for the reading and writing program.

4.2 Use a large supply of books, technology-based information, and nonprint materials representing multiple levels, broad interests, and cultural and linguistic backgrounds.

4.3 Model reading and writing enthusiastically as valued lifelong activities.

Introduction

Of all the language arts, writing is the most complex for children to learn and the most difficult for teachers to teach. As Newman (1985, p. 17) states, "Writing develops in many directions at once; it develops continually, sometimes inconspicuously, sometimes in dramatic spurts." Not only must the writer have an idea about a chosen subject, but the writing must be organized, presented with clarity, written legibly, contain correct spelling, and be free of grammatical errors. In addition, the writer must consider the readers, or audience, who will read the piece, including their interpretations and any biases that they may have. Such orchestration of many kinds of skills is a formidable task indeed. As Dyson and Freedman (2003, p. 975) point out, when a student writes an essay, "The writer must solve subproblems of how to form letters, how to punctuate and spell, how to construct felicitous written sentences, how to get ideas, how to order those ideas, and so on. Some of these processes become quite automatic and unconscious as the writer matures, while others take time, attention, and skill, even for experienced adults."

Whereas the student experiments with various writing experiences and techniques, the teacher must constantly evaluate student progress in the area of writing knowledge. Rather than demanding performance and ultimately confining both the writer and product, a teacher must set the classroom tone for writing. In doing so, the teacher must stress the importance of the writing process and the resulting satisfaction of sharing personal writings with peers.

According to Kerry Ridolfi (1997), a middle school teacher in New Hampshire, students are impacted by their own and their classmates' writing in addition to that of established writers. Ridolfi writes, "It is powerful to learn that you can make sense of the world through words; it is powerful to learn that you can persuade, entertain, inform, and touch the heart" (p. 41). Writing can be contagious, with students becoming excited over topics and sharing their work. Regrettably in many classrooms students have very limited opportunities to share their compositions with their peers, depriving them of the joy of authorship as well as limiting the scope and breadth they gain from the writings of their peers.

Many feelings are evoked as one writes. Teachers must be aware of the hills and valleys of writing. Calkins and Harwayne (1991, p. 99) put it this way:

> Magical writing is contagious. . . . But good writing classrooms are not filled with success stories alone; they are also filled with heartache and struggle, with bravado and jealousy, with students who think they have nothing to say and with students who spend more time on their margins and handwriting than on the content of their writing.

Writing offers children ways to develop social awareness. Teachers should be "rewarded for recognizing moments when children share differing views and values with their peers through writing" (Dyson, 1994, p. 1). For young children, the classroom writing climate should be one of enthusiasm and acceptance, where correct language use and precision (correct spelling, punctuation, and grammar) take second place to reflection and expression (Walley, 1991).

Emphasis has shifted from product-oriented writing assignments in which little or no prior instruction was provided to process-oriented writing in which students are taught how to write. Writing is recursive and cyclical, with writers moving back and forth through a series of stages that generally include prewriting, drafting, revising, and editing. As writers progress through a series of drafts, ideas are collected, discarded, and refined. "A process writing classroom is arranged so that students are free to talk, share, brainstorm, and write, so clusters of students are grouped together and allowed to share their work and use peers as resources. This arrangement promotes a socially oriented interactive experience and ownership of the writing process" (Buss & Karnowski, 2000, p. 2). This chapter gives an overview of the writing process and what to expect as a teacher at the different grade levels.

Initial Attempts at Writing

In a literate society, children make conscious strides toward successful reading and writing relatively early in life. Preschool-age children eagerly maneuver their pens and pencils in order to "write" on walls, magazines, tables, and other objects. Such creative marks reveal the youngsters' recognition that jottings and scrollings serve as symbols of meaning. Through these markings, a child proclaims, "Here I am world. I have something worth sharing!"

Scribbling is the child's initial experimentation with writing. As the child begins to explore, some recognizable forms emerge: lines, circles, and crosses

(Clay, 1987). Such shapes are eventually combined to represent familiar, tangible objects and people within the child's life: the family dog, siblings, parents, home, and so on. Yet children do learn quickly that drawing is distinguishable from writing; drawing conveys meaning through pictures, whereas writing conveys meaning through a combination of representative symbols and is therefore more adultlike in nature. Letters of the alphabet and other symbols come to represent complete words for youngsters and will often accompany the drawings of two- and three-year-olds. According to Harste, Woodward, and Burke (1984), when three-year-old children are given a pen, about 75 percent of them will use the implement for writing or scribbling, while presentation of a crayon is recognized by the same age-group as a tool for drawing.

Among the first to conduct research concerning young children's early encounters with writing was Marie Clay (1975). She demonstrated that children's early writings precede any formal instruction in either reading or writing. Similarly, in a study designed to examine children's acquisition of speech sounds, Read (1971) described the key young children use to understand spelling. He discovered that young children "invented" the spelling of words, with the spellings becoming progressively more rule based and predictable (see chapter 11). According to Teale (1986), children as young as two or three years of age have "specific ideas about what written language is, and how the processes of reading and writing work." Indeed, some language arts authorities propose that reading and writing require either identical or analogous cog-

After celebrating Johnny Appleseed's birthday in September, Mrs. Phyllis Richardson's class made story chains. The students each wrote and illustrated the major events in Johnny Appleseed's life.

nitive processes, knowledge, skills, and strategies (Laminack, 1990; Tierney & Pearson, 1983). Because reading and writing develop concurrently and are so interrelated, both should be taught in the early grades. Graves (1983) believes that teachers should provide daily writing opportunities for children as early as the first grade. Calkins (1995) extends this theory in recommending that writing be undertaken daily for one hour. However, in most elementary and middle school classrooms, 40 to 45 minutes devoted to writing each day is more realistic.

If children are going to learn writing methods, they must actively participate in writing tasks that hone their writing skills. Personal letters, reports, thank-you notes, journals, poetry, and stories serve as appropriate subjects for classroom assignments because they allow children to practice and develop their writing techniques. Simply put, children learn to write by writing.

The Writing Process

During the past 20 years, researchers have refocused their attention on the writing process itself rather than on the writing product. The overall result has been the discovery of the writing process as an event, not an act. Writing is a process that takes place over time and requires substantial blocks of uninterrupted time. The role of writing should be recognized as both functional and self-educative (Harste et al, 1984). Skills involved in the writing process are:

1. Recollection of experiences—vicarious and real
2. Knowledge of words, sentences, paragraphs, etc.
3. Familiarity with literature of varying genres (reading and discussing skills)
4. Questioning skills (research skills)
5. Dictionary skills
6. Organization skills
7. Spelling skills
8 Handwriting skills/keyboarding skills

Research findings indicate that the writing process used by the professional writer is quite similar to the writing process used by the novice six-year-old author (Murray, 1980). This four-step or four-stage process, which includes the sequence of prewriting, writing, rewriting, and publishing, is described in the following sections.

Prewriting

Prewriting includes collecting thoughts and information, experimenting with new ideas, and eventually adopting an appropriate course or map that outlines the route to be followed in a piece of writing. Murray (1980) refers to prewriting as "rehearsal."

As a readiness stage, prewriting involves both preparation and reflection. Connections are made through the linkage of ideas, thoughts, and newly discovered knowledge. Classification, association, analysis, and evaluation are important processes for this opening stage and further foster divergent thinking, questioning, and probing. Brainstorming, clustering, interviewing, listing, and mapping are related behaviors that assist children in discussing their ideas with each other. Smith (1982, p. 12) notes, "We do not think and then write, at least not without putting an unnecessary handicap on ourselves. We find out what we think when we write, and in the process put thinking to work—and increase its possibilities." Similarly, Abel, Hauwiller, and Vandeventer (1989) describe writing as a tool of thought, necessary for developing ideas and promoting thinking.

Motivation and stimulation are important components of the prewriting stage because it is much easier to write if one is excited about the task. Such enthusiasm is most likely to occur when the writer is permitted to undertake subjects that he views as relevant or even personal. The research of Donald Graves (1983) further suggests that teachers should devote more attention to the individual interests and concerns of their students, for any successful attempts at writing will more often than not revolve around those interests and concerns. Gahn (1989) asserts that what is taught in the classroom should be linked with the "real" world if writing is to be used as a tool in children's developing and retaining knowledge.

Prewriting also focuses on editing to some extent because the writer consciously adopts and rejects ideas by weighing the value of each against its negative aspects. Research indicates that by the time the prewriting stage is completed, most of the elements that the writer will include in the piece are present (Emig, 1971).

During this rehearsal or "warm-up" stage, teachers rely on activities that provide background experiences: field trips, hands-on science experiments, films, guest speakers, and so forth. In addition, teachers may focus on common personal experiences, such as a favorite tangible object, a project each student designed and completed without assistance, or a humorous incident.

Writing

The second step or stage of the *writing* process is writing, actually composing the piece. Within this stage, the writer is primarily concerned with content, while mechanics and spelling are a second priority. This writing, or drafting, is accomplished with a distinct purpose in mind and for a specified audience.

As the writer transforms thoughts and ideas into sentences, some editing automatically takes place; words, sentences, and ideas are discarded or modified. Indeed, the organization of the entire piece of writing may be altered if the writer elects to relocate whole paragraphs.

Rewriting

Rewriting is commonly referred to as editing and revising. Generally, this is the step or stage most dreaded by teachers and students, for now the piece must be polished; the writer must reread and evaluate the work in terms of both content and the conventions of language.

Rewriting requires the writer to move from the role of author to that of reader. The writer therefore begins to evaluate the piece in terms of communication of the main idea, number of examples, clarity of descriptions, repetition of ideas, attractiveness of the title, length of sentences, paragraph division, and ease of reading. Although the author should clean up the mechanics of grammar and spelling before sharing the finished product with the teacher, the teacher should not place too much emphasis on spelling and grammar at the expense of content (Abel & Abel, 1988).

After the writer has objectively evaluated the piece, she must make several decisions regarding content. The writer must consider possible adjustments in the organization of the material, the clarification of meanings, and the expansion of general ideas. Similarly, original "lead-in" sentences and the conclusion may need to be reworked to make them stronger and, ultimately, more attractive to readers. At this juncture, the writer must also analyze and correct punctuation, spelling, and usage errors.

Although rewriting may occur without assistance or feedback from others, a writer may exchange drafts with a classmate or writing partner. Along the same line, writers may share and discuss their papers within small groups. When the writing is a "work in progress," that is, actively being reviewed, the opinions and responses of others can help the author further refine the writing.

Publishing

Publishing is the final step or stage of the writing process and involves sharing a completed piece of writing with an audience, typically one's classmates. Indeed, a variety of established publishing forms exist: reading the piece aloud to a small group or the entire class; participating in individually prepared books, class books, a class literary newspaper, or a bulletin board display (see figure 8.1); recording the piece on a cassette; and so on.

A special place for the sharing of writing—the "Author's Chair"—should be designated within the classroom (Graves and Hansen, 1983). The Author's Chair serves as a formal place where a writer sits and reads a personally chosen selection to the class. The selection may be the writer's own work or that of a professional author. Once the writer has completed the reading, the listeners can react to the piece. Initial reactions must be positive and accepting. After this courtesy, members of the audience may ask the author more challenging questions concerning the piece.

In upper-elementary and middle school classrooms, Hansen (1992) suggests that children both support and challenge, but not confront, their classmates. By doing so, the children learn about themselves and their writing as well as become better judges of their own and others' work.

Figure 8.1   A first grader's story about a dinosaur

Writer's Workshop

The center of writing instruction is writer's workshop, a period of between 30 minutes for primary-grade students to 1 hour and 15 minutes for middle school students. Nancie Atwell, a middle school teacher, is one of the major advocates of writer's workshop. According to Atwell (1998, p. 71), the writer's workshop is "a way of teaching and learning uniquely suited to [students] . . . of every ability." During writer's workshop the teacher presents a *mini lesson* on an aspect of writing, conducts a *read aloud* of a book or a portion of a book, and the students engage in *writing* and *sharing*.

The writer's workshop needs to be structured with set procedures, such as having a set daily routine. For example:

- *A read aloud of a book, a portion of a book, or an entire poem by the teacher* with the class (a poem may be placed on a chart for primary students; on an overhead transparency for intermediate and middle school students). After the teacher has read the poem, the class may read it along with the teacher.

- *Mini lesson on a skill or strategy* needed by most of the class. At other times, students may be grouped for specific skill and strategy lessons.

- *Status of the class survey* by the teacher using a clipboard with a class list. As each student's name is called out, the student responds with the "status" of her current piece of writing. For instance, Emily may be drafting a story about a mouse who lives in a cupboard and Michael is revising his story about a pirate. The teacher may use a code system (D—drafting, E—Editing, R—Revising, CR—conducting research) to simplify record keeping.

- *Independent writing and conferencing* by the students. During this time the classroom resembles a beehive with pencils flying across paper and brief conferences between peers taking place. By the time students reach middle school, this portion of writer's workshop almost resembles a social event with the sharing and discussing that takes place. According to Atwell (1998), this is a natural aspect of adolescence that we teachers should use to our own advantage in teaching writing.

- *Group meetings (but not every day)* may take place to discuss a particular topic, to have friends write on a topic of their own choosing, to help low-ability students grasp a concept, to assist ELL students learn the conventions of English that are not a part of their own languages, or to challenge gifted students to write on a specific topic.

Mini Lessons

Mini lessons are brief direct instruction lessons used "to introduce and highlight concepts, techniques, and information that will help writers and readers grow up" (Atwell, 1998, p. 149). A mini lesson may be as short as 5 minutes with kindergartners or as long as 30 minutes with intermediate-elementary and middle school students. In writing, mini lessons focus on writing skills and strategies. Mini lessons are perfect for introducing the conventions of language: capitalization, punctuation, usage, spelling patterns, and so forth.

For kindergartners and first graders, the "Morning Message" that the teacher writes on the chalkboard each day is the beginning of mini lessons. Students can provide content for the teacher to include in the "Morning Message" (e.g., "My mom is going to have a baby." "We're going to the zoo on Saturday." "I got stung by a wasp."). By second semester of first grade, mini lessons are usually based on specific skill development, such as learning how to write a descriptive piece about an animal, like the classroom or family pet.

Mini lessons should not be dominated by the teacher. Through careful planning, the teacher can set up a constructivist approach to mini lessons in which students must "discover" how writing works. For example, the teacher may ask the students to bring their library books to writer's workshop. Students can take turns reading the first sentence or two of their books to determine what makes a great "hook" to motivate the reader to continue.

The teacher can use mini lessons to model appropriate writing behavior, as with the "hook" mini lesson described above. The teacher should occasionally demonstrate how she thinks as she writes. By writing about a topic on an overhead transparency, the teacher can then voice her thoughts out loud. Here she can state where she is going with the draft, things she wants to change or add or move, and so on. This greatly enhances students' understanding of how they, themselves, should go about writing. If the teacher isn't certain how to spell a word, she circles it to come back to later and continues on to get her message down. Later, the teacher uses the same piece to edit and revise. Thus, students recognize the need to focus first on content, then on revising and polishing their own work.

Gail Tompkins (2004, p. 58) suggests that a mini lesson contain five steps:

1. Introduce the strategy or skill.
2. Demonstrate the strategy or skill.
3. Provide guided practice using the strategy or skill.
4. Review the strategy or skill.
5. Apply the strategy or skill.

Tompkins believes the above five steps provide for scaffolding and a transfer of responsibility from the teacher to the students. They will then apply the skills and strategies in their own writing.

Writing Consideration

Audience

Writing revolves around more than content and the conventions of language (punctuation, spelling, and usage). The writer must also be able to organize and describe ideas in such a way as to ensure clarity and the understanding of a message. In view of this, the writer must consider audience. *Audience* refers to those who will read (or listen to) the piece. Direct awareness of the readers' degree of knowledge and types of personal experiences can aid the writer in choosing appropriate descriptions.

Graves (1985, p. 36) notes that "writing makes sense of things for oneself, and then for others." "Audience awareness in writing typically means being sensitive to the expectations, demands, and background of those reading the composition" (Bright, 1995, p. 71). For elementary children, four types of audiences exist: (1) self, (2) teacher, (3) known, and (4) unknown. Children's writing tends to be influenced by their sense of the audience, "the manner in which the writer expresses a relationship with the reader in respect to the writer's understanding" (Britton et al., 1975, pp. 65–66). According to Bright (1995, p. 12), "students' perceptions about both the value of audience and its composition undoubtedly influence the processes and products of their writing."

Self

Self, as audience, results in a very private type of writing because no one else is expected to read the message or text. The writing is done for one's own enjoyment and pleasure; therefore, diaries, journals, and personal notes exemplify writing for self. Poetry, stories, song lyrics, and ideas for problem solving may also fall within this category if the writer's purpose is to compose a piece without sharing it with anyone else. It should be noted that a piece originally intended for self may later be developed for a wider audience.

Teacher

The teacher is undoubtedly the most familiar type of audience for students. Historically, the student's role has always been to undertake and complete writing tasks assigned by and for the teacher. Whether or not this is consciously understood, the teacher as audience is often brought to mind when children write. First and second graders have a strong desire to please teachers with their writing, whereas older children may attempt to demonstrate newly developed proficiencies. The teacher can avoid the creation of excessive student dependence by converting the classroom into a writing community. By sharing their writing with one another in pairs and in writing groups, children learn to appreciate, value, and critique one another's works. Eventually, students will learn to seek advice about their writing from one another as well as from the teacher.

Known Audience

The *known audience* is just that—a person (or people) with whom the writer is familiar. Five-year-olds are very much aware of the known audience; if a kindergartner draws a picture and is asked who the picture is for, the child will respond with the name of a person, typically "Mommy" or "Daddy."

A known audience helps the writer select and control the type of writing. In view of the writer's familiarity with the reader, a common knowledge base is available. Little or no degree of clarification is needed when a known audience is acquainted with the experience being described. The known audience may be a sibling, a good friend, or a grandparent, for example. Writing that is intended for a known audience is of a semiprivate nature, for the author will share certain thoughts and feelings with only a very restricted group of readers or perhaps only one reader.

Unknown Audience

For the fourth type of audience, the *unknown audience*, writers must create pieces along more public lines. This type of audience is usually made up of more people than any of the other types and also expects more from a piece of writing. The revising and polishing of a piece to be read by an unknown audience necessitates that a writer understand and follow the conventions of language. Thus, written communications to be shared with students in other classrooms, business letters, and thank-you notes sent to museum guides after a field trip, for example, all require careful writing and editing.

Below is a summary of types of audiences.

Self:	Only the writer is the audience; no one else is to read what is written. The written piece may be practical, such as a grocery list, or personal, such as a poem or a biographical statement.
Teacher:	The most familiar audience for students is the classroom teacher, who not only makes the writing assignments but reads the pieces as well.
Known:	A known audience is one with whom the author is familiar. This type of audience is often composed of a single friend or relative.
Unknown:	An unknown audience is one that is unfamiliar to the writer. This type of audience is usually made up of several people and expects more from a piece of writing than the other types of audiences.

Voice

Voice refers to how a piece of writing is presented, how a story is told. For example, does it reflect the writer's own experiences, views, and interests, or does it objectively describe how to do something? Voice for young children is generally expressive within written works because youngsters attempt to write in the same bouncy, rambling way in which they tell a story. In the following example of use of the expressive voice, Stacie relates a visit to a friend's house:

> Yestrday I went to Susies house and we playd
> with her new doll. She naemd it Mande but
> it looks more like a Tifene.

Writing usually reflects one of three primary voices: narrative, expository, and poetic. Emergent writers tend to write in the narrative as they share stories about their family, friends, and pets. Beginning writers venture further afield into expository and poetic writing as they describe how to cook a particular dish, outline the steps in making an art project, or record observations of the classroom guinea pig. Their poetry may consist of two- or three-line rhymes. As children progress in their writing skills, they include more description, better organization, improved transitions, and greater awareness of their reader audience. We now take an in-depth look at voice in terms of elementary and middle school students and their writing.

Narrative Writing

Narrative writing is sometimes referred to by teachers as "story writing" in which the child writes a tale. It may be an adventure, a piece of fantasy, or even a folktale. Young children do this naturally. And why not? Children, and adults alike, live in the narrative. When they talk about an event that happened to them or something they'd like to occur, they are "telling a tale." They invent characters, sometimes enhancing their own abilities so that they, themselves, are characters in their stories. Plots are mapped out and settings devised. Feelings and emotions are charged and then, ta da! A story is spun on the page.

Expository Writing

The primary goal of narrative writing is to entertain the reader. However, *expository writing* takes a different route—that of informing the reader. The two main categories of expository writing are: descriptive and explanatory. It is helpful for the teacher to introduce students to various types of nonfiction through read alouds and model different inquiry strategies (Tower, 2000).

Descriptive writing requires that the writer point out exactly what took place without any bias. Children may write a descriptive piece that paints a portrait of their family dog or that summarizes a basketball game or video. It may describe the events that took place on a field trip or the observation of a science experiment. The key is that the writer remain objective in presenting the information.

The second category of expository writing is *explanatory* in which the writer outlines the steps or details of a process. For instance, the writing may explain how to draw a bicycle or how to make a vegetable car from an ear of corn, toothpicks, and wheels. The writer must keep in mind the sequence of events and present any directions accurately and completely.

Persuasive Writing

Persuasive writing involves presenting a belief, want, or desire and then giving ample reasons why that belief is appropriate or that the want or desire should be fulfilled. The closing statement repeats the request. Figure 8.2 shows a semantic map that students may use as a guide for their persuasive writing.

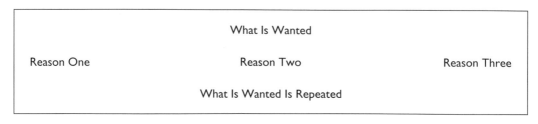

Figure 8.2   Persuasive writing map

Children have been found to actively explore techniques for persuading their classmates and family members through writing. They go beyond the models and examples provided by their teachers and develop their own persuasive writing strategies that they use within social interaction.

Poetic Voice

The *poetic voice* is the least used writing style of children. The poetic voice is used in writing both prose and poetry that can be appreciated intrinsically. Early-childhood-level children often believe—wrongly—that all poetry must rhyme or follow a rhyming pattern. In fact, there are several types of poetry. Many are discussed in the following chapter.

Prose is distinguished from poetry by its close correspondence to the patterns of everyday speech, whereas poetry is rhythmic verse. However, writers of both poetry and prose use the poetic voice. Heard (in Calkins, 1995) lists four characteristics of poetry:

1. Poetry uses condensed language. Every word is important.
2. Usually the language of poetry is figurative. It contains simile, metaphor, and imagery.
3. Poetry is rhythmical.
4. Just as the units of organization in prose are the sentence and the paragraph, the units of organization in poetry are the line and the stanza.

Poetry is popular provided that it comments on the aspects of life that are meaningful to children (Huck et al., 1997). Writing poetry often appeals to children because it is nonthreatening. As Kormanski (1992, p. 189) states, "Poetry is the natural language of children." Because of the relative shortness of poems, children can get immediate satisfaction from and responses to their writing efforts (Kirby & Liner, 1981).

The voices of writing are summarized as follows:

Narrative: The narrative, or expressive voice, reflects the feelings and personality of the writer and includes the frequent use of the pronoun "I." The primary goal of narrative writing is to entertain the reader.

Expository: Expository writing is informational writing and can be descriptive, explanatory, or persuasive.

Descriptive writing requires the writer to present only the facts and the details.

Explanatory writing requires that the writer present the steps or details of a process.

Persuasive: Persuasive writing requires that the writer try to influence the reader to accept a particular way of thinking by using facts.

Poetic: Poetic voice reflects the sensitivity, thoughts, and word selection of the writer through either poetry or prose.

The Development of Children's Writing

Jeff, age 3 1/2, was going shopping with his mother and her friend Jenny. While his mother was busy in a dressing room, Jeff engaged in a conversation with Jenny.

"We're going shopping," Jeff said.

Jenny replied, "Yes, at the shopping mall."

Jeff nodded knowingly, "I know a great place to eat. Give me a pencil, and I'll write it down for you."

Hoping to keep Jeff amused, Jenny searched through her purse and found a pen and some paper, both of which she gave to Jeff. Jeff's writing is shown in figure 8.3.

"Can you read it?" Jeff asked.

"Of course," replied Jenny, somewhat surprised that she could indeed read what such a young child had written. "It says 'McDonald's.'"

Jeff beamed, "Yeah, we'll eat at McDonald's. They've got great hamburgers and french fries there."

Although their scribblings are often undecipherable, some emergent writing can be easily recognized and understood. Consider, for example, Jenny's interpretation of Jeff's *M* (for McDonald's) when it is viewed in the context of lunch. Through the use of similar invented spellings, a young child actively engages in writing as a way to share thoughts and ideas with others. Although youngsters begin by drawing, they quickly proceed to scribbling, which serves as writing's precursor.

Figure 8.3   Jeff's writing about McDonald's

Kindergarten

Kindergarten children exhibit a wide range of writing abilities. Some children enter school knowing how to read and having been encouraged to write at home; others have no or only limited knowledge of sound-symbol relationships; and still others are unaware that the alphabet even exists. According to Sulzby (1992), most kindergarten children do not use conventional forms of writing. Many are still in the scribbling and drawing stage. However, by the second semester, many kindergartners do enjoy writing. This writing may consist mainly of drawings, which also convey messages, or it may be advanced to the point where an adult can actually recognize the words and read the story.

Initially, children only draw pictures of objects, never considering the use of accompanying labels. Lists are also popular with children of this age. Figure 8.4 is a list of events to take place in a neighborhood Olympics. Later, as children begin to create pictures depicting action, they use sound-symbol relationships to supply their drawings with appropriate phrases and sentences. Graves (1983) refers to such writing preceded by illustration as a "rehearsal" process inasmuch as a child is preparing for writing ventures.

Some teachers consider writing to be an unteachable skill at the kindergarten level. However, Calkins (1995) asserts that children who have a rudimentary knowledge of print tend to perceive themselves as writers. In this way, they quickly learn conventions of written language. Therefore, Calkins encourages both kindergarten and first-grade teachers to promote stimulating writing situations: for example, providing paper and envelopes for letter writing or

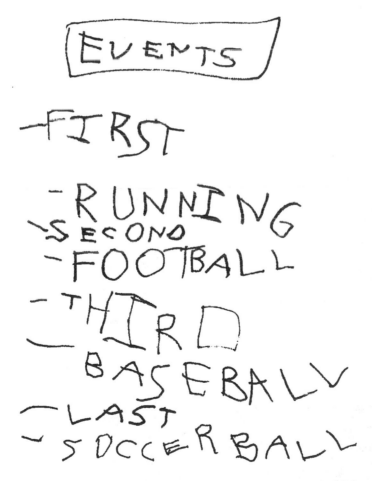

Figure 8.4   Beginning writers like to make lists. Here is a list of events to be included in a neighborhood Olympics as developed by a 5 1/2 year-old.

index cards for labeling objects in the room. Box 8.1 is a checklist of emergent writing skills.

First Grade

As children leave kindergarten's socialized world and enter the more academically oriented first-grade classroom, they often have a sense of "I can do it; I am a writer." At age six, few children are reluctant to attempt anything that the teacher suggests. Along the same line, first graders rarely encounter "writer's block" because they always have something to put down on paper even when

---

8.1   In the Classroom: Teaching Hint

Checklist of Emergent Writing Skills

Name: _____   Teacher: _____

Age: _____   Grade: _____   Date: _____

	Always	Sometimes	Never
Can differentiate between writing and drawing			
Uses pencil, marker, or pen for writing			
Writes in scribbles			
Uses letters in writing			
Uses letter strings in writing			
Uses invented spelling in writing			
Uses conventional (correct) spelling in writing			
Can print own first name —In all capital letters —Using capital and lowercase letters			
Expresses interest in writing (i.e., writes notes, keeps lists, makes cards)			
Writes from left to right			
Attempts to copy words and sentences			
Attempts to write independently			
Asks how to spell words			
Asks to dictate words/sentences/stories to someone who writes them down			
Teacher comments:			

they realize that their work is to be shared with others. In living for the moment and giving little consideration to yesterday or tomorrow, first graders want to write, write, write, and write some more. Their writing projects seem to flow as if off a production line without any quality control; and as soon as one first draft is written, these youngsters are anxious to begin another. Within any single writing session, it is not unusual for an eager first grader to write three or four new stories rather than to develop and perfect the first story. First graders are persistent in getting their ideas down on paper and moving on to the other ideas that are burning in their minds. Box 8.2 is a checklist of beginning writing skills.

For first-grade writers, editing is either very limited or essentially nonexistent until they recognize that polishing a piece of writing can make reading easier. Even at this point, the strong urge to begin and finish a piece within a very brief period still exists. It therefore becomes something of a momentous occasion for a child when he or she erases or crosses out a line of text for the first time. The first grader has now formally identified the piece as a draft that requires reworking to improve the text and ultimately to please the "writer."

8.2 In the Classroom: Teaching Hint

Checklist of Beginning Writing Skills

Name: _____   Teacher: _____

Age: _____   Grade: _____ Date: _____

	Always	Sometimes	Never
Expresses interest in writing (i.e., writes notes, keeps lists, makes cards, writes letters, makes sports cards)			
Talks with others about own writing			
Talks with others about his/her writing			
Writes on lines			
Makes capital letters correctly			
Makes lowercase letters correctly			
Leaves space between words			
Leaves space between sentences			
Uses periods and question marks appropriately			
Uses commas appropriately			
Uses quotation marks for dialogue			
Teacher comments:			

Although first graders show growth in all the conventions of language, the most dramatic growth occurs in the area of spelling. They often will write in capital letters or trace over and darken letters in an attempt to emphasize specific words or phrases. Punctuation marks—in particular exclamation points, question marks, and periods—are soon incorporated into their writing. The use of quotation marks is not popular at the beginning of first grade, but as the students gain exposure to dialogue in stories, they begin to incorporate quotation marks into their own writing.

Even at this young age, children notice that responsibility accompanies writing. To reinforce this sense of responsibility, the teacher can take attendance by having the children sign in each morning as they enter the classroom (Harste et al., 1984). The names of those both present and absent is an important piece of information that classroom teachers must collect every school day. After tabulating the data, the teacher forwards the information to the principal's office, which compiles all class attendance data and sends the compilation on to the central office of the school district. For first graders, then, signing in becomes both a responsibility and a morning writing ritual from the very beginning of the school year.

First graders should begin with writing pattern stories. That is sentences serve as templates for their ideas with students filling in blanks where the words are missing. Narrative, or story, writing is usually the first kind of sentence we introduce to students. Speech patterns are shared with which students are familiar. For example:

A _____ is blue.
A _____ is blue.
But a _____ is not blue.

Many children's books have repetition that can be used for patterned writing. Using the familiar "Brown bear, brown bear, what do you see? I see a red bird looking at me" (Martin, 1964; 1983, unpaged) as a pattern, students can write their own version in "_____ _____, what do you see? I see a _____ _____ looking at me." Kyle, age six, wrote, "Green frog, green frog, what do see? I see a yellow cat looking at me." The "Very" series of books by Eric Carle (1969; 1984; 1990; 1995) (e.g., *The Very Hungry Caterpillar, The Very Busy Spider, The Very Quiet Cricket,* and *The Lonely Firefly*), Douglas Florian's (2000) *A Pig Is Big,* Martin Waddell's (1993) *Farmer Duck,* and Sue Williams's (1990) *I Went Walking* all offer patterns that beginning writers find appealing to adopt as starting points for their own writing.

Expository, or informational, writing can be done in a similar fashion as students describe what they saw on a field trip to the apple orchard in September to commemorate Johnny Appleseed's birthday. "We went to the apple orchard. Apples taste _____. Apples can be _____. I like to eat _____."

After doing patterned writing, students venture farther into the world of writing. They may imitate stories the teacher shares as read alouds. In so doing, it is important to remember that students need not only ideas but words as they write. Mary Gardener supplies her charges with words in a fun way. She

8.3   In the Classroom: Teaching Hint

Supplies for Writing

Before the school year begins, the teacher can acquire writing supplies to make the writing process both organized and interesting for students. The following suggested items can help provide a variety of writing experiences:

Paper
- Butcher paper
- Computer paper
- Drawing paper
- Envelopes (small and legal size)
- Graph paper
- Index cards (3″ × 5″; 5″ × 7″)
- Legal pads of various colors and sizes
- Lined paper of various sizes and types
- Newsprint
- Postcards
- Post-it Notes
- Stationery (note cards, notepaper, and envelopes)

Writing instruments
- Colored pencils
- Computer and printer
- Crayons
- Felt-tipped pens (fine, medium, and broad tipped)
- Ink pens
- Markers of various colors
- Pencils
- Poster paints and brushes
- Typewriter (manual)
- Watercolor paints and brushes

Office Supplies
- Brass fasteners
- Clipboards
- Date stamp and pad
- Duct tape
- Erasers (pencil and ink)
- File folders (including colored folders for special projects)
- Paper clips
- Paper punch
- Poster board

- Scissors
- Stapler and staples
- Tagboard
- Three-hole punch
- Transparencies
- Transparency markers
- Scotch tape
- Stickers (blank circles of various colors)
- Vinyl adhesive letters

Reference Materials
- *Add It, Dip It, Fix It: A Book of Verbs* (R. M. Schneider, Boston: Houghton Mifflin, 1995)
- Almanac
- Atlas of the world
- Dictionaries
- Encyclopedia (e.g., *Pocket Encyclopedia*, A. Jack, New York: Random House, 1988)
- Examples of letter formats for friendly and business letters
- Franklin Spelling Ace
- Magazines
- Thesaurus
- *Time to Rhyme: A Rhyming Dictionary* (M. Terban, Honesdale, PA: Wordsong, 1994)

Storage Containers
- Cardboard boxes to hold books to be published
- Desktop In/Out boxes (editing box, publishing box)
- File cabinet
- Floppy disk storage box
- Milk cartons (half gallon) to serve as mailboxes (one for each student and one for the teacher)
- Plastic milk crates for writing folders
- Shoeboxes

collects key rings that tie in with a book (dog, cat, bear, moose, etc.). Then she finds words in the picture book that will empower a child's writing. After writing the words on small pieces of tagboard, Mary laminates and punches a hole in them before attaching them to the key ring. After sharing the book in a read aloud, both the book and the key ring of words is then placed in the writing center for students to use as a writing resource. For *Olivia* (Falconer, 2000), she jotted down these words for the Olivia key ring: Olivia, mother, father, brushes, kiss, teeth, hair, read, beach, dance, dressed, and castle.

Word Walls (see chapter 11) are a means to share spelling patterns or words for writing. A Word Wall can include words with common spelling chunks (e.g., *day, fan*) or they can feature words that pertain to a specific area of study (e.g., frog, eggs, tadpole, swim, tail). A Word Wall can also consist of all the names of students in the class. Yet another kind of Word Wall is that which is comprised of words from a particular read aloud selection. Consider the Word Wall for the hilarious *Click, Clack, Moo: Cows that Type* (Cronin, 2000) in figure 8.5.

A	B	C	D	E
	believe brought barn boring blankets board busy	click clack cows cold	dear demand deal diving	electric eggs emergency exchange
F farmer furious	G growing gathered	H heard hens	I impossible impatient	J
K knocked	L	M milk meeting morning	N night note neutral	O
P problem party pond	Q quack quite	R	S sincerely strike sorry snoop	T type typewriter
U ultimatum	V	W work waited	X	Y & Z

Figure 8.5   Word Wall for *Click, Clack, Moo: Cows that Type*

After hearing the book read aloud a couple of times and talking about animals that live on farms and in zoos, students were given a copy of the Word Wall words for their writing folders. They then wrote their own version of what an animal might write with a typewriter after brainstorming a list of animals the teacher wrote on the white board as possibilities (e.g., "Click, Clack, Arf! Dogs that Type," "Click, Clack, Hisssss! Snakes that Type," "Click, Clack, Roar! Lions that Type!" and "Click, Clack, Gobble! Turkeys that Type").

A study of exemplary first-grade literacy instruction found that children wrote every day and used many different forms of writing (Morrow et al. 1999). Writing activities included daily journals that sometimes contained spelling words and "special words." The first graders also wrote about topics that interested them. Another important aspect was the "Morning Message" that was written neatly by the teacher in manuscript on the board as the students dictated the message. (The Morning Message is discussed in more detail on pp. 335–336.) This was followed by a story being read by the teacher with the students then given a writing assignment based upon the story. For example, after reading *Swimmy* (Lionni, 1973), a story about how a school of fish worked together for protection, the students were asked to write about when a friend helped them. Writing extended across the curriculum as students recorded science experiments in journals and wrote words and sentences that related to math (i.e., a list of classroom items that relate to geometric concepts such as a clock, cookie, and paper plate for the concept of circle). Writing activities also were included as part of social studies with the concept of cooperation as with the activity accompanying the reading of *Swimmy* described above. Figures 8.6 through 8.8 on pp. 320–323 are examples of first graders' writing.

A teacher can best distinguish and evaluate the immense changes in writing that occur during the first-grade year by dating samples of each student's work and storing the samples sequentially in writing folders (see figure 8.8 on pp. 322–323). On a regular basis, the teacher should sit down with individual students to discuss and reflect on their growth and progress.

Second Grade

Writing in second-grade classrooms can be quite diversified. Some children continue to write as confidently and enthusiastically as they did in first grade, producing pages of stories that describe happenings in their lives. For other children, writing becomes a dreaded, anxious activity as they wrestle for perfection with every pencil stroke. One misspelled word in the middle of an otherwise error-free paper may cause a student to wad up and throw away the piece before he attempts the project again. Similarly, even a minor stray mark may result in a child's discarding the work and beginning anew.

As children leave the egocentric world of the preoperational stage and enter the stage of concrete operations, they begin to notice that some things are acceptable while others are not. First graders rarely fret over their writing because they give all their attention to enjoyment of the writing activity rather than to the audience's reaction. For second graders, on the other hand,

Figure 8.6 Eric's book for his first-grade teacher. "My teacher's book. My teacher's tree. My teacher's boat. Teacher you are my favorite teacher in the whole wide world. The end."

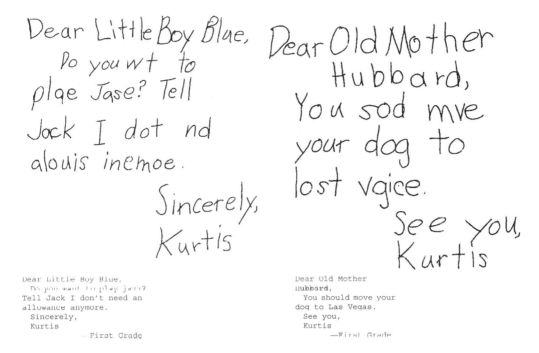

Dear Little Boy Blue,
   Do you want to play jacks?
Tell Jack I don't need an
allowance anymore.
   Sincerely,
   Kurtis
      —First Grade

Dear Old Mother
Hubbard,
   You should move your
dog to Las Vegas.
   See you,
   Kurtis
      —First Grade

Figure 8.7 Kurtis, a first grader, was given the assignment to write letters to nursery rhyme characters. Notice his humor as he suggests Old Mother Hubbard should move to "Lost" Vegas because she can't find a bone for her dog.

approval and acceptance become increasingly important. For example, if the teacher praises Victoria's story about her stuffed monkey, the other students may elect to attempt similar stories about their stuffed animals in hope that the teacher will praise their work as well. Similarly, a sense of authorship begins to evolve during second grade.

When second graders write about an incident, they want to include everything: "And then" such and such occurred, "and then" such and such happened, "and then. . . ." The writing is somewhat like an objective report of an event: It contains little or no personal reflection. Every aspect of the event, trivial or otherwise, is given equal attention, and few, if any, underlying interpretations are provided.

Children at this age frequently produce "bed-to-bed" stories, which are narratives of the occurrences that take place from the time they awaken in the morning until they fall asleep at night (Calkins, 1995). Even if the purpose of the writing is to describe a child's birthday or Christmas, the opening of presents typically receives the same amount of attention as do eating breakfast and preparing for bed.

At the second-grade level, the teacher continues to use the "Morning Message" to teach writing skills. Spelling, grammar, capitalization, and punctua-

continued

Figure 8.8   Samples of an average first grader's writing in September and November

tion are pointed out. As with all grade levels the teacher models the writing strategy or skill first, then assigns the students to write using the strategy. Lots of quality literature is shared, just as with the other grade levels.

Third Grade

Like their second-grade counterparts, third graders are still struggling to find that self-confidence they had in first grade. They have already become aware of the importance of spelling and usage, but now they are expected to write in the cursive handwriting style that they only recently learned.

In addition, third graders demonstrate an increased awareness of the influence of authorship. For example, after experimenting with two or three written drafts, third graders will produce final drafts of "books," which they feel are worthy of fine leather binding and gold lettering. Likewise, after careful

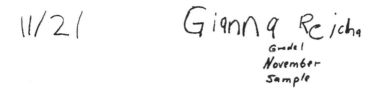

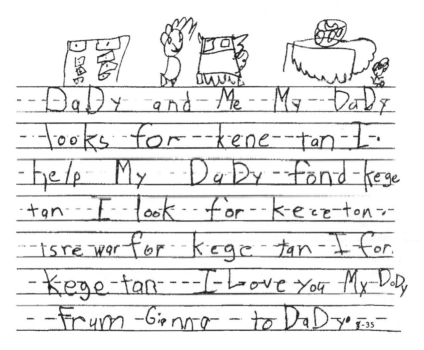

Figure 8.8   *(continued)*

examination of several different books, they often will write their own dedications. Generally, a dedication is to a writer's parents, rarely to brothers and sisters. When brothers and sisters are included in the dedication, grandparents and all the family pets are also likely to be named. After all, because writing a book is a major effort, the family should identify with the youngster's sense of pride in publishing the piece of writing. Of course, such a masterpiece will often describe the author in a brief section entitled "About the Author." The students will write about themselves—but use the third person—including information on their birthday, interests, and hobbies. These students spend a great amount of time on their autobiographical statements.

Third graders continue to include every detail in their description of an incident. Considering the overall development of their oral language skills, however, this is true to form. For example, in describing a recent movie or television program, the children review every scene because they do not understand any reason for beginning a description or summary in the middle of an action. A story must start at the beginning; thus, bed-to-bed stories will continue to be produced.

Although narrative writing still predominates, third graders begin to experiment with some forms of poetry and to write informational and factual reports about science experiments and social studies topics. Children of this

Students in grades three and up may write their drafts on the computer and then revise. They become proficient in moving text, inserting words or phrases, and deleting undesired words or sentences.

age are also able to create story problems as a way of better understanding mathematical concepts.

Editing is troublesome for many third graders. One student referred to revising and editing as "fighting with myself." Some simply cannot distinguish between what is correct and what is incorrect within their writing. Indeed, critiquing a peer's work may become synonymous with criticizing every mistake, whether it be a major error or a minor oversight. When this happens, the teacher must quickly clarify this activity's goal: to positively assist one's classmates without condemning every fault. Editing someone else's work may be an impossible task unless it is attempted as a group.

A majority of third-grade students are adept at developing simple sentences and paragraphs. However, their stories almost universally contain a straightforward, predictable style of writing with little or no embellishment. This results in a stiff, robotlike product with relatively few mechanical errors (see box 8.4 for a suggested writing activity).

8.4 In the Classroom: Mini Lesson

Using Literature to Compare Human Traits

Don't Fidget a Feather by Erica Silverman (1994) is a delightful story of friendship, stubbornness, and love. Gander and Duck are best friends who do everything together. One day they decide to have a contest to see which of them is the best. Duck wins the swimming contest but Gander wins the flying contest. Then they decide to determine the "champion of champions" by seeing which of them doesn't "fidget a feather." Silently, Gander and Duck stand in the barnyard for hours until a Fox appears. Both fowl have a strong streak of stubbornness and neither yields as Fox tucks them into his sack and heads off to his house. When Gander is picked up by Fox to plop into his stewpot, Gander still doesn't move. But Duck can't bear to lose his friend, so he is the first to fidget; he pinches Fox and rescues Gander.

This story is a good one to share with first through third graders. They can write about how they have done a good deed for a friend or family member. Then, they can write about a time they were a bit stubborn. Kindergartners can also engage in this activity by illustrating a picture of their good deed.

Silverman, E. (1994). *Don't fidget a feather* (S. D. Schindler, Illus.). New York: Macmillan.

Fourth Grade

Unlike third graders, fourth graders tend to project their individuality through writing. Consider that even a child's handwriting at this age may evolve into an expressive message of its own when curls, loops, and hearts replace the dots over *i*'s, a common practice in this age group. Likewise, their stories become more worldly as their experiential backgrounds expand through reading, talking, traveling, and "living" in general. Informational reporting is also used more frequently (see figures 8.9 and 8.10 on p. 326).

Revising and editing are more palatable now because fourth graders want to share their work with others. (Box 8.5 on pp. 327–328 offers a writing checklist for fourth through sixth grades.) Because they are more venturesome

I have a calf named Mac Kenzie. He has a black face with a sort-of white triangle on his forehead, knobby knees, short tail and he is is mostly black. My calf has a tongue like a snake. It feels like sandpaper on top.

He likes to suck your fingers. Mac Kenzie also likes to have one hind foot in the hay bunk and three in the straw.

When he hears me stirring milk, he holds his head up high. If you wonder what a calf's bottom chin going into his neck looks like, it is oval shaped.

The thing I like about Mac Kenzie is that he gives love to the cats.

Figure 8.9   Sample of a fourth grader's expository writing. Notice the description presented.

Moosl Men of the Wrld

For 13 yers Men hav Bene punping iron for the USA Moosl Man cantest event. Moovestors are capeting in this avent. you will see if teh moovestors: the winr is the evilop ples. Arnold sors anger.

—Robert, a sixth grader

Muscle Men of the World

For 13 years men have been pumping iron for the USA Muscle Man contest event. Movie stars are competing in this event. You will see fifty movie stars: the winner is (the envelope please) Arnold Schwarzenegger.

—Robert, a sixth grader

Figure 8.10   Students often write about topics that interest them. Here, an LD student, Robert, writes about his hobby, weight lifting.

8.5   In the Classroom: Teaching Hint

Writing Checklist: Grades 4–6

Name: _____   Teacher: _____

Age: _____   Grade: _____   Date: _____

	Always	Sometimes	Never
Expresses a desire to engage in writing (i.e., is eager to join in writing activities, writes without being prompted)			
Can write in various forms —narrative			
—expository			
—persuasive			
—descriptive			
—poetic			
Can brainstorm for ideas using variety of techniques (i.e., semantic webs, questions to be answered, interviews)			
Uses resources to find information (i.e., literature, reference materials, interviews with people)			
Keeps a writing journal of ideas, vocabulary, mechanics, spelling, character traits, etc.			
Can write good first draft			
Has a good writing vocabulary			
Can sequence and organize ideas			
Can write a paragraph with a topic sentence and supporting ideas			
Is willing to edit own work			
Is willing to have others edit work			
Can edit writing through adding, deleting, and moving text			
Can locate spelling errors			
Can correct spelling errors			
Can locate punctuation errors			
Can correct punctuation errors			
Can locate grammar errors			

continued

	Always	Sometimes	Never
Can correct grammar errors			
Is interested in listening to peers read their work			
Can accept criticism from peers			
Can accept criticism from teacher			
Can give appropriate criticism to peers			
Is proud of own writing			
Is supportive of the writing of peers			
Can use the vocabulary of writers in discussing own or others' writing			
Writes so the audience can understand			
Writes to peak audience interest			
Writes legibly			
Composes with a computer			
Keeps a writing portfolio with writing samples, writing goals, and self-critiques of work			
Teacher comments:			

in writing, their creations become more fluent and flamboyant. Drafts become messier than they were in the primary grades as the students use erasures, eradicating marks, and arrows to refine and improve their writing.

Most fourth graders don't spend much time writing outside of school. This is true even if they enjoy writing. Thus, it is crucial that the classroom teacher provide opportunities to write, keying in on student interests.

Fifth and Sixth Grades

Fifth and sixth graders have diverse abilities, skills, interests, and concerns, and each of these may be reflected in their writing (see figures 8.11–8.13 on pp. 329–330). Hansen (1986) believes that such variability is an asset in the teaching of writing. Students discover that everyone has personal strengths and weaknesses and that individuals must pursue those areas that highlight their own uniqueness. According to Hansen, by "celebrating, challenging, and defending" their own writing as well as that of their peers and familiar authors of children's literature, children can begin to develop pride and confidence in themselves and each other as they become "real authors."

Because fifth and sixth graders are more confident in their own writing and have had experience in deliberating their work with other students and with the classroom teacher in conferences, they tend to discuss writing problems and concerns among themselves quite freely. A type of authorship bond seems to emerge within the classroom. In an effort to rework a piece until it is in its best form, a youngster may use a different audience for each of several drafts. Moreover, writers in the intermediate grades will make insertions and deletions in their own work more readily than will younger authors. Lines with arrows now indicate the repositioning of entire sentences and paragraphs in initial drafts. Even when the writer is convinced that the piece is well written, he or she may still make a few changes. Although mechanical skills are becoming more refined, organizational thoughts and ideas continue to be troublesome for fifth and sixth graders.

Bright (1995) found that fifth and sixth graders consider good writers to be familiar with the subjects they write about, to read a lot, to know the meanings of various words, to listen to others, and to write in a way that is interest-

---

I Can't Whishel

One day my friends asked me if I would like to be in there club. I said I would be glad to be in there club. But there were so many people in the club they decided to only let the people who could wishel in the club I had to go because I couldn't whistle.

My next store neighbor said to suck something sour to pucker my mouth up I tryed some pickels but it didn't help. I thought I would never be able to wistle

But that day I went to the store to get some sour cherries. They were realy sour.

That night I lost a tooth. I put it under my pillow so I would get a dollar.

I got into bed and had a sour cherry. I tryed to wistle. I could finally do it. I got to be in the club after all.

Figure 8.11   Sample of a fifth grader's writing. Notice how the student reveals her feelings of disappointment and later joy in this piece.

How Monkey got its Tail

One day in the jungle there was a little monkey. Monkey was jumping from tree to tree.

Then a big leopard jumped right behind Monkey. Monkey started jumping really fast. The leopard was right behind Monkey. Then Lion roared loud. The leopard looked down and saw him. The leopard jumped down and ran away. Monkey got down from the tree and thanked Lion for saving him. From then on Monkey stayed with Lion for protection.

One day Monkey was walking along and thought that Lion was behind him. A big tiger was sneaking up behind Monkey. The tiger bit Monkey's little tail. Monkey started running. The tiger was hanging on tight to Monkey's tail. The tiger let go and Monkey's tail was real long. Since then, Monkeys tails have been long.

—Troy, 5th grade

Figure 8.12   After studying fables, Troy wrote his own.

The Kite and the Sun

Once there was a kite who flew high in the sky. But one day he saw the sun who was the highest thing in the sky.

The kite was jealous of the sun. Each day he tried to fly higher and higher so he could be the highest in the sky.

One day the sun was no where to be seen. That made the kite happy. He thought he had finally conquered the sun. Just then the sun came out from behind a cloud. This made kite furious. He was determined to be the highest.

Kite flew higher and higher and higher still. Then he got too close to sun and got burned. Kite fell down and down and could no longer fly at all.

It was then that kite realized that he should have liked himself for just what he was. And that's the way people should be.

—Kristy, 6th grade

Figure 8.13   After studying fables, Kristy wrote her own.

---

ing to others. Good writers are also hard, determined workers and write often, according to students in the study.

Seventh and Eighth Grades

Seventh and eighth graders are capable of screening information. They can research a topic and take notes. In addition, these students rely on previously gained knowledge as they write. Their level of sophistication as writers sometimes surprises their teachers as these students can present very polished and well-organized final writing pieces. Writer's workshop, outlined in the chapter that follows, is used to select the aspects of writing that students need to hone (e.g., development of ideas, organization, word selection, writing conventions).

As with all grade levels, sharing examples of exemplary writing from quality literature is critical if middle schoolers are to improve their own writing. Translate this into sharing informational books, passages from novels and plays, and selections of poetry. Reader's response journals (see chapter 4) can aid in students gaining a better grasp of the fine points and subtleties of narrative writing. Considering different examples of informational books will aid in writing expository reports. Plays and poetry will aid word choice and embellishment of vocabulary.

Dialogue journals—a written exchange between students and their teacher about something they have read recently (e.g., a novel, a magazine or newspaper article, or an informational piece)—are done on a weekly basis when the school year begins. Assignments may be turned in either by class section or by alternating weeks with morning classes and afternoon classes to limit the number of journals the middle school teacher has to read each day. Some teachers collect dialogue journals on Mondays through Thursdays only, which provides a needed breather from reading student responses and writing thoughtful, provocative responses in return. According to Morretta and Ambrosini (2000, p. 24):

The dialogue journal provides genuine conversation and communication between students and teacher about reading literature. A written dialogue with a real audience is an interactive conversation that gives students practice writing and communicating. In this scenario student and teacher are equal participants; two minds unite to bring about new understanding, ideas, and possibilities to each other. Frequently, as students learn from the teacher, the teacher also learns from them.

Morretta and Ambrosini (2000, p. 24) go on to suggest that teachers provide sample questions for the students to respond to as they read. For instance,

Topic: What is the topic of the piece? What was this section (or chapter) about?

Connection: Can you connect an event in the book to an event in your life? What happened? How are they alike? How are they different?

Grace of language: Did the sentences flow? Were they choppy? Did you notice yourself thinking about how well a particular line worked?

The development of children's writing from kindergarten through eighth grade is summarized in box 8.6 on p. 332. Note the changes that occur in the various stages of writing.

The Teacher's Role in the Writing Process

Teachers play a significant role in helping students develop their writing skills. By providing writing models and holding conferences with children about their individual work, teachers help students understand and learn the craft of writing more thoroughly. Teachers need to also understand how children acquire writing skills at different developmental levels (see box 8.6). Teaching writing includes modeled writing, shared writing, interactive writing, guided writing, and independent writing.

The Teacher as a Writing Model

When teachers do not write in class, they cannot serve as models. Many classroom teachers lack the confidence to share personal writing with students because of memories of their own school years. They may readily recall their pieces of writing returned to them filled with red marks. As Smith (1981, p. 797) points out, "Children will learn what they are taught, and the teacher who perceives writing as a tedious chore with trivial applications will teach just those things." Such perceptions are unfortunate, for when teachers can share their own writing with their students, they can transform an ordinary classroom into a writing community. Generating a draft on an overhead projector and doing a think aloud as you write, gives students a framework of how their own thinking and writing go hand in hand. Stopping to ponder organization, word choice, or a subdetail of the idea about which you are writing, lets students know that thinking and incubating are very much a part of writing. Rereading the piece aloud is something all authors—even award winning

8.6 The More You Know

Development of Writing

	Kindergarten–First Grade	Second Grade	Third Grade	Fourth–Sixth Grades	Seventh–Eighth Grades
Prewriting (Rehearsal)	Pretend to write Draw pictures Talk about pictures Use pictures to convey much of the meaning	Use increased oral language May talk with peers about writing	Discuss writing (ideas, etc.) Problem solve Focus on single topic	Focus on single topic Think in more abstract terms, need less concrete examples Engage in self-questioning	Think abstractly Research information Use effective organization of notes Screen information Use previous knowledge
Writing (Draft)	Need variety of writing materials Need regular, set time to write Teacher-student conferences help develop ideas Skill lessons focus on basic punctuation (use of periods, capital letters, quotation marks, etc.)	Create short pieces Often include information that doesn't fit Write about start of day to end of day (bed-to-bed) Grow as writers	Select personal experiences Write sequentially Use little reflection/ thought	Write from different points of view/ voice/mood Show audience awareness May begin story in middle of action Exhibit empathy Show growing awareness of elements of good writing Can write, read, and edit	Are more sophisticated writers Are sensitive to reader/audience Consider organization of piece
Rewriting (Revision)	Put stories in book format Share writing with others Begin rereading for content Ask editing questions	Want to change wording (cut and paste-"sloppy copy")	Make simple corrections only Dread revising	Self-edit Internalize mechanics Consider the reader of the piece	Present very polished final products

Elements the Teacher Must Provide at All Grade Levels

Modeling of the writing process
Brief skill lessons
One-to-one teacher-student conferences
A classroom atmosphere of trust and support
Recognition of writing growth for all students
A variety of writing materials
Sharing of quality children's literature with the class

ones—do. They want to know how the piece they are creating sounds to the ear. Thus this is quite appropriate for young writers as they polish their own works.

Modeled writing is the level of greatest support for students. This can be done with the entire class of third graders writing a persuasive letter, a group of gifted first graders first trying to write with dialogue, a group of eighth graders needing transitions between paragraphs, or a group of struggling writers at any grade level. Modeling writing enables the teacher to demonstrate a new type of writing activity before having students engage in the activity or to demonstrate writing conventions (grammar, usage, capitalization, or punctuation).

The sharing of writing allows a teacher to send a message to students: Writing is a demanding but valuable skill to acquire. In referring to their own pieces of writing, teachers can be honest in conveying the personal feelings of success, frustration, and uncertainty that often accompany the writing process. As Smith (1981, p. 797) also states, teachers who write and share their compositions with their students "demonstrate what writing does, and how to do it."

Most children believe that writing develops naturally for adults. They believe that when an adult puts a pencil to paper, the words flow like water in a river until the adult decides to end the piece. Except for watching their parents write grocery lists and letters to relatives and friends, children rarely see adults actively engaged in the writing process—brainstorming, making prewriting decisions, drafting, editing, and sharing the final product.

Teachers can frequently model writing through planned activities. For example, a teacher may choose to gather primary-grade students into a semicircle on the floor for a more relaxed writing demonstration in which she uses chart paper and a felt-tipped marker. In a similar fashion, teachers may use an overhead projector in their writing presentations to increase eye contact between themselves and their students.

Before the teacher actually begins to write, a major classroom rule needs to be emphasized. No interruptions will be allowed during the writing period. Thus, no one is permitted to ask a question concerning the due date of a project or to whisper to classmates during the activity. All attention must be focused on the teacher's writing.

The most natural way for a teacher to begin writing is to talk about events that have actually taken place. Typically, seemingly commonplace occurrences are often intriguing to children. In choosing appropriate topics, a teacher should be certain that an event is authentic and neither spectacular nor unusual. Here are some events that almost every teacher has experienced and that children will find interesting as writing topics:

- Cutting your own hair or that of a sibling when you were a child
- Dressing up a pet
- Following a recipe and leaving out a crucial ingredient
- Learning to ride a bicycle
- Venturing into the local "haunted" house with your childhood friends

- Swinging for a long time during the day and then awakening in the middle of the night with the sensation that you are still swinging
- Learning how to roller skate
- Camping out
- Reading or performing before an audience for the first time
- Using certain shortcuts as a child to hasten completion of your household chores

When a teacher can demonstrate skill in writing about an everyday occurrence, children will come to realize that in having experienced similar situations, they have the potential to write. Because daily occurrences in their own lives are equally interesting, real, and relevant, students do not feel a need to write only of stabbings, shootings, or poisonings. Common happenings are just as worthy of being shared and are appreciated by audiences.

After briefly suggesting three or four possible writing topics, a teacher should select one as the writing model. By deliberating over a topic, a teacher demonstrates that beginning a piece of writing is very difficult, even for an adult. In this same way, the teacher should continue to verbalize and share thoughts while the writing is taking place. Once the draft is finished, the teacher should read the entire piece to the class. At the next writing session, the teacher should demonstrate editing techniques as the first draft is revised and the final work is produced.

While it is impossible to participate in every student writing assignment, it is critical that the teacher write about the same topics as the students both regularly and frequently. Although there is little need for such modeling on a daily basis, a teacher can reach the same goal by working on a journal or a science essay with the students. In such an exercise, both teacher and students should write simultaneously without interruption. After all class members have completed their final drafts, the students and the teacher should share their individual works.

Shared Writing

In shared writing, the teacher and the students work together to write a composition with the teacher jotting down the piece. The teacher may write on chart paper, white board, or the computer with the image being projected on a screen for all to see. Shared writing can also be done for creating a class book. Using shared writing enables the teacher to demonstrate how writing works. It is also a means of recording students' ideas. Both the language experience approach (LEA) and *Morning Message* are shared writing experiences.

LEA

The language experience approach (LEA) in which the student dictates his own experiences, such as a field trip to the grocery store or Dairy Queen as the teacher writes it down, is a variation of shared writing. LEA is used with beginning readers and English language learners to create texts the children can read. For content area subjects, such as science and social studies, LEA offers an opportunity to write the ideas or information shared by students on chart paper, which can then be used as a resource.

Morning Message

The importance of the *Morning Message* in the primary grades (K–3) should not be overlooked. As the teacher writes on the chalkboard what is dictated by the students, several important language concepts are being shared during the Morning Message:

- The teacher is using correct and neat manuscript or, if cursive has been introduced, cursive letter forms. The students are able to visualize the phoneme-grapheme relationship. Later, usually at the beginning of third grade, students learn how to read cursive handwriting via the Morning Message.
- The teacher can use the Morning Message to introduce patterns for spelling that can be added to the Word Wall (see chapter 11).
- The teacher can ask students how a word begins, ends, the middle sound, and so on.
- The teacher may elect to write only the initial and vowel sounds in the Morning Message and have students volunteer to add the final sounds.
- After the students have gained proficiency in working with vowel sounds, the teacher may write only the consonants in the Morning Message and have students volunteer to add the vowels.
- The teacher can ask about punctuation such as apostrophes, commas, periods, question marks, quotation marks, and exclamation marks.
- The teacher may refer to the students regarding what words need to start with capital letters.
- After the Morning Message has been written, the students can be encouraged to look for words that contain the same spelling patterns.
- Students' vocabulary is expanded via the Morning Message.
- The Morning Message encourages speaking, listening, and reading as part of the routine. This aids all students but in particular assists special needs and ELL learners.

Here is an example of a Morning Message:

Today is Monday, March 20, 2004.
It is the first day of spring. Flowers grow
in spring. We fly kites and play ball.
Tracey lost a tooth today. Timmy saw
a skunk on the way to school.

At the intermediate level (Gr. 3–5), the Morning Message can become more sophisticated as students share current events such as news, weather, and sports (i.e., local, state, national, or international). These can be typed into the computer and projected on a screen for the students to view. As with the primary level, the Morning Message enhances spelling, grammar, and vocabulary development and keeps the students aware of what is happening in their community, state, and the world.

Interactive Writing

"Sharing the pen" is one way to describe interactive writing as both the teacher and students write the text on chart paper, an overhead transparency, or the white board. The composition is generated by the group of students with the teacher guiding them as they write the text word-by-word for all to see. The students take turns writing known words and filling in known punctuation. The teacher guides them with spelling, grammar, capitalization, and punctuation, often by questioning, pointing out similarities, or having the students look around the room for a common word chunk that might be viewable on another chart or on the Word Wall. Unlike shared writing, students in interactive writing actually do all of the writing but under the guidance of the classroom teacher.

Interactive writing allows the teacher to demonstrate how to write words, phrases, sentences, and, eventually, paragraphs. It also permits the teacher to instruct students in grammar, capitalization, and punctuation as well as applying phonemic awareness in their spelling. Content may be refined as the teacher can ask questions of the students about what they intend to write.

Interactive writing can begin in the middle of the kindergarten year. When children are capable of writing some words fluently, interactive writing can be done in small groups. Each student can be given a different colored marker. When they complete the piece they can sign their names and the teacher will know who wrote what sentence of the composition.

Guided Writing

Guided writing is a kind of scaffolded writing in which the teacher works with small groups of students to support their writing. The teacher plans a structured writing lesson, such as writing a book patterned after one that has been shared in a read aloud or having upper-elementary students write Haiku or cinquain poetry. The teacher designs the lesson so students in the class will be successful in developing their writing skills.

The teacher can provide samples of others' writing that the students can use as examples to follow. Guided writing is often used to introduce aspects of a writing project, such as editing and revising. New skills and strategies of writing are also introduced through guided writing as it gives the teacher the opportunity to closely supervise the students as they encounter a new procedure or concept.

Independent Writing

Independent or free writing is when the students write by themselves. They may do this at the writing center, during a portion of writer's workshop, or at the computer. The end result may be a book about insects, a story about their birthday party, a journal entry, or a rhyming poem. Since the child selects her own topic to write about, anything goes! It is important that such writing be encouraged and supported. By promoting independent writing, we authenticate that writing is a valuable and desired skill. Just as we desire to produce lifelong readers, we need to produce lifelong writers, too!

To encourage students to do independent writing with expository text (informational writing), Andrea Rogers posts a vocabulary calendar in her fifth-grade classroom. Each day students learn two new vocabulary words taken from their content area reading (e.g., science, social studies, or math). Since there are only five days each school week, students learn about 40 words a month or 360 new words each year.

Conferencing with Students

The term *conferencing* evolved from secondary school and college writing courses built around the idea of a writing workshop. Murray (1968) believes that students must discuss their writings with someone if they are to learn to write. Actually, elementary teachers have been "conferencing" with their students for many years; the typical teacher walks around the classroom, responding to questions and talking at random with the students as they write. They key is that the teacher listens and responds to the young writers.

"Honeybee" Conferences

"Honeybee" conferences take place when the teacher flitters about the room from student to student responding to questions much like a honey bee descends upon a flower blossom for a fleeting moment before taking ascent and alighting on another bloom: twenty seconds to help Jasmine with a subject-verb agreement question, a minute to help Zack line up some additional resources for his report on tree frogs, half a minute to answer Alissa's inquiry about her report's organization. Brief, concise, and succinct responses from the teacher, which often also entail the teacher asking questions, comprise the "honeybee conference." (What direction do you want your report to take? Does your problem statement make sense? Have you checked the Internet and the school library's resources? Did you first look at the reference format we use for informational reports? Or, for narrative writing, questions such as these: You've developed the protagonist well. Can you do the same for the other main character? Can you flush out more details about the setting? Can you tell less and show more so the reader of your story puts the pieces together for himself?). "Honeybee conferences" occur immediately after the mini lesson in Writer's Workshop as students pull out their notebooks and begin to write.

Structured Conferences

Writing conferences that are more structured and formal in nature are likewise important (Murray, 1968). The typical conference between teacher and student lasts an average of three to five minutes, although a longer or shorter meeting occasionally takes place. During this time, the teacher asks the student how the work is progressing. The student, in turn, may either ask for assistance with some part of the piece or just share a favorite paragraph or sentence with the teacher. In any event, the teacher should be careful to respond initially to content rather than to mechanics. Although simple questions that encourage student reflection and thinking are preferable to those that only require a yes or no answer, the teacher must avoid overusing such questions and potentially dominating the discussion. Instead, the student should be an active participant in the conference and actually talk more than the teacher (Mack & Farris, 1992). Anecdotal records of writing conferences should be kept by the teacher either in a notebook or on index cards and filed in the student's portfolio (Tierney et al., 1991; Tompkins, 2004). Some basic conference guidelines are listed in box 8.7.

Conferences can be set up for a variety of purposes and to address students' individual needs. The following are some examples of the different types of conferences that can be helpful to students during their writing project.

8.7   In the Classroom: Teaching Hint

Teacher-Student Conference Guidelines

- The teacher should attempt to make the writing conference nonthreatening. For example, by sitting next to rather than across from a child, a teacher can be looked upon as a helper rather than an antagonist.

- The teacher should use the child's first name.

- The student and teacher should be at the same eye level when seated. Eye contact serves to highlight the teacher's support of the child's effort through nonverbal means.

- The student shares the piece of writing with the teacher. The teacher should not write on the piece or take it from the student because the work belongs to the child.

- The teacher should ask open-ended questions that are based on meaning and that the student can respond to freely. Even as the questions become increasingly challenging, the student still should be able to respond to them.

- The teacher should give the student ample time to formulate a response to a question. Even though some questions can be answered quickly, others require more thought on the part of the youngster and a longer corresponding waiting time for the teacher. Usually, the teacher can determine whether a student needs some additional time in which to prepare a response.

- The teacher should ask questions that demonstrate a natural curiosity about the work. For instance, asking, "What kind of fish did you catch?" followed by "What are some of the special things you do to catch [kind of fish]?" allows the student to describe the techniques of fishing for a particular kind of fish. The student may even begin to compare and contrast fish and the ways in which they are caught.

- The teacher should never attempt to control the conference by requiring the student to change the focus of the work or to elaborate on something that is of particular interest to the teacher.

- The teacher should keep the conference brief, no longer than three to five minutes.

- The teacher should attempt to discuss only one or two concerns per conference. To attempt to resolve more is fruitless because the student will become confused.

- The conference should always end on a positive note.

- *Drafting conferences* can be having students come individually to a table or the teacher's desk with specific writing problems. These conferences are quite brief, perhaps one to three minutes per student.

- *Revising conferences* may be done in small groups (four to eight students) when each student shares aloud his work and his peers ask questions to help tighten up the composition.

- *Editing conferences* have students reading over each other's work for spelling, punctuation, capitalization, and grammatical errors and are often done in pairs or trios. Caution has to be taken so the better editing student doesn't get swamped or overburdened by her peers' writing deficiencies, thereby taking time from her own writing to get the rest of her group's compositions polished.

- *Skill conferences* are short, 10–15-minute conferences with those students who are at a particular point in their writing that they will benefit from instruction in a specific area, such as creating a relative clause or using the semicolon.

- *Class conferences* should be held periodically for a variety of reasons. New assignments are outlined for everyone, a new type of writing is introduced (e.g., a new form of poetry), a large portion of the class has problems with the current writing task, or collaborative writing tasks for the class on a specific topic are assigned and monitored to their completion (e.g., recycling, interviews with senior citizens, Civil War reports, science fair expository reports).

Conferences can be used to help students at various stages of their writing project, such as selecting a topic and writing the report. Examples of questions the teacher might consider asking, as well as comments expressing interest, are listed below.

- *Conferences to select a writing topic* can include questions or comments such as:
    Tell me about your family (or friends, neighbors, pets).
    What do you like?
    What do you dislike?
    What is your favorite sport?
    What kind of hobbies do you have?
    What is your favorite book?
    Do you have a favorite author?
    Was there something you wanted to do for a long time that you finally got to do?
    What is the funniest thing that you have ever seen happen?
    What is the strangest thing that you have ever seen?

- *Conferences while writing is in progress* can include questions or comments that teachers can use during individual or small group conferences while a work is still being written:
    Tell me about your work.
    How is your writing coming along?

Do you have a favorite part? Read it to me.

How did you decide on your title?

Does the beginning make people want to read what you are writing?

What convinced you to write about this topic?

You seem to be very familiar with this topic. How could you find out even more about it?

What is the most exciting part of what you are writing?

What additional details would make this part [specify the part] clearer? Is there anything that you have repeated and you can therefore take out? Are there any other important details that you should add?

Does the ending fit with how you want the reader to feel? Have you run into any problems that I can help you with?

Group Conferences

Group conferences can promote the development of editing skills and provide students with associated global learning activities. Each work read during a conference usually provides some new information, insight, or knowledge for the other members of the group, either about the writing process or the topic itself. For example, Mrs. Duncan's third-grade class chose pets and their care as a writing topic. Dawn decided to present facts about her older brother's pet parrot. The other third graders were amazed to learn that parrots can live to be 80 years old and that all birds ingest small bits of gravel on a daily basis. Sam, another member of the class, wrote about his brother's pet boa constrictor, which only needed to be fed every two or three weeks. The other children wrote about the daily exercise needs of dogs, the independent nature of cats, and the swimming habits of goldfish. Obviously, then, children are capable of sharing their accrued knowledge with others through group conferencing.

A group writing conference might even begin with a student reading a draft of a work in progress. As the work is being read, other group members write down any questions they may have. These questions may provide the writer with useful ideas for improving her writing project. Upon completion of the reading, the students are allowed to make comments and to ask questions about the work in accordance with one major ground rule: The initial comments must be positive, direct, and specific. Following this criterion, one can say, "I liked what you wrote because it . . ." and then specify the reason. This eliminates the tendency to attack a writer for mistakes while allowing the writer to gain further insight into those areas that prove to be strengths or weaknesses.

Group conferencing cannot be successful unless students trust both the teacher and each other. Therefore, until a majority of students feel secure and at ease within the classroom, conferencing is best accomplished on a one-to-one basis. In undertaking this venture, a teacher must prove to be trustworthy, kind, and helpful.

Another form of group conferencing can occur for cooperative writing projects on specific content area topics. The teacher may first elect to have students engage in a fun cooperative writing activity such as the one in box 8.8.

8.8   In the Classroom: Mini Lesson

Roulette Writing

A cooperative writing activity in which all students can take part is "roulette writing," developed by Farris (1988). For this activity, the teacher divides the class (grades three and up) into groups of five students and joins one of the groups (a different group each time). The teacher becomes one of the members of the group, thereby promoting teamwork in this cooperative learning activity. Everyone is given the same topic about which to write. The topic should be an open-ended one, for example, "The Day Our School Burned Down." The teacher instructs everyone to begin writing about the topic, allows ample time for students to complete about three sentences, and then announces that the students are to finish the sentence they are working on and pass the story to the person on their right. This pattern continues until the fifth writer receives the story. The fifth, or last, writer must bring the story to a conclusion. As the papers are exchanged, the amount of time between exchanges increases so that the new writer has an opportunity to read the work of the preceding authors. An example of roulette writing is shown below.

It was a hot fall day. Bugs, the class troublemaker was writing a fantasy piece. He was really into it. He said something about a fire.

Suddenly I smelled smoke coming from the front of the room. A wastebasket had caught on fire.

Tina screemed, "Help!" "Fire!" I RAN to my LUNCHBox FOR my HI-C JuiceBox. I ripped THE ToP OFF AND POURED IT on THE FIRE. THE FLAMES ROSE EVEN HIGHER.

Everyone started to get nervous. Next, the fire bell went off and we all started filing out.

Well it was a happy ending. Bugs wrote this story for class, and it was so realistic that everyone sat spell bound. I never knew Bugs could write this well. Of course with Bugs around one never knew when this story could become reality.

Farris, P. J. (1988). Roulette writing. *The Reading Teacher, 41* (1), 91.

Next the teacher may have the students evaluate their finished products to select the best one. Finally, students must determine what made it a good piece of writing (interesting topic sentence, organization, details, etc.). Then students are ready to begin a group writing task.

Special Needs Learners

As teachers, we can look at children's writing and we can determine their reading ability. Special needs students struggle with reading as well as writing their ideas on paper. Many special needs students in the primary grades have language problems that may include limited vocabulary and an inability to articulate well. These problems transfer into limited writing vocabulary and spelling errors because of the inability to correctly identify phoneme-grapheme relationships. Below are examples of writing by two third-grade boys from the same classroom. The class was told to write about their families and pets. Corey is learning disabled and Lukasz is an above-average-ability student. Corey's writing appears on the left and the accurately written version on the right.

I haf two dogs and I	I have two dogs and I
hav a fsh in mY rom	have a fish in my room.
I nam it emow. and we	I named it Elmo. And we
osol haf ann nuthr fish	also have another fish
don sthrs and we hav brs	downstairs and we have birds
in sid a caju in sid my hos	inside a cage inside my house.
hers hos men pepol aer in	Here's how many people are in
my famuley My sir is 14	my family. My sister is 14
yers old and hr nam is hethr	years old and her name is Heather.
My mom is 31 hr nam is	My mom is 31 her name is
Deanu. My Das nam is Wotr	Deana. My Dad's name is Walter.
My haf bruthr nam is Erik.	My half brother's name is Erik.
—Corey, age 8	

Next is Lukasz's writing:

I like to play basketball. I have one sister that's 3 years old. She's really anoying. I am 8. 1 am going to be 9 in November. My favorite thing to do after school is to play sports with my friends.
—Lukasz, age 8

By comparing these two writing samples you can see that the classroom teacher has different challenges for writing instruction for each of these students. Corey needs to work on conventions of language and spelling patterns. He'll need lots of direct instruction and much practice to master these areas. Corey will need to be reminded to use the Word Wall as a resource when he writes. Corey needs to have several opportunities to write as well. The teacher must stress the need for Corey to put content first as he writes. From Corey's writing sample, we see that he tends to write in set patterns, which do convey his message. He needs to develop other word patterns to stretch him as a writer. Sharing enjoyable, frolicking, humorous books, such as those written by Pamela Duncan Edwards and Judith Viorst (see chapter 6) with Corey will provide him with appropriate writing examples suitable for encouraging him to write his own thoughts and ideas and helping him to find writing to be an enjoyable experience.

Lukasz is well on his way as a writer. He needs to learn about different forms of writing and the concept of audience (and perhaps to tolerate his "anoying" younger sister!). Like Corey, he needs to have lots of enjoyable writing activities. The teacher seeks out children's books that interest Lukasz to provide ideas for his future writings.

Direct instruction in writing is essential for special needs students. Through explicit instruction, they can grasp writing skills and concepts. Often it is best to group lower-ability writers together to explain certain concepts in a concrete fashion. For instance, when talking about quotation marks, you might describe them as a "fence" for what characters in a story say.

English Language Learners

Writing can be frustrating for English as a second language learners if the teacher fails to recognize the importance of having the students write for content first and then consider spelling and mechanics. As ELL students learn to write, they have a strong tendency to incorporate sounds of their first language. Below are writing samples from three ELL seven- and eight-year-old students whose first language is Spanish. Notice the Spanish articulation influence that appears in their spelling.

Ay si A owl en th book en de owl is en de Forest —Osmar, age 7	I see a owl in the book and the owl is in the forest.
the Owl Lif an the forec en America the foag lif an the ouchen. —Rocio, age 8	The owl live in the forest in America The frog live in the ocean.
A lorn about burts and spars and laribogs and barflais and bis and snecs dlfins and charcs. —Elizabeth, age 7	I learn about birds and sparrows and ladybugs and butterflies and bees and snakes dolphins and sharks.

Clearly Elizabeth is more advanced in her acquisition of English compared with Osmar, who has difficulty distinguishing short vowels and final consonant sounds. Elizabeth also has a wider English vocabulary than do Osmar and Rocio. Below is a sample from another student in the same class.

The snake lef ande desiert.   The snake lives in the desert.
—Gabriel, age 7

When reading Gabriel's sentence aloud, it is easy to understand how "in the" is translated into Gabriel's "ande." The sounds to an ELL learner are quite similar. When teaching ELL students, there must be opportunities for the students to hear their writing read with a standard English pronunciation if they are to make the connection to how the words should be articulated properly. This gives the students a "sound" model for them to use.

Modeling writing, mentioned earlier in this chapter, works well with ELLs. Gibbons (2002) suggests that teacher provide different models of compositions for students to examine before being divided into small groups to collaboratively create a composition. The next step is having students write their own composition. This scaffolding approach permits the teacher to demonstrate writing strategies and skills, assist students in widening their knowledge about the writing craft, and expand ELL students' linguistic capabilities.

Summary

The writing process is comprised of four stages: prewriting, writing, rewriting, and publishing. Rather than being a linear process, with strategies and skills being refined and new ones acquired, writing is recursive in nature, with strategies and skills continually be acquired and honed.

The prewriting stage, also referred to as rehearsal, enables a writer to prepare for the writing task by brainstorming, gathering information, and playing with thoughts and ideas. During the writing stage, the writer puts developed thoughts and ideas down on paper in the form of sentences and paragraphs. In the rewriting stage, the writer revises the draft; although limited editing and revising occur during prewriting and writing, in the rewriting stage, the writer refines, clarifies, and reorganizes ideas to a much greater extent. In the last stage, that of publishing, the writer shares what she has written with others.

When undertaking a writing project, the student should consider the audience, or who will read the work. For elementary children, four types of audiences exist: (1) self, (2) teacher, (3) known, and (4) unknown. Voice is yet another aspect of the writing process. Young children naturally write in the narrative voice, but they acquire the expository and poetic voices as time passes and experiences change.

When instructing students in the writing process, the effective teacher serves as a writing model and writes on the same topics that are assigned to students. By conferring with children both individually and in groups, the teacher can gain insight into their development as writers and their understanding of the writing process. Such conferences work best if they revolve around an individual piece of writing, addressing its strengths and weaknesses, and if the teacher is nonjudgmental about the piece.

Questions

1. Writing is referred to as the most complex language art for children to learn and for teachers to instruct. Give rationale to support this statement.
2. Define the four types of voice and write an example of each.
3. What role does the teacher play in the development of children's writing skills?
4. In what ways can children be introduced to the different types of audiences?
5. In what ways are teacher-student conferences similar to teacher-small group conferences? How do they differ?

Reflective Teaching

Flip back to the beginning of the chapter to the teaching vignette entitled "Peering into the Classroom." After rereading the vignette, consider the following questions: What characteristics (either implied or directly exhibited) does the teacher possess that you would like to develop? What strengths and weaknesses are revealed for the students described in this section? How would you meet the needs of students such as these?

Activities

1. Observe a four- or five-year-old beginning writer. Compare the child's actions with those of a first or second grader.
2. Develop a list of questions for conferencing with children at a particular grade level.
3. Develop and videotape a model writing lesson. Critique the videotape prior to presenting the lesson to a group of students.
4. Conference with three children who vary from low to high in their writing abilities. Try to use many of the same questions with all three students. Compare their responses to the questions and descriptions of their works.
5. Compare and contrast the diverse writing found within second grade classrooms with the egocentric writing of first graders.

Further Reading

Atwell, N. (1998). *In the middle: New understandings about writing, reading, and learning with adolescents* (2nd ed.). Portsmouth, NH: Heinemann.

Behymer, A. (2003). Kindergarten writing workshop. *The Reading Teacher, 57* (1), 85–88.

Buss, K, & Karnowski, L. (2002). *Reading and writing nonfiction genres.* Newark, DE: International Reading Association.

Christenson, T. (2002). *Supporting struggling writers in the elementary classroom.* Newark, DE: International Reading Association.

Dorn, L., & Soffos, C. (2001). *Scaffolding young writers: A writer's workshop approach.* Portland, ME: Stenhouse.

Ehrenworth, M. (2003). Literacy and the aesthetic experience: Engaging children with the visual arts in the teaching of writing. *Language Arts, 81* (1), 43–51.

Ernst, G., & Richard, K. J. (1994/1995). Reading and writing pathways to conversation in the ESL classroom. *The Reading Teacher, 48* (4), 320–327.

Morrow, L. M., Tracey, D. H., Woo, D. G., & Pressley, M. (1999). Characteristics of exemplary first-grade literacy instruction. *The Reading Teacher, 52* (5), 462–476.

Tompkins, G. E., & Collom, S. (2004). *Sharing the pen: Interactive writing with young children.* Upper Saddle River, NJ: Prentice/Merrill.

References

Abel, J. P., & Abel, F. J. (1988). Writing in the mathematics classroom. *Clearing House, 62* (2), 155–158.

Abel, F. J., Hauwiller, J. G., & Vandeventer, N. (1989). Using writing to teach social studies. *Social Studies, 80* (1), 17–20.

Atwell, N. (1998). *In the middle: New understandings about writing, reading, and learning with adolescents* (2nd ed.). Portsmouth, NH: Heinemann.

Bright, R. (1995). *Writing instruction in the intermediate grades.* Newark, DE: International Reading Association.

Britton, J., Burgess, T., Martin, N., McLeod, A., & Rosen, H. (1975). *The development of writing abilities (11–18).* London: Schools Council Publications.

Buss, K., & Karnowski, L. (2000). *Reading and writing literary genres.* Newark, DE: International Reading Association.

Calkins, L. M. (1995). *The art of teaching writing* (2nd ed.). Portsmouth, NH: Heinemann.

Calkins, L. M., & Harwayne, S. (1991). *Living between the lines.* Portsmouth, NH: Heinemann.

Clay, M. (1975). *What did I write?* London: Heinemann.

Clay, M. (1987). *Writing begins at home.* Portsmouth, NH: Heinemann.

Dyson, A. H. (1994). *Negotiating a permeable curriculum: On literacy, diversity, and the interplay of children's and teachers' worlds* (NCTE Concept Papers No. 9). Urbana, IL.

Dyson, A. H., & Freedman, S. W. (2003). Writing. In J. Flood, D. Lapp, J. R. Squire, & J. M. Jensen's (Eds.), *Handbook of research on teaching the English language arts.* New York: Macmillan.

Emig, J. (1971). *The composing process of twelfth graders.* Urbana, IL: National Council of Teachers of English.

Gahn, S. M. (1989). A practical guide for teaching writing in the content areas. *Journal of Reading, 32* (6), 525–531.

Gibbons, J. (2002). *Scaffolding language, scaffolding learning.* Portsmouth, NH: Heinemann.

Graves, D. (1983). *Writing: Teachers and children at work.* Portsmouth, NH: Heinemann.

Graves, D. (1985). *Write from the start.* New York: Dutton.

Graves, D., & Hansen, J. (1983). The author's chair. *Language Arts, 60* (2), 176–183.

Hansen, J. (1986). *When writers read.* Portsmouth, NH: Heinemann.

Hansen, J. (1992). The language of challenge: Readers and writers speak their minds. *Language Arts, 69* (2), 100–105.

Harste, J. C., Woodward, V. A., & Burke, C. L. (1984). *Language stories and literacy lessons.* Portsmouth, NH: Heinemann.

Hillocks, G. (1986). *Research on written composition.* Urbana, IL: National Council of Teachers of English.

Huck, C., Hepler, S., & Hickman, J. (1997). *Children's literature in the elementary school* (6th ed.). New York: Holt, Rinehart, & Winston.

Kirby, D., & Liner, T. (1981). *Inside out.* Montclair, NJ: Boynton/Cook.

Kormanski, L. M. (1992). Using poetry in the middle grades. *Reading Horizons, 32* (3), 184–190.

Laminack, L. (1990). "Possibilities, Daddy, I think it says possibilities": A father's journal of the emergence of literacy. *The Reading Teacher, 43* (8), 536–541.

Mack, B., & Farris, P. (1992). Conferencing in the writing process, a primer. *Illinois Reading Council Journal, 20* (4), 17–23.

Morretta, T. M., & Ambrosini, M. (2000). *Practical approaches for teaching reading and writing in the middle schools.* Newark, DE: International Reading Association.

Morrow, L. M., Tracey, D. H., Woo, D. G., & Pressley, M. (1999). Characteristics of exemplary first-grade literacy instruction. *The Reading Teacher, 52* (5), 462–476.

Murray, D. (1968). *A writer teaches writing: A practical method of teaching composition.* Boston: Houghton Mifflin.

Murray, D. (1980). How writing finds its own meaning. In T. R. Donovan & B. W. McClelland, (Eds.), *Eight approaches to teaching composition.* Urbana, IL: National Council of Teachers of English.

Newman, J. M. (1985). *Whole language: Theory in use.* Portsmouth, NH: Heinemann.

Read, C. (1971). Pre-school children's knowledge of English phonology. *Harvard Educational Review, 41* (1), 1–14.

Ridolfi, K. (1997). Secret places. *Voices from the Middle, 4* (1), 38–41.

Smith, F. (1981). Myths of writing. *Language Arts, 58* (5), 792–798.

Smith, F. (1982). *Writing and the writer.* New York: Holt, Rinehart, & Winston.

Sulzby, E. (1992). Research directions: Transitions from emergent to conventional writing. *Language Arts, 69* (3), 290–297.

Teale, W. H. (1986). The beginnings of reading and writing: Written language development during the preschool and kindergarten years. In M. R. Sampson (Ed.), *The pursuit of literacy: Early reading and writing.* Dubuque, IA: Kendall/Hunt.

Tierney, R. J., Carter, M. A., & Desai, L. E. (1991). *Portfolio assessment in the reading-writing classroom.* Norwood, MA: Christopher-Gordon.

Tierney, R. J., & Pearson, P. D. (1983). Toward a composing model of reading. *Language Arts, 60* (5), 568–581.

Tompkins, G. E. (2004). *Teaching writing: Balancing process and product* (4th ed.). Upper Saddle River, NJ: Merrill.

Tower, C. (2000). Questions that matter: Preparing elementary students for the inquiry process. *The Reading Teacher, 53* (7), 550–557.

Walley, C. W. (1991). Diaries, logs, and journals in the elementary classroom. *Childhood Education, 67* (3), 149–154.

Children's Literature

Carle, E. (1969). *The very hungry caterpillar*. New York: Philomel.

Carle, E. (1984). *The very busy spider*. New York: Philomel.

Carle, E. (1990). *The very quiet cricket*. New York: Philomel.

Carle, E. (1995). *The very lonely firefly*. New York: Philomel.

Cronin, D. (2000). *Click, clack, moo: Cows that type* (B. Lewin, Illus.). New York: Simon & Schuster.

Falconer, I. (2000). *Olivia*. New York: Atheneum.

Florian, D. (2000). *A pig is big*. New York: Greenwillow.

Lionni, L. (1973). *Swimmy*. New York: Random House.

Martin, B. (1964; 1983). *Brown bear, brown bear, what do you see?* (E. Carle, Illus.). New York: Holt, Rinehart, & Winston.

Waddell, M. (1993). *Farmer duck* (H. Oxenbury, Illus.). Cambridge, MA: Candlewick.

Williams, S. (1990). *I went walking* (J. Vivas, Illus.). San Diego: Harcourt Brace.

Writing
Narrative, Poetry, Expository, and Persuasive

> A sense of authorship comes from the struggle to put something big and vital into print, and from seeing one's own printed words reach the hearts and minds of readers.
>
> —Lucy McCormick Calkins
> *The Art of Teaching Writing*

PEERING INTO THE CLASSROOM
JOURNAL WRITING

It is 8:15 AM and spiral notebooks are open as Deanna White's seventh graders write in their personal journals, something they do two days a week—Tuesdays and Thursdays for this class and Mondays and Wednesdays for her other section of seventh graders. Some students fill two or three pages with their thoughts in the 15 minutes Deanna gives them, whereas others write more slowly as the thoughts trickle forth. Usually Deanna writes in her journal at the same time and occasionally shares her writing along with her students.

Bemoaning the lack of more time for students to write in their journals, Deanna proclaims, "Sometimes really great stuff just pours from these kids. Like when we're studying poetry, some students fill page after page with poems—some sad, some hilarious, some very deep for a young adolescent to compose. I get to know my students so much better through journaling than just teaching them in class, grading their work, and passing them in the hallway. If we had more time, I'd have the kids journal at least three days a week for 15 minutes each day. Unfortunately we have so much material to cover if we are going to meet state objectives and those are also very important. Time quickly evaporates."

Journal writing translates into lots of reading by the classroom teacher. Deanna has a method that aids her: she takes home one-fourth of each class's journals every day except Friday. With this approach she reads each student's journal entries once every two weeks. If students need to talk with Deanna about a particular issue, they can make appointments during Writer's Workshop or e-mail her. Taking the journals home four nights a week means that Deanna is free Friday evening through Monday morning. As Deanna says, "Even language arts teachers need a life!!!! I'm a better teacher by being well read and well rounded. My students tease me when they see me with my family at the movie complex or exercising at the Y. But I give them everything I've got during the week and I ask them to give 110 percent to me. And they pretty much do. So I don't give homework over weekends unless they start slacking off. A writing assignment over a three-day weekend is the absolute worst assignment that seventh graders can bear to endure. The following week is always a most productive week."

Chapter Objectives

The reader will:

✓ understand the different purposes for writing.

✓ learn ways to teach narrative writing.

✓ develop ways to teach poetry.

✓ learn techniques in teaching expository writing.

✓ learn techniques in teaching persuasive writing.

✓ discover how technology can aid writing.

✓ learn different ways to evaluate student writing.

Standards for Professionals

The following Standards will be addressed in this chapter:

Standard 1: Foundational Knowledge and Dispositions

1.1 Demonstrate knowledge of psychological, sociological, and linguistic foundations of reading and writing processes and instruction.

Standard 2: Instructional Strategies and Curriculum Materials

2.1 Use instructional grouping options (individual, small-group, whole-class, and computer based) as appropriate for accomplishing given purpose.

2.2 Use a wide range of instructional practices, approaches, and methods, including technology-based practices, for learners at differing stages of development and from differing cultural and linguistic backgrounds.

2.3 Use a wide range of curriculum materials in effective reading instruction for learners at different stages of reading and writing development and from differing cultural and linguistic backgrounds.

Standard 3: Assessment, Diagnosis, and Evaluation

3.1 Use a wide range of assessment tools and practices that range from individual and group standardized tests to individual and group informal classroom assessment strategies, including technology-based assessment tools.

3.2 Place students along a developmental continuum and identify students' proficiencies and difficulties.

3.3 Use assessment information to plan, evaluate, and revise effective instruction that meets the needs of all students, including those at different developmental stages and those from differing cultural and linguistic backgrounds.

3.4 Effectively communicate results of assessments to specific individuals (students, parents, caregivers, colleagues, administrators, policy makers, policy officials, community, etc.).

Standard 4: Creating a Literate Environment

4.1 Use students' interests, reading abilities, and backgrounds as foundations for the reading and writing program.

4.2 Use a large supply of books, technology based information, and nonprint materials representing multiple levels, broad interests, and cultural and linguistic backgrounds.

4.3 Model reading and writing enthusiastically as valued lifelong activities.

Introduction

Writing is a learning vehicle that enables children and adults to become more aware of personal beliefs, to nurture their techniques of evaluation and interpretation, and ultimately to formulate related decisions. "One develops as a writer each time one engages in the process" (Newman, 1983, p. 860). Writing is a medium not only for learning, but also for teaching students *how* to learn (Abel & Abel, 1988). Each time children write, a period of discovery ensues; they gain new knowledge about writing, language conventions, reading, and thinking, in addition to a better understanding of themselves. The part of the student's writing experience that belongs to the teacher is that of facilitator. According to Wendy King (1997, p. 28), a teacher in Canada, "a teacher's role is to authenticate where a student is, and nudge that student along the path a little. But the path is not smooth and straight, and while some of our students wear roller blades, others are barefoot!"

As mentioned previously, children do not develop as writers in a linear progression, for writing is recursive. As they struggle to experiment with and incorporate new techniques into their writing repertoires, their writing can seemingly deteriorate. For every upward gain, the line reflecting their writing development may form a plateau or even turn downward.

Writing facilitates learning in two ways. First, in the prewriting stage, a child gains control over the development of ideas. Second, writing requires discipline to do the tasks necessary from start to finish so that the final product is the child's best effort; the child must engage in the ongoing assessment of the product by responding, questioning, defining, formulating, generalizing, and theorizing. Thus, writing empowers the child during the learning process.

As children write, a natural division occurs in the type of material produced: Narrative and poetry writing are deeply personal and represent the private side of a child; feelings, beliefs, interests, desires, and innermost thoughts will be expressed and described. Expository and persuasive writing, on the other hand, are used as a child plans, organizes, summarizes, expands, and elaborates upon beliefs, ideas, or information.

If children are to grow through their writing, the teacher must continually evaluate their progress. Children, too, should critique their own writing by objectively reviewing and editing their work. Such teacher evaluation and self-evaluation should also be accompanied by peer evaluation. In discussing their work with other children, youngsters not only gain the respect of their peers but also develop a more thorough understanding of their own perspectives and interpretations.

This chapter discusses writing strategies, tools for evaluation of student writing, and the use of word processing in the elementary classroom. An overview is given of writing strategies for narrative, poetry, expository, and persuasive writing, along with other writing genres such as letter writing and writing a biography.

Writing Strategies and Skills

Like using strategies to solve math problems or comprehension difficulties in reading, writers depend on strategies. For those who use writing strategies, the writing process becomes a welcome challenge rather than an arduous task. To become competent writers, students need ideas, organization, words, connections, and the conventions of the English language (grammar, usage, spelling, capitalization, and punctuation).

Ideas

Ideas are the essence of the composition itself. An idea can come from a myriad of places—something observed on the way to school, a story in a book, a science experiment, or a humorous news event might trigger an idea that can evolve into a marvelous writing piece. Often students possess terrific ideas, but they are too afraid or timid to go with them and put them down on paper. A list of writing ideas that students compile throughout the school year should be part of the students' writing folders. Janiel Wagstaff, a second-grade teacher, models how she gets writing ideas for her own writing by talking about the ideas with her students before and jotting them down in a corner of the chalkboard so her entire class can view them. Whether Janiel has taken a trip to New York, gotten a new bike, been walloped in the forehead from a softball, or had an encounter with her mischievous pet cat and dog, Janiel lets her students know that writing ideas can come from anywhere. She also keeps lots of quality literature in her classroom for her students to read, using a number of such books as read alouds during her writing workshop. Quality literature provides an excellent model of good writers.

Struggling writers may feel that they lack sufficient experiences to share. Some may rely on television shows or movies for characters and plots in their narrative writing. Such writing may transpire into "blood and guts" writing by the end of second grade as they describe the gory details of stabbings and beatings they create in their stories. Banning characters from television, movies, and popular children's literature series (e.g., Captain Underpants, Harry Potter) as subjects of students' writing, while at the same time acknowledging that these are indeed interesting characters, can be a challenge for the teacher, who needs to convey the importance of the student producing his own unique characters and plot.

Ideas must make sense to the writer's audience and compel the reader to read beyond the first few sentences. If the reader is disinterested, the writer never gets to share the story. The composition must demonstrate, at the very start, that the writer knows the topic, and including interesting or intriguing details conveys this. Hence, the opening one or two sentences must be compelling enough to pull the reader in.

Organization

How the composition hangs together depends on its organization. The writer may use a cluster, web, list, note cards, or outline to gather and organize the ideas and information. In writing, the piece should open by hooking the reader, then continue to build interest before it ends so the reader has a fulfilling literary experience that has given him pause to think.

Beginning writers can use large and small circles as a means of writing down their ideas. Each large circle is the bigger idea with two smaller circles depicting support for that particular big idea. Some teachers have students use different colored note cards for each heading in an expository paper. The note cards have a hole punched in the upper left-hand corner enabling them to be attached to a key ring. Once the student has the cards organized, the ring makes a kind of flip book of her notes and resources from which she can then move to writing the first draft. Box 9.1 on p. 356 contains an example of how younger elementary students can organize ideas to produce a classroom writing project.

Transitioning from one paragraph to another or one scene to the next is difficult for many writers. Good writers smoothly transition from one idea to the next. Young writers need to see this modeled in quality literature. They

9.1   In the Classroom: Mini Lesson

Organizing a Writing Project

One activity that aids the development of organizational skills is to read aloud, over a four-day period, picture book biographies about the same individual (e.g., Johnny Appleseed, Christopher Columbus, Helen Keller, Martin Luther King, Jr.). Each day have five or six students dictate or write on a sentence strip one fact they learned from listening to the book read that day. At the end of the week, have the students get into groups as to when their fact occurred in the person's life (beginning, middle, or end). The class then spreads out the sentences and decides what order they should be in. Next, the sentence strips are numbered and handed back to the students who copy down their statement on art paper before they illustrate the scene. The teacher then compiles the pages into a class book.

also need a display of transition words. Below is such a list for beginning writers that should be posted on a chart in the classroom:

Transition Words

first	last week	yesterday	today
second	next month	tonight	in the morning
third	before lunch	noon	in the afternoon
next	then	lastly	finally
before	prior to	ahead	earlier
previously	later	evening	night

Students can readily use these words in steps for explanatory writing or in their narrative story.

Words

As one reads the work of a great author, the exquisiteness of word choice stands out. Good writers show but don't tell their readers. Eloquent use of words transforms the piece. As young writers hone the craft of writing they need to learn the subtleties of finding the precise word. Rather than writing, "My neighborhood is noisy," they *show* the noisy neighborhood. "Six barking dogs, eleven rowdy kids, and a yellow tomcat that meows at midnight live in my neighborhood" paints a far more descriptive image in the reader's mind.

By using specific, precise words that create vivid pictures, writers make the reader's job easier. Careful selection of nouns and verbs by the writer enhances the composition or poem. Mini lessons on general nouns and nouns that offer specificity as well as verbs and vivid verbs—those that create images in the reader's mind—are essential if students are to write rich passages. As part of the mini lessons, word charts can be posted around the room. Students should make a mini-thesaurus to put in their writing folder. Below are some examples of nouns, adjectives, and verbs that can be used in writing to provide richness and variety.

Noun	Verb	Adjective
ball:	*said:*	*happy:*
sphere	screamed	joyful
orb	yelled	delighted
soccer ball	whispered	content
baseball	cried	thrilled
basketball	exclaimed	glad
rubber ball	groaned	pleased
trees:	*walked:*	*beautiful:*
grove	trudged	pretty
forest	hiked	gorgeous
woods	strode	attractive
glen	marched	lovely
woodlands	paraded	sumptuous

"To be" verbs such as *is, are, was,* and *were* drain a composition of its energy. Write the sentence "The boy was on the hill" on the overhead transparency and then demonstrate possible alternatives: "The boy sat cross-legged on the pinnacle of the hill." "The boy perched on the hilltop." "The boy peered down from the hill."

Descriptive words need to be colorful and add "pizzazz." Remind students that adjectives modify and describe nouns. Too many adjectives strangle the sentence. Rather than "the extremely large, colossal, gigantic, huge, humongous, monster," "the massive monster" might better suffice to convey the message. Likewise, adverbs, those words that frequently end in *-ly,* generally describe the action of the verb. Consider, "the girls trudged down the trail" with "the girls trudged confidently down the trail." Or, "the bike swerved away from the curb" with "the bike swerved briskly away from the curb."

By third grade, students can readily use a thesaurus, provided it is set up as a dictionary. Word XP has a thesaurus that can be found by clicking "tools" then "language" then "thesaurus." However, there are several bound versions that offer more word selections and choices for students. Purchasing dictionary/thesaurus software such as Merriam Webster is best for middle school, as students can access the thesaurus or dictionary as they compose. Every classroom from grades three through eight should have at least three bound thesauruses and dictionaries with one of each kept in the writing center.

Connections

Writers need to be able to make connections, such as a personal connection, a connection to a particular author's style in what's called a text-to-text connection, or a connection to the world. Personal responses are important in writing autobiographical pieces. A third-grade boy responded to his teacher's read aloud of *The Relatives Came* (Rylant, 1985) by writing, "My relatives drove all the way from Boston to see us last summer. They talked funny. But they told great jokes. Later we went to the park and played softball. Then we had a cookout and everyone ate brats and hot dogs. I love my relatives."

While the above example demonstrates a personal connection, quality literature can bring about text-to-text connections. A student may attempt to model their own writing on that of a favorite author such as Beverly Cleary, Joan Bauer, Anne Fine, Steven Kellogg, Richard Peck, Patricia Polacco, or Jerry Spinelli.

Yet another type of connection is text to world. The student may create an opening hook that has a universal connection that is so compelling, that all readers will not be able to resist reading the composition. Examples of such hooks are listed below:

Question:	What goes up must come down. Or does it?
Quote:	"It was the best of times. It was the worst of times."
Series of Verbs:	Fast! Furious! Exciting!
Fact:	For every dollar spent at Wal-Mart, two cents goes for shoplifting expenses.
Riddle:	Which came first, the chicken or the egg?
Proverb:	A penny saved is a penny earned.

Text-to-world connections can relate an expository topic to current events such as a report on Taser guns that includes protecting passengers on airplanes and trains.

Conventions

Lastly, all writers need to be proficient users of the conventions of language. They need to use correct spelling, grammar, capitalization, and punctuation for the ease of the reader. Without correctly using such conventions, the writer is destined to lose in her audience. Certainly a job application with grammatical and spelling errors stands out, often resulting in no offer of even an interview. Conventions of English are covered in chapters 10 and 11.

Narrative Writing

Narrative writing is the telling of our own personal stories and those we create in our minds. Through such writing children often share their beliefs, feelings, thoughts, or concerns with others. A child's first strokes on paper signify the beginning of personal writing, for these unrefined markings are actually an extension of the child. In advancing from simple scribbling to drawing lines and circles that represent people and objects and finally to forming letters, a child continues to demonstrate that the act of "writing" remains highly personal. Narrative writing is that found in picture storybooks, chapter books, historical fiction, and high fantasy. We read of Junie B. Jones, Cam Jansen, Rodzina, and the creatures of Redwall as narrative characters and follow them through plots we find enthralling and spellbinding.

To encourage primary-grade children to write a narrative piece, the teacher might share Joan Lowery Nixon's *If You Were a Writer* (1988) with them. This is a warm, humorous book that describes a mother's explanations of commonplace, everyday events of family life as she urges her daughter to search for ideas, imagine characters, and use descriptive words in her writing. In the end, the mother gives her daughter a pencil and paper and tells her to record her stories, which she can either keep to herself or share with everyone. A companion book is Martin Selway's (1992) *Don't Forget to Write*, which describes how a young girl writes a letter to her mother when she stays on her grandfather's farm for a week.

Kate Duke's (1992) classic *Aunt Isabel Tells a Good One* outlines how a good story is written from the characters, to the setting, to the conflict, and to the final resolution. Although it is a rather wordy book, by hearing it read aloud quickly in one setting to first graders at mid-year, the children can begin to organize their own story writing. Below is a worksheet they would complete prior to writing their own story.

Title of Story:_____

Main Character:_____

Character:_____

Character:_____

Setting—Place:_____

Setting—Time:_____

Problem:_____

Resolution:_____

For children, a narrative piece of writing might describe a recent family incident, the arrival of a new puppy, or an extension of a picture storybook read by the teacher. Narrative writing is important to children as seen in their strong desire to share beliefs, thoughts, and ideas with others through writing. Such high motivation provides for growth in writing skills because fluency in writing depends on the opportunity to write.

There are several children's literature selections that model narrative writing skills for budding young writers. Below are a few:

Blume, J. (1974). *The pain and the great one*. New York: Dell. (Ideas—comparing and contrasting two people)

Brett, J. (1996). *Comet's nine lives*. New York: Putnam. (Organization—using cause and effect and strong transitions to sequence a story)

Bruss, D. (2001). *Book! Book! Book!* (T. Beeke, Illus.). New York: Arthur A. Levine Books. (Organization—sequencing a story; Word choice—effective use of alliteration)

Cooney, B. (1982). *Miss Rumphius*. New York: Dial. (Ideas and Word Choice—developing a strong character)

Cowley, J. (1998). *Big moon tortilla* (D. Strongbow, Illus.). Honesdale, PA: Boyds Mill Press. (Conventions—vivid verbs; Word choice—use of metaphors)

Fox, M. (1985). *Wilfred Gordon McDonald Partridge* (J. Vivas, Illus.). San Diego: Harcourt. (Sentence development—using effective lead sentences)

Johnson, D. B. (2000). *Henry hikes to Fitchburg*. Boston: Houghton Mifflin. (Ideas—clever ways of problem solving)

Leedy, L. (2004). *Look at my book: How kids can write and illustrate terrific books*. New York: Holiday House. (Ideas—Creating a book at a child's level)

McDonald, M. (1999). *The night iguana left home* (P. Goembel, Illus.). New York: DK Ink. (Organization—sequence of events)

Tomlinson, J. (2001). *The owl who was afraid of the dark* (P. Howard, Illus.). Cambridge, MA: Candlewick. (Ideas—developing a main character; Organization—demonstrating story resolution)

Wong, J. (2002). *You have to write* (T. Flavin, Illus.). New York: Simon & Schuster. (Ideas—Who, what, when, where of writing)

The teacher must provide beginning writers as well as the more sophisticated writers with experiences that will familiarize them with the many examples of narrative writing, including journals, personal letters and e-mails, and

---

9.2 In the Classroom: Teaching Hint

Pocket Books

Children like to fold paper. Just imagine how many paper airplanes have been produced by students over the years! Pocket books are one way to engage children in folding paper with a positive literary result for both narrative and expository writing. Give each student four sheets of 8 1/2" × 11" white or colored paper. Place the paper on the desk, positioned as if the students were going to write on it. Have them bring the bottom of the paper one-third of the way up and fold. Next, fold the sheet of paper in half lengthwise, with the "pockets" on the outside. Do this for the other three sheets of paper, then staple the sides away from the folds together into a book.

One variation is to make angled pockets. This is done by folding the top corners into the center of the paper and then folding the paper in half as though you were going to make a paper airplane. Next, open the paper and fold it in half with the pockets on the outside. Finally, staple the open sides together to make a two pocket book.

Additional sheets of folded paper may be added to make a book with the number of pockets you want. Larger paper makes for larger pocket books. Tagboard covers can be decorated and stapled to ordinary white paper to give the book durability.

These pocket books can be used for a variety of purposes. For instance, after hearing *The Very Hungry Caterpillar* by Eric Carle (1970), students can label the pockets in their pocket books the days of the week. Another good book to use is *Is This a House for Hermit Crab?* by Megan McDonald (1990). The students can use tagboard or old manila file folders and markers to make the various objects in these books. By drawing lines on the bottom of the paper and photocopying the paper, the pockets of the book will have lines on which the students can write a story.

Older students can use the pocket books for regional studies of the states or of countries. For instance, they can draw a map of the state on the top of the page and write facts about the state on an index card that slides into the pocket.

Science concepts can be written on index cards and questions on the pockets themselves. Students can then exchange their pocket books and insert their index cards into the pockets with the matching questions.

Carle, E. (1970). *The very hungry caterpillar*. New York: Philomel.

McDonald, M. (1990). *Is this a house for hermit crab?* (S. D. Schindter, Illus.). New York: Orchard.

autobiographies. Reader response journals, in which the students write to dialogue with the teacher or a peer about the book they are reading, are important for two reasons. They provide motivation for reading quality fiction and an opportunity to share ideas in a written format.

Dialogues

Dialogues provide a child with an opportunity to participate in a written conversation with someone else, such as the teacher or a classmate. Unlike letter writing, dialogue writing is more informal and unstructured (Farris, 1989) and can be likened to a two-way diary. A child writes a brief message of perhaps only one or two sentences, and beneath this message on the same piece of paper, the correspondent writes a response. Introducing children to dialogue writing at the beginning of the school year encourages them to write. If the teacher serves as the correspondent, he may gain insights about each student from the various messages exchanged.

The use of dialogue writing can also function as a motivational technique for slow learners or children with learning disabilities. Consider Larry, a fourth grader with weak written communication skills. During the time in which his teacher, Miss Davis, read Steven Kellogg's (1971) book *Can I Keep Him?* to the class, Larry developed a dialogue with Miss Davis via a computer. Although he had access to the classroom computer during the school day, Larry arrived early every day for a week to use the computer. Each morning before class, the computer disk with Larry's dialogue would appear on Miss Davis's desk. Likewise, every afternoon, Larry would check his desk for the computer disk, which now contained Miss Davis's reply. While Kellogg's book is about a young boy's desire to acquire a pet, Larry focused his writing on his desire to obtain a sporty vehicle. A portion of Larry's written dialogue with Miss Davis follows:

> Der Miss Davs,
>   Twoday I fnd a red crvtt car on my way to shol. It is reel cool and gos reel fast. Can I keep it?
>   Larry

> Dear Larry,
>   I think red Corvettes are beautiful cars. They do go very fast and look cool. But you don't have a driver's license so you could not drive it. No, you can't keep the red Corvette.
>   Your friend,
>   Miss Davis

The next day the following correspondence took place:

> Dear Miss Davs,
>   Twoday I fnd a Hrly Davisn bike. It is cool and gos faster thn a corvet. Can I keep it?
>   Your friend, Larry

> Dear Larry,
>   Harley Davidson motorcycles are cool. They run in motorcycle races because they are so fast. But you need a driver's license to ride a motorcy-

cle, and you are still too young to apply for a license. No, Larry, you can't keep the Harley Davidson.
  Your friend,
  Miss Davis

Journals

Like dialogue writing, journal writing is informal and often unstructured. Essentially serving as diaries, *journals* are a means by which children record events and their feelings about those events. Journals serve as a means of moving from personal to public writing, thereby making journals an important part of the writing curriculum. For children who have already been introduced to dialogue writing, journal writing is the next stage in a natural progression. Even though kindergartners and first graders have yet to acquire writing skills, their drawings of a day's primary events can serve as journal writing. Later, as they develop some writing talent, they can move to a combination of illustrations and words.

Initially, a thin spiral notebook makes a good, sturdy journal. Although intermediate children sometimes prefer to use two- or three-ring notebooks that allow them to insert and remove pages, such notebooks are often cumbersome and require additional storage space.

Because children in the primary grades find it a great deal easier to direct their writings to a specific audience, the teacher may ask the students to pretend that they are writing the journal for a friend outside the immediate classroom (see figure 9.1). Getting older children to write in a journal can be frustrating for a teacher at first because intermediate-grade students' seemingly enthusiastic initial attempts may yield only bland writing at best. Children at this age are suspicious of open-ended and unstructured assignments, and they simply lack experience in keeping a journal. To encourage students to take some liberties in recording life events, a teacher may share portions of another person's journal or diary with them. Beverly Cleary's (1983) *Dear Mr. Henshaw* and its 1991 sequel, *Strider,* are examples of one child's dialogue writing that evolved into journal writing. Still another introductory and motivational approach is the sharing of excerpts from the teacher's own journal with the class.

Some teachers encourage students to write in their journals on a daily basis for a short period of time, such as five minutes. Along with their students, these teachers write in a journal during the designated period. However, time constraints may prohibit some teachers from pursuing such a daily schedule. When this is the case, the teacher may decide that writing two or three times a week is sufficient, the journal can still function as a continuous log over some selected period of time.

At times, students may actually express a desire to write in their journals. One sixth-grade teacher, Mrs. Murphy, was asked by a student whether class members could have time to write in their journals. When Mrs. Murphy replied that journal writing was not scheduled for that day, the student exclaimed, "But I just *have to* write today!" Because she was a flexible teacher and recognized the student's distress at being unable to record her thoughts,

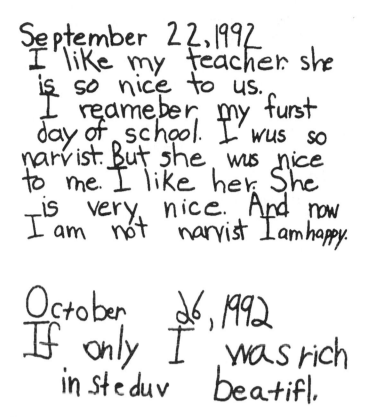

September 22, 1992
I like my teacher. she
is so nice to us.
I reameber my furst
day of school. I wus so
narvist. But she wus nice
to me. I like her. She
is very nice. And now
I am not narvist I am happy.

October 26, 1992
If only I was rich
in stе duv beatifl.

Figure 9.1   Journal entries of a second grader

Mrs. Murphy rearranged the day's schedule to include journal writing. Later the student shared her journal entry for that day with Mrs. Murphy; it revealed the child's concern about a serious problem she had had with one of her friends who was considering suicide. In this instance, journal writing allowed the child to work out a potential solution to the problem. Teachers have a legal obligation to report such information as shared by students in their journals. In this case, the teacher notified her principal who referred the situation to the school counselor. Child abuse also is sometimes shared in students' journals.

On a regular basis, teachers should collect the journals and read the students' entries. Some teachers collect all the journals and read the entries once every week or two. Other teachers elect to collect and read a few journals each day. The latter scheme results in better time management because teachers can set aside a small amount of time each day for entry reading. This can be easily done by dividing the class into five groups corresponding to the five days of the school week.

Because journal writing is considered personal, a teacher must respect a student's entries and maintain confidentiality. In some instances, a child may not want the teacher to read all of the entries because some are so personal. In such specific cases, the teacher and student should establish a coding system: The student might attach a red dot at the beginning of a very private entry and a green dot at the point where the teacher may continue reading. This coding system ensures the child's freedom and privacy but keeps the journal intact.

Journal writing goes hand in hand with literature response journals. In journal writing the focus is upon the thoughts, impressions, and feelings of the child as the writer. For literature response journals, the focus is on the child as the reader and the "lived-through literary experience and experiences, thoughts, feelings, images, and associations which are evoked" (Many, 1992, p. 169).

Letters and E-Mails

Like journal writing, letter writing evolves from dialogue writing. Unlike dialogues and journal entries, however, letters must be structured and planned by the writer. Letter writing is motivational in that all children are eager to receive letters in the mail. Having young children write letters is an easy way to arouse their writing enthusiasm because they cannot resist the chance to communicate with those around them. This is evident in student whispering and in the passing of notes within the classroom. As children learn to share their experiences and thoughts in such notes, they are actually developing their skills in clarity as well as in organizational writing. In view of this, teachers should encourage note passing by establishing a mailbox for each student. Likewise, a letter writing station can be established in the classroom and supplied with ample and appropriate writing supplies: pencils, pens, paper, and envelopes. The class may even wish to design its own stationery, with a unique logo, class motto, or marginal design. Similar group efforts, such as writing thank-you notes to room parents and invitations to other classes to share special events, not only support the development of writing skills but also function as models of appropriate social behavior (figure 9.2).

Modeling is an appropriate approach to the teaching of letter writing. For example, a teacher can use an overhead projector while writing a friendly letter so that the class is able to observe the process. With this goal in mind, the teacher should first speculate about the letter: To whom shall it be written? What will it contain? How familiar is the audience with the planned topics? How will the contents be organized? After sharing the decision as to who will receive the letter, the teacher must express some general thoughts about the topic(s) to be covered and the audience's familiarity with the subject(s). As the discussion proceeds, the teacher may take notes pertaining to the topic(s) as part of the prewriting activity. At this point, the teacher is able to begin writing the initial draft of the letter.

Pen pals are very popular with children. Youngsters enjoy finding out about other children and are especially pleased to develop a writing relationship with someone of the same age or grade level (see figure 9.3 on p. 366). To eliminate postal expenses, a teacher who has students who want to write letters to pen pals can seek pen pals from another school in the same district. Such an arrangement can be very satisfying, particularly if the two neighboring classes can meet for a joint field trip or picnic at the end of the school year.

Dear Second Grade,

One of my favorit animals
is a spider. It is a pet in
our classroom. Come visit us
Tvsday and learn about spiders.

Your friend,
Aeron

Figure 9.2 Writing letters gives each student the chance to share experiences and organize thoughts.

The U.S. Postal Service encourages writing to pen pals by suggesting how to establish a postal system within the school itself. A videotape entitled *Wee Deliver: Stamp Out Illiteracy* and an accompanying booklet explain how to set up a postal system by using different sections of the school as towns and having each classroom serve as a street. Each student is assigned his or her own street number. Students serve as the postmaster or postmistress and postal workers after applying for various jobs and successfully passing a modified version of the civil service exam (for example, being able to determine correct and incorrect addresses on envelopes). The workers change jobs each month, and every morning before school begins, the mail is delivered. More information about this program can be obtained by writing to the following address:

Stamp Out Illiteracy Program Office of Literacy
U.S. Postal Service
470 L'Enfant Plaza SW, Room 4102E
Washington, DC 20260-3110

Young pen pals from different geographical areas can help each other foster letter-writing abilities and develop social studies skills, particularly when they are in the intermediate grades. The World Pen Pals organization establishes formal networks between children of various nationalities. For further information on international pen pals, write to the following address:

World Pen Pals
1694 Como Avenue
St. Paul, MN 55108

Scholastic also has a pen pal program for subscribers to *Weekly Reader*.

Friendly and business letters have a set structure (see figures 9.4 and 9.5).

Children need to be taught the proper conventions for sending e-mail messages. Unlike paper and pencil letters, e-mail is brief and to the point and consists of essential points, much like the telegrams of yesteryear. Unlike

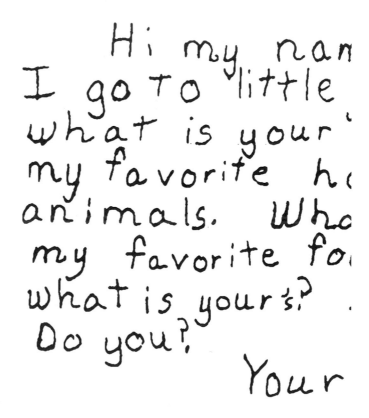

Figure 9.3 A letter from a second grader to a pen pal in Mexico

friendly letters, a complimentary closing may or may not be included in a friendly e-mail message. The widespread use of e-mail has led to abbreviations being used for certain words and phrases. Here are some examples:

- BTW: By the way
- CU: See you
- F2F: Face to face
- FAQ: Frequently asked questions

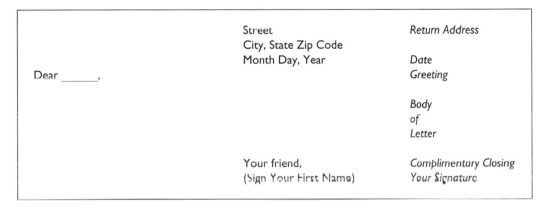

Figure 9.4   Form of a friendly letter

Figure 9.5   Form of a business letter

- GMTA: Great minds think alike
- H&K: Hugs and kisses
- DK: I don't know
- SOSO: Same old, same old
- IMHO: In my humble opinion
- JAM: Just a minute
- WFM: Works for me
- :) Smile (happy)
- :(Frown (sad)

Normally these abbreviations are not used in a business e-mail. Figures 9.6 and 9.7 show a friendly and business e-mail, respectively.

First Name of Person,	*Greeting*
	Body of E-mail
Your First Name	*Your Name*

Figure 9.6   Format for a friendly e-mail

First Name of Person,	*Greeting*
	Body of E-mail
Sincerely, Your Name (Last Name Optional) Street Address City, State Zip Code	*Complimentary Closing* *Your Name* *Address*

Figure 9.7   Format for a business e-mail

Poetry

What exactly is poetry anyway? Jared Hayslip, a student of Wendy King's (1997, p. 28) writes that "'poetry is like stealing a piece of the world and hiding it in words . . . because in every poem you read, you must find the secret message, and in every poem you write, you must hide a message. I guess poetry is the art of becoming a shadow.'" Like all writing, writing poetry is a developmental process.

Unfortunately, teachers are less apt to share poetry, particularly their own, than narrative works with children. As a result, children often lack enthusiasm for or become indifferent to poetry. Sharing a variety of literature including poetry raises the level of students' language and vocabulary development. The vicarious experiences provided by and the expressive nature of poetry serve to increase students' awareness and sensitivity to the world around them. "When teachers share a variety of poems with children several times a day, children develop positive attitudes about this genre of literature" (Kormanski, 1992, p. 189). Unfortunately, "the poetry that children prefer often lacks the subtle imagery, interesting rhythms, and clever plays on words that characterize the really good examples of this genre" (McClure, 1995, p. 118). Thus, it is up to the teacher to share a variety of forms of poetry with students. Poetry should be included naturally in the classroom, both purposefully and spontaneously. Stewig (1988) points out three misconceptions children have about poetry: (1) poetry *must* rhyme, (2) poetry must be beautiful and pretty, and (3) nothing occurs in poetry because the writing is predominately descriptive.

Students need to play with and manipulate words, combining them in new and unusual ways. Denman (1988) calls this "wordsmithing," or an awareness of the resources of language. This means that attention is given to a phrase because of its repetition of a particular sound, to the element of surprise that can be achieved by unusual combinations of words, to the power and effect of a few well selected words, or to the insights made possible by the use of metaphor.

Poetry permits a teacher to encourage children to experiment with words as well as with a wide variety of formats: lyric, narrative, limerick, rhyming, free verse, haiku, cinquain, and so on. Children almost universally prefer rhyming poetry as a style because it is the one they have encountered the most. For example, Jack Prelutsky's (1984, 1990, 1996) *The New Kid on the Block, Something Big has Been Here, Monday's Troll,* and Shel Silverstein's (1974, 1981) *Where the Sidewalk Ends* and *A Light in the Attic* typically fit into this category. However, a teacher should expose children to the other forms of poetry as well.

Children find it easiest to write about what is familiar to them. Poetry about daily life and ordinary objects provides children with an opportunity to examine and relate their own personal experiences.

In order for children to write poetry, they need to have it read to them and to read it themselves. Cullinan, Scala, and Schroder (1995, p. 3) wrote that "poetry is especially appropriate for language learning because it contains language used in its most beautiful forms. . . . Children wrap it easily around their tongues and play with its sounds." Some teachers use poetry as a base from which each school day evolves. For instance sharing poetry that relates to a topic the class is studying. According to Kathy A. Perfect (1999, p. 728), a third-grade teacher, "I could not imagine teaching a day without poetry in my classroom. It starts our day, shapes our day, and sometimes helps us get through the day. It doesn't take long for students to be captivated by the allure of poetry once it begins to weave its magic in the classroom."

Three good sources of suggestions and activities for teaching poetry are Ralph Fletcher's (2002) *Poetry Matters*, Georgia Heard's (1998) *Awakening the Heart: Exploring Poetry in Elementary and Middle School*, and Paul Janeczko's (1999) *How to Write Poetry*. These are filled with suggestions and ideas pertaining to a wide variety of poetry forms. A good book for upper-elementary and middle school students is Janeczko's (2002) *Seeing the Blue Between: Advice and Inspiration for Young Poets*. Tips on topics, word selection, style, and more are contained in this book.

Poetry about various topics should also be shared with children to encourage them to write about similar topics. Holidays, humor, nature, and scary things are some of the topics to which children naturally relate. Children enjoy reading *Sweet Corn* by James Stevenson (1995) which has poems entitled "Tree House," "Cows," "Snow," "Bus Stop," and "The Dancer." Through these and similar poems, children learn that poetry can be found in common things, such as sweet corn and clotheslines.

Poetry writing should be part of writing across the curriculum. Jim Ronan, a fifth-grade teacher, includes poetry writing in his social studies units. For instance, he reads a descriptive scene from a piece of historical fiction and then has his students work in pairs or alone to write a poem about that scene.

Poetry is often about the ordinary; that is, everyday things and occurrences that are taken for granted. Consider, for example, "Bug Catcher," a poem by Rick Walton (1995) in which a child attempts to catch several different insects—a ladybug, a caterpillar, a butterfly, a cricket, and a fly—but to no avail. Every child has had a similar experience and can easily relate to this poem.

Collections of poetry to have in the classroom for reading to students and for students to explore on their own include the following:

Adoff, A. (1991). *In for winter, out for spring* (J. Pinkney, Illus.). San Diego: Harcourt Brace.

Adoff, A. (Ed.). (1997). I *am the darker brother: An anthology of modern poems by African-Americans*. New York: Simon & Schuster.

Alarcón, F. X. (1997). *Laughing tomatoes and other spring poems (Jitomates risueños y otros poemas de primavera)*. San Francisco: Children's Book Press.

Appelt, K. (2002). *Poems from homeroom: A writer's place to start*. New York: Henry Holt.

Dakos, K. (1990). *If you're not here, please raise your hand: Poems about school*. New York: Four Winds Press.

Esbensen, B. J. (1996). *Echoes for the eye: Poems to celebrate patterns in nature*. New York: HarperCollins.

Gollub, M. (1998). *Cool melons turn to frogs: The life and poems of Issa*. New York: Lee & Low.

Greenfield, E. (1991). *Night on neighborhood street*. New York: Dial.

Harrison, M. (1989). *Splinters: A book of very short poems* (S. Heap, Illus.). New York: Oxford University Press.

Harrison, D. L. (1996). *A thousand cousins: Poems of family life*. Honesdale, PA: Wordsong/Boyds Mills.

Hopkins, L. B. (1993). *Extra innings: Baseball poems*. San Diego: Harcourt Brace.

Hopkins, L. B. (1994). *April bubbles chocolate: An ABC of poetry*. New York: Simon & Schuster.

Hopkins, L. B. (1996). *Opening days: Sports poems*. San Diego: Harcourt Brace.

Hopkins, L. B. (1996). *School supplies: A book of poems*. New York: Simon & Schuster.

Hopkins, L. B. (Ed.) (1998). *Families, families*. New York: Sadlier-Oxford.

Hopkins, L. B. (2004). *Wonderful words: Poems about reading, writing, speaking, and listening* (K. Barbour, Illus.). New York: Simon & Schuster.

Huang, T. (1992). *In the eyes of the cat: Japanese poetry for all seasons* (Demi, Illus.). New York: Henry Holt.

Hughes, L. (1986). *The dream keeper and other poems* (H. Sewell, Illus.). New York: Knopf.

Janeczko, P. (Ed.). (1987). *This delicious day*. New York: Orchard.

Janeczko, P. (Ed.). (1990). *The place my words are looking for*. New York: Bradbury.

Levy, C. (1991). *I'm going to pet a worm today and other poems* (R. Himler, Illus.). New York: McElderberry.

Lewis, J. P. (1991). *Earth verses and water rhymes*. New York: Atheneum.

Lyne, S. (2004). *Soft hay will catch you: Poems by young people* (J. Monk, Illus.). New York: Simon & Schuster.

Mavor, S. (Ed.). (1997). *You and me: Poems of friendship*. New York: Orchard.

Merriam, E. (1986). *A sky full of poems*. New York: Dell.

Merriam, E. (1989). *Chortles: New and selected wordplay poems*. New York: Morrow.

Morrison, L. (1977). *The sidewalk racer and other poems of sports and motion*. New York: Lothrop, Lee, & Shepard.

Morrison, L. (Ed.). (1997). *At the crack of the bat*. New York: Hyperion.

Myers, W. D. (1997). *Harlem* (C. Myers, Illus.). New York: Scholastic.

Prelutsky, J. (1983). *The Random House book of poetry for children* (A. Lobel, Illus.). New York: Random House.

Prelutsky, J. (1984). *The new kid on the block*. New York: Greenwillow.

Prelutsky, J. (1993). *A nonny mouse writes again!* New York: Knopf.

Rosen, M. (1996). *Food fight*. San Diego: Harcourt Brace.

Schwartz, A. (1992). *And the green grass grew all around: Folk poetry from everyone*. New York: HarperCollins.

Shields, C. D. (1996). *Lunch money* (P. Meisel, Illus.). New York: Dutton.

Thomas, J. C. (1993). *Brown honey in broomwheat tea*. New York: HarperCollins.

Wood, N. (1993). *Spirit walker*. New York: Doubleday.

Yolen, J. (1996). *Sky scraper/city scape: Poems for city life*. Honesdale, PA: Wordsong/Boyds Mill.

Elements of Poetry

Through writing poetry, children discover the importance of word choice, as finding exactly the right word to use is more critical in poetry than in prose.

Thus, students' writing and speaking vocabularies often increase as a result of incorporating more poetry into the curriculum.

Rhyme is one of the most well-known elements of poetry. A good rhyme is almost like a piece of music, but rhyme must be used appropriately. Sometimes children, and adults, overuse rhyme. Some children write lengthy rhyming poems—thoroughly enjoying the challenge of finding words that rhyme—but the rhyme is often forced and unnatural.

Alliteration is another component of poetry. Consider "Peter Piper picked a peck of pickled peppers." The constant repetition of a sound, such as [p] in this Mother Goose rhyme, is called *alliteration*. When the alliteration is the repetition of a sound within words, such as in "Fuzzy Wuzzy was a bear," it is referred to as *hidden alliteration*.

Like alliteration, onomatopoeia is based on the use of sound. For *onomatopoeia*, the poet uses words or phrases that imitate sounds. These include such words as *buzz, hiss, sigh, bang, ring, scratch, crunch,* and *tick-tock*.

Rhythm is the beat or pattern of a poem. Poems are often based on a cadence that is predictable. This is referred to as *meter*. Perfect meter is almost a singsong verse such as that found in many commercially developed greeting cards.

The poet uses the above aspects in writing but also incorporates figures of speech, including simile, metaphor, and personification. The *simile* compares one thing to another using *as* or *like*. The following phrases are similes: "big as a barn," "sweet as honey," and "crazy like a loon." A *metaphor* is used when the writer says that one thing is something else, for instance referring to bulldozers as "gigantic beasts." *Personification* assigns human qualities to nonhuman things, such as "the dog's eyes reflected wisdom" or "spring does her decorating, rolling out emerald green carpeting with yellow daffodils and red tulips tucked along the sides of her room."

By becoming familiar with the different writing techniques that can be incorporated into writing poetry, students can hone their general writing skills as well.

Types of Poetry

There are numerous types of poetry that children enjoy both writing and reading. Some of these are described in the paragraphs that follow.

List poems offer children an introduction to poetry and free verse. These are easy to introduce to a class by using the chalkboard or an overhead projector and having the students brainstorm to generate a list about a particular topic. For instance, a first-grade class brainstormed to create the following list poem about rabbits, which one reads in this order—left column, middle column, and finally right column:

Rabbits

white	hiding	lettuce
furry	tame	stretching
brown	wild	nibble
paws	chewing	wriggly nose
foot	grass	Rabbits
hopping	carrots	

They then went on to write the following list poem about their classroom:

Our Classroom

books	lots of kids	helping dads
journals	helpers	centers
Peedee, the guinea pig	reading buddies	calendar
warm	library books	clock
yellow	art projects	windows
loud desks	Mrs. Simpson	trays
free time	helping moms	our best work

All responses the students offer are appropriate to include in a list poem. This helps give them confidence in writing their own list poem, regardless of their grade level.

Free verse does not follow any structure or rules. Thus, it is a collection of the poet's thoughts that may ramble about on the page. By being introduced to free verse, children discover that not every poem has to rhyme or follow a strict poetic structure. List poems are actually free verse.

Concrete poetry is sometimes referred to as shape or pattern poetry. Livingston (1991) calls concrete poetry "a picture poem" because it combines both. The poem may consist of one word written over and over again in the shape of an object, for instance writing "dog" several times to outline a dog's body. Or the poem may include words that are written or drawn in an artistic manner (see figure 9.8).

Often children find it difficult to begin to write a poem. For some, the first line can seem overwhelming. For such students, a *poetry starter* can be

Figure 9.8   Example of a concrete poem

helpful in removing that initial writer's block. Some examples of poetry starters are as follows:

- Yesterday I was . . .
- My pet . . .
- When _____ was alive . . . (fill in the blank with a historical figure)
- Can he (or she) ever play! (the student focuses on a baseball, basketball, football, or other sports star)
- Don't forget _____. (fill in the blank—could be a person, place, or thing)
- Green is . . . (or any color the child selects)

Students enjoy the challenge of using a *name or a word* and transforming it into a poem. They can take their first name and make it into a poem, such as the following:

JASON
Joking
Awesome
Soccer player
Only child
Neat (Not!!!)
JASON

To begin this type of writing the teacher can either use the school's name and have the class develop a class poem, or have each student develop her own poem.

Couplets are two-line poems that rhyme whereas *triplets* are three-line poems that rhyme. These are fairly easy for students to write, even for those in the lower grades. Children enjoy them because they are pleasing to the ear (Livingston, 1991). To help students start writing these kinds of poems, the teacher may want to provide the first line of a poem and have the students complete it. Here is an example of a triplet that a fourth grader completed upon being given the first line:

The Mouse
There once was a mouse
Who lived in a house
With his little spouse.

Haiku is a three-line poem with nature as its subject. This short, 17-syllable poem is a popular poetic form with elementary students. The first and third lines contain five syllables, and the second line seven syllables. "Haiku" means "beginning phrase" in Japanese. The author of haiku always writes about the here and now in nature. Thus, haiku is always written in the present tense. Below is an example of haiku:

Lonely yellow leaf
Floating downward to the earth
Autumn has arrived.

Writing haiku is a real challenge, but children have, for some reason, adopted this challenge. Perhaps it is because writing haiku is like fitting together a puzzle that comes from within.

Cinquain is another popular poetic form with children. Like haiku, cinquain has a set structure. The five-line poem consists of two syllables in the first line, four in the second, six in the third, eight in the fourth, and two again in the fifth.

Here is a cinquain about the ocean written by a fifth grader:

Ocean
Big, deep
Expanse of blue
Home to fish, sharks, whales
Beautiful, peaceful, splashing waves
Giving.

A *diamante* poem consists of seven lines. The poem begins with one subject and ends with its opposite. The second and sixth lines contain two adjectives with the third and fifth lines containing three verbs. The fourth line contains four nouns. Here is an example of a diamante poem:

Fawn
Small, awkward
Falling, crashing, learning
Baby, deer, female, adult
Bounding, leaping, jumping
Tall, graceful
Doe
                          —Deana, Fifth Grade

There are numerous ways to include poetry. Box 9.3 on p. 376 is another example of weaving poetry into the curriculum.

Informational/Expository Writing

Expository writing entails using the composing process to satisfy some utilitarian need, such as knowledge acquisition, comprehension, or concept development. The focus is getting information down in a palatable manner so that the reader will gain new knowledge. This doesn't mean that expository writing has to be boring. Far from it! Nonfiction writing can stir up interests in topics and spur students to read and write more about the topic.

There are many ways to structure expository writing. For example, it can be descriptive, as in telling what penguins look like, where they live, what they eat, different kinds, and so forth. It can also be organized around a sequence of events such as steps needed to build a birdhouse or the life cycle of a frog. In some instances, an expository piece can compare and contrast two things such as a moth and a butterfly. Using cause and effect is yet another way to structure expository writing (e.g., what causes a volcano to erupt or an earthquake to take place). Problem and solution is still another type of expository writing. In this case, a problem is posed and several possible resolutions are explored (e.g., how to prevent water pollution in the Great Lakes).

Some kindergarten and first-grade teachers prefer to introduce expository writing before narrative writing, because expository writing is based on facts and is easier to structure than narrative writing. Hence, students write about a trip to the pumpkin patch or apple orchard, how to take care of the classroom hamster or fish, and so on. By the intermediate grades, students have an

---

9.3 In the Classroom: Mini Lesson

Poetry in the Content Areas

Poetry needs to be a part of the entire curriculum, including content area subjects. By reading aloud a portion from a picture book, a historical novel, or a piece of nonfiction, children can be motivated to write a poetic reflection. After the scene describing the slave auction in *Nettie's Trip South* by Ann Turner (1987) had been read to a class of seventh graders, their teacher put them into groups of three to write a poem based on what had been read to them and what they had learned about slavery through the Civil War unit they were currently studying. Below is the poem that one group of three boys wrote:

Auctions Today
Walked into town from home, with my sister
Hetta holt my hand and wouldn't let go.
It's dusty in the pen.
Waiting.
Tompkins' men pushed us up.
Platform's got splinters.
Hetta holt my hand and wouldn't let go.
Tompkins yelled out, "Two youths,
From Will Jackson's place,
What am I bid?"
Yellin' numbers and dollars.
Hetta holt my hand and wouldn't let go.
"Boy Sold! For nine dollars."
Hetta holt my hand and wouldn't let go.
Yellin' numbers and dollars.
Hetta holt my hand and wouldn't let go.
"Girl Sold! For five dollars."
Hetta holt my hand and wouldn't let go.
One of Tompkins' men took my arm.
Hetta holt my hand and wouldn't let go.
Tompkins took Hetta's arm.
Hetta holt my hand and wouldn't let go.
With a heave, Tompkins flung Hetta off the platform.
Hetta don't hold my hand no more.

Turner, A. (1987). *Nettie's trip south* (R. Himler, Illus.). New York: Macmillan.
From Pamela J. Farris, *Elementary and Middle School Social Studies: An Interdisciplinary and Multicultural Approach*, 4th ed., Boston: McGraw-Hill. Copyright © 2004.

awareness of the different kinds of expository writing, and they apply this knowledge as they write informational papers and make booklets for science and social studies. By middle school, expository writing becomes relatively refined and sophisticated for most students if they have had ample opportunities to explore it (see figure 9.9 on pp. 378–381 for an example of a fifth grader's expository descriptive writing for a science project). Typically middle schoolers only turn in expository pieces that they have polished and produced with a word processing program.

In addition to descriptive and explanatory writing, informational writing includes academic learning logs, informational reports, business letters, autobiographies, biographies, and note taking. Most of these are discussed in the remainder of this section.

Academic Learning Logs

Academic learning logs are interpretative journals in which children explain a concept or topic through their writing. Therefore, such logs serve as records of children's understandings and, because they are written in the children's own words, can help to clarify their thoughts about a particular subject. As Boyer (1983, p. 90) writes, "clear writing leads to clear thinking."

Using the academic learning log in a content area as reflective writing has proved to help students become more aware of their problem-solving methods (Brady, 1991; Hand & Treagust, 1991). Students discover which learning strategies are most effective for them.

The academic learning log can be applied to various subject areas. For example, such a log can provide explanations of scientific experiments or relay a deeper understanding of social studies concepts. Even for mathematics, such logs are beneficial in helping children gain understanding, as shown in a fourth grader's description of the steps involved in long division (see figure 9.10 on p. 381).

Cudd and Roberts (1989) have developed a modified academic learning log for use by primary-grade students. This version of the log is designed to enhance content area learning through writing. Cudd and Roberts use sequentially organized paragraphs so that students can easily recognize and use this type of paragraph structure in their own writing. The teacher begins instruction by modeling the writing of a simple paragraph in a series of seven steps:

1. Write a short, simple paragraph about a topic that lends itself to sequential ordering, using the sequencing terms *first, next, then,* and *finally.* Examples of topics include the development of a frog from an egg to a tadpole to a young frog to an adult frog, a bear entering and emerging from hibernation, and so on. (See the following example.)

   Hibernation
   First, a bear eats lots of food during the summer. Next, the bear finds a cave or hollow tree to sleep in. Then the bear falls asleep for the winter. Finally, it wakes up in the spring.

2. Write the sentences on sentence strips or transparency strips.

BATTERIES

BY ASHLEY CAMMACK

TABLE OF CONTENTS

STATEMENT OF PURPOSE

I wanted to learn how a battery worked, what kinds of batteries there are, and who invented the first battery.

HYPOTHESIS

I predict that the celery will create more voltage than the other vegetables.

Figure 9.9   An example of an expository piece of writing done on a computer by an above-average ability fifth-grade student

KEEPS GOING AND GOING AND GOING

BATTERIES

Batteries are connected cells that store electricity. They change chemical energy into electric energy. Batteries have one or more units. The units are called electric cells. Batteries also have positive and negative charges. Batteries are used in appliances such as televisions, radios, and car engines. There are two main types of batteries, primary and secondary cell.

In a primary cell battery there are two parts. The anode, which has a negative charge, and the cathode, which has a positive charge. There are three major types of primary cell batteries, carbon-zinc oxide cell, alkaline cell, and mercury cell. The carbon-zinc oxide cell is used in flashlights and toys. The alkaline cell is like the carbon-zinc oxide cell but, the alkaline cell is used in bicycle lights and walkie-talkies not flashlights and toys. The mercury cell is used in small things such as hearing aids and sensitive devices. Most primary cell batteries are dry cell or nonspillible.

A secondary cell battery can be recharged or used again after it has been charged. All secondary cell batteries take their own time to recharge. There are two major types of secondary batteries, lead-acid storage batteries and nickel-cadmium storage batteries. Lead-acid storage batteries are used for powering submarines. They can be used for four years. Nickel-cadmium storage operate like a lead-acid storage. They are used in portable equipment such as drills and garden tools. They are also used in space satellites.

Solar batteries make electricity by the photoelectric conversion process. Solar batteries can be used for a very long time. They can be used to operate space equipment on a space craft.

The first battery was developed by Count Alessandro Volta in the 1790's. It was called the voltaic cell. In 1836 John F. Daniell made a more advance primary cell. Gaston Plante' made the first secondary cell battery in 1856.

There are many different kinds of Alkaline, rechargeable, and heavy-duty batteries. The cost of all the kinds vary. The costs are listed on Chart A. As the chart shows, the rechargeable batteries cost the most and the heavy-duty costs the least.

Some of the good batteries you could look for when you go to the store are Duracell, Energizer, and Sears Die hard. Duracell and Energizer are good batteries but, they cost alot. Sears Die hard is a good battery and also has a good price. One of the batteries that is not good is Rayovac.

Batteries help us in lots of ways. They are still changing to meet our needs. People will always be trying to make a better battery.

Figure 9.9   *(continued)*

Cost	Alkaline	Rechargeable		Heavy-duty	
$4.00					
$3.50					
$3.00					
$2.50					
$2.00					
$1.50					
$1.00					
$0.50					
$0.00					
	Duracell	Radio Shack	GE Charge	Millenium	Evereacy	Sears

Cost of Batteries

CHART A

MATERIALS

1 piece of celery
1 piece of a carrot
1 potato
1 lemon
1 lime
galvanometer
12″ strip of copper
12″ strip of nickel

PROCEDURE

Stick the copper and the nickel into a piece of food. Let the copper and the nickel sit in the piece of food for one to two minutes. Use the galvanometer find the voltage. Record the results. Repeat this two or three times. Do the same to the other foods.

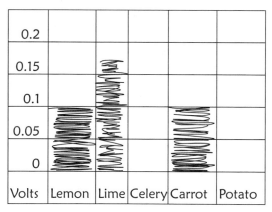

0.2					
0.15					
0.1					
0.05					
0					
Volts	Lemon	Lime	Celery	Carrot	Potato

Volts created by Foods

CHART B

RESULTS

The lime created the most volts. The lemon and the carrot had the second most volts. The potato and the celery created the least volts. Chart B shows the actual volts for each vegetable. I learned that electricity travels best through some kind of liquid.

Figure 9.9 *(continued)*

BIBLIOGRAPHY

Leon, de Lucenary, George, <u>The Electricity Story</u>, New York City, New York, Arco Publishing, 1983.

"Batteries: Disposable or Rechargeable", <u>Consumer Reports</u>, November 1991, pgs. 20-23.

"Battery", <u>McGraw Hill Encyclopedia of Science and Technology</u>, 1992 Edition, Vol. 2, pgs. 487-488.

"Battery", <u>Microsoft Encarta</u>, 1993, Microsoft Corporation.

"Battery", <u>World Book Encyclopedia</u>, 1992 Edition, Vol. 2, pgs. 168-171.

Figure 9.9   *(continued)*

---

3. Review the topic and the logical sequence of events with the entire class or group.

4. Have the children arrange the sentence strips in the correct order in a pocket chart or on the overhead if transparency strips are used.

5. Have the entire class or group read the paragraph together.

6. Have the children reorder the paragraph on their own and write it in paragraph form.

7. Have the students illustrate the details of the paragraph (Cudd & Roberts, 1989, p. 394).

$$\begin{array}{r}
282 \\
3\,\overline{)846} \\
6 \\
\hline
24 \\
24 \\
\hline
06 \\
6 \\
\hline
0
\end{array}$$

To divide in long division. First you take the 3 into the 8. It goes two times. Write the 2 above and multiply 2 times 3. Then you subtract 6 from 8 and get 2. Then you bring down the next number, a 4. You then take 3 into 24. It goes eight times. Write down 8 next to the 2 and multiply 8 times 3. You get 24. Then you subtract 24 from 24 and get 0. Bring down the 6 and divide 3 into 6. It goes two times. Write 2 next to the 8. Then subtract 6 from 6. You have nothing left. You can check the answer by multiplying 3 times 282. You get 846.

Figure 9.10   A fourth grader's description of steps in long division

Children recall in greater detail and completeness information that is presented with pictorial support. Therefore, having children illustrate their paragraphs and research reports is important to the students' comprehension of the topics covered.

Autobiographies

Autobiographical writing permits children to share their individual life experiences with others. Such writing helps the author gain new and often deeper perspectives on relationships and events.

An *autobiography* may describe one's entire lifetime, from birth to the present, or it may provide information only on selected portions of that lifetime, such as special events and remembrances. For children in kindergarten through the second or third grade, a modified autobiography, whereby a child may draw or write about likes and dislikes, may be more appropriate. A good book to share with children before they write such an autobiography is Susan Pearson's (1988) *My Favorite Time of Year.* Kelly, the young girl in the book, describes autumn as her favorite time of the year and then points out that each of the other seasons also holds some special joy for her and her family.

An appealing autobiography to share with second and third graders as well as upper-elementary special needs students is Tomie dePaola's (1999) *26 Fairmount Avenue.* In his short (57 pages) autobiography, Tomie dePaola describes his family and his early school experiences—sometimes humorous, sometimes sad. In turn, this presents young writers with ideas of how to share their own personal histories as they write their own autobiographies.

Typically, intermediate-grade children and middle schoolers find the writing of autobiographies to be quite appealing. By this age, they have read both biographies and autobiographies about famous people, and they have also had some practice in writing "About the Author" sections, short synopses in which they describe themselves on the jacket covers of their "published books." "The subject matter of autobiographies is ideal for middle school students, who are naturally inclined to write about topics that concern them and their place in the world. In addition to providing positive role models, this type of nonfiction gives students a powerful mechanism for self-reflection" (Gazin, 2000, p. 49). The teacher can also model autobiographical writing for this age group by reading a portion of a personal, self-written statement.

In particular, children are interested in learning about their favorite authors. *When I Was Your Age: Original Stories about Growing Up* (Ehrlich, 1996) is a collection of childhood memories by several popular children's authors. Both Lois Lowry and Jerry Spinelli have written their own autobiographies (see list below), something sure to please their adoring readers. Jean Fritz's (1982) *Homesick,* a book to which almost every child can relate, describes the emptiness of longing for the familiar surroundings of home, family, and friends. An unusual autobiography is Eloise Greenfield and Lessie Jones Little's (1979) *Childtimes: A Three Generation Memoir* in which a grandmother, mother, and daughter describe the events they experienced "growing up."

Below is a list of autobiographies. In the case of *I, Columbus* (Roop & Roop, 1990), the book is based upon Christopher Columbus's diary entries.

Angelou, M. (1993). *I know why the caged bird sings*. New York: Bantam. (Grades 7–8)

Appleman-Jurman, A. (1990). *Alicia, my story*. New York: Bantam. (Grades 7–8)

Bruchac, J. (1999). *Seeing the circle*. Albany, NY: Richard C. Owen. (Grades 3–5)

Keller, H. (1993). *Helen Keller, the story of my life*. New York: Watermill. (Grades 5–8)

Lowry, L. (1998). *Looking back*. Boston: Houghton Mifflin. (Grades 4–8)

Parks, R. (1997). *I am Rosa Parks*. New York: Penguin. (Grades 5–8)

Peet, B. (1989). *Bill Peet: An autobiography*. Boston: Houghton Mifflin. (Grades 2–5)

Roop, P., & Roop, C. (1990). *I, Columbus*. New York: Walker. (Grades 4–8)

Spinelli, J. (1998). *Knots in my yo-yo string*. New York: Knopf. (Grades 5–8)

Biographies

Biographies require children to conduct research before they write about a person's life. Although a biography need not cover an individual's entire life span, it should describe a selected portion of it. Children's literature provides a wealth of examples of biographies for students. David Adler and Jean Fritz are master biographers for primary- and intermediate-level students to read. Russell Freedman is a terrific biographer to serve as a model for middle school students. These authors combine exacting research findings with colorful language to weave stories about famous historical figures. Such qualities result in books that are highly motivating.

Beginning any composition is a challenge for all writers; however, initiating a biographical sketch can be especially difficult for children. Because children have problems establishing a frame of reference for a setting (both time and place), their biographies often fail to describe a distinct period and locale. As a result, it is not unusual for a child's biography about a historical figure or famous athlete to begin with "Once upon a time, there was a boy [girl] named. . . ." There exists a plethora of quality biographies within literature that can serve as models for more realistic depiction of characters and setting. An example of a book in which the opening sentences entice the reader to continue reading is Jean Fritz's (1973) *And Then What Happened, Paul Revere?* In this book, Fritz opens with a description of the setting, Boston, which becomes critical in considering the Revolutionary War.

In undertaking biographical sketches, children should become aware of significant factors in an individual's life, for such factors are necessary elements for biographies. When the student biographer knows the subject's interests and values, he or she should be encouraged to include these in the biography as well. Following are several biographies that serve as good models for grades 1–8.

Adler, D. A. (1989). *A picture book of Martin Luther King, Jr.* New York: Holiday. (Grades 1–4)

Adler, D. A. (1990). *A picture book of Thomas Jefferson.* New York: Holiday. (Grades 1–4)

Adler, D. A. (1996). *A picture book of Davy Crocket.* New York: Holiday. (Grades 1–4)

Adler, D. (2000). *America's champion swimmer: Gertrude Ederle.* New York: Gulliver. (Grades 1–3)

Adler, D. (2003). *Dwight David Eisenhower.* New York: Holiday House. (Grades 1–4)

Anderson, L. H. (2002). *Thank you, Sarah: The woman who saved Thanksgiving.* New York: Simon & Schuster. (Grades 2–4)

Cooney, B. (1996). *Eleanor.* New York: Viking. (Grades 3–6)

Freedman, R. (1987). *Lincoln: A photobiography.* Boston: Clarion. (Grades 4–8)

Freedman, R. (1992). *Franklin Delano Roosevelt.* Boston: Clarion. (Grades 4–8)

Freedman, R. (1996). *The life and death of Crazy Horse.* Boston: Clarion. (Grades 4–8)

Freedman, R. (1997). *Eleanor Roosevelt: A life of discovery.* Boston: Clarion. (Grades 5–8)

Freedman, R. (1999). *Babe Didrikson Zaharias.* Boston: Clarion. (Grades 6–8)

Fritz, J. (1973/1998). *And then what happened, Paul Revere?* (M. Tomes, Illus.). New York: Coward McCann. (Grades 2–5)

Fritz, J. (1975/1998). *Who's that stepping on Plymouth Rock?* (J. B. Handelsman, Illus.). New York: Coward McCann. (Grades 2–4)

Fritz, J. (1976/1996). *What's the big idea, Ben Franklin?* (M. Tomes, Illus.). New York: Coward McCann. (Grades 2–4)

Fritz, J. (1989). *The great little Madison.* New York: Putnam. (Grades 5–8)

Fritz, J. (1991). *Bully for you, Teddy Roosevelt.* New York: Putnam. (Grades 5–8)

Fritz, J. (1994). *Harriet Beecher Stowe and the Beecher Preachers.* New York: Putnam. (Grades 7–8)

Fritz, J. (1997). *Traitor: The case of Benedict Arnold.* New York: Paper Star. (Grades 5–8)

Fritz, J. (1999). *Why not, Lafayette?* (R. Himler, Illus.). New York: Putnam. (Grades 5–8)

Golenbock, P. (1990). *Teammates.* San Diego: Harcourt Brace. (Grades 3–5)

Hodges, M. (1997). *The true story of Johnny Appleseed.* New York: Holiday. (Grades 1–3)

Jakes, J. (1986). *Susanna of the Alamo.* San Diego: Harcourt Brace. (Grades 2–5)

Pinkney, A. (2002). *Ella Fitzgerald.* New York: Hyperion. (Grades 5–7)

Sis, P. (1991). *Follow the dream: The story of Christopher Columbus.* New York: Knopf. (Grades 1–4)

Stanley, D. (1992). *Bard of Avon: The story of William Shakespeare.* New York: Morrow. (Grades 5–8)

Stanley, D. (1996). *Leonardo da Vinci.* New York: Morrow. (Grades 5–8)

Stanley, D. (1998). *Joan of Arc.* New York: Morrow. (Grades 5–8)

Stanley, D. (1999). *Cleopatra.* New York: Morrow. (Grades 5–8)

Tames, R. (1989). *Anne Frank.* New York: Franklin Watts. (Grades 5–8)

Wallner, A. (1997). *Laura Ingalls Wilder.* New York: Holiday. (Grades 2–4)

Gathering Information: Note Taking

Children typically find note taking difficult because they lack the ability to be selective. Generally, youngsters are unable to distinguish between important information and that of little significance. When given proper instructions, however, children can become proficient note takers at a relatively early age. *The New York Public Library Kid's Guide to Research* (Heiligman, 1998) is a book worth having in every fourth- through eighth-grade classroom. A variety of tips are given specifically addressing a number of different kinds of research and where to locate information. A portion of the book is devoted to the Internet including not only how to retrieve information from the Internet but Internet safety—something teachers and parents need to be cognizant of.

One approach to the development of note-taking skills is teacher modeling, whereby students can actually see how important information is selected (see chapter 7). For example, with second or third graders, a teacher might choose a book about an animal to read to the class. Before proceeding with the book, however, the teacher writes four questions about the animal on the chalkboard: (1) What does it eat? (2) Where does it live? (3) What does it look like? (4) Are there any interesting facts about the animal? After sharing the book with the students, the teacher uses an overhead projector to show four boxes labeled "food," "habitat," "appearance," and "interesting facts." Next, the teacher writes information provided by the students about the animal in the appropriate box as shown in figure 9.11 (Farris, 1988). Finally, the teacher

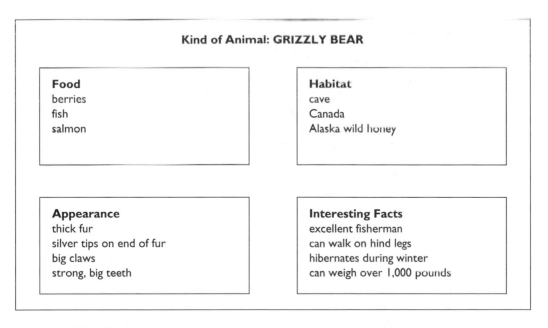

Figure 9.11   This represents the note-taking portion of a class-generated report on grizzly bears. The categories were put on an overhead transparency and filled in by the students.

uses the information the students have provided to write a report about the animal. For each of the four areas (food, habitat, appearance, and interesting facts), the teacher uses a separate sheet of paper and leaves enough space for an illustration. Figure 9.12 shows a sample report entitled "Grizzly Bears."

Following such teacher modeling, the class generates a list of what makes a good report. Sneed (2002) believes this step is important as is sharing copies of the books used to make the original class report. The list could look like the one below:

A good report on animals should tell:

1. What the animal looks like.

2. Where the animal lives.

3. What the animal's habitat looks like.

4. What the animal eats.

5. Interesting or unusual facts about the animal.

By generating a list, students are better able to take notes and then write their own animal reports. Each child selects an animal book from among those the teacher checked out of the library. The students are given about two days in which to read the books. By the third day, students are taking notes about the animal's food, habitat, appearance, and other interesting facts. On the fourth day, the students begin their first drafts by writing about and illustrating the food the animal eats. On the fifth, sixth, and seventh days, the students write about and illustrate the animal's habitat, the animal's appearance, and interesting facts about the animal, respectively. On the eighth and ninth days, the students revise their entire reports. On the tenth day, the authors recopy their writing and redraw their illustrations to produce their final products for publication and sharing with classmates (Farris, 1988).

This same note-taking approach can be used with children in the intermediate grades by increasing the sophistication of the task. By selecting narrower subject areas, students can gather information that will result in more specific, well-defined research topics. For example, a unit on World War II may yield term papers with various general themes: causes of the war, political leaders, generals, famous battles, the D-Day invasion of Normandy, types of weapons, and so forth. Any chosen theme may then be divided into more specific topics. For example, given the general theme of World War II political leaders, one student may wish to focus on Adolph Hitler's youth, work, rise to power, and death. Another student may choose to do the same with Franklin Roosevelt, a third with Winston Churchill, and a fourth with Joseph Stalin, and so on.

Intermediate-grade students can use different books and periodicals as references in gathering notes for their term papers. For each piece of information used, the student must record in the body of the term paper both the name of the author(s) and the publication date of the book from which the information came. The student must also include an alphabetical list of all references at the end of the paper. Each source entry must contain the author's name, date of publication, title of book, city of publication, and name of publisher.

TITLE: GRIZZLY BEARS
AUTHORS: Mrs. Carpenter's
                   Second Grade Class
ILLUSTRATOR: Mrs. Carpenter

FOOD
Grizzly bears eat fish and berries.
They especially like to eat salmon.
Wild honey is a special treat because
grizzly bears have a sweet tooth like
people do.

HABITAT
Grizzly bears live in Alaska and
Canada. They live in caves to keep
them warm in the winter and cool in
the summer.

APPEARANCE
They have huge claws and strong
teeth. Their fur is thick and has a
silver tip on the end of each hair.

INTERESTING FACTS
Grizzly bears are large. They weigh
over 1,000 pounds. They can stand
on their hind feet. Grizzly bears eat a
lot in the summer and fall so they can
hibernate in the winter.

Figure 9.12   This is the final draft of the report on grizzly bears as dictated to the teacher by the class.

Children can easily take notes on material presented in textbooks. The headings and subheadings of most textbooks serve as summaries for chapter sections and subsections. By using these headings and subheadings as note-taking categories, a student can jot down important phrases or sentences while simultaneously reading the material. Once a chapter is completed, the student can review the headings, subheadings, and notes and ultimately check for comprehension by answering any section- and chapter-end questions.

Persuasive Writing

For many students, persuasive writing is perhaps the most challenging genre of writing. Persuasive writing involves presenting ideas that motivate the reader to do something or believe something that the writer wants by first stating an opinion and then giving reasons for taking that position. The "reasons" should "persuade" the reader to agree with the writer. Elementary and middle school writers can generally grasp three persuasive techniques, or appeals, used in persuasive writing (and also in persuasive speaking). The most common is the appeal to reason, which requires that the writer support his argument with factual information; this is an appeal to the reader's intellect. The second technique that students may use in their writing is an appeal to character, which entails convincing the reader that the writer's ideas are credible and acceptable, for example they are noble or wise and have a positive effect on the greater good; they are not intended for the personal gratification of the writer. The last way to persuade is to appeal to emotions, to arouse the reader's fear, compassion, anger, or another emotion in order to convince the reader to accept or act on the ideas presented. Often political ads are based on an appeal to readers' emotions.

When second and third graders attempt persuasive writing, they sometimes drift away from their original position statements, often giving the opposite stance in their concluding statement. Hence, students at this level need to see models of a position statement followed by strong justification (see figure 8.2 on p. 310). Primary-grade students will enjoy writing persuasive letters after listening to Mark Teague's (2002) delightful *Dear Mrs. Teague: Letters from Obedience School.* After tolerating typical doggie mischief when her pet eats food intended for her own dinner and chews on clothing, Mrs. Teague ships her dog off to be properly trained at a well-known canine school, only to receive persuasive letters from her pooch begging to return home.

An activity to share with upper-elementary and middle school students deals with naming products. As a mini lesson, read aloud a book or a chapter from a novel about names. Some examples would be Gloria Houston's (1992) *My Great Aunt Arizona*, who got her name from her brother who sent a letter from the territory of Arizona where he was stationed as an Army cavalry soldier; the first chapter of *Because of Winn-Dixie* (DiCamillo, 2000), which describes how a mongrel dog was named for a grocery store chain; *My Name is Jorge, On Both Sides of the River* (Medina, 1999), the story of a young Hispanic boy who must learn to live in two different cultures; or *Locomotion* (Woodson, 2003), a book in prose that tells how an African American boy was named Lonnie Collins Motion (Lo Co Motion) after a dance described in a song ("Everybody's doing a brand new dance now. Come on baby, do the locomotion."). Talk about how people and pets get names—how the students each got their own name(s) or how they named pets they've owned. Then discuss how products are named (i.e., Nike was named after a mythical god after first being called the "Blue Shoe Company"; Toll House chocolate chips were named after the small wayside restaurant where chocolate chip cookies were first created). Next have the students create a product to sell and select a name for it. The students then write a persuasive paragraph about the product, accompanied by a poster to promote their product.

Technology and Writing

Recent advances in technology have provided students and teachers with access to a vast amount of information beyond that contained in books and periodicals on the library shelves. Some elementary schools, for example, have CD-ROM (compact disc-read only memory) and interactive video. CD-ROM is a slightly scaled down optical disc that can store a tremendous amount of information. The first type of compact disc was used to hold audio information, or music. Because the discs are touched by only a beam of light when being read, they are far more durable than traditional records. One CD-ROM disc has the capacity to store approximately 250,000 pages of text. Thus, its use permits access to a wealth of information. By having a CD-ROM disc that contains an encyclopedia, for example, and using a computer with a CD-ROM drive, a student can search and locate information in as little as two seconds. The use of CD-ROM and the Internet allows intermediate-grade students access not only to reference materials but to recently published materials as well.

Interactive video can be used at all grade levels, depending on the content and purpose of the video program. With interactive video, the teacher or a group leader may stop the video at any point to permit class discussion of the content. Students are able to further develop their knowledge, experiential background, and thinking skills when such technology is appropriately included as part of language arts instruction, especially in the area of writing.

Writing with a word processor involves the same steps as writing with pencil and paper: prewriting, writing, rewriting, and publishing. In bypassing the "traditional" writing implements, children are freed from the problem of illegible handwriting, and some are therefore better able to concentrate on the content of the piece (see figure 9.13 on p. 390). When an initial draft appears clean, without distracting marks and erasures, some children are motivated to write more. Similarly, revision is easier on a word processor than on a handwritten piece of work because the word processor enables a writer to revise text by inserting, deleting, rearranging, retrieving, and replacing words and even moving entire sentences and paragraphs around.

timmy d march 2

wus a pon a tom thar wuz

dinosr ho ludtoploa

gamz likmunoble

`(Timmy D. March 2`

`Once upon a time there was a`

`dinosaur who liked to play`

`games like Monopoly.)`

Figure 9.13   A 5-year-old's story written on a word processor

After learning basic keyboarding skills, many children find word processing to be a quicker writing method than using pencil and paper. As implied earlier, by removing the problems of handwriting, a word processor makes writing more enjoyable for some children; because they do not need to concentrate on forming legible letters, they are more free to write their thoughts and ideas. Once primary ideas are formulated and put into the computer, an author can easily remove unnecessary details, mechanical errors, and misspellings. In addition, the final product is more polished than a handwritten piece and looks like that of the professional author.

Word processing programs allow for a variety of student writing interactions. For instance, children may engage in cooperative story writing by pairing up with a classmate and actually composing a piece together at the keyboard. The pair may write notes or letters to each other, sharing a common "mailbox" or classroom bulletin board. A weekly class newspaper is yet another writing activity. By selecting an editor and a group of reporters each week, students can learn the various aspects and responsibilities of writing columns about classroom activities.

Several word processing programs have been developed for primary-level children and intermediate-level students. Middle school students can use adult-level software such as *Microsoft Word* and *Office 2003*. In addition, a variety of programs such as grammar and spelling checkers, thesaurus programs, and word counters are constantly being updated and new software products are becoming available almost weekly. A list of computer electronic software and programs for the classroom is offered in box 9.4.

9.4   The More You Know

Computer, Electronic, and Software Programs

Program	Title	Company
Bundled Software	*Microsoft Office 2003*	Microsoft
	Microsoft Word 2003	Microsoft
Desktop Publishing	*Pagemaker*	Adobe
	Publish It!	Microsoft
Digital Cameras	*Photo Smart*	Hewlett Packard
	Xap Shop	Canon
Drawing/Painting	*Kid Pix*	Broderbund
Graphics	*Printshop Deluxe*	Broderbund
Hypermedia	*HyperCard*	Apple
	HyperStudio	Roger Wagner
Keyboarding Instruction	*JumpStart Typing*	Knowledge Adventure
	Mavis Beacon Teaches Typing I	Mindscape
	Slam Dunk	The Learning Company
Presentation Software	*Kid Pix SlideShow*	Broderbund
	PowerPoint	Microsoft

Style checkers, which students can use to check for grammatical and punctuation errors, indicate awkward expressions, incorrect usages, and clichés. A few of these programs actually locate a specific error, thereby helping students identify areas in which they need further practice. Similarly, spelling checkers may be used to ensure correct spelling.

Advances in telecommunications can now enable a school in one state to communicate with a school thousands of miles away via classroom computers and the Internet. By means of such technology, information and ideas as well as school newspapers, class projects, and so on, can be exchanged quickly and efficiently.

Evaluating Student Writing

Evaluating the development of children's writing skills must be constant and ongoing. There are several different means of assessing children's writing, and they should be used in combination to give the truest picture of each child's writing development. As Valencia (1990, p. 339) writes, "No single test, single observation, or single piece of student work could possibly capture the authentic, continuous, multidimensional interactive requirement of sound assessment." Several different kinds of assessment measures, both formal and informal, are discussed here.

Portfolios

A *portfolio* is a "systematic and organized collection of evidence used by the teacher and student to monitor growth of the student's knowledge, skills, and attitudes in a specific subject area" (Varvus, 1990, p. 48). Teachers have discovered that portfolios better demonstrate a student's growth over time than do test scores.

In the elementary classroom, folders with pockets or expandable accordion files may serve as portfolios. The expandable accordion files allow for computer discs, cassette tapes, or even videotapes to be a part of the portfolio. For instance, a child may share a piece of work using the "Author's Chair" format and have it videotaped for future reference (Graves & Hansen, 1983). Other possibilities include audiotapes of choral reading of a poem that the students wrote together, a dramatic presentation of a play written by a group of students, or even a presentation put together by a student using a computer and hypercard technology. Portfolios allow for a wide variety of media to be used in the evaluation process, rather than only paper and pencil.

Some teachers prefer students to have a "working" portfolio for weekly work and a "showcase" portfolio that parents view and is kept as the "official" assessment instrument (Miller, 1995). Other teachers prefer to have a single portfolio for the language arts and one for each of the content areas. Because most of the writing in science and social studies tends to be expository, one could argue for a single portfolio for each student covering all of the content areas. How it is organized is up to the individual teacher, but what is most important is that portfolios with dated work are maintained for every class member. Ideally, with some supervision by the classroom teacher, the students themselves keep track of their work, date it, and deposit it in their portfolio.

For writing, the portfolio should include a variety of samples. Narrative, expository, and poetic writing should all be represented (Tierney et al., 1991). In addition, literature response journals, dialogue journals, academic learning logs, and writing about different literary components can all be a part of the student's portfolio. Notes written by the teacher during conferences should be dated and included in the portfolio as well. In addition, preliminary drafts of works can be dated, paper clipped together with the final copies, and deposited into the portfolio (Tompkins & Friend, 1988).

In order to maintain some organization within the portfolio itself, it is important to include a list of what it contains stapled directly to the inside cover of the portfolio. Box 9.5 contains an example of a "Portfolio Inventory Sheet" for fourth grade.

Other lists and checklists may also be included, such as an attitude survey, a personal interest inventory, and a reflective work habits survey. Because reading interests influence writing, a list of books read by the child should be kept, even those books merely attempted but not completed. Children's literature selections read as part of assigned reading should also be noted. Books that have been shared in class (i.e., read by the teacher) should be kept on a separate list.

9.5   In the Classroom: Teaching Hint

Portfolio Inventory Sheet

Name: _____

1. Cursive Handwriting Sample
   _____ Sept.   _____ Jan.
   _____ Oct.   _____ Feb.

2. Writing Samples
   _____ Narrative
   _____ Expository
        _____ Descriptive
        _____ Explanatory
   _____ Persuasive
   _____ Poetic

3. Journals
   _____ Dialogue
   _____ Literature Response

Checklists
_____ Reflective Work Habits Survey
_____ Personal Interests Survey
_____ Books Read for Class
_____ Books Read Independently
_____ Books Read for Literature Circle

4. Social Studies Informational Reports
   _____ Questioning Strategies
   _____ Research

5. Science Writing
   _____ Written "Observations"
   _____ Data Collection
   _____ Scientific Process Experiment

At least once a month, the student and the teacher can sit down together to review the contents of the portfolio and evaluate the student's progress. Because the student and the teacher work together in selecting the pieces of writing that are placed in the portfolio, student input is crucial (Cress & Farris, 1992). The student must formulate goals, evaluate strengths and weaknesses, and assess progress. For, as Lamme and Hysmith (1991) note, "If children are to become autonomous learners, they must learn to assess what they have learned and how they learn best" (p. 632). After conferencing with the teacher regarding the portfolio's contents, the student then must create new goals that are written down and stored in the portfolio until the next conference occurs.

Children should be encouraged to critique each selection when they add it to their portfolio. A 4" × 6" index card stapled to the top of each piece of writing can be used by the student to describe the value of the piece and indicate what writing skill was developed or enhanced. The teacher can jot down a reaction to the student's work, as well.

By collecting samples of work and then assessing them along with considering learning goals, portfolios can serve as a diagnostic-reflective evaluative measure (Courtney & Abodeeb, 1999). Such portfolios require the following:

- Diagnosis of the student's strengths and weaknesses in order to plan and guide literacy instruction
- Collection of student work by the student and teacher
- Sorting through the collection of sample work by the student
  Example:
  —Select two math papers that demonstrate you can write out the steps to solve a story problem.
  —Select an entry from your book log that best explains why you liked a book you read.
  —Select a piece of narrative writing that shows you know how to write dialogue.
- Goal setting by the student under the guidance of the teacher. The goals must be realistic and appropriate. The goals are established at the beginning of each grading period or term.
- Reflection and construction occurs with a teacher-student conference at the end of the grading period or term. The student reflects back on each piece of work in terms of what, why, and how learning has taken place.
- Sharing of the portfolios with parents and guardians three times a year. The student does the sharing/explaining of the portfolio at home after having practiced with a school mate in the classroom.

Diagnostic-reflective portfolios are useful during parent-teacher conferences. They are quite helpful for those students who have individualized educational plans (IEPs).

Responding to Children's Writing

Teachers must formally respond to children's writing efforts frequently, positively, and honestly so that students begin to recognize their individual strengths and weaknesses. In acknowledging a child's work, a teacher may want to respond either orally, as in a writing conference, or by way of a written note attached directly to the piece. When writing conferences are used, the evaluation process and response are simplified because the teacher is familiar with the piece and has observed its development throughout the writing process. Sometimes writing a note entails more time than a brief discussion with the child about the piece. Whichever method is used, the teacher must be aware that generalities do not help the child to grow as a writer; rather, direct, specific comments will guide the child in improvement and refinement of writing skills.

Positive responses should far outweigh negative comments about students' written work. If a teacher can highlight what students do correctly while pointing out two or three types of errors, children can direct their energies toward overcoming a small number of deficiencies instead of being overwhelmed by them.

Conferences are important. Here the teacher is questioning the student about the changes in her drafts of a writing task.

Anecdotal Records and Checklists

Informal evaluation techniques can be used effectively to note children's writing progress. The teacher may jot down information on a clipboard throughout the school day, filing the information in the appropriate student's writing folder at the end of the day. Checklists noting skills mastered and new skills being attempted are also effective and require little time to manage (see figure 9.14 on pp. 396–397). Besides keeping anecdotal records and checklists, photographs of accompanying projects may also be tucked into a child's portfolio (Fueyo, 1991).

Cambourne and Turbill (1990) recommend that teachers use a hardcover, three-ring binder to hold notes from student writing conferences; four pages should be allotted for each student. Notes from both formal (i.e., a statement made by a student during a regularly planned conference) and informal (e.g., a question asked by a student as the teacher moves around the room assisting students while they are writing) conferences should be placed in the notebook.

Students need to be aware of their own progress as writers. Cambourne and Turbill (1990) suggest that older students, those in the middle- and upper-elementary grades, keep their own "reflective journals." Students can use these to evaluate their own abilities in both reading and writing. When students can see for themselves what they can do well and what is, to them, a good piece of writing, they become better writers (see figure 9.15 on p. 398). At this point, real growth and learning occur at all levels of their writing.

Children need to question their writing as part of the editing process. The form in box 9.6 on p. 399 is appropriate for third through eighth graders to use for self-evaluation of their writing. Such use of checklists and self-questioning are important for writing growth.

Most school districts use rubrics for writing assessment. Examples of such rubrics were presented in chapter 1. Box 9.7 on p. 400 contains a rubric that a school district uses for fifth grade writing.

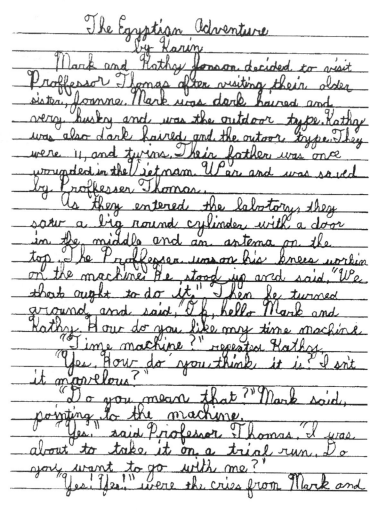

Figure 9.14   An example of a student's narrative writing and the accompanying teacher-student conference record

Kathy,
    "O.K. Get in!" said the proffesser as he was stepping inside.
    When Kathy and Mark got there, Professer Thomas said, "Where do you want to go?"
    "Ancient Egypt!" they chorused. So the proffesser turned a dilal and they heard a great roaring sound. Neat thing they knew they were on a camel headed for Cyro. Just when they were about to enter Cyro, three guards came up and one of them said, "You are strange people. We are going to take you to the Great Cleopatra." Then the other two gaurds said, "Hail Cleopatra! Hail!" Then the first gaurds said, "Didn't you hear them? Hail, boy huid."
    Then, Mark swiftly braugt out a little laser and turned it on. He said to the suprised gaurds, "This will hurt you if you don't let us go." While they were still suprised Mark, Kathy, and Proffessor Thomas leaped into the time machine and went back to the twentieth century.

Writing Conference Record

Name: _Karin G._   Grade: _5_

Date	Title of Place	Skills Used Properly	Skill Taught	Skills to be Attained
9/14	The Egyptian Adventure	Dialogue – began new paragraph with new speaker	Write out numbers less than 25 as word	Forming complex sentences versus compound sentences -Clauses
9/17	The Greatest Band	Transitional sentences to	Development of relative	Leave out unnecessary details

Figure 9.14   (continued)

Temptation

The sight of that long straight stretch of hallway seems to have a dire influence on our feet. It is not we who are racing pell-mell though the hall; we are just the unwary victims of exceptionally mischievous feet. They play dual roles. Usually they play the role of our friends, walking us quietly within the buildings. But at the sight of that long corridor they turn into rogues. With a dash and a slide they sail us trough the hall. We get blamed, we face the battle, they just dangle out of sight under our desks probably planing another hectic scramble from the room, a dash down the hall, and a leap through the door. And so goes the cycle of the normal child against the abnormal feet.

WRITING FORMATIVE EVALUATION FORM

Student: *David*   Grade: *6*

Date: *11-6*   Type of Writing: *Reflective*

Title: *Temptation (sp) = "Temptation"*

Comments: *Excellent vocabulary. Vivid images are created in this piece. Well organized. Parallel construction is good. Strong writing*

Strengths: *Vocabulary — dire, rogues, exceptionally, unwary, well developed*

Weaknesses: *Spelling, Paragraphing, Run-On Sentences*

Date: _____ Type of Writing: _____

Title: _____

Comments:

Strengths:

Weaknesses:

Date: _____ Type of Writing: _____

Title: _____

Comments:

Strengths:

Weaknesses:

Figure 9.15 A student's "reflective journal" entry and the teacher's feedback

Holistic Evaluation

To determine the writing skills of two or more classes of students at a particular grade level, *holistic evaluation* can be used as a quick, effective technique. Two or three teachers at the same grade level agree to work together to evaluate their students' writing. The teachers first decide on a topic and an appropriate writing time frame. By way of a trial session, the teachers themselves write about the topic in the specified amount of time. If they can address the topic adequately within the designated time period, they give the topic to the students. If, on the other hand, the topic proves to be too difficult or time-consuming, the teachers select another topic and repeat the pretesting.

All student papers are coded according to some preestablished numbering system; subsequently, 10 papers are randomly selected from the entire group. The teachers then read each of the papers and, using a 5-point rating scale

9.6   In the Classroom: Teaching Hint

Writing Self-Evaluation—grades 3–8

Name: _____   Date: _____

Writing Topic: _____

Poor	**Getting Better**	**Better**	**Pretty Good**	**Good**	**Great**
I	2	3	4	5	6

Focus—6 Points
Did you make your idea clear to the reader?
Did you stay on the subject from the beginning to end?
Is there a topic sentence that explains what the paragraph is about?
Did you react to the idea and tell how you felt?
Is there a closing sentence or end to the idea?

Support—6 Points
Did you give enough reasons or examples to prove your idea?
Did you explain the ideas with details so the reader really understands?

Organization—6 Points
Did you plan the writing so the reader does not get mixed up?
Are all your ideas written in the right order?

Conventions—6 Points
Did you:
   Use good English?
   Write good sentences?
   Spell all the commonly used words correctly?
   Spell the best you could on difficult words?
   Indent the beginning of the paragraph?
   Use capital letters and punctuation where they are needed?

Integration—6 Points
Is the paragraph interesting to the reader?
As a complete paragraph, will the reader feel this is well written?

Score
I received _____ out of a possible 30 points.

Developed by Dr. Elizabeth Taglieri, teacher, May Whitney Elementary, Lake Zurich, Illinois.

such as the one suggested in box 9.8 on p. 400, rate each paper according to the criteria listed.

Because a gestalt approach is used, the teacher should take no more than 1 minute per paper for analytic holistic evaluation. Once each of the 10 papers has been rated, the teachers compare their respective scores, which should differ by no more than 3 points for each writing sample. Any significant discrepancies pertaining to criteria should be discussed prior to the evaluation of the remaining papers. After all the student ratings have been tabulated, an average total score can be obtained for the entire group and for each individual class. The teachers may then elect to find the average score for each of the 10 crite-

9.7   In the Classroom: Teaching Hint

Rubric for Fifth Grade Writing

The piece is:

6 points   very focused
well organized
good transitions
has beginning, middle and end
well developed
variety of word use

5 points   focused
organized
some transitions
has beginning, middle and end
well developed
variety of word use

4 points   fairly focused
organized
weak transitions
has beginning, middle and end
developed somewhat
some variety of words used

3 points   somewhat focused
loosely organized
no transitions
has beginning, middle, and end
weak development
weak variety of word choice

2 points   weak focus
poorly organized
no transitions
has beginning and end
poorly developed
weak variety of word choice

1 point   no focus
poorly organized
no transitions
beginning but no real middle or ending
poorly developed
poor word choice

9.8   In the Classroom: Teaching Hint

Holistic Evaluation

	High		Average		Low
Content					
1. Quality of ideas	5	4	3	2	1
2. Organization of ideas	5	4	3	2	1
3. Word choice	5	4	3	2	1
4. Clarity	5	4	3	2	1
5. Support of ideas	5	4	3	2	1
Mechanics					
6. Capitalization	5	4	3	2	1
7. Grammar usage	5	4	3	2	1
8. Spelling	5	4	3	2	1
9. Punctuation	5	4	3	2	1
10. Handwriting	5	4	3	2	1

ria. Below-average scores on any individual criterion indicate the need for additional instruction. For instance, if students in one of the classes averaged 3.7 on organization but only 2.5 on paragraph structure, the teacher would be wise to devote additional class time to paragraph structure.

To be most effective, analytic holistic evaluation should be performed three times a year: September, January or February, and May. If the teachers remain consistent in their scoring methods, this scheme will provide them with information on how the classes are performing as a group over time, a type of summative evaluation. Whenever teachers undertake holistic evaluation, they should reread the original 10 papers and recheck the established criteria to ensure consistency in their ratings. Figure 9.16 is a child's writing sample for you to practice the analytic holistic evaluation process. Have a peer do the evaluation process with you before discussing your results.

The Blizzard

Oouullmm. . . ." Colleen yawned as she stretched and swung her feet out of bed.

She pulled a yellow jogging suit and flannel socks out of a drawer and sleepily trudged down the creaky stairs.

Her mother and Aunt Martha were seated at the breakfast table They looked up from their magazines when Colleen reached the ground floor

"You're late," Aunt Martha told her. "Its seven forty five. Get dressed and serve yourself some breakfast. Hurry or you'll be tardy for school!"

Colleen obediently changed from her sleepwear to her school clothes and tennis shoes. Then she seated herself at the breakfast table and ate a bowl of cereal.

The bitter cold Canadian wind whipped harshly at the small country cottage. Sleet pelted against the windows and banged on the roof.

Colleen quickly put on her warm winter coat, slipped her boots over her shoes, wrapped a scarf tightly around her face, and tugged on a pair of mittens.

"Be careful on your way to class. Its terrible weather out there, "Mrs. Jakllnn warned.

"I will, mom," Colleen answered. "Don't worry."

Colleen arrived at school out of breath and freezing cold from the wind but she was all right.

The morning passed slowly from subject to subject until noon when the lunch bell rang.

Colleen was the only one who lived out of the small village of Carterville except for Zachery Molston, who was home sick with the flu.

Colleen looked out the window as she went to get coat and boots. The snow was about two feet deep and was still falling heavily!

There were many shouts as the children exited the school A lot of them hung around and played with each other in the snow But Colleen hurried to get on her way. She was a little worried. It was over three miles to her house and in this weather she didn't know if she would get home in time for lunch.

She trudged through the heavy snow with great effort.

continued

Figure 9.16 Writing sample for a holistic evaluation

One mile from the school Colleen reached the Nelson store She just had to stop in to take a rest and warm up She found a nickel in her coat pocket and bought a cup of hot chocolate. She quickly gulped it down and put on all of the winter gear she was taken off to get comfortable Mr. Nelson had asked if Colleen had wanted to stay awhile but she had insisted she had better be on her way

The snow was being whipped around and was much deeper. It got harder and harder to walk. By the time Colleen reached the abandoned barn which was the half-way mark she could barely walk. But she plodded on. Her legs were becoming stiff and her face was numb and frost bitten. Finally she couldn't go any further. Colleen wished she had stayed at the Nelson store where it was warm and dry There she could stay until the wind died down. Her whole body shook violently. Her head whirled and her vision was going . . .

The children back at the Carterville school had already begun class, but no one noticed that Colleen was missing.

"About one o'clock Colleen's mother called the school to see why Colleen hadn't come home for lunch. Mrs. Archer the secretary, had said Colleen didn't come back to school when she left for home.

Aunt Martha called the police. They told her they would ride to the school and then to their house on horseback.

No one knew anything at the school, but when they rode further up towards the Jaklinn's house, about a mile away they found Colleen She lay pale and unconcious in cold Canadian snow.

The police quickly unmounted and set Colleen on one of the horses rumps. They rode back to the school. Then the police called Mrs. Jaklinn and Aunt Martha to tell them what happened and to come quickly, just after they called the hospital.

First the ambulance came. It was a large horsedrawn wagon. A couple of nurses hoisted Colleen up onto the cart and wrapped her in many blankets. Next Mrs. Jaklinn and Aunt Martha arrived on horseback. They were ordered to follow the ambulance to the hospital.

The ambulance drove up to the emergency entrance. A doctor rushed out of the building followed by two men carrying a stretcher. They laid Colleen on it and hurried away back into the hospital.

When Colleen's mother and aunt arrived, Colleen was gaining conciousness in a second floor hospital room. Four policemen were there, and a doctor to make sure she recovered all right.

"Oh, Honey!" Mrs. Jaklinn cried. "I'm so relieved you're all right!" and she kissed Colleen's forehead.

"Just no school for a week and hot tea everyday for one month," the doctor said. "I'll also give you a medication."

Colleen recovered just fine. Soon she was up and healthy. But she decided from then on to ride horseback to school winter day.

Figure 9.16   *(continued)*

Summary

Writing can be personal, practical, or both. Through writing, students can enhance and develop their thinking skills. Writers can gain knowledge and understanding as well as new insights into personal opinions, beliefs, and interests.

To evaluate student writing effectively, teachers must be both objective and compassionate. Portfolios offer an insightful approach to evaluation because they allow teachers to note growth over a period of time. Constructive criticism by both the teacher and a student's peers ought to be genuine and include positive statements about the writing. Only one or two major faults should be highlighted at a time so that young writers can focus simultaneously on correcting their errors and developing their writing skills. Holistic evaluation can aid in determining an entire class's strengths and weaknesses in their writing.

Questions

1. In what ways does writing enhance a child's learning?
2. Why does personal writing tend to be more motivational than practical writing?
3. How can journal writing benefit children?
4. What are the advantages and disadvantages of using word processing with elementary level students?
5. Why should teachers adopt an ongoing process for evaluating writing?

Reflective Teaching

Flip back to the beginning of the chapter to the teaching vignette entitled "Peering into the Classroom." After rereading the vignette, consider the following questions: What characteristics (either implied or directly exhibited) does the teacher possess that you would like to develop? What strengths and weaknesses are revealed for the students described in this section? How would you meet the needs of students such as these?

Activities

1. Apply the analytic holistic evaluation criteria to the piece in figure 9.16.
2. Develop a set of criteria for evaluating students' writing at a particular grade level.
3. Keep an academic learning log for one of your classes. In addition, keep a journal for jotting down thoughts about everyday occurrences. After a month has passed, reread your writing in both notebooks and make a list of observations about your learning and personal feelings that emerged from these two types of writing.
4. Prepare a poetry writing lesson in which a poem that you have written is used as an example.
5. Write a three- or four-page autobiographical sketch about an elementary school experience.
6. For two weeks, keep daily lists of things to do. Then determine whether you were more efficient as a result of this form of practical writing.

Further Reading

Button, K., Johnson, M. J., & Furgerson, P. (1996). Interactive writing in a primary classroom. *The Reading Teacher, 49* (6), 446–455.

Cudd, E. T., & Roberts, L. (1989). Using writing to enhance content area learning in the primary grades. *The Reading Teacher, 42* (4), 392–405.

Harvey, S. (2002). Nonfiction inquiry: Using real reading and writing to explore the world. *Language Arts, 80* (19), 12–22.

Heffernan, L. (2004). *Critical literacy and writer's workshop: Bringing purpose and passion to student writing*. Newark, DE: International Reading.

Hubbard, R. & Shorey, V. (2003). Worlds beneath the words: Writing workshop with second language learners. *Language Arts, 81* (1), 52–61.

Parsons, L. (2001). *Response journals revisited: Maximizing learning through reading, writing, viewing, discussing, and thinking*. Portland, ME: Stenhouse.

Richgels, D. (2003). Writing instruction. *The Reading Teacher, 56* (4), 364–368.

Sneed, T. (2002). *Is that a fact? Teaching nonfiction writing, K–3*. Portland, ME: Stenhouse.

References

Abel, J. P., & Abel, F. J. (1988). Writing in the mathematics classroom. *Clearing House, 62* (4), 155–158.

Boyer, E. (1983). *High school: A report of the Carnegie Foundation for the Advancement of Teaching*. New York: Harper & Row.

Brady, R. (1991). A close look at student problem solving and the teaching of mathematics: Predicaments and possibilities. *School Science and Mathematics, 91* (4), 144–151.

Cambourne, B., & Turbill, J. (1990). Assessment in whole-language classrooms: Theory into practice. *Elementary School Journal, 90* (3), 337–347.

Courtney, A. M., & Abodeeb, T. L. (1999). Diagnostic-reflective Portfolios. *The Reading Teacher, 52* (7), 708–714.

Cress, E. & Farris, P. J. (1992). An assessment alternative: The portfolio approach. *Florida Reading Quarterly, 284* (4), 11–15.

Cudd, E. T., & Roberts, L. (1989). Using writing to enhance content area learning in the primary grades. *The Reading Teacher, 42* (6), 392–404.

Cullinan, B., Scala, M. C., & Schroder, V. C. (1995). *Three voices: An invitation to poetry across the curriculum*. York, ME: Stenhouse.

Denman, G. A. (1988). *When you've made it your own: Teaching poetry to young people*. Portsmouth, NH: Heinemann.

Farris, P. J. (1988). Developing research writing skills in elementary students. *Florida Reading Quarterly, 25*, 6–9.

Farris, P. J. (1989). Storytime and story journals: Linking literature and writing. *New Advocate, 2*, 179–185.

Fletcher, R. (2002). *Poetry matters*. New York: HarperCollins.

Fueyo, J. A. (1991). Reading "literate sensibilities": Resisting a verbocentric writing classroom. *Language Arts, 68* (8), 641–649.

Gazin, A. (2000). Focus on autobiography. *Scholastic Instructor, 109* (5), 49–50.

Graves, D., & Hansen, J. (1983). The author's chair. *Language Arts, 60* (2), 176–183.

Hand, B., & Treagust, D. F. (1991). Student achievement and science curriculum development using a constructive framework. *School Science and Mathematics, 91* (4), 172–176.

Heard, G. (1998). *Awakening the heart: Exploring poetry in elementary and middle school.* Portsmouth, NH: Heinemann.

Janeczko, P. (1999). *How to write poetry.* New York: Scholastic.

Janeczko, P. (2002). *Seeing the blue between: Advice and inspiration for young poets.* Cambridge, MA: Candlewick.

King, W. (1997). Stealing a piece of the world and hiding it in words. *Voices in the middle, 4* (1), 22–29.

Kormanski, L. M. (1992). Using poetry in the intermediate grades. *Reading Horizons, 32* (3), 184–190.

Lamme, L. L., & Hysmith, C. (1991). One school's adventure into portfolio assessment. *Language Arts, 68* (8), 629–639.

Livingston, M. C. (1991). *Poem-making: Ways to begin writing poetry.* New York: Harper-Collins.

Many, J. E. (1992). Living through literacy experiences versus literary analysis: Examining stance in children's literature. *Reading Horizons, 32* (3), 169–183.

McClure, A. A. (1995). Fostering talk about poetry. In N. L. Roser & M. A. Martinez (Eds.), *Book talk and beyond.* Newark, DE: International Reading Association.

Miller, W. (1995). *Authentic assessment in reading and writing.* Englewood Cliffs, NJ: Prentice Hall. 305–306

Newman, J. (1983). On becoming a writer. *Language Arts, 60* (1), 860–870.

Perfect, K. A. (1999). Rhyme and season: Poetry for the heart and head. *The Reading Teacher, 52* (7), 728–737.

Sneed, T. (2002). *Is that a fact? Teaching nonfiction writing, K-3.* Portland, ME: Stenhouse.

Stewig, J. W. (1988). *Children and literature.* Boston: Houghton Mifflin.

Tierney, R. J., Carter, M. A., & Desai, L. E. (1991). *Portfolio assessment in the reading-writing classroom.* Norwood, MA: Christopher-Gordon.

Tompkins, G. E., & Friend, M. (1988). After your students write: What's next? *Teaching Exceptional Children, 20,* 4–9.

Valencia, S. (1990). A portfolio approach to classroom assessment: The whys, whats, and hows. *The Reading Teacher, 43* (4), 338–340.

Varvus, L. (1990). Put portfolios to the test. *Instructor, 100* (1), 48–53.

Children's Literature

Cleary, B. (1983). *Dear Mr. Henshaw.* New York: Morrow.

Cleary, B. (1991). *Strider.* New York: Morrow.

dePaola, T. (1999). *26 Fairmount Avenue.* New York: Putnam.

DiCamillo, K (2000). *Because of Winn-Dixie.* Cambridge, MA: Candlewick.

Duke, K. (1992). *Aunt Isabel tells a good one.* New York: Penguin.

Ehrlich, A. (1996). *When I was your age: Original stories about growing up.* Boston: Candlewick.

Fritz, J. (1973). *And then what happened, Paul Revere?* New York: Coward, McCann.

Fritz, J. (1982). *Homesick.* New York: Dell.

Greenfield, E., & Little, L. J. (1979). *Childtimes: A three-generation memoir.* New York: Crowell.

Heiligman, D. (1998). *The New York Public Library kid's guide to research.* New York: Scholastic.

Houston, G. (1992). *My great aunt Arizona* (S. C. Lamb, Illus.). Boston: Houghton Mifflin.

Kellogg, S. (1971). *Can I keep him?* New York: Dial.

Medina, J. (1999). *My name is Jorge, on both sides of the river* (F. Vandenbrock, Illus.). Honesdale, PA: Boyds Mills Press.

Nixon, J. L. (1988). *If you were a writer* (B. Degen, Illus.). New York: Four Winds.

Pearson, S. (1988). *My favorite time of year.* New York: Harper & Row.

Prelutsky, J. (1984). *The new kid on the block* (J. Stevenson, Illus.). New York: Greenwillow.

Prelutsky, J. (1990). *Something big has been here* (J. Stevenson, Illus.). New York: Greenwillow.

Prelutsky, J. (1996). *Monday's troll* (P. Sis, Illus.). New York: Morrow.

Rylant, C. (1985). *The relatives came* (S. Gambell, Illus.). New York: Bradbury.

Selway, M. (1992). *Don't forget to write.* Nashville, TN: Ideals.

Silverstein, S. (1974). *Where the sidewalk ends.* New York: HarperCollins.

Silverstein, S. (1981). *A light in the attic.* New York: HarperCollins.

Stevenson, J. (1995). *Sweet corn.* New York: Greenwillow.

Walton, R. (1995). *What to do when a bug climbs in your mouth* (N. Carlson, Illus.). New York: Lothrop, Lee, & Shepard.

Woodson, J. (2003). *Locomotion.* New York: Putnam.

Grammar

> Grammar is at once the most controversial of the aspects of the language arts and the least understood.
>
> —Barbara Stoodt
> *Teaching Language Arts*

PEERING INTO THE CLASSROOM
TEACHING GRAMMAR TO FIRST AND SECOND GRADERS

Second-grade teacher Kyra Fetchina (Hinchey et al. 1999), working with two other primary-grade teachers and a professor from Pennsylvania State University, kept track of the type of writing lessons she taught to her charges during a 28-day period. Kyra averaged teaching a grammatical lesson each day. During the 28 days, Kyra taught 17 different skills, primarily at the second-grade level or above. These included lessons on pronouns, plurals, inflectional endings, and possessives.

Whenever the opportunity arises Kyra likes to take advantage of "teachable moments," that is, teaching skills spontaneously as students ask questions or as errors occur. Kyra has found that some of the books used in her school district's curriculum give her solid ways to introduce skills. For instance, *Over in the Meadow* (Langstaff & Rojankovsky, 1989) demonstrates how to use quotation marks when a character is speaking. *When I Was Young in the Mountains* (Rylant, 1992) is written in first person, thus giving the opportunity to introduce first person as a writer's voice to her second graders. *The Nap-*

ping House (Wood, 1984) is useful when she has her students look up synonyms in a primary-level thesaurus.

Down the hall, Kyra's colleague Sally also introduces her first graders to language and usage skills via children's literature. Sally uses *Have You Seen My Cat?* (Carle, 1988) to point out the purpose of quotation marks. *City Cats, Country Cats* (Hazen, 1969) provides the opening to talking about antonyms. Possessives are a natural extension discussion upon sharing the book *Cookie's Week* (Ward, 1988).

By seeing grammar and usage in action in books they enjoy, students develop a better understanding of their purposes. Use of quality literature as model writing helps children adopt correct usage in their own writing and speaking—and makes teaching much easier.

Chapter Objectives

The reader will:

✓ understand the difference between grammar and usage.

✓ understand the historically different ways of teaching grammar and usage.

✓ be aware of methods of teaching grammar.

Standards for Professionals

The following Standards will be addressed in this chapter:

Standard 1: Foundational Knowledge and Dispositions

1.1 Demonstrate knowledge of psychological, sociological, and linguistic foundations of reading and writing processes and instruction.

1.3 Demonstrate knowledge of language development and reading acquisition and variations related to cultural and linguistic diversity.

Standard 2: Instructional Strategies and Curriculum Materials

2.3 Use a wide range of curriculum materials in effective reading instruction for learners at different stages of reading and writing development and from differing cultural and linguistic backgrounds.

Standard 3: Assessment, Diagnosis, and Evaluation

3.1 Use a wide range of assessment tools and practices that range from individual and group standardized tests to individual and group informal classroom assessment strategies, including technology-based assessment tools.

3.3 Use assessment information to plan, evaluate, and revise effective instruction that meets the needs of all students, including those at different developmental stages and those from differing cultural and linguistic backgrounds.

Standard 4: Creating a Literate Environment

4.1 Use students' interests, reading abilities, and backgrounds as foundations for the reading and writing program.

4.2 Use a large supply of books, technology-based information, and nonprint materials representing multiple levels, broad interests, and cultural and linguistic backgrounds.

4.3 Model reading and writing enthusiastically as valued lifelong activities.

Introduction

Grammar is an integral part of language. Preschoolers use grammar without knowing, let alone understanding, the rules that accompany it, just as they run, breathe, or toss a ball without understanding the processes that make such physiological functions possible. Children in the primary grades continue to speak and write without having been formally exposed to the nuances of grammar.

Grammar is the structure of a language. Thus, every language has a grammar. English, Spanish, Cantonese, Swahili, and Cherokee all have their own grammar as do all other languages on our planet. In short, grammar is the rules of word and sentence formation. Usage is often confused with grammar. Usage refers to the selection of the appropriate word in a sentence as dictated by society. The distinction between grammar and usage has best been defined as follows: "Grammar is the rationale of language; usage is its etiquette" (Fraser & Hodson, 1978, p. 52). In other words, grammar refers to the rules of language and usage is the preferred word choice or use by society.

Teachers must keep in mind that grammar and punctuation, like spelling, are writing conventions. They fail to enhance the meaning of the piece of writing; rather, they help the reader to better understand what the writer is saying (Graves, 1995). For instance, when a writer begins a sentence with a capital letter, practices subject-verb agreement, includes an apostrophe in a contraction such as can't, uses commas to separate a series of items, and places a period at the end of a sentence, he is using writing conventions.

By gaining familiarity with grammar, a child discovers how to speak and write more effectively, efficiently, and precisely. The child learns to use conventions through trial and error as well as discovery until she can apply such conventions naturally in speaking and writing. Such knowledge results in the child's becoming a more confident speaker and writer. Experimenting with words, something preschoolers do naturally, is often curtailed during the elementary school years but resurfaces as children discover the wide variety of language possibilities. However, to understand the rules of grammar, a child must be able to think in abstract terms. Most children fail to possess this cognitive skill until age 11 or 12, or even later. Donovan (1990) believes that forcing abstract concepts on youngsters before they are ready may result in their disinterest in language study. As a result, they may be reluctant to write or engage in public speaking activities. McCraig (1977, pp. 50–51) suggests the following:

> By literal count, good sixth grade writing may have more errors per word than good third grade writing. In a Piagetian sense, children do not master things for once and for all. A child who may appear to have mastered sen-

tence sense in the fourth grade may suddenly begin making what adults call sentence errors all over again as he attempts to accommodate his knowledge of sentences to more complicated constructions.

Research findings also point out that grammar should not be taught in the artificial world of English grammar exercises but in the context of speaking and writing, which take place daily in the classroom. It is best to teach grammar or punctuation conventions in a mini lesson, one at a time, thus reducing possible confusion. Children should be informed a few days in advance of a mini lesson so they can begin practicing the convention in their own writing.

This chapter discusses the various systems of grammar and the importance of teaching grammar in a relevant manner at an appropriate time as children develop their cognitive skills. Suggestions are also made for assisting students in refining their grammar skills. Teaching the conventions of language becomes not less but more difficult as children progress through the grades, because their thought processes become increasingly more complex.

Standard and Non-Standard English

Standard English is the most widely accepted, or preferred, use of the English language. Geographic, ethnic, and socioeconomic distinctions do not exist in Standard English; to some, this implies elitism.

In many communities, children hear non-Standard English in the home and neighborhood, and they hear Standard English in the classroom and at church. According to Smith (1988a, p. 20),

> Every child learns a very specialized grammar. Children may not learn to talk the way their schoolteachers talk, but they do not see themselves as teachers. Children learn to talk like the people they see themselves as being. They learn to talk the way their friends talk.

In recent years, some media personalities have become more relaxed in the use of Standard English—except in newscasts and documentaries, both of which are rarely viewed by children. When surrounded by adults and peers who speak non-Standard English, children often find it difficult to distinguish between what is and is not "correct."

Systems of Grammar

Grammar consists of basic patterns or rules of a language. In essence, *grammar* is a theory that, when applied, explains the natural knowledge of a language that is possessed by every native speaker of the language (Dale, 1976). The rules of grammar dictate whether a group of words constitutes a viable sentence or is merely a collection of words.

Different grammatical systems have been devised to classify or categorize the workings of the English language. Traditional, structural, and transformational generative grammars influenced the way grammar was taught in elementary and secondary schools in the twentieth century. Today traditional grammar reigns in classrooms. Using computer technology, researchers continue to search for a universal grammar that can be applied to all languages.

Traditional Grammar

During the eighteenth century, most teachers taught traditional grammar. *Traditional grammar* is Latin based; that is, its precise rules are derived from Latin, a language Priestly and Lowth, prominent grammarians of the nineteenth century, considered to be perfect. As such, traditional grammar is prescriptive in nature.

From traditional grammar came the parts of speech: nouns, pronouns, verbs, adverbs, adjectives, conjunctions, prepositions, articles, and interjections. Sentences are classified as simple, compound, complex, and compound/complex. Sentence types are also defined by traditional grammar as declarative, interrogative, imperative, and exclamatory. These terms are still used today in elementary- and secondary-level English grammar textbooks. Basic sentence patterns are:

Pattern	Example
N-V	Puppies bark.
N-V-N	The puppy searched the house.
N-LV-N	Puppies are pets.
N-LV-Adj	Puppies are loyal.
N-V-N-N	Puppies give owners pleasure.

Most of traditional grammar textbooks also contain "cookbook" exercises that require students to identify the parts of speech. The word "cookbook" is used to refer to these exercises because every exercise is based on a sentence that has been carefully crafted in terms of the rules of grammar—in effect, a recipe of sorts. A similar concept, sentence diagramming, evolved from parsing, an eighteenth-century method of showing the relationship of words in a sentence. Such diagramming transformed grammar from the abstract to the concrete.

Unfortunately, children perceive traditional grammar that has been taught in the form of textbook exercises as having little to do with grammar in their own writing. Meyer, Youga, and Flint-Ferguson (1990, p. 66) believe, as a result, that "traditional grammar instruction is bound to fail because it is given without any realistic context."

Structural Grammar

Unlike traditional grammar, which is prescriptive, *structural grammar* is descriptive. Propounded by Leonard Bloomfield, a prominent linguist of the early 1900s, structural grammar attempts to separate the study of syntax (structure) from the study of semantics (meaning). Rather than classifying words according to their meaning (for example, a noun is a person, place, or thing) as is done in traditional grammar, in structural grammar, words are classified according to their use or function. As a result, the term *slotting,* which refers to the "slot" or function of a word in a particular sentence, evolved. For instance, consider the following sentence:

_____ car is red with black seats.

Only a possessive noun or pronoun will correctly complete the sentence, or fill the slot. Now consider another sentence:

Tobblin is blit.

By replacing *Tobblin* with a slot, other words may be inserted. Adjectives, adverbs, and verbs are inappropriate; only a noun or pronoun is appropriate. By replacing *blit* with a slot and inserting other words, children will eventually discover that only an adjective, or descriptive word, fits. Such experimentation with words assists students in understanding the parts of speech.

Transformational Generative Grammar

Transformational generative grammar incorporates both syntax and semantics, or surface and deep structure. Transformational generative grammar is based chiefly on the work of one man, Noam Chomsky, and his research in the late 1950s and early 1960s. Like traditional grammar, transformational generative grammar has exact, precise rules. The basic theory behind transformational generative grammar is that a kernel sentence (a simple declarative sentence) can be transformed to generate new sentences.

Chomsky's work with surface and deep structure suggests that a sentence may have an underlying meaning. For instance, consider this sentence:

Visiting relatives can be fun.

In first reading the sentence, the reader may interpret the writer's words as meaning conversing with relatives in their homes is enjoyable. Careful analysis, however, may yield entirely different interpretations—that conversing with relatives is rarely an enjoyable experience or that relatives who appear at the writer's doorstep can be enjoyable. The actual intent of a sentence is easier to determine when it is spoken because the listener hears the speaker's intonation. A reader, however, must consider information that surrounds the sentence.

As defined by the rules of transformational generative grammar, kernel sentences can be expanded and combined. Research by Mellon (1969), Hunt and O'Donnell (1970), and O'Hare (1971) indicates that practice in combining sentences enables students to improve their own writing. Thus, rather than producing short, choppy sentences, students are able to write longer sentences, each of which conveys more meaning.

Children are first exposed to sentence combining in kindergarten as part of classroom oral language activities. A child is told to combine two short sentences into one sentence—for instance, to combine the first two sentences below:

The bike is red.
The bike has stripes.
Combined sentence:
The red bike has stripes.
or
The bike is red and has stripes.

As students progress through elementary school, sentence combining becomes more complex. By using examples from children's literature, students can gain insight into the effects of different sentences.

A long compound and/or complex sentence can be meaningful; a simple sentence or a short compound or complex sentence can also be powerful. Children should be encouraged to rewrite an author's original sentences, using adjectives and adverbs to expand sentences and conjunctions to combine two or more sentences. For example, consider the sentence "Puppies bark." The list below provides examples of how this kernel sentence (noun phrase + verb phrase) can be transformed.

Simple Transformation	Example
Negation	Puppies don't chase cars.
Yes/no question	Do puppies chase cars?
Wh-question	Why do puppies chase cars?
Imperative	Chase cars, puppies!
There	There are puppies who chase cars.
Passive	The cars were chased by the puppies.

Grammar Instruction

As mentioned earlier, children should not be expected to learn grammar by completing exercises in English grammar textbooks. Research studies conducted over the last 40 years have failed to support the benefit of such activities in developing grammatical skills. As Smith (1988b, p. 18) writes, "Punctuation, capitalization and other 'rules' of grammar are essentially circular and meaningless to anyone who cannot already do what is being 'explained.'" Yet children *do* need to become familiar with grammar; they need to know what a noun, pronoun, and verb are and how to use each effectively to refine and improve their speaking and writing.

For many children—and adults—a lack of knowledge of grammar can result in personal embarrassment. For instance, after Larry Bird, the basketball superstar, graduated from Indiana State University, he confided to his mother that he had been uneasy about his lack of preparation in grammar when he entered college. "I didn't know a noun from a pronoun. I was ashamed" (Levine, 1988, p. 177).

In introducing students to grammar, teachers should remember that grammar is a convention of writing and thus a sensitive area of study. Children, like adults, are typically uneasy when placed in a position in which they lack confidence and with which they have little familiarity. It is far more effective to have students start with an analysis of sentences selected from children's literature than from their own writings, which may reflect their own shortcomings.

As mentioned in the introduction, grammar is best taught in short mini lessons. If students are given three to four days notice prior to a mini lesson on a particular grammar convention, they will have had an opportunity not only to experiment with that convention in their own writing but also to find examples of it in their reading of children's literature. By encouraging students to bring such examples to the mini lesson, they will be more eager to engage in the mini lesson. Furthermore, the examples provided by the students will give the teacher some insight as to the level of understanding of that particular convention each child possesses. Graves (1995, p. 41) suggests it is best to "keep the tone of each mini lesson as one of discovery, rather than of preoccupation with accurate use of the convention."

After a mini lesson, a wall chart or handout can be made as a reference for the students. In addition, children can keep their own record of their use of writing conventions in grammar, punctuation, and spelling as shown in box 10.1.

Another effective approach to the teaching of grammar includes the following five steps:

1. Introduce children to passages from children's literature.
2. Present passages from the classroom teacher's own writings.
3. Present passages from an anonymous child at the same grade level.
4. Present passages from a self-confident student in the class.
5. Present passages from all students in the class on a regular basis.

Such a succession of selections ensures that students will not lose confidence in their own abilities. Ironically, it is usually not the students but the classroom teacher who becomes the most anxious in the sharing and analyzing of one's own writing.

Three great sources of grammar, punctuation, and word selection mini lessons are *A Fresh Approach to Teaching Punctuation* (Angelillo, 2002), *The Revision Toolbox* (Heard, 2002), and *Reviser's Toolbox* (Lane, 1999). These books provide numerous practical mini lessons that break down the complexity of writing so that elementary and middle school students can gain revision skills.

10.1   In the Classroom: Teaching Hint

My Grammar Conventions

Date	Convention	Writing Piece	First Time Used	Usually Accurate
9/27	+es—to make plural (tomatoes)	Joe's Lunchbox	x	
9/27	Caps. Name of People	Joe's Lunchbox		x
9/27	Period at end of sentence	Joe's Lunchbox		x
9/27	subject/verb agreement—"was," "were"	Joe's Lunchbox		x
9/29	comma in series	The Last Soccer Game	x	

Teaching Punctuation

The first convention of grammar that children understand is punctuation, because punctuation is noticeable in both oral and written language. For instance, in revising a piece of writing, children are able to determine where to insert a period by noticing where a pause occurs when the piece is read aloud. When a first grader is asked where a period goes, she will probably say, "At the end of the line." Because first graders' sentences are usually short, a period usually does go at the end of the line in most of their writings. According to Ronald Cramer (2003, p. 477), "If children write three or more hours per week and if punctuation and capitalization are taught through modeling, revision, and mini-lessons with the context of writing, significant progress can be made, though progress varies widely from child to child. Punctuation clarifies writing, and this is an important concept for children."

Periods, Question Marks, and Exclamation Points

Periods, question marks, exclamation points, apostrophes, commas, and quotation marks are the essential punctuation marks with which primary-grade students need to be familiar. Periods are used at the ends of sentences that make a statement or express a command, after abbreviations, and after initials in proper names. Question marks are used at the ends of sentences that ask a question. For the reader, a question mark signifies that the voice is to be raised for the last word. Like question marks, exclamation points signify a change of voice for the final word, in this case, for emphasis. First graders typically learn readily when to use periods and question marks as stipulated here. Once they have been introduced to the exclamation point, however, many first graders demonstrate that this is the one punctuation mark for which they have been waiting; no other punctuation mark will do for their writing. Hence, some first graders' writing appears to be nothing short of a series of adamant statements, their importance dictated by exclamation points (see figure 10.1).

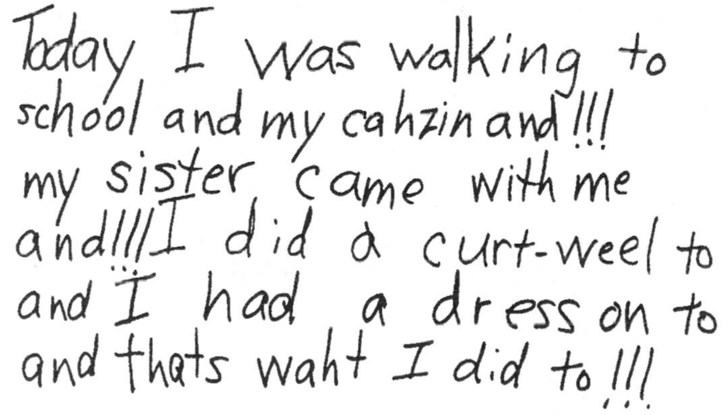

Today I was walking to school and my cahzin and!!! my sister came with me and!!!I did a curt-weel to and I had a dress on to and thats waht I did to!!!

Figure 10.1   A second grader beginning to use exclamation points in her writing

Apostrophes

First graders should be introduced to the apostrophe early on because they frequently encounter it in their basal readers and library books. They need to learn that an apostrophe and the letter *s* are used to indicate possession and that apostrophes are used to indicate missing letters in contractions. Contractions are particularly difficult for students who are not native English speakers and for some students with learning disabilities. Therefore, special attention needs to be devoted to the functions of the apostrophe. Intermediate-grade students need to learn that the apostrophe can also be used to indicate the omission of a number, as in a date (the '96 Summer Olympics or the Great Depression of the '30s).

Commas

By the end of first grade, teachers should introduce the comma. This usually comes after seeing two or three pieces of writing that consist of a series of "_____ and _____ and _____ and _____ and" or an entire page composed of one sentence in which "and then" is used to connect a multitude of thoughts.

Children often find the comma confusing. Even well-educated adults will debate whether a comma should be used before the word *and* when more than two items are listed in series. Unfortunately, comma use has been cyclical in terms of grammatical instruction; the comma is used either sparingly or profusely. However, students have been consistently taught to use a comma (or commas) in the following situations:

- After the salutation of a letter: Dear Ron,
- After the close of a letter: Your friend, Mike
- To separate the name of a city from its state: Fort Worth, Texas
- To separate the day from the year in a date: February 12, 2000

Primary-grade children find the foregoing rules to be clear and understandable. They also have no problems placing commas between words in a series.

- To separate words in a series: The garden had beans, lettuce, radishes, and tomatoes.

Placing a comma before the conjunction clarifies the meaning of the sentence.

The following rules for the use of commas should be introduced to intermediate-grade students:

- To set apart a direct quotation: "Throw me the ball," called Jenny.
- Between parts of a compound sentence that are joined by a conjunction: The car was repaired, and they continued on their trip.
- After an introductory clause: While the car was being fixed, they drank a can of soda.
- Before and after an appositive: The manager, Tommy McPherson, let the customers in early.
- Before and after a nonrestrictive clause: That player, who has a bandaged left hand, is the best scorer on the team.

After teaching a grammar or punctuation skill, it is good to have students find examples in trade books or textbooks. This helps reinforce the concept.

Quotation Marks

Quotation marks rank with exclamation points in terms of popularity among second graders. By including quotation marks in their writing, they demonstrate that they can write like adults. Upon encountering dialogue in the stories they are reading or in Big Books that they read together as a class, some first graders eagerly attempt to write their own dialogue because they insist upon having characters in their stories speak, just as the characters do in books written by professional authors. Graves (1983), in his study of beginning writers, found that a third of the first graders used quotation marks accurately. Quotation marks are used to encompass directly spoken words. For example, consider the following:

"The weatherman said to expect rain," Grandpa said as his eyes cast about the skies, looking for clouds.

By the second or third grade, students learn that quotation marks are used around the title of a poem and that titles of books are underlined (or italicized in print).

Punctuation marks that are introduced later than those described above include the colon, semicolon, and hyphen. By the fifth grade, children typically use these punctuation marks frequently in their writing. Still, other conventions of the English language remain for students to learn.

Teaching Grammar

Upon entering school, children become aware of their own grammatical errors largely through writing. Flood and Salus (1984) advocate that children should write often in a pressureless situation, because time devoted to writing is more conducive to improvement of written language than time devoted to learning the concepts and terminology associated with grammar.

The six parts of speech with which elementary students need to become familiar are noun, pronoun, verb, adjective, adverb, and conjunction, and are defined as follows:

Noun: In traditional grammar, a noun identifies a person, a place, a thing, or an idea. A noun may be singular or plural, and it may also be possessive.
Singular Nouns:
Fix the *radio* in my *car*.
He has *integrity*.
The *pilot* headed toward *Birmingham*.
Plural Noun:
The blue swallowtail *butterflies* flutter among the flowers.
Possessive Noun:
The *bike's* fender is damaged.

Pronoun: A pronoun is a word that is used to take the place of a noun or another pronoun. Like nouns, pronouns refer to people, places, things, or ideas. Unlike nouns, pronouns change form according to their use.
She likes to play golf.
It is *her* game.

Verb: A verb expresses an action or links the subject of a sentence with its description. The most common linking verbs are *am, are, be, being, been, is, was,* and *were*.
Terrance *rode* a skateboard. (Action verb)
The house *was* once an old hotel. (Linking verb)

Adjective: An adjective is a word that modifies, or describes, a noun or pronoun. The *soft, white* snow fell silently.

Adverb: An adverb is a word that modifies a verb, an adjective, or another adverb. An adverb tells how, when, where, or to what extent.
The woman worked *methodically*.
Rags was a *very* happy dog.
He prints *really* well.

Conjunction: A conjunction is a word that connects words or groups of words.
The puppy *and* the older dog chased each other.
Labron James is a professional basketball player, *but* he also enjoys playing golf.

Upon entering kindergarten, children already possess and consistently use each of these parts of speech in their speaking vocabulary. In grades K–2, instruction should focus on how a word is used in a sentence. For example, descriptive words such as *huge, blue,* and *spotted* are not initially introduced as adjectives; the precise labeling comes after students understand the concept of words that can be used to describe people, places, or things (see box 10.2).

Teachers can demonstrate the use of the parts of speech through poetry and song. "I Like Bugs" by Margaret Wise Brown (1999) can be shared with first and second graders to teach adjectives, descriptive words that specify and beautify our writing. Using the poem as a pattern, the teacher and students can rewrite it as "I Like Dogs," as a mini lesson in descriptive words. Teachers can also use it with third and fourth graders to teach prepositional phrases. The poem can likewise be rewritten as "I Like Chocolate" for upper-grade students who are struggling writers to develop adjectives and prepositional phrases.

I Like Bugs*	I Like Dogs	I Like Chocolate
I like bugs,	I like dogs,	I like chocolate,
Black bugs,	_____ dogs,	_____ chocolate,
Green bugs,	_____ dogs,	_____ chocolate,
Bad bugs,	_____ dogs,	_____ chocolate,
Mean bugs,	_____ dogs,	_____ chocolate,
Any kind of bug,	Any kind of dog.	Any kind of chocolate,
I like bugs.	I like dogs.	I like chocolate.

*"I Like Bugs" from *I Like Bugs* by Margaret Wise Brown. Copyright © 2000 by Golden Books. Permission granted by Random House.

10.2   In the Classroom: Mini Lesson

Parts of Speech

Objective: To introduce nouns, verbs, adjectives, and adverbs to fourth graders.

Collect pictures of famous individuals with whom students can identify (for example, media, political, or sports figures). Select four of the pictures to be used for the lesson and paste them in a single column on the left side of a sheet of paper turned sideways. Make and label four other vertical columns, one for each part of speech included in the lesson: nouns, verbs, adjectives, and adverbs. Then make four horizontal columns, separating the four pictures. On the chalkboard, write the definition and an example of each of these four parts of speech. Select one of the pictures to use in a model exercise for the class, for example, a caricature of the president of the United States or prime minister of Canada. After reviewing the definition of a noun, have the students give examples of nouns that relate to that person (president, prime minister, leader, commander-in-chief, father, husband, and so on). After completely filling the first box with nouns, follow the same procedure for verbs, adjectives, and adverbs.

After the class has completed the row for the first picture, divide the students into pairs and have them select one of the three remaining personalities and give examples of each of the parts of speech that characterize that individual. After finishing the exercise, the students should write a short story using as many of the words as possible from the lists they created.

This exercise may be modified to include only political leaders, scientists, characters from children's literature, or the like.

A bug on the sidewalk,	A dog on the _____,	Chocolate in _____,
A bug in the grass,	A dog in the _____,	Chocolate on _____,
A bug in the rug,	A dog under the _____,	Chocolate over _____,
A bug in a glass,	A dog in the _____,	Chocolate inside _____,
I like bugs!	I like dogs!	I like chocolate!
Round bugs,	_____ dogs,	_____ chocolate,
Shiny bugs,	_____ dogs,	_____ chocolate,
Fat bugs,	_____ dogs,	_____ chocolate,
Buggy bugs,	_____ dogs,	_____ chocolate,
Big bugs,	_____ dogs,	_____ chocolate,
Lady bugs,	Any kind of dog,	Any kind of chocolate,
I like bugs!	I like dogs!	I like dogs!

Ruth Heller has a delightful series of language books for children that provide examples of the parts of speech. These colorful books include *Merry-Go-Round: A Book about Nouns, A Cache of Jewels and Other Collective Nouns, Kites Sail High: A Book about Verbs,* and *Up, Up, and Away: A Book about Adverbs* (Heller, 1990a, 1989, 1990b, 1990c). Whereas kindergartners and first graders will enjoy the beautiful illustrations and prose, upper-elementary and middle school students can use Heller's books as reference books for their own writing. Another helpful piece of children's literature, appropriate for kindergarten through second grade, is R. M. Schneider's (1995) *Add It, Dip It, Fix It: A Book of Verbs.* This simple alphabet book is a playful way to introduce the concept of verbs.

Substituting words to make a sentence more powerful and/or effective is good practice for children. Consider the following two sentences from *The Trumpet of the Swan* by E. B. White (1970, p. 18) which Mrs. Bridges, a fourth-grade teacher, wrote on the chalkboard to share with her students:

When the swan had laid five eggs, she felt *satisfied.* She gazed at them *proudly.*

Mrs. Bridges asked her students to suggest substitute words for the word *satisfied.* The students volunteered *happy, pleased, wonderful,* and *relieved.* For *proudly,* they came up with *lovingly, peacefully,* and *happily.* Mrs. Bridges then had her students reread the current drafts of the stories they were writing to suggest words they might substitute for words they had already chosen.

Because children's literature displays a rich use of language, children should be encouraged to find and share passages that show how an author has weaved sentences together to express a certain mood or to achieve a certain tone. Then the students should examine their own stories during revision to see whether they can combine sentences or substitute words to make their stories more effective.

Grammar instruction is most effective when students are required to use inductive reasoning to discover what works and what does not. Through experimentation with language, grammatical knowledge is advanced and skills are enhanced.

Grammar for English Language Learners (ELLs)

Upon their arrival in the United States or Canada, children and adults who speak a language other than English quietly observe other children and adults speaking English. This goes on for an extended length of time, usually several months, before they attempt to speak or write in English (Krashen, 1982). However, those who can read in their first language apply those same skills to "survival reading" of English words: For instance, in learning to read street signs, *st* stands for *street* and *ave* stands for *avenue*. Logos of prominent businesses and products may also be quickly learned—Wal-Mart, McDonald's, Coke, Exxon, and Tide. The exception is when the company's name has unfamiliar letter combinations, such as *Shell*, which has an *sh* beginning, a combination that is not found in Spanish.

Initially, the English used by English language learners is quite simple and usually grammatically incorrect. Two or three word sentences are commonplace. For instance, children may say "no book" for "I don't have a book" or "pencil" for "I need a pencil." They also overgeneralize, for instance labeling all vehicles "car" or all grown-ups at school "teacher." ELLs need the opportunity to use language for meaningful, functional, and genuine purposes (Urzua, 1980). For example, ELL children often learn a great deal of English from their classmates and playmates as they interact socially on the playground. This is especially important since many such children hear only their first or "home" language spoken in their homes and neighborhoods.

As ELLs begin to use English, they are very deliberate in their speech. They enunciate their words clearly and speak slowly. As they acquire more knowledge of syntactic structures, they become more confident and use more complex language. Figure 10.2 on p. 424 contains a chart of the stages of grammar acquisition of second-language learners.

In teaching the structure of the English language to ELL children, the teacher must point out the importance of noun and verb agreement and of proper placement of adjectives and adverbs. By introducing such concepts orally and having the students engage in concrete activities with language, they will more quickly learn the grammatical structures of English. One such activity is to have the students listen to directions, repeat them, and then follow them. Here are some suggestions for such directions:

Put the book under the chair.
Put the book on the chair.
Put the book beside the chair.
Pick up the chair.
Pick up the book and give it to me.
Pick up the chair and put it by the table.
Put the crayon on the desk.
Put the crayon under the chair.

ELLs often engage in codeswitching, or the combining of their native language and their second language (Lara, 1989). They may use English nouns but Cantonese verbs, for example.

Stage 1

Yes-no answers

Positive statements

Subject pronouns (e.g., *he, she*)

Present tense/present habitual verb tense

Possessive pronouns (e.g., *my, your*)

Stage 2

Simple plurals of nouns

Affirmative sentences

Subject and object pronouns (*all*)

Possessive (*'s*)

Negation

Possessive pronouns (e.g., *mine*)

Stage 3

Present progressive tense (*-ing*)

Conjunctions (e.g., *and, but, or, because, so, as*)

Stage 4

Questions (*who? what? which? where?*)

Irregular plurals of nouns

Simple future tense (*going to*)

Prepositions

Stage 5

Future tense (*will*) questions (*when? how?*)

Conjunctions (e.g., *either, nor, neither, that, since*)

Stage 6

Regular past-tense verbs

Questions (*why?*)

Contractions (e.g., *isn't*)

Modal verbs (e.g., *can, must, do*)

Stage 7

Irregular past-tense verbs

Past-tense questions

Auxiliary verbs (*has, is*)

Passive voice

Stage 8

Conditional verbs

Imperfect verb tense

Conjunctions (e.g., *though, if, therefore*)

Subjunctive verb mood

From Gonzales, Phillip C. (1981, November). Beginning English reading for ESL students. *The Reading Teacher, 35* (2), 154–162. Reprinted with permission of Phillip Gonzales and the International Reading Association. All rights reserved.

Figure 10.2   Stages in second-language acquisition

After speaking and reading English for 1 1/2 to 2 years, an ELL can carry on a conversation. But it takes several years before an ELL student becomes proficient in all the language arts—reading, writing, listening, and speaking.

The Revision Process

Understanding the various parts of speech and learning how to write better sentences are assets to a writer. However, the effective writer must also develop good proofreading and editing skills.

Proofreading

In revising a written draft, the student needs to pay close attention to both content (ideas and organization) and mechanics (grammar, usage, and spelling). A checklist for proofreading is helpful to students. For first graders, the proofreading list may be very simple:

Does the story make sense?

Have I left out anything?

Do all of the sentences begin with a capital letter?

Do all names begin with a capital letter?

Do all of the sentences end with a period or a question mark?
Are all the words spelled correctly?

For intermediate-grade students, the proofreading checklist might include the items from the earlier list written at a higher level of sophistication, along with new rules. A fourth-grade checklist, for example, might appear as follows:

Is the main idea clear?
Is the story well organized so the reader doesn't get lost?
Have I used clear words and phrases?
Does anything take away from the story and need to be removed?
Have I used any run-on sentences?
Are all punctuation marks used correctly?

Editing

Editing requires the writer to reread with different lenses. That is, the writer must consider the piece as a reader would view it. The writer in effect distances himself from the piece and asks critical questions. Is the grammar correct? Is the piece organized? Are there transitions from one paragraph to the next? If it is a narrative piece, are the characters well developed? What about setting, time and place? For expository pieces, are the descriptions and explanations clear?

To demonstrate how to proofread, the teacher can take a draft of her own writing and place it on the overhead projector and read it aloud to the class as they follow along. The draft should be written on alternate lines allowing ample space to write in corrections. The teacher then rereads the piece looking for spelling errors. When a word is misspelled or the teacher is uncertain if it was spelled correctly, she circles it. The third time the teacher rereads for grammatical errors, making the changes by marking out the error and inserting the correction (e.g., were for was). The fourth read-through is to correct for punctuation. The teacher uses the proofreaders' marks, using green ink to indicate errors. Samples of anonymous students' work, preferably students from previous years' classes, are good sources to demonstrate the proofreading skills students need to acquire as writers.

In addition to using a proofreading checklist, students need to use the editing marks proofreaders' use to assist them in revising their drafts. Even the beginning writer can use a pencil to circle words that are misspelled and three lines to indicate a letter needs to be capitalized. Figure 10.3 on p. 426 contains a list of editing marks for elementary students.

Involving students in the editing process through peer editing not only reduces the amount of teachers' paperwork, but also improves children's writing. Research suggests that peer editing improves mechanics and overall writing fluency more than teacher editing alone (Weeks & White, 1982). Peer editing provides feedback for the writer and helps the editor sharpen skills, as well. Peer editing may be done on a one-on-one basis or by editing committees assigned to critique one or more specific areas, such as mechanics or content.

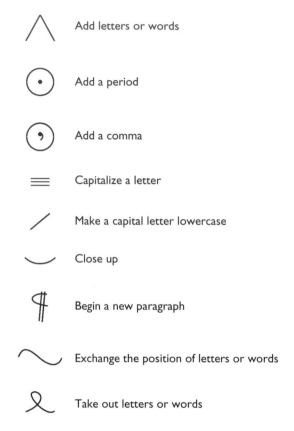

Figure 10.3 Editing symbols

The writer first edits her own work before exchanging it with that of another student or giving it to a committee. In each instance, the editor reads the paper, writes something about the paper that he liked, and then makes suggestions about how the writer might improve the paper. Finally, the editor provides the writer with a list of misspelled words and their correct spellings (Harp, 1988).

Summary

To avoid the teaching of isolated pieces of information, grammar must be taught as part of the listening, speaking, reading, and writing activities that occur daily in the elementary classroom. Teachers must provide children with examples of well-constructed sentences, paragraphs, and works. By sharing specific portions of well-written children's literature, students can better understand grammar and how to improve their own writing and speaking.

Thus, mini lessons can play an important role in the teaching of grammar. To be effective speakers, writers, listeners, and readers, children must be fluent in their use of both oral and written language and must therefore be knowledgeable about the workings of grammar.

Questions

1. Compare and contrast traditional, structural, and transformational generative grammar.
2. What role does writing play in the learning of Standard English grammar?
3. In what ways can children's literature be used to enrich students' language use?
4. Do elementary students need to know the names and definitions of the parts of speech? Why or why not?
5. How should editing be included in the writing process?

Reflective Teaching

Flip back to the beginning of the chapter to the teaching vignette entitled "Peering into the Classroom." After rereading the vignette, consider the following questions: What characteristics (either implied or directly exhibited) does the teacher possess that you would like to develop? What strengths and weaknesses are revealed for the students described in this section? How would you meet the needs of students such as these?

Activities

1. Observe a first- or second-grade class as students are engaged in a writing activity. What punctuation marks do they use?
2. Observe a writing lesson being taught to a group of children for whom English is a second language. What grammar problems emerge?
3. Videotape a 3-minute clip of a variety of television programs (local news, sports, home repair, and so on) and show the video to a fifth- or sixth-grade class. Have each student note obvious grammatical errors. Replay the tape, stopping it to discuss the errors as they occur.
4. Develop a lesson plan to improve fifth-grade students' ability to write complex sentences.
5. Review two English grammar series for elementary students. How is writing incorporated? In what ways are students given the opportunity to improve their grammar skills independently of "cookbook" exercises?
6. Develop and implement a lesson that includes grammar but requires knowledge in a content area, as well.

Further Reading

Angelillo, J. (2002). *A fresh approach to teaching punctuation*. New York: Scholastic.

Casteel, J., Roop, L., & Schiller, L. (1996). "No such thing as an expert": Learning to live with standards in the classroom. *Language Arts, 73* (1), 30–35.

Haussamen, B. (2003). *Grammar alive! A guide for teachers*. Urbana, IL: NCTE.

Heard, G. (2002). *The revision toolbox: Teaching techniques that work*. Portsmouth, NH: Heinemann.

Hinchey, P. H., Adonizio, S., DeMarco, N., & Fetchina, K. (1999). Sketching a self-portrait of skills instruction: Classroom research and accountability. *Language Arts, 77* (1), 19–26.

Invemizzi, M. A., Abouzeid, M. P., & Bloodgood, J. W. (1997). Integrating word study: Spelling, grammar, and meaning in the language arts classroom. *Language Arts, 74* (3), 185–192.

Lane, B. (1999). *Reviser's toolbox*. Shoreham, VT: Discover Writing Press.

Simmons, J. S., & Baines, L. (Eds.). (1998). *Language study in middle school, high school, and beyond*. Newark, DE: International Reading Association.

Umstatter, J. (2001). *Grammar grabbers: Ready to use games and activities for improving basic writing skills*. New York: Prentice Hall.

References

Angelillo, J. (2002). *A fresh approach to teaching punctuation*. New York: Scholastic.

Cramer, R. L. (2003). *The language arts: A balanced approach to teaching reading, writing, listening, talking, and thinking*. Boston: Allyn & Bacon.

Dale, P. S. (1976). *Language development: Structure and function* (2nd ed.). New York: Holt, Rinehart, & Winston.

Donovan, J. M. (1990). Resurrect the dragon grammaticus. *English Journal, 79* (1), 62–65.

Flood, J., & Salus, P. (1984). *Language and the language arts*. Englewood Cliffs, NJ: Prentice Hall.

Fraser, I. S., and Hodson, L. M. (1978). Twenty-one kicks at the grammar horse. *English Journal, 67*, 49–53.

Graves, D. (1983). *Writing: Teachers & children at work*. Portsmouth, NH: Heinemann.

Graves, D. (1995). Sharing the tools of the writing trade. *Instructor, 105* (4), 38–41.

Harp, B. (1988). When the principal asks? Why aren't you using peer editing? *The Reading Teacher, 41* (8), 828–830.

Heard, G. (2002). *The revision toolbox: Teaching techniques that work*. Portsmouth, NH: Heinemann.

Hinchey, P. H., Adonizio, S., DeMarco, N., & Fetchina, K. (1999). Sketching a self-portrait of skills instruction: Classroom research and accountability. *Language Arts, 77* (1), 19–26.

Hunt, K. W., & O'Donnell, R. C. (1970). *An elementary school curriculum to develop better writing skills*. Washington, DC: U.S. Government Printing Office.

Krashen, S. (1982). *Principles and practices of second language acquisition*. Oxford: Pergamon.

Lane, B. (1999). *Reviser's toolbox*. Shoreham, VT: Discover Writing Press.

Lara, S. M. (1989). Reading placement for code-switchers. *The Reading Teacher, 42*, 278–282.

Levine, L. D. (1988). *Bird: The making of an American sports legend*. New York: McGraw-Hill.

McCraig, R. A. (1977). What research and evaluation tells us about teaching written expression in the elementary school. In C. Weaver & R. Douma (Eds.), *The language arts teacher in action* (pp. 46–56.) Urbana, IL: National Council of Teachers of English.

Mellon, J. C. (1969). *Transformational sentence combining: A method for enhancing the development of syntactic fluency in English composition* (NCTE Research Report No. 10). Urbana, IL: National Council of Teachers of English.

Meyer, J., Youga, J., & Flint-Ferguson, J. (1990). Grammar in context: Why and how. *English Journal, 79* (1), 66–70.

O'Hare, F. (1971). *Sentence combining: Improving student writing without formal grammar instruction* (NCTE Research Report No. 15). Urbana, IL: National Council of Teachers of English.

Smith, F. (1988a). *Insult to intelligence.* Portsmouth, NH: Heinemann.

Smith, F. (1988b) *Joining the literacy club: Further essays into education.* Portsmouth, NH: Heinemann.

Weeks, J. O., & White, M. B. (1982). *Peer editing versus teacher editing: Does it make a difference?* Urbana, IL: National Council of Teachers of English. (ERIC Document Reproduction Service No. ED 224014)

Urzua, C. (1980). Doing what comes naturally: Recent research in second language acquisition. In G. S. Pinnell (Ed.), *Discovering language with children* (pp. 33–38). Urbana, IL: National Council of Teachers of English.

Children's Literature

Brown, M. W. (1999). *I like bugs.* New York: Golden Books.

Carle, E. (1988). *Have you seen my cat?* New York: HarperCollins.

Hazen, B. S. (1969). *City cats, country cats.* New York: Golden Press.

Heller, R. (1989). *A cache of jewels and other collective nouns.* New York: Putnam.

Heller, R. (1990a). *Kites sail high: A book about verbs.* New York: Putnam.

Heller, R. (1990b). *Merry-go-round: A book about nouns.* New York: Putnam.

Heller, R. (1990c). *Up, up and away: A book about adverbs.* New York: Putnam.

Langstaff, J., & Rojankovsky, F. (1989). *Over in the meadow.* San Diego: Harcourt Brace.

Rylant, C. (1992). *When I was young in the mountains.* New York: Dutton.

Schneider, R. M. (1995). *Add it, dip it, fix it: A book of verbs.* Boston: Houghton Mifflin.

Ward, C. (1988). *Cookie's week.* New York: Putnam.

White, E. B. (1970). *The trumpet of the swan.* New York: Harper & Row.

Wood, A. (1984). *The napping house.* San Diego, CA: Harcourt Brace.

Spelling, Word Study, and Handwriting

Writing is, for most, laborious and slow. The mind travels faster than the pen.

—William Strunk, Jr. and E. B. White
The Elements of Style, 4th edition

PEERING INTO THE CLASSROOM
SPELLING DEMONS OR SPELLING PATTERNS?

Stephanie taps her pencil against her head. It is Monday and her teacher is giving a spelling pretest to find out what words and spelling patterns the students need to develop and understand. Today the words include *believe, weigh,* and *receive.* She knows these words have an *ei* or an *ie* combination, but she has no idea which combination goes where. Suddenly Stephanie perks up. Quickly she erases the *ei*s and *ie*s from her paper. She makes two loopless *e*s, which could be read as i or e, and strategically places a dot between them. If she doesn't know where the *i* goes, Stephanie thinks, then maybe her new fourth-grade teacher can figure it out.

Stephanie's teacher, Taylor Myers, knows that the *ei* and *ie* combinations can be difficult. After having her students self-score their own spelling tests, she encourages her students to find words in their reading with the two different combinations. They set aside a portion of the bulletin board to list *ie* words in one column and *ei* words in another.

Here are the words they discovered:

ie	ei
believe	sleigh
relief	weigh
belief	height
piece	receive
niece	freight

After the words were gathered, the class poured over them looking for a pattern.

Shreika beamed and raised her hand.

Mrs. Myers called on her. "I found one! When the word has *ei* before *gh* it sounds like along *a*."

"Let's try it out, class," Mrs. Myers said. "Shreika, you point to the word and we'll say it out loud."

The class joined in. "Sleigh, weigh, height, freight."

"It doesn't work for height," Salam said.

The class agreed but then Mrs. Myers covered up the *t* in height and had the students pronounce the word.

"It does work!" announced Jerome.

"Let's look for another pattern," Mrs. Myers said. "Who sees one?"

"Oh!" exclaimed Erica. "I've got one."

"What pattern have you discovered?" asked Mrs. Myers.

"That when *ie* is in a word it sounds like a long *e*."

"Okay, class, let's give this pattern a whirl. Erica, point to the words and we'll say them."

"Believe, relief, belief, piece, niece."

"Boys and girls, I think we've solved the spelling mystery. Here's an old saying that my teacher taught me. See if it works: *i* before *e* except after *c* or when it sounds like *a*, as in neighbor and weigh."

"Yeah!"

"That's it!" says Stephanie.

"But we figured it out all by ourselves," said Jeremy smugly. "Nobody told us."

"I guess you boys and girls are just smarter than I was when I was your age." Huge smiles spread across 23 faces with a few heads nodding an affirmative. Deep inside, Taylor smiles to herself, knowing that she's the wiser teacher for having her students discover the spelling patterns on their own rather than having them memorize a rule that would otherwise be meaningless.

Chapter Objectives

The reader will:

✓ understand the developmental stages of spelling.

✓ be able to teach frequently used English spelling patterns.

✓ be able to analyze spelling errors and suggest appropriate instruction.

✓ be able to assist ELL and special needs students in developing their spelling skills.

✓ be able to evaluate manuscript and cursive handwriting.

✓ be able to assist right- and left-handed children in becoming fluid in their handwriting.

Standards for Professionals

The following Standards will be addressed in this chapter:

Standard 1: Foundational Knowledge and Dispositions

1.4 Demonstrate knowledge of the major components of reading (phonemic awareness, word identification and phonics, vocabulary and background knowledge, fluency, comprehension strategies, and motivation) and how they are integrated in fluent reading.

Standard 2: Instructional Strategies and Curriculum Materials

2.2 Use a wide range of instructional practices, approaches, and methods, including technology-based practices, for learners at differing stages of development and from differing cultural and linguistic backgrounds.

2.3 Use a wide range of curriculum materials in effective reading instruction for learners at different stages of reading and writing development and from differing cultural and linguistic backgrounds.

Standard 3: Assessment, Diagnosis, and Evaluation

3.1 Use a wide range of assessment tools and practices that range from individual and group standardized tests to individual and group informal classroom assessment strategies, including technology-based assessment tools.

3.2 Place students along a developmental continuum and identify students' proficiencies and difficulties.

3.3 Use assessment information to plan, evaluate, and revise effective instruction that meets the needs of all students, including those at different developmental stages and those from differing cultural and linguistic backgrounds.

Standard 4: Creating a Literate Environment

4.3 Model reading and writing enthusiastically as valued lifelong activities.

Introduction

Within society, the ability to correctly spell words identifies the educated person. Because society places such importance on accurate spelling, some people actually form positive or negative opinions about an individual solely on the basis of the spelling skills she displays in written communication.

Reading plays a major role in the development of spelling. Good readers are often good spellers, but, unfortunately, poor readers are usually poor spellers. Wide reading helps children to recognize the visual shapes of words. They may be able to remember the way a word looks as they write the word, determining whether or not it is spelled correctly. Knowledge of phonemic awareness of the common letter patterns found in English also aids spelling. In writing instruction, spelling is a problem for both children and teachers. As Wilde (1990, p. 276) writes, it would be ideal if learning to spell were "analogous to learning how to speak the language" and "ultimately be as natural, unconscious, effortless, and pleasant as learning to speak." Such is usually not the case, for although children are eager to record their thoughts on paper as quickly as possible, they are not concerned with correct spelling until they reach the revising stage of the writing process. In effect, proper spelling serves as a courtesy to the writer's audience, the reader, because the correct spelling of words eases the entire reading process. Therefore, the child as writer must be intrinsically motivated to spell words correctly.

Another problem for both children and teachers is the fact that many words in the English language have been borrowed from other languages and thus have irregular spellings. In fact, over 600 different ways to represent the 42 phonemes in English have been documented (Pitman & St. John, 1969). Moreover, the same English words may be spelled differently by different groups: Compare, for example, the British and Canadian spellings of *colour* and *labour* with the American *color* and *labor*. Then, too, new words are constantly being invented; some of these are based on acronyms (for example, *scuba,* from *self*-contained *u*nderwater *b*reathing *a*pparatus), and others develop as hybrids of consumer-oriented products (Xerox and Palm Pilot, for example). Nevertheless, 86.9 percent of all the words in the English language are phonetically rule based (Anderson & Lapp, 1988). Thus, the relationship between a letter and the sound it represents is of a systematic nature.

In addition to phonology, one must also consider morphology, syntax, and semantics if correct spelling is to occur. For instance, the position of a word within a sentence may indicate the appropriate spelling. Such is the case when choosing among *to, two,* and *too.* Emerging trends in spelling instruction suggest that expectations of perfect spelling in young children's writing are unrealistic and inappropriate considering the developmental nature of spelling ability.

Current instructional emphasis in spelling is on the discovery by students of the *patterns,* or *chunks,* of letters that can be found in the sounds, structures, and meanings of words (Templeton & Morris, 1999). The more students understand about words, the more efficient and fluent their reading will be (Perfetti, 1992). Or, to put it another way, "spelling knowledge is the engine that drives efficient reading as well as writing" (Templeton & Morris, 1999, p. 103). This chapter will explore current instructional trends and assessments in spelling.

Along with good spelling, good handwriting is an important factor in conveying a written message. This chapter discusses the development of manuscript and cursive handwriting skills.

English Spelling

English spelling has three primary informational characteristics that children need to learn in order to spell conventionally. These different layers of spelling information are referred to as *alphabetic, pattern,* and *meaning* (Henderson & Templeton, 1986). Each of these layers is described by Templeton and Morris (1999, p. 105) below:

- *Alphabetic* refers to the fact that there *are* a good number of words in English for which the spelling is primarily left to right and there is a fairly straightforward linear matching of letters and sounds. (Examples: *cat, ham, bit, run)*

- The *pattern* layer provides information about (1) sounds that a group or pattern of letters represents *within* a syllable—for example, the signaling of long vowels by silent letters; and (2) patterns *across* syllables, as in the closed VCCV pattern of *kitten* and *helmet* and the open VCV pattern of *pilot* and *hotel.*

- The *meaning* layer provides information through the consistent spelling of *meaning elements* within words, despite sound change, as in *solemn/solemnity* and *critic/criticize.*

The question then becomes, How do students learn to spell? The next section examines this important issue.

Children begin to attempt to write words as early as age three or four. During this emergent literacy stage, they are acquiring much knowledge about how print works. As they discover the names of the letters of the alphabet, children create or invent their own spelling. They produce their written "words" on the basis of how they sound to them. For instance, Farhana wrote "GM AT" next to her illustration of an old woman with a birthday cake. What did GM AT represent? Grandma [is] 80. When children are in the "letter name" stage, the teacher has to "sound out" the letters by their names as well as keep in mind the context in which each child is writing in addition to using any pictorial clues.

The *alphabetic* layer of information is indicative that the children know that words are written in a left-to-right sequence, with sounds matching their respective letters. Thus they can "sound out" words going from left-to-right as they attempt to write or read them.

"When the speller learns how *patterns* work the possibilities for correct spelling increase significantly because the speller has more information that can be brought to bear in order to generate conventional spelling" (Templeton & Morris, 1999, p. 104). The *pattern* layer is more advanced than is the *alphabetic* layer. At this point children recognize what adults have long known about English spellings: some words do not always work in a right-to-left manner because certain letter combinations form particular sounds. The most common example is the "silent *e*" rule in words such as *cake, bike, dude,* and *lame.* The student must "skip to the end of the word and think in a left-to-right fashion, grasping the notion that a letter can in fact not stand for a sound itself but provide information about the sound of another letter in the word. This understanding means that children grasp that the vowel/consonant/silent *e* functions as a single pattern or unit" (Templeton & Morris, 1999, p. 105). As students learn this concept, they apply it to their writings often by placing the "silent *e*" immediately after the letter it changes the sound of. For instance, the word game becomes GAEM, late becomes LAET, and time becomes TIEM.

Other *patterns* include:

- *igh* as in *right, night,* and *high;*
- doubling of the final consonant/e-drop before adding a suffix to a base word such as *hit* becoming *hitting* but race changes to *racing;*
- VC/V across syllables, the vowel is long as in *hotel, student;*
- VC/CV pattern across syllables, the vowel is in a closed syllable and is short as in *mitten* and *helmet.*

See the examples on pp. 459–460 for additional spelling patterns and generalizations.

The *meaning* layer requires that children be able to recognize the common spelling of derivationally related words. This could be one of the most efficient and effective means of becoming aware of and organizing spelling concepts that share a common base (Fowler & Liberman, 1995). Here are some examples of words:

human	*fresh*	*sleep*	*medicine*
humanity	*freshen*	*sleeping*	*medical*
humane	*refresh*	*sleeper*	*medic*
posthumous	*refreshing*	*sleepover*	*medicate*
humus	*freshening*	*sleepwalk*	*medicinal*
exhume	*freshener*	*sleepy*	*medication*
		sleepyhead	*medicare*

By considering the common spelling chunks, children can begin to see the conceptual linkages of derivationally related words.

Stages of Spelling Development

Read's (1971) classic study discovered that preschool children tend to "invent" the spellings of words they use in their writing. He also discovered that these inventions are predictable rather than random and that consonant sounds are used quite consistently. Current research findings based on Read's work indicate that children progress through several developmental stages before they actually master the intricacies of learning to spell (Bissex, 1980; Henderson & Beers, 1980). Studies by Gentry (1981) and Henderson (1985) suggest the existence of five developmental stages: (1) precommunicative, (2) prephonetic, (3) phonetic, (4) transitional, and (5) conventional spelling. Children go through "temporary" spelling as they develop their auditory and sound/symbol relationship skills prior to moving on to conventional spelling. These developmental stages are described in figure 11.1 and illustrated in figure 11.2 on pp. 438–439.

Children begin to write words in much the same way as they begin to learn to speak them; that is, they rely on experimentation (Clay, 1975). They move from invented, temporary spelling to correct spelling. Very young children draw and scribble as an attempt to represent actual writing patterns. Although children scribble for pure pleasure and enjoyment at age two, by age three they begin to imitate their adult counterparts by perfecting their circular and linear drawings. From this point onward, children view writing as an entire process, not just as a combination of individual letters and words. Between the ages of three and five years, children move from the imitative stage to one of creation, forming real letters to write messages for adult readers. At this time, children are not only discovering the finer features of writing but are also becoming more aware of the variations found within written language (Atkins, 1984).

Three- to five-year-olds in the *precommunicative stage* of spelling invent the spellings of words by developing both capital letter and numerical symbols and later grouping such symbols together in a variety of combinations. Eventually, however, only the capital letters are grouped together as children discover the concept of "word"—a combination of letters used to represent

Stage	Characteristics	Significance	Examples
1. Precommunicative	Letters are used randomly.	Child recognizes that words are made up of letters.	RbTz for car
2. Prephonetic	Generally, one to three letters that represent consonant sounds are used.	Child uses some consonant sounds to spell entire words.	KR for car KT for cat
3. Phonetic	Letters used closely resemble sounds contained in a word.	Child adds some vowel sounds and more consonant sounds to the word.	ustuliv for used to live bot for boat
4. Transitional	Vowels are contained in every syllable.	Child is ready for formal instruction in spelling.	gurbul for gerbil
5. Conventional	Spelling is generally accurate; few spelling errors are made.	Child can edit his or her own writing for spelling errors. Child continues to participate in formal spelling instruction.	

Figure 11.1   Developmental spelling chart

meaning. In Henderson's (1985) view, this concept serves as a major bench-mark in literacy acquisition. When children can consider a word as a concrete object, they are then able to examine words systematically and to detect the spelling patterns that occur.

Initial attempts to write words at this stage result in the use of letters that are not normally found in a particular word. For instance, a child may write "TRX" to represent "Sandy," the name of the family's dog. This is in accordance with the fact that one's ability to discriminate between actual words and nonwords does not usually appear until age five or six (Brownell et al., 1978).

Within their own home settings, young children practice and play with graphic symbols as a way to both organize their world and express their thoughts and feelings (Piazza & Tomlinson, 1985). In Hall's (1985) view, parents should encourage their young children to use invented or temporary spellings in their writing to promote an atmosphere of acceptance for such creation; at the same time, parents should reassure the young writers that they, too, will develop the perceptual ability needed to distinguish correct from incorrect spelling.

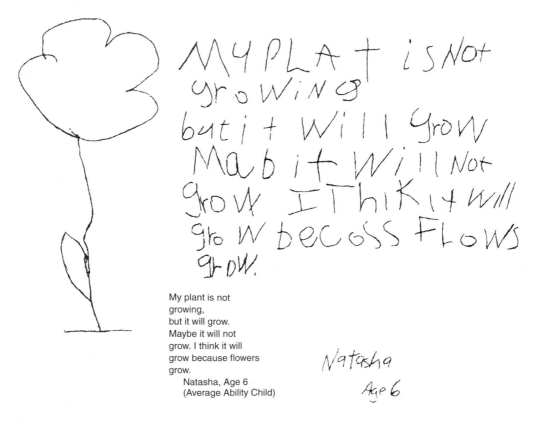

My plant is not
growing,
but it will grow.
Maybe it will not
grow. I think it will
grow because flowers
grow.
    Natasha, Age 6
    (Average Ability Child)

Figure 11.2 Spelling samples from 6-, 7-, and 8-year-olds are represented here. Use the developmental spelling chart to classify the different stages of spelling of these three students.

u bowt my brThday

cristy Sed hoLd up heThre didit Say enything

Akila Age 7

About my birthday
Christy said, "Hold up three [fingers]."
He didn't say anything.
Akila, Age 7
(Below Average Ability Child)

April 11, 1992
Dear Peter Rabbit
How are you doing
I. weh I cod see you But I
like your story and wen
I ron in a grdn I
never get my cot and hos
clt and I hope you never
get cttagen

Mike
Age 8

Dear Peter Rabbit,
    How are you doing? I wish I could see you. But I like your story, and when I run in a garden, I never get my coat and hose caught, and I hope you never get caught again.
        Mike, Age 8
        (Average Ability Child)

Figure 11.2   *(continued)*

Typically, during kindergarten or first grade, children begin to match letters with sounds. First graders should explore the left-to-right letter/sound correspondence within words as well as learn the common short vowel spellings and simple consonant blends and diagraphs (Templeton, 1991). Because the children already understand the concept of "word" and can identify the names and shapes of most, if not all, of the letters of the alphabet, the youngsters next attempt to spell words that are used in conversations with others. Even though these children have only a limited knowledge of print, they can consider themselves to be "writers," for they quickly become attuned to the needs of their readers and the conventions of written language. Children will advance rapidly from the deviant stage to the prephonetic stage because of the confidence they possess as writers.

The *prephonetic stage* could also be referred to as the letter-name stage because children begin to display an exactness in their association of letters with the corresponding sounds of a word. In this stage, children are generally dependent upon the use of capitalized consonants: for example, Bissex's (1980) young son, in an attempt to get attention, wrote, "GNYS AT WRK" (correctly translated as "genius at work"). Furthermore, although long vowels are used with great accuracy by the letter-name speller, short vowel sounds are difficult for the child to use accurately. Typically, a child will substitute the long vowel sound that is most similar to the short vowel sound that he or she hears. This being the case, the letter *a*, as a long vowel, might be substituted for the short vowel *e* in *ten*.

During the prephonetic stage, children initially spell an entire word with only a single letter. A second letter, which they add later, usually represents the final sound of the word. Yet as children develop finer auditory discrimination, they begin to identify sounds contained within the word itself. When this happens, children are ready to enter the phonetic stage.

In the *phonetic stage*, children's spelling reflects a more perfect match between a word's letters and associated sounds (as in the writing of "klok" for clock). As children advance toward the transitional stage, the classroom teacher finds reading their writing relatively easy because vowels now represent each of the syllables in a word (see figure 11.3).

During the *transitional stage*, the spelling is very close to correct and is recognizable by the reader. The student in the transitional stage is rapidly moving from temporary, invented spelling to conventional, correct spelling.

October 30,
to day I did
not get to have
ABC cereler.
becose tharer was
non. so I had to
have capten croch
and ten.

Figure 11.3 An example of writing by a student in transitional stage. Notice that the child writes "and ten," words he knows how to spell rather than "instead," a word he uses in his oral but not written vocabulary.

Children's progression to the *conventional stage* is demonstrated through their use of common letter patterns, such as *ing, ap, et, amp, ent,* and so on. In addition, prefixes, suffixes, and root words are recognized by children in this stage. Thus, over time, children refine their spelling as they adopt spelling conventions and spell words correctly (Wilde, 1992).

As children proceed through school, they have increasingly more experiences with both reading and writing. Such word encounters enable children to familiarize themselves with groups of words that share phonological, morphological, and syntactic features. As a result, both older children and adults learn to go beyond the use of phoneme-grapheme strategies to spell words correctly.

Henderson and Templeton (1986) observed children as they progressed through the developmental stages of spelling. The researchers concluded that the developmental theory is valid and that it provides a "rationale for the pacing and maintenance of instruction in a more detailed and clearly stated manner than has been possible before" (p. 314). Examining how children move through the stages of spelling development can therefore be helpful in terms of providing guidelines for spelling instruction.

A Simple Spelling Test for Kindergartners and First Graders

Teachers of kindergartners and first graders can test students' spelling abilities by giving a simple spelling test consisting of ten words: *back, feet, step, junk, picking, mail, side, chin, dress,* and *road.* To administer the test, ask the students what sound they hear at the beginning of the word *map.* Next ask what letter comes next in *map.* Then ask what is the last sound they hear in *map.* Since *m* is a sound introduced early in first grade, *map* is a good example for the test. The ten words of the test are then given with the same directions, with the teacher asking what is the first, middle, and last sound of the word as each child writes the letters. Scoring is 1 point if the word has at least the beginning and final consonant (e.g. *feet* spelled FT, FAT, FTE, or FET would be worth one point.). Other spellings would not receive any points (e.g. *feet* spelled F, FA, R, or T would receive zero points.). The test scores can range from 0 to 10 and each score is converted to a percentage of correct answers (Morris, Bloodgood, Lomax, & Perney, 2003). Teachers can then readminister the same spelling test at midyear and at the end of the year to determine how the students are progressing.

Initially, students at the kindergarten level may only give the initial consonant sound, such as B for *back.* Many five-year-olds will not be able to give the initial consonant sound for any of the words on the list. A few will be able to spell some of the words correctly. However, by end of first grade, the same students should be able to successfully spell all ten words, as these words represent common English spellings with phonetic patterns students frequently encounter in their reading. If the teacher applies careful, systematic instruction to teaching alphabetic knowledge and phoneme awareness, the students will gain skill in spelling and progress more rapidly through the developmental spelling process. Thus it is important to link phoneme awareness in spelling to beginning reading instruction, as well as to provide students with opportunities to write.

As previously mentioned, the Morning Message can be a means of shared writing to support the teaching of alphabetic knowledge and phoneme awareness. In kindergarten, the teacher should write a message in front of the students each day. The message may include such things as the date, day of the week, weather, birthdays, special events for the day (e.g., PE, art, convocation), and other information. It should also include a sentence or two about one of the students (e.g., getting a new kitten, moving away to another school, taking a trip to Disney World). By the end of a month, all of the students should have had at least one sentence written about them in a Morning Message. By late October or early November, students can use a spiral notebook to copy part of the Morning Message, such as the day of the week and the date, and then write their own thoughts in their notebooks. At the first- and second-grade levels, the teacher incorporates the Morning Message with language and spelling lessons. Together with the class the teacher writes the Morning Message on the board with the students spelling out the words and indicating which letters are to be capitalized, what kind of punctuation is needed, and where the punctuation marks are to be placed, as well as sharing information about their own lives. Students can participate by taking turns writing one word at a time, marking the punctuation, or being involved with other aspects of creating the Morning Message, making it a shared writing experience.

High-Frequency Words

English contains a number of words that we use over and over again in our speaking and writing. These are known as high-frequency words. An adult's writing typically consists of 50 percent or more of the 100 most frequently used words. Beginning writers rely heavily on high-frequency words. Unfortunately, many of the 100 most frequently used words cannot be spelled by the *alphabetic* pattern. The best way for children to learn these words is to see them repeatedly and have ready access to them when they write. First and second graders should have the list of 100 high-frequency words laminated and taped to their desks. Another copy should be inside their writing folders, so that once a word is mastered it can be checked off the list. By the second half of first grade, students should be held responsible for correctly spelling all 100 words in the final draft of their writing. After all, they have the words literally "right in front of them." Some teachers prefer to put the words on a Word Wall in the classroom rather than taping the list on desks. Because 6–8-year-olds are still growing, their eyeballs are as well. Hence many first and second graders cannot focus their eyes on the distant Word Wall and refocus to look at the paper on their desks to write the word. It is not unusual for a child to misspell a word in the process of looking up and looking down until the word is completed. It is far better to have the high-frequency words at hand so no refocusing is needed. Figure 11.4 contains a list of the 100 high-frequency words.

a	be	didn't	had	I	make	our	than	to	what
about	because	do	has	in	me	out	that	too	when
after	big	don't	have	is	my	over	the	up	where
all	but	down	he	it	new	people	their	us	which
am	by	eat	her	just	no	run	them	very	who
an	can	find	here	know	not	said	then	was	will
and	can't	for	him	like	of	saw	there	way	with
are	come	from	his	little	on	see	they	we	would
as	could	get	house	long	or	she	thing	went	you
at	did	go	how	look	other	some	this	were	your

Figure 11.4   List of the 100 high-frequency words. Note that most of these words are function words.

Spelling and Word Study Instruction

As children move from temporary spelling to become conventional spellers, they acquire an awareness of how words are formed. Although researchers have yet to determine precisely when students should be expected to no longer use developmental spelling, students at the second- and third-grade levels should be making significant progress toward spelling words in their writing correctly. According to Tompkins (2000, p. 112), "by the time children enter fourth grade they should be conventional spellers; that is, they should spell 90 percent or more of the words they write correctly." Children who fail to reach the 90 percent goal should be permitted to continue writing with invented spelling so that they will eventually learn both visual and morphological spelling strategies rather than memorize spelling words. To determine a child's readiness for spelling instruction, teachers can administer the Yopp-Singer Test of Phonemic Awareness (Yopp, 1995). This test is administered individually and is appropriate for students in kindergarten through second grade.

If children find words to be part of things they find pleasurable, then they will be more apt to acquire the skills they need to use in their writing and reading according to Yopp and Yopp (2000). They believe teachers of preschoolers and kindergartners should have activities that focus on rhyme, syllable manipulation, onset-rime manipulation, and phoneme manipulation in order for children to acquire the essential phonemic awareness skills they need for decoding in reading and spelling in writing. *Rhyme* activities include reading books such as *The Hungry Thing* (Slepian & Shepard, 2001), the story of a creature who asks people in the town to "FEED ME" when it points to the sign on its chest. When the townspeople inquire as to what the creature desires to eat, it responds, "Schmancakes!" Confused, the townspeople are frustrated until a small boy says, "Schmancakes sounds like fancakes sound like pancakes to me!" Whereupon the townspeople feed the creature pancakes. The creature then asks for other foods, each time slightly mispronounced so the townsfolk have to guess what it wants. As a read aloud, students have to listen carefully to predict what food the creature wants. As a follow-up activity, the teacher can bring out various foods and mispronounce them. Students can then correct the teacher. For example, "napes" instead of "grapes," "sudding" instead of "pudding," "mogurt" rather than "yogurt," and "tizza" instead of "pizza." In each instance, the context in which the food is presented yields clues (e.g., "I love to eat a bowl of sudding." "Ah, strawberry mogurt. My favorite!" or, "This yellow kanana has a slippery peel.").

The use of rhyme in song is encouraged by Yopp and Yopp (2000). A good example is "The Ants Go Marching." After learning the song, students can make up their own verses.

The Ants Go Marching
The ants go marching one by one,
Hurrah! Hurrah!
The ants go marching one by one,
Hurrah! Hurrah!
The ants go marching one by one,
The little one stops to have some fun,
And they all go down to the ground,
To get out of the sun.
Boom! Boom! Boom!

Another popular song that children enjoy and can add their own verse is "Down By the Bay."

Down By the Bay
Down by the bay,
Where the watermelons grow,
Back to my home I dare not go.
For if I did,
My mother would say,
Did you ever see a goat,
Rowing a boat,
Down by the bay?

Other verses include:

Did you ever see a pig,
With a curly wig,
Down by the bay?

Did you ever see a moose,
Kissing a goose,
Down by the bay?

Activities with syllable manipulation suggested by Yopp and Yopp (2000) include having students clap their hands for each syllable. It is best to begin with two-syllable words before moving to three- and then four-syllable words. Students can also clap to the number of syllables in names of classmates or the teacher (e.g., Tony, Eric, Madison, Allison, Israel) and afterwards construct a picture of themselves using a colored rectangle piece of construction paper for each syllable in their name. They would glue the rectangle(s) on a separate piece of paper and then use crayons or colored pencils to create their picture.

Onset-rimes break down a syllable by separating everything that appears before the vowel (onset: *c* in *cat*) and the vowel and everything after it (rime: *at* in *cat*). Activities with onset-rime manipulation can include having pictures of objects with one-syllable words (cat, dog, street, brick) on cards. A shoebox is covered with colored paper and made into a mailbox. Each child is then given a card with a one-syllable object picture. The teacher then segments the onset and rime as he says it aloud (e.g., c-at, d-og, str-eet, br-ick). The child with the card then deposits it into the mailbox.

Phoneme manipulation can be a simple as a scavenger hunt for letters. Students are put into pairs and given a paper bag with a letter on the outside and a picture of an object that begins with that letter (e.g., D and a drawing of a dog; H and a picture of a horse). The students then have to find objects in the classroom that begin with their designated letter.

Yopp and Yopp (2000) assert that teachers must provide linguistically rich classrooms for students. Language must be explored and valued by teachers with their students. Teachers should say, "Look at the way I write this." "Wasn't that an interesting word?" "My, listen to all the sounds in this word." "Your two names both start with the same sound." "What a sense of humor this author has! Notice the way he plays with words in this section" (Yopp & Yopp, 2000, p. 143). Pointing out the interesting combinations in words helps to make students alert to phonemic awareness and to apply it on their own.

A framework for spelling instruction in the elementary grades is offered by Templeton (1991). He believes that first graders should begin their study of spelling by examining simple letter patterns in sight words (i.e., consonant–short vowel–consonant, as in *cat*, *did*, and *fun*; consonant–long vowel–consonant–silent *e*, as in *cake*, *bike*, and *poke*; consonant blends, as in *drip*, *flap*, and *slip*; and consonant digraphs, as in *phone* and *right*).

Second and third graders should acquire basic vowel patterns and simple syllable patterns. Beginning in the fourth grade, children need to compare and contrast spelling/meaning relationships in words in addition to syllable patterns. In Templeton's opinion, the examination of word meanings is important at the intermediate and middle school levels.

Bloodgood (1991) supports integrated instruction of spelling in a literature-based curriculum. Bloodgood suggests the use of pattern books for word study by first and second graders. For example, *Polar Bear, Polar Bear, What Do You Hear?* (Martin, 1991) provides children with repetitive use of the phrase "What do you hear?" The children can also begin to identify words that depict the names of the animals in the book.

In addition, Bloodgood (1991) believes that third through fifth graders should compare different versions of folktales or fairy tales as part of word study at this level. She gives the example of *Cinderella* (Brown, 1954), *Moss*

Gown (Hooks, 1987), and *Princess Furball* (Huck, 1989). Students in third grade and up could read a book in small groups. As they read, they can be given word study assignments for each chapter. For instance, a group reading a novel about the Civil War could look for words in a chapter that relate to a specific concept (e.g., the cause of the war). Another chapter may be used for the study of grammatical units (e.g., verbs that express action) or unusual vocabulary (e.g., words used during the 1860s that are not in common use today).

Spelling Research

Graham (1983) reports that 100 words account for 50 percent of all the words children use in their writing, 1,000 words for 89 percent, and 3,000 words for 97 percent. The 100 words to which Graham refers are largely function words and verbs: *a, is, are, have, had, that, this, there, was, were,* and so forth. Children tend to use such words frequently as they begin writing in sentences.

Read's (1971) discovery of invented spelling led to the reexamination of formal spelling programs. Research conducted by Hammill, Larsen, and McNutt (1977) compared the spelling of fourth- through eighth-grade students who received formal instruction through a basal spelling textbook series with the related spelling of a similar group of students who received no formal spelling instruction. Their findings indicated that there was no significant difference between the two groups of students in terms of their spelling ability. An earlier study by Manolakes (1975) found that the average child in grades 2–6 could already spell 75 percent the words contained in a randomly chosen spelling textbook lesson before receiving any instruction for that particular word list. By the end of the eighth grade, students often encountered a common core of 2,800 to 3,200 words in a spelling textbook series. Still, in considering grade placement and sequence, teachers should not hesitate to alter the words within particular lessons to meet student needs.

The current trend is to promote the integration of spelling and writing instruction. Many schools no longer use a formal spelling textbook series; instead, teachers are encouraged to forge a stronger link between writing and spelling instruction. One advocate of this approach is Hillerich (1977), who believes that the reason children learn to spell is to write. Thus, children must engage in lots of writing in order for them to not only maintain but also further develop their spelling skills. Wilde (1992) believes that children should be questioned during the writing conference as to how they know how to spell certain words and what they use to help themselves spell correctly.

Gentry and Henderson (1978, pp. 23–24) recommend that early-childhood-level teachers incorporate the following three steps in their spelling instruction:

1. Encourage writing in order that a child may actively participate in the acquisition of written language. By permitting a child to experiment with and to manipulate words, the youngster becomes directly involved with those cognitive operations that are essential to competent learning.

2. Deemphasize standard spelling for the beginning speller; in this way, children can develop their reasoning powers in order to ascertain why a particular spelling is used.

3. Respond to nonstandard spelling in an appropriate manner and provide for the smooth transition from one developmental strategy to the next.

In order for conventional spelling to be developed by children they need to have a relevant use for it. In other words, students must write frequently on topics in which they are interested. According to Hughes and Searle (2000, p. 203):

> What too often appears to be missing in planned spelling instruction, especially as children move beyond their first two or three years in school, is a continuous emphasis on "the second R"—writing—specifically writing for which children have a personal investment and commitment. Such writing supports learning to spell in some very specific ways. Essentially, writing challenges children to use their knowledge of print to express their thoughts on paper. Writers may spell correctly or incorrectly, but they cannot avoid spelling. Moreover, the process of generating words, making choices about which letters to put down on paper, requires writers to pay attention to the internal details of words in ways that readers do not have to. Writing also creates a purpose for learning to spell correctly by developing a sense of audience. When writers care about what they are writing and about how their ideas are received by readers, they are more apt to understand how readers are influenced by correct and incorrect spellings. As a consequence, committed writers are more likely to strive to become good spellers.

Gay Su Pinnell and Irene C. Fountas (1998, p. 150), point out that children need strategies for spelling and reading. Here are five they suggest:

Strategies for Solving Words

Sound
You can read or write some words by thinking about the sounds *(man, dog)*.

Look
You can read or write some words by thinking about the way they look *(the, pie)*.

Mean
You can read or write some words by thinking about what they mean *(unpack, two, sandwich)*.

Connect
You can use what you know about a word to figure out a new word *(tree, my,—try)*

Inquire
You can use materials to learn more about words *(list, dictionary, chart, computer)*.

Spelling Activities

Making Words

Making Words is an approach developed by Patricia M. Cunningham (1992; 2000) who believes that children need to discover the common phonetic chunks that exist in English spelling if they are to become proficient spellers. Unlike invented spelling, Making Words is used along with regular writing activities to help children improve their decoding skills. According to Cunningham and Cunningham (1992, p. 107),

> Making Words is an activity in which children are individually given some letters that they use to make words. During the 15-minute activity, children make 12–15 words, beginning with two-letter words and continuing with three-, four-, five-letter, and longer words until the final word is made. The final word (a six-, seven-, or eight-letter word) always includes all the letters they have that day, and children are usually eager to figure out what word can be made from all these letters. Making Words is an active, hands-on manipulative activity in which children discover sound-letter relationships and learn how to look for patterns in words. They also learn that changing just one letter or even the sequence of the letters changes the whole word.

To conduct a Making Words lesson, the teacher must decide which word will be the final word in the lesson. Cunningham and Cunningham (1992) suggest these six steps:

1. Select the "final word." Consideration should be given to:
   - number of vowels;
   - letter-sound patterns the children need;
   - student interests;
   - curriculum tie-ins.

2. After the final word has been selected, write down a list of the shorter words that can be made from the letters of that word.

3. From the words listed, pick the following:
   a. words that meet the pattern(s) you want to emphasize in the spelling lesson;
   b. little words and big words so the lesson is developmental in nature (i.e., meets the needs of special needs, ELL, low, average, above-average, and gifted students);
   c. words that can be made with the same letters in different places (e.g., *bran* and *barn; ride* and *dire*);
   d. a proper name (or two) to remind students to use capital letters;
   e. words that most students have in their listening vocabularies.

4. Write all the words on index cards and order them from the shortest word to the longest.

5. After putting the two-letter, three-letter, etc., words together, then order them as in number 3 (patterns, words with same letters, etc.).

6. Store the cards in an envelope. Write on the outside of the envelope the words in order and the patterns you will have the students sort for at the end of the lesson. Inside the flap of the envelope, write the "final word" to prevent the students from seeing the word and to assist yourself in remembering the different words for the various Making Words lessons.

Cut out 2-inch square cards to use in a pocket chart or, 3-inch square cards if you use the ledge of a chalkboard. On each of the cards is a letter from the "final word." Have a designated student give out the cards to classmates until all are gone. The same child will collect the letters after the lesson and place them in a resealable, plastic bag. Direct the students to make two-letter words. For instance, if the final word is *table*, the students may come up with *at* and *be*. The students holding these letters place them in order in the pocket chart or on the chalkboard ledge. For each word, the students say it and spell it along with the teacher. Then one student uses it in a sentence. This reinforces both phonetics and semantics. The next step of the lesson is to have the students work together to make three-letter words such as *tab, lab, get, let, gab,* *bet,* and *let.* Again, for each word, the students say and spell it. Then a student uses the word in a sentence. If students are unclear as to a word's meaning, the lesson stops while the teacher explains and uses the word in yet another sentence. This process continues until a student, or students, figures out the "final word." At this point, the teacher praises the students by saying, for example, "You boys and girls are terrific (or marvelous or fantastic or incredible or awesome) spellers!" If the final word stumps them, the teacher says

---

11.1   The More You Know

Spelling Software Programs

Students enjoy practicing their spelling with various computer software programs. Two such programs are described below.

"Super Solvers Spellbound" is a program designed by teachers and sold through The Learning Company, 6493 Kaiser Drive, Fremont, California 94555. The program is very flexible in that it comes with 1,000 different words that are sorted into several different topics, such as "planets." Teachers and/or students can add up to an additional 3,000 words. By playing three different spelling games (Word Search, Criss Cross, and Flash Card), students become engaged in a spelling bee program. The program gets more difficult as a student becomes more proficient. The sound effects are superb so that the pronunciation of the words is very clear. The program is available on CD-ROM for both IBM compatible and Apple computers. Suggested age levels are 7 to 12.

"Spelling Jungle" is a program created by Sierra On-Line, P.O. Box 85007, Bellevue, Washington, 98007. This program focuses on words that children often have difficulty spelling. It includes a tricky maze that even adept video game players will find challenging. The program is limited in that additional words cannot be added. It is available on CD-ROM for both Apple and IBM compatible computers. Suggested age levels are 7 to 10.

Both of the above programs give students suggestions for spelling rules.

something like, "Today's final word is a tricky one. You have to be wily like a fox or as wise as an owl to get this one. Put all the letters together and make the word _____ [or in this lesson *vegetable*]." Later as students become more proficient, the teacher may give hints such as the beginning letter(s) of the final word if it proves to be difficult to unlock.

After doing this activity as a group, students move to doing it individually at their desks. This requires that each student have all the cut out letters for the final word. The best way to prepare for this is to decide what the final words will be in advance (over summer vacation or during a holiday break). Use a computer with a large font size to make the letters. Prior to cutting the letters apart, laminate them. This will allow repeated use of letters with little wear. Place the letters of the final word into plastic resealable sandwich bags, one for each student in the class. Because students often drop letters off their desks, you may want to alternate the color of the paper. For instance, use light blue, yellow, and light green paper, being consistent that all the letters in each packet are the same color. Thus when a child drops a light green letter, he knows that it belongs to him and not his classmate who is working with yellow letters today. Commercially prepared letters and small trays are also available. Keep the packages of letters (sealed, of course) in the master envelope described earlier. Such envelopes fit nicely inside a file drawer.

Using the Making Words model of Cunningham (2000) and Aiken and Bayer (2002) link books so that first graders have a rich language framework for their Making Words. Each October, Lisa introduces the Making Words instructional strategy to her first graders. She presents two lessons using the phonograms *ap* and *at*, as these combinations are in several possible words (e.g., *cap, map, tap,* and *bat, cat, hat*). A letter holder and a plastic bag containing a set of letters *(a, c, l, m, n, p, t)*, each written on a small tile square, are given to each child. The vowel is written in green with the consonants in black. Lisa then tells the students they are going to Make Words. She starts with the word *cap* and has the students make the word on their letter holder. Next she has a student come to the front of the room and write *cap* on the board. They continue with that phonogram with students creating the words at their desks before one of them goes to the board to write the word. Other words using the *ap* phonogram are *lap, map, nap, tap*.

Further developing her students' spelling and writing skills, Lisa relies upon such books as *Brown Bear, Brown Bear, What Do You See?* (Martin, 1968; 1983) and *I Love You, Sun, I Love You, Moon* (dePaola, 1994), Lisa presents the books as read alouds. After reading the book for the day, Lisa then has the students write their own book using the same sentence pattern. She then has the students read a poem in unison, analyzing it for rhyming words and words with a common vowel or consonant sound, such as the long *a* sound or the consonant cluster *ch*.

Word Walls

Word Walls are another creation of Patricia Cunningham (1992, 2000). By putting words on large wall charts that are in alphabetical order, the students can quickly locate the words they need for their writing. For instance, the A chart may contain such words as *at, ate, apple, and, ant, animal,* and *applesauce.* New words are added throughout the school year.

Word Walls may also include spelling patterns or chunks. Janiel Wagstaff (1998), a second-grade teacher, refers to *Key Words,* or words that contain spelling patterns or chunks we encounter often in our reading and writing. Such Key Words may be *feet* for the *ee* combination or *pail* for the *ail* pattern. Each time the pattern is underlined so the students will not forget the pattern later when they search for it on their own. Words that begin with common blends such as *brown* for *br* or *pretty* for *pr* are also put on the Key Word charts with each blend underlined. Words that begin with common digraphs such as *ch, sh,* and *th* are placed on yet another Key Word chart. Likewise, words that end in such blends are added to the same chart later on during the school year. Like the Word Wall, the Key Word charts remain on the walls throughout the year and are added to as the students develop their spelling skills.

For intermediate and middle school students, Word Walls can serve as content area vocabulary and spelling lessons for units of study. For instance, words such as *democracy, freedom, traitor, revolution, monarchy,* and *independence* may accompany a fifth-grade unit on the Revolutionary War. A fourth-grade unit on electricity might include such words as *generate, electric, turbine, transmit, battery, current, magnetic, resistance, watt,* and *voltage.* Word Walls for upper elementary and middle school can include those difficult to spell words that students sometimes consider to be "tricky" (e.g., a lot, all right, buy-by-bye, because, experience, neighbor, physical, their-there-they're, threw-through, watch, weather-whether).

Word Study Activities

Word study requires that students group words into categories of similar or different words (Bear et al., 2000). The words are categorized on the basis of "spelling, meaning, and use patterns in order to better understand how spelling represents a word's meaning and grammatical function" (Invernizzi et al., 1997, p. 185). Children acquire the features of words developmentally. First they recognize letter-to-sound correspondences. Next they become aware of the patterns of consonants and vowels such as VCV and VCCV. This stage is followed by students becoming aware of structures within words, such as closed syllables contain short vowels and open syllables contain long vowels (e.g., *pi-lot:* the *pi-* is an open syllable; *lot* is a closed syllable). The last stage is the derivational stage in which the words can be traced to their Greek and Latin roots and stems.

Examples of how spelling points out differences in word meaning are *homophones.* Here are some examples of *homophones,* words that sound the same but have different meanings:

here	hear	tail	tale
sail	sale	pail	pale
there	their	blue	blew
where	wear	bail	bale

Students in third grade through eighth grade need to engage in such word studies of homophones. The homophones of *there, their,* and *they're, here* and *hear,* as well as *wear* and *where* should be introduced by second semester of first grade.

Unlike homophones, *homographs* are spelled the same but are pronounced differently based on the part of speech. Because *homographs* are given different syllable stresses, or accents, depending upon word function, students need to listen carefully to determine how the word is used in conversation. Invernizzi, Abouzeid, and Bloodgood (1997, p. 186) provide categories of the common relationship between syllable stress and word function.

Stress in First Syllable		Stress in Second Syllable	
Word	*Part of Speech*	*Word*	*Part of Speech*
subject	(noun, adjective)	subject	(verb)
conduct	(noun, adjective)	conduct	(verb)
rebel	(noun, adjective)	rebel	(verb)
console	(noun, adjective)	console	(verb)

From this, students can see the language pattern evolve. If the two-syllable word stresses the first syllable, the word is likely to be a noun or adjective. If the second syllable is stressed, the word is probably a verb.

Spelling Study Methods

Of all the spelling study methods currently available, the most widely accepted relies on student self-discipline. In the "look, say, cover, write, and compare" approach, which has been used for generations, a student looks at a word, says and spells the word aloud softly, covers up the word, writes it on a sheet of paper, and then finally compares the original and attempted spellings. This same sequence is then repeated until the word is spelled correctly *and* the student is confident of having mastered the word. Although this study technique has proved to be quite effective, teachers must routinely reiterate the five study steps to prevent students who use it from becoming lax in its application.

Spelling Errors

Students' spelling errors should be classified as well as evaluated by the classroom teacher. Because there is more than one way to make a spelling error, an analysis of the exact nature of the mistake can aid a teacher in developing a plan for instruction (Henderson, 1985). Often, a pattern of errors seems to emerge; a child may continually delete one of a pair of consonants from a word ("tenis" for *tennis* and "batle" for *battle).* From an instructional point of view, such repetition of errors highlights the particular spelling skills a student needs to practice. Some common spelling errors are listed below. These error categories can assist the classroom teacher in choosing instructional tactics.

Categories of Spelling Errors

Error Category	Example	Correct Spelling
1. Vowel omission	familis	families
2. Vowel substitution	elephunt	elephant
3. Vowel addition	develope	develop
4. Consonant omission	poses	possess
5. Consonant substitution	chrok	truck
6. Consonant addition	askt	asked
7. Letter reversal	hrap	harp

To assess error patterns, a teacher must first acquire a sample of a student's spelling. For students in grade 3 and above, this can easily be accomplished through the administration of either a grade-level spelling test of 25 to 50 words or a word-by-word dictation of particular sentences or paragraphs. Although student spelling errors are much more consistent across word lists (DeMaster et al., 1986), sentence and paragraph writing does offer greater flexibility in spanning content area topics and materials (e.g., mathematics, science, and social studies).

Students often provide insights about their word perceptions through conversation. For example, during a writing conference with her first-grade teacher, Amber was asked whether she knew how to spell the word *banana*. She replied, "Oh, yes. I can spell banana. I just don't know when to stop" (see figure 11.5).

Good and poor spellers differ in the strategies they use to tackle difficult words. A study by Radebaugh (1985) found that good spellers thought of possible spellings syllable by syllable, whereas poor spellers attempted to "sound out" the word one or two sounds at a time. None of the poor spellers in Radebaugh's study reported using visual imagery when considering possible spellings of a word.

Students in grades 2 through 8 can keep spelling logs to assist them in improving their spelling skills. A spelling log needs to be frequently used if it is to be effective. This technique works best if the student writes down the reason(s) a word confuses her as well as suggestions and tips to help her remember the correct spelling. Spelling logs have been around since the late 1970s. Figure 11.6 on p. 454 is an example of a commonly used format for a spelling log.

Spelling logs are very effective with students who have dialects that are different from the area in which they live. Such logs are invaluable in aiding ELL and special needs students as well, including gifted students. By the student's own identification of the spelling error and a suggestion as to how to remedy it, spelling improves greatly.

Figure 11.5   Amber's spelling of banana

My Spelling Log			
Correct Spelling	My Misspelling	Why the Word Confuses Me	Helps to Remember the Correct Spelling
demonstrate	demenstrate	I use e instead of o.	A demo is used to demonstrate.
separate	seperate	I say it wrong.	"par" as in golf
principal	principle	The ending is like another word.	Principal at school is my "pal."
coarse	course	I get it mixed up with course as a class.	a = coarse is hard.
meant	ment	I spell it like I think it sounds.	It's the past of *mean*.

Figure 11.6   Excerpt from upper-grade student's spelling log

Assisting Children with Spelling

Students progress as spellers when teachers support them as readers and writers (Bartch, 1992; Scott, 1994). In particular, the teacher must help the student form links between reading and spelling. "Specific incidents in which the child focuses on the spoken and written word simultaneously may enhance the acquisition of the spellings of phonemes and of whole words" (Griffith, 1991, p. 232). Good spellers tend to be those who are wide readers and who have ample writing opportunities within which to use their spelling.

In addition, children's attitudes toward spelling are important. According to Jill Scott (1994, p. 189), a first-grade teacher, a classroom atmosphere that promotes "words and spelling as interesting and enjoyable can only be an advantage to the student. When risk taking and invented spelling are treated as natural and desirable, the students will write more and thus become more knowledgeable about words."

Scott suggests the following activities to promote spelling in early-childhood classrooms:

Teacher Modeling. The teacher demonstrates how adults determine the proper spelling of a word, for instance by pronouncing a word and then asking students to help spell it or by looking words up in a dictionary.

Labeling the Classroom. Objects and materials can be labeled using markers and tagboard. These become spelling references for young writers. Time of day can be taught this way as well; the teacher may hold up the proper sign for different activities during the day, including signs for recess, lunch, art, music, and gym, as well as time to go home.

Word Categories. Lists of words organized into categories can be hung around the room. These may include lists of words for family members, colors, animals, etc.

Pattern Charts. Charts should be displayed that demonstrate the patterns that occur in words. For example, *br* in *brick, brown,* and *bright* and *ing* in *ring, bring,* and *thing.*

Interesting Words. Bring students' attention to interesting words, such as compound words (*ladybug, fireplug,* and *gun-shy*), family words (*featherbed, featherhead, featherbrain,* and *featherweight*), and word histories (*bigwig* comes from the colonial period when the more powerful politicians wore large powdered wigs).

Word Sorts. Each student is given word cards and asked to sort them into spelling patterns. For instance, beginning spellers could be given *bin, in, tin, red, bed, fed, cat, sat,* and *bat.* Avoid using words that don't fit into the categories.

Bulletin Board Dictionary. Have the students write down words on index cards and arrange them in alphabetical order on the bulletin board. With young children, the teacher can make squares for each of the 26 letters of the alphabet. The child can then place the word in the square of the letter that starts the word.

Routman (1991) suggests the following additional ideas for improving spelling:

Spelling Big Book. The pattern and word charts can be laminated and put together in a class Big Book, which becomes a kind of class dictionary. This book can be placed near a writing center for students to use as a reference when they write.

Have-a-Go. "Have-a-go" spelling originated in Australia as children attempted to spell unknown words, or to "have a go at it." Students select three words from their writing that may be misspelled. Next the students make three attempts at spelling their words properly, each attempt resulting in a different way to spell the word until they believe they have spelled the word correctly. Each attempt is written on a "Have-a-Go Sheet" that is taken with them when they meet with the teacher for a writing conference. The Have-a-Go Sheet may be modified for emergent spellers by including three different headings used to indicate how the students determined the correct spelling of a word. The headings are as follows: "My try," "Help from a friend," and "Help from the teacher or aide."

Suggestions for Parents to Help Their Children Grow as Spellers

More than any other subject, expect perhaps math, spelling is an area in which parents are willing to devote time to assist their children. Help with review of spelling words for a weekly test, for instance, gives parents the feeling of being supportive as well as involved in their children's learning. Below are suggestions to give parents in order to help their children develop spelling skills (Chandler & Mapleton Teacher-Researcher Group, 2000, p. 228):

- Help children write out labels for objects in the home.
- Ask children to make shopping lists or write menus for a meal.

- Have even young children write their own thank-you notes (perhaps with translation of invented spelling penciled in underneath for the recipient's convenience).
- Read, sing, and learn nursery rhymes together. Familiarity with nursery rhymes helps build knowledge of word families.
- Have scavenger hunts with words—for example, "Find me three things that begin with a T" or "find three things that rhyme with 'can.'"
- Make tedious time—doing dishes, folding clothes, riding in the car—quality time by playing word games. Generate lists of antonyms and synonyms, words that start with the same letter, or words listed alphabetically in a particular category (e.g., armadillo, baboon, cat).
- Play word games such as Boggle, Scrabble, and Upwords.

Children in grades 3 through 8 enjoy playing games on the computer. Scrabble and Wheel of Fortune are games they can play alone, with friends, or even with others across the country or world via the Internet. Although not specifically a spelling game, Jeopardy requires that the spelling of the response either be correct or closely approximate the correct spelling. Hence, while developing skills in the content areas such as science and social studies, Jeopardy also offers spelling as an additional skill area.

Spelling Development of English Language Learners (ELLs)

English language learners acquire spelling through the relationship between sound and symbol patterns as well as with semantics. It is not unusual for spelling patterns of the first language to be infused into the English spellings. Here is the writing of a seven-year-old ELL student whose primary language is Spanish. The student was told to write about where animals live.

Marro wrote:

What aminos lives here?	What animal lives here?
da frog	the frog
da Bee	the Bee
da turo	the turtle
da chark	the shark
da esnaik	the snake
da fich	the fish

It is important for the teacher to consider what elements of spelling Marro has already acquired. For instance the words frog and bee are spelled correctly. Turtle has the initial *tur* spelling pattern with o substituted for the final syllable of *tle*. Because words in Spanish do not start with an *s + consonant* as a blend, Marro has substituted *ch* for *sh* in shark. Likewise, an *e* has been added to the *sn* blend to form the word *esnaik* for *snake*. Marro repeated the substitution of *ch* for *sh* in the word fish. By considering the child's first language and how it influences his second-language spelling, the teacher can better assist the student to look for letter-sound patterns in English.

Because spelling is developmental in nature for all children, the teacher needs to point out patterns of letters that occur. For instance, CVC as in *cat, hit, red,* and *tap* and CVCE as in *bake, cute, gate,* and *kite.* ELLs need more time to acclimate to the spelling patterns because they often lack the refined auditory acuity needed to differentiate between sounds. By combining visual and auditory spelling activities, they will develop such skills. Thus, the more word-sorts and making-words types of activities they engage in the better their English spelling will be. Writing activities that are relevant to the child will also aid spelling development.

Spelling Development of Special Needs Learners

Spelling is learned by special needs learners in the same developmental steps as with other children. However, the teacher must make certain the words the child is being asked to learn for spelling each week contain the spelling patterns that the child is capable of understanding and recognizing. For instance, a child who consistently writes *runing, swiming,* and *hiting* is ready to be introduced to the concept that a consonant is doubled before adding the suffix *ing.* The student should be encouraged to find words in her reading where this spelling pattern applies and write them down in her spelling folder. A reduced number of words on the weekly spelling list aids the student as well.

With learning disabled (LD) students, spelling can be a more severe problem inasmuch as the child may not be able to distinguish between one English spelling pattern and another similar one. For example, *pre* as a prefix can appear to a LD child as *per.* The child must learn the sequence of the letters from left to right in both spelling patterns. This will usually take more time than with other students of the same developmental level. Many LD students have auditory discrimination difficulties in that they may not hear certain tonal qualities. This is also true of hearing impaired students.

Students with learning disabilities tend to score lower than those without such disabilities on spelling tests of both predictably and unpredictably spelled words (Carpenter & Miller, 1982). In addition, children with learning disabilities are apt to demonstrate poor visual short-term memory and often have problems with auditory and/or visual long-term memory (Wallace & McLoughlin, 1988). In order to assist such students, as well as students with other mental handicaps, spelling instructional time may be increased and additional assistance provided through peer tutoring, word lists displayed on the student's desk, increased use of the spelling words in other content areas during the week the words are being studied, and other appropriate instructional steps.

One suggestion for assisting special needs learners with spelling is to say the word slowly and have the students repeat it. As the word is said the students listen to the sounds and write them in order on paper or on a slate board with chalk. A variation is to have the students say the word and clap the syllables. Students need to be reminded that each syllable must contain a vowel or a *y.*

Students should be encouraged to think about how the word looks, what spelling pattern does it have? What are other words that have the same spelling pattern? Is the pattern on the Word Wall?

Semantics plays an important role as well. Students should be encouraged to think about what the word means. How is it used in the sentence or paragraph?

The *multisensory approach* of Grace Fernald (1943) is appropriate for use with spellers who have disabilities or those who lack confidence in their spelling ability. The teacher writes the word on a card in large letters (manuscript for first and second graders and cursive for higher grade levels). Then the teacher shows the card to the student while pronouncing the word. The student repeats the word. The teacher holds the child's hand while the child traces the letters with the index and middle fingers of the writing hand and pronounces the syllables aloud. Next, the child turns the card over and writes the word without looking at it. The child then verifies the spelling. If the word was spelled correctly, the child then writes and rechecks the word three more times. If the word was spelled incorrectly, the child repeats the finger tracing and verbalization of the word. The child may not erase any part of the word; it must be written correctly, letter by letter, or the word is considered to be incorrect. On the following day, the child is tested for the words presented the previous day.

One teacher who had several students with severe spelling problems found that this approach resulted in fewer words learned but increased correct spelling by 80 percent (Norton, 1989). The multisensory approach is time-consuming for both the teacher and the student; however, its use with students with special needs has met with much success since Fernald first developed it over 50 years ago.

Gifted students pose another instructional dilemma for the teacher as often they focus on the content of their writing and are unconcerned about their spelling errors. Getting such students to edit effectively for spelling can be a trying task at best. When gifted students come to their own realization that they must spell correctly to convey their messages, at that point they are willing to devote more attention to their spelling progress as they polish their works.

Spelling Generalizations

The link between the sound a letter represents and spelling is a strong one. Whereas kindergartners and first graders tend to spell a word the way they hear it said aloud, older children and adults apply spelling generalizations to unfamiliar words. As Adams (1990, p. 103) states:

> Clearly, the connections between sound patterns and spelling patterns must enhance our ability to remember or figure out how a new word is spelled. They must enhance our ability to recognize a printed rendition of a word once having heard it. And they must enhance our ability to recognize a spoken rendition of a word once having seen it in print.

By second grade, most students have already amassed some spelling generalizations or rules, including those of capitalization, prefix and suffix addition, and phonic generalizations. Second graders usually know that the first letter of a proper name is capitalized and that the addition of an *s* changes most nouns into the plural form.

Nevertheless, formal instruction in spelling rules should begin only after a child is cognitively able to understand the generalizations being taught (Allred, 1977). Beers (1980) and Templeton (1991) suggest that teachers should wait to introduce these rules until a child possesses a strong sight vocabulary; it is at this point that a child has a large repertoire of words within which to compare and contrast once phonics instruction is initiated. Allred's (1977) findings have yielded the following guidelines for spelling instruction:

- Rather than teaching students all of the generalizations, only a few rules should be taught. Rules that have an exception should not be taught.
- Only one rule should be taught at a time.
- A rule should be taught when there is a direct need for it.
- Rules should be taught inductively via various word examples.

Following is a list of spelling generalizations that children should know by the fourth grade.

Plurals

1. Plurals of most nouns are formed by adding an *s*: dog, dogs; bed, beds; car, cars.
2. Plurals of nouns ending in *ch, s, sh,* or *x* are usually formed by adding *es*: church, churches; bus, buses; dress, dresses; brush, brushes; box, boxes.
3. When a noun ends in a *y* that is preceded by a consonant, the plural is formed by changing the *y* to an *i* and adding *es*. fly, flies; baby, babies; candy, candies.
4. Plurals of a small number of nouns are formed by changing their singular form: man, men; woman, women; goose, geese; mouse, mice; child, children.

Possessives

5. Possessives of most singular nouns are formed by adding an apostrophe followed by an *s*. boy, boy's; dog, dog's.
6. Possessives of most plural nouns are formed by adding an apostrophe: girls, girls'; ladies, ladies'.
7. Possessives of a small number of plural nouns are formed by adding an apostrophe followed by an *s*: men, men's; children, children's.

Suffixes

8. A word that ends in a "silent *e*" usually keeps the *e* when a suffix beginning with a consonant is added: grace, graceful; nine, ninety; hate, hateful.
9. A word that ends in a "silent *e*" usually drops the *e* when a suffix beginning with a vowel is added: bake, baking.
10. A word that ends in a single consonant preceded by a vowel usually doubles the final consonant before a suffix beginning with a vowel is added: tag, tagged; put, putting; big, bigger.

11. A word ending in a *y* that follows a consonant usually changes the *y* to *i* before a suffix is added, unless that suffix begins with *i*: battery, batteries; silly, silliness.

Vowels

12. An *o* at the end of a word usually represents the long /ō/ sound: tobacco, potato.

13. When an *r* follows a vowel, the sound of the vowel is neither long nor short but is "*r*-controlled," meaning that the *r* influences the sound of the vowel that precedes it.

Capitals

14. Proper nouns begin with capital letters: Jim, English, Smith, New York.

These generalizations are best learned through children's own inductive reasoning processes. For instance, if students are able to determine whether or not the suffix *-ed is* pronounced with the /d/, /t/, /ed/, or /id/ sound, they should begin their inquiry by providing examples of words that actually end in *-ed*. The teacher simultaneously writes these words on an overhead transparency or the chalkboard and then asks the class to identify the words that are pronounced with the /d/ sound. At this time, students are to look for any common features among the words. The students then follow the same sequence of steps to examine the words pronounced with the /t/ sound. Such a list might include the following words:

dogged	bragged	coughed
stretched	bobbed	started
dipped	handed	pointed

Once the activity has been completed, students should have formed various conclusions. In our sample list, for example, words that end in *d*, *g*, and *t* are pronounced with the /d/ sound after the *-ed* suffix is added, whereas words that end in *ch*, *gh*, and *p* are pronounced with the /t/ sound after the suffix is added.

Dictionary Skills

Teaching children how to use a dictionary will give them a sense of writing freedom. In recent years, dictionaries written specifically for children have been greatly improved. Colorful picture dictionaries that enable young children to make picture-word associations in their quests for the correct spellings of specific words are motivational for primary-grade students. Such early experiences help students understand the importance of the dictionary as a reference tool for writing.

Children also need to learn how to use a dictionary to discover the meanings of words, as well as their pronunciations. Proper use of a dictionary's pronunciation key will enable children to pronounce any word correctly, including placing the accent on the proper syllable of a multisyllabic word. Dictionaries on CD-ROMs, such as Merriam-Webster's, are more thorough than typical

11.2   In the Classroom: Mini Lessons

Alphabetical Order

Objective: Teaching the alphabetical order of words that begin with different letters.

The first skill required in dictionary use is alphabetical sequencing. Although children may know the "alphabet song," they may have little knowledge of the placement of letters relative to one another (e.g., that *m* is the middle of the alphabet whereas *w* is close to the end). Certain activities can eliminate this uncertainty. With flash cards that contain words beginning with different letters, students can practice arranging words in their proper alphabetical order on their desks under the teacher's guidance. The trading of flash cards allows for repetition of the activity. Once the students have mastered this skill, they can be introduced to the alphabetizing of words beginning with the same letter; this can be followed by activities involving the alphabetizing of words that begin with the same two letters, and so on.

After learning alphabetical order, students should be instructed in the use of guide words. For example, the teacher distributes word flash cards to each student. When the teacher displays two chosen guide words, the students raise the flash cards containing the words that alphabetically come between the two guide words.

elementary-level dictionaries but are easy to use. They are especially helpful in that the words are pronounced correctly so students can hear and imitate the proper pronunciation of a word. This feature is especially beneficial to ELL and special needs students.

Besides the familiar picture dictionaries and elementary-level dictionaries, other types of dictionaries are available for use by elementary school students. Children who have difficulty with spelling or who have learning disabilities may benefit from using handheld spelling computers. With these, the child spells a word phonetically, and the computer then produces the correct spelling. However, homonyms such as *there, their,* and *they're* remain a problem because the handheld devices fail to differentiate among the meanings of such words. Most handheld computers contain up to 75,000 words.

Word processing software usually contains programs that check spelling. As with the handheld spelling computers, however, most of these programs cannot discern the proper homonym. Although such computerized devices can aid students in their spelling, students should not be allowed to become totally dependent upon them. Children still need to develop spelling skills to aid them in their writing.

Handwriting

As four-year-old Kurtis and his mother were driving home from his childcare center, she asked him what he did at school that day.

"Oh," he answered, "We made letters."

Very slowly and deliberately he said, "We made *A*. We made *B*. We made *C*." Then he suddenly perked up as he enthusiastically and proudly announced, "I'm a good *C*-er!"

Handwriting is the making of symbols that, when placed together, represent words. When young children first begin making letters, they find some letters easier to form than others. For instance, Kurtis found the letter *C* much easier to make than *A* or *B*. Despite the prevalence of both typed and word-processed material, handwriting is an important skill for children to master; it is used for writing drafts of compositions and letters, for taking class and source notes, and for making lists.

When children construct words slowly and laboriously on paper, they are less effective in their overall development of compositions because they frequently lose important thoughts and ideas in the process. Thus, poor, handwriting can be said to inhibit the creative, productive writer (Graves, 1978).

Young children typically initiate handwriting attempts when they are able to distinguish between pictures (or drawings) and print. For most children, this occurs at about age four, when experiments with marking instruments and paper generally begin. Formal instruction in handwriting may profitably start either at the end of kindergarten or at the beginning of first grade. Because young children differ in their acquisition of motor skills, most teachers wait for an appropriate signal from a child before introducing handwriting. Such a signal often consists of the child's production of his or her own name. Not only does this action indicate that the child is ready to learn handwriting, but it serves to identify the point in time when a child understands that a word actually conveys meaning (Clay, 1975) (see figure 11.7).

Children are introduced to the manuscript, or print, method before learning the cursive method at the end of the second or the beginning of the third grade. In the intermediate grades, handwriting receives less emphasis as part of the writing process. Because ideas flow much more quickly than does the recording of those ideas on paper, young authors often sacrifice legibility. Not until the writing of a final draft is the quality of handwriting considered a priority.

We now examine the various aspects of handwriting acquisition and instruction and offer suggestions for evaluating and improving handwriting in the various grades.

Children's Handwriting Development

By age three, children produce drawings that are composed of the same basic lines that constitute manuscript letters: (1) vertical lines, (2) horizontal lines, and (3) circles (Harste et al., 1984). Because of such early experience, most six- and seven-year-olds can create these vertical and horizontal lines more easily than the relatively complicated connections associated with D'Nealian manuscript or cursive handwriting. Because vertical lines are made with a straight up-and-down motion and horizontal lines by a left-to-right motion, they are made by using predominately already acquired gross motor skills.

Nevertheless, preschoolers and primary-grade students need to engage in activities that will develop fine motor skills. In working with modeling clay, finger paints, beads and string, and interlocking construction toys such as Lincoln Logs, Legos, or Wee Waffle Blocks, children begin to refine the move-

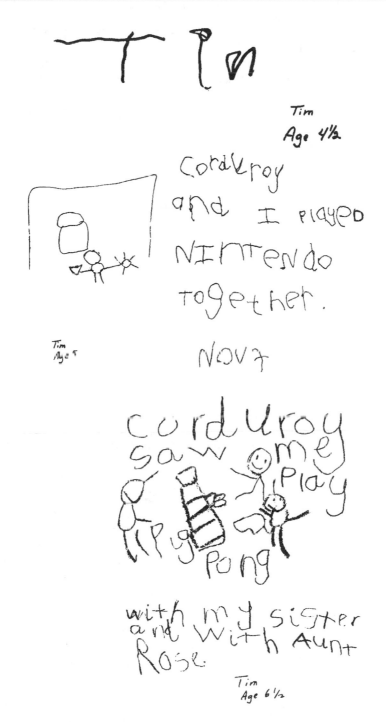

Figure 11.7   Tim's handwriting development as a preschooler and after direct handwriting instruction in kindergarten and first grade

ment of their fingers and hands and thus to develop precise maneuvers required for handwriting.

Eye-hand coordination, like fine motor control, is still being developed by children in early childhood. Connecting lines and closing circles are considered difficult tasks for many of these children. Furthermore, the eye continues to develop until children reach the age of about eight. Thus, six- to eight-year-old students either struggle in their attempts to copy assignments from the chalkboard or find such tasks impossible because they are unable to refocus their eyes from long to short distances (i.e., from the chalkboard to their desks).

By the time students reach the middle childhood or intermediate level, grades four through six, they can handwrite much more quickly and reduce the size of their letters. At this time, legibility becomes a primary concern. Many students are attempting to express their own individuality, such as the way in which they dot their *i*'s and incorporate extra loops and other frills. Although teachers should permit individuality and creativity, these traits must not interfere with legibility; slovenly handwriting should not be accepted (Graham & Miller, 1980).

Instruction in Handwriting

Handwriting is an important tool for communicating and thus needs to be addressed instructionally. Children need to become both legible and fluent in their handwriting. Handwriting instruction may be either formal, direct instruction or incidental instruction.

> Direct instruction is more efficient while incidental instruction is more in line with the philosophy of whole language. However, without being introduced to and given instruction in the basic handwriting writing skills such as letter formation, alignment, slant, and size, children are left to discover such skills on their own. As such they develop inappropriate techniques, and legibility suffers. (Farris, 1991, pp. 313–314)

As noted earlier, formal handwriting instruction should begin either at the end of kindergarten or at the beginning of first grade. In areas of the country where a majority of children attend preschool before entering kindergarten, such formal instruction may be undertaken even earlier. However, unless these children are able to differentiate between letter forms and to develop the motor skills needed to hold a pencil and have the associated eye-hand coordination, they are simply not prepared for formal handwriting instruction.

Young children should be given plenty of opportunities to use pencils, crayons, and felt-tipped markers in their scribbling, drawing, and writing attempts before their formal introduction to handwriting (see figure 11.8 on p. 465). In choosing paper for such experimentation, teachers have found that blank sheets of paper are much more effective than lined sheets; the lines prove to be frustrating in that the preschooler lacks eye-hand coordination and therefore is not capable of producing letters that stay between linear boundaries. The same holds true for kindergarten children and for many beginning first graders.

Figure 11.8   Example of an early attempt at handwriting by a four-year-old. Notice the stiffness in the handwriting.

Six-year-olds can more easily learn to write manuscript letters that fall between lines if the selected paper contains actual folds 1 1/4 inches apart. Teachers can prepare for this exercise in advance by creasing paper at the standard 1 1/4-inch intervals. In this way, children will rely on tactile sensation rather than sight to write the letters within the top and bottom lines.

If handwriting instruction is to be effective, the teacher must include four strategies in every lesson: (1) allow the students to observe the letter as it is formed, (2) describe for the students the steps needed to make the letter, (3) have the students describe the stepwise procedure as they create the letter, and (4) conclude the lesson by having the students apply the newly acquired handwriting skill in a meaningful context (such as by writing a letter to a pen pal). Because these strategies depend on the visual, auditory, and kinesthetic learning modalities, children are better able to recall proper letter formation when it is re-created in other settings. Likewise, if the letter is used in a meaningful context, teachers can actually reinforce the skill that was taught.

The classroom teacher should present new letters to beginning writers while simultaneously helping them visually identify the ways in which these letters compare or contrast with other letters of the alphabet. By asking students simple questions about letter size, shape, and required strokes, a teacher can promote a kind of visual analysis that will help the students gain insight into letter construction. The teacher should write the letter on the chalkboard using proper form and making it large enough to be visible to students in the back of the classroom without grossly misrepresenting the letter. Accordingly, capital letters should be between three and four inches in height and lower-case letters no less than two inches high.

As the teacher models the correct way to make the letter, a formal description of the necessary steps or movements should be included. After this, the students should use pencils and paper to form the letter at their own desks while individually describing the techniques used. Each student can then compare the letter she created with that produced by the teacher before the instruction is resumed. Because this process necessitates interaction, the teacher should actively circulate among the students, thereby offering both encouragement and objective criticism (Tompkins, 1998).

The practicing of previously taught letters should be constantly encouraged. This can best be done by including many practical writing activities in class. Successful exercises might include writing greeting card verses for classmates or relatives, preparing and sending invitations to other classes or parents for special events, or developing posters for upcoming activities.

Writing Instruments

Years ago, people believed that children should learn to write with large, child-sized pencils. Generally, first graders would use their "fat pencils" at school and standard, adult-sized pencils at home because few of their homes possessed sharpeners large enough for the bigger pencils. We now know that although children with severe eye-hand coordination problems can benefit from writing with larger pencils, most children can use the more readily available, standard-sized pencil without difficulty. In fact, Lamme (1979) found that children may actually have better handwriting overall when they use standard pencils from the beginning.

Children should be given many opportunities to write with a variety of writing instruments, such as felt-tipped pens and markers, ink pens, and chalk. Just like adults, children will quickly find a writing implement that they prefer to use. Although felt-tipped pens are popular because their ink flows easily, the ones that release harmful odors should be avoided.

Gripping the Pencil

Children are often not taught the correct way to hold a pencil or have somehow adopted their own improper approaches to doing so, especially when they enter kindergarten never having had the opportunity to hold a writing utensil. These children are usually easy to identify because they typically curl all their fingers around the pencil in a fistlike position. As a result, it is not unusual to see a student grip a pencil in a tight, almost choking manner and in turn develop large calluses on the middle finger of the writing hand. Other children tend to point the eraser straight up into the air, and still others hold the pencil between the index and middle forgers. Despite such awkwardness, many teachers devote little attention to the manner in which students hold their pencils, even though this is crucial to the development of legible handwriting.

The proper way in which to grip a pencil can be explained methodically. A child begins by placing a sharpened pencil on a desk, with the point of the pencil pointing towards the child's midsection. If the child is right-handed, he then picks up the pencil with the right hand's thumb and index finger at the point where the paint and sharpened wood meet. By using the other hand, the child can gently pull the eraser end of the pencil upward so that the pencil rests on the hand between the thumb and index finger. Left-handed students follow the same procedure except that the pencil should be grasped with the thumb and index finger of the left hand about 1/4 inch above the line where the paint and the sharpened wood meet. Regardless of the hand used, the grip should be somewhat loose and free of tension.

Manuscript Handwriting

Manuscript handwriting, often referred to by parents as printing, requires the use of independent strokes to form letters. There are two popular manuscript styles. The first, the *Zaner-Bloser* manuscript style, emphasizes circles and lines in the forming of the 26 letters of the alphabet (see figure 11.9 on p. 468). The Zaner-Bloser circles and lines are found most commonly in environmental print (e.g., McDonald's, Lowes, Wal-Mart, and Target signs) and somewhat similar to the fonts used in picture books. In the second style, the *D'Nealian* manuscript style, letters more closely resemble italic, cursive letters than print in books (e.g., *Walgreens*). The pencil rarely leaves the paper as circles, lines, and curves are used in D'Nealian letter construction.

Kindergartners were found to have four times more difficulty recognizing and identifying D'Nealian manuscript letters than Zaner-Bloser letters (DeWitz & Kuhl, 1994). Because of children's greater familiarity with the Zaner-Bloser letter formation, which closely resembles printed text, many schools use it instead of the newer D'Nealian style of curved manuscript letters.

In experimenting with handwriting and writing instruments, young children first produce capital manuscript letters. Once they begin to write their own pieces, they start to use the lowercase manuscript alphabet more frequently.

Because children are so eager to write and to share their recorded ideas and feelings with others, students accept manuscript handwriting lessons quite readily. Unfortunately, by the end of first grade or the beginning of second grade, this enthusiasm is offset by the fact that children have often come to accept only perfection in their work. Thus, the second grader who writes several lines perfectly before making a minor error will likely wad up the paper and stomp off to the wastebasket only to return to attempt another "perfect" paper.

Some children continue to use manuscript writing throughout their school years and even beyond. Ten percent of adults print their signatures (Sedgwick, 1996). The reasons for this vary. Some students may never be introduced to cursive writing through formal instruction. This can happen, for instance, when a second grader initially attends a school district in which the transition to cursive handwriting occurs in the third grade, but the child subsequently moves to another school district where the transition to cursive occurs in the second grade. In cases such as this, the child may attempt to make an informal, independent transition, but this may or may not prove to be successful. Thus, the child is more likely to continue to rely on the more familiar manuscript handwriting style.

Children may also come to rely solely on manuscript handwriting because they find the connecting of cursive letters to be difficult. Moreover, because some children simply write more legibly in the manuscript style, the classroom teacher may no longer insist that such students use cursive handwriting at all times. This may be the best resolution, particularly if a fifth or sixth grader is uncomfortable with cursive handwriting and this discomfort hinders composition writing. When this is the case, cursive handwriting may be required for the final draft, but the other drafts may be allowed in manuscript handwriting.

Zaner-Bloser Simplified Manuscript Font

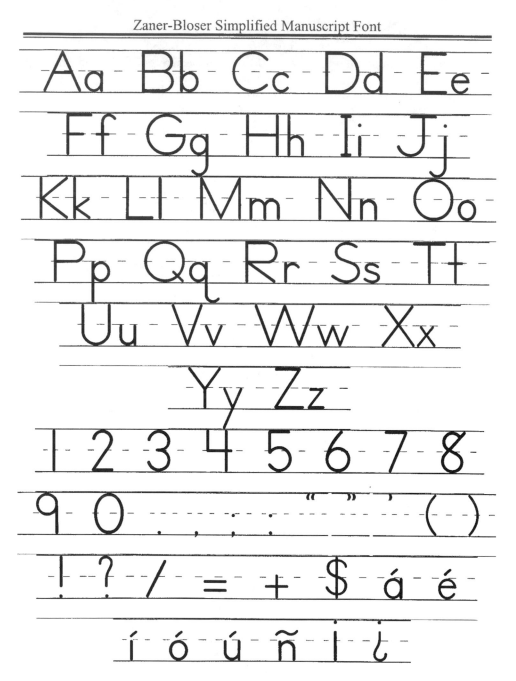

Figure 11.9   Example of Zaner-Bloser manuscript handwriting

Letter Reversals

Young children frequently make letter reversals as they learn manuscript handwriting. Such reversals may involve confusing two letters, such as *b* and *d*, or actually writing a letter backward. Furthermore, *mirror writing*, or writing entire words backward so that when held up to a mirror they can be read correctly, is commonplace among first graders. Some researchers believe that although all children produce such reversals, only a small number of children will continue to make these inversions over a long period of time; for those who do, instructional intervention by the teacher is necessary.

To help reduce the number of letter reversals, kindergarten and first-grade teachers should introduce letters that are similar in different lessons scheduled several days or even weeks apart. For example, children often confuse the letters *p* and *q*; by introducing the letter *p* first, the teacher provides students with an opportunity to acquaint themselves with this letter before they are presented with the less frequently used letter *q*.

By making sure that children know correct letter formation and use proper beginning and ending points, teachers can help students reduce letter reversals. Likewise, the use of simple mnemonic devices can also be helpful. For instance, using both hands, children can form two circles with their thumbs and index fingers. By holding the remaining fingers up and touching the thumbnails together, they can form and then visualize the letters *b* and *d*, as in *bed*. Such an activity creates a vivid impression on youngsters as they seek to recall proper techniques.

Regardless of whether the D'Nealian or Zaner-Bloser handwriting approach is used, children produce reversals. Similarly, regardless of approach, some children were found to write the letter *s* in mirror fashion (Farris, 1994). Nevertheless, research indicates that D'Nealian-instructed students have significantly fewer reversals than students taught by the other approaches (Farris, 1994; Trap-Porter et al., 1984). On the other hand, D'Nealian-instructed students interchange letters other than those traditionally interchanged; for example, *f* and *t* are often confused by these children.

Cursive Handwriting

Instruction in cursive handwriting differs from that of the manuscript technique, for children must be taught to read the flowing cursive style before attempting to produce letters and words in a similar fashion. Cursive writing maintains a continuous, linear motion of pencil on paper from the first to the last letter of a word (see figure 11.10 on p. 470). Despite this basic criterion, some children insist on stopping in the middle of a word to dot an *i* and cross a *t*.

Typically, children are expected to make the transition from manuscript to cursive handwriting during the second semester of the second grade or the first semester of the third grade. When children are older, such as beginning third or fourth grade, the transition takes place more quickly, usually within six to eight weeks, and is more lasting. By waiting to introduce cursive at the beginning of third grade or even later, fewer students revert to using manuscript in upper-elementary and middle school. By the beginning of third grade,

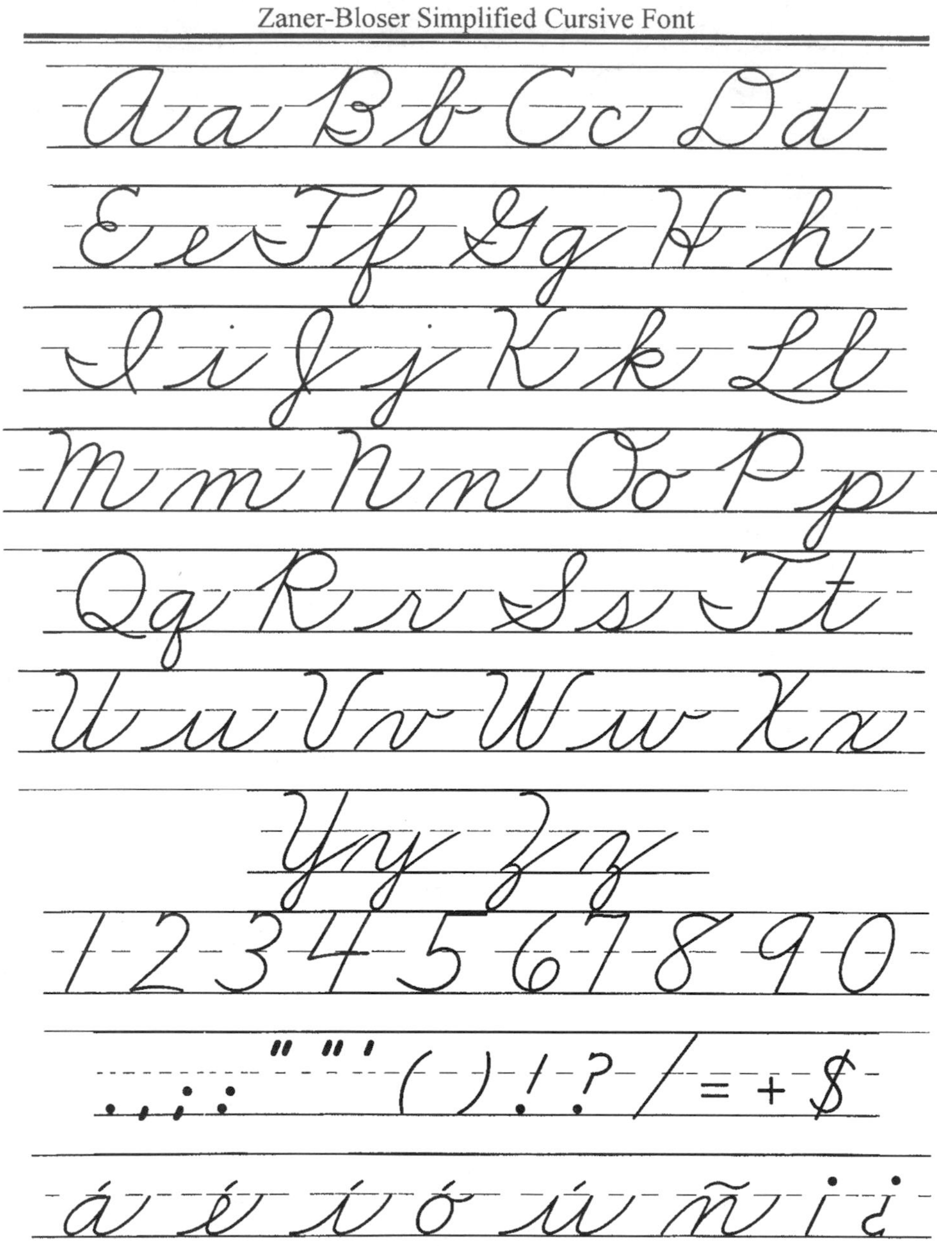

Zaner-Bloser Simplified Cursive Font

Figure 11.10   Example of Zaner-Bloser cursive handwriting

fine motor skills are much more developed than they were nine months earlier at the beginning of second semester of second grade.

Children tend to equate the mastering of cursive handwriting with being adultlike, and they are highly motivated to leave the "childish" manuscript behind in order to advance to what they perceive as the "grown-up" handwriting style. A second benefit to introducing cursive handwriting at a later age is that boys, who generally lag behind in fine motor skill development, may be more developmentally prepared to learn the new style in third grade rather than second grade.

Because children vary in the development of their handwriting skills, teachers should be aware of individual student progress in the use of manuscript handwriting. For example, Penny, a second-semester first grader, wrote her name in the kind of condensed cursive style shown in figure 11.11, an indication that she was ready for the transition to cursive. In this regard, a teacher must address the unusual advances of a certain class member so as not to hinder overall handwriting development.

Figure 11.11   Six-year-old Penny's attempt at cursive handwriting

As mentioned earlier, some children move from one school district to another without receiving cursive handwriting instruction. Other children will develop fine motor control later than their peers and thus will require special guidance in the acquisition of cursive skills. In either case, educators should pay particularly close attention to both student backgrounds and individual talents in evaluating students' needs for direction.

Legibility

Legibility is an important factor in both manuscript and cursive handwriting methods. Yet legibility plays a greater role in the cursive method because the connections between various letters and the letter formations themselves affect overall clarity to a greater extent.

Teachers who accept papers that are barely readable are not inspiring students to appreciate handwriting as an essential skill, and without other, more formal standards, students often lack personal goals in this regard. The teacher who feels a sense of inadequacy about his own handwriting may also place less emphasis on the importance of legibility for students. Therefore, it is essential that all teachers become masters of the craft.

Six letters account for 30 percent of all illegibilities in cursive handwriting: *h, i, k p, r,* and *z.* Of these, *r* accounts for 12 percent of the overall illegibility total (Horton, 1970). Keeping this in mind, teachers must make certain that children are aware of the need for correct letter formation in their writing of these six troublesome letters.

Cursive handwriting that has a smooth beginning and ending stroke increases legibility, whereas abruptly beginning or ending the word decreases legibility. The stroke should start on the baseline and then move to begin the letter formation. Likewise, the stroke for the last letter of a word should continue with a flowing motion to the baseline. By including such strokes for each letter, legibility is increased by as much as 25 percent (Froese & Straw, 1981). This can be demonstrated by the fact that a hastily made *a* might look like an *o* when incorrect stroking techniques are used.

Some children develop bad habits either because they have never learned correct letter formation procedures or because they have created their own shortcuts to save time. However, if such habits are quickly corrected, children are less likely to insist on using them in the future and therefore will eliminate them from any potential lifetime repertoire.

Motivating intermediate-grade children to improve their handwriting techniques can be difficult. One successful approach has been to introduce entire classes to the art of calligraphy. Simple calligraphy books can be purchased at most bookstores, and inexpensive felt-tipped pens are available in a variety of colors at most office supply stores. One or two projects using basic calligraphy skills as part of an art class can result in students' increased attention and devotion to their own handwriting (see box 11.3).

Left-Handed Children

Hand dominance is usually established before children enter kindergarten, and sometimes by the age of two. Still, some children enter kindergarten using

---

11.3 In the Classroom: Mini Lesson

Introducing Calligraphy

Calligraphy is elegant handwriting that requires much patience, time, and skill to learn. Breakthroughs in writing instruments such as felt-tipped pens have made calligraphy more accessible for intermediate-level students. Felt-tipped pens are available in several colors and are relatively inexpensive. The teacher may want to obtain a supply of such pens, calligraphy paper, and an easy-to-follow calligraphy guide and place these materials on a table where students can have access to them. Then, over a period of a few days, the teacher reads *The Strange Night Writing of Jessamine Colter,* a mystery by Cynthia DeFelice (1988). This book is about a calligrapher, or "fancy writer," who over a period of 50 years makes posters, diplomas, birth and marriage announcements, and death notices for people in her community. As she grows older, Jessie discovers that she has the ability to foresee the future—to write about events before they occur.

After listening to the story, students are encouraged to use calligraphy to make their own posters and announcements that will predict future events. Students may wish to refer to examples of calligraphy in the DeFelice book.

DeFelice, C. C. (1988). *The strange night writing of Jessamine Colter.* New York: Macmillan.

both hands for coloring, drawing, and manipulating eating utensils. One kindergarten teacher, Mrs. James, expressed concern over Kyle, a student who possessed superior verbal and mathematical abilities as compared to the other students in the class. She observed Kyle in the process of coloring a picture he had drawn. He used his right hand to color from the bottom of the page to the top and his left hand to color from the top down. Mrs. James asked him to explain why he used his crayons in such a unique way. Kyle responded, "'Cause when I color up, I like to use my right hand and when I color down, I like to use my left hand." These habits obviously made sense to him. Later on, Mrs. James had the opportunity to talk with Kyle's parents and discovered that they actually encouraged him to use both hands in hopes that such ambidextrous talent would help Kyle in athletics as he grew older.

Some children continue to use both hands for writing for a year or even longer. This is particularly true of the child who breaks his writing arm. In other cases, children write ambidextrously simply because they have never been forced to choose one hand over the other. Mrs. Volkman, a third-grade teacher, complained about one student's illegible handwriting style. Although it was April and she had introduced the transition from manuscript to cursive handwriting at the beginning of the school year, Mrs. Volkman could barely read Terry's cursive handwriting. Upon closer observation, she noticed that

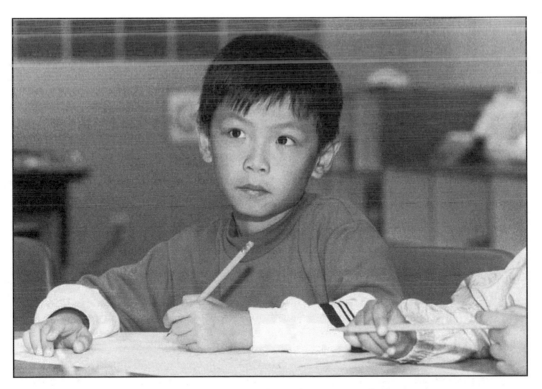

Left-handed students need special attention in letter formation and slant.

Terry would begin to write with his right hand but ultimately would switch the pencil to his left hand. After witnessing this sequence several times, Mrs. Volkman asked Terry, "Why don't you write with just one hand instead of changing hands?" Terry looked up at her and responded, "When one hand gets tired, I let it rest while I write with the other one." Again, this was a perfectly logical response in view of the child's perceptions of the situation.

Wasylyk (1989) estimates that between 10 and 15 percent of students in a typical class show left-hand dominance and that the rate of incidence is increasing. These children require special instruction in the areas of pencil grip, paper position, and handwriting slant because each of these varies from those of their right-handed counterparts.

As already noted, left-handed students need to grip writing instruments about 1/4 inch higher than do right-handed students. Doing this allows left-handers to avoid dragging their hand across the page, thereby smearing recently written letters and also gives them a better overall view of what they are writing. The writing instrument should be positioned so that it points over the writer's left shoulder. As is true for right-handed students, left-handed students should keep their grip both flexible and relaxed.

The writing paper needs to be slanted to the right for left-handed students. However, each of these students must find the best location for the paper because both an individual's height and the slant of the desk necessitate some adjustment in paper position. For students in grade three and up, "left-handed notebooks" are recommended; such notebooks have the spiral on the right side rather than on the left.

Grouping left-handed students together for formal handwriting instruction helps prevent the confusion that often occurs when a teacher attempts to instruct both right- and left-handed students simultaneously. In addition, teachers should provide a suitable amount of time for the completion of in-class writing assignments because left-handed students write more slowly than right-handed students when first gaining handwriting experience.

Special Problems

Whereas some children never acquire the fine motor skills needed for legible writing, others have legibility problems caused by gripping a pencil too tightly. Teachers need to address these and other special problems through individual guidance. A lack of fine motor control may require a student to use a larger pencil. In the case of severe shaking of the hand, a teacher may have a child hold a pencil between the index and middle finger; by pointing the eraser end of the pencil toward the shoulder of the writing hand and resting the pencil on the thumb, the child achieves a more thorough command of handwriting despite the use of such an unorthodox grip. Some children simply write best by using manuscript forms.

When a child insists on gripping a pencil too tightly, the teacher can have the child use a plastic or rubber grip that slides over the pencil. The triangular-shaped grip fits comfortably in a child's hand and reduces the tension that develops between the pencil and child's fingers. Should a child continue to grip the pencil too tightly, a piece of tape wrapped around the first knuckle of the index finger may lessen the pressure of the grip. If a student clenches the pencil in a fistlike grip, holding a ball of wadded paper in the palm of the hand while writing will help to release tension (Wasylyk, 1989).

Some students in grades four to eight, particularly boys, prefer to print rather than to use cursive. Generally these children were introduced to cursive before they had sufficient fine motor skills.

When a teacher notices a sudden deterioration in a child's handwriting, the teacher should be alerted to other possible changes that might be occurring within the child. The student may be physically ill or worried about family problems at home. Researches have found that handwriting is closely linked to an individual's emotions. It should be noted that students who produce extremely small letters are usually shy and withdrawn, whereas those who write large letters tend to be more outgoing. Because of this, some corporations have initiated a policy that requires job applicants to submit a handwriting sample for analysis.

Evaluating Handwriting

In evaluating both manuscript and cursive handwriting, the teacher should consider six primary factors: letter formation, spacing, slant, alignment, line quality, and size. Correct letter formation is, of course, extremely important (Hackney, 1993). The teacher should evaluate this according to the handwriting method taught. The space between letters should be consistent, that is, neither too large nor too small. Likewise, the distance between words should be appropriate so that readers are readily able to identify individual words. The slant of the letters should be uniform and not overly dramatic. In general, the writing of right-handed students should slant to the right, whereas that of left-handed students should either be vertical or slant to the left. The criteria for evaluating handwriting are summarized as follows:

Letters should be of even height. For example, the lowercase manuscript or cursive letters *a, c, e, g, i, j, m, n, o, p, q, r, s, u, v, w, x, y,* and *z* should all be of the same height, with i and j being dotted slightly above the other letters. Such proper alignment greatly aids readability. The size of the letters should also allow for easy reading. Students who produce microscopic-size letters should be encouraged to increase overall letter size. Students who can only fit a few words on a line because they use extremely large letters should gain practice in reducing letter size. In addition, line quality should not be too faint or too bold. Rather, lines should be of an even thickness throughout the writing.

Letter formation: The shape of the letters should correspond to the handwriting method taught.

Spacing: Letters should not be cramped together or strung out across the page. Spacing should be consistent between letters and between words.

Slant: All letters should be consistent in terms of slant. That is, letters may slant slightly to the left or to the right or they may have no slant at all just as long as they all do the same thing.

Alignment:	Comparable letters (for example, a and c or h and l) should be the same height.
Line quality:	The writing instrument should be held correctly and in a relaxed manner. The lines should be steady and unwavering, with an even thickness.
Size:	Letters should be neither too small nor too large to be read easily, and the size should be consistent.

After gaining some practical handwriting experience, children should be encouraged to evaluate their own handwriting by circling their best letters according to the six criteria. Because of its major significance, however, correct letter formation should be the first criterion they consider.

Summary

Spelling and handwriting are conventions of writing and should be taught in that context. Teachers must be aware of the five stages of spelling development (precommunicative, prephonetic, phonetic, transitional, and conventional), including the characteristics of each stage. The first stages of spelling development are temporary; they last only until the student learns the conventions of writing. It is important that teachers assess students' spelling error patterns so that specific instruction can be determined and implemented for each student.

The successful acquisition of both manuscript and cursive handwriting skills is important for children because such skills provide them with the freedom to write as they wish. A lack of handwriting skills can both hinder and frustrate a child, thereby reducing writing productivity.

Manuscript handwriting, which utilizes a combination of circles and lines in the formation of letters, is usually introduced in late kindergarten or early first grade. The transition to cursive handwriting generally occurs during the second semester of second grade or the beginning of third grade. In planning instructional procedures, the teacher should consider writing grip, paper position, and the handedness of the child. The criteria for evaluating handwriting are letter formation, spacing, slant, alignment, line quality, and size.

Teachers must provide opportunities for children to write frequently if spelling and handwriting skills are to be maintained and further developed. In addition, students must realize that good spelling and handwriting help to effectively convey the written message.

Questions

1. What are the stages of temporary or invented spelling? What are the characteristics of and instructional strategies for each stage?
2. What is the best method for studying spelling? Why don't all students succeed with this approach?

3. What are the components of a good spelling program? What can a teacher do to improve students' spelling?

4. How does manuscript handwriting differ from cursive handwriting?

5. Compare and contrast the D'Nealian and Zaner-Bloser handwriting styles.

6. What suggestions would you give to the parent of a four-year-old who shows left-hand dominance?

Reflective Teaching

Flip back to the beginning of the chapter to the teaching vignette entitled "Peering into the Classroom." After rereading the vignette, consider the following questions: What characteristics (either implied or directly exhibited) does the teacher possess that you would like to develop? What strengths and weaknesses are revealed for the students described in this section? How would you meet the needs of students such as these?

Activities

1. Each content area tends to have vocabulary words that are associated with that particular area. Using an intermediate-level mathematics, science, or social studies textbook, design a spelling lesson that incorporates the use of such vocabulary.

2. Make a list of words that are difficult for you to spell. Tape the list to your refrigerator and use the "look, say, cover, write, and compare" study technique to master the spelling of the words.

3. Analyze the spelling of an elementary or middle school student. Can you detect any error patterns?

4. Compare the handwriting skills of elementary or middle school students and then ask their teacher to rate each student according to reading ability (good, average, or poor). Are the good readers necessarily better in handwriting as well?

5. Observe the body language of children as they practice handwriting. How does it compare with their body language as they write in their journals?

6. Evaluate your own handwriting according to the criteria used with children.

Further Reading

Aiken, A. G., & Bayer, L. (2002). They love words. *The Reading Teacher, 56* (1), 68–74

Brand, M. (2004). *Word savvy: Integrating vocabulary, spelling, and word study, grades 3–6.* Portland, ME: Stenhouse.

Cunningham, P. M. (2000). *Phonics they use* (3rd ed.). New York: Addison-Wesley.

Farris, P. J. (1991). Handwriting instruction should not become extinct. *Language Arts, 68* (4), 312–314.

Hughes, M., & Searle, D. (2000). Spelling and the second "R." *Language Arts, 77* (3), 203–208.

Martin, C. (2003). *Word crafting: Teaching spelling, grades K–6.* Portsmouth, NH: Heinemann.

Templeton, S., & Morris, D. (1999). Questions teachers ask about spelling. *Reading Research Quarterly, 34* (1), 102–112.

Wasylyk, T. M. (1989). Teaching left-handers the right stuff. *The Reading Teacher, 42* (6), 446–447.

Wilde, S. (1990). A proposal for a new spelling curriculum. *Elementary School Journal, 90* (3), 275–290.

References

Adams, M. J. (1990). *Beginning to read: Thinking and learning about print.* Urbana, IL: Center for the Study of Reading.

Aiken, A. G., & Bayer, L. (2002). They love words. *The Reading Teacher, 56* (1), 68–74.

Allred, R. A. (1977). *Spelling: The application of research findings. The curriculum series.* Washington, DC: National Education Association. (ED 135 003).

Anderson, P. S., & Lapp, D. (1988). *Language skills in elementary education* (4th ed.). New York: Macmillan.

Atkins, C. (1984). Writing: Doing something constructive. *Young Children, 40* (1), 3–7.

Bartch, J. (1992). An alternative to spelling: An integrated approach. *Language Arts, 69,* 404–408.

Bear, D. R., Invernizzi, M., Templeton, S., & Johnson, F. (2000). *Words their way: Word study for phonics, vocabulary, and spelling instruction.* Upper Saddle River, NJ: Merrill.

Beers, C. (1980). The relationship of cognitive development to spelling and reading abilities. In E. H. Henderson & J. W. Beers, *Developmental and cognitive aspects of learning to spell.* Newark, DE: International Reading Association.

Bissex, G. (1980). *GNYS AT WRK: A child learns to write and read.* Cambridge. MA: Harvard University, Press.

Bloodgood, J. W. (1991). A new approach to spelling instruction in language arts programs. *Elementary School Journal, 92* (2), 203–211.

Brownell, C. A., Drozdal, J. G., Hopmann, M. R., Pick, A. D., & Unze, M. G. (1978). Young children's knowledge of word structure. *Child Development, 49* (3), 69–80.

Carpenter, D., & Miller, L. J. (1982). Spelling ability of reading disabled LD students and able readers. *Learning Disability Quarterly, 5* (2), 65–70.

Chandler, K., & Mapleton Teacher-Research Group. (2000). Squaring up to spelling: A teacher-research group surveys parents. *Language Arts, 77* (3), 224–229.

Clay, M. (1975). *What did I write?* Portsmouth, NH: Heinemann.

Cunningham, P. M. (2000). *Phonics they use* (3rd ed.). New York: Addison-Wesley.

Cunningham, P. M., & Cunningham, J. W. (1992). Making Words: Enhancing the invented spelling-decoding connection. *The Reading Teacher, 46* (2), 106–115.

DeMaster, V., Crossland. C., & Hasselbring, T. (1986). Consistency of learning disabled students' spelling performance. *Learning Disability Quarterly, 9* (1), 89–96.

DeWitz, P. A., & Kuhl. D. (1994, April). *The effect of handwriting style on alphabet recognition in kindergarten.* Paper presented at American Education Research Association, New Orleans, LA.

Farris, P. J. (1991). Handwriting instruction should not become extinct. *Language Arts, 68* (4), 312–314.

Farris, P. J. (1994). Learning to write the ABC's: A comparison of D'Nealian and Zaner-Bloser handwriting styles. *New Mexico Journal of Reading, 14* (2), 13–20.

Fernald, G. (1943). *Remedial techniques in basic school subjects.* New York: McGraw-Hill.

Fowler, A. E., & Liberman, I. Y. (1995). The role of phonology and orthography in morphological awareness. In L. B. Feldman (Ed.), *Morphological aspects of language processing* (pp. 157–188). Hillsdale, NJ: Erlbaum.

Froese, V., & Straw, S. B. (1981). *Research in the language arts.* Baltimore. MD: University Park Press.

Gentry, J. R. (1981). Learning to spell developmentally. *The Reading Teacher, 34* (4), 378–381.

Gentry, J. R., & Henderson. E. S. (1978). Three steps to teaching beginning readers to spell. *The Reading Teacher, 31* (6), 632–637.

Graham, S. (1983). Effective spelling program. *Elementary School Journal, 83* (5), 560–569.

Graham, S., & Miller, L. (1980). Handwriting research and practice: A unified approach. *Focus on Exceptional Children, 13* (2), 1–16.

Graves, D. (1978). Handwriting is for writing. *Language Arts, 55* (3), 393–399.

Griffith, P. (1991). Phonemic awareness helps third graders remember correct spellings, *Journal of Reading Behavior, 23,* 215–232.

Hackney, C. (1993). *Handwriting: A way to self expression.* Columbus. OH: Zaner-Bloser.

Hall, S. E. (1985). Oad Mahr Gos and writing with young children. *Language Arts, 62* (3), 262.

Hammill, D. D., Larsen, S., & McNutt, G. (1977). The effects of spelling instruction: A preliminary study. *Elementary School Journal, 78* (1), 67–72.

Harste, J., Woodward, V. A., & Burk, C. (1984). *Language stories and literacy lessons.* Portsmouth, NH: Heinemann.

Henderson, E. (1985). *Teaching spelling.* Boston: Houghton Mifflin.

Henderson, E., & Beers, C. (1980). *Developmental and cognitive aspects of learning to spell.* Newark, DE: International Reading Association.

Henderson, E., & Templeton, S. (1986). A developmental perspective of formal spelling instruction through alphabet, pattern, and meaning. *Elementary School Journal, 86* (1), 305–316.

Hillerich, R. (1977). Let's teach spelling-not phonetic misspelling. *Language Arts, 54* (3), 301–307.

Horton, L. W. (1970). Illegibilities in the cursive handwriting of ninth-graders. *Elementary School Journal, 70* (8), 446–450.

Hughes, M., & Searle, D. (2000). Spelling and the second "R." *Language Arts, 77* (3), 203–208.

Invernizzi, M. A., Abouzeid, M. P., & Bloodgood, J. W. (1997). Integrating word study: Spelling, grammar, and meaning in the language arts classroom. *Language Arts, 74* (3), 185–192.

Lamme, L. (1979). Handwriting in an early childhood curriculum. *Young Children, 35* (1), 20–27.

Manolakes, G. (1975). The teaching of spelling: A pilot study. *Elementary English, 52* (2), 243–247.

Morris, D., Bloodgood, J. W., Lomax, R. G., & Perney, J. (2003). Developmental steps in learning to read: A longitudinal study in kindergarten and first grade. *Reading Research Quarterly, 38* (3), 302–329.

Norton, D. E., (1989). *The effective teaching of language arts* (3rd ed.). Columbus, OH: Merrill.

Perfetti, C. (1992). The representation problem in reading acquisition. In P. Gough, L. Ehri, & R. Treiman (Eds.), *Reading acquisition* (pp. 145–174). Hillsdale, NJ: Erlbaum.

Piazza, C., & Tomlinson, C. (1985). A concert of writers. *Language Arts, 62* (2), 150–158.

Pinnell, G. S., & Fountas, I. C. (1998). *Word matters: Teaching Phonics and spelling in the reading/writing classroom.* Portsmouth, NH: Heinemann.

Pitman, Sir J., & St. John, J. (1969). *Alphabets and reading.* London: Pitman.

Radebaugh, M. R. (1985). Children's perceptions of their spelling strategies. *The Reading Teacher, 38* (6), 532–536.

Read, C. (1971). Preschool children's knowledge of English phonology. *Harvard Educational Review, 41* (1), 1–34.

Routman, R. (1991). *Invitations: Changing as teachers and learners.* Portsmouth, NH: Heinemann.

Scott, J. (1994). Spelling for readers and writers. *The Reading Teacher, 48* (2), 188–190.

Sedgwick, J. (1996, March 18). Call the script doctor. *Newsweek,* 62.

Templeton, S. (1991). Teaching and learning the English spelling system: Reconceptualizing method and purpose. *Elementary School Journal, 92* (2), 185–201.

Templeton, S., & Morris, D. (1999). Questions teachers ask about spelling. *Reading Research Quarterly, 34* (1), 102–112.

Tompkins, G. (2000). *Teaching writing* (3rd ed.). Columbus, OH: Merrill.

Tompkins, G. (1998). *Language arts: Content and teaching strategies* (3rd ed.). Columbus, OH: Merrill.

Trap-Porter, J., Cooper, J., Hill, D., Swisher, J., & LaNunziata, L. (1984). D'Nealian and Zaner-Bloser manuscript alphabets and initial transition to cursive handwriting. *Journal of Educational Research, 77* (6), 343–345.

Wagstaff, J. M. (1998). Building practical knowledge of letter-sound correspondences: A beginner's Word Wall and beyond. *The Reading Teacher, 51* (4), 298–304.

Wallace, G., & McLoughlin, J. A. (1988). *Learning disabilities: Concepts and characteristics* (3rd ed.). Columbus, OH: Merrill.

Wasylyk, T. M. (1989). Teaching left-handers the write stuff. *The Reading Teacher, 42* (6), 446–447.

Wilde, S. (1990). A proposal for a new spelling curriculum. *Elementary School Journal, 90* (3), 275–290.

Wilde, S. (1992). *You kan red this!* Portsmouth, NH: Heinemann.

Yopp, H. K. (1995). A test for assessing phonemic awareness in young children. *The Reading Teacher, 49* (1), 20–29.

Yopp, H. K., & Yopp, R. H. (2000). Supporting phonemic awareness development in the classroom. *The Reading Teacher, 54* (2), 130–143.

Children's Literature

Brown, M. (1954). *Cinderella.* New York: Macmillan.

Hooks, W. H. (1987). *Moss gown.* Boston: Clarion.

Huck, C. (1989). *Princess Furball* (A. Lobel, Illus.). New York: Greenwillow.

Martin, B. (1968; 1983). *Brown bear, brown bear, What do you see?* (E. Carle, Illus.). New York: Holt, Rinehart, & Winston.

Martin, B. (1991). *Polar bear, polar bear, What do you hear?* (E. Carle, Illus.). New York: Henry Holt.

Pandell, K., & dePaola, T. (1994). *I love you, sun, I love you, moon.* New York: G. P. Putnam's Sons.

Slepian, J., & Shepard, A. (2001). *The hungry thing.* New York: Scholastic.

Reading
Interaction Between Text and Reader

If you give a child a book, he's going to want to read it.

And as he reads, he's going to think about what he's reading.

And as he thinks, he's going to recall what he already knows and similar experiences he's had.

And as he thinks about those experiences, he's going to want to write.

And as he writes, he's going to want to talk to his friends and share his thoughts and ideas with them.

And as he talks with others, he's going to want to learn and discover more.

So, chances are he'll find another book to read,

And then another,

And another.

And as he reads more books, he'll discover books that make him smile, laugh, cry, angry, curious, frustrated, contented, thoughtful, happy.

And then, as time passes, he'll become a lifelong reader.

Thanks to a teacher who gave a child a book.

—Pamela J. Farris © 1995

PEERING INTO THE CLASSROOM
CREATING A READING ENVIRONMENT

Craig Sherwood is a brand-new second-grade teacher. He loves working with seven-year-olds. "They have the best humor—really corny jokes. They are so bad you have to laugh. And the kids respect your role as teacher. When they come into the classroom in the morning, they are so excited! And I pounce on their enthusiasm with lots of interesting activities about things they are interested in. Cha ching!!! The next thing you know they are so busy learning they don't even think about getting off task or into mischief."

The classroom is filled with picture books that Craig has placed in colorful milk crates. Each row of crates is marked with the genre it represents—information books, folktales, chapter books, and so forth. Over the summer, Craig devoted several early Friday and Saturday mornings poking through garage sales for his library. "Lots of people get rid of old books when their kids outgrow them. But one garage sale was the best. A first-grade teacher had just retired and I loaded up with lots of great books, even Caldecott winners. It was great! I found some software for the classroom computer, "Little Critter" and "Arthur," stuff the kids love. The "Little Critter" software even contains both English and Spanish versions. I have a Spanish-speaking student this year so that may be helpful."

An overstuffed chair with an area rug—more garage sale purchases—occupy one corner of the classroom. According to Craig, "The kids enjoy sitting in the 'author's chair' when they read their own writing. I use it to start reader's or writer's workshop when I share a book with the class."

A basket of books sits nearby. "When I was an undergraduate, I had a professor who read to us every class session, fiction and informational books. And we loved it! The professor said we should bring in ten books a week and do quick book talks. I put the books in the basket and share them every Monday. The students are then free to read the books. This means that with every Scholastic or Trumpet book order I'm spending about $30 on new books for the classroom. But the kids do read the books after I talk about or read a couple of pages from them as part of a book talk. So it does work."

Chapter Objectives

The reader will:

✓ learn about balanced literacy instruction.

✓ understand different approaches to reading instruction.

✓ learn major aspects of phonics instruction.

✓ understand ways to teach reading to special needs students.

✓ understand the best methods of teaching second-language learners to read.

✓ develop reading assessment strategies.

Standards for Professionals

The following Standards will be addressed in this chapter:

Standard 1: Foundational Knowledge and Dispositions

1.1 Demonstrate knowledge of psychological, sociological, and linguistic foundations of reading and writing processes and instruction.

1.2 Demonstrate knowledge of reading research and histories of reading.

1.3 Demonstrate knowledge of language development and reading acquisition and variations related to cultural and linguistic diversity.

1.4 Demonstrate knowledge of the major components of reading (phonemic awareness, word identification and phonics, vocabulary and background knowledge, fluency, comprehension strategies, and motivation) and how they are integrated in fluent reading.

Standard 2: Instructional Strategies and Curriculum Materials

2.1 Use instructional grouping options (individual, small-group, whole-class, and computer based) as appropriate for accomplishing given purpose.

2.2 Use a wide range of instructional practices, approaches, and methods, including technology-based practices, for learners at differing stages of development and from differing cultural and linguistic backgrounds.

2.3 Use a wide range of curriculum materials in effective reading instruction for learners at different stages of reading and writing development and from differing cultural and linguistic backgrounds.

Standard 3: Assessment, Diagnosis, and Evaluation

3.1 Use a wide range of assessment tools and practices that range from individual and group standardized tests to individual and group informal classroom assessment strategies, including technology-based assessment tools.

3.2 Place students along a developmental continuum and identify students' proficiencies and difficulties.

3.3 Use assessment information to plan, evaluate, and revise effective instruction that meets the needs of all students, including those at different developmental stages and those from differing cultural and linguistic backgrounds.

3.4 Effectively communicate results of assessments to specific individuals (students, parents, caregivers, colleagues, administrators, policy makers, policy officials, community, etc.).

Standard 4: Creating a Literate Environment

4.1 Use students' interests, reading abilities, and backgrounds as foundations for the reading and writing program.

4.2 Use a large supply of books, technology-based information, and nonprint materials representing multiple levels, broad interests, and cultural and linguistic backgrounds.

4.3 Model reading and writing enthusiastically as valued lifelong activities.

4.4 Motivate learners to be lifelong readers.

Standard 5: Professional Development
5.1 Display positive dispositions related to reading and the teaching of reading.

Introduction

Reading has received more attention over the years than all of the other language arts. The importance of knowing how to read is immeasurable, for reading provides a means of acquiring not only information, but pleasure and enjoyment as well. As the noted children's author, Natalie Babbitt (1987, p. 582) writes, "Honey, you know, is actually good for us nutritionally. So is peanut butter. But they taste so good that we forget about the nutrition. Reading is like that."

As children learn to read, they devour, like honey and peanut butter, book after book. And they don't realize or care that the process of reading, like honey and peanut butter, is good for them. Undoubtedly, the goal of a successful teacher should be to have every student become a "blanket reader"—a child who deftly hides under the blanket in bed, reading by flashlight a book that's just too good to put down. In short, students "learn to read, and to read better, by reading" (Eskey, 2002, p. 8) whether they are good readers, struggling readers, or English Language Learners (ELLs).

Reading is more than word recognition and the gleaning of concepts, information, and ideas from text. Reading is the processing of words, concepts, information, and ideas put forth by the author as they relate to the reader's previous experiences and knowledge. Only a portion of information is included by the author of a passage; it falls upon the reader to interpret the remaining information. No written text is completely self-explanatory. According to Palincsar, Ogle, Jones, Carr, and Ransom (1985), reading comprehension consists of three important parts: (1) an active, constructive process; (2) a thinking process before, during, and after reading; and (3) an interaction of the reader, the text, and context of the reading.

The type of reading material also influences the reading process. As Pam Bradley, a fourth-grade teacher, said in an interview, "Reading a book is different from reading a story. You have to follow one thread and remember it from day to day. You have to read books in order to know how to read books" (Whitney & Hubbard, 1986). Certainly reading a fictional piece differs greatly from reading an informational book, which adds yet another dimension to the act of reading. Both narrative and expository text are critical and must be part of daily reading tasks undertaken by students. "Readers use their knowledge of narrative and expository text features to make predictions about text organization and content" as well as to "answer questions and synthesize text for themselves and others" (Mills, 2002, p. 155).

Research supports Bradley's statement. In comparing out-of-school activities such as watching television, participating in sports, listening to music, and reading books, researchers have found that the strongest association with reading proficiency is reading books and that a significant increase in reading achievement occurs when a child reads for at least 10 minutes a day. The same study found that students who ranked at the fiftieth percentile or lower in reading achievement read fewer than five minutes per day outside of school (Anderson, Wilson, & Fielding, 1988).

The goals in teaching reading in elementary and middle school are first to teach students how to read and then to entice them to want to read. According to Purves (1990, p. 105), "Children should be made aware from an early stage that the world of text is a rich one indeed." To be good readers, children must have time to read, at least have temporary ownership of the material they are reading, and be allowed to respond to the material while and after reading it (Atwell, 1998). This chapter discusses various approaches to the teaching of reading in elementary school, including ways to integrate reading into the elementary curriculum.

Teachers as Professionals

What do teachers do to provide appropriate reading instruction for their students? The majority of classroom teachers rely on an eclectic approach; that is, they select what they believe are the best instructional practices, depending on the needs of their students. To do so, the teachers must stay current with instructional methods and materials. This means being a member of the International Reading Association and attending local, state, and occasionally national reading conferences as well as participating in local professional staff development opportunities. Maria Walther, a first-grade teacher, joins with two other teachers in her school district for Tuesday-night team meetings as they plan for the following week of instruction. By hashing out ideas, creating interesting lesson plans, sharing new children's literature, and discussing professional books, these teachers reflect on their own instructional practices and seek answers to teaching challenges they face every day. Through such professional discussions and activities, the Tuesday-night team become exemplary teachers as they strive to meet the needs of all of their students.

A major study of exemplary teachers was conducted by Richard Allington (2002) who found six common factors that he dubbed the six Ts: time, texts, teaching, talk, tasks, and testing.

Time: Ample time was provided for students to engage in meaningful reading and writing activities during the school day.

Texts: The reading material in the classroom was plentiful and at the proper reading level of the students, thereby aiding fluency and comprehension.

Teaching: Exemplary teachers were found to model good reading and writing strategies for their students. They were active teachers who instructed as needed, nurturing and prodding when appropriate.

Talk: Students of exemplary teachers were encouraged to talk to their peers and to the teacher, sharing ideas, criticizing text, and discussing what they've read.

Tasks: Tasks were designed to provide students with choices. Such activities increasingly kept students engaged for longer periods of time and to encourage self-monitoring of one's own work.

Testing: Student work was assessed more for effort and improvement than for achievement.

Allington (2002) summed up his research study by pointing out that exemplary teachers taught children while typical teachers taught programs. The more teachers rely on a program, the less knowledgeable they are about reading instruction. Typical teachers were less able to discuss current instructional practices and develop tasks that would best produce growth in reading. As Aristotle, the Greek philosopher said, "We are what we repeatedly do. Excellence, then, is not an act, but a habit." If we are to be exemplary teachers, we must know reading and writing strategies and apply them as our students need them.

The six Ts as defined by Allington provide us with an excellent guide to classroom reading instruction. As teachers, we should reflect each week on how we've met each of the six Ts in our own instructional practices. For those we believe we haven't accomplished but feel we should have, we need to plan ways to ensure that those areas are covered for the upcoming week.

Approaches to the Teaching of Reading

Instruction in reading may be planned or unplanned. Durkin (1990, pp. 473–474) writes that *planned* instruction occurs

> when a teacher selects materials and procedures for the purpose of attaining a prespecified goal. Instruction can also be unplanned as when a teacher is wise enough to respond in helpful ways to students' questions, misinterpretations, overgeneralizations, and the like. Other things being equal, unplanned instruction has a better chance of succeeding than planned instruction because the reason that prompts it is obvious to students. That makes the instruction inherently meaningful.

Every teacher must thoroughly plan each day's reading instruction. However, when the unexpected question arises or unfamiliar word is encountered during a child's reading, the teacher must be able to think on her feet and react to the teachable moment. Holdaway (1986, p. 42) agrees, stating "The teacher of reading is a skilled attendant to the natural language processing abilities of children." This is referred to by Yetta Goodman as "kid watching" as the teacher must have her thumb on the pulse of every reader in the classroom and react accordingly. Thus, decision making and evaluation are ongoing processes, and the teacher must be constantly alert for "teachable moments."

In 1938, Louise Rosenblatt introduced the transactional theory of reading. She believed that the reader not only brings meaning to the reading act through previous experiences and other reading but that the reader's feelings add to what is taken away from the text, as well. Rosenblatt believed that people read for two purposes: for enjoyment and to get information. She called these aesthetic and efferent reading stances. Today, educators recognize the importance of reading for pleasure and to gain new information. Motivating students has become an important aspect of reading instruction (see chapter 3).

In the 1980s, the four blocks reading program became widespread in the primary grades as teachers put up Word Walls above chalkboards and phonics once again came to the forefront of reading. The four blocks program includes independent reading, guided reading, and writing along with working with word instruction (Cunningham & Hall, 1998). In the 1990s, guided reading (Fountas & Pinnell, 1996; 1999; 2001) grew in popularity as teachers in grades K–8 used think alouds to demonstrate reading strategies as they read aloud with their students following along with the text. Classroom libraries were coded by reading level according to the readability difficulty. Inferential reading instruction is emphasized in the early 2000s as students are encouraged to write any facts, questions, or responses to narrative and expository text as they read and use small group discussions to probe further. Think alouds modeled by the teacher to demonstrate reading strategies for different kinds of text became yet another element in the teacher's repertoire of reading instructional practices (Harvey & Goudvis, 2000).

Basal readers remain the major components of most reading programs in elementary schools in the United States, despite the increasing number of followers of the transactional view of reading. Until recently, basal readers depended upon skills and subskills taught through workbook and worksheet exercises that accompanied selections, actual or condensed, from children's literature. Research findings in literacy development have led publishers to modify their basal reading series to incorporate children's literature and word strategies as well as an interactive model of reading, writing, and discussing. However, workbooks and worksheets are still integral parts of basal reading programs.

Reading in a Balanced Literacy Program

A *balanced literacy program* integrates phonics in grades K–2 and continues with word study through eighth grade, along with the reading of quality literature. Opportunities to write reflectively and objectively abound. Students in a balanced literacy program "experience both broad and deep reading. The breadth of all types of literature . . . makes broad reading possible. When literature itself provokes thought and reflection through profound themes, characters challenged by problems, and plots linked by events that are held together by an appealing style, then readers can engage in deep reading" (Burke, 1999, p. 67).

In considering a balanced approach to teaching reading, Jill Fitzgerald (1999, p. 103) suggests that the approach is based on a set of beliefs:

• There are equally important multiple kinds of knowledge about reading that children should attain. Local knowledge about reading is important, such as being able to read words at sight, knowing how to use various strategies to figure out unknown words, and knowing word meanings. Global knowledge about reading is important, such as understanding, interpreting, and responding to reading. Love of reading is important.

- There are equally effective multiple knowledge sources, including the teacher, parents, and other children.
- There are equally important multiple ways of learning through which children can attain the varied sorts of knowledge about reading.

In Fitzgerald's view, by considering the above philosophical beliefs, teachers can then determine which forms of reading instruction children need. Balanced literacy instruction includes shared reading, guided reading, self-selected or independent reading, and literature study. These go hand in hand with shared writing, guided writing, and independent writing.

Shared Reading and Think Alouds

Shared reading involves having the text available for the students to follow along as the teacher reads it aloud. Students may each have a copy of the actual text or the text may be on chart paper or projected on an overhead transparency. At the kindergarten and first-grade levels, the teacher may have a big book so that all students can easily see the words. As the teacher reads aloud, students follow along. The teacher first introduces the book by talking about the title and the illustration on the book's cover. If the book is a picture book, a picture walk is done to cue the students as to what may be forthcoming. Next the teacher reads aloud, modeling his thinking strategies. Occasionally he will invite a student to share his thinking. Shared reading permits the teacher to reveal his thought processes in "think alouds" (see chapter 3) as he examines various aspects of the text. The teacher shares how he does word analysis and comprehends the text, and unlocks meaning for unfamiliar words (Harvey & Goudvis, 2000). For average and struggling readers, this process may need to be modeled repeatedly throughout the school year for each reading strategy presented. Above average readers may only need an occasional refresher for each reading strategy. When the text is finished, the students then reread it independently to practice their reading skills. Many teachers have the students reread the text at least once at school and again at home.

In reading narrative text, the teacher may speak to the protagonist's behavior or how she visualizes the action in the story. An unfamiliar word receives a musing as to how to determine its meaning through use of context clues while a multisyllabic word is highlighted as to how to divide it into syllables. For expository text, the teacher might demonstrate how to skim through the text and illustrations to focus on key concepts for the passage. By reading aloud the headings and picture captions while noting words in bold print, the teacher can demonstrate how her own reading antenna is alerted. As she reads, she then relates her previous knowledge to the newly gained knowledge found in the text. Because the students are following along with the text, the teacher may stop from time to time and have one of the students reread aloud a section for the group to discuss.

Guided Reading

Guided reading was popularized by Irene Fountas and Gay Su Pinnell (2001) who believe that students should engage in small group instruction of three to eight students as they read the same text. The group is homogeneous as the children read at about the same level of difficulty, have the same or similar reading behaviors, and have similar instructional needs. Nevertheless, the groups are temporary as some students may progress more rapidly than their peers. The teacher selects the material that the guided reading group is to read and has the students read it silently and independently. As they read the text at the reading table, the teacher may ask each student to read briefly aloud four or five sentences to do a fluency check. Each student's fluency is then noted by the teacher in her anecdotal records. If the text seemed too difficult, the student might be moved to a lower level text for the next guided reading lesson. If too easy, the student could be moved to one with increased difficulty. Marie Clay (1991) suggests that students should be able to read 91 to 94 percent of the words of a text for a guided reading lesson to be successful. The text may be narrative or expository, depending upon the reading strategy being taught that day.

Reading strategies are introduced explicitly to the group to enable the students to read fiction and nonfiction, informational text. The teacher jots down problems the students are having and then tailors future guided reading lessons to their needs. Extension activities assigned by the teacher may involve group discussion, individual writing responses, or other tasks.

Unlike readability formulae that assign a grade level such as 2 or 2.5, texts used for guided reading have been more precisely leveled by Fountas and Pinnell (1996; 1999; 2001). Below is a listing of a few fiction trade books for the A to Z (easiest to most difficult) categories by Fountas and Pinnell (1996; 1999; 2001). Most school libraries will have these books as part of their collection.

Level

A	Burningham, J. (1985). *Colors.* New York: Crown.
B	Carle, E. (1987). *Have you seen my cat?* New York: Picture Book Studio.
C	Williams, S. (1989). *I went walking.* Orlando, FL: Harcourt Brace.
D	Peek, M. (1985). *Mary wore her red dress.* New York: Clarion.
E	Hill, E. (1980). *Where's Spot?* New York: Putnam.
F	Hutchins, P. (1968). *Rosie's walk.* New York: Macmillan.
G	Shaw, N. (1986). *Sheep in a jeep.* Boston: Houghton Mifflin.
H	Kraus, R. (1970). *Whose mouse are you?* New York: Macmillan.
I	Wood, A. (1984). *The napping house.* San Diego: Harcourt Brace.
J	Rylant, C. (1987). *Henry and Mudge: The first book.* New York: Scholastic.
K	Williams, V. (1987). *Three days on a river in a red canoe.* New York: Scholastic.
L	Allard, H. (1985). *Miss Nelson is missing.* Boston: Houghton Mifflin.
M	Park, B. (1992). *Junie B. Jones and the stupid smelly bus.* New York: Random House.
N	Danziger, P. (1994). *Amber Brown is not a crayon.* New York: Putnam.
O	Cleary, B. (2002). *Ramona's world.* New York: HarperCollins.
P	Sobol, D. (1978). *Encyclopedia Brown takes the case.* New York: Scholastic.
Q	Howe, D., & Howe, J. (1979). *Bunnicula.* New York: New York: Atheneum.
R	Reynolds, P. R. (1991). *Shiloh.* New York: Atheneum.

S   Paterson, K. (1984). *The great Gilly Hopkins*. New York: Hearst.

T   Curtis, C. (1999). *Bud, not Buddy*. New York: Delacorte.

U   Lowry, L. (1989). *Number the stars*. Boston: Houghton Mifflin.

V   Sachar, L. (1999). *Holes*. New York: Farrar, Straus & Giroux.

W   Yep, L. (1993). *Dragon's gate*. New York: HarperCollins.

X   Farmer, N. (1996). *A girl named Disaster*. New York: Orchard.

Y   Collier, J., & Collier, C. (1994). *With every drop of blood*. New York: Delacorte.

Z   Myers, W. D. (1988). *Scorpions*. New York: Harper & Row.

Self-Selected, Independent Reading

Self-selected, independent reading requires that students choose their own reading material. Kindergartners and first graders typically select picture books, both fiction and nonfiction, while second graders drift to the chapter books. Third graders and on up tend to explore a wide variety of genres—contemporary fiction, fantasies, informational books, mysteries, and the like. Middle schoolers may select magazines and computer game code books for leisure reading. The teacher's role is multifaceted as she must demonstrate a few times each semester how to select a book and once a week give book talks to "sell" the books to her students (see chapter 4). And she must know each student's interests—a rather arduous task at any level but even more so at the middle school level.

Students should be encouraged to consider a number of things in selecting a book to read. Covers that are attractive appeal to students. Hence displaying books with the covers clearly visible enhances the likelihood that such books will be selected. Familiarity with an author also increases the potential for a book to be taken off a shelf and read. Having the student flip to the middle of the book and read from the top of the page to the bottom, counting the number of unknown or unfamiliar words with fingers on one hand can roughly determine the readability. If the student gets to his thumb before reading to the end of the page, the book is most likely too difficult. This is known as the "rule of thumb."

Literature Study

Students need to read and discuss different literary genres, and literature study is one way to accomplish that goal. As we saw in chapter 4, there are different ways to conduct literature study. Grand conversations, literature circles, and literature response offer heterogeneous groupings so that the literary piece can be explored from different facets (i.e. characters, plot, setting, theme) via a literary discussion. Struggling readers and diverse learners may have the book read to them or listen to books on tape so they, too, can engage in their group's discussion. By having students complete assigned reading and writing tasks for their group, students learn to compromise and to assist one another. A kind of shepherding of lower ability readers and writers takes place as the discussion leader strives to make certain everyone is on task and up to speed with the material being covered.

The more children read, the better readers they become. This Hispanic student is enjoying a humorous trade book during SSR time. Teachers must continually assess each student's needs and base their instruction on those needs.

Literature study enriches readers with a deeper understanding of the text. By listening to each other's interpretations of the piece of literature, they gain new insights and appreciation. According to Fountas and Pinnell (2001, p. 47), "literature study helps students connect complex concepts and ideas to their own lives and encourages them to become lifelong readers."

Four Blocks Reading Program

Reading in the primary grades can be divided into four blocks: guided reading, self-selected reading, writer's workshop, and working with words (Cunningham & Hall, 1998). *Guided reading* involves reading a selection from a basal reader section by section. After the students read the section or entire story silently, the children are randomly asked to read aloud the story or portions of the story. The basis of the actual guided reading portion of the lesson is the development of comprehension derived by questions the teacher asks about the story. *Self-selected reading* occurs when students read books of their own choosing, either from the teacher's own classroom library or books checked out from the school's library. The teacher's role is to assist students in locating books that interest them and that are at their independent reading level. *Writer's workshop* in the primary grades consists of the same components as in grades four to eight: sharing a piece of literature, doing mini lesson on some aspect of writing, evaluating the status of the class, having students do on-task writing, sharing of student work, and assigning group work as needed. *Working with words* involves having children engage in word sorts, making words, seeking patterns in words, and developing class Word Walls.

The Four Blocks of Reading approach is considered by many to be a balanced approach. It involves the development of comprehension, free reading of children's literature, writing, and word study. The two goals of the program are to "combine the major approaches to reading" and to provide "for a wide range of literacy levels without ability grouping" (Cunningham & Hall, 1998, p. 35).

Reader's Workshop

Reader's workshop follows the same structure as writer's workshop with five main components: sharing time, mini lesson, status of the class, student reading, and student sharing.

Sharing time is a brief, five- to ten-minute period in which teachers read aloud a piece of children's literature (e.g., patterned books, folktales, opening pages of a chapter book, a section of a nonfiction book, poetry). Typically the piece shared ties into the goals of the curriculum. For instance, sharing descriptive writing, a form of expository writing, in a book by Gail Gibbons or Seymour Simon. The students can then discuss what makes a piece of descriptive writing interesting and informative.

After sharing time, the teacher presents a *mini lesson* on a reading strategy. Topics for mini lessons vary but usually are based on current student needs so that the instruction is developmental in nature. Required reading skills as included in the school district's curriculum and state reading goals are also mini lesson possibilities. From time to time the mini lesson will focus on activities designed to help students with reading a particular kind of genre or how to read to gather information for content area subjects.

After the mini lesson, the teacher takes the *status of the class* in which he uses a clipboard with a list of student names and boxes for each day of the week to jot down notations as to the type of reading the student is doing. To speed up the process, often codes are used: SSB—self-selected book; CRB—class required book; LC—literature circle group; LR—literature response; RK—record keeping; RC—reading conference; GRC—group reading conference; PR—portfolio review; GS—goal setting; BOB—bailed out of book (failed to finish reading the book). Some teachers even manage to squeeze in the title and/ or author of the book the student is reading. This is a nice anecdotal record for the teacher because it indicates who is an avid reader and who is a plugger.

After the status of the class is taken, usually a 3-minute task, the teacher has the students read for 15 to 40 minutes, depending upon the grade level of the students. When starting with first graders around the middle of the school year, 10 minutes is long enough for them to read independently. Four different activities take place during the student reading portion of reader's workshop: self-selected reading, literature response, literature circles, and individual reading conferences.

Self-selected reading occurs when students read books they have picked out for pleasure reading. This fosters the love of reading as students become involved in the aesthetics of the book. Chapter books by favorite authors are devoured during such times. Some students, particularly gifted students, prefer reading nonfiction books for pleasure as they really do enjoy learning for learning's sake. They love discovering ideas that are new to them. For such children, there is no difference between aesthetic and efferent reading.

Literature response involves the student reading and reacting to what she is reading by writing down thoughts in a journal. *Literature circles* require that students work in groups and take active roles. Group discussion, or grand conversations, of the textual material(s) is an integral part of literature circles Both literature response journals and literature circles are discussed in detail in chapter 4.

Individual reading conferences also take place during student reading time. Each day, the teacher meets individually with a few students. Ideally, the teacher will meet once every two weeks with each student. This develops a close student-teacher relationship and can help alleviate problems early. During the individual reading conference, the student and teacher review the student's reading portfolio as well as discuss any concerns or problems. It is a good time for the teacher to ask short, provocative questions that require long, thoughtful answers regarding the content of the books the child is reading. Most of the talking during these conferences should be done by the student, with the teacher taking a few brief, to-the-point notes.

Reader's workshop concludes each day with five to ten minutes of *student sharing*. This permits students to engage in a free discussion about what they have just read. Often it is a time when a student shares his enthusiasm for a book that becomes contagious among classmates. It is also a time to discuss literary elements, point out interesting passages, or question an author's decision.

Transactional View of Reading

As readers read a text they construct meaning based on their own previous experiences and background knowledge (Rosenblatt, 1938; 1978). According to the *transactional view* of reading, readers change their interpretations as they read the text. Thus in reading, the constructed meaning is fluid and ever-changing. Langer (1990, p. 238) believes that readers start by "being out of and stepping into" their own personal "envisionment" of the text. As they move through this envisionment, they often step back and rethink or reconsider their previous understandings. They may raise questions about what they thought they knew as well as about what the text is presenting. The last stage occurs when the readers step out of this envisionment and react to the total reading experience. According to Langer, this process occurs with all types of texts, but the emphasis and reasoning processes differ depending on whether the text is informative or narrative.

Efferent and Aesthetic Reading

In 1938, Louise Rosenblatt described reading as consisting of two stances, aesthetic and efferent. Rosenblatt asserted that we read for two primary purposes: enjoyment, or *aesthetic reading*, and to be informed, or *efferent reading*. According to Cullinan and Galda (1999, p. 43), this view of creating meaning as one reads "involves connecting life and text. And the act of creating meaning while reading a story or poem is at once highly individual and intensely social. This creation, however, always begins with a reader." Thus children and adults approach the act of reading differently, depending upon their purpose for reading. Aesthetic reading enables readers to focus on the feelings, thoughts, and images evoked as they read. Associations with characters and reactions to similar events in the readers' own lives may be made. For instance, *Uncle Jed's Barbershop* (Mitchell, 1993) may remind readers of getting their own haircuts, whereas reading *Julius, Baby of the World* (Henkes, 1990) allows readers to explore the sibling rivalry that occurs when a new baby arrives and the strong family ties that arise when someone criticizes a family member. In contrast, the poetry in *Thirteen Moons on Turtle's Back: A Native American Year of the Moons* (Bruchac & London, 1992) may sensitize readers to the different seasons and Native Americans' appreciation and respect for nature.

In efferent reading, readers want to take away information and therefore concentrate on the "practical purpose of gaining knowledge from the text" (Cullinan & Galda, 1999, p. 43). In reading about Emperor and Adelie penguins in Helen Cowcher's (1990) *Antarctica*, readers learn how penguins survive and what frightens them, while William Jay Jacob's (1990) *Ellis Island: New Hope in a New Land* gives readers background information on immigration in America beginning with Native Americans through the establishment of Ellis Island as an immigration center.

Aesthetic and efferent stances of reading are not at different ends of the spectrum, but rather are both often included in reading. Aesthetic reading relates to private, affective aspects of meaning—to the lived-through experience—whereas efferent reading primarily relates to public, cognitive aspects of meaning (Rosenblatt, 1991). A student studying about the war between the states may read *The Boys' War: Confederate and Union Soldiers Talk about the Civil War* (Murphy, 1990). The student will not only get a better understanding of the number of young men and boys who served on both sides, but also of the roles they played as drummer boys, flag bearers, and soldiers. This represents the efferent stance of reading; however, the same student may feel a tug of emotion when considering the number of boys who died of dysentery and inadequate medical care or when reading about the bartering of tobacco for coffee and the occasional letter writing between soldiers of the two opposing sides.

Evaluation in the Transactional Reading Program

Literature circles and literature response journals are important tools of evaluation in a transactional reading program. Journals may include simulated or character journals in which the reader pretends to be a favorite character and writes from that person's viewpoint, dialogue journals in which the reader writes to another student or the teacher about the book as it is read, or a literature response journal that the reader shares in a small group discussion. The teacher jots down notes about the student's journal responses and his contributions to group discussions. Rather than giving letter grades, a written description is given of the student's progress and growth as a reader.

Basal Reading Program

Basal readers have been extremely popular ever since the success of William McGuffey's *McGuffey's Reader*, which was handed down from sibling to sibling and parent to child beginning in the mid-1800s. A typical basal reading series includes a readiness workbook for emergent readers and a preprimer, a primer, and a first "reader" as introductory materials for beginning readers. For second and third graders, there are two readers with accompanying workbooks, whereas fourth through eighth graders receive one reader and an optional workbook. The teacher's manual that accompanies each level of reader provides a rigid format that precisely defines how the students are to be instructed. Discussion questions and follow-up activities are included so that the teacher does not need to prepare these in advance.

Basal reading programs have been criticized for their lack of flexibility. In addition, the narrative stories and informational selections may not be of interest to the students in a particular classroom. Regardless of the criticisms, however, basal reading programs remain a popular approach to reading instruction.

Evaluation in the Basal Reading Program

Typically, a classroom teacher takes an informal reading inventory of each student to determine her reading level before assigning a basal reader to the student. The informal reading inventory may be one developed by the publisher of the basal reading series used by the school district, by someone within the school district, or by the teacher. It consists of graded paragraphs and comprehension and vocabulary questions pertaining to each paragraph. As the student reads a paragraph orally, the teacher notes word recognition errors. After the student has completed the paragraph the teacher removes the text from the student's view and asks the comprehension and vocabulary questions.

In addition to providing informal reading placement inventories, publishing companies provide unit tests for students to take after they have completed each instructional unit of the reader. Such tests are usually designed to determine the reading achievement of the student at each point in terms of skill and subskill attainment. Some school districts use the results of such tests to determine whether a student will be retained or promoted to the next grade.

Instructional Practices for Emergent and Beginning Readers

Children exhibit the rudimentary beginnings of reading in their attentiveness to a story as it is read aloud and in their recognition of a sign advertising a favorite fast-food restaurant. This section examines emergent reading more closely and describes instructional practices for use with beginning readers.

Emergent Reading

As soon as a baby is brought home from the hospital, he is surrounded by stimulating materials: toys, household objects, television, and so on. Even the essentials needed to care for the baby are put in colorful, inviting packages. As the child grows older, training pants and underwear featuring the antics of favorite cartoon characters may be worn. Videos and computer software programs are available for children as young as 18 months. An abundance of printed materials is also available to stimulate children, including children's books, children's magazines (as well as those for grown-ups), and colorful advertisements and brochures.

Growing up in such an environment, a child's literacy development begins early, as exemplified by the three-year-old who recognizes brands of cereal, soup, and toothpaste during the weekly grocery shopping excursion with Dad or Mom. This early literacy acquisition was emphasized in a story shared by Yetta

A working father may fit in reading a storybook to his child before heading to the kitchen to prepare dinner, doing chores, or running errands.

Goodman at an international symposium focusing on preschoolers. Goodman said that in a study of over 5,000 four-year-olds, it had been impossible to find an American child who could not read the word "McDonald's" (Smith, 1986).

A study of early readers conducted by Durkin (1966; 1972) indicated that the children did not learn to read by themselves, but that they learned in a developmental and natural way. Durkin found that early readers had four things in common: (1) their parents conversed with them, (2) the children asked many questions, (3) the parents responded to the children's questions, and (4) the children frequently asked, "What is that word?" Durkin's research has been supported by findings by Heath (1983), Lartz and Mason (1988), Snow (1983), and Taylor (1983), which show that a child's awareness of and desire to demonstrate literacy result from meaningful communication with regard to literacy. Putting notes on the refrigerator, writing a thank-you note to Aunt Mary for a birthday present, dropping a postcard to a friend who has moved away, and reading bedtime stories are all informal activities in which a parent can assist the youngster in acquiring literacy.

According to Holdaway (1979), parents do not typically read to their children out of a sense of duty or to ensure that their child has an educational advantage; they do so for the satisfaction and enjoyment that their child gets from the situation. Holdaway states that during such informal reading time,

> the parent makes no demands on the child, but is deeply gratified by the lively responses and questions that normally arise. It provides a stimulus for satisfying interaction between parent and child, different, richer, and more wide-ranging than the mundane interactions of running the house. (p. 39)

Being read to can have a major effect on children's attitudes toward reading (Lartz & Mason, 1988). A study of four preschoolers who were read to on a regular basis found that they associated the sharing of books with a positive, secure, and enjoyable environment (Doake, 1981). Indeed, the warm and comfortable sense of sharing while reading to his children led one father to say, "You don't even have to listen to the words; it's that kind of rapport" (Teale, 1984, p. 72).

Writing also plays a significant role in early reading (Calkins & Harwayne, 1991). According to Clay (1982, p. 208), writing is a "synthetic experience where letters are built into words which make up sentences. . . . [Thus] when a child writes she has to know the sound-symbol relationship inherent in reading." Through writing, children learn to organize and discover the features of written language.

Clay (1982) further explains that when children share their own stories with their classmates, a framework and purpose for writing evolve. Research indicates that children who write before they enter school are more apt to be better readers (Clark, 1976; Durkin, 1966). Other research studies (Bissex, 1980; Heath, 1983; Schickedanz & Sullivan, 1984) show that the beginning of writing is contemporaneous with the emergence of reading.

The increasing number of working women has changed the role of kindergarten as a transition or socialization process between home and school. Today youngsters attend day care, nursery schools, and/or preschools; this results in their being socialized prior to entering kindergarten. In some communities, the language arts curriculum has been changed to include reading instruction that in the 1950s and 1960s was reserved for the first grade. Some research studies indicate that formal, structured "reading readiness" programs are beneficial; other studies indicate that informal, well-developed programs are just as effective for the emergent reader (Bissex, 1980; Durkin, 1974–1975; Edwards, 1991; Meyer et al., 1983).

Children who enter school with a familiarity of books and how they should be handled have been observed to possess the following reading behaviors: (1) identification of letters, (2) identification of words, (3) retelling of a story, (4) indication of where to begin reading on a page, and (5) awareness of the direction of print, left to right (Wiseman & Robeck, 1983).

Evaluating Emergent Reading

Children enter school having encountered different experiences, each developing at his or her own pace; it is therefore important for kindergarten and first-grade teachers to determine the degree of emergence of reading so that they can plan instruction accordingly. Unfortunately, one study of kindergarten programs revealed a heavy reliance on developmental and academic tests, with little evidence that the tests were used to determine the suitability of the instructional programs for the children. Rather, in most schools the children were expected to adjust to the program instead of an adjustment of the program to meet the students' needs (Durkin, 1987).

The following simple questionnaire for emergent reading evaluation can be used soon after the start of the school year:

1. Can the child listen attentively to a 5-minute story?
2. Can the child play/work independently for short periods of time?
3. Is the child interested in books?
4. Does the child ask for word meanings?
5. Can the child tell a story without confusing the order of events?
6. Does the child recognize that letters make up words?
7. Does the child attempt to write?
8. Does the child draw pictures to illustrate an idea?
9. Can the child remember the main parts of a story?
10. Does the child enter into group and/or class discussions freely?
11. Can the child identify the letters of the alphabet?
12. Does the child know directionality of books (left to right, top to bottom)?

These 12 items reflect the essentials for learning to read. "Yes" answers to 9 of the questions suggest that the child is an emergent reader and should be given opportunities to engage in simple reading activities. For instance, the teacher needs to share pattern books with the child so that after listening to the text a few times, the child will be able to join in the rereading of the book.

Other activities include listening to a cassette recording of a picture book and following along with the text, learning simple songs and poetry, learning finger plays and rhymes, and using writing instruments.

Children who fail to meet this informal cutoff need to be given lots of opportunities to develop oral language skills; to have quality literature read to them, especially predictable literature that allows the child to anticipate upcoming events; and to use crayons and pencils freely for drawing and writing.

One out of every 600 children enters kindergarten knowing how to read (Lapp & Flood, 1983). For such a child, pattern books soon become too predictable and easy to read. More challenging material must be provided for the child at this point. Concept picture books such as *The Last Dinosaur* by Jim Murphy (1987), which describes the habits of these extinct creatures, often enthrall such a child. Narratives also delight early readers; the unforgettable *Frog and Toad Are Friends* (Lobel, 1970) series of books is a popular example.

Instruction for Children as They Begin to Read

As children leave the emergent reading stage and enter the beginning reading stage, they are enthusiastic about reading and eager to stretch their world through encounters with printed text. In a study of exemplary first-grade literacy instruction, Morrow, Tracey, Woo, and Pressley (1999) discovered that many types of reading experiences were carried out daily. These experiences included daily read alouds of high-quality children's literature by the teacher as well as reading with a partner. Guided reading in which children of similar reading needs are grouped was also done each day. The teachers provided time for independent reading of self-selected books. This activity was supported by having elaborate literacy centers in each first-grade classroom with lots of quality children's literature from which the students could choose. The books were categorized by genre and placed in easily accessible baskets or bins. The following are methods of teaching the beginning reader.

Shared Book Experiences

Kindergarten and first graders in the emergent reading stage and the beginning reading stage benefit from the experience of sharing books. "Shared reading is one way of immersing students in rich, literary-level language without worrying about grade level or reading performance. For young children who have had limited exposure to the language of storybooks, shared reading and discussion of stories provide a framework for literature and language" (Routman, 1991, p. 33). The teacher devotes a half-hour each day to sharing simple stories that the children easily understand and enjoy. This is in addition to the amount of time set aside for reading instruction either with a basal reader or a whole language program. Each month 20 to 30 books are shared, including three or four *Big Books*, popular books that have been enlarged by the publisher so that children can easily read the print from 12 to 15 feet away as they sit in a semicircle around the teacher.

Holdaway (1979) believes that a shared reading experience should meet three criteria: (1) the books read should be ones children love to hear; (2) children need to see the print themselves; and (3) the teacher must display genuine enjoyment in reading the books aloud.

Adams (1990, p. 69) refers to the sharing of Big Books as the "classroom version of bedtime stories, and like bedtime stories, they are meant to be read over and over, as often as they are enchanting." A typical half-hour shared book activity includes the singing of a simple song or choral speaking of a simple poem or rhyme. This is followed by the introduction of a Big Book that the teacher reads, using a pointer so that the children are aware of exactly where the teacher is as the story is being read. The teacher then rereads the story and encourages the children to join in. The teacher may select a small group to act out the story as it is read for a third time. The activity usually ends with the teacher reading a new book or perhaps rereading a class favorite (Holdaway, 1979).

The shared book activity may begin the first day of kindergarten and continue through third grade. It is appropriate for use with either a literature-based whole language program or a developmental, basal reading program (box 12.1).

A beginning reader reads with oral fluency after having been read a story several times and modeling the classroom teacher's reading. In Routman's (1988) view, such fluency transforms the child into a reader because the child reads with emotion, inflections, and enjoyment, and the emphasis is on reading for meaning. According to Clay (1991, p. 264), "A child who already enjoys shared reading can be encouraged to become more independent as a reader if new stories are introduced before he tries to read them for himself. A good introduction makes the new text more accessible to the reader."

12.1 In the Classroom: Teaching Hint

Shared Book Experiences (K–3)

Students engage in shared book experiences as they become involved in reading a *Big Book*, one that has large enough print so that everyone in the class can see the words. The procedure summarized below was developed in New Zealand by Don Holdaway (1979).

1. The teacher introduces the book to the students. (This introduction typically occurs on Monday and the book is used daily for the remainder of the week.)

2. The teacher asks students to predict what the book will be about.

3. The teacher reads the book to the students. The book is usually placed on an easel or held so that the students can see the words and illustrations. The teacher also points to the words as they are read.

4. The teacher may stop periodically to encourage students to tell what they think will happen next in the story.

5. The teacher rereads the book, encouraging the students to read along with him or her.

6. On subsequent readings, a student may read a page individually or join with another student in reading a portion of the book aloud.

7. All members of the class read the book together every day for a week.

The classroom teacher is a major influence on children's reading according to research by Anderson, Wilson, and Fielding (1988). This is an important finding for every teacher, at every grade level. For example, when children enter kindergarten, it falls upon the teacher to provide a literacy-rich environment with ample opportunities for all students to engage in meaningful conversations about reading and writing. Because not every five-year-old has had an abundance of literary experiences—being read to, having books to browse through, talking about stories—the teacher must share quality literature informally in the classroom so that students will be motivated to engage in discussion and eager to explore books on their own. The shared book activity provides the teacher with a positive instructional opportunity.

Language Experience Approach (LEA)

The *language experience approach* (LEA) is sometimes viewed as a precursor to the whole language approach. Emphasizing the relationships between thought, oral language, and written language, the LEA builds on a child's interests and oral language. As mentioned earlier, five- and six-year-olds are eager to share thoughts, ideas, and feelings with others. The LEA capitalizes on this personal and, to some extent, social need by having children share their own thoughts and experiences through both verbal and written interchanges. A prominent advocate of the language experience approach, Allen (1976) stresses the need for reading materials that grow out of children's oral expressions rather than published materials.

A language experience lesson is comprised of the following five steps:

1. Discuss a shared experience with the class: what may happen, what they may see or feel, what preparations they must make, and so forth.

2. Have the shared experience with the students (for example, cooking breakfast or visiting a museum or zoo).

3. Discuss what took place during the activity.

4. Have the students write about the experience.

5. Have the students share what they wrote with the class.

For the child who lacks the skills needed to write, the teacher or an aide should write down exactly what the child says during the language experience so that she can make the sound-print connections. This enables the child to read a piece correctly in her own words.

When firsthand experiences are not possible, the teacher must rely on vicarious experiences. For example, a poem and a book about kangaroos, a video about how sheep are raised in New Zealand, a filmstrip about pioneers traveling on flatboats down the Ohio River, and a DVD film about making kites are all vehicles for sharing and can enrich children's experiences and knowledge without requiring them to leave the classroom. Although vicarious experiences may be effective, firsthand experiences, such as seeing a sheep sheared or making a kite from plastic garbage bags and bamboo strips, followed by writing about such activities will usually be more vividly recalled by children and for a longer period of time.

As part of the language experience approach, each student creates a dictionary for reading and writing called a *word bank*. Using 3" × 5" index cards, the student creates word categories according to how the words are used: words for people, words for colors, action words, and the like. The student may cut out a picture from a magazine or draw an appropriate illustration so that each word will be recognized. After attaching a picture and writing the word, the student places the card in a plastic card file, a mobile container that he may carry around the classroom or take home to write about personal experiences involving family or friends.

Shared Story Reading and Beginning Readers

Shared story reading evolved out of cross-age tutoring. In shared story reading with beginning readers, students at different grade levels are paired up as partners. Once a week, time is set aside during the school day for shared story reading in which the older child reads a book to the younger child and the younger child reads a book to the older child. Both students select books they believe their partner will enjoy; both practice reading their selections aloud before the sharing time. This type of sharing increases children's familiarity with children's literature and builds self-confidence. The social interaction is an added plus.

When simple pattern books are used, even the beginning reader who only recognizes a few words can participate in this activity. When wordless picture books are used, the beginning reader can describe the actions that occur in the illustrations.

Phonics Instruction

Phonics instruction involves teaching relationships between letters and the sounds they represent. Once children are able to identify the letters of the alphabet, the teacher can introduce rhyming words and words that have the same beginning or ending consonant sound. Some phonics programs require students to know 25 to 30 sight words, or words they recognize when seen in isolation, such as on a piece of tagboard or the chalkboard. At that point, words with the same beginning consonant sound are introduced. Later, short and long vowel sounds and then consonant blends are introduced as part of the instruction. The introduction of each sound and accompanying letter should begin with several examples of words with which the students are familiar. Proper names should be avoided because of their wide variation in spelling and pronunciation.

Phonics instruction should begin early and accompany meaningful text. After reviewing, evaluating, and integrating several research studies, Adams (1990, p. 578) came to the following conclusions about how children learn to read:

> The vast majority of the studies indicated that approaches [that include] intensive, explicit phonics instruction resulted in comprehension skills that are at least comparable to, and word recognition and spelling skills that are significantly better than those that do not. . . . Approaches in which systematic code instruction is included along with meaningful connected reading result in superior reading achievement overall.

"Many of the activities of the early elementary classrooms already incorporate elements that heighten phonemic awareness" (Griffith & Olson, 1992, p. 520). However, upon completion of the second grade, a child need not receive phonics instruction unless a specific need for such instruction has been diagnosed (Anderson et al., 1984).

Every student learns about letter-sound correspondences, or phonics, as part of learning to read, regardless of the type of reading instruction they receive (Stahl, 1992). "There is substantial evidence that phonemic awareness is strongly related to success in reading and spelling acquisition" (Yopp, 1995, p. 21). Phonics involves not only learning about letter-sound relationships, but learning about words, as well. It has been suggested that children go through three stages in learning about words. Initially they learn about words in whole units, such as when a child can identify a Burger King or Wal-Mart sign. This is the *logographic stage*. The next stage for the emergent reader is the *alphabetic stage* in which children use individual letters and sounds to identify words, such as "luv" for *love* or "tu" for *to*. The third stage is the *orthographic stage*, within which children see patterns in words, or word families, and use these patterns to identify words without attempting to sound them out. For instance, a child who knows the words *boy* and *toy* can then pronounce *joy*. In this last stage, children develop the ability to recognize words automatically without pausing to think about how they are constructed or spelled (Frith, 1985).

In regard to teaching phonics, Stahl (1992, p. 620) points out that "letter-sound instruction makes no sense to a child who does not have an overall conception of what reading is about." Stahl suggests the following nine guidelines for exemplary phonics instruction:

1. Build on the child's concepts about word formation (i.e., the arrangement of letters in predictable patterns).

2. Build on a foundation of the child's phonemic awareness.

3. Be clear and direct.

4. Integrate phonics instruction into the total reading program.

5. Focus on reading words rather than learning phonics rules.

6. Include instruction of onsets, the part of the syllable before the vowel, and *rimes*, the part of the syllable from the vowel onward. For instance, in the word *meat*, *m* is the onset and *eat* is the rime. If the child knows the *eat* rime, the child can then transfer that knowledge to *wheat* and *beat* in decoding those words.

7. Include practice with invented spelling.

8. Develop independent word recognition strategies, focusing instruction on the internal structure of words or word patterns.

9. Develop automatic word recognition skills so that the students can focus on comprehension of the text and not the words themselves.

Common rimes are presented in box 12.2 on p. 506.

The Yopp-Singer Test of Phoneme Segmentation (Yopp, 1995) measures a child's ability to separately articulate—in order—the sounds of a spoken word.

12.2 In the Classroom: Teaching Hint

Common Rimes

Rime	World that Uses the Rime	Rime	Word that Uses the Rime
-ack	back, sack, track	-ick	brick, sick, trick
-ail	sail, mail, nail	-ide	hide, ride, side
-ain	pain, rain, train	-ight	bright, fright, night
-ake	cake, make, snake	-ill	fill, hill, pill
-ale	pale, sale, whale	-in	chin, twin, win
-ame	came, game, name	-ine	fine, nine, shine
-an	can, man, ran	-ing	king, sing, thing
-ank	bank, drank, thank	-ink	pink, sink, think
-ap	cap, map, trap	-ip	lip, ship, sip
-ash	cash, mash, trash	-ir	fir, sir, stir
-at	cat, hat, that	-ock	block, lock, sock
-ate	hate, late, plate	-oke	joke, poke, woke
-aw	jaw, paw, saw	-op	hop, mop; shop
-ay	day, play, say	-ore	more, shore, store
-eat	beat, seat, wheat	-uck	duck, luck, truck
-ell	bell, sell, shell	-ug	bug, hug, rug
-est	best, chest, west	-ump	bump, jump, lump
-ice	mice, rice, twice	-unk	bunk, junk, sunk

For instance, for the word *sat*, the child should respond with the following: /s/ -/a/-/t/. Students who answer most of the items correctly are considered phonemically aware. On the other hand, students who answer with random sounds (e.g., /b/-/d/ for *cat*) lack phonemic awareness. If a student spells the word rather than presenting the individual sounds, the teacher can determine the degree of letter-sound correspondence for a given word (see box 12.3).

A balanced or combined approach to reading includes the strengths of a whole language, literature-based program with those of a phonics program. Thus, the skills of reading in context are included along with decoding, or phonics, skills (Adams, 1990). Trachtenburg (1990) uses a three-step combined approach with kindergarten through second-grade students. The steps are whole-part-whole as follows:

1. **Whole:** The students read, comprehend, and enjoy an entire quality literature selection.

2. **Part:** The teacher provides instruction in a high-utility phonic element by drawing from an appropriate, quality literature selection.

3. **Whole:** The students apply the new phonic skill when reading and enjoying another quality literature selection.

As Adams (1990, p. 17) notes in her findings, "Perhaps the single most striking characteristic of skillful readers is the speed and effortlessness with which they can breeze through text. In particular they appear to recognize

12.3   In the Classroom: Teaching Hint

Yopp-Singer Test of Phoneme Segmentation

Student's name _____   Date _____

Score (number correct) _____

Directions: Today we're going to play a word game. I'm going to say a word and I want you to break the word apart. You are going to tell me each sound in the word in order. For example, if I say "old," you should say "/o/-/l/-/d/." (*Administrator: Be sure to say the sounds, not the letters, in the word.*) Let's try a few together.

Practice items: (Assist the child in segmenting these items as necessary.) ride, go, man

Test items: (*Circle those items that the student correctly segments; incorrect responses may be recorded on the blank line following the item.*)

1. dog _____
2. keep _____
3. fine _____
4. no _____
5. she _____
6. wave _____
7. grew _____
8. that _____
9. red _____
10. me _____

11. sat _____
12. lay _____
13. race _____
14. zoo _____
15. three _____
16. job _____
17. in _____
18. ice _____
19. at _____
20. top _____
21. by _____
22. do _____

The author, Hallie Kay Yopp, California State University, Fullerton, grants permission for this test to be reproduced. The author acknowledges the contribution of the Late Harry Singer to the development of this test.

Test from Yopp, Hallie Kay. (1995, September). A test for assessing phonemic awareness in young children. *The Reading Teacher, 49* (1), 20–29. Reprinted with permission of Hallie K. Yopp and the International Reading Association. All rights reserved.

whole words at a glance, gleaning their appropriate meaning at once." This level of skill is the goal of teachers in the instruction of phonics and comprehension.

Oral activities such as songs, games, and riddles can draw children's attention to the basic elements of language—phonemes and graphemes. Such activities should supplement rather than replace children's interactions with relevant and meaningful language, both oral and written (Yopp, 1992). By combining phonics with a whole language approach, that is, with the use of quality literature as the primary reading material, teachers can apply the best of both instructional approaches (see box 12.4 on p. 508).

12.4   In the Classroom: Teaching Hint

Phonics Generalizations and Rules

Consonants

1. A consonant cluster consists of two (or three) consonants that appear together and are blended when pronounced.

b*lip*	b*rat*	c*lip*	c*row*	d*rag*	f*log*	f*rame*	g*low*	p*lane*
p*ride*	s*coop*	s*kip*	s*late*	s*mut*	s*tream*	s*tamp*	s*wim*	t*rim*
be*nt*	coa*st*	gra*sp*	me*lt*	bo*ld*	ma*sk*			

2. A consonant digraph consists of two consonants that appear together and result in one consonant sound when pronounced.

*ch*ip	*ch*ur*ch*	*th*igh	*th*ey	*wh*ip	si*ng*

Vowels

1. A vowel is short if it is in a closed syllable (a syllable that ends in a consonant).
   bĕd, crăb, bŏx, păst, jŭmp
2. A vowel is long if it is the last vowel in an open syllable (a syllable that ends in a vowel).
   trēē, crādle
3. A vowel digraph consists of two vowels that together represent one vowel sound.
   tr*ai*n   br*ea*d   c*ou*gh
4. A vowel diphthong consists of one of the following four vowel combinations: oi, oy, ou, ow.
   s*oi*l   pl*oy*   h*ou*se   t*ow*el
5. When e appears at the end of a one-syllable word, the first vowel in the word is usually long.
   cāpe, māde, rōbe, drāpe, pīne

Syllabication

1. A syllable must have a vowel sound: tan, med/i/um, flex/i/ble
2. A final e in a word is usually silent: mane, fine, dance
3. An open syllable is a syllable that ends with a vowel other than a "silent e":   o/bey, bu/reau
4. A closed syllable is a syllable that ends with a consonant: *um*/pire, ba/*boon*
5. When a consonant appears between two vowels, the word is divided between the first vowel and the consonant: a/far i/deal
6. When two consonants appear between two vowels, the word is divided between the consonants: ham/mer fis/cal
7. When a word ends with a consonant and the letters *le*, the word is divided immediately before the consonant preceding *le*:   ca/ble dou/ble
8. A compound word is divided between the two words: fire/arm base/ball flash/light

Comprehension

Comprehension instruction has many facets with each holding challenges and possibilities (Pressley, 2000). This section of the chapter will describe some of the comprehension strategies elementary and middle school students need to understand text.

Repeated Exposure to Different Genres

Different genres have different kinds of writing for the reader to discern. A biography may begin with the a famous person's birth and follow that individual through the end of her life culminating at the last page of the book. A fantasy novel may have flashbacks. A sports article in the newspaper may give a synopsis of the scoring by a baseball team. A poem about nature may cause one to stop and ponder an insect on a maple tree leaf. An instruction manual about the codes in a video game may be extremely complex while a newspaper cartoon may require the reader to notice subtleties in a phrase or visual. Reading isn't simply reading, just as driving isn't simply driving. Although many of the same skills are used to drive to the convenience store, to a shopping mall, or to a stadium to watch a football game, other skills are also used depending on the context of the situation. Driving to the neighborhood convenience store may require watching for pedestrians. Driving on the interstate requires ability to safely pass other vehicles and return to one's lane. And driving in congested traffic around a stadium requires being alert in bumper to bumper traffic while watching for police officers as they direct traffic.

As seen in chapter 4, children's literature offers a variety of genres. Usually for reading instruction we categorize a genre as being either narrative, expository, or poetic. With young readers we stress the illustrations of picture books as we take a picture walk to introduce a book or story from a basal reader. Informational books provide the chance to read photo captions and headings.

Visual Structures to Support Comprehension

Narrative literature offers the opportunity to study characters, setting, and plot. The teacher can help students make a story plot of a book by graphing the major dramatic events that occur in the story. Candace Fleming's (2002) *Muncha! Muncha! Muncha!* is the tale of three mischievous bunnies who yearn for the veggies in Mr. McGreely's garden. To fend them off, Mr. McGreely puts up a small wire fence to no avail. Next he constructs a tall wooden fence but the bunnies manage to dig under it and get into the garden. A moat is dug without success. Finally out of desperation, Mr. McGreely builds a fortress around his beloved vegetable garden. The bunnies can't possibly scale its walls or dig under it. But they manage to reach the veggies when they hide in Mr. McGreely's basket. Using large chart-size sticky paper attached to the wall, the class can chart the book's actions beginning on the left side of the page with the action on the cover of the book. At the beginning of the book, the action is low as Mr. McGreely thinks about planting a garden. The action increases as the bunnies find the veggies so the graph spikes a bit. It increases more when they must get over the fence. Then the graph moves higher as the bunnies conquer the taller wooden fence and so on until the resolution of the story when Mr. McGreely decides to share his veggies with the determined bunnies at which point the graph moves downward as the story has ended (see figure 12.1 on p. 510).

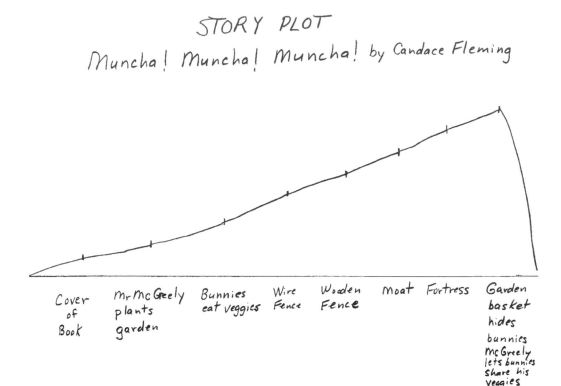

Figure 12.1   Student's graph depicting action in *Muncha! Muncha! Muncha!*

Informational books also provide opportunities to use visuals. Some, such as charts, bar graphs, time lines, and diagrams, may be present in the text itself. Graphic organizers, as we saw in chapter 3, can be useful visual tools to compare and contrast or convey cause and effect.

Making Predictions

Having students consider the cover of a book and its title then make a prediction as to what the book is about is an important comprehension strategy as it activates prior knowledge. For instance, *Muncha! Muncha! Muncha!* (Fleming, 2002) may conjure up thoughts of Peter Rabbit by a child whose grandmother had read that classic to him while another child may have a rabbit as a pet and knows that rabbits like to eat carrots and lettuce leaves. As the teacher reads along, she should stop from time to time to have the students predict what they think will happen next. Obviously the bunnies have to outthink Mr. McGreely, while Mr. McGreely must outmaneuver those dexterous rabbits if he's to keep them out of his garden. Likewise in reading a novel, students need to anticipate what the characters will do next and what twists and turns the plot will take.

For informational text such as Margery Facklin's (2001) *Spiders and Their Web Sites*, readers need to predict what new information the author plans to share. Headings and subheadings serve as guides for the reader of expository text just as chapter titles may give clues to what is coming ahead in a novel.

Sequencing

Putting the events of a story or informational text in order is an important reading skill. After doing a read aloud of a picture book, you may want to list five events out of order on the chalkboard and have the class discuss their proper sequence. Cutting up old basal stories and pasting them on construction paper can be the makings of a sequencing activity for first and second graders. After reading aloud a story, students can illustrate a story circle by jotting down each event in a clockwise direction with the illustration being outside of the circle of events.

Biographies are good books for developing sequence as they usually begin at birth and go through until death or from one age to a later age of the individual. *One-Eyed Tree Frog* (Cowley, 1999) is an informational book that is excellent for sequencing.

Comparing and Contrasting

Explaining how two things are alike or how they differ can be introduced with a weave chart. The chart has different headings to accommodate for what is different (things, people, places, or ideas). Below is a weave chart created for the book *Talking Walls* (1992).

Wall	Location	Construction	Purpose
Great Wall of China	China	large stones and boulders	keep invaders out of China
Berlin Wall	Berlin, Germany	concrete and iron rods	divide Berlin to separate Eastern Europe (Communist) and Western Europe (free elections)
City of the Sun	Cuzco, Peru	large, huge stones moved by levers	to celebrate with song and dance
Vietnam Veterans Memorial Wall	Washington, DC	black granite with names of soldiers who died during the war	to remember those who gave their lives in the war

Younger readers may need a more concrete way of comparing and contrasting. As suggested in chapter 3, Venn diagrams are excellent means of comparing and contrasting. Two hula hoops can serve a physical Venn diagrams when they are overlapped on the floor. Strips of paper can be used to write the comparisons and contrasting elements with the students placing the comments in the appropriate location, either how the two are alike or how they differ.

Locating Details

Finding specific information in a text is best taught when the detail being sought is located within the text on a single page. This helps struggling and beginning readers stay focused as they are confined to a small passage. Once students can locate details on one page of text, have them use a double-wide page spread as found in most picture books to locate details. Jim Arnosky's (2000) *All About Turtles* is a good book to use with primary students while Lynn Curlee's (2002) *Seven Wonders of the Ancient World* is intriguing for upper-grade and middle schoolers to find descriptive details.

Cause and Effect

The cause of an event and resultant effect is yet another reading skill students need to master. Whether it be the decline in value of products and drought during the Great Depression that led to massive unemployment, the sale of the Louisiana Purchase to the United States by Napoleon to fund his French army, resulting in the emergence of a nation stretching across North America between the Mississippi River and the Rockies, the action of a lever and pulley system in science, or the behavior of two characters in a book after a major event takes place in the plot, cause and effect are important aspects of reading. *An American Plague: The True and Terrifying Story of the Yellow Fever Epidemic of 1793* (Murphy, 2002) describes the fear that struck Americans. Because the source of the disease was unknown, as was the cure, many mistakes were made in seeking resolution from this terrible disease. Prominent citizens fled the cities to the countryside to escape the dreaded illness.

Problem and Solution

Finding the solution to a problem is something every person must do from time to time. Children can use books to analyze the problem-solving process, something inventors and scientists do every day. From the simple *Muncha! Muncha! Muncha!* (Fleming, 2002), beginning readers can understand how the farmer devises a plan to protect his vegetables from the rabbits. They can also do an analysis of how the bunnies undermine his efforts. Middle-elementary grade readers will delight in Amelia Bloomer's solution to keeping one's skirt out of the way when taking part in physical activities such as riding a bike as they read *You Forgot Your Skirt, Amelia Bloomer* (Corey, 2000).

Instructional Strategies for Primary, Intermediate, and Middle School Readers

For children who possess more than beginning reading skills, the teacher may select from other instructional methods, according to the appropriateness of the learning situation. Effective teachers of reading plan, implement, monitor, and evaluate each lesson or instructional activity. Some teachers keep tally sheets for every lesson, noting which portions of the lesson were successful and possible ways to improve on the lesson when working with other children.

Short selections of text are efficient ways to teach reading strategies. According to Harvey and Goudvis (2000), short passages of narrative or informational text:

- are well-crafted and contain vivid language, striking illustrations, and/or photographs;
- provide a complete set of thoughts, ideas, and information;
- focus on issues of critical importance to the reader;
- are easily read aloud and are easy for students to follow along at their desk if they have a copy or a copy is projected via the overhead or an Elmo projector, thereby giving a common experience for everyone in the room;
- are easily reread for deeper meaning, increasing comprehension;
- are accessible to all kinds and ability of readers;
- provide a realistic model for writing by students;
- are authentic and prepare students for real-world reading.

Teachers should be strategists in reading instruction and teach their students to be strategic readers using the following methods:

1. provide assistance during reading instead of suggesting a reading procedure or assessing the child's progress;
2. help a student to know how he or she knows;
3. make conscious connections to previous and future learning;
4. emphasize the context in which new skills will be applied;
5. make invisible cognitive skills tangible;
6. respond to student confusion with advice about how to think strategically (Paris, 1985).

In guiding children to become strategic readers, the teacher must be familiar with a variety of instructional techniques. Questioning, Book Clubs, the directed reading activity (DRA), and the directed reading-thinking activity (DR-TA) are techniques that have proved effective with elementary and middle school students.

Questioning

Teachers must not only ask effective questions, but they must model such behavior so that students can develop a questioning technique that they can use independently. The quality of students' answers and the degree to which students actively participate in the discussion are influenced by the quality of the questions the teacher asks (Norton, 1985). The type and quality of the text material used also influence the quality of student responses. For example, a simple, straightforward text might not provide the teacher with sufficient material to develop higher-order questions, whereas a good realistic fiction book may provide such material (Monson, 1992).

Teachers can help students develop their cognitive skills by asking them questions designed for different levels of thinking. Literal, inferential, and critical questions should all be asked with equal frequency. It is best, however, to begin with literal, or knowledge-level, questions in order to build the students' self-confidence. Some teachers refer to literal questions as $.25 or "skinny" questions with critical questions being "fat" or $2 questions. Modeling such questions during a read aloud helps students to understand the difference. Soon they'll be referring to "skinny" and "$2" questions.

Literal questions are based on facts that students can readily recall or locate in a specific passage. Such questions typically refer to main ideas, story details, and sequences of events.

Inferential questions require students to be familiar with the text at the literal level but also to think beyond the printed word. By using previously gained knowledge along with information acquired from the text, students are able to make inferences. Comparing and contrasting, drawing conclusions, formulating generalizations, recognizing relationships, and predicting outcomes are all types of inferential thinking.

Critical thinking requires students to make judgments. Unless students can effectively think at the literal and inferential levels, their critical thinking ability will be quite limited. In thinking critically, students must objectively view the material and withhold final judgment until they have evaluated enough information to form that judgment.

Question-Answer Relationship (QAR)

A reading strategy developed by Taffy Raphael (1986) is called question-answer relationship (QAR), which teaches students to recognize a taxonomy of relationships between specific kinds of questions and their answers. Raphael divides questions as follows:

Category One: In the Book or Story

Right There: Answers to literal-level questions can be answered from information *right there* in the book or story.

Think and Search: The answer is in the story, but the reader must pull it together from two or more sentences in different parts of the text.

Category Two: In My Head

On My Own: The answer is *not* in the text. The reader uses his own background experiences to answer the question. It is possible to answer the question without ever reading the text.

Author and Me: The answer is *not* in the story. It is found in the reader's own background knowledge and from what the author offers in the text. The reader infers, or reads between the lines, to produce the correct response.

To introduce QAR, the teacher differentiates for the class the two basic categories, those answers that can be found "In the Book or Story" and those "In My Head." Modeling these kinds of answers by using a text projected on an overhead projector, the teacher then uses guided practice as students do likewise with other questions from the text. After the students show they can do these types of questions over a period of a couple days, the teacher demonstrates "Right There" and "Think and Search" questions, again using a text that the students either have at their desks or projected for them to easily follow along. Finally a few days later, the teacher models the "On My Own" and "Author and Me" responses. The teacher may want to use the same text to demonstrate each of these tasks and then do a follow-up with a different text the next day. Focusing on one aspect, particularly "Author and Me," which requires inferencing skills, should be done once a week with different kinds of texts, narrative and expository, until the students develop their understanding of and demonstrate a proficiency in using this skill.

For introducing QAR at the first-grade level, usually during the second semester, a fitting book is Mem Fox's (1994) *Tough Boris*. At the second- and third-grade levels, a good book to use to introduce QAR is *The Lotus Seed* (Garland, 1993), particularly as it requires a substantial degree of inferencing. Upper-elementary and middle school teachers will find *Martin's Big Words: The Life of Dr. Martin Luther King, Jr.* (Rappaport, 2001) a ready vehicle for demonstrating QAR.

Book Clubs

Reading, writing, student-led discussion groups, and whole-class discussions are included in the *Book Club*, a literature-based reading program. Originated by Taffy Raphael and Susan McMahon (1994), the Book Club requires that the teacher locate good literature with an identifiable theme, such as the Revolutionary War, westward expansion, famous inventors, or the Great Depression. The teacher then discusses with the class the differences between talking about books in a group discussion/conversation and answering questions about books. Next, the students are given guidelines for using reading logs as they read the books. Finally, the teacher and the class discuss what makes good speakers and good listeners, making a wall chart of characteristics of each.

As students read their books, they keep a vocabulary sheet that has the title of the book and the student's name on the top. The sheet is divided into four columns: date, word, page number, and meaning of the word. As the students read, they record the vocabulary information. After reading the book or an assigned portion, such as two or three chapters in a novel, the students write in their reading logs. Below are some possible reading log examples (Raphael & McMahon, 1994):

Character Map. The student thinks about a character that he or she liked or didn't like and makes a map of the character. The map shows what the character looked like, things the character did, what was interesting about the character, how the character interacted with other characters, etc.

Wonderful Words. New, unusual, or descriptive words are jotted down. These are words that the student may want to use in her own writing. The student also writes a short explanation of why the word was chosen.

Pictures. The student draws a picture depicting a scene and writes a brief reason for including the picture.

Book/Chapter Critique. The student writes what he thinks is good or could be improved about the book or a chapter of the book.

Sequences. The student keeps a sequence of events chart, adding to the chart as she reads the book. For each event listed, the student writes a brief reason why it was included.

Special Story Part. The student writes down a phrase or sentence that begins a special part of the book, as well as the page number on which it appears.

Author's Crafts. The student writes down special words, descriptive or funny phrases, dialogue examples, etc., that make the book appealing to the reader.

Me and the Book. The student relates an event or character in the book to his own life.

The students then form their Book Clubs and discuss what they have read. When initiating Book Clubs, the teacher offers guidelines and models how discussion groups work. Students are encouraged to prepare a couple of questions in advance to bring with them to their Book Club. The teacher floats from Book Club to Book Club and notes the progress and problems that arise. The teacher doesn't interrupt the groups unless an unusual circumstance arises or the students ask for clarification or assistance with a problem. Later the teacher uses the information gathered from her own observations of the Book Clubs to use in entire class instruction.

In addition to the reading log, the students keep "What I Learned" sheets in which they briefly summarize, in one to three sentences, what they learned from each book they read within the thematic unit. These sheets are used as part of the assessment of the student's work.

Directed Reading Activity

The *directed reading activity* (DRA) has been a part of basal reading programs for decades. It consists of six steps:

1. Establish a purpose for reading.
2. Develop background information.
3. Introduce new vocabulary.
4. Provide students with questions to serve as reading guides.
5. Read the passage silently or aloud.
6. Ask follow-up questions.

In establishing a purpose for reading, the teacher's role is that of a promoter and motivator, often bringing in related materials and items for the students.

Directed Reading-Thinking Activity

The *directed reading-thinking activity* (DR-TA) (Stauffer, 1969) engages students in the reading process by having them make predictions as they read.

The teacher breaks the text into appropriate sections or stopping points, where the students discuss the text. The students are given more control of the discussion in the DR-TA than in the DRA. In making a prediction about what will happen in upcoming text, a student relies on two sources of information: personal knowledge and the text material.

The DR-TA begins with the teacher outlining the purpose for reading and the students analyzing the title of the material to be read. The text may be a narrative, such as a story from a basal reader or a chapter in a fiction book, or descriptive writing, such as that found in a science or social studies textbook. The students discuss what they already know from previous experiences and from the title itself, then they make predictions about what will happen in the text. After the students resume reading, the teacher has the students stop at a predetermined point, and the students confirm or reject their predictions and form new hypotheses based on the newly acquired information. The process is one of formulating questions, testing those questions for affirmation or denial, and generating new questions based on the information gathered (Moore et al., 1982).

Content Area and Expository Reading

Increasingly, children's literature is being used to teach content areas such as science, social studies, and even math as informational books become prevalent in classroom reading instruction. Such literature can be used to introduce students to different viewpoints. For instance, "Selected picture books can offer older students new insights into historical perspectives" (Farris & Fuhler, 1994, p. 383). While stories in basal readers are predominately realistic fiction or narratives, content area textbooks contain predominately nonfiction or expository material. Students need to develop different strategies for reading expository prose than for narration because each content area makes use of specific vocabulary and concepts. For instance, Saul (1992, p. 1) writes, "Science books may help children realize the pleasures, potential, and limits of science. The best of these do far more than inform; they give voice to the beauty, the intricacy, and the connectedness of physical existence."

Marjorie Hancock (2004) relies on informational books to introduce access features of nonfiction such a table of contents, bibliography, diagrams, graphs, sidebars, maps, source notes, index, and endpapers. A few of the informational books she suggests are Gail Gibbons's (2002) *Tell Me, Tree*, a book for grades one through three that features diagrams; Laurence Pringle's (1997) *An Extraordinary Life: The Story of a Monarch Butterfly*, which has sidebars with information; and James Cross Giblin's (2000) *The Amazing Life of Benjamin Franklin*, a perfect book to share table of contents, index, maps, and other access features depending upon the level of reading sophistication of the group.

Box 12.5 on pp. 518–520 is a thematic unit for intermediate students on weather. Figure 12.2 on p. 521 contains a graphic organizer for the unit and figure 12.3 on p. 522 shows a student's final report for the weather unit of study. The remainder of this section describes instructional approaches designed to assist students in content area reading.

12.5   In the Classroom: Mini Lesson

Weather—A Theme Cycle

Informational Books

See the bibliography.

Read Alouds

Where the River Begins by Thomas Locker—picture book
The Night of the Twisters by Ivy Ruckman—novel
Many of the informational books are suitable for read alouds, too.

Choral Reading

Tornado! by Arnold Adoff—poems
Weather by Lee Bennett Hopkins—poems

Interview

The class will interview a meteorologist from the National Weather Service in Joliet, IL.

Word Wall

Both the students and the teacher contribute to the Word Wall. Some possibilities are as follows:

weather vane	accumulation	condensation	humidity
thermometer	high pressure	meteorologist	cold front
anemometer	low pressure	evaporation	warm front
rain/snow gauge	Fahrenheit	frigid	wind sock
hygrometer	Celsius	precipitation	water cycle
barometer	predict	wind chill factor	psychrometer

Charts and Maps

Using outline maps of the United States, the students will take turns recording the progress of cold and warm fronts as they move across the United States. Newspapers provide these maps in their daily weather sections. Each day's map will be compared to the previous maps and used to predict and discuss weather changes.

Project

In small groups the students will assemble and use a weather instrument such as a barometer, weather vane, snow/rain gauge, anemometer, hygrometer, or psychrometer.

Learning Log

Twice a day for the duration of the theme cycle all students will record in their learning logs the findings of the instruments they assembled (see Project) along with the findings of the "real" instruments within the classroom and outside the school. The students will also note the current weather and cloud conditions and make predictions as to any weather changes they believe will occur and why. The learning logs are also used to reflect upon other scientific information learned throughout the unit.

Computers/Technology

Each day one group of students will prepare a weather report using the *Weatherschool* program on the computer. Using daily weather information, the group will present the weather using the visuals provided by the computer.

Research

Each student or pair of students will choose a weather-related question to research. The research will be compiled to form a class report explaining why and how different types of weather occur and how weather can be helpful or harmful. Some possible questions are as follows:

- How do oceans affect weather?
- What is the water cycle?
- What causes lightning and/or thunder?
- What part does evaporation (or condensation, precipitation, or accumulation) play in the water cycle?
- What does low pressure (or high pressure) mean?
- How does a low (or high) pressure system affect the weather?
- What is a tornado?
- What is a hurricane?
- How is wind formed?

Art

The students will design and make wind socks. They will write a description of how the wind sock works in their learning log.

Bibliography

Informational Books

Barrett, N. (1989). *Picture library: Hurricanes and tornadoes*. New York: Watts.

Bartlett, M. F. (1973). *Where does all the rain go?* (P. Collins, Illus.). New York: Coward, McCann, & Geoghegan.

Bramwell, M. (1994). *Earth science library: Weather* (C. Forsey, Illus.). New York: Watts.

Branley, F. M. (1983). *Rain & hail* (H. Barton, Illus.). New York: HarperCollins.

Branley, F. M. (1985). *Flash, crash, rumble, and roll* (B. & E. Emberley, Illus.). New York: HarperCollins.

Branley, F. M. (1987). *It's raining cats and dogs* (T. Kelley, Illus.). Boston: Houghton Mifflin.

Branley, F. M. (1988). *Tornado alert* (G. Maestro, Illus.). New York: Crowell.

Cole, J. (1986). *The magic school bus at the waterworks* (B. Degen, Illus.). New York: Scholastic.

Compton, G. (1981). *What does a meteorologist do?* New York: Dodd, Mead.

Cooper, J. (1992). *Wind: Science secrets*. Vero Beach, FL: Rourke.

Day, J. A. (1998). *Peterson first guide to clouds and weather*. Boston: Houghton Mifflin.

dePaola, T. (1975). *The cloud book*. New York: Holiday.

DeWitt, L. (1991). *What will the weather be?* (C. Croll, Illus.). New York: HarperCollins.

Fradin, D. B. (1982). *Disaster! Tornadoes*. Chicago: Children's Press.

Gibbons, G. (1987). *Weather forecasting* (G. Gibbons, Illus.). New York: Four Winds.

Gibbons, G. (1990). *Weather words and what they mean* (G. Gibbons, Illus.). New York: Holiday.

Lambert, D. (1990). *Our planet: Weather* (M. Camm, Illus.). New Mahwah, NJ: Troll.

Martin, C. (1987). *I can be a weather forecaster*. Chicago: Children's Press.

Martin, J. B. (1998). *Snowflake Bentley* (Mary Azarian, Illus.). Boston: Houghton Mifflin.

Murphy, J. (2000). *Blizzard: The storm that changed America*. New York: Scholastic.

Parker, S. (1990). *Fun with science: Weather* (K. K. Chen & P. Bull, Illus.). New York: Warwick.

Simon, S. (1989). *Storms*. New York: Scholastic.

Singer, M. (2000). *On the same day in March: A tour of the world's weather* (F. Lessac, Illus.). New York: HarperCollins.

Steele, P. (1991). *Weather watch: Snow causes and effects*. New York: Watts.

Ward, A. (1992). *Project science: Sky and weather* (A. Pang & R. Turvey, Illus.). New York: Watts.

Webster, V. (1982). *A new true book: Weather experiments*. Chicago: Children's Press.

continued

Fiction

Adoff, A. (1977). *Tornado! Poems* (R. Himler, Illus.). New York: Delacorte.

Hopkins, L. B. (1994). *Weather* (M. Hall, Illus.). New York: HarperCollins.

Hershenhorn, E. (1998). *There goes Lowell's party* (J. Rogers, Illus.). New York: Holiday.

Locker, T. (1984). *Where the river begins* (T. Locker, Illus.). New York: Penguin.

Ruckman I. (1984). *Night of the twisters*. New York: HarperCollins.

Teacher Resources

Williams, J. (1992). *The weather book: An easy-to-understand guide to the U.S.A.'s weather*. New York: Random House.

Yaros, R. A. (1991). *Weatherschool*. Chesterfield, MO: Yaros Communications.

Web Sites

www.accuweather.com—AccuWeather (radar)

www.fema.gov/kids—FEMA for Kids

www.weatherbug.com—Weatherbug

www.weather.com—The Weather Channel

Study Skills

Students need to develop their own reading strategies and to become less dependent upon the teacher for establishing purposes for reading. Thus, students must become adept at formulating questions and making predictions about the text without teacher or classmate assistance.

To learn to generate questions independently, students must practice this skill with their classmates. For instance, the teacher may ask the class what questions they have about the Underground Railroad and write those questions on an overhead transparency. After viewing these questions, students will begin suggesting additional questions about the same topic. It is probably best to demonstrate such question generation for texts used in both science and social studies, rather than to assume that students will be able to formulate good questions for both content areas, since reading strategies for science are different from those used for social studies.

SQ3R

One strategy for prereading is the SQ3R process developed by Robinson (1983). *SQ3R* consists of five steps: survey, question, read, recite, and review. The student surveys the passage to be read by reading the headings, highlighted items, italicized words and phrases, questions at the end of the sections and chapter, and the introductory and concluding paragraphs. The student formulates questions based on the headings and then reads the passage to find the answers to the questions. Next, the student recites what was read. In the last step, review, the student looks back over the text as well as any notes jotted down while reading and determines the author's major points. The SQ3R process must be practiced on a regular basis if students are to use it effectively.

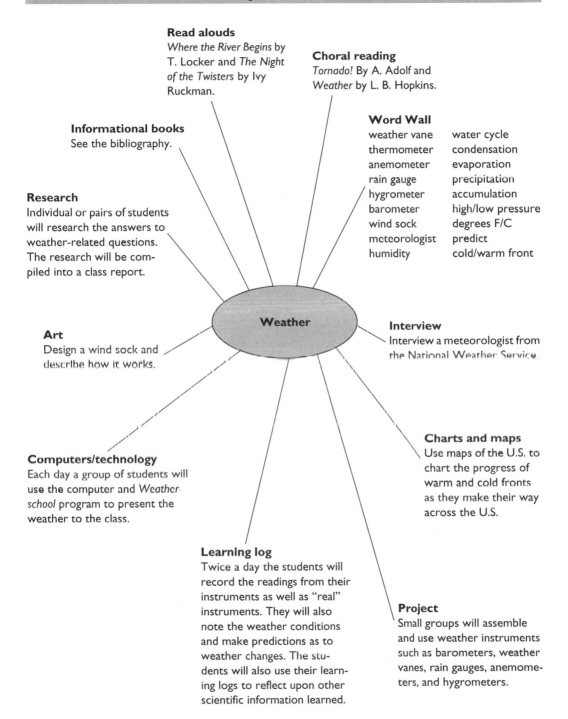

Read alouds
Where the River Begins by T. Locker and *The Night of the Twisters* by Ivy Ruckman.

Choral reading
Tornado! By A. Adolf and *Weather* by L. B. Hopkins.

Informational books
See the bibliography.

Word Wall

weather vane	water cycle
thermometer	condensation
anemometer	evaporation
rain gauge	precipitation
hygrometer	accumulation
barometer	high/low pressure
wind sock	degrees F/C
meteorologist	predict
humidity	cold/warm front

Research
Individual or pairs of students will research the answers to weather-related questions. The research will be compiled into a class report.

Weather

Interview
Interview a meteorologist from the National Weather Service.

Art
Design a wind sock and describe how it works.

Charts and maps
Use maps of the U.S. to chart the progress of warm and cold fronts as they make their way across the U.S.

Computers/technology
Each day a group of students will use the computer and *Weather school* program to present the weather to the class.

Learning log
Twice a day the students will record the readings from their instruments as well as "real" instruments. They will also note the weather conditions and make predictions as to weather changes. The students will also use their learning logs to reflect upon other scientific information learned.

Project
Small groups will assemble and use weather instruments such as barometers, weather vanes, rain gauges, anemometers, and hygrometers.

From Lisa Vogt, Weather: A Theme Cycle. Reprinted by permission.

Figure 12.2   Graphic organizer for a thematic unit on weather

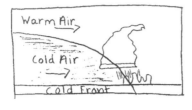

Fronts

Some front cause dangerous storms and may cause serious damage to property. What are fronts? What are the different kinds of fronts? How do they affect weather? Fronts help you plan your everyday activities.

A front is the interface between air masses at different temperatures When cold air and warm air meet they form a front. The air masses can make two kinds of fronts which are cold fronts and warm fronts. In a cold front, the edge of the mass of cold air moves under the warm air. Then the warm air is pushed upward while the cold air moves down to ground level. In a warm front, the edge of the air moving toward the cold air goes over the old air that is moving away. The warm air takes the place of the cold air at ground level.

Most of the changes in the weather happen along fronts. The moving of the fronts depend on the shape of the pressure systems. Cyclones push fronts along at twenty to thirty miles per hour. An anticyclone is where the air mass moves in the opposite direction of a cyclone and rotates arond the center of high barometric pressure. Anticyclones go into an area after a front has passed.

Cold fronts cause quick changes in weather. The kinds of changes rely alot on the amount of moisture that is being replaced. If the air is dry, it may cause the weather to be partly cloudy but no rainfall. If the air is humid, then the weather could be cloudy and maybe bring rain or snow. The precipitation caused by most cold fronts are pretty heavy but doesn't last long. Cold fronts also could bring strong winds. When cold fronts pass, most of them bring a fast drop in temperature, quickly clearing skies, and a drop in humidity.

From Anne McKibben. Used by permission.

Warm fronts make a slower change in the weather than cold fronts do. The changes rely mostly on the humidity of the oncoming warm air. If the air is dry, thin clouds could form and little or no precipitation would fall. If the air is humid, the sky will turn gray. Light steady rain or snow could fall for a couple of days. Sometimes fog may come. Most warm fronts have light winds. When warm fronts pass, they bring a quick rise in temperature, clearing skies, and a rise in humidity.

Cold fronts travel twice as fast as warm fronts do. So when a cold front meets a warm front, it forms an occluded front: cold front occlusions and warm front occlusions. In a cold front occlusion, the air behind the front is cooler than the air in front of the warm front. A cold front occlusion is like a cold front and has similar weather conditions. In a warm front occlusion, the air in the back of the cold front is warmer than the air ahead of it. A warm front occlusion is like a warm front and has similar weather conditions. But occluded fronts cause less violent weather than warm and cold fronts.

Another kind of front starts when a cold air and warm air mass meet, but they move very little. This kind is called a stationary front. It may stay in one area for a couple of days. The weather of a stationary front is usually moderate.

Fronts can be dangerous. They also affect the weather and people. Fronts have alot to do with our lives and what we do during the day.

Bibliography

The World Book Encyclopedia Volume 21 W. X. Y. Z. Copywrited by World Book Inc. 1990
The World Book Encyclopedia Volume 21 W. X. Y. Z. Copywrited by World Book Inc. 1983

Figure 12.3 A report by Anne McKibben (11 years old—above average student) on "fronts," which she researched as part of the weather unit

RESPONSE

Another study strategy is the RESPONSE approach created by Jacobson (1989). Like SQ3R, RESPONSE encourages students to generate questions about the text, but unlike SQ3R, RESPONSE requires students to categorize their questions. For this reason, it is most appropriate for students in grades four through six. A RESPONSE form is shown in box 12.6.

The RESPONSE form is an interactive device in that the student is given the opportunity to ask questions and to request immediate responses to those questions. After completing the RESPONSE form, the student gives it to the teacher, who notes the questions, names, vocabulary, concepts, and the like that have asterisks (*) next to them. The teacher then "responds" to those items, either in class discussion or in writing. By having the students record the page numbers that accompany the questions, names, and so on, the teacher can go directly to the appropriate section, thereby making the process more efficient.

12.6   In The Classroom: Teaching Hint

RESPONSE Form

Name: _____   Date: _____

Reading assignment: _____

Important points: As you read, list essential information and state important ideas; cite page numbers.

Questions: As you read, note questions that occur to you. Cite page numbers of their source. Some questions will be ideas for discussion. For others, you will want an immediate answer; star * these.

New terms/concepts/vocabulary/names: List words, phrases, technical terms, names of people, basic ideas that are new to you. Cite page numbers. Star * items you would like to have defined or explained.

The RESPONSE technique, originated by Jeanne M. Jacobson, is described in the winter '89 issue of Reading Horizons.

Reciprocal Teaching

Reciprocal teaching may be used with intermediate and middle school students and older students with learning disabilities. It requires students to use four strategies in summarizing content area material. First, the student reads the passage and then summarizes it in one sentence. Second, the student asks one or two high-level questions about the material read. Third, the student clarifies any difficult portions of the passage. Fourth, the student predicts what will occur in the next paragraph or portion of the text to be read.

Reciprocal teaching places less emphasis on teacher explanation and focuses more on the teacher and student collaborating in an attempt to bring meaning to the text. "At the heart of reciprocal teaching is a dialogue about the meaning of the text" (Palincsar & Brown, 1989, p. 33). In essence, reciprocal teaching is a type of individual DR-TA in that the student must use previously gained knowledge along with information gathered from the passage being read to formulate questions and to make feasible predictions. Research findings support the use of such strategies with low-ability intermediate-grade students and seventh and eighth graders with learning disabilities (Palincsar & Brown, 1985). It is essential that the classroom teacher model reciprocal teaching and then encourage students with a great deal of positive feedback as they implement the strategies in their reading of content area materials.

"Students read with greater purpose when they know they are expected to frame questions about their reading" (Hashey & Connors, 2003, p. 227). In her middle school classroom, Diane Connors introduces levels of questions as "skinny" if the query is literal in nature and "fat" if the question posed requires complex thought processes. "Skinny" questions might start with *Who, What, Where,* or *List.* "Fat" questions might begin with *Predict,* or *Why do you think . . .* After students have demonstrated an understanding of these two different levels, Diane then has the students generate questions on their own (Hashey & Connors, 2003). Modeling questioning helps students. So does modeling responses to both "skinny" and "fat" questions. Otherwise students my provide "skinny" responses to "fat" questions and not think deeply about what they've read.

Clarification is often needed as students read a passage of text. Typically competent readers will seek clarification—either rereading a particular section of text, asking another student, or querying the teacher. However, average and struggling readers often fail to search out clarification thereby hindering their understanding. To get students to seek clarification, the teacher might ask the class what they would do if they took a trip to a large city and found themselves lost. What would they look for? Perhaps it would be the tallest building. A museum? A particular street? In other words, landmarks. As they read, they need to locate landmarks, too. These may be semantic, syntactic, or grammatical. Rereading the passage is similar to retracing their steps when lost in a large city. Asking someone for guidance is yet another way to clarify, to find their way (Hashey & Connors, 2003).

Students need to be able to summarize the material. Having them read a number of well-written summaries that the teacher has selected in advance will assist them as they write their own summary of a short story or short expository piece such as an article in the *Scholastic News.*

12.7   In the Classroom: Mini Lesson

Comparing Different Versions of Folktales

Many folktales have been written and rewritten in several versions. Children may find one version of a folktale in their basal reader and another version of the same folktale in their school library. Analyzing how the versions are similar and how they differ can result in an excellent discussion about what makes a good folktale.

Among the folktales that are available in several versions are *The Little Red Hen, The Three Billy Goats Gruff, Chicken Little, Snow White and the Seven Dwarfs, Beauty and the Beast, Little Red Riding Hood, The Three Little Pigs, The Gingerbread Man, The Fisherman's Wife,* and *The Anasi Tales.* The teacher should bring to class as many versions of the same folktale as possible and encourage the students to do likewise.

The teacher divides the class into groups of three or four students and gives each group two versions of the same folktale to compare and contrast. The children should compare the literary elements of character, plot, setting (time and place), theme, and author's style. They should also note the differences in language use (words, phrases, and so on) that enrich the two versions of the folktale.

Children can create their own charts to compare the differences between the two versions. The individual literary elements and the different uses of language can serve as the headings for such charts. Here is an example of a comparison chart for *The Three Little Pigs.*

Title	Characters	Setting	Problem	Resolution
The Three Little Pigs	3 pigs wolf	Country	Wolf blows down houses of pigs.	Pigs are safe in brick house. When wolf tries to climb down chimney, he burns his tail and leaves.
The True Story of the Three Little Pigs	3 pigs wolf	Country	Wolf's cold makes him sneeze causing him to blow down the pigs' houses. Then he eats the pigs.	Wolf is arrested for murdering the three little pigs.
The Three Little Wolves and the Big Bad Pig	3 wolves big bad pig	Country	Big bad pig destroys homes of wolves.	Big bad pig becomes friend of three wolves.

Moser, B. (2001). *The three little pigs.* New York: Little, Brown.
Scieszka, J. (1989). *The true story of the three little pigs* (L. Smith, Illus.). New York: Viking.
Trivizas, E. (1993). *The three little wolves and the big bad pig* (H. Oxenbury, Illus.). New York: Scholastic.

Vocabulary Acquisition

Vocabulary is first cousin of comprehension for without the knowledge of words we cannot begin to understand text. Thus, it is critical that we teach vocabulary hand in hand with comprehension. Research from the National

Institute of Child Health and Human Development (2000) indicates that a determinant of poor comprehension is the possession of a poor vocabulary. Achievement in reading and writing is largely determined by one's vocabulary, and cognitive ability tests rely heavily on one's knowledge and use of words. Avid readers expand their vocabulary through their reading. And those avid readers who are interested in a variety of literary genres enhance their word familiarity even more. Students who possess a keen interest in word acquisition through reading and including new words in their own speaking and writing clearly have the advantage over their peers who find word study to be dull and boring. Students who detest reading and writing are doomed to lag behind such peers in vocabulary as well as comprehension. Teachers must create excitement and curiosity about words if students are to greatly expand their vocabulary.

The Importance of Vocabulary Development

Vocabulary is sometimes referred to as "knowing a word." This implies several things as the individual may know the word's literal meaning, its various connotations, the different sorts of syntactic constructions in which it appears in grammar, the morphological possibilities it may possess, and the various array of semantic family members (antonyms, synonyms, words with closely related but contrasting meanings, etc.) (Carlo et al, 2004). Actually learning a word and making it part of one's reading and listening vocabularies requires numerous encounters with the word itself. The student must then be willing to attempt to make it part of his expressive language in terms of including the newly gained word when speaking and writing opportunities arise.

Hart and Risley's (1995) classic study of word knowledge of children underscores the need to develop vocabulary when children are preschoolers as well as when they are students in elementary through high school and beyond. Hart and Risley labeled children of middle-socioeconomic status families as being the "fortunate group," as by age three they had heard 30 million more words than their counterparts from low-socioeconomic status families, members of the "unfortunate group." By the end of high school, despite the instruction they had received in reading and vocabulary development, the unfortunate group was four times behind that of the fortunate group. Even more discouraging is that the parents of the unfortunate group had a lower vocabulary than did the three-year-olds in the fortunate group. Children in the fortunate group enter school with 6,000 more words in their vocabulary than the unfortunate group. Add in that successful school curricula enlarge students' vocabulary by about 300 words a year (Stahl & Fairbanks, 1986), it would seem that extra emphasis on word acquisition is vital for preschoolers and elementary and middle school students if they are to be adequately prepared for the reading and writing demands of high school.

As mentioned earlier, avid readers acquire new vocabulary incidentally, through their reading. However, research points out that a new word has to be encountered eight times to be learned (Kuhn & Stahl, 1998). In short, expecting our students to acquire new vocabulary through their reading without any instruction is unrealistic—and even more so with average and struggling readers. If over 2 percent of the words in a text are unfamiliar, the reader's comprehension is blocked (Carver, 1994). English language learners (ELLs) encounter even greater difficulty in vocabulary growth as they lack full command of English grammar and are more apt to encounter a higher proportion of words they do not know (Carlo et al., 2004).

Vocabulary Instruction Techniques

Piquing the curiosity of students is a great way to develop vocabulary. The classroom teacher not only has to be interested in words but enthusiastic about sharing them! A bulletin board can be changed each week based on new words students encounter in guided and independent reading in addition to those discovered in the teacher's daily read alouds.

There are a number of engaging, fun vocabulary activities that enliven the vocabulary acquisition process. Here are a few.

- Chart new vocabulary words on 18 by 24 art paper along with a brief definition. Then hang the chart in the classroom so students may familiarize themselves with the new terms for reading and include in their own writing.

- Designate a bulletin board for a two-week study of words by category. For instance, one week the categories may be "beautiful" and "ugly." The students search to find words for each category, writing them on strips of construction paper and stapling them to the board. They note where they found each word as well as their own name on the strip. Each student is limited to one word per category the first week. Each day, the teacher reviews the words with the students, noting any new additions to the listing. The second week, students can put up as many words as they can locate.

- Have a favorite word day in which students dress up as a "Super Vocabulary Word." Good words to use as examples are porous, gnawed, ghoulish, and overindulgent.

- Have a vocabulary chart for a nonfiction read aloud. A terrific book for grades 6–8 for such a chart is *Phineas Gage: A Gruesome But True Story About Brain Science* (Fleishman, 2002).

- Interview a word. Give each student a different word. In groups of four, have the students interview each "word." The student with the word gives responses as though he was that word. For instance if the word is "pollution" the interview might go like this:

What do you like?	Lots of trash and stuff people can't use.
What do you do?	I gunk up water and earth.
How do you do this?	I encourage people to toss cups and food wrappers out their car windows and hope an oil tanker springs a leak.
Do people like you?	Messy people don't even acknowledge me.

Vocabulary instruction never ends as students discover new words daily. Sharing words from newspapers and magazines and sources other than books is also important as it models to the class that words are everywhere.

Instructional Approaches for Struggling Readers

Struggling readers come from different backgrounds. High-risk students are students who may graduate or drop out of school without having attained sufficient skills to function successfully in society. Typically, such students come from low socioeconomic backgrounds, are low achievers, have poor attendance records, and may demonstrate behavior problems. English language learners (ELLs) are children for whom English is a second language. Special needs students are children with a mental or physical disability or who are mentally or physically challenged in some way and are often mainstreamed in inclusion programs. Some students may come from affluent homes with well-educated parents but still find reading to be a difficult challenge. Struggling readers need additional attention and observation by the teacher. This section of the chapter will offer some insights about strategies for teaching struggling readers, which the classroom teacher can put into practice.

High-Risk Students

Children from low socioeconomic backgrounds have been studied extensively in terms of reading achievement (Adams, 1990). As Allington (1991, p. 237) writes, "It is the children of poverty who are most likely to have literacy-learning difficulties." Programs for high-risk students have been available for many years. Among them are Head Start, a program designed for deprived preschoolers, and Chapter 1, a remedial reading, writing, and mathematics program for elementary and secondary students. These programs were heavily funded by the federal government in the 1960s, and the 2002 No Child Left Behind Act increased federal funding to the highest fiscal funding in history. However, schools that continually fail to increase reading achievement of such students receive reduced funding.

Some states have adopted their own programs to assist high-risk students. Indiana, Nevada, and Tennessee, among other states, have encouraged school districts to have smaller classes for first, second, and third graders. Other states help fund all-day, everyday kindergarten. Such programs are not directed solely at the high-risk population but include all students.

Slavin and Madden (1989) found that all effective programs for high-risk students had a comprehensive approach. According to Slavin and Madden, an overall school plan for these students should include (1) a statement that the school is responsible for ensuring that every student succeeds, (2) recognition that a successful program requires substantial fiscal and personnel resources, (3) an emphasis on prevention rather than remediation, (4) an emphasis on classroom change that includes follow-up programs, and (5) reliance on remedial programs as a final resort.

Another program to aid beginning readers is Reading Recovery, a program for promising potential (at-risk) first graders that focuses on intensive reading instruction provided by a specially trained teacher. Research on the long-term effects of the Reading Recovery program suggests that students in the program read at levels substantially higher than those students who receive no assistance. Although the gains diminished over a two-year period, they remained significant even though the Reading Recovery students received no assistance after first grade (DeFord et al., 1987). One drawback is the high cost of the program.

Reading Recovery is one approach to working with high-risk students; other ways of developing reading strategies with such students include the language experience approach and literature-based instruction. In the language experience approach, described earlier in this chapter, the child dictates a story to the teacher or an aide who writes it down exactly as the child tells it. The teacher or aide reads the story back to the child, and the child then reads it aloud. This occurs until the child literally memorizes the story and the words. The child will write several stories in this fashion. Then the teacher introduces the child to pattern books, which are also read repeatedly to and with the child until they are memorized.

The literature-based approach with high-risk students provides a wide variety of options (Indrisano & Paratore, 1992). For the beginning reader, pattern books are often used. For the student who has some reading proficiency, literature response journals can be used. In these, a student shares her reactions with the teacher, who writes comments and questions back to the child on a daily basis. The literature-based approach is good for pairing up students with similar interests. For example, two or three students at different reading levels who are interested in basketball may each read a book selected from a text set, a set of books on the same theme (basketball in this case). The students meet daily to discuss their books. Thus, the low-ability student has the opportunity to share a similar interest and discuss it with students who have greater reading ability.

Another technique includes pairing a high-risk student with a student of higher reading ability in a shared reading task and having them read a book or short story to each other. The students take turns reading the sentences. This enables the lower-ability reader to hear an average or good reader read aloud (modeling of good oral reading) while the lower-ability student follows the phonological/graphemic relationship of the printed page. It also forces the low-ability reader to keep up and not lose his place.

English Language Learners (ELLs)

ELL students are often considered to be high-risk candidates. When a bilingual student in a regular classroom has difficulty with reading or writing, she should be given appropriate tests to determine whether the problem in learning is due to second-language acquisition or to a learning disorder in the child's native, or first, language. If a child has a learning or language disorder within her native language, instruction should not continue in a second language.

ELL students need to develop language proficiency, cognitive proficiency, and academic proficiency in a positive classroom setting (Ovando & Collier, 1998). With second-language learners, the emphasis should be on comprehension rather than phonics instruction inasmuch as the students may be able to pronounce the words successfully but fail to have a clue as to their meaning (Freeman, 1999). This is not to say that phonics is never taught. It is taught in the context of reading literature. The stress should be on having students "read to learn" their newly acquired language. If they are forced to learn how to decode words or nonsense syllables apart from reading actual text, their academic development will be delayed (Cummins, 1996). According to David Freeman (1999, p. 246), "It's as ridiculous to claim that teachers who use literature never teach skills or phonics as it is to say that students in bilingual classes never hear a word of English."

When phonics is taught, the teacher should be aware that whole-to-part phonics is most effective with some second-language learners. For instance "in learning to read Spanish, children are better able to make letter-syllable correspondences than letter-phoneme correspondences" (Moustafa & Maldonado-Colon, 1999, p. 455). They give the example of "Finding an Egg," a Spanish finger play for young children similar to "The Eensy Weensy Spider" and "Five Little Ducks."

"Finding an Egg"	**"Hallando un Huevo"**
This little boy found an egg.	Este niño halló un huevo.
This one cooked it.	Este lo coció.
This one peeled it.	Este lo peló.
This one salted it.	Este le echó la sal.
This fat little one ate it.	Este gordo chaparrito se lo comió.
He became thirsty	Le dió sed
and he went to look for water.	y se fue a buscar agua.
He looked and looked	Buscó y buscó
and here he found it	y aquí halló
and drank and drank and drank.	y tomó y tomó y tomó.

Some of the letters Moustafa and Maldonado-Colon (1999) suggest children should be made aware of would be as follows:

Word	*Highlight*
Este	[Es]te, Es[te]
lo	[lo]
buscar	[bus]car, bus[car]
sed	[sed]
gordo	[gor]do, gor[do]
tomó	[to]mó, to[mó]
agua	[a]gua, a[gua]

Effective bilingual programs have been found to have common elements. Here are a few as identified by Collier (1995):

1. Integrated schooling, with English speakers and ELLs learning each other's languages.

2. Perceptions among teachers, administrators, students, and parents that the program is a "gifted and talented program" with high expectations for student performance.

3. Equal status of English and the minority language(s) as much as possible so that ELLs develop self-confidence.

4. Sound and healthy involvement by parents of both first- and second-language learners. This results in closer home-school cooperation.

5. Continuous staff development for teachers, administrators, and aides in the following areas:

   • Literature-based instruction

   • Cooperative learning

   • Interactive and discovery learning

   • Cognitive complexity for all proficiency levels

With ELLs, parental involvement can be difficult to initiate and maintain. Many second-language learners live in extended families in cramped apartments or houses with their parents earning minimum wages and often working two or more jobs. Alessandra Kennedy (1999), a bilingual teacher, visited all of her students in their homes early in the school year. Initially she was viewed with skepticism as some of the parents thought she was trying to determine if they were illegal aliens. Once she convinced them that her visit was based on her concern as a teacher for her students, parents opened up to her. She found that one of her students delivered newspapers each morning and missed school sometimes to work at odd jobs to help provide for his family. Another parent worked three low-paying jobs and found it difficult to encourage her children to do their homework. One mother had eight children, all by different fathers. She had little interest in what school could provide for her children other than a free meal and being out of the small apartment in which they lived for part of the day. After beginning the year optimistically, Alessandra became frustrated. "Who am I, a teacher, to say to these parents that schooling is more important than providing food on the table and a place for their families to live?"

Teachers often falsely assume that parents of ELLs are literate in their first language. This is not true. Alessandra found that over one-third of her students' parents could not read Spanish, their primary language. Thus, there exists a lack of support and motivation from home for the children to become literate.

The language experience approach has been found to be a most effective strategy to use with ELLs who are initially acquiring English. Keep in mind that code switching, combining English with their first language, is indicative of language growth in English. Other reading instructional practices that are helpful include books on tape, which students can follow along as they read. Both shared reading and listening to a book on tape provides English language learners with "an opportunity to hear language while observing its corresponding phonological representation" (Drucker, 2003, p. 24). Books printed in two languages so that the child can see both languages side by side can be beneficial. Such a book is Jane Medina's (1999) picture book, *My Name is Jorge: On Both Sides of the River,* which contains the text in both English and Spanish. Providing books with familiar subjects such as Mary-Joan Gerson's (2001) *Fiesta Femenina: Celebrating Women in Mexican Folktales* or Robert D. San Souci's (2000) *Little Gold Star: A Spanish American Cinderella Tale* can entice ELL students to read.

Cultural schema and background knowledge of ELLs need to be taken into consideration. It is particularly helpful if ELLs have heard folktales that are translations of stories in their native language. Also ELLs more readily relate to books that depict characters who are similar to themselves (Drucker, 2003). For instance, *Red Is a Dragon* and *Round Is a Mooncake* (Thong, 2000, 2002) contain delightful drawings of Asian children accompanied by simple text that introduces colors and shapes in these two concept books.

Regular classroom teachers can address the needs and interests of ELL students by following the guidelines below (Canney et al, 1999).

- Learn as much as possible about each student's culture.
- Encourage students to share their histories, culture, and language with the class.
- Invite the parents of all your students to take any active role in their children's education.
- Keep the students in the regular classroom. They are just as capable of learning as the other students.
- Employ the same literacy teaching strategies used with the rest of the class.

These suggestions are simple and practical for the elementary teacher to incorporate but much more difficult for the middle school teacher who has so many students.

Other suggestions include audiotaping all content area textbooks and permitting the students to take the tapes and an inexpensive cassette recorder home. If a student walks a distance or rides the bus, the student can complete a science or social studies chapter during the trip to and from school. Don't underestimate the need to read aloud to ELLs. Research found that when teachers read aloud a story to students just three times a week vocabulary scores of ELLs increased by 40 percent (Freeman & Freeman, 2000).

Struggling Readers and Special Needs Students

Over the past decade, the number of struggling readers and special needs students in the regular classroom has increased for a variety of reasons. No longer are special needs students taught in self-contained special education classrooms. The increased mobility of our society has resulted in some students moving frequently from school to school, thereby falling through the cracks in the educational system as their needs are barely identified by a school before they move once again. Struggling readers have certain characteristics when compared with good readers. Richard Allington (2001) found that struggling readers are more likely to:

- Be reading material that is too difficult resulting in poor fluency
- Be requested by the teacher to read aloud
- Be interrupted by the teacher when they miscall a word
- Pause at a word and then wait for the teacher to prompt
- Be told by the teacher to sound out a word
- Be interrupted while reading aloud sooner than an average or good reader

Allington (2001) found in comparison that good readers are more likely to:

- Be reading materials of appropriate difficulty resulting in good fluency
- Be asked by the teacher to read silently
- Be expected to self-monitor and self-correct
- Be interrupted by the teacher only after a wait period or at the end of a sentence
- Be asked by the teacher to reread a passage or cross check when interrupted

Working with struggling readers led Allington (2001) to assert that such readers need a "double dose of reading." That is to say, students having difficulty reading need to read at least twice as much as the typical reader if they are to catch up to be reading at or above grade level. For the teacher, this means finding appropriate texts, providing needed instruction, and making sufficient time available for the struggling reader to read, read, READ! Rereading a text aids word identification, comprehension, and fluency. Thus, the student may first read the passage silently then reread it later. Parental support can really help the student if the child takes the book home and reads to a parent three or four times each week.

A study of test scores on achievement and diagnostic reading tests led Valencia and Buly (2004) to suggest that struggling readers may not be receiving the proper reading instruction. Each assessment must be considered as instruction is designed for that particular child. If a child has good comprehension but poor word analysis skills, then the instructional emphasis should be placed on word analysis and phonemic awareness while encouraging the student to read children's literature during independent reading time. A student who reads slowly but with good comprehension would benefit from having fluency tasks such as choral reading or shared reading with a buddy. A student with average comprehension but poor word identification and fluency would likely benefit from word analysis and phonemic awareness along with fluency exercises.

A student with special needs may be emotionally challenged, have a learning disability, a hearing or visual impairment, some other physical impairment, a speech or language problem, or be mentally challenged. Most of these students read below the average reading level of their peer group, and they typically lack practice in reading because they are poor readers. Such students need positive experiences with reading—and many of them. Using children's literature with such students is helpful because literature shapes events into some kind of meaning. According to Bruner (1990), literature is the driving force in language learning.

The old saying—"use it or lose it"—is true when it comes to special needs students. Research has shown that special needs students need lots of repetition and practice in gaining reading skills. Beginning readers should have numerous opportunities to put into use newly introduced phonics skills. Reading and rereading familiar stories is quite appropriate for special needs students.

Comprehension can be enhanced by using graphic organizers such as those described in chapter 3. This gives special needs students a visual element in addition to the text. By having the students discuss the material with a partner or in small groups, comprehension will be improved. Intermediate-level and middle school students should be encouraged to engage in reciprocal teaching as described earlier in this chapter.

Putting text on auditory tape does improve comprehension for special needs students; it also increases their dependency on listening and reduces their desire to learn how to read. Using books on tape is a good way for those who struggle with reading to participate in literature circles, but there is an appropriate time for them to read a book on their own, too. Science and social studies textbooks are appropriate for audiotaping for special needs students. Students should be encouraged to follow the text as they listen as well as to utilize visual aids such as photos, maps, charts, and graphs in the textbook to further aid their comprehension.

Students with learning disabilities (LD students) may have difficulty remembering what they have seemingly already learned. This can be discouraging, both for the student and the classroom teacher. Success with LD students typically occurs when a reading program is individually tailored for each child and an underlying support system to develop the child's self-concept is in place. Such a program meets with less resistance by LD children. One-to-one adaptive instruction can generally be used to overcome learning difficulties (Vellutino & Scanlon, 2002).

An essential ingredient for working with any student with a special need is to provide many opportunities for small and large group involvement in which the child contributes in a positive way to the learning environment and is not considered an outcast within his own classroom.

Reading Assessment

"In theory, assessment is about gathering and interpreting data to inform action. In practice, data interpretations are constrained by our views of literacy and students, the assessment conversations that surround us, and the range of 'actions' we can imagine" (Johnston, 2003, p. 90). Thus, assessment of student reading is not based solely on formal tests or standardized measurements. Such measures lend themselves to skills orientation. Most states mandate formal evaluation of reading competence at specified grade levels to determine which schools and school districts are meeting state reading standards. Formal testing usually includes state tests as well as commercially developed standardized tests. Without standardized reading achievement tests, teachers and school

12.8   The More You Know

Reading Recovery

Reading Recovery began in New Zealand as a means of helping young children who failed to respond to literacy instruction during their first year of schooling. Created by Marie Clay (1996), Reading Recovery is an intensive, individualized instructional program. A regular classroom teacher who is specially trained in the Reading Recovery methodology devotes part of the school day to working with Reading Recovery students on a one-to-one basis.

Reading Recovery teachers assist low-achieving six- and seven-year-old students to reach average or close to average classroom achievement levels. The materials used are simple: a magnetic chalkboard, magnetic letters, felt-tipped pens, simple storybooks, and exercise books. Lesson plans are created daily, not a week in advance as for a typical class.

Record keeping for each child includes notes on the lesson plans used, records and graphs on reading accuracy, vocabulary charts, and a record of books selected by the teacher for the child to read. A child may be in the program for 12 to 16 weeks or longer if necessary.

In an attempt to explain why Reading Recovery programs work and traditional remedial reading programs fail, Spiegel (1995) offers the following 15 reasons:

1. Intervention must take place early.
2. Reading instruction should focus on the comprehension of connected text, not the fragmented study of isolated skills.
3. Children should spend time reading rather than completing worksheets.
4. Both the teacher and the child should be aware of the goals of instruction.
5. Children must have the opportunity to learn.
6. Children should be given materials to read that are appropriate for their reading level.
7. Children should be taught reading strategies and how to transfer those strategies to new situations.
8. Writing should be an integral part of a beginning reading program.
9. A beginning reading program should include phonemic awareness as part of the curriculum.
10. The intervention program should be congruent with the classroom reading program.
11. Direct instruction should be part of the program.
12. Instruction in special reading programs should be individualized.
13. Children's attempts to make meaning of text should be monitored and reinforced.
14. Children most at risk should be taught by the best teachers.
15. Children who have fallen behind need a program that accelerates their progress.

Clay, M. M. (1996). Why is an in-service programme for Reading Recovery teachers necessary? *Reading Horizons, 31* (5), 355–372.

Spiegel, D. L. (1995). A comparison of traditional remedial programs and Reading Recovery: Guidelines for success for all programs. *The Reading Teacher, 49* (2), 86–96.

administrators often have difficulty convincing parents—who themselves were taught according to the isolated skills approach—that their child is performing at an appropriate level. The classroom teacher can instruct students so they will become "test wise." The focus of assessment should be to document student progress, using the results to guide instructional practice in the classroom.

Nevertheless, assessment of reading progress relies on a combination of techniques, including teacher observation and analysis of records kept over a period of time. Teachers should be concerned with children's interests, level of functioning, and literacy development as evidenced through student evaluation and classroom activities. According to Routman (1991, p. 305) evaluation should include five components that occur interactively; "that is, the observation, activity, test, or task must be relevant, authentic, and part of the teaching-learning process by informing the learner and furthering instruction." Noticing and recording literate knowledge and practice of children is a critical component of assessment as is what children know and can do. It is likewise important that we as teachers analyze the classroom learning environment as we make our assessment (Johnston, 2003). Failure to have an adequate classroom library or an insufficient amount of independent reading time can be factors that result in lower student reading achievement. Routman (1991) believes that a classroom library should consist of 2,000 books—an expensive and extensive collection for even an experienced teacher.

The teacher must observe the student working individually, in small groups, and in whole-class activities to determine the child's ability to use language, solve problems, and work cooperatively with peers. The teacher must also interact with the student through conferences, questioning, and written dialogues to assess the student's knowledge level and approaches to problem solving. Finally, the teacher must analyze the student's oral and written reactions to written material, both published books and the student's own pieces, to evaluate the student's knowledge of language and its use (Goodman, 1988).

By means of checklists, anecdotal records, journals, and portfolios, the classroom teacher can monitor the learning and development of each student. A monthly review of each student's reading growth, such as a comparison of anecdotal records and checklists over several weeks, helps the teacher determine the types of experiences and activities that have been successful and unsuccessful for each child. The use of journals enables teachers to reflect on their own teaching as well as the learning of each student.

The classroom teacher should also encourage students to evaluate themselves. By keeping lists such as "Books I Have Read" and "Things I Can Do in Writing," and dating such lists to indicate progress, students can self-monitor their efforts. By determining what they already know and do not know, they can direct their learning to new and unfamiliar areas. Thus, students take control of their own learning.

The evaluation of a student's reading should be a continuous process in that every day a teacher will likely observe a new skill being acquired by the student. She may discover that a skill thought to have been mastered by another student has yet to be acquired. By using both formal and informal measures, the classroom teacher can effectively gauge the reading ability of all students in the class.

Formal Evaluation Measures

Formal evaluation measures include standardized tests and the tests that accompany basal reader series, such as unit tests. Many formal measures are either norm referenced or criterion referenced. A *norm-referenced test* compares a student's test results with those of other students who have previously taken the same test. A *criterion-referenced test* compares the student's test result with a set performance, or criterion. For example, standardized achievement tests are norm-referenced tests, whereas a written examination for a driver's license is a criterion-referenced test.

Norm-referenced tests are useful to the classroom teacher in terms of reading evaluation. By administering a norm-referenced standardized achievement test each year and comparing student results with those of the previous year's students, teachers can evaluate their current students' progress. Furthermore, when the scores of all students in a school or a school district are compiled together according to grade level, the overall effectiveness of the school's or district's reading program can be measured.

Criterion-referenced tests are frequently used to determine whether or not students have mastered specific skills. For instance, a criterion-referenced test may contain 10 items pertaining to syllabication rules; if a student successfully completes 8 of those items, that student is considered competent in syllabication. Criterion-referenced tests are also useful in working with high risk students. For example, a teacher may construct a criterion-referenced test to measure a specific behavior. The student is evaluated on her own work, and the results are not compared with those of other students.

Teachers must continually assess each student's needs and base their instruction on those needs.

Reading Readiness Tests

Typically, formal reading readiness tests are administered to young children before they enter elementary school. Such tests include subtests to evaluate the emergent literacy skills of young children in such areas as auditory discrimination, letter identification, letter-sound association, letter copying, and following directions. In selecting a readiness test, a teacher must be careful to choose one that can effectively identify language-delayed, high-risk children.

Diagnostic Tests

As students progress through elementary school, formal diagnostic tests may be administered to determine individual skill competency. Such tests are usually given when a child has difficulty with a particular reading skill, such as the ability to recognize consonant or vowel sounds, consonant blends and diphthongs; the ability to sequence events; or the ability to comprehend what is read. Diagnostic tests are administered individually and require careful scoring and interpretation of the results.

A proliferation of commercial reading tests has resulted in the "overtesting" of students. One superintendent complained that some teachers in his district were administering unit reading tests before the students had even completed the unit being evaluated. When the students scored poorly, one teacher told his class: "That's okay. We haven't covered the material so I didn't expect you to do well on the test." Obviously, such misuse of tests should be avoided.

Informal Evaluation Measures

Many teachers believe that to make reading instruction more effective, they should find out all they can about their students: their interests, attitudes, preferences, and abilities. Such teachers have students keep lists of things they like and don't like, of what they would like to do during their free time, of what their hobbies are, and so forth. In addition, the students keep lists of the books they have read as well as those they would like to read, and these teachers routinely peruse the students' lists in an attempt to keep up with their current interests and reading activities.

Other teachers prefer to informally measure student attitudes and interests in reading by means of inventories or checklists. Still other teachers arrange time for informal *reading interviews*, audiotaped interviews within which the student shares a "special" passage from a favorite book. The teacher then questions the student about the book and other reading interests.

Anecdotal Records

Anecdotal records are notations made by the classroom teacher about a student after observing the student. Routman (1991, p. 309) defines anecdotal records as being

> dated, informal observational notations that describe language development as well as social development in terms of the learner's attitudes, strengths, weaknesses, needs, progress, learning styles, skills, strategies

used, or anything else that seems significant at the time of the observation. These records are usually brief comments that are very specific to what the child is doing and needs to be doing. They provide documented, accumulated information over time and offer an expanded view of the student's development of literacy.

Anecdotal records can be about a variety of things. For instance, they can be about "written products or can include information about both process and product" (Rhodes & Nathenson-Mejia, 1992, p. 502). Rhodes and Nathenson-Mejia further state that "taken regularly, anecdotal notes become not only a vehicle for planning instruction and documenting progress, but also a story about an individual" (p. 503).

Unlike checklists, anecdotal records are time consuming for the classroom teacher. However, the records can provide valuable information, particularly when viewed with other evaluation measures. Anecdotal records are especially important for providing the teacher with insightful information during student-teacher and parent-teacher conferences.

Reading Portfolios

A reading portfolio should contain a running list of the books a child has read, including the date on which each book was finished, and a running list of books the child would like to read. Vocabulary words can also be maintained and dated in a list kept in the portfolio.

During the primary grades (beginning in January with first graders), a record should be kept of the number of words each child can read from a simple children's book in one minute's time. The record should be updated three times a year. The children's book should be one that no student can finish, and the same book should be used for the entire class so that the teacher can gauge the progress of all the students (Pils, 1991).

The breadth of different reading experiences (reading stories; reading poetry, songs, and other material; and reading across content areas while working on projects) should be shared in a literacy portfolio. In addition, it should contain a record of how reading and writing are used in combination to solve problems, communicate with others, make new connections and discoveries, and pursue projects both in and out of school (Tierney, Carter, & Desai, 1991). The teacher should review and evaluate the portfolio periodically, at least once a month. This assessment should indicate types of reading and writing selections and their content. For instance, how does the child analyze literary elements in his literature response journal over a period of time? Does one author (or topic) seem to captivate the student's reading interests? After evaluating the portfolio, the teacher should have a conference with the student to discuss the portfolio, including how the student is progressing and what the student's current reading interests are compared to what they were at the beginning of the school year. The student should feel free to examine his strengths and weaknesses in a candid manner during the conference. Some teachers exchange portfolios of four different-ability students (one superstar, one average, one struggling, and one puzzling or inconsistent) and then write a brief synopsis of the progress of each of the four students. The resultant assessments are then discussed as the teachers go over the respective student's portfolio (Gillespie et al., 1996). This aids teachers in keeping their judgments reliable and valid. Reading can be assessed in combination with writing to provide a wider literacy assessment as students' interests and patterns evolve from both their reading and writing.

Technology has made portfolios more efficient and less time consuming: writing samples can be scanned by computer, records can be downloaded from handheld computers to laptops, short video clips of plays can be stored on CDs, and so forth. The speed and efficiency that result from using computers allow teachers to assess a wide range of activities and get a better gauge of each student's literacy progress.

Diagnostic-Reflective Portfolios

By collecting samples of work and then assessing them along with considering learning goals, portfolios can serve as a diagnostic-reflective evaluative measure (Courtney & Abodeeb, 1999). Such portfolios require the following:

- Diagnosis of the student's strengths and weaknesses in order to plan and guide literacy instruction
- Collection of student work by the student and teacher
- Sorting through the collection of sample work by the student:

  Select two math papers that demonstrate the student can write out the steps to solve a story problem.

  Select an entry from the book log that best explains why the student liked a book he/she read.

  Select a piece of narrative writing that shows the student knows how to write dialogue.

- Goal setting by the student under the guidance of the teacher:

  The goals must be realistic and appropriate.

  The goals are established at the beginning of each grading period or term.

- Reflecting back on each piece of work in terms of what, why, and how learning has taken place:

  Reflection and construction occurs when the teacher sits down with the student at the end of the grading period or term.

- Sharing the portfolios with parents and guardians:

  This is done three times a year.

  The student does the sharing/explaining of the portfolio at home after having practiced with a schoolmate in the classroom.

Diagnostic-reflective portfolios are useful during parent-teacher conferences. They are quite helpful for those students who have individualized educational plans (IEPs).

Summary

Until recently, reading was the primary focus of language arts instruction. The balanced approach to literacy instruction combines phonics instruction with the basal reader or whole language approach for young children who are beginning to learn how to read.

The reading field has witnessed recent interest in the area of emergent literacy as researchers seek to examine how children acquire literacy. Along with this has come a renewed interest in sharing books with preschoolers and extending this practice into the primary and intermediate grades. Reader's workshop is used from first through eighth grades.

A variety of reading methodologies exist for both beginning and experienced readers. Moreover, several study techniques are available for reading in the content areas. Finally, there are a number of formal and informal methods for evaluating children's reading progress.

Questions

1. Compare the guided reading approach with how you learned to read. What are the advantages and disadvantages of each?
2. What are the characteristics of a child in the emergent reading stage?
3. How does the shared book activity compare with your own experiences of having the teacher read to you during "story time"?
4. Compare and contrast the different study skill techniques. Suggest a strength and a weakness of each.

Reflective Teaching

Flip back to the beginning of the chapter to the teaching vignette entitled "Peering into the Classroom." After rereading the vignette, consider the following questions: What characteristics (either implied or directly exhibited) does the teacher possess that you would like to develop? What strengths and weaknesses are revealed for the students described in this section? How would you meet the needs of students such as these?

Activities

1. Observe four children of different ages varying between age four and age nine while they are reading. Make a chart to indicate when children possess the specific reading skills (e.g., left-to-right directionality, top-to-bottom directionality, and use of picture clues).
2. Find a book that would be appropriate for a guided reading activity. Develop and implement a guided reading lesson for a group of six to eight elementary students who are reading at that instructional level.

3. Help an English language learner write a language experience story.

4. Adopt one of the study skill techniques described in this chapter for one of your own classes. Use it for at least a month and then compare their progress.

For Further Reading

Ainsle, D. (2000/2001). Word detectives. *The Reading Teacher, 54* (4), 360–362.

Allington, R. L. (2002). What I've learned about effective reading instruction from a decade of exemplary elementary teachers. *Phi Delta Kappan, 83* (10), 740–747.

Barton, J., & Sawyer, D. M. (2003/2004). Our students *are* ready for this: Comprehension instruction in the elementary school. *The Reading Teacher, 57* (4), 334–347.

Cunningham, P. (2000). *Phonics they use* (3rd ed.). New York: Addison-Wesley.

Drucker, M. J. (2003). What reading teachers should know about ESL learners. *The Reading Teacher, 57* (1), 24–29.

Freeman, D. E., & Freeman, Y. S. (2000). *Teaching reading in multicultural classrooms*. Portsmouth, NH: Heinemann.

Gambrell, L. B., Morrow, L. M., Neuman, S. B., & Pressley, M. (Eds.). (1999). *Best practices in literacy instruction*. New York: Guilford.

Johnston, P. (2003). Assessment conversations. *The Reading Teacher, 57* (1), 90–93.

Morrow, L. M, Tracey, D. H., Woo, D. G., & Pressley, M. (1999). Characteristics of exemplary first-grade literacy instruction. *The Reading Teacher, 52* (5), 462–476.

Moss, B. (2004). Teaching expository text structures through information trade book retellings. *The Reading Teacher, 57* (8), 710–719.

Moustafa, M., & Maldonado-Colon, E. (1999). Whole-to-parts phonics instruction: Building on what children know to help them know more. *The Reading Teacher, 52* (5), 448–458.

Stewart, M. T. (2004). Early literacy instruction in the climate of No Child Left Behind. *The Reading Teacher, 57* (8), 732–743.

Valencia, S. W., & Buly, M. R. (2004). Behind test scores: What struggling readers *really* need. *The Reading Teacher, 57* (6), 520–533.

Vellutino, F. R., & Scanlon, D. M. (2002). The interactive strategies approach to reading intervention. *Contemporary Educational Psychology, 27,* 573–635.

References

Adams, M. J. (1990). *Beginning to read: Thinking and learning about print*. Urbana, IL: Center for the Study of Reading.

Allen, R. V. (1976). *Language experiences in communication*. Boston: Houghton Mifflin.

Allington, R. L. (1991). Children who find learning to read difficult: School responses to diversity. In E. H. Hiebert (Ed.), *Literacy for a diverse society: Perspectives, practices, and policies*. New York: Teachers College Press.

Allington, R. L. (2001). *What really matters for struggling readers: Designing research based programs.* New York: Wiley.

Allington, R. L. (2002). What I've learned about effective reading instruction from a decade of exemplary elementary classroom teachers. *Phi Delta Kappan, 83* (10), 740–747.

Anderson, R. C., Hiebert, E. H., Scott, J. A., & Wilkinson, I. A. G. (1984). *Becoming a nation of readers: The report of the Commission on Reading.* Washington, DC: National Institute of Reading.

Anderson, R. C., Wilson, P. T., & Fielding, L. G. (1988). Growth in reading and how children spend their time outside of school. *Reading Research Quarterly, 23,* 285–303.

Atwell, N. (1998). *In the middle: New understandings about writing, reading, and learning* (2nd ed.). Portsmouth, NH: Heinemann.

Babbitt, N. (1987). Boston Globe Award speech. *The Horn Book, 63,* 582–585.

Bissex, G. (1980). *GNYS AT WORK: A child learns to read and write.* Cambridge, MA: Harvard University Press.

Bruner, J. (1990). *Acts of meaning.* Cambridge, MA: Harvard University Press.

Burke, E. M. (1999). Literature in a balanced reading program. In S. M. Blair-Larsen & K. A. Williams (Eds.), *The balanced reading program* (pp. 53–71). Newark, DE: International Association.

Calkins, L. M., & Harwayne, S. (1991). *Living between the lines.* Portsmouth, NH: Heinemann.

Canney, G. F., Kennedy, T. J., Schroeder, M., and Miles, S. (1999). Instructional strategies for K–12 limited-English proficiency students in the regular classroom. *The Reading Teacher, 52* (5), 540–545.

Carlo, M. S., August, D., McLaughlin, B., Snow, C. E., Dressler, C., Lippman, D. N., Lively, T. J., & White, C. E. (2004). Closing the gap: Addressing the vocabulary needs of English language learners in bilingual and mainstream classrooms. *Reading Research Quarterly, 39* (2), 188–215.

Carver, R. P. (1994). Percentage of unknown vocabulary words in text as a function of the relative difficulty of the text: Implications for instruction. *Journal of Reading Behavior, 26,* 413–437.

Clark, M. (1976). *Young fluent readers: What can they teach us?* Portsmouth, NH: Heinemann.

Clay, M. M. (1982). *Observing young readers: Selected papers.* London: Heinemann.

Clay, M. M. (1991). Introducing a new storybook to young readers. *The Reading Teacher, 45* (4), 264–273.

Collier, V. (1995). Acquiring a second language for school. *Directions on Language and Education* [online]. Available: http://www.ncbe.gwu.edu/ncbepubs/directions/dir14.htm

Courtney, A. M., & Abodeeb, T. L. (1999). Diagnostic-reflective portfolios. *The Reading Teacher, 52* (7), 708–714.

Cullinan, B. E., & Galda, L. (1999). *Literature and the child* (3rd ed.). Fort Worth: Harcourt Brace.

Cummins, J. (1996). *Negotiating identities: Education for empowerment in a diverse society.* Ontario, CA: California Association of Bilingual Education.

Cunningham, P. M., & Hall, D. (1998). The four blocks: A balanced framework for literacy in primary classrooms. In K. Harris, S. Graham, & M. Pressley (Eds.), *Teaching every child every day* (pp. 32–76). Cambridge, MA: Brookline Books.

DeFord, D. E., Pinnell, G. S., Lyons, C. A., & Young, P. (1987). *Ohio's Reading Recovery Program: Vol. 3. Report of the follow-up studies.* Columbus: Ohio State University.

Doake, D. (1981). *Book experience and emergent reading in preschool children.* Unpublished doctoral dissertation, University of Alberta, Alberta, Canada.

Drucker, M. (2003). What reading teachers should know about ESL learners. *The Reading Teacher, 57* (1), 22–29.

Durkin, D. (1966). *Children who read early: Two longitudinal studies.* New York: Columbia Teachers College Press.

Durkin, D. (1972). *Teaching young children to read.* Boston: Houghton Mifflin.

Durkin, D. (1974–1975). A six-year study of children who learned to read in school at the age of four. *The Reading Teacher, 10* (1–5), 9–61.

Durkin, D. (1987). Testing in the kindergarten. *The Reading Teacher, 37,* 766–770.

Durkin, D. (1990). Dolores Durkin speaks on instruction. *The Reading Teacher, 43* (7), 472–477.

Edwards, P. A. (1991). Fostering early literacy through parent coaching. In E. H. Hiebert (Ed.), *Literacy for a diverse society: Perspectives, practices, and policies.* New York: Teachers College Press.

Eskey, D. E. (2002). Reading and teaching of L2 students. *TESOL Journal, 11* (1), 5–9.

Farris, P. J., & Fuhler, C. J. (1994). Developing social studies concepts through picture books. *The Reading Teacher, 47* (5), 380–387.

Fitzgerald, J. (1999). What is this thing called "balance"? *The Reading Teacher, 53* (2), 100–107.

Fountas, I. C., & Pinnell, G. S. (1996). *Guided reading: Good first teaching for all children.* Portsmouth, NH: Heinemann.

Fountas, I. C., & Pinnell, G. S. (1999). *Matching books to readers: Using leveled books in guided reading.* Portsmouth, NH: Heinemann.

Fountas, I. C., & Pinnell, G. S. (2001). *Guiding readers and writers: Grades 3–6.* Portsmouth, NH: Heinemann.

Freeman, D. (1999). The California Reading Initiative: A formula for failure for bilingual students? *Language Arts, 76* (3), 241–248.

Frith, U. (1985). Beneath the surface of developmental dyslexia. In K. E. Patterson, K. C. Marshall, & M. Coltheart (Eds.), *Surface dyslexia: Neuropsychological and cognitive studies of phonological reading.* Hillsdale, NJ: Erlbaum.

Gillespie, C. S., Ford, K. L., Gillespie, R. D., & Leavell, A. G. (1996). Portfolio assessment: Some questions, some answers, some recommendations. *Journal of Adolescent and Adult Literacy, 39* (6), 480–491.

Goodman, Y. (1988). *Evaluation of students: Evaluation of teachers.* In K. Goodman,

Goodman, Y., & Hood, W. (Eds.), *The whole language evaluation book.* Portsmouth, NH: Heinemann.

Griffith, P. L., & Olson, M. (1992). Phonemic awareness helps beginning readers break the code. *The Reading Teacher, 45* (7), 516–525.

Hart, B., & Risley, T. R. (1995). *Meaningful differences in the everyday experience of young American children.* Baltimore, MD: Paul H. Brooks.

Harvey, S., & Goudvis, A. (2000). *Strategies that work.* Portland, ME: Stenhouse.

Hashey, J. M., & Connors, D. J. (2003). Learn from our journey: Reciprocal teaching action research. *The Reading Teacher, 57* (3), 224–232.

Heath, S. B. (1983). *Ways with words: Language, life, and work in communities and classrooms.* Cambridge, England: Cambridge University Press.

Holdaway, D. (1979). *The foundations of literacy.* Sydney, Australia: Ashton Scholastic.

Holdaway, D. (1986). Guiding a natural process. In D. R. Tovey & J. E. Kerber (Eds.), *Roles in literacy learning: A new perspective.* Newark, DE: International Reading Association.

Indrisano, R., & Paratore, J. R. (1992). Using literature with readers at risk. In B. E. Cullinan (Ed.), *Invitation to read: More children's literature in the reading program*. Newark, DE: International Reading Association.

Jacobson J. M. (1989). RESPONSE: An interactive study technique. *Reading Horizons, 29*, 86–92.

Johnston, P. (2003). Assessment conversations. *The Reading Teacher, 57* (1), 90–93.

Kennedy, A. (1999). *Home visits as part of an elementary bilingual program*. Unpublished masters paper, Northern Illinois University, De Kalb, IL.

Kuhn, M. R., & Stahl, S. A. (1998). Teaching children to learn word meanings from context: A synthesis and some questions. *Journal of Literacy Research, 30* (1), 19–38.

Langer, J. A. (1990). The process of understanding: Reading for literary and informative purposes. *Research in the Teaching of English, 24*, 229–260.

Lapp, D., & Flood, J. (1983). *Teaching reading to every child* (2nd ed.). New York: Macmillan.

Lartz, M. N. & Mason, J. M. (1988). Jamie: One child's journey from oral to written language. *Early Childhood Research Quarterly, 3*, 193–208.

Meyer, L. A., Gersten, R. M., & Gutkin, J. (1983). Direct instruction: A Project Follow Through success story. *Elementary School Journal, 84* (2), 241–252.

Mills, D. (2002). *Reading with meaning. Teaching comprehension in the primary grades* Portland, ME: Stenhouse.

Monson, D. L. (1992). Realistic fiction and the real world. In B. Cullinan (Ed.), *Invitation to read: More children's literature in the reading program*. Newark, DE: International Reading Association.

Moore, D. W., Readence, J. E., & Rickelman, R. J. (1982). *Prereading activities for content reading and learning*. Newark, DE: International Reading Association.

Morrow, L. M., Tracey, D. H., Woo, D. G., & Pressley, M. (1999). Characteristics of exemplary first-grade literacy instruction. *The Reading Teacher, 52* (5), 462–476.

Moustafa, M., & Maldonado-Colon, E. (1999). Whole-to-parts phonics instruction: Building on what children know to help them know more. *The Reading Teacher, 52* (5), 448–458.

National Institute of Child Health and Human Development. (2000). *The report of the National Reading Panel. Teaching children to read: An evidence-based assessment of the scientific literature on reading and its implications for reading instruction*. Washington, D.C.: U.S. Government Printing Office.

Norton, D. E. (1985). *The effective teaching of language arts* (2nd ed.). Columbus, OH: Merrill.

Ovando, C., & Collier, V. (1998). *Bilingual and ESL classrooms: Teaching in multicultural contexts*. New York: Macmillan.

Palincsar, A. S., & Brown, A. L. (1985). Reciprocal teaching: Activities to promote "reading" in your mind. In T. L. Harris & E. J. Cooper (Eds.), *Reading, thinking, and concept development* (pp. 147–158). New York: College Board Publications.

Palincsar, A. S., & Brown, A. L. (1989). Instruction for self-regulated learning. In L. B. Resnick & L. E. Klopfer (Eds.), *Toward the thinking curriculum: Current cognitive research*. Washington, DC: Association for Supervision and Curriculum Development.

Palincsar, A. S., Ogle, D. S., Jones, B. F., Carr, E. G., & Ransom, K. (1985). *Facilitators' manual for teaching reading as thinking*. Washington, DC: Association for Supervision and Curriculum Development.

Paris, S. G. (1985). Using classroom dialogues and guided practice to teach comprehension strategies. In T. L. Harris & E. J. Cooper (Eds.), *Reading, thinking, and concept development* (pp. 133–146). New York: College Board Publications.

Pils, L. J. (1991). Soon anofe you tout me: Evaluation in a first-grade whole language classroom. *The Reading Teacher, 45* (1), 46–50.

Pressley, M. (2000). What should comprehension instruction be the instruction of? In M. Kamil et al. (Eds.), *Handbook of reading research.* Hillsdale, NJ: Erlbaum.

Purves, A. C. (1990). *The scribal society.* New York: Longman.

Raphael, T. E. (1986). Teaching question-answer relationship, revisited. *The Reading Teacher, 39* (6), 516–523.

Raphael, T. E., & McMahon, S. I. (1994). Book Club: An alternative framework for reading instruction. *The Reading Teacher, 48* (2), 102–117.

Rhodes, L. K., & Nathenson-Mejia, S. (1992). Anecdotal records: A powerful tool for ongoing literacy assessment. *The Reading Teacher, 45* (7), 502–511.

Robinson, H. A. (1983). *Teaching reading, writing, and study strategies: The content areas* (3rd ed.). Boston: Allyn & Bacon.

Rosenblatt, L. (1938). *Literature as exploration.* New York: Noble & Noble.

Rosenblatt, L. (1978). *The reader, the text, the poem: The transactional theory of the literary work.* Carbondale, IL: Southern Illinois University.

Rosenblatt, L. (1991). Literature—S.O.S.! *Language Arts, 68,* 444–448.

Routman, R. (1988). *Transitions: From literature to literacy.* Portsmouth, NH: Heinemann.

Routman, R. (1991). *Invitations: Changing as teachers and learners, K–12.* Portsmouth, NH: Heinemann.

Saul, W. (1992). Introduction. In W. Saul & S. A. Jagusch (Eds.), *Vital connections: Children, science, and adults.* Portsmouth, NH: Heinemann.

Schickedanz, J., & Sullivan, M. (1984). Mom, what does U-F-F spell? *Language Arts, 61* (1), 7–17.

Shannon, P. (1989). *Broken promises.* Granby, MA: Bergin & Gavey.

Slavin, R. E., & Madden, N. A. (1989). What works for students at risk: A research synthesis. *Educational Leadership, 46* (5), 4–13.

Smith, F. (1986). *Insult to intelligence: The bureaucratic invasion of our classrooms.* Portsmouth, NH: Heinemann.

Snow, C. E. (1983). Literacy and language: Relationships during the pre-school years. *Harvard Educational Review, 53* (2), 165–189.

Stahl, S. A. (1992). Saying the "p" word: Nine guidelines for exemplary phonics instruction. *The Reading Teacher, 45* (8), 618–625.

Stahl, S. A., & Fairbanks, M. (1986). The effects of vocabulary instruction: A model-based meta-analysis. *Review of Educational Research, 56,* 72–110.

Stauffer, R. G. (1969). *Directing reading maturity as a cognitive process.* New York: Harper & Row.

Taylor, D. (1983). *Family literacy.* Portsmouth, NH: Heinemann.

Teale, W. H. (1984). Reading to young children: Its significance for literacy development. In H. Goelman, A. Olberg, & F. Smith (Eds.), *Awakening to literacy.* Portsmouth, NH: Heinemann.

Tierney, R. J., Carter, M. A., & Desai, L. E. (1991). *Portfolio assessment in the reading-writing classroom.* Needham, MA: Christopher-Gordon.

Trachtenburg, P. (1990). Using children's literature to enhance phonics instruction. *The Reading Teacher, 43* (9), 648–654.

Valencia, S. W., & Buly, M. R. (2004). Behind test scores: What struggling readers *really* need. *The Reading Teacher, 57* (6), 520–533.

Whitney, J., & Hubbard, R. (1986). *Time and choice: Key elements for process teaching* (videotape). Portsmouth, NH: Heinemann.

Wiseman, D. E., & Robeck, C. P. (1983). The written language behavior of two socio-economic groups of preschool children. *Reading Psychology, 4* (2), 349–363.

Yarington, D. (1978). *The great American reading machine.* Rochelle Park, NJ: Hayden.

Yopp, H. K. (1992). Developing phonemic awareness in young children. *The Reading Teacher, 45* (9), 696–703.

Yopp, H. K. (1995). A test for assessing phonemic awareness in young children. *The Reading Teacher, 49* (1), 20–29.

Children's Literature Books

Arnosky, J. (2000). *All about turtles.* New York: Scholastic.

Bruchac, J., & London, L. (1992). *Thirteen moons on turtle's back: A Native American year of the moons* (T. Locker, Illus.). New York: Philomel.

Corey, S. (2000). *You forgot your skirt, Amelia Bloomer.* (C. McLaren, Illus.). New York: Scholastic.

Cowcher, H. (1990). *Antarctica.* New York: Farrar, Straus, & Giroux.

Cowley, J. (1999). *Red-eyed tree frog.* New York: Scholastic.

Curlee, L. (2002). *Seven wonders of the ancient world.* New York: Atheneum.

Facklin, M. (2001). *Spiders and their web sites* (A. Male, Illus.). New York: Little, Brown.

Fleishman, J. (2002). *Phineas Gage: A gruesome but true story about brain science.* Boston: Houghton Mifflin.

Fleming, C. (2002). *Muncha! Muncha! Muncha!* (G. B. Karas, Illus.). New York: Atheneum.

Fox, M. (1994). *Tough Boris.* San Diego: Harcourt Brace.

Garland, S. (1993). *The lotus seed.* San Diego: Harcourt Brace.

Gerson, M-J. (2001). *Fiesta Femenina: Celebrating women in Mexican folktales* (M. C. Gonzales, Illus.). New York: Barefoot.

Gibbons, G. (2002). *Tell me, tree.* New York: Little, Brown.

Giblin, J. C. (2000). *The amazing life of Benjamin Franklin* (M. Dooling, Illus.). New York: Scholastic.

Henkes, K. (1990). *Julius, baby of the world.* New York: Greenwillow.

Jacob, W. J. (1990). *Ellis Island: New hope in a new land.* New York: Macmillan/Scribner.

Lobel, A. (1970). *Frog and Toad are friends.* New York: Harper & Row.

Medina, J. (1999). *My name is Jorge: On both sides of the river* (F. Vandebrock, Illus.). Honesdale, PA: Boyds Mills.

Mitchell, M. K. (1993). *Uncle Jed's barbershop* (J. Ransome, Illus.). New York: Scholastic.

Murphy, J. (1987). *The last dinosaur.* New York: Scholastic.

Murphy, J. (1990). *The boys' war: Confederate and Union soldiers talk about the Civil War.* Boston: Houghton Mifflin.

Murphy, J. (2002). *An American plague: The true and terrifying story of the Yellow Fever Epidemic of 1793.* New York: Clarion.

Pringle, L. (1997). *An extraordinary life: The story of a monarch butterfly* (B. Mastall, Illus.). New York: Orchard.

Rappaport, D. (2001). *Martin's big words: The life of Dr. Martin Luther King, Jr.* (B. Collier, Illus.). New York: Hyperion.

San Souci, R. D. (2000). *The little gold star: A Spanish American Cinderella tale* (S. Martinez, Illus.). New York: Harper/Collins.

Thong, R. (2000). *Round is a mooncake.* San Francisco: Chronicle Books.

Thong, R. (2002). *Red is a dragon.* San Francisco: Chronicle Books.

Extending the
Language Arts Curriculum

From the standpoint of the child, the great waste in school comes from his inability to utilize the experience he gets outside of school in any complete and free way.

—John Dewey
School and Society

PEERING INTO THE CLASSROOM
AFTER THE KIDS GO HOME

Karen Adams sits at the keyboard e-mailing her students over the winter break. Some students will get the e-mails at home; others won't have the opportunity to read them until they return to school. For those students, Karen has also jotted a note on a postcard and dropped it in the mailbox. A terrific communicator, Karen says she teaches with a capital "T." "I'm an avid reader and I love to talk. So naturally I've incorporated lots of reading and talking into my classroom and outside my classroom. My sixth graders have to learn interview skills, conduct interviews of local individuals, and write reports to share. I've learned that the more involved I become with my students, the more they learn. For instance, I call every child's parent or caregiver at least once a month. I first started this with my students who were struggling or who had gotten into trouble. Then I realized all parents deserve to know how their children are doing. And kids need to know they deserve a pat on the back. My colleagues refer to me as the "bouquet and thorns" teacher. I toss bouquets to students who demonstrate improvement or have shown effort was put forth but I also deliver thorny messages whenever a student goofs off. I call parents from my cell phone in the classroom and have the child tell them he got an A on a project or a test. The kids love it and so do their parents. And somehow I've been able to do it for all of my students. They burst with pride as I dial the number.

"Part of the curriculum has to revolve around what I call 'real world.' Sixth graders know a lot about what is taking place. Some of my students are pretty savvy and streetwise. I make an attempt to draw in volunteers who share their experiences and stories so my students can see that what we do in the classroom pays off in the end. I even bring in high school dropouts who returned to school to get their GEDs and then went on to college. I point out that Wendy's founder Dave Thomas was a high school dropout who later returned to school to get his GED degree. And big-name sports heroes like Ahmad Green and Shaquille O'Neal returned to college to get their degrees. That can shake a few of the kids up and get them on task."

Chapter Objectives

The reader will:

✓ learn the importance of home-school links and how to enhance those connections.

✓ learn how to recruit and use classroom volunteers.

✓ discover how to expand classroom experiences.

✓ explore ways to incorporate technology into language arts instruction.

Standards for Professionals

The following Standards will be addressed in this chapter:

Standard 2: Instructional Strategies and Curriculum Materials

2.2 Use a wide range of instructional practices, approaches, and methods, including technology-based practices, for learners at differing stages of development and from differing cultural and linguistic backgrounds.

2.3 Use a wide range of curriculum materials in effective reading instruction for learners at different stages of reading and writing development and from differing cultural and linguistic backgrounds.

Standard 3: Assessment, Diagnosis, and Evaluation

3.4 Effectively communicate results of assessments to specific individuals (students, parents, caregivers, colleagues, administrators, policy makers, policy officials, community, etc.).

Standard 4: Creating a Literate Environment

4.1 Use students' interests, reading abilities, and backgrounds as foundations for the reading and writing program.

Standard 5: Professional Development

5.1 Display positive dispositions related to reading and the teaching of reading.

5.2 Continue to pursue the development of professional knowledge and dispositions.

5.3 Work with colleagues to observe, evaluate, and provide feedback on each other's practice.

5.4 Participate in, initiate, implement, and evaluate professional development programs.

Introduction

Elementary school is an extension of the local community. Just as the supermarket, park, and library should be familiar territories, children need to feel comfortable in the classroom if they are to enjoy the learning experience. This is not possible if the school fails to include the community as a whole, thereby suggesting that learning occurs only in the school setting and is not applicable outside it. Learning is a social phenomenon that takes place everywhere, whether it be in a classroom, an airport, a supermarket, or the neighborhood Taco Bell. In promoting such learning, the support the teacher and local school provide plays a vital role.

Because learning is a social phenomenon, children learn from those around them: parents, siblings, peers, teachers, and other adults. As Smith (1989) notes, children in the company of music lovers learn about music; those who join gangs learn the nuances of gang activities and rules. The classroom teacher must incorporate into the school community the community at large, and even the world. This chapter discusses ways to connect the school community with the larger community and beyond. Parental involvement, senior citizen participation as classroom volunteers, and school-school and school-business partnerships are examined in terms of language arts instruction.

Family Literacy

When one becomes a parent, one becomes a teacher. "Family is the root of a child's early literacy experiences" (Darling & Lee, 2003, p. 382). Research has found that parent-child literacy activities in the home, such as helping children recognize letters of the alphabet, helping children learn beginning sounds of objects, reading with children, or helping children with reading and writing assignments, not only improves their literacy and language skills but amplifies their interest in books (Primavera, 2000). Involving parents in the teaching of language arts through family literacy programs has long been promoted by educators as parents and caregivers must be our partners in instructing children. The acquisition of literacy begins in the home; therefore, it is logical to promote activities in which parents can contribute to their child's literacy development. Indeed, a strict, linear approach to the teaching of literacy can reduce children's opportunities for literacy learning in their own homes in that their parents are alienated and thus made to feel inadequate about their own literacy knowledge and abilities (Heath, 1980).

Feelings of inadequacy can extend to children as they examine their own abilities. Consider, for example, homogeneous ability grouping for reading instruction. Research indicates that such grouping results in the overrepresentation of students from working-class, poor, and minority families in the lower-ability reading group, and the overrepresentation of students from middle- and upper-class families in the higher-ability group (Cummins, 1986; Routman, 1991; 2000). Instruction differs between the high and low groups, with more time devoted to silent reading in the higher groups. Moreover, the teacher asks more higher-level questions and interrupts students less to correct oral reading errors in the higher groups. Thus, children in the lower groups are not provided with the same opportunities for learning to read. Indeed, increased interruptions have been found to inhibit the development of students' self-correction strategies (McNaughton, 1981), as well as to impair their ability to answer questions (Wilson, 1988). Obviously, teachers need to reexamine the logic of this instructional practice if the goal is to help students become literate.

Students provide the strongest link between the school and the home. They must be respected, and they must clearly recognize that they are respected. Otherwise, they and their parents will have little regard for learning, and that feeling will eventually permeate the community. Studies of parental involvement in schools suggest that without such involvement, overall student achievement will not improve (Henderson, 1988; Taylor et al., 2002). Typically, parents are most willing to assist their children during the primary grades, but parental involvement at the intermediate and junior and senior high levels has also been shown to increase student achievement.

Teachers need to try to involve all parents in the schools. Henderson (1988) found in her review of the research that it is minority children from low-income families who benefit most when their parents are involved in the schools. Henderson also discovered that parents do not have to be well educated for student achievement to improve. Teachers may find that such parents possess feelings of inadequacy. For instance, a parent who was a high school dropout may associate school with failure but still want his child to graduate.

Some parents may find it difficult to get to the school—babysitters cost money, bosses don't always allow time off during working hours, transportation is not always readily available, and so on. Furthermore, gone are the days when mothers stayed at home with their children and families consisted of two parents living under the same roof. Nevertheless, the classroom teacher must reach out to parents so that students are given ample opportunities to become literate. It is up to the individual teacher to find creative ways of involving parents in the learning process. The need to reach the caretaker-parent is critical and more difficult today than at any other time in the history of American education. Following are some suggestions for assisting and encouraging parents to take a greater role in their children's literacy acquisition.

Sherrell Shanahan (2004) is a reading specialist who, along with her teaching colleagues at El Sierra School in Downers Grove, Illinois, has built strong parent-school ties over the past decade. Some of the ideas that El Sierra School has used include a parent (or caregiver)/child learning night. Parents of kindergartners gather with their children in a learning center where they participate together in activities, such as putting the alphabet in order using letter cards glued to clothespins and a clothespin line; an ABC bean bag toss using two mats with the 26 letters of the alphabet and a basket of hand size bean bags; a beginning-sound object sort; and forming a letter on top of a magnetic plastic letter using Wikki Stix letters. First- and second-grade parents attend a workshop with their children while third through fifth graders attend a workshop tailored for working at home with older students.

The school involves parents in their children's reading incentive program. Each year the school strives to have the students read at least ten minutes a day. Students take home a simple chart with the child's name, teacher's name, and class listed at the top. The parent records ten minutes of reading the child has done by writing the title of the book, the page numbers, the date, and the parent's initials on the sheet. The students return their sheets to the classroom teacher, and the sheets are tallied by parent volunteers.

Some of the themes established for the reading incentive program have been: "Read the Oceans" (a *Finding Nemo* theme in which students learn about each of the oceans in their classes throughout the school year), "Take the Lead! Read for the Gold!" based on the 2004 Summer Olympics, and "Million Minutes of Reading," in which the school totaled the number of minutes students, teachers, and staff read. Milestones are established each month but are not cumulative so that students who may not have read as much in one month may have a greater sense of accomplishment in another month. Creative accountability measures help keep the students interested (i.e., a passport is made for each student for "Read the Oceans" and stored in a pocket chart). Simple awards such as certificates made on the computer or inexpensive prizes can be handed out. Local businesses may donate prizes such as theater tickets, free french fries, and so forth. Paperback books are great prizes as well. When the final goal is met, an afternoon celebration takes place. A parade is organized with each grade level having a banner decorated by students from that grade and indicating how many total minutes the students read, such as "Third Grade 70,000 minutes."

Parents and caregivers can be supportive of students by having their child engage in the ten-minute read. Shanahan and Johnson (2004) suggest some guidelines for the ten-minute read:

1. Preview the book by looking at and talking about the title, chapter titles, and illustrations. Make predictions with your child as to what the book is about.

2. Sit in a comfortable place where you can both comfortably see the book easily.

3. Have the child read orally for 10 minutes.

4. If the child hesitates on a word, after 5 seconds tell her the word.

5. If the child misreads a word that interrupts the meaning of the sentence, wait until the child gets to the end of the sentence and say, "That doesn't make sense. Try it again."

6. If the meaning is NOT changed by a misread word, do not interrupt the child.

7. At the end of the 10 minutes, record the progress on the chart and discuss what was read.

8. The next day start at the beginning of the chapter again and repeat steps 4–7.

Because parents do not always have the financial resources to subscribe to a variety of magazines, a classroom teacher may recycle current issues of magazines by sending them home with a student for a specified period of time, such as two nights, so students can take turns taking the recent magazine issues home. Older issues can be sent home separately. A helpful "magazine

Students should be encouraged to learn from all family members. This student, for her report on Women's History Month, interviewed her grandmother about the hardships she encountered during World War II, including rationing, clothing shortages, and war bond drives.

pack" might include special-interest magazines geared to various family members—for example, magazines with recipes, consumer reports, auto repair tips for parents and older siblings, and those with games and activities for children—as well as a newsmagazine. Fridays are good days to send home such magazine packs because most families have more time to spend reading together on weekends.

Another possibility is to arrange for class subscriptions to a local or nearby large-city newspaper. To increase subscriptions, many newspapers offer low- or no-rate subscriptions for students for a short period of time. Through a class's subscription to such newspapers, students can use the newspapers both at school and at home. In addition, the students' families can read the newspapers. Parents can encourage their children to read the grocery ads and cut out coupons, a practical, real-life literacy activity that also saves the family money.

A family projects curriculum was designed by Andrea L. Burkhart (1995) for her class. This enabled her students to work with their parents on a variety of different activities, such as tracing family roots and sharing an object that represented the family, such as food, music, dance, literature, or clothing. December was designated "biography month," when the students interviewed a family member and wrote a biography about that person. Other monthly features included weather, plants, measurement, poetry, and simple machines.

Providing materials for parents and caregivers to use in the home is yet another means of aiding the students. Mary Kay Merema makes little books for the students to read over the summer and sends them home with her students. A second-grade teacher in a neighborhood school, Julie Kranz, invites all of her students assigned to her classroom for the fall to join her once a week at the public library branch located two blocks from the school. She sends the parents a letter at the end of school inviting them to a briefing at the library where they can get a library card for their child. Julie and the librarian hold storytelling and read aloud sessions plus a sleep over at the library during the summer months. By fall her students can't wait to get to school.

The government can be a great source of not only information but also materials for parents and caregivers. The U.S. Department of Education has published a series entitled *Helping Your Child Become a Reader*. The information is available in English and Spanish, and is appropriate for ages infancy through six years. Kindergarten and first-grade teachers can go to the Web site and get free copies of this booklet, which offers practical suggestions about how to help children learn to read, for each child's parents by logging on to *www.ed.gov/parents/academic/help/reader/reader.pdf*.

Teachers should keep parents informed of what is occurring in the classroom and what their children are currently studying. Mrs. Markgraft did this by having her students take turns working in pairs as classroom reporters and newspaper editors. The students wrote brief paragraphs to describe each day's activities, Monday through Friday, and edited and revised their "articles" for the "final edition." On the following Monday, copies were sent home for the parents to read (see figure 13.1 on pp. 556–557).

Figure 13.1   Weekly class newspaper. Each day, two students are assigned to write, edit, and produce completed articles for the newspaper.

Wednesday

We had early dismissal today. We started a Latin america Study. We got science test notes on Heat energy. In gym we are going to play with tennis balls, yarn balls, and punching balloons.

By Rob Cucchi
Bill Lypkoff

Thursday

Today we had an assembly with African dancers, and drummers. We all participated in learning african dances. Our seats got changed, too. The Bio-poems are in the Hall of fame.

BY: Yolanda Karas

Friday

Today is St Patrick's Day. Our mystery ads for book reports are due today. Our Journals are going to collected and graded today. We have our unit 25 Test today. Also miss Bernhard, our student teacher, is going to start teaching us the science lessons.

by, Barbara Pizzi
&
Joey Gerari

Figure 13.1   *(continued)*

Parents should also be included in as many on-site, school-related activities as possible. Research indicates participants in family literacy programs have significant reading and writing gains (Philliber et al., 1996). For example, Mrs. Kilgard, a first-grade teacher in Texas, has several students whose parents are migrant workers. During the time that there is no field work because of the climate, she arranges activities for her students that include their parents. Early in February, for instance, her students write and mail invitations to their parents, inviting them to an afternoon tea. Mrs. Kilgard's students politely greet their parents at the classroom door, serve tea and cookies, and read the books they have written. Each child wears a large yellow button that says, in both English and Spanish, "Ask me for my autograph; I'm an author." The next day, the students again write short notes to their parents, this time thanking them for attending the tea.

Activities such as those just described promote parental involvement in literacy in a special, yet nonthreatening way. In general, parents are proud of their children and want to do more to help them but often do not know how or do not believe they have the time or the means to do so.

Classroom Volunteers

Opening the classroom to volunteers from the community is important, but such assistance is becoming more difficult to obtain. Because of the increasing number of working mothers and single-parent families, parent volunteers are becoming fewer in number. Senior citizens, however, make up a steadily increasing population of potential volunteers. The involvement of senior citizens in the classroom can serve a dual purpose by providing assistance for students and fulfilling the need of senior citizens to keep active and involved.

Many senior citizens are very active in volunteer work in the community and with their social and travel activities. Some enjoy physical activities, such as hiking, golf, and tennis. Many are active and involved in local community activities such as singing in church choirs, bowling in leagues, working as hospital volunteers, and the like. After retiring from one career, many individuals begin a new career because increased leisure time has allowed them to develop new interests and hobbies. Such individuals are excellent candidates for inclusion in school activities. Involving senior citizens in the classroom usually results in an enriched curriculum because they are able to share lifetime experiences as well as their skills. Storytelling, for instance, is a natural way in which senior citizens can describe local historical events that have occurred over the years. They can share old photographs of area landmarks and old newspaper clippings that the students can analyze and compare in terms of community growth or decline. Many senior citizens are involved in "Generation to Generation," in which they correspond with students via the Internet or through America Online. The students and seniors write stories together as well as share historical and other information.

One fourth-grade class invited senior citizens from a nearby retirement center to participate in an activity each month of the school year. The monthly activities included the following:

September: Watermelon festival to celebrate the opening of school. Students were paired with senior citizens, and each pair made a time capsule from an empty paper towel roll to open at the end of the school year.

October: A harvest festival for which some of the senior citizens taught the class how to square dance. Activities included a taffy pull, bobbing for apples, a three-legged race (student and senior citizen pairs), and other games from the 1800s.

November: The class prepared a Thanksgiving Day feast for the senior citizens.

December: The class performed their version of Dickens's *A Christmas Carol* and gave the retirement center a framed print purchased with funds from a bake sale.

January and February: Pen pal months. Because most of the senior citizens were vacationing in a warmer climate, the students and senior citizens exchanged letters.

March: Kite building and flying contest.

April: Favorite book character day. Each person dressed up as his or her favorite character from a children's book.

May: Spring planting of flowerbeds and a flowering crab tree purchased by the class for the school. Students volunteered to give up recess for a day to clean up trash and litter on the school playground before the spring planting day.

June: The senior citizens hosted a picnic for the students at the retirement center. Students were allowed to fish in the center's pond and play games in the morning. The afternoon was devoted to skits and storytelling by both students and senior citizens.

There are other ways to involve senior citizens. Because there are many senior citizen travel groups, teachers may contact the local senior citizens club or a travel agency and arrange to have the senior citizens serve as pen pals during one of their upcoming trips. Even if a trip is no more than a one–day shopping trip to a nearby big city, receiving a picture postcard of the city's skyline or famous landmark with a brief note written on the back can mean a great deal to a child who has never been to that city. On longer trips, the tourists may keep a travel log, writing down events as they occur to send to their student pen pals on a regular basis.

Inviting guest speakers is still another way to link the classroom with the community. Because today's children are predicted to change jobs at least eight times during their lives, it is important that they discover what careers are currently available. Having people from a wide variety of career areas share some of their work experiences adds to a child's knowledge base. Rather than setting aside one day as "Career Day" and bringing in 20 people to speak, it is far more effective to invite one person at a time to speak to the class. This frees the speaker from having to compete for the audience's attention and allows the students to study one career at a time and to formulate questions for the speaker before the presentation.

Asking people who live near the school to speak to the class is relevant to students because those individuals are a part of the community, and children see many of them in the neighborhood, in local stores, and at church. Involving such people promotes a sense of belonging for children and thereby strengthens the community. When inviting local people into the classroom, the teacher should spend some time helping them to decide on an appropriate speaking topic. For example, if the teacher can suggest one of the skills that an individual uses daily in her work and that the students will be able to understand and appreciate, both the students and the guest speaker will benefit (see box 13.1). Skills that local merchants might possess include the following:

Banker:	determining a client's credit standing; explaining the different types of accounts
Beautician:	determining appropriate hairstyles; pleasing hard-to-please customers
Gas Station Owner:	handling flammable materials; locating engine problems; giving directions to strangers
Grocery Store Manager:	displaying merchandise; estimating costs; handling perishables
Hardware Store Manager:	understanding customers' problems in order to sell them the right parts; predicting seasonal sales

---

13.1   In the Classroom: Mini Lesson

Bringing Community History into the Classroom

Barbara Cooney's (1988) *Island Boy* tells the story of Matthias, who was born on Tibbetts Island off the coast of Maine. As a boy, Matthias became a cabin boy on his uncle's schooner, the Six Brothers, and years later he became the captain of the ship. However, he couldn't forget the island, and he returned there to live and raise a family. As Matthias grew older, he shared the stories of the island with his grandson, who also loved Tibbetts Island. The book ends with Matthias's drowning in rough seas. The theme of the book is repeated throughout: "It is good to see the world beyond the bay, then you will know where your heart lies."

After reading the book to the class, have a member of the local historical society visit the class to tell about two of the community's early founders. Students can then write a "fictionalized" biography about one of the two and his or her life in the area.

Cooney, B. (1988). *Island boy*. New York: Viking.

A local naturalist with the U.S. Department of the Interior was a guest of Mr. Bauman's fourth-grade class. The class had been studying the flora and fauna of the area, and the naturalist explained the effects of the Ice Age and glacial movement in geological terms, showing slides to demonstrate his points. A few days after the naturalist's presentation, one student made a flora and fauna web for the book *Sarah, Plain and Tall* by Patricia MacLachlan (1985) (see figure 13.2).

Another way to include community members with upper-elementary and middle school students is via a unit on history. By combining state, national, or international history with the local community's role, children get a better perspective of their own roots. In so doing, it is critical to have students interview community members and research historical information at the library.

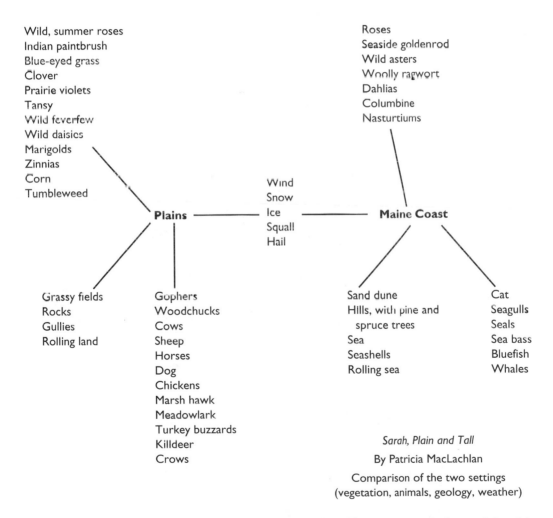

Figure 13.2   A web comparing the flora and fauna of the Maine coast with those of the plains

To facilitate the learning of history is to read aloud historical fiction books at the beginning of the unit and have a class discussion on how the authors of such books convey facts through the plot and actions of characters. Such authors of historical fiction as Ann Turner can bring her readers into the past to see life through the eyes of people who lived then, and she can bring characters from the past into the present so her readers can examine them as real people who are shaped by their time and temporal environment. This gives readers the ability to compare their own lives with the realistic characters from the past (Fraser & White, 2000, p. 355). Read alouds and library research also help students to formulate questions to ask community members about the period of time being studied. After the interviews have taken place, the students can write their reports as part of Writer's Workshop.

The Classroom and Beyond

Demonstrating genuine and sincere caring for and interest in students must be an essential element of every teacher. This involves going beyond the minimum requirements of the school district. It requires spending personal resources—a weekend doing curriculum work, every other Wednesday after school working on lesson plans with teachers from the same grade level, buying children's books for the classroom library, purchasing gutters from the home improvement store and screwing them into the wall under the white board to display books for students to read, and more. Concerned teachers pay their own way to attend a professional development conference, develop their own professional library, share information with colleagues, and enroll in graduate coursework that is rigorous and demanding of themselves as learners in order that they better understand and meet the instructional needs of all students. Genuine caring for all learners, especially minority students, should be "accompanied by instructional practices that support successful literacy learning. These practices include nurturing lively discussions, immersing children in drama, supporting lifetime literacy efforts, building resilience in literacy learners, and supporting better connections between schools and families" (Sanacore, 2004, p. 750).

In surveying research findings of factors distinguishing effective and successful schools, Lipson, Mosenthal, Mekkelsen, and Russ (2004) found the following to make a significant difference between a successful and an unsuccessful school in terms of literacy achievement:

- Strong and determined leadership by the building principal
- Schoolwide efforts to improve instruction and student achievement, not just a few teachers involved
- Orderly classrooms with effective classroom management techniques incorporated by the teachers
- Effective and efficient use of instructional time
- High expectations for student performance; a commitment to excellence

- Collaborative effort among teachers (classroom, reading specialists, and special education), principal, and district curriculum leaders; a sense of professional community
- Effective home communication
- Extensive and effective professional development
- Specific instructional practices to meet student needs

In short, exemplary practices in schools make a difference in the literacy performance of students.

Orderly classrooms with set classroom management procedures are critical to keep students on task and prevent the frittering away of precious minutes for discipline or transition between learning activities. Having three or four simple classroom rules (e.g., respect each other's property, be respectful of everyone, turn things in on time) helps to maintain order and not make every incident a major issue. Thomas Dutton (2004), an older, returning preservice teacher, noted the importance of having good instructional techniques during his teaching observations. Dutton wrote "of the classes I have observed, those where worksheets were a substitute for instruction had the most behavior management problems" (p. 36).

Transitioning from one activity to the next is more efficient if at the end of the first activity, the students are told exactly what they will need for the next activity, such as their literature circle book, notebook, pencil, and ruler. Then the students put away the materials currently out on their desks or tables and pull out the literature circle materials. Having one person at each set of desks or tables retrieve basal readers or content area textbooks and put them in bins next to the cluster of desks can be an efficient means of using time and space in a classroom. Groups can be identified by the color of the bins (i.e., purple, blue, green, red, or yellow).

Diane Bradley gives every one of her third graders a task to do each week—pencil sharpener, assignment keeper for those who are absent, paper tray filler (for computers), computer engineer (to help students with computer problems), mail sorter, mail delivery person, fish feeder, hamster feeder, weather monitor, office runner, paper passer outer, and so on. While these tasks are assigned on a weekly basis, Diane selects a student to serve as "teaching assistant" for each school day. The teaching assistant does odd tasks such as taking any new students around the school so they won't become lost, finding the janitor if the aquarium has leaked, and so forth. The child who is assigned to be the teaching assistant also sits next to Diane during guided reading so that Diane can listen to and assess the student's reading progress.

Experienced teachers agree that the first week of school sets the tone for the year. Having a classroom door decorated with a lively poem that is illustrated, displaying colorful posters around the classroom, posting students' names on their desks, along with the first learning task of the day, putting colorful real flowers on your desk, placing candy in an oversized jar, and playing classical music softly in the background as you greet your new charges at the door will start the school year off in a positive mode. Being highly organized and overplanning for lessons helps prevent anxiety on your part. From day one, let students know the learning bar is set high and then encourage them to reach it. Also let them know learning is fun. Choose a read aloud with a humorous picture or trade book. Have humorous incidents captured by news photographers for newspapers or magazines made into transparencies for a shared writing experience (e.g., a photo of a car or horse in a swimming pool, a dog or cat in an unusual position, a young child playing with a sprinkler). Don't forget the critical "Morning Message," as a warm, enticing message can hook students into this critical aspect of literacy learning. Sharing a joke or riddle with younger students or a question that requires a bit of research by older students can pique their interest.

Dividing students into small groups for instruction provides greater opportunity for the teacher to know each child as a learner, to scaffold appropriate learning experiences for each student, and provide engaging activities that motivate each learner. In order to have time to work with small groups, the teacher needs to create learning centers for independent work by the remaining students while the teacher does guided reading or writing conferences with small groups. Ford and Opitz (2002) suggest five guidelines for successful learning centers:

1. Each learning center must be grounded in the teacher's knowledge about the students as readers, writers, and learners. To what degree can they work independently? Surprisingly even kindergartners can work independently for short periods of time once they understand the parameters. Some teachers announce when they are going to work with a small group that they aren't to be interrupted unless "someone is bloodied." In other words, students are to follow classroom procedures regarding sharpening pencils, going to the rest room, and so on but not interrupt the teacher unless it is an absolute emergency.

   Each learning center needs to be demonstrated to the class via a mini lesson. The learning center's mini lesson should have

   • a focus or purpose for the lesson;

   • an explanation for the purpose;

   • guided practice by the students (i.e., role playing);

   • direct application so that the information can be used while at the learning center.

2. The activities must be tasks students can engage in and complete on their own while advancing their knowledge about literacy. The superior learning center creates excitement about literacy, not just cutting, pasting, and drawing after doing a bit of reading and writing.

3. The task must be developed under the guise of school district and state standards. The teacher may even want to code the list of district standards with the learning centers that meet each benchmark.

4. The learning center must engage the learner in an activity that they can be successful doing and that if the student completes the task, the out-

come or product will be valued and recognized by the teacher. Like the successful piano teacher who knows that along with learning scales, if students learn a simple song melody each lesson, they will be eager to return the following week, the classroom teacher must create a learning morsel that is challenging but ever so appealing to the student.

5. There must be a consistent infrastructure of instruction away from the teacher so that students won't need to continually ask questions. Ford and Opitz (2002) suggest that the learning center activities

- must facilitate independent use by children;

- operate with minimal transition time and management concerns;

- have equal value for all students and be of equal value: all students need to participate in all of the activities even if they find one more pleasurable than another;

- have a simple accountability system (for example, for younger learners the teacher makes an index card divided into 11 boxes. One box contains the student's name and date. Each of the remaining ten boxes has the task listed along with a crude illustration depicting the purpose of that particular learning center [e.g., an ear for the listening center, a pen for the writing center, a notebook for pocket charts, an eyeball for read the room, two stick figures for buddy reading, one stick figure for independent reading, the ABCs for ABC games, a large question mark for choice of activity, a book for poetry-book sharing with buddy, and pencil and paper for letter writing to a book character]. Older students' charts would contain boxes for reader's theatre, scavenger hunts for words, solving mystery questions from science or social studies, and so on. Index charts can be stored in a pocket chart with a pocket for each student. A rubber stamp or hole punch can be stored at each center to designate completion of the task);

- be practical in terms of the time and energy required for teacher preparation;

- fit in naturally with class routines.

Literacy centers can entail a variety of activities and resources, including listening, reader's theatre, reading the room, writing the room, pocket charts with sentences to sequence events in a story or lines of a poem, story packs, poetry packs, big books, responding to literature through art with precut art projects and materials, writing, and reading activities. An example of a listening center activity may be an informational picture book that the teacher has recorded over the summer break and developed three or four accompanying activities that the students engage in upon completion of listening and following along with the book. If the teacher has incorporated appropriate background music and given an introduction that heightens student curiosity, student motivation is increased. For example, a first-grade teacher might play the "Flight of the Bumble Bee" to open the tape for *The Bee-Man of Orn* (Stockton, 2004), then have students illustrate a beehive and a bee, writing three or four sentences about how to take care of bees, and then have the children taste honey on a small piece of bread and describe its taste along with the texture and structure of honeycomb.

Another example for third- or fourth-grade teachers would be to play softly "Those Magnificent Men in their Flying Machines" as an introduction to the tape of *Touching the Sky: The Flying Adventures of Wilbur and Orville Wright* (Bordon & Marx, 2003). Upon listening to the tape as they followed along with the text, the students could do a map activity relating Kitty Hawk, North Carolina, to Dayton, Ohio; write a biopoem for either Wilbur or Orville Wright; and construct a paper airplane to be used in a paper airplane contest in the gym after all the students have completed the learning center. The song "Freight Train," "Wabash Cannonball," "Orange Blossom Special," or "I've Been Working on the Railroad" would be a good opener for *I Dream of Trains* (Johnson, 2003) for fifth graders. Activities might include math activities involving story problems, reading a train schedule, and doing choral reading with a partner from a selection of poems about trains.

The writing center needs to captivate the learner as a writer. This requires ample stimulation to create ideas. Second and third graders may find reading a portion of *The Diary of a Worm* (Cronin, 2003) to turn on their creative juices. Consider when worms do the "Hokey Pokey" they "put their heads in, they put their heads out, they put their heads in and shake them all about, they do the hokey pokey and they turn themselves around"—and that's the end of the song since they don't possess any other body parts to put in and shake about. Such a learning center should accompany a science unit on the study of mealworms.

Often overlooked are opportunities for students to be e-mail buddies with students at the same grade level in a school in the same school district. If both schools feed into the same middle school or high school, this can be particularly beneficial. Diana Williamson, a fourth-grade teacher, has the students e-mail her and she passes along the e-mails. She requires her students to write out their e-mail responses in a rough draft before saving them as a Word document for her to send to the other teacher to distribute. At the middle school level, students will want to e-mail or instant message each other directly, something some teachers may not want their students to do.

Arranging to have teleconferences with classes in other states two or three times a year can foster cooperative learning. Common interests can be pursued by sending letters, poetry, reports, riddles, jokes, and stories back and forth via e-mail and traditional mail. Students in schools along the Mississippi River e-mailed students attending a school in Oregon along the Lewis and Clark trail to share information they had garnered in their study of this major scientific and historical event. Both groups read *This Vast Land: A Young Man's Journal of the Lewis and Clark Expedition* (Ambrose, 2003), based on the notes of one of the members of the expedition. Students can become dialogue journal partners, despite being in classrooms that are 500 miles apart. Students from a northern state can read the same historical novel about the Civil War as students in a southern state. Such activities expand students' worlds by widening the scope of their interests and their goals. Two teachers met in a graduate class and teamed up sections of their middle school language arts classes as they read a trilogy of mysteries during a grading period by Margaret Peterson Haddix, *Among the Hidden* (1999), *Among the Imposters* (2000), and *Among the Betrayed* (2002). Such reaching out to other teachers and students in other locations makes students realize that their own interests are shared by people in other parts of the country and world.

The Language Arts and the Internet

The Internet can be a vast sea of information or a vast waste of time. If you plan to demonstrate how to locate Web sites, make certain that you get to school early and log on to the Web site prior to your demonstration. Demonstrating how to locate Web sites early in the day increases the likelihood of reaching the Web site, as more people access sites later in the day, often shutting out instructional opportunities.

The Internet can be used in a wide variety of ways. Web quests are tasks that have been tailored for students to complete individually, in pairs, or in small groups. Students go to several different links to gain information and perform tasks as part of a unit of study. Web quests have been popularized in science and social studies. Their drawback is the amount of time required to successfully accomplish the tasks. Generally Web quests are used with students in grades four and up since some keyboarding proficiency is needed to reduce the time of the tasks.

Search Engines

You've probably used search engines to locate information on the Internet. Depending on the search tool used, the search results will vary greatly in relevancy, quantity, and quality of information. Thus it is important that students learn how to refine their searches to limit the amount of information and increase its quality (Jackson, Smolin & Lawless, 2004). Younger students should use search directories that are based on age appropriateness. Such search directories include Yahooligans *(http://yahooligans.com)* and KidsClick *(http://kidsclick.org)*. Some search engines filter the sites for children so that inappropriate material won't suddenly appear on the screen. These include Ask Jeeves for Kids *(www.ajkids.com)* and Onekey *(www.onekey.com)*. Middle schoolers usually possess far more sophisticated computer and Internet skills and can rely on Ask Jeeves *(www.askjeeves.com)* or Google *(www.google.com)*. The Ask Jeeves Web site has a sponsored link called Fastpapers.com, which sells research papers, reports, and the like for a fee. Hence, teachers may find students purchasing papers rather than producing them.

Web Sites

Literally a plethora of Web sites exists for language arts. Below are a few of the sites along with the suggested grade levels and focus.

Aesop's Fables Online Collection: *www.pacificnet.net/~johnr/aesop*
Over 650 of Aesop's fables and 125 of Hans Christian Anderson's fairy tales are narrated by a young child. Some images accompany the fables and fairy tales. This makes a great listening center activity. (Gr. 2–8)

Reading Zone: *www.ipl.org/div/kispace/browse/rzn0000*
This is the Internet Public Library Youth Division Web site, which contains picture books, short stories, and poetry. (Gr. 4–8)

Story Place: *www.storyplace.org*
This Web site is designed as an educational activity center for children as it comprises stories that have both sound and animation along with fun activities for children. (Gr. K–3)

Children's authors jumped on the Internet with Web pages and Web sites. Here is a sampling of a variety of different authors.

Jan Brett: *www.janbrett.com*
Probably one of the most engaging author Web sites, teachers and students will find books written by the author and can jot a quick e-mail off to the author. (Gr. K–3)

Beverly Cleary: *www.beverlycleary.com*
This site is maintained by a publisher, not the author so it may not endear as many readers. However, it does provide Beezus, Henry, and Ramona fans with information about these characters. (Gr. 2–5)

Sharon Creech: *www.sharoncreech.com/index.html*
Creech has written picture books and young adult novels, including the Newbery Award winner, *Walk Two Moons* (1994). This site has suggestions for teachers who use her books as well as audio files of some book excerpts. (Gr. 1–8)

Roald Dahl: *www.roalddahl.com*
The unusual and quirky nature of one of the most beloved children's authors, Roald Dahl, is shared on this Web site. Dahl, once the husband of actress Patricia Neal, passed away a few years ago and this site is maintained by his daughter. An audio of an interview with Dahl in which he discusses some of his ideas for books (i.e. *James and the Giant Peach*, 1961) can be accessed at this site. (Gr. 3–8)

Tomie dePaola: *www.tomie.com/main.html*
This Web site provides a closer look at who this engaging author is. Among the many features are Tomie dePaola's insights about the creative process of writing and illustrating a book. (Gr. K–3)

Lois Lowry: *www.loislowry.com*
Lowry's Web site gives snippets of her books for students while teachers may be enlightened by reading some of her speeches. She shares her own personal tragedy of how her son died in an accident. (Gr. 6–8)

Megan McDonald: *www.meganmcdonald.net*
The delightful author of the Judy Moody series along with numerous picture books, Megan McDonald responds to e-mails from teachers and students. Best to generate a class e-mail and send it along. (Gr. 1–3)

Linda Sue Park: *www.lindasuepark.com*
This Web site details the author's works including her Newbery Award winning book, *A Single Shard* (2001), which has a visual representation of the twelfth-century celadon pottery upon which the book's plot is based. (Gr. 6–8)

Katherine Paterson: *www.terabithia.com*
The warmth of Katherine Paterson's personality exudes from this Web site. Students and teachers alike will come away with a an appreciation for this writer's numerous wonderful works. (Gr. 4–8)

Gary Paulsen: *www.randomhouse.com/features/garypaulsen*
This site describes adventures Gary has engaged in from running the Iditarod to white-water rafting. Students can e-mail questions about his novels. (Gr. 5–7)

Patricia Polacco: *www.patriciapolacco.com*
The author/illustrator of over 30 heart-warming picture books, Polacco has a fantastic Web site for both teachers and students. (Gr. 1–6)

J. K. Rowling: *www.scholastic.com/HarryPotter*
One of several Harry Potter Web sites, this one is sponsored by Scholastic. (Gr. 4–8)

Often teachers use expository books and topic Web sites to enrich the reading or content area experience. Certainly teachers should keep the following list of Web sites available as support sites for instruction.

Field Museum: *www.fieldmuseum.org*
This museum has ancient artifacts from China and Egypt and of Native Americans, as well as the dinosaur Sue.

National Geographic: *www.nationalgeographic.com*
National Geographic has marvelous links to information about different countries and aspects of science. A superb resource for both social studies and science.

Public Broadcasting Service: *www.pbs.org*
A good site for teachers as it often has supportive teaching activities for special programming.

ReadWriteThink: *www.readwritethink.org*
Top quality lesson plans for grades K–12 based on NCTE and IRA Standards for the English Language Arts that have been developed by classroom teachers are available from the Web site. Subjects covered include reading and writing workshop, drama, children's and young adult literature, and critical literacy.

These and other Web sites offer a way to enrich the language arts curriculum and motivate discussion, reading, and writing by students.

Summary

Through a variety of means, students can discover how the language arts are a major part of everyday life. By interacting with classroom guests and volunteers, children learn from the experiences of adults. By helping to keep students abreast of events occurring in their communities and throughout the United States and the world, teachers encourage their students' sensitivity to other cultures and countries. As a result, students are more likely to become active citizens and lifelong learners—a worthy goal for a language arts program.

Questions

1. Why do elementary students need to be aware of the world outside their classroom?
2. In what ways can teachers involve parents in classroom activities?
3. The school dropout rate is high among minority children. What can be done to reduce this trend? How are the language arts involved?
4. How can a community's involvement in the activities of a class benefit students' language arts skills?

Reflective Teaching

Flip back to the beginning of the chapter to the teaching vignette entitled "Peering into the Classroom." After rereading the vignette, consider the following questions: What characteristics (either implied or directly exhibited) does the teacher possess that you would like to develop? What strengths and weaknesses are revealed for the students described in this section? How would you meet the needs of students such as these?

Activities

1. Develop a unit that incorporates the teaching of the language arts and involves individuals, businesses, or groups from outside the school setting.
2. Write to a relative in a distant state or foreign country and ask the relative to give you the name and address of the principal of the elementary school in his or her neighborhood. After you receive the information, write a letter to the principal to arrange a pen pal program for your students.
3. Make a list of potential guest speakers who could provide insight into their fields of work.
4. Brainstorm for ways in which students can interact with local businesses in your area.

For Further Reading

Akroyd, S. (1995). Forming a parent reading-writing class: Connecting cultures, one pen at a time. *The Reading Teacher, 48* (7), 580–587.
Dalton, B. (2000). Exploring literacy on the Internet. *The Reading Teacher, 53* (8), 684–693.

Darling, S., & Lee, J. (2003). Linking parents to reading instruction. *The Reading Teacher, 57* (4), 382–384.

Edwards, P. A. (1991). Fostering early literacy through parent coaching. In E. H. Hiebert (Ed.), *Literacy for a diverse society: Perspectives, practices, and policies.* New York: Teachers College Press.

Fowler, R. C., & Corley, K. K. (1996). Linking families, building community. *Educational Leadership, 53* (7), 24–26.

Klobukowski, P. (1996). Parents, buddy journals, and reader response. *The Reading Teacher, 49* (4), 349–350.

U.S. Department of Education. (2002). *How to help your child read.* Washington, D. C.: U.S. Government Printing Office.

References

Burkhart, A. L. (1995). Breaking the parental barrier. *The Reading Teacher, 48* (7), 634–635.

Cummins, J. (1986). Empowering minority students: A framework for intervention. *Harvard Educational Review, 56* (1), 18–36.

Dutton, T. J. (2004). The real costs of worksheets . . . on our students. *Illinois Reading Council Journal, 32* (2), 34–37.

Ford, M. P., & Opitz, M. F. (2002). Using centers to engage children during guided reading time: Intensifying learning experiences away from the teacher. *The Reading Teacher, 55* (8), pp. 710–717.

Fraser, J. W., & White, D. E. (2000). Ann Turner: The person, the writer, and her historical works. *Language Arts, 77* (4), 353–360.

Heath, S. B. (1980). The functions and uses of literacy. *Journal of Communications, 30,* 123–133.

Henderson, A. (1988). Parents are a school's best friend. *Phi Delta Kappan, 70* (1), 148–153.

Jackson, G., Smolin, L. I., & Lawless, K. A. (2004). SearchSmart: Helping students search the Web in smart ways. *Illinois Reading Council Journal, 32* (2), 58–63.

Lipson, M. Y., Mosenthal, J. H., Mekkelsen, J., & Russ, B. (2004). Building knowledge and fashioning success one school at a time. *The Reading Teacher, 57* (6), 534–542.

McNaughton. S. (1981). The influence of immediate teacher correction on self-corrections and proficient oral reading. *Journal of Reading Behavior, 13* (1), 367–371.

Philliber, W. W., Spillman, R. E., & King, R. E. (1996). Consequences of family literacy for adults and children: Some preliminary findings. *Journal of Adolescent and Adult Literacy, 39* (7), 558–565.

Primavera, J. (2000). Enhancing family literacy competence through literacy activities. *Journal of Prevention and Intervention in the Community, 20,* 85–101.

Routman, R. (1991). *Invitations: Changing as teachers and learners, K–12.* Portsmouth, NH: Heinemann.

Routman, R. (2000). *Conversations: Strategies for Teaching, Learning, and Evaluating.* Portsmouth, NH: Heinemann.

Sanacore, J. (2004). Genuine caring and literacy learning for African American children. *The Reading Teacher, 57* (8), 744–753.

Shanahan, S. (June 11, 2004). One school's answer to "How can I help my child read better?". Sugar Grove, IL: Northern Illinois Reading Council Summer Reading Conference.

Shanahan, S., & Johnson, M. (2004). Ten minute read. Downers Grove, IL: El Sierra School.

Smith, F. (1989). Overselling literacy. *Phi Delta Kappan, 70* (5), 353–359.

Taylor, B. M., Peterson, D. S., Pearson, P. D., & Rodriguez, M. C. (2002). Looking inside classrooms: Reflecting on the "how" as well as the "what" in effective reading instruction. *The Reading Teacher, 56,* (3), 270–279.

U.S. Department of Education. (2002). *How to help your child learn to read.* Washington, D.C.: U.S. Government Printing Office.

Wilson, P. T. (1988). *Let's think about reading and reading instruction: A primer for tutors and teachers.* Dubuque, IA: Kendall/Hunt.

Children's Literature Books

Ambrose, S. (2003). *This vast land: A young man's journal of the Lewis and Clark expedition.* New York: Simon & Schuster.

Bordon, L., & Marx, T. (2003). *Touching the sky: The flying adventures of Wilbur and Orville Wright* (P. Fiore, Illus.). New York: McElderry.

Creech, S. (1994). *Walk two moons.* New York: HarperCollins.

Cronin, D. (2003). *Diary of a worm* (H. Bliss, Illus.). New York: HarperCollins.

Dahl, R. (1961). *James and the giant peach* (N. E. Burkert, Illus.). New York: Knopf.

Haddix, M. P. (1999). *Among the hidden.* New York: Simon & Schuster.

Haddix, M. P. (2000). *Among the imposters.* New York: Simon & Schuster.

Haddix, M. P. (2002). *Among the betrayed.* New York: Simon & Schuster.

Johnson, A. (2003). *I dream of trains* (L. Long, Illus.). New York: Simon & Schuster.

MacLachlan, P. (1985). *Sarah, plain and tall.* New York: Harper & Row.

Park, L. S. (2001). *A single shard.* Boston: Houghton Mifflin.

Stockton, F. R. (2004). *The bee-man of Orn* (P. J. Lynch, Illus.). Cambridge, MA: Candlewick.

Appendix
Additional Resources and
Award-Winning Children's Literature

Professional Journals

Book Links

American Library Association
50 E. Huron Street
Chicago, IL 60611

An excellent source of information about new books, the columns within this journal focus on the use of children's literature with students and provide background information about authors and books.

Journal of Adolescent and Adult Literacy

International Reading Association
800 Barksdale Road, P.O. Box 8139
Newark, DE 19714-8139

This journal is appropriate for middle school teachers and above.

Language Arts

National Council of Teachers of English
1111 Kenyon Road
Urbana, IL 61801

This journal covers the language arts from preschool through grade 6. Each issue contains a column on current research in the language arts plus a list of children's books.

The New Advocate

Christopher-Gordon Publishers
480 Washington Street
Norwood, MA 02062

This quarterly journal provides in-depth information about children's literature, including articles and book reviews.

Reading Horizons

Reading Center and Clinic
Western Michigan University
Kalamazoo, MI 49008

Published five times a year, this outstanding journal contains a bevy of articles that link theory and practice and is very reasonably priced.

The Reading Teacher

International Reading Association
800 Barksdale Road, P.O. Box 8139
Newark, DE 19714-8139

An old standard for elementary teachers, it includes articles on research in reading and writing, practical classroom ideas, and children's literature.

WEB (Wonderfully Exciting Books)

Martha L. King Center for Language and Literacy
The Ohio State University
Columbus, OH 43210

Recently published children's books and their role in the classroom are shared in this journal.

Web Sites

CBC Features

http://www.cbcbooks.org

A Web site of the Children's Book Council, a nonprofit organization, it features children's literature and literacy-related materials for children through young adults.

Great Sites for Kids

http://www.ala.org/greatsites

This Web site sponsored by the American Library Association is terrific for kids AND teachers as well as parents. Links to hundreds of sites that students can navigate are included. Each linked Web site is coded by level (preschool, elementary, middle school/high school). Headings of the various topics include animals, the arts, history and biography, literature and languages, look it up, mathematics and computers, sciences, and social sciences. A teacher designing a unit of study should definitely use this source.

Library of Congress

http://www.loc.gov

The Library of Congress Web site bulges with information. Every book printed in the U.S. is sent to the Library of Congress along with recordings and videotapes that are copyrighted. A historical depository for the U.S., this site has tremendous value for intermediate elementary and middle school grade level teachers who use interdisciplinary units of study. For instance going to http://www.memory.loc.gov will yield actual audio recordings of survivors of the 1888 blizzard that struck the east coast. Coupling this with Jim Murphy's (2000) informational book, *Blizzard!* and going to http://www.weatherchannel.com makes a terrific combination for part of a weather unit on snowstorms for upper elementary and middle school students. This same Web site has other recordings of citizens, entertainers, and political leaders during major historical events such as the Great Depression, World War II, and so on.

International Reading Association

http://www.reading.org

The official Web site of the International Reading Association, it contains information about lesson plans, new books published by the organization, and IRA sponsored conferences.

Storycart Press: A Readers Theater Subscription Service

http://www.storycart.com

Log on for information and a free readers theater script. Subscribers receive three scripts every month during the school year that are appropriate for grades 1–6, thus reflecting the different reading abilities in a classroom. Curricular themes, holidays, and literary genres are reflected in the different scripts.

Caldecott Medal and Honor Books (2004–1980)

Caldecott Award Web site http://www.ala.org/ala/alsc/awardsscholarships/literaryawds/caldecottmedal/caldecotthonors/caldecottmedal.htm

The Caldecott Medal is presented annually to the best illustrated picture book in the U.S.

2004: *The Man Who Walked Between the Towers* by Mordicai Gerstein
Honor Books: *Ella Sarah Gets Dressed* by Margaret Chodos-Irvine; *What Do You Do with a Tail Like This?* by Robin Page and Steve Jenkins, illustrated by Steve Jenkins; *Don't Let the Pigeon Drive the Bus* by Mo Willems

2003: *My Friend Rabbit* by Eric Rohmann
Honor Books: *The Spider and the Fly* by Mary Howitt, illustrated by Tony DiTerlizzi; *Hondo & Fabian* by Peter McCarthy; *Noah's Ark* by Jerry Pinkney

2002: *The Three Pigs* by David Wiesner
Honor Books: *The Dinosaurs of Waterhouse Hawkins* by Barbara Kerley, illustrated by Brian Selznick; *Martin's Big Words: The Life of Martin Luther King, Jr.* by Doreen Rappaport, illustrated by Bryan Collier; *The Stray Dog* by Marc Simont

2001: *So You Want to Be President?* By Judith St. George, illustrated by David Small
Honor Books: *Casey at the Bat: A Ballad of the Republic sung in the Year 1888* by Ernest Lawrence Thayer, illustrated by Christopher Bing; *Click, Clack, Moo: Cows that Type* by Doreen Cronin, illustrated by Betsy Lewin; *Olivia* by Ian Falconer

2000: *Joseph Had a Little Overcoat* by Simms Taback
Honor Books: *Sector 7* by David Wiesner; *The Ugly Duckling* by Hans Christian Anderson, illustrated by Jerry Pinkney; *A Child's Calendar* by John Updike, illustrated by Trina Schart Hyman; *When Sophie Gets Angry—Really, Really Angry* by Molly Garret Bang

1999: *Snowflake Bentley* by Jacqueline Briggs Martin, illustrated by Mary Azarian
Honor Books: *Duke Ellington* by Andrea Davis Pinkney, illustrated by Brian Pinkney; *No. David!* by David Shannon; *Snow* by Uri Shulevitz; *Tibet: Through the Red Box* by Peter Sis

1998: *Rapunzel* by Paul O. Zelinsky
Honor Books: *The Gardener* by Sarah Stewart, illustrated by David Small; *Harlem* by Walter Dean Myers, illustrated by Christopher Myers; *There Was an Old Lady Who Swallowed a Fly* by Simms Taback

1997: *Golem* by David Wisniewski
Honor Books: *Hush! A Thai Lullaby* My Minfong Ho, illustrated by Holly Meade; *The Graphic Alphabet* by Neal Porter, illustrated by David Pelletier; *The Paperboy* by Dav Pilkey; *Starry Messenger: Galileo Galilei* by Peter Sis

1996: *Officer Buckle and Gloria* by Peggy Rathmann
Honor Books: *Alphabet City* by Stephen Johnson; *Zin! Zin! Zin!: A Violin* by Lloyd Moss, illustrated by Marjorie Priceman; *The Faithful Friend* by Robert San Souci, illustrated by Brian Pinkney; *Tops and Bottoms* by Janet Stevens

1995: *Smoky Night* by Eve Bunting, illustrated by David Diaz
Honor Books: *Swamp Angel* by Anne Issacs, illustrated by Paul O. Zelinsky; *John Henry* by Julius Lester, illustrated by Jerry Pinkney; *Time Flies* by Eric Rohmann

1994: *Grandfather's Journey* by Allen Say
Honor Books: *Peppe the Lamplighter* by Elisa Barton, illustrated by Ted Lewin; *In the Small, Small Pond* by Denise Fleming; *Owen* by Kevin Henkes; *Raven: A Trickster Tale from the Pacific Northwest* by Gerald McDermott; *Yo! Yes?* by Chris Raschka

1993: *Mirette on the Highwire* by Emily Arnold McCully
Honor Books: *Seven Blind Mice* by Ed Young; *The Stinky Cheese Man Other Fairly Stupid Tales* by Jon Scieszka, illustrated by Lane Smith; *Working Cotton* by Sherley Anne Williams, illustrated by Carole Byard

1992: *Tuesday* by David Wiesner
Honor Book: *Tar Bleach* by Faith Ringgold

1991: *Black and White* by David Macaulay
Honor Books: *Puss in Boots* by Fred Marcellino; *"More, More, More," Said the Baby: Three Love Stories* by Vera B. Williams

1990: *Lon Po Po: A Red-Riding Hood Story from China* translated by Ed Young
Honor Books: *Bill Peet, an Autobiography* by Bill Peet; *Color Zoo* by Lois Ehlert; *Hershel and the Hanukkah Goblins* by Eric Kimmel, illustrated by Trina Schart Hyman; *The Talking Eggs* by Robert D. San Souci, illustrated by Jerry Pinkney

1989: *Song and Dance Man* by Karen Ackerman, illustrated by Stephen Gammell
Honor Books: *The Boy of the Three-Year Nap* by Dianne Snyder, illustrated by Allen Say; *Free Fall* by David Wiesner; *Goldilocks* retold and illustrated by James Marshall; *Mirandy and Brother Wind* by Patricia C. McKissack, illustrated by Jerry Pinkney

1988: *Owl Moon* by Jane Yolen, illustrated by John Schoenherr
Honor Book: *Mufaro's Beautiful Daughters: An African Tale* by John Steptoe

1987: *Hey, Al* by Arthur Yorinks, illustrated by Richard Egielski
Honor Books: *Alphabatics* by Susie MacDonald; *Rumpelstiltskin* retold and illustrated by Paul O. Zelinsky; *The Village of Round and Square Houses* by Ann Grifalconi

1986: *The Polar Express* by Chris Van Allsburg
Honor Books: *King Bidgood's in the Bathtub* by Audrey Wood, illustrated by Don Wood; *The Relatives Came* by Cynthia Rylant, illustrated by Richard Egielski

1985: *St. George and the Dragon* retold by Margaret Hodges, illustrated by Trina Schart Hyman
Honor Book: *Hansel and Gretel* retold by Rika Lesser, illustrated by Paul O. Zelinsky

1984: *The Glorious Flight: Across the Channel with Louis Bleriot* by Alice and Martin Provensen
Honor Books: *Ten, Nine, Eight* by Molly Bang; *Little Red Riding Hood* retold and illustrated by Trina Schart Hyman

1983: *Shadow* by Blaise Cendrars, illustrated by Marcia Brown
Honor Books: *When I Was Young in the Mountains* by Cynthia Rylant, illustrated by Diane Goode; *Chair for My Mother* by Vera B. Williams

1982: *Jumanji* by Chris Van Allsburg
Honor Books: *A Visit to William Blake's Inn: Poems for Innocent and Experienced Travelers* by Nancy Willard, illustrated by Alice and Martin Prov-

ensen; *Where the Buffaloes Begin* by Olaf Baker, illustrated by Stephen Gammell; *On Market Street* by Arnold Lobel, illustrated by Anita Lobel; *Outside Over There* by Maurice Sendak

1981: *Fables* by Arnold Lobel
Honor Books: *The Bremen-Town Musicians* by Ilse Plume; *The Grey Lady and the Strawberry Snatcher* by Molly Bang; *Mice Twice* by Joseph Low; *Truck* by Donald Crews

1980: *Ox-Cart Man* by Donald Hall, illustrated by Barbara Cooney
Honor Books: *Ben's Trumpet* by Rachel Isadora; *The Treasure* by Uri Shulevitz; *The Garden of Abdul Gasazi* by Chris Van Allsburg

Newbery Medal and Honor Books (2004–1980)

Newbery Award Web site http://www.ala.org/ala/alsc/awardsscholarships/literaryawds/newberymedal/newberywinners/medalwinners.htm

The Newbery Award is given annually to the best children's book based on the quality of the writing.

2004: *The Tale of Despereaux* by Kate DiCamillo
Honor Books: *Olive's Ocean* by Kevin Henkes; *An American Plague: The True and Terrifying Story of the Yellow Fever Epidemic of 1793* by Jim Murphy

2003: *Crispin: The Cross of Lead* by Avi
Honor Books: *The House of the Scorpion* by Nancy Farmer; *Pictures of Hollis Woods* by Patricia Reilly Giff; *Hoot* by Carl Hiaasen; *A Corner of the Universe* by Ann M. Martin; *Surviving the Applewhites* by Stephanie S.Tolan

2002: *A Single Shard* by Linda Sue Park
Honor Books: *Carver: A Life in Poems* by Marilyn Nelson; *Everything on a Waffle* by Polly Horvath

2001: *A Year Down Under* by Richard Peck
Honor Books: *Because of Winn-Dixie* by Kate DiCamillo; *Hope Was Here* by Joan Bauer; *Joey Pigza Loses Control* by Jack Gantos

2000: *Bud, Not Buddy* by Paul Curtis
Honor Books: *Getting Near to Baby* by Audrey Couloumbis; *26 Fairmount Avenue* by Tomie dePaola; *Our Only May Ameila* by Jennifer L. Holm

1999: *Holes* by Louis Sachar
Honor Book: *A Long Way from Chicago* by Richard Peck

1998: *Out of the Dust* by Karen Hesse
Honor Books: *Ella Enchanted* by Gail Carson Levine; *Lily's Crossing* by Patricia Reilly Giff; *Wringer* by Jerry Spinelli

1997: *The View from Saturday* by E. L. Konigsburg
Honor Books: *A Girl Named Disaster* by Nancy Farmer; *Moorchild* by Eloise McGraw; *The Thief* by Megan Whalen Turner; *Belle Prater's Boy* by Ruth White

1996: *The Midwife's Apprentice* by Karen Cushman
Honor Books: *What Jamie Saw* by Carolyn Coleman; *The Watsons Go to Birmingham, 1963* by Christopher Paul Curtis; *Yolanda's Genius* by Carol Fenner; *The Great Fire* by Jim Murphy

1995: *Walk Two Moons* by Sharon Creech
Honor Books: *Catherine, Called Birdy* by Karen Cushman; *The Ear, the Eye, and the Arm* by Nancy Farmer

1994: *The Giver* by Lois Lowry
Honor Books: *Crazy Lady* by Jane Leslie Conly; *Eleanor Roosevelt: A Life of Discovery* by Russell Freeman; *Dragon's Gate* by Laurence Yep

1993: *Missing May* by Cynthia Rylant
Honor Books: *What Hearts* by Bruce Brooks; *The Dark-Thirty: Southern Tales of the Supernatural* by Patricia C. McKissack; *Somewhere in the Darkness* by Walter Dean Myers

1992: *Shiloh* by Phyllis Reynolds Naylor
Honor Books: *Nothing But the Truth* by Avi; *The Wright Brothers: How They Invented the Airplane* by Russell Freedman

1991: *Maniac Magee* by Jerry Spinelli
Honor Book: *The True Confessions of Charlotte Doyle* by Avi

1990: *Number the Stars* by Lois Lowry
Honor Books: *Afternoon of the Elves* by Janet Taylor Lisle; *Shabanu, Daughter of the Wind* by Susan Fisher Staples; *The Winter Room* by Gary Paulsen

1989: *Joyful Noise: Poems for Two Voices* by Paul Fleischman
Honor Books: *In the Beginning: Creation Stories from around the World* by Virginia Hamilton; *Scorpions* by Walter Dean Myers

1988: *Lincoln: A Photobiography* by Russell Freedman
Honor Books: *After the Rain* by Norma Fox Mazer; *Hatchet* by Gary Paulsen

1987: *The Whipping Boy* by Sid Fleischman
Honor Books: *A Fine White Dust* by Cynthia Rylant; *On My Honor* by Marion Dane Bauer; *Volcano: The Eruption and Healing of Mount St. Helens* by Patricia Lauber

1986: *Sarah, Plain and Tall* by Patricia MacLachlan
Honor Books: *Commodore Perry in the Land of the Shogun* by Rhoda Blumberg; *Dogsong* by Gary Paulsen

1985: *The Hero and the Crown* by Robin McKinley
Honor Books: *Like Jake and Me* by Mavis Jukes; *The Moves Make the Man* by Bruce Brooks; *One-Eyed Cat* by Paula Fox

1984: *Dear Mr. Henshaw* by Beverly Cleary
Honor Books: *The Sign of the Beaver* by Elizabeth George Speare; *A Solitary Blue* by Cynthia Voigt; *The Wish Giver* by Bill Brittain

1983: *Dicey's Song* by Cynthia Voigt
Honor Books: *Blue Sword* by Robin McKinley; *Dr. Desoto* by William

Steig; *Graven Images* by Paul Fleischman; *Homesick: My Own Story* by Jean Fritz; *Sweet Whisper, Brother Rush* by Virginia Hamilton

1982: *A Visit to William Blake's Inn: Poems for Innocent and Experienced Travelers* by Nancy Willard

Honor Books: *Ramona Quimby, Age 8* by Beverly Cleary; *Upon the Head of the Goat: A Childhood in Hungary, 1939–1944* by Aranka Siegal

1981: *Jacob Have I Loved* by Katherine Paterson

Honor Books: *The Fledgling* by Jane Langton; *A Ring of Endless Light* by Madeleine L'Engle

1980: *A Gathering of Days: A New England Girl's Journal 1830–32* by Joan Blos

Américas Award

Américas Award Web site http://www.uwm.edu/Dept/CLA/outreach_americas.html

This children's book award is presented annually to the most outstanding book by a Latino/a author.

2002: *Before We Were Free* by Julia Alvarez
2001: *A Movie in My Pillow* by Jorge Argueta
2000: *The Composition* by Antonio Skármeta
1999: *Crashboomlove* Juan Felipe Herrera
1998: *Barrio: José's Neighborhood* by George Ancona
1997: *The Circuit* by Francisco Jiménez
1996: *In My Family/En Mi Familia* by Carmen Lomas Garza
1995: *Tonight, by the Sea* by Frances Temple
1994: *The Mermaid's Twin Sister* by Lynn Joseph
1993: *Vejigante Masquerader* by Lulu Delacre

Pura Belpé Award Winners

This children's book award is given in even years to a Latino/Latina writer (for best narrative) and illustrator whose work best portrays, affirms, and celebrates the Latino cultural experience. The award is named for the first Latina librarian in the New York City Public Library.

2000: Narrative: *Under the Royal Palms* by Alma Flor Ada

Honor Books: *From the Bellybutton of the Moon and Other Summer Poems/ Del Ombligo De Luna Y Otro Poemas De Verano* by Francisco X. Alarcón; *Laughing Out Loud, I Fly* by Juan Felipe Herrera

Illustration: *Magic Windows* by Carmen Lomas Garza, Harriet Rohmer, and David Schecter, illustrated by Carmen Lomas Garza

Honor Books: *Barrio: José's Neighborhood* by George Ancona; *The Secret Stars* by Joseph Slate, illustrated by Felipe Davalos; *Mama and Papa Have a Store* by Amelia Lau Carling

1998: Narrative: *Parrot in the Oven: Mi Vida* by Victor Martinez
Honor Books: *Laughing Tomatoes and Other Spring Poems (Jitomates Risueños y Otros Poemas de Primavera)* by Francisco X. Alarcón, illustrated by Maya Christina Gonzales; *Spirits of the High Mesa* by Floyd Martinez
Illustration: *Snapshots from the Wedding* by Gary Soto, illustrated by Stephanie Garcia
Honor Books: *In My Family/En Mi Familia* by Carmen Lomas Garza; *The Golden Flower: A Taino Myth From Puerto Rico* by Nina Jaffe, illustrated by Enrique O. Sánchez; *Gathering the Sun: An Alphabet in Spanish and English* by Alma Flor Ada, illustrated by Simón Silva

1996: Narrative: *An Island Like You: Stories of the Barrio* by Judith Ortiz Cofer
Honor Book: *Baseball in April and Other Stories* by Gary Soto
Illustration: *Chato's Kitchen* by Gary Soto, illustrated by Susan Guevara
Honor Books: *The Bossy Gallito: A Traditional Cuban Folktale*, retold by Lucia M. Gonzalez, illustrated by Lulu Delacre; *Pablo Remembers: The Fiesta of the Day of the Dead*, written and photographed by George Ancona; *Family Pictures/Cuadros de Familia* by Carmen Lomas Garza

Coretta Scott King Award Winners

Coretta Scott King Award Web site
http://www.ala.org/ala/srrt/corettascottking/corettascott.htm
The Coretta Scott King Award is given annually to an African American author, and in recent years, a separate award has been given to an African American illustrator. The award is to sponsor peace and brotherhood.

2004: Narrative: *The First Part Last* by Angela Johnson
Illustration: *Beautiful Blackbird* by Ashley Bryan

2003: Narrative: *Bronx Masquerade* by Nikki Grimes
Illustration: *Talkin' About Bessie: The Story of Aviator Elizabeth Coleman* by Nikki Grimes, illustrated by E. B. Grimes

2002: Narrative: *The Land* by Mildred Taylor
Illustration: *Goin' Someplace Special* by Patricia and Frederick McKissack, illustrated by Jerry Pinkney

2001: Author: *Miracle's Boys* by Jacqueline Woodson
Illustration: *Let It Shine! Stories of Black Women Freedom Fighters* by Andrea Davis Pinkney; illustrated by Bryan Collier

2000: Narrative: *Bud, Not Buddy* by Christopher Paul Curtis
Honor Books: *Black Hands, White Sails: The Story of African-American Whalers* by Patricia C. McKissack and Frederick L. McKissack; *Monster* by Walter Dean Myers; *Francie* by Karen English
Illustration: *In the Time of the Drums* by Kim L. Siegelson, illustrated by Brian Pinkney
Honor Books: *My Rows and Piles of Coins* by Tololwa M. Mollel, illustrated by E. B. Lewis; *Black Cat* by Christopher Myers

1999: Author: *Heaven* by Angela Johnson
Illustrator: *i see the rhythm* by Toyomi Igus, illustrated by Michele Wood

1998: Author: *Forged by Fire* by Sharon M. Draper
Illustrator: *In Daddy's Arms I Am Tall* by Javaka Steptoe

1997: Author: *Slam!* by Walter Dean Myers
Illustrator: *Minty: A Story of Young Harriet Tubman* by Alan Schroeder, illustrated by Jerry Pinkney

1996: Author: *Her Stories: African American Folktales* by Virginia Hamilton, illustrated by Leo & Diane Dillon
Illustrator: *The Middle Passage: White Ships Black Cargo* by Tom Feelings

1995: Author: *Christmas in the Big House, Christmas in the Quarters* by Patricia McKissack and Frederick McKissack, illustrated by John Thompson
Illustrator: *The Creation* by James Weldon Johnson, illustrated by James Ransome

1994: Author: *Toning the Sweep* by Angela Johnson
Illustrator: *Soul Looks Back in Wonder*, compiled and illustrated by Tom Feelings

1993: Author: *The Dark-Thirty: Southern Tales of the Supernatural* by Patricia McKissack
Illustrator: *Origins of Life on Earth: An African American Creation Myth* by David A. Anderson, illustrated by Kathleen Atkins Smith

1992: Author: *Now Is Your Time! The African-American Struggle for Freedom* by Walter Dean Myers
Illustrator: *Tar Beach* by Faith Ringgold

1991: Author: *Road to Memphis* by Mildred D. Taylor
Illustrator: *Aida*, retold by Leontyne Price, illustrated by Leo and Diane Dillon

1990: Author: *A Long Hard Journey* by Patricia and Frederick McKissack
Illustrator: *Nathaniel Talking* by Eloise Greenfield, illustrated by Jan Spivey Gilchrist

1989: Author: *Fallen Angels* by Walter D. Myers
Illustrator: *Mirandy and Brother Wind* by Patricia McKissack, illustrated by Jerry Pinkney

1988: Author: *The Friendship* by Mildred D. Taylor, illustrated by Max Ginsberg
Illustrator: *Mufaro's Beautiful Daughters: An African Tale*, retold and illustrated by John Steptoe

1987: Author: *Justin and the Best Biscuits in the World* by Mildred Pitts Walter
Illustrator: *Half Moon and One Whole Star* by Crescent Dragonwagon, illustrated by Jerry Pinkney

1986: Author: *The People Could Fly: American Black Folktales* by Virginia Hamilton
Illustrator: *Patchwork Quilt* by Valerie Flournoy, illustrated by Jerry Pinkney

1985: Author: *Motown and Didi* by Walter Dean Myers
Illustrator: No award

1984: Author: *Everett Anderson's Good-Bye* by Lucille Clifton
Illustrator: *My Mama Needs Me* by Mildred Pitts Walter, illustrated by Pat Cummings

1983: Author: *Sweet Whispers, Brother Rush* by Virginia Hamilton
Illustrator: *Black Child* by Peter Mugabane

1982: Author: *Let the Circle Be Unbroken* by Mildred D. Taylor
Illustrator: *Mother Crocodile: An Uncle Amadou Tale from Senegal,* adapted by Rosa Guy, illustrated by John Steptoe

1981: Author: *This Life* by Sidney Poitier
Illustrator: *Beat the Story-Drum, Pum-Pum* by Ashley Bryan

1980: Author: *The Young Landlords* by Walter Dean Myers
Illustrator: Cornrows by Camille Yarbrough, illustrated by Carole Byard

1979: Author: *Escape to Freedom* by Ossie Davis
Illustrator: *Something on My Mind* by Nikki Grimes, illustrated by Tom Feelings

1978: Author: *Africa Dream* by Eloise Greenfield
Illustrator: The same title, illustrated by Carole Byard

1977: Author: *The Story of Stevie Wonder* by James Haskins
Illustrator: No award

1976: Author: *Duey's Tale* by Pearl Bailey
Illustrator: No award

1975: Author: *The Legend of Africana* by Dorothy Robinson. Johnson
Illustrator: The same title, illustrated by Herbert Temple

1974: Author: *Ray Charles* by Sharon Bell Mathis
Illustrator: The same title, illustrated by George Ford

1973: *I Never Had It Made* by Jackie Robinson as told to Alfred Duckett

1972: *17 Black Artists* by Elton C. Fax

1971: *Black Troubadour: Langston Hughes* by Charlemae Rollins

1970: *Martin Luther King, Jr.: Man of Peace* by Lillie Patterson

Name/Title Index

Subject Index

Academic diversity, 57–58
Academic learning logs, 377–382
Achievement tests, standardized, 26
Aesthetic appreciation, 24
Aesthetic reading, 496
African American children's literature, 143–144
Age, influence on learning and achievement, 44
Alliteration, 372
Alphabetic stage of word learning, 505
Alphabetical sequencing, 461
Ambidexterity, 473
Analytical listening, 279, 281–283
Anecdotal record keeping
    photo album method of, 28
    reading evaluation and, 538–539
    student assessment and, 25
Appreciative listening, 272–273
Apprenticeships, 82–83
Articulation
    English language learners and, 259
    pronunciation and, 203
    second language learners and, 343–344
    storytelling and, 239
Asian American children's literature, 144–145
Asian-influenced English, 216–217
Assessment. *See also* Evaluation
    anecdotal record keeping, 25, 28, 538–539
    diagnostic-reflective, 540

individualized educational plans (IEPs)
    and, 30
language arts and, 25–30
language development, 218–219
listening, 270
methods of, 29, 82
minorities, instruments for, 13
oral presentations, 26
portfolios, 26–27, 392–394, 539–540
reading, 534–540
rubrics and, 25–27, 396, 400
standardized achievement tests, 26
writing, 391–401
Attention deficit hyperactivity disorder
    (ADHD), 61–62
Attentive listening, 274–278, 289
Audience, 307–309
Ausubel's theory of organizers, 93
Author Web sites/Web pages, 569
Author's Chair, 1, 3, 282, 304, 392
Autobiographies, 382–383
    genre of, 135
    importance of connections in, 357
    list of recommended, 383

Babbling, 200
Background listening, 271–272
Balanced literacy instruction theory, 7, 18
Balanced literacy programs, 489–493

About the Author

Writing in "snitches and snatches," Dr. Pamela J. Farris leads a busy life as she teaches undergraduate and graduate methods courses in the Department of Literacy Education at Northern Illinois University where she serves as Distinguished Teaching Professor. Formerly, Pam served as Coordinator of NIU's School-University Partnership Program and was an elementary teacher before becoming Title I reading director. An avid reader and prolific author, she has written over 175 articles in such journals as *Language Arts, The Reading Teacher, Journal of Reading,* and *The Middle School Journal.* Her books include *Elementary and Middle School Social Studies: An Interdisciplinary, Multicultural Approach* (2004), *Teaching Reading: A Balanced Approach for Today's Classrooms* (2004), with Carol Fuhler and Maria Walther, and *Teaching, Bearing the Torch* (1999). Pam has presented at conferences throughout North America, Europe, and Australia. Her expertise has been sought out by school districts throughout the United States. Her husband, Richard, is a former school superintendent, and her son attends local public schools. During her free time, Pam enjoys gardening, reading, long walks, and traveling.